Rick Steves'®

LONDON 2006

Rick Steves & Gene Openshaw

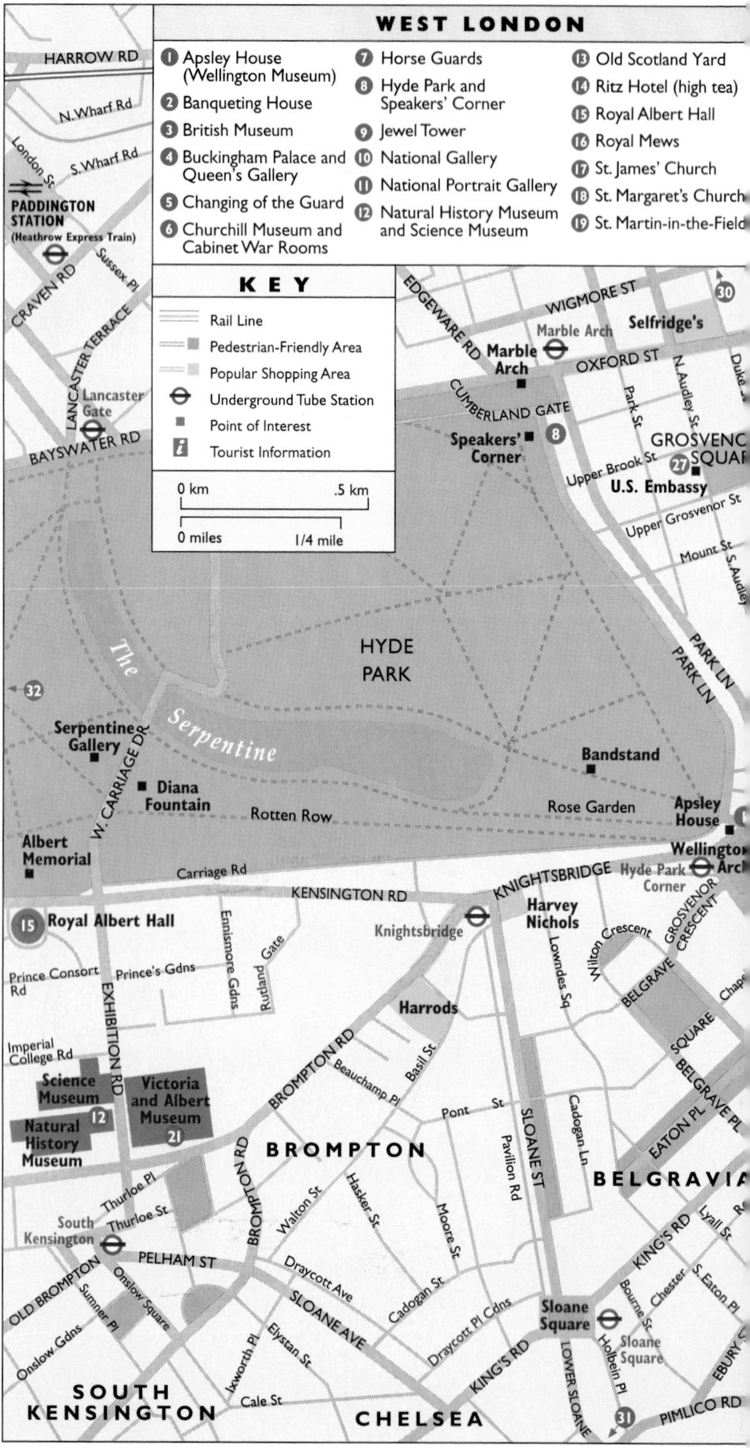
WEST LONDON
1 Apsley House (Wellington Museum)
2 Banqueting House
3 British Museum
4 Buckingham Palace and Queen's Gallery
5 Changing of the Guard
6 Churchill Museum and Cabinet War Rooms
7 Horse Guards
8 Hyde Park and Speakers' Corner
9 Jewel Tower
10 National Gallery
11 National Portrait Gallery
12 Natural History Museum and Science Museum
13 Old Scotland Yard
14 Ritz Hotel (high tea)
15 Royal Albert Hall
16 Royal Mews
17 St. James' Church
18 St. Margaret's Church
19 St. Martin-in-the-Field
KEY
Rail Line
Pedestrian-Friendly Area
Popular Shopping Area
Underground Tube Station
Point of Interest
Tourist Information
0 km
.5 km
0 miles
1/4 mile
HARROW RD
N. Wharf Rd
S. Wharf Rd
London St
PADDINGTON STATION
(Heathrow Express Train)
Sussex Pl
CRAVEN RD
LANCASTER TERRACE
Lancaster Gate
BAYSWATER RD
EDGEWARE RD
WIGMORE ST
Marble Arch
Selfridge's
OXFORD ST
CUMBERLAND GATE
Park St
N. Audley St
Duke St
Speakers' Corner
GROSVENOR SQUARE
Upper Brook St
U.S. Embassy
Upper Grosvenor St
Mount St
S. Audley St
HYDE PARK
PARK LN
The Serpentine
Serpentine Gallery
W. CARRIAGE DR
Diana Fountain
Rotten Row
Bandstand
Rose Garden
Apsley House
Wellington Arch
Albert Memorial
Carriage Rd
KENSINGTON RD
KNIGHTSBRIDGE
Hyde Park Corner
Harvey Nichols
Knightsbridge
Royal Albert Hall
Ennismore Gdns
Rutland Gate
Lowndes Sq
Wilton Crescent
GROSVENOR CRESCENT
Prince Consort Rd
Prince's Gdns
EXHIBITION RD
Harrods
BELGRAVE SQUARE
Chapel St
Imperial College Rd
BROMPTON RD
Beauchamp Pl
Basil St
BELGRAVE PL
Science Museum
Victoria and Albert Museum
Natural History Museum
Pont St
SLOANE ST
Pavilion Rd
Cadogan Ln
EATON PL
BROMPTON
BELGRAVIA
Thurloe Pl
Thurloe St
South Kensington
Walton St
Hasker St
Moore St
Lyall St
KING'S RD
PELHAM ST
Draycott Ave
Cadogan St
Chester Row
S. Eaton Pl
OLD BROMPTON
Sumner Pl
Onslow Square
SLOANE AVE
Draycott Pl Gdns
Sloane Square
Bourne St
Onslow Gdns
Ixworth Pl
Elystan St
KING'S RD
LOWER SLOANE
Holbein Pl
EBURY ST
SOUTH KENSINGTON
Cale St
CHELSEA
PIMLICO RD

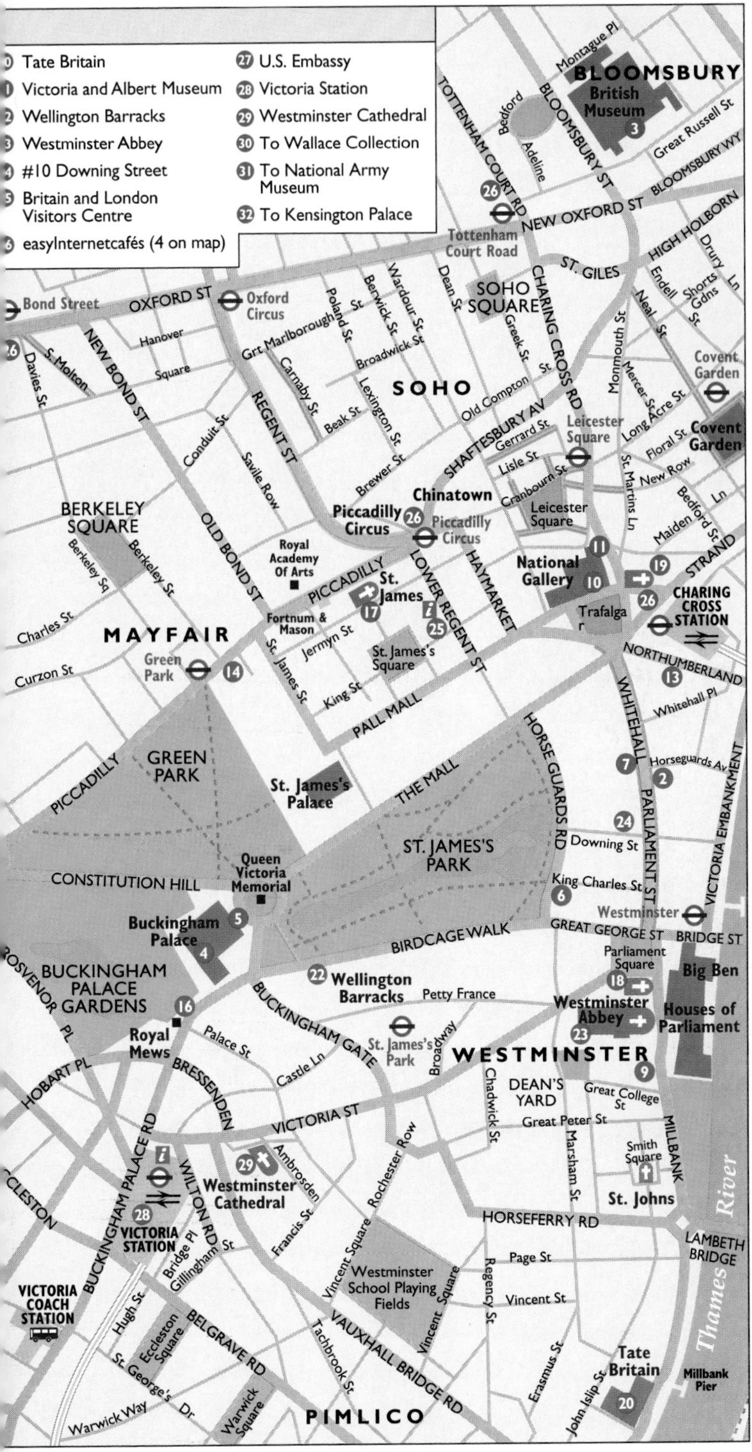

Tate Britain
Victoria and Albert Museum
Wellington Barracks
Westminster Abbey
#10 Downing Street
Britain and London Visitors Centre
easyInternetcafés (4 on map)
27 U.S. Embassy
28 Victoria Station
29 Westminster Cathedral
30 To Wallace Collection
31 To National Army Museum
32 To Kensington Palace
BLOOMSBURY
British Museum
SOHO
SOHO SQUARE
MAYFAIR
BERKELEY SQUARE
Chinatown
Piccadilly Circus
Royal Academy Of Arts
St. James
Fortnum & Mason
St. James's Square
National Gallery
Trafalgar
CHARING CROSS STATION
Covent Garden
Leicester Square
GREEN PARK
St. James's Palace
ST. JAMES'S PARK
Queen Victoria Memorial
Buckingham Palace
BUCKINGHAM PALACE GARDENS
Royal Mews
Wellington Barracks
WESTMINSTER
Westminster Abbey
Big Ben
Houses of Parliament
Parliament Square
DEAN'S YARD
St. Johns
Smith Square
Westminster Cathedral
VICTORIA STATION
VICTORIA COACH STATION
Westminster School Playing Fields
Tate Britain
Millbank Pier
PIMLICO
Thames River
OXFORD ST
NEW OXFORD ST
REGENT ST
PICCADILLY
PALL MALL
THE MALL
WHITEHALL
STRAND
VICTORIA ST
VAUXHALL BRIDGE RD
HORSEFERRY RD
MILLBANK
LAMBETH BRIDGE
BIRDCAGE WALK
CONSTITUTION HILL

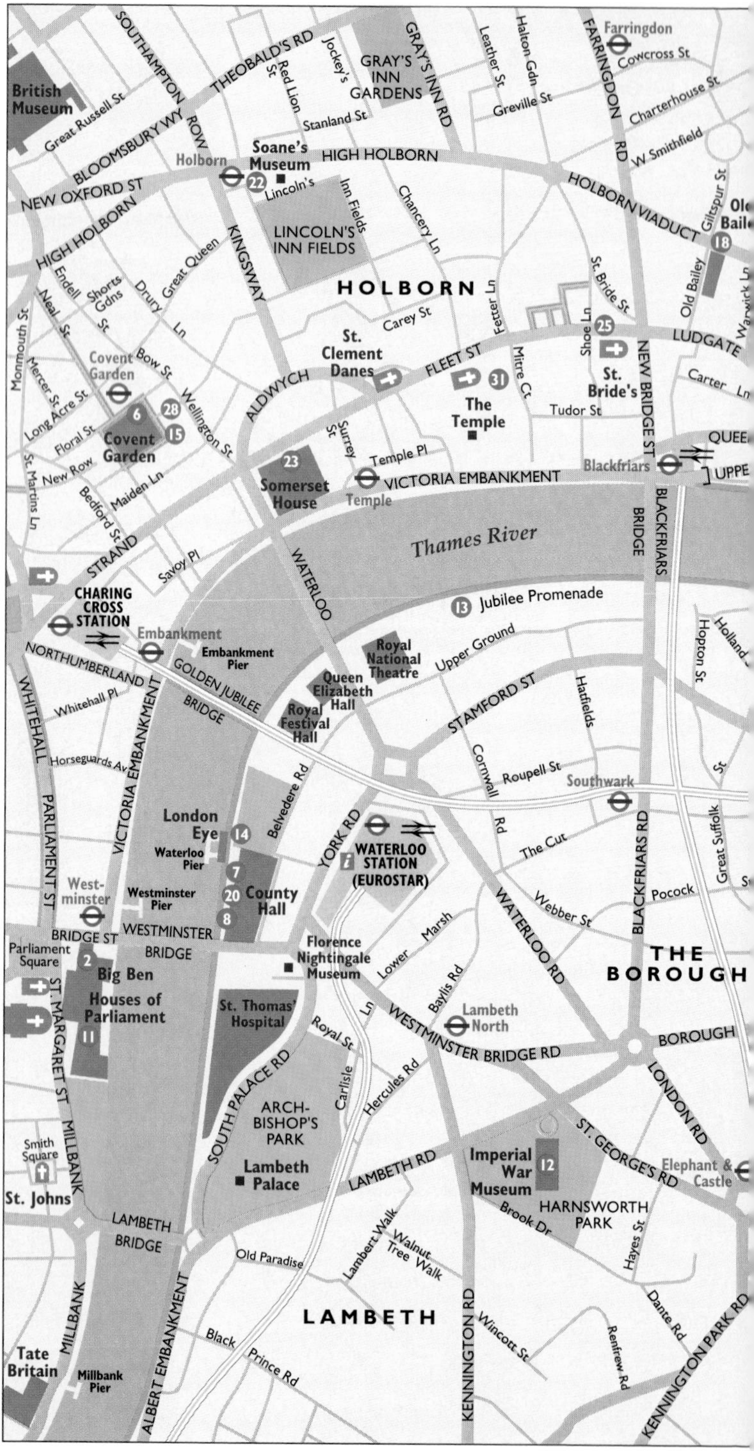
British Museum
Great Russell St
SOUTHAMPTON ROW
THEOBALD'S RD
Red Lion St
Jockey's
GRAY'S INN GARDENS
GRAY'S INN RD
Leather St
Halton Gdn
FARRINGDON RD
Farringdon
Cowcross St
Charterhouse St
Greville St
W Smithfield
BLOOMSBURY WY
Stanland St
Soane's Museum
HIGH HOLBORN
Holborn
22
Lincoln's Inn Fields
NEW OXFORD ST
HIGH HOLBORN
LINCOLN'S INN FIELDS
Chancery Ln
HOLBORN VIADUCT
Giltspur St
Old Bailey
18
Old Bailey
Warwick Ln
KINGSWAY
HOLBORN
Fetter Ln
St. Bride St
Endell
Shorts Gdns
Drury Ln
Great Queen St
Neal St
Monmouth St
Mercer St
Carey St
Shoe Ln
25
LUDGATE
St. Clement Danes
FLEET ST
31
Mitre Ct
St. Bride's
Carter Ln
Covent Garden
Bow St
ALDWYCH
Long Acre St
6
28
15
Covent Garden
Wellington St
The Temple
Tudor St
NEW BRIDGE ST
Floral St
Surrey St
QUEEN
New Row
St. Martins Ln
Temple Pl
Blackfriars
UPPER
23
Somerset House
VICTORIA EMBANKMENT
Temple
Maiden Ln
Bedford St
BLACKFRIARS BRIDGE
Thames River
STRAND
Savoy Pl
WATERLOO
CHARING CROSS STATION
13
Jubilee Promenade
Embankment
Embankment Pier
Royal National Theatre
Upper Ground
Hopton St
Holland St
NORTHUMBERLAND
GOLDEN JUBILEE BRIDGE
Queen Elizabeth Hall
STAMFORD ST
Hatfields
WHITEHALL
Whitehall Pl
Royal Festival Hall
Horseguards Av
VICTORIA EMBANKMENT
Belvedere Rd
Cornwall Rd
Roupell St
Southwark
St
PARLIAMENT ST
London Eye
14
Waterloo Pier
YORK RD
WATERLOO STATION (EUROSTAR)
The Cut
BLACKFRIARS RD
Great Suffolk
West-minster
Westminster Pier
7
20
County Hall
8
Webber St
Pocock
BRIDGE ST
WESTMINSTER BRIDGE
Florence Nightingale Museum
Lower Marsh
WATERLOO RD
Parliament Square
2
Big Ben
Houses of Parliament
11
THE BOROUGH
St. Thomas' Hospital
Baylis Rd
Lambeth North
Ln
Royal St
WESTMINSTER BRIDGE RD
BOROUGH
LONDON RD
ST. MARGARET ST
SOUTH PALACE RD
Carlisle
Hercules Rd
ARCH-BISHOP'S PARK
ST. GEORGE'S RD
Smith Square
MILLBANK
St. Johns
Lambeth Palace
LAMBETH RD
Imperial War Museum
12
Elephant & Castle
HARNSWORTH PARK
Brook Dr
Hayes St
LAMBETH BRIDGE
Old Paradise
Lambert Walk
Walnut Tree Walk
Dante Rd
LAMBETH
ALBERT EMBANKMENT
KENNINGTON RD
Wincott St
Renfrew Rd
KENNINGTON PARK RD
Black Prince Rd
Tate Britain
MILLBANK
Millbank Pier

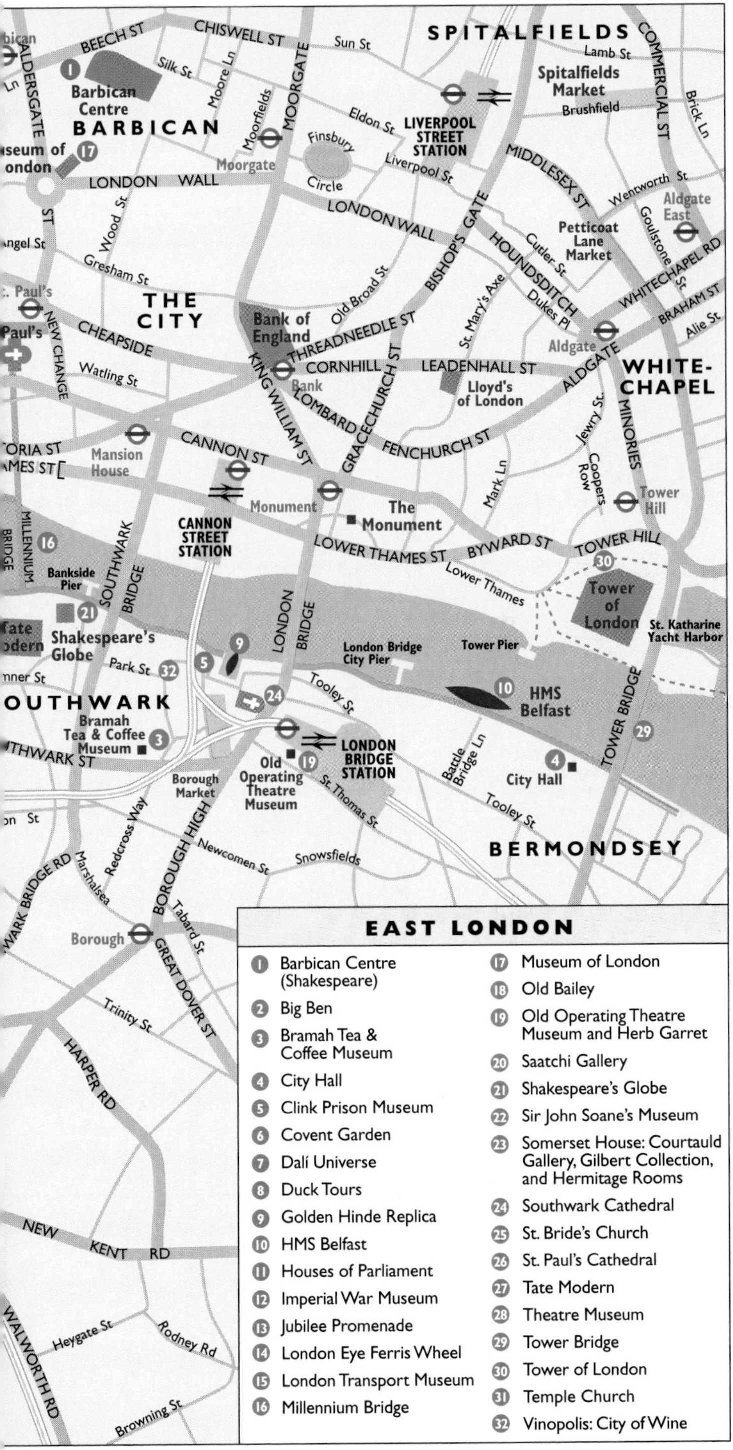
SPITALFIELDS
BARBICAN
THE CITY
WHITE-CHAPEL
SOUTHWARK
BERMONDSEY
Barbican Centre
Museum of London
Spitalfields Market
LIVERPOOL STREET STATION
Bank of England
Lloyd's of London
Petticoat Lane Market
The Monument
CANNON STREET STATION
LONDON BRIDGE STATION
Tower of London
St. Katharine Yacht Harbor
HMS Belfast
City Hall
Shakespeare's Globe
Bankside Pier
London Bridge City Pier
Tower Pier
Bramah Tea & Coffee Museum
Borough Market
Old Operating Theatre Museum
BEECH ST
CHISWELL ST
Sun St
Lamb St
COMMERCIAL ST
Brick Ln
Brushfield
Silk St
Moore Ln
Moorfields
MOORGATE
Moorgate
ALDERSGATE
Eldon St
Finsbury Circle
Liverpool St
MIDDLESEX ST
Wentworth St
Aldgate East
LONDON WALL
Wood St
Gresham St
Goulstone St
Cutler St
HOUNDSDITCH
BISHOP'S GATE
Old Broad St
St. Mary's Axe
Dukes Pl
WHITECHAPEL RD
BRAHAM ST
Alie St
Aldgate
ALDGATE
CHEAPSIDE
NEW CHANGE
Watling St
THREADNEEDLE ST
CORNHILL
LEADENHALL ST
Bank
KING WILLIAM ST
LOMBARD
GRACECHURCH ST
FENCHURCH ST
Jewry St
MINORIES
Mansion House
CANNON ST
Mark Ln
Coopers Row
Tower Hill
Monument
LOWER THAMES ST
BYWARD ST
TOWER HILL
Lower Thames
MILLENNIUM BRIDGE
SOUTHWARK BRIDGE
LONDON BRIDGE
TOWER BRIDGE
Park St
Tooley St
Battle Bridge Ln
St. Thomas St
Redcross Way
BOROUGH HIGH
Newcomen St
Snowsfields
Marshalsea
Tabard St
Borough
GREAT DOVER ST
Trinity St
HARPER RD
NEW KENT RD
WALWORTH RD
Heygate St
Rodney Rd
Browning St
EAST LONDON
1 Barbican Centre (Shakespeare)
2 Big Ben
3 Bramah Tea & Coffee Museum
4 City Hall
5 Clink Prison Museum
6 Covent Garden
7 Dalí Universe
8 Duck Tours
9 Golden Hinde Replica
10 HMS Belfast
11 Houses of Parliament
12 Imperial War Museum
13 Jubilee Promenade
14 London Eye Ferris Wheel
15 London Transport Museum
16 Millennium Bridge
17 Museum of London
18 Old Bailey
19 Old Operating Theatre Museum and Herb Garret
20 Saatchi Gallery
21 Shakespeare's Globe
22 Sir John Soane's Museum
23 Somerset House: Courtauld Gallery, Gilbert Collection, and Hermitage Rooms
24 Southwark Cathedral
25 St. Bride's Church
26 St. Paul's Cathedral
27 Tate Modern
28 Theatre Museum
29 Tower Bridge
30 Tower of London
31 Temple Church
32 Vinopolis: City of Wine

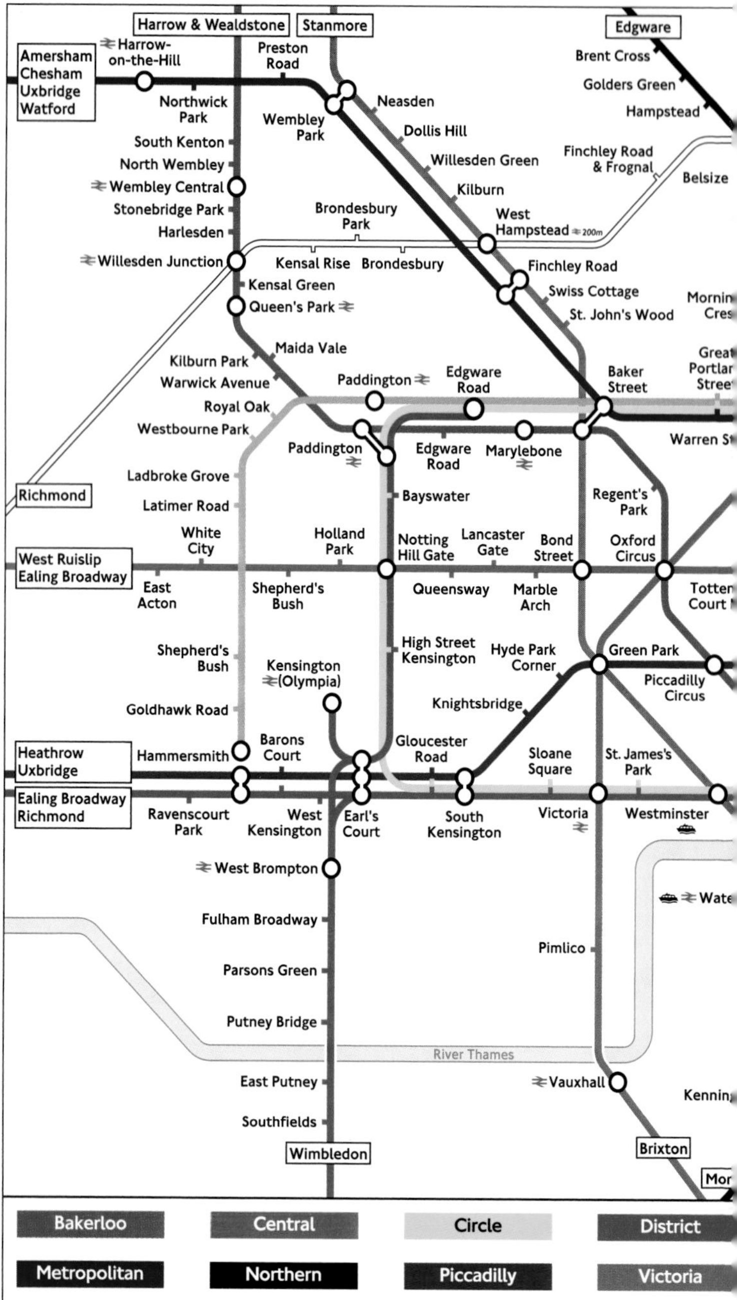
Harrow & Wealdstone
Stanmore
Edgware
Amersham
Chesham
Uxbridge
Watford
Harrow-on-the-Hill
Preston Road
Northwick Park
Wembley Park
Neasden
Dollis Hill
Willesden Green
Kilburn
Brent Cross
Golders Green
Hampstead
Finchley Road & Frognal
Belsize
South Kenton
North Wembley
Wembley Central
Stonebridge Park
Harlesden
Willesden Junction
Brondesbury Park
West Hampstead
200m
Kensal Rise
Brondesbury
Finchley Road
Swiss Cottage
St. John's Wood
Kensal Green
Queen's Park
Maida Vale
Kilburn Park
Warwick Avenue
Paddington
Edgware Road
Baker Street
Great Portlar Stree
Royal Oak
Westbourne Park
Paddington
Edgware Road
Marylebone
Warren St
Ladbroke Grove
Latimer Road
Richmond
Bayswater
Regent's Park
White City
Holland Park
Notting Hill Gate
Lancaster Gate
Bond Street
Oxford Circus
West Ruislip
Ealing Broadway
East Acton
Shepherd's Bush
Queensway
Marble Arch
Totten Court
Shepherd's Bush
Kensington (Olympia)
High Street Kensington
Hyde Park Corner
Green Park
Piccadilly Circus
Goldhawk Road
Knightsbridge
Heathrow
Uxbridge
Hammersmith
Barons Court
Gloucester Road
Sloane Square
St. James's Park
Ealing Broadway
Richmond
Ravenscourt Park
West Kensington
Earl's Court
South Kensington
Victoria
Westminster
West Brompton
Wate
Fulham Broadway
Pimlico
Parsons Green
Putney Bridge
River Thames
East Putney
Vauxhall
Kennin
Southfields
Wimbledon
Brixton
Mor
Bakerloo
Central
Circle
District
Metropolitan
Northern
Piccadilly
Victoria

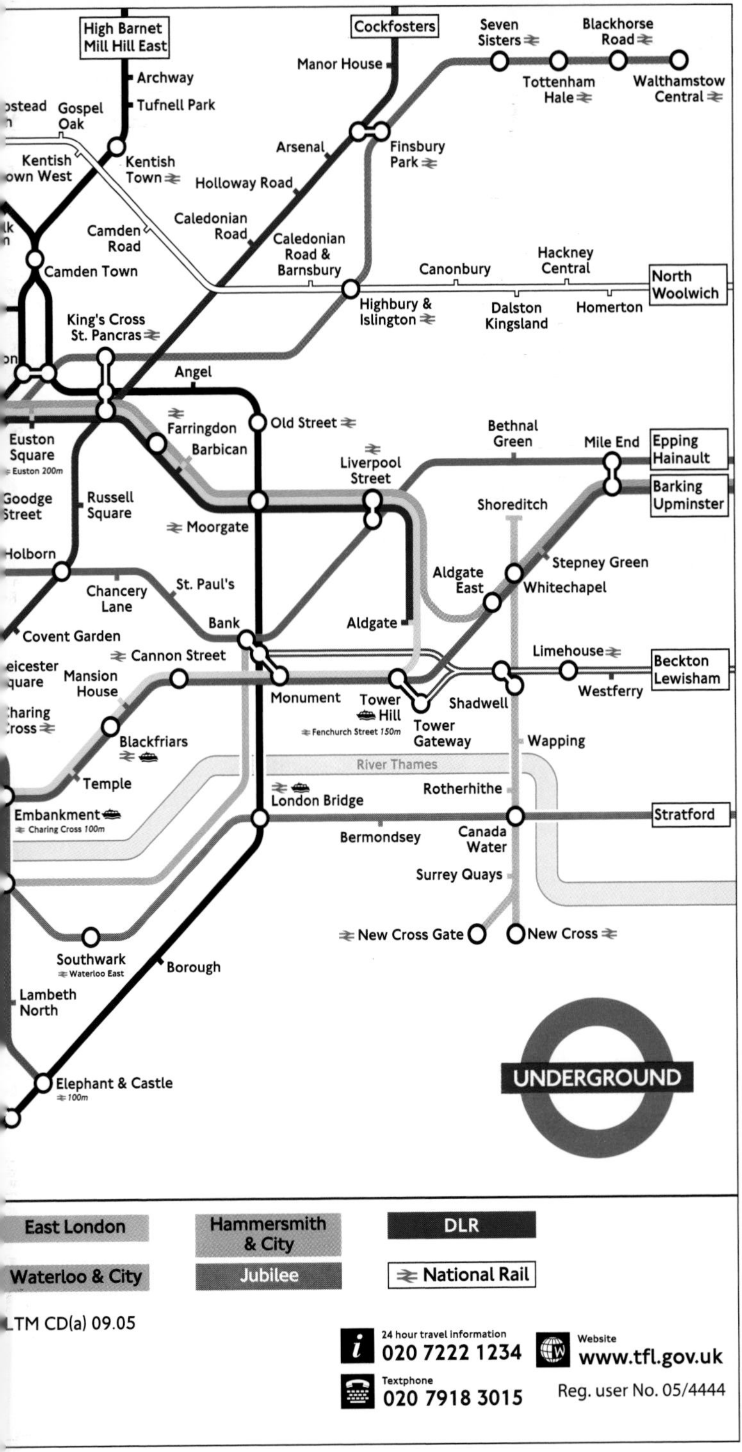
High Barnet
Mill Hill East
Archway
Tufnell Park
Cockfosters
Manor House
Seven Sisters
Blackhorse Road
Tottenham Hale
Walthamstow Central
Gospel Oak
Kentish Town
Kentish Town West
Arsenal
Finsbury Park
Holloway Road
Caledonian Road
Camden Road
Camden Town
Caledonian Road & Barnsbury
Canonbury
Hackney Central
North Woolwich
Highbury & Islington
Dalston Kingsland
Homerton
King's Cross St. Pancras
Angel
Farringdon
Old Street
Barbican
Euston Square
Euston 200m
Goodge Street
Russell Square
Moorgate
Liverpool Street
Bethnal Green
Mile End
Epping
Hainault
Barking
Upminster
Shoreditch
Holborn
Chancery Lane
St. Paul's
Aldgate East
Stepney Green
Whitechapel
Covent Garden
Bank
Aldgate
Cannon Street
Leicester Square
Mansion House
Limehouse
Beckton
Lewisham
Westferry
Monument
Tower Hill
Shadwell
Tower Gateway
Charing Cross
Fenchurch Street 150m
Blackfriars
Wapping
River Thames
Temple
Rotherhithe
London Bridge
Embankment
Charing Cross 100m
Stratford
Bermondsey
Canada Water
Surrey Quays
New Cross Gate
New Cross
Southwark
Waterloo East
Borough
Lambeth North
Elephant & Castle
100m
UNDERGROUND
East London
Hammersmith & City
DLR
Waterloo & City
Jubilee
National Rail
LTM CD(a) 09.05
24 hour travel information
020 7222 1234
Textphone
020 7918 3015
Website
www.tfl.gov.uk
Reg. user No. 05/4444

Rick Steves'®

LONDON 2006

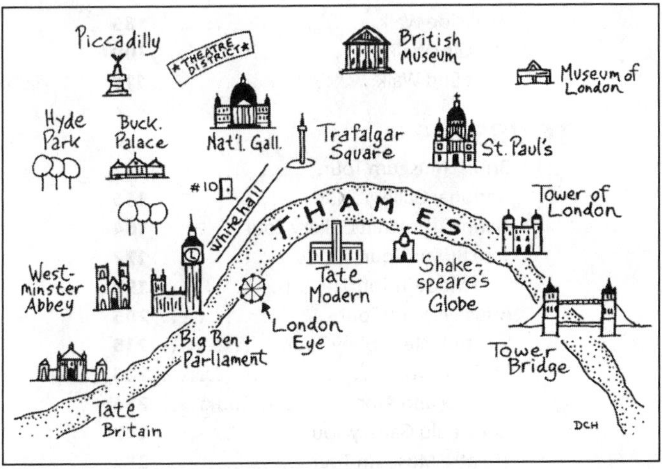

AVALON TRAVEL

CONTENTS

London

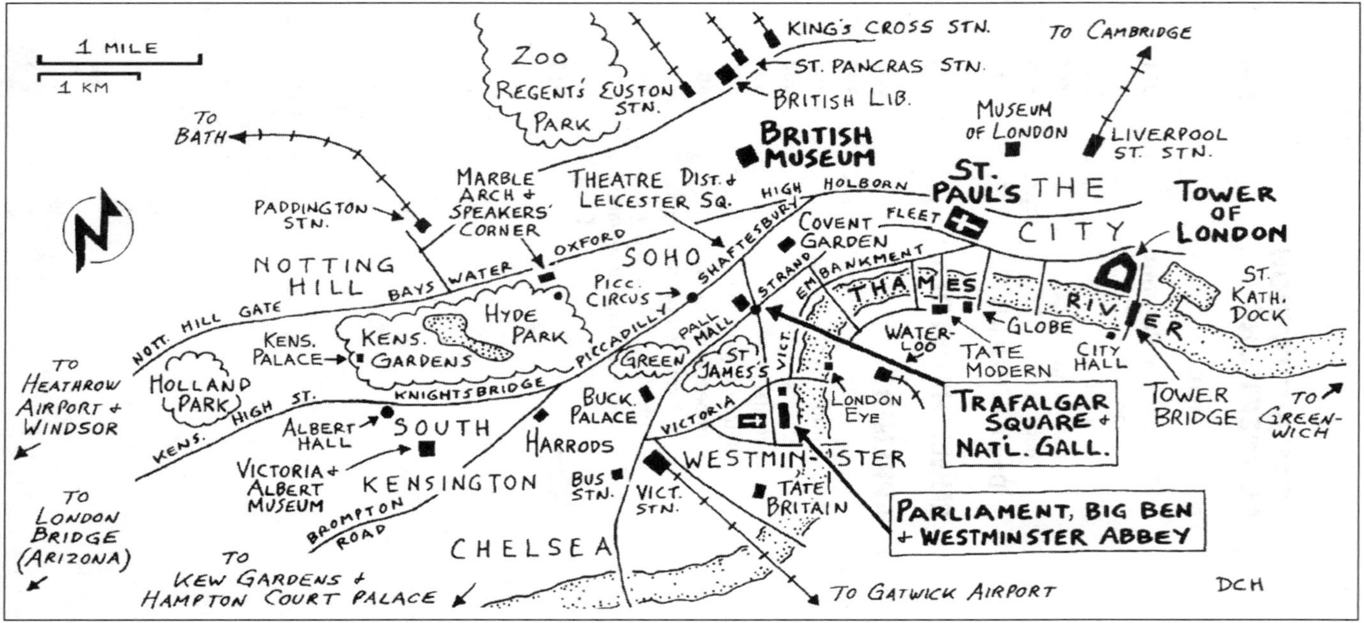
1 MILE
1 KM
ZOO
REGENT'S PARK
EUSTON STN.
KING'S CROSS STN.
ST. PANCRAS STN.
BRITISH LIB.
TO CAMBRIDGE
MUSEUM OF LONDON
LIVERPOOL ST. STN.
TO BATH
BRITISH MUSEUM
MARBLE ARCH + SPEAKERS' CORNER
THEATRE DIST. + LEICESTER SQ.
HIGH HOLBORN
ST. PAUL'S
THE CITY
TOWER OF LONDON
PADDINGTON STN.
COVENT GARDEN
FLEET
SHAFTESBURY
OXFORD
SOHO
NOTTING HILL
BAYS WATER
PICC. CIRCUS
STRAND
EMBANKMENT
THAMES RIVER
ST. KATH. DOCK
NOTT. HILL GATE
HYDE PARK
KENS. GARDENS
KENS. PALACE
PICCADILLY
PALL MALL
GREEN
ST JAMES'S
VICT.
WATER-LOO
TATE MODERN
GLOBE
CITY HALL
TO HEATHROW AIRPORT + WINDSOR
HOLLAND PARK
KNIGHTSBRIDGE
BUCK. PALACE
LONDON EYE
TRAFALGAR SQUARE + NAT'L. GALL.
TOWER BRIDGE
TO GREENWICH
KENS. HIGH ST.
ALBERT HALL
SOUTH KENSINGTON
HARRODS
VICTORIA
WESTMINSTER
VICTORIA + ALBERT MUSEUM
BUS STN.
VICT. STN.
TATE BRITAIN
PARLIAMENT, BIG BEN + WESTMINSTER ABBEY
TO LONDON BRIDGE (ARIZONA)
BROMPTON ROAD
CHELSEA
TO KEW GARDENS + HAMPTON COURT PALACE
TO GATWICK AIRPORT
DCH

INTRODUCTION

Blow through the city on the open deck of a double-decker orientation tour bus and take a pinch-me-I'm-in-London walk through the West End. Ogle the crown jewels at the Tower of London, hear the chimes of Big Ben, and see the Houses of Parliament in action. Cruise the Thames River and take a spin on the London Eye Ferris Wheel. Hobnob with the tombstones in Westminster Abbey, enjoy Shakespeare in a replica of the Globe Theatre, and stand in awe over the original Magna Carta at the British Library. Visit with Leonardo, Botticelli, and Rembrandt in the National Gallery. Whisper across the dome of St. Paul's Cathedral and rummage through our civilization's attic at the British Museum. And sip your tea with pinky raised and clotted cream dribbling down your scone.

You can enjoy some of Europe's best people-watching at Covent Garden and snap to at Buckingham Palace's Changing of the Guard. Just sit in Victoria Station, Piccadilly Circus, or a major Tube station and observe. Tip a pint in a pub with a yacky local, and beachcomb the Thames. Spend one evening at a theater and the others catching your breath.

London is more than its museums and landmarks. It's a living, breathing, thriving organism...a coral reef of humanity. The city has changed dramatically in recent years, and many visitors are surprised to find how "un-English" it is. Whites are now a minority in major parts of the city that once symbolized white imperialism. Arabs have nearly bought out the area north of Hyde Park. Chinese take-outs outnumber fish-and-chips shops. Many hotels are run by people with foreign accents (who hire English chambermaids), while outlying suburbs are home to huge communities of Indians and Pakistanis. With the English Channel Tunnel making travel between Britain and the Continent easier than ever, many locals see even more holes in their bastion of Britishness. London is learning—sometimes fitfully—to live as a microcosm of its formerly vast empire.

This Information Is Accurate and Up-to-Date

This book is updated every year. Most publishers of guidebooks that cover a city from top to bottom can afford an update only every two or three years (and even then, it's often by e-mail or fax). Since this book is selective, covering only the sights that make the top week or so in and around London, I can update it in person each summer. The telephone numbers, hours, and prices of the places listed in this book are accurate as of mid-2005. Even with annual updates, things change. Still, if you're traveling with the current edition of this book, I guarantee you're using the most up-to-date information available in print. For the latest, visit www.ricksteves.com/update. Also at my Web site, you'll find a valuable list of reports and experiences—good and bad—from fellow travelers who have used this book (www.ricksteves.com/feedback).

Use this year's edition. People who try to save a few bucks by traveling with an old book are not smart. They learn the seriousness of their mistake...in London. Your trip costs about $10 per waking hour. Your time is valuable. This guidebook saves lots of time.

About This Book

Rick Steves' London is a personal tour guide in your pocket. Better yet, it's actually two tour guides in your pocket: The co-author of this book is Gene Openshaw. Since our first "Europe through the gutter" trip together as high-school buddies almost 30 years ago, Gene and I have been exploring the wonders of the Old World. An inquisitive historian and lover of European culture, Gene wrote most of this book's self-guided museum tours and neighborhood walks. Together, Gene and I will keep this book up-to-date and accurate. For simplicity, from this point, "we" will shed our respective egos and become "I."

This book is organized in the following way:

Orientation includes tourist information and public transportation. The "Planning Your Time" section offers a suggested schedule with thoughts on how best to use your limited time.

Sights provides a succinct overview of London's most important sights, arranged by neighborhood, with ratings: ▲▲▲—Don't miss; ▲▲—Try hard to see; ▲—Worthwhile if you can make it; No rating—Worth knowing about.

The **Walks** take you through Westminster (from Big Ben to Trafalgar Square), Bankside (on the South Bank through

Shakespeare's world to the Tate Modern), The City (the financial district—banks, churches, and courts busy with barristers and baristas), and the West End (it's the thee-ah-ter district, darling, with restaurants and shops galore, from Leicester Square to Covent Garden with Piccadilly Circus as the finale).

The **Tours** lead you through London's most fascinating museums and sights: the British Museum, National Gallery, National Portrait Gallery, Tate Britain, Tate Modern, British Library, Westminster Abbey, St. Paul's Cathedral, Victoria and Albert Museum, Courtauld Gallery, Theatre Museum, and the Tower of London.

Day Trips covers nearby destinations: Greenwich, Windsor, Cambridge, Bath, and even Paris.

Sleeping is a guide to my favorite good-value hotels, in several pleasant London neighborhoods.

Eating offers a wide assortment of restaurants ranging from fun, inexpensive eateries to classy splurges.

London with Children includes my top recommendations for keeping your kids (and you) happy in London.

Shopping gives you tips for shopping painlessly and enjoyably, without letting it overwhelm your vacation or ruin your budget.

Entertainment is your guide to fun, including theater, music, walks, and cruises.

Transportation Connections covers connections by train (including the Eurostar to Paris) and by plane (with detailed information on London's two major airports), laying the groundwork for your smooth arrival and departure.

London History, which gives the background of this historic city, has a timeline and a *Who's Who* list of British notables.

The **appendix** is a traveler's toolkit, with telephone tips, a climate chart, and a fun British–Yankee dictionary.

Throughout this book, when you see a ✪ in a listing, it means that the sight is covered in much more depth in a self-guided walk or one of my museum tours—a page number will tell you just where to look to find more information.

Browse through this book and choose your favorite sights. Then have a great trip! Traveling like a temporary local, you'll get the absolute most out of every mile, minute, and dollar.

PLANNING

Trip Costs

Five components make up your trip costs: airfare, surface transportation, room and board, sightseeing/entertainment, and shopping/miscellany.

Airfare: Don't try to sort through the mess. Find and use a good travel agent. A round-trip, U.S.–London flight costs $400 to $1,000 (even cheaper in winter), depending on where you fly from and when.

Surface Transportation: For a typical one-week visit, allow about $50 for Tube tickets (for a 1-week pass or 2 Carnets for 20 single rides). The cost of round-trip train rides to day-trip destinations is about $6 for Greenwich (cheaper by Tube), $30 for Cambridge, $65 for Bath, and $140 (round-trip Standard Leisure "value fare" ticket) for Paris on the Eurostar. (Save money by taking buses instead of trains, and see the Transportation Connections chapter for tips on how to get the cheapest Eurostar tickets.) Add $100 if you plan to take a couple of taxi rides between London's Heathrow Airport and your hotel (or save money by taking the Tube, train, or airport bus).

Room and Board: London gets my vote for Europe's most expensive city. But if you're careful, you can manage comfortably in London on $120 a day per person for room and board. A $120-a-day budget allows $15 for lunch, $25 for dinner, and $80 for lodging (based on 2 people splitting the cost of a basic $160 double room that includes breakfast). That's doable. Students and tightwads do it on $45 a day ($30 for hostel bed, $15 for groceries).

Sightseeing and Entertainment: Fortunately, many of the best sights in London are free (though they usually request donations): the British Museum, National Gallery, Tate Britain, Tate Modern, British Library, Imperial War Museum, Natural History Museum, and the Victoria and Albert Museum. Figure on paying $14–40 for the major sights that charge admission (e.g., Westminster Abbey-$14, Tower of London-$26, Madame Tussaud's Waxworks-$40), $10 for guided walks, and $30 for bus tours and splurge experiences (plays range from $10–65). An average of $40 a day works for most. Don't skimp here. After all, this category is the driving force behind your trip—you came to sightsee, enjoy, and experience London.

The British Heritage Pass, which covers your entry fees into more than 600 British Heritage and National Trust properties, doesn't make sense for a London visit, but is worth considering if you'll be traveling extensively throughout Britain (£28/$50 for 4 days, £39/$70 for 7 days, £52/$94 for 15 days, £70/$125 for 30 days; sold at the Britain and London Visitors Centre on Lower Regent Street in London and at the various for-profit TIs at the major train stations and airports; don't get the pass for kids, since they get discounts on admissions but not on the pass).

Shopping and Miscellany: Figure $1–2 per postcard, tea, or ice-cream cone, and $4 per beer. Shopping can vary in cost from nearly nothing to a small fortune. Good budget travelers find that this category has little to do with assembling a trip full of lifelong and wonderful memories.

When to Go

July and August are the peak-season months—my favorite time—with very long days, the best weather, and the busiest schedule of tourist fun. Prices and crowds don't go up as dramatically in Britain as they do in much of Europe. Still, travel during "shoulder season" (May, early June, Sept, and early Oct) is easier and a bit less expensive. Shoulder-season travelers get minimal crowds, decent weather, and the full range of sights and tourist fun spots. Winter travelers find absolutely no crowds and soft room prices, but shorter sightseeing hours. The weather can be cold and dreary, and nightfall draws the shades on sightseeing well before dinnertime. While England's rural charm falls with the leaves, London's sights are fine in the winter.

Plan for rain no matter when you go. Just keep going and take full advantage of "bright spells." Conditions can change several times in a day, but rarely is the weather extreme. Daily averages throughout the year range between 42° and 70° Fahrenheit. Temperatures below 32° or over 80° cause headlines. (For more information, see the climate chart in the appendix.) July and August are not much better than shoulder months. May and June can be lovely. While sunshine may be rare, summer days are very long. The summer sun is up from 6:30 to 22:30 (10:30 p.m.). It's not uncommon to have a gray day, eat dinner, and enjoy hours of sunshine afterward.

Trip Tips and Travel Arrangements

If you're planning to stay in Bath as well as London, consider a gentler, small-town start in Bath (the ideal jet-lag pillow) and visit London afterward, when you're rested and accustomed to travel in Britain. Heathrow Airport has direct connections to Bath and other cities.

You could make these travel arrangements before your trip:

- Reserve your room. For my recommended hotels, see the Sleeping chapter.
- To book a play, you can call from the U.S. as easily as from London, using your credit-card number to pay for your tickets. For the current schedule and phone numbers, visit www.officiallondontheatre.co.uk, or if your hometown library carries a London newspaper, photocopy the theater section. For simplicity, I book plays while in London. For more information, see the Entertainment chapter.

- If you want to attend the pageantry-filled Ceremony of the Keys in the Tower of London, write for tickets (see page 63).
- If you'll be day-tripping to Paris on the Eurostar train, consider ordering a ticket in advance (or buy it in Britain); for details, see "Crossing the Channel," page 327.

Travel Smart

A smart trip is a puzzle—a fun, doable, and worthwhile challenge. Reading this book before you leave, and rereading as you travel, will enhance your enjoyment and save you time and money. The British Museum is much more entertaining, for instance, if you've boned up on mummies the night before.

Buy a phone card and use it for reservations and confirmations. You speak the language—use it! Enjoy the friendliness of the local people. Ask questions. Most locals are eager to point you in their idea of the right direction. Pack along a pocket-size notebook to organize your thoughts. Get a map. Understand and use public transportation. Take advantage of audioguides at sights and local guided tours. Plan ahead for laundry, Internet stops, and picnics. Every traveler needs slack days. Pace yourself. Assume you will return.

Design an itinerary that enables you to hit the various sights at the best possible times. For example, if you like to free up your busy days, note that Westminster Abbey is open and empty Wednesday evenings. Visit The City (London's old center) during the day on weekdays when it's lively, not at night and on weekends when it's dead. The two-hour orientation bus tour is best on Sunday morning (when some sights are closed) or evenings (when it costs half as much). There are no plays on Sunday nights. Treat Saturday as a weekday, except for transportation connections outside of London (can be less frequent than on Mon–Fri, and downright meager on Sun). Be aware of upcoming holidays that could affect your trip (see page 10).

RESOURCES

British Tourist Office in the U.S.

The **Visit Britain** office is a wealth of knowledge. You can contact them at: tel. 800/462-2748, fax 212/986-1188, 551 Fifth Ave. #701, New York, NY 10176, www.visitbritain.com, travelinfo@visitbritain.org. Ask for free maps of London and Britain and any specific information you may want (such as regional information, a garden-tour map, urban cultural activities brochures, and so on).

London has a fine tourist information office, called the Britain and London Visitors Centre (see page 22). Note that tourist information offices are abbreviated "TI" in this book.

Web Sites: To study ahead, also visit www.timeout.com/london, www.thisislondon.com, and www.londontown.com.

Rick Steves' Guidebooks, Public Television Show, and Radio Show

Rick Steves' Europe Through the Back Door gives you budget-travel skills, such as minimizing jet lag, packing light, planning your itinerary, traveling by car or train, finding rooms, changing money, avoiding rip-offs, buying a mobile phone, hurdling the language barrier, staying healthy, taking great photographs, using a bidet, and much more. The book also includes chapters on 38 of my favorite "Back Doors," six of which are in Great Britain.

Country Guides: These annually updated books offer you the latest on the top sights and destinations, with tips on how to make your trip efficient and fun. Here are the titles:

Rick Steves' Best of Europe
Rick Steves' Best of Eastern Europe
Rick Steves' England (new in 2006)
Rick Steves' France
Rick Steves' Germany & Austria
Rick Steves' Great Britain
Rick Steves' Ireland
Rick Steves' Italy
Rick Steves' Portugal
Rick Steves' Scandinavia
Rick Steves' Spain
Rick Steves' Switzerland

City and Regional Guides: Updated every year, these focus on Europe's most compelling destinations. Along with specifics on sights, restaurants, hotels, and nightlife, you'll get self-guided, illustrated tours of the outstanding museums and most characteristic neighborhoods.

Rick Steves' Amsterdam, Bruges & Brussels
Rick Steves' Florence & Tuscany
Rick Steves' London
Rick Steves' Paris
Rick Steves' Prague & the Czech Republic
Rick Steves' Provence & the French Riviera
Rick Steves' Rome
Rick Steves' Venice

Rick Steves' Phrase Books: In much of Europe, a phrase book is as fun as it is necessary. This practical and budget-oriented series covers French, German, Italian, Spanish, Portuguese, and French/Italian/German. You'll be able to make hotel reservations over the phone, chat with your cabbie, and bargain at street markets.

And More Books: *Rick Steves' Europe 101: History and Art for the Traveler* (with Gene Openshaw) gives you the story of Europe's people, history, and art. Written for smart people who were

Begin Your Trip at www.ricksteves.com

At www.ricksteves.com you'll find a wealth of **free information** on destinations covered in this book, including fresh European travel and tour news every month and helpful "Graffiti Wall" tips from thousands of fellow travelers.

While you're there, the **online Travel Store** is a great place to save money on travel bags and accessories designed by Rick Steves to help you travel smarter and lighter, plus a wide selection of guidebooks, planning maps, and DVDs.

Traveling through Europe by rail is a breeze, but choosing the right railpass for your trip—amidst hundreds of options—can drive you nutty. At www.ricksteves.com, you'll find **Rick Steves' Annual Guide to European Railpasses**—your best way to convert chaos into pure travel energy. Buy your railpass from Rick, and you'll get a bunch of free extras to boot.

Travel agents will tell you about mainstream tours of Europe, but they won't tell you about **Rick Steves' tours.** Rick Steves' Europe Through the Back Door travel company offers more than two dozen itineraries and 300 departures reaching the best destinations in this book...and beyond. You'll enjoy the services of a great guide, a fun bunch of travel partners (with group sizes in the twenties), and plenty of room to spread out in a big, comfy bus. You'll find trips to fit every vacation size, from weeklong city getaways to longer cross-country adventures. For details, visit www.ricksteves.com or call 425/771-8303 ext 217.

sleeping in their history and art classes before they knew they were going to Europe, *101* helps Europe's sights come alive. However, this book has far more coverage of the European continent than of Britain.

Rick Steves' Easy Access Europe, geared for travelers with limited mobility, covers London, Paris, Bruges, Amsterdam, and the Rhine River Valley.

Rick Steves' Postcards from Europe, my autobiographical book, packs 25 years of travel anecdotes and insights into the ultimate 2,000-mile European adventure.

My latest book, *Rick Steves' European Christmas,* covers the joys, history, and quirky traditions of the holiday season in seven European regions, including England.

Public Television Show: My series, *Rick Steves' Europe,* keeps churning out shows (more than 60 at last count), including several featuring the sights in this book.

Radio Show: My new weekly radio show, which combines

call-in questions (à la *Car Talk*) and interviews with travel experts, airs on public radio stations. For a schedule of upcoming topics, an archive of past programs, and details on how to call in, see www.ricksteves.com/radio.

Other Guidebooks

If you're like most travelers, this book is all you need. But racks of fine London guidebooks are sold at bookstores throughout London. The *Michelin Green Guide to London,* which is somewhat scholarly, and the more readable Access guide for London, are both well-researched. *Let's Go: London* is youth-oriented, with good coverage of nightlife, hosteling, and cheap transportation deals. London's TIs hand out a useful, free, monthly *London Planner* (includes a listing of sights and lots of London tips). Newsstands sell the excellent weekly entertainment magazine, *Time Out,* which has good maps and a concise and opinionated rundown on sightseeing, shopping, entertainment, and eats (£3, www.timeout.com/london). If you'll be traveling elsewhere in Britain, *Rick Steves' Great Britain 2006* will come in handy.

Recommended Books and Movies

To get the feel of London past and present, check out a few of these books or films:

Nonfiction: *A History of London* (Stephen Inwood), *A Traveller's History of London* (Richard Tames), *London: The Biography* (Peter Ackroyd), *Elizabeth's London: Everyday Life in Elizabethan London* (Liza Picard), *Secret London* (Andrew Duncan), *The Princes in the Tower* (Alison Weir), *Letters from London* (Julian Barnes), *Notes from a Small Island* (Bill Bryson), *84 Charing Cross Road* and *The Duchess of Bloomsbury Street* (both by Helene Hanff), and *My Love Affair with England* (Susan Allen Toth).

Fiction: *Pygmalion* (George Bernard Shaw), *Persuasion* (Jane Austen, partially set in Bath), *Oliver Twist* (Charles Dickens), *London* and *Sarum* (both by Edward Rutherfurd), *In the Presence of the Enemy* (Elizabeth George), *Lucia in London* (E.F. Benson), the *Jeeves & Wooster* series (P.G. Wodehouse), *Murder in Mayfair* (Robert Barnard), *A Study in Scarlet* (Arthur Conan Doyle), and *Bridget Jones's Diary* (Helen Fielding).

Flicks: *Shakespeare in Love; Elizabeth; Royal Wedding; Waterloo Bridge; Howard's End; The End of the Affair; To Sir, with Love; Mary Poppins; Four Weddings and a Funeral; A Man for All Seasons; Anne of a Thousand Days; The Elephant Man; Topsy-Turvy; My Fair Lady; A Little Princess; The Madness of King George; My Beautiful Launderette; Secrets and Lies; Sliding Doors; Alfie* (1966 version); *Plenty; Mrs. Dalloway; A Hard Day's Night; Blow-up; Passport to*

Pimlico; Georgy Girl; An Ideal Husband; 84 Charing Cross Road; Persuasion; A Fish Called Wanda; Notting Hill; Bridget Jones's Diary; Bend It Like Beckham; and *Vanity Fair.*

Maps

The black-and-white maps in this book, drawn by Dave Hoerlein, are concise and simple. Dave, who is well-traveled in London and Britain, has designed the maps to help you quickly orient and painlessly get to where you want to go. Once in London, simply consult the color city map and handy Tube map at the front of this book, and you're ready to travel. For more detail, buy a city map at a London newsstand (the excellent *Bensons Mapguide*, £3, is better than the TI's map and the vending-machine maps sold in Tube stations). Before you buy a map, look at it to make sure it has the level of detail you want.

PRACTICALITIES

Red Tape: You need a passport, but no visa or shots, to travel in Britain. It's a good idea to pack a photocopy of your passport in your luggage in case the original is lost or stolen.

Time: In London—and in this book—you'll use the 24-hour clock. It's the same through 12:00 noon, then keep going: 13:00, 14:00, and so on. For anything over 12, subtract 12 and add p.m. (14:00 is 2:00 p.m.).

Britain is five/eight hours ahead of the East/West Coasts of the U.S., and one hour behind the rest of Europe.

Business Hours: Most stores are open Monday through Saturday from roughly 10:00–18:00, with a late night on Wednesday or Thursday (until 19:00 or 20:00), depending on the neighborhood. On Sunday, when some stores are closed, street markets are lively with shoppers.

Holidays: Bank holidays bring most businesses to a grinding halt on Easter Monday (April 17 in 2006), the first and last Mondays in May (May 1 and 29), and the last Monday in August (Aug 28).

Many businesses, as well as many museums, close on Good Friday (April 14), Easter (April 16), and New Year's Day. On Christmas, virtually everything closes down, even the Tube (taxi rates are high). Museums are also generally closed December 24 and 26; smaller shops are usually closed December 26.

Shopping: Shoppers interested in customs regulations and VAT refunds (the tax refunded on large purchases made by non-EU residents) can refer to the Shopping chapter on page 305.

Discounts: While I don't list discounts (called "concessions" in Britain), nearly all British sights are discounted for seniors (loosely defined as anyone retired or willing to call themselves a "senior"), youths (ages 8–18), students, groups of 10 or more, and families (with 2 full-fare parents, kids go for about half-price).

Watt's Up? If you're bringing electrical gear, you'll need an adapter plug. Britain's plugs have three square-shaped prongs (not the 2 round prongs used by continental Europe). You may also need a converter to deal with the increased voltage. Travel appliances often have convenient, built-in converters; look for a voltage switch marked 120V (U.S.) and 240V (Europe).

News: Americans keep in touch in Europe with the *International Herald Tribune* (published almost daily via satellite). Every Tuesday, the European editions of *Time* and *Newsweek* hit the stands with articles of particular interest to European travelers. Sports addicts can get their fix from *USA Today*. Good Web sites include www.europeantimes.com and http://news.bbc.co.uk.

MONEY

Banking

Bring plastic (ATM, credit, or debit cards) along with several hundred dollars in hard cash as an emergency backup. Traveler's checks are a waste of time and money. Since fees are charged per exchange, and most ATM screens top out at £200, save money by pushing the "other amount" button and asking for a higher amount.

Before you go, verify with your bank that your card will work, inquire about fees (can be up to $5 per transaction), and alert them

Exchange Rate

I list prices in pounds (£) throughout this book.

1 British pound (£1) = about $1.80

While the euro (€) is now the currency of most of Europe, Britain is sticking with its pound sterling. The British pound (£), also called a "quid," is broken into 100 pence (p). Pence means "cents." You'll find coins ranging from 1p to £2 and bills from £5 to £50.

London is so expensive that some travelers try to kid themselves that pounds are dollars. But when they get home, that £1,000-pound Visa bill isn't asking for $1,000...it wants $1,800. To avoid this shock, double British prices to estimate dollars. By overshooting it, you'll spend less...maybe even less than you budgeted (good luck).

Damage Control for Lost or Stolen Cards

If you lose your credit, debit, or ATM card, you can stop people from using your card by reporting the loss immediately to the respective global customer-assistance centers. Call these 24-hour U.S. numbers collect: Visa (tel. 410/581-9994), MasterCard (tel. 636/722-7111), and American Express (tel. 336/393-1111).

Have, at a minimum, the following information ready: the name of the financial institution that issued you the card, along with the type of card (classic, platinum, or whatever). Ideally, plan ahead and pack photocopies of your cards—front and back—to expedite their replacement. Providing the following information will allow for a quicker cancellation of your missing card: full card number, whether you are the primary or secondary cardholder, the cardholder's name exactly as printed on the card, billing address, home phone number, circumstances of the loss or theft, and identification verification (your birthdate, your mother's maiden name, or your Social Security number—memorize this, don't carry a copy). If you are the secondary cardholder, you'll also need to provide the primary cardholder's identification verification details. You can generally receive a temporary card within two or three business days in Europe.

If you promptly report your card lost or stolen, you typically won't be responsible for any unauthorized transactions on your account, although many banks charge a liability fee of $50.

that you'll be making withdrawals in Europe; otherwise, the bank may not approve transactions if it perceives unusual spending patterns. Bring an extra card in case one gets demagnetized or gobbled up by a machine.

Credit (or debit) cards are handy for booking rooms and theater and transportation tickets over the phone, and necessary for renting a car. In general, Visa and Mastercard are far more widely accepted than American Express.

Even in jolly olde England, you should use a money belt (a pouch with a strap that you buckle around your waist like a belt and wear under your clothes). Thieves target tourists. You can carry lots of cash safely in a money belt, and given bank and ATM fees, you should.

Don't be petty about changing money; it's not efficient to visit ATMs and banks frequently to withdraw a minimum amount of cash each time. Change a week's worth of money, get big bills, stuff them in your money belt, and travel!

Tips on Tipping

Tipping in Britain isn't as automatic and generous as it is in the U.S., but for special service, tips are appreciated, if not expected. As in the U.S., the proper amount depends on your resources, tipping philosophy, and the circumstance, but some general guidelines apply.

Restaurants: At pubs where you order at the counter, don't tip. At a pub or restaurant with wait staff, check the menu or your bill to see if the service is included; if not, tip about 10 percent (for details, see page 290).

Taxis: To tip the cabbie, round up. For a typical ride, round up to a maximum of 10 percent (to pay a £4.50 fare, give £5; or for a £28 fare, give £30). If the cabbie hauls your bags and zips you to the airport to help you catch your flight, you might want to toss in a little more. But if you feel like you're being driven in circles or otherwise ripped off, skip the tip.

Special Services: Tour guides at public sites often hold out their hands for tips after they give their spiel. If I've already paid for the tour, I don't tip extra, though some tourists do give a pound, particularly for a job well done. I don't tip at hotels, but if you do, give the porter about 50p for carrying bags and leave a pound in your room at the end of your stay for the maid if the room was kept clean. In general, if someone in the service industry does a super job for you, a tip of a pound or two is appropriate...but not required.

When in doubt, ask. If you're not sure whether (or how much) to tip for a service, ask your hotelier or the tourist information office; they'll fill you in on how it's done on their turf.

TRANSPORTATION

Transportation concerns within London are limited to the Tube (subway), buses, and taxis, all of which are covered in the Orientation chapter. If you have a car, stow it. You don't want to drive in London. If you need convincing, here's one more reason: In order to fight traffic congestion, the London city government charges drivers an £8/day fee to enter central London during peak hours (Mon–Fri 7:00–18:30, no charge Sat–Sun and holidays). Traffic cameras photograph and identify every vehicle that enters the fee-zone; if you get spotted and don't pay up by 22:00 that day, you'll get socked with a £50 penalty. (Pay at public parking lot self-service machines, convenience stores, and gas stations, or online at www.cclondon.com; see Web site for more details.)

Transportation to day-trip destinations is covered in the Day Trips and Transportation Connections chapters.

For all the specifics on transportation throughout Great Britain by train or car, see *Rick Steves' Great Britain 2006.*

COMMUNICATING

Telephones

Smart travelers learn the phone system and use it daily for making hotel/restaurant reservations, verifying hours at sights, and phoning home. London is a big city. Always use the telephone to confirm tour times, book theater tickets, or make reservations at fancy restaurants. If you call before heading out, you'll travel more smoothly.

Types of Phones

You'll encounter various kinds of phones in Britain.

British **public pay phones** are great, easy-to-use, and everywhere. Phones clearly list which coins they'll take (usually from 10p to £1, with a minimum toll of 30p; some new phones even accept euro coins), and a display shows how your money supply's doing. Only completely unused coins will be returned, so put in biggies with caution. (If money's left over, rather than hanging up, push the "make another call" button.) You can also pay for calls on these phones with a major credit card (see "Paying for Calls," below).

The only tricky public payphones you'll use are the expensive, coin-op ones in bars and B&Bs. Some require money before you dial, while others wait until after you're connected. Many have a button you must push before you begin talking. But all have clear instructions.

Hotel room phones are fairly cheap for local calls, but pricey for international calls, unless you use an international phone card (see below).

American mobile phones work in Europe if they're GSM-enabled, tri-band (or quad-band), and on a calling plan that includes international calls. With a T-Mobile phone, you can roam using your home number, and pay $1–2 per minute for making or receiving calls.

Some travelers buy a **European mobile phone** in Europe. For about $125, you can get a phone that will work in most countries once you pick up the necessary chip (about $30) per country. Or you can buy a cheaper, "locked" phone that only works in the country where you purchased it (about $100, includes $20 worth of calls). If you're interested, stop by any European shop that sells mobile phones (such as Vodafone, O2, and Orange); you'll see prominent store window displays. You aren't required to (and shouldn't) buy a monthly contract—buy prepaid calling time instead (as you use it up, buy additional minutes at newsstands or mobile-phone shops). If you're on a budget, skip mobile phones and use phone cards instead.

Some London hotels will lend you a free mobile phone, but you'll pay a 50 cents-a-minute usage fee. Ask your hotel about this if you're interested.

Paying for Calls

You can spend a fortune making phone calls in Britain...but why would you? Here's the skinny on different ways to pay, including the best deals.

You can use a **major credit card** to pay for both domestic and international calls from a public pay phone. Just insert the card into the phone and dial away (minimum charge for a credit-card call is 50p). This is a handy way to make quick calls, but the rates are high, so avoid long chats.

Prepaid **international calling cards** are the cheapest way to make international calls from Britain (for under 20 cents a minute to the U.S.). These and are sold at most newsstands, mini-marts, and exchange bureaus in denominations of £5, £10, and £20.

There are many different brands, so ask the clerk which one has the best rates to wherever you're calling (Unity has a reputation for having the cheapest per-minute rates). Because cards are occasionally duds, avoid the high denominations.

Since you don't insert these cards into the phone, you can use them from anywhere, including your hotel room, avoiding pricey hotel rates. You'll actually get more minutes per card if you call from your hotel rather than phone booths, which come with a hefty surcharge. Make sure, however, that your hotel isn't overcharging you to dial the access number (it's free to dial from phone booths).

To use a card, scratch off the back to reveal your code. After you dial the access phone number, the message tells you to enter your code and then dial the phone number you want to call. (If you have several access numbers listed on your card, you'll save money overall if you choose the one starting with 0800 rather than 0845 or 0870.) To call the U.S., see "How to Dial," on page 16. To make calls within Britain, dial the area code plus the local number; when using an international calling card, the area code must be dialed even if you're calling across the street. These cards work only within the country of purchase (e.g., one bought in Britain won't work in France).

To make numerous, successive calls with an international calling card without having to redial the long access number each time, press the keys (see instructions on card, usually ##) that allow you to launch directly into your next call. Remember that you don't need the actual card to use a card account, so it's sharable. You can write down the access number and PIN (Personal Identification Number) in your notebook and share it with friends.

Dialing direct from your hotel room without using an international calling card is usually quite expensive for international calls. I always ask first how much I'll be charged. Keep in mind that you might have to pay for local and occasionally even toll-free calls.

Receiving calls in your hotel room is often the cheapest way to keep in touch with the folks back home—especially if your family has an inexpensive way to call you (either a good deal on their long-distance plan, or a prepaid calling card with good rates to Europe). Give them a list of your hotels' phone numbers before you go. As you travel, send your family an e-mail or make a quick payphone call to set up a time for them to call you, and then wait for the ring.

U.S. calling cards (such as the ones offered by AT&T, MCI, or Sprint) are the worst option. You'll nearly always save a lot of money by paying with a British phone card.

How to Dial

Calling from the U.S. to Britain, or vice versa, is simple—once you break the code. The European calling chart on page 400 will walk you through it. Remember that British time is five/eight hours ahead of the East/West Coasts of the U.S. and one hour behind the rest of Europe.

Dialing within Britain: Britain, like much of the U.S., uses an area-code dialing system. If you're dialing within an area code, you just dial the local number to be connected; but if you're calling outside your area code, you have to dial both the area code (which starts with a 0) and the local number.

Area codes are listed by city on phone-booth walls or are available from directory assistance (dial 192, free from phone booths). It's most expensive to call within Britain from 8:00–13:00 and cheapest from 17:00–8:00. Still, a short call across the country is inexpensive; don't hesitate to call long distance.

Dialing International Calls: For a listing of country codes, see the appendix. When making an international call to Britain, first dial the international access code of the country you're in (011 from the U.S. or Canada, 00 if you're calling from Europe), then Britain's country code (44), then the area code (without its initial 0) and the local number. For example, London's area code is 020. To call one of my recommended London B&Bs from the U.S., dial 011 (U.S. international access code), 44 (Britain's country code),

Send Me a Postcard, Drop Me a Line

If you enjoy a successful trip with the help of this book and would like to share your discoveries, please fill out the survey at www.ricksteves.com/feedback. I personally read and value all feedback.

20 (London's area code without its initial 0), then 7730-8191 (the B&B's number).

To dial out of Britain, start your call with its international code (00), then dial the country code of the country you're calling, then the number you're calling. To call my office from Britain, I dial 00 (Britain's international access code), 1 (U.S. country code), 425 (Edmonds' area code), then 771-8303.

E-mail and Mail

E-mail: Internet cafés are easy to find in London; for more information, see "Helpful Hints" in the Orientation chapter). Many hotels have a dedicated computer for guests' e-mail needs. Small places are accustomed to letting clients sit at their desk for a few minutes just to check their e-mail, if you ask politely.

Mail: Get stamps at the neighborhood post office, newsstands within fancy hotels, and some mini-marts and card shops. To arrange for mail delivery, reserve a few hotels along your route in advance and give their addresses to friends. Allow 10 days for a letter to arrive. Phoning is so easy that I've dispensed with mail stops altogether.

TRAVELING AS A TEMPORARY LOCAL

We travel all the way to Europe to enjoy differences—to become temporary locals. You'll experience frustrations. There are certain truths that we find God-given and self-evident, such as cold beer, ice in drinks, bottomless cups of coffee, "the customer's always right," easy shower faucets, and driving on the right-hand side of the road. One of the benefits of travel is the eye-opening realization that there are logical, civil, and even better alternatives. A willingness to go local ensures that you'll enjoy a full dose of English hospitality.

If there is a negative aspect to the image the British have of Americans, it is that we are big, aggressive, impolite, rich, loud, superficially friendly, and a bit naive. Americans tend to be noisy in public places, such as restaurants and trains. Our raised voices can demolish Britain's reserved and elegant ambience. Talk softly. While the British look bemusedly at some of our Yankee excesses—and worriedly at others—they nearly always afford us individual travelers all the warmth we deserve.

Judging from all the happy postcards I receive from travelers who have used this book, it's safe to assume you'll enjoy a great, affordable vacation—with the finesse of an independent, experienced traveler. Thanks, and have a brilliant holiday!

BACK DOOR TRAVEL PHILOSOPHY

From *Rick Steves' Europe Through the Back Door*

Travel is intensified living—maximum thrills per minute and one of the last great sources of legal adventure. Travel is freedom. It's recess, and we need it.

Experiencing the real Europe requires catching it by surprise, going casual..."Through the Back Door."

Affording travel is a matter of priorities. (Make do with the old car.) You can travel—simply, safely, and comfortably—anywhere in Europe for $100 a day plus transportation costs (allow more for London). In many ways, spending more money only builds a thicker wall between you and what you came to see. Europe is a cultural carnival, and, time after time, you'll find that its best acts are free and the best seats are the cheap ones.

A tight budget forces you to travel close to the ground, meeting and communicating with the people, not relying on service with a purchased smile. Never sacrifice sleep, nutrition, safety, or cleanliness in the name of budget. Simply enjoy the local-style alternatives to expensive hotels and restaurants.

Extroverts have more fun. If your trip is low on magic moments, kick yourself and make things happen. If you don't enjoy a place, maybe you don't know enough about it. Seek the truth. Recognize tourist traps. Give a culture the benefit of your open mind. See things as different but not better or worse. Any culture has much to share.

Of course, travel, like the world, is a series of hills and valleys. Be fanatically positive and militantly optimistic. If something's not to your liking, change your liking. Travel is addictive. It can make you a happier American as well as a citizen of the world. Our Earth is home to six billion equally important people. It's humbling to travel and find that people don't envy Americans. They like us, but, with all due respect, they wouldn't trade passports.

Globe-trotting destroys ethnocentricity. It helps you understand and appreciate different cultures. Regrettably, there are forces in our society that want you dumbed down for their convenience. Don't let it happen. Thoughtful travel engages you with the world—more important than ever these days. Travel changes people. It broadens perspectives and teaches new ways to measure quality of life. Many travelers toss aside their hometown blinders. Their prized souvenirs are the strands of different cultures they decide to knit into their own character. The world is a cultural yarn shop. And Back Door travelers are weaving the ultimate tapestry. Come on, join in!

ORIENTATION

London is more than 600 square miles of urban jungle. With nine million people—who don't all speak English—it's a world in itself and a barrage on all the senses. On my first visit, I felt extremely small. To grasp London more comfortably, see it as the old town in the city center without the modern, congested sprawl.

The Thames River runs roughly west to east through the city, with most of the visitor's sights on the north bank. Mentally, maybe even physically, trim down your map to include only the area between the Tower of London (to the east), Hyde Park (west), Regent's Park (north), and the Thames (south). (This is roughly the area bordered by the Tube's Circle Line.) This three-mile stretch between the Tower and Hyde Park (about a 90-min walk) looks like a milk bottle on its side (see map on page 21) and holds 80 percent of the sights mentioned in this book.

London is a collection of neighborhoods:

The City: Shakespeare's London was a walled town clustered around St. Paul's Cathedral. Today, "The City" is the modern financial district.

Westminster: This neighborhood includes Big Ben, Parliament, Westminster Abbey, and Buckingham Palace, the grand government buildings from which Britain is ruled.

The West End: Lying between Westminster and The City (that is, at the "west end" of the original walled town), this is the center of London's cultural life. Trafalgar Square has major museums. Piccadilly Circus and Leicester Square host tourist traps, cinemas, and nighttime glitz. Soho and Covent Garden are thriving people-zones housing theaters, restaurants, pubs, and boutiques.

The South Bank: Until recently, the entire south bank of the Thames River was a run-down, generally ignored area, but now it's the hottest real estate in town, with upscale restaurants, major

London's Neighborhoods

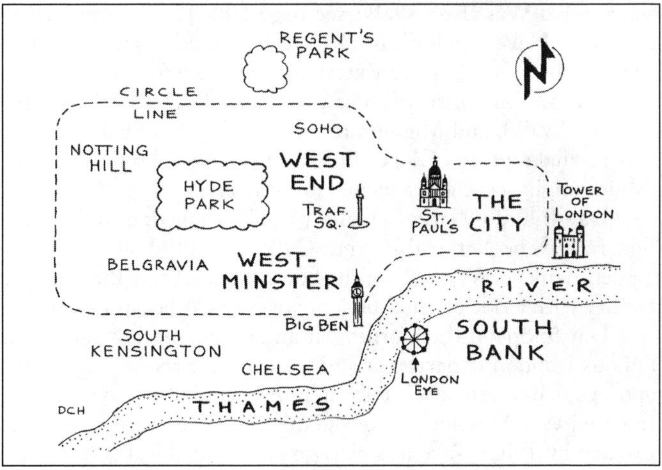

new sightseeing attractions, and pedestrian bridges allowing easy access from the rest of London.

Residential Neighborhoods to the West: Though they lack major tourist sights, the neighborhoods of Mayfair, South Kensington, Notting Hill, Chelsea, and Belgravia are home to the city's wealthy and trendy, as well as many shopping streets and enticing restaurants.

With this focus and a good orientation, you'll get a sampling of London's top sights, history, and cultural entertainment, and a good look at its ever-changing human face.

Planning Your Time

London's a super one-week getaway. Its sights can keep even the most fidgety traveler well entertained for a week. After considering London's major tourist destinations, I've covered just my favorites in this book. You won't be able to see all of these, so don't try. You'll keep coming back to London. After dozens of visits myself, I still enjoy a healthy list of excuses to return.

Here's a suggested schedule:

Day 1: 9:00–Tower of London (Crown Jewels first, then Beefeater tour, then White Tower); 12:30–Munch a sandwich on the Thames while cruising from Tower to Westminster Bridge; 14:00–Tour Westminster Abbey, coffee in the cloisters; 15:30–Follow the self-guided Westminster Walk.

Day 2: 9:00–Take a double-decker hop-on, hop-off London sightseeing bus tour (start at Victoria Street and hop off for the Changing of the Guard); 11:30 at Buckingham Palace (guards change most days, but worth confirming); 13:00–Covent Garden for lunch, shopping, and people-watching (consider following the self-guided West End Walk; see page 118); 15:00–Tour British Museum. Have a pub dinner before a play, concert, or evening walking tour (for ideas, see Entertainment chapter).

Day 3: Tour British Library, St. Paul's Cathedral (following the City Walk), and Museum of London. Enjoy a Shakespearean play at Shakespeare's Globe (19:30). Dive into Soho for London's liveliest night scene and a memorable dinner.

Day 4: 10:00–National Gallery and lunch on or near Trafalgar Square and the National Portrait Gallery; 14:00–Follow the self-guided Bankside Walk along the South Bank of the Thames. Cap the day with a ride on the London Eye Ferris Wheel (open late).

Day 5: Spend the morning at an antique market and visit a famous London department store. In the afternoon, depending upon your interests, choose from Tate Britain, Tate Modern, the Imperial War Museum, or Kew Gardens (cruise to Kew, return to London by Tube). Take in a play, go on a guided walk, or watch a concert tonight.

Day 6: Cruise to Greenwich, tour the town's salty sights, then Tube back to London. With extra time in the afternoon, drop by the Victoria and Albert Museum.

Day 7: For a one-week visit to London, I'd spend a day or two side-tripping. To keep an English focus, head out to Windsor, Cambridge, or Bath for one day. For maximum travel thrills, consider a Paris getaway. With the zippy English Channel train, Paris is three hours away and can even be worth a long day trip. To pull this off, see the Day Trip to Paris chapter.

Arrival in London

By Train: London has eight train stations, all connected by the Tube (subway) and all with exchange offices and luggage storage. From any station, ride the Tube or taxi to your hotel.

By Bus: The bus ("coach") station is one block southwest of Victoria Station, which has a TI and a Tube entrance.

By Plane: For detailed information on getting from London's airports to downtown London, see the Transportation Connections chapter on page 320.

Tourist Information

The Britain and London Visitors Centre, just a block off Piccadilly Circus, is the best tourist information service in town (Mon–Fri 9:00–18:30, Sat–Sun 10:00–16:00, phone not answered after 17:00 Mon–Fri and not at all Sat–Sun, booking service, 1 Lower Regent Street, tel. 020/8846-9000, www.visitbritain.com, www.visitlondon.com). If you're traveling beyond London, take advantage of the Centre's well-equipped England desk. Bring your itinerary and a checklist of questions. At the London desk, pick up these free publications: *London Map and Guide*, *London Planner* (a great free monthly that lists all the sights, events, and hours), walking-tour schedule fliers, a theater guide, *Central London Bus Guide,* and the Thames River Services brochure. After you've grazed through the great leaflet racks, head upstairs for the inviting tables and Internet access (with disk-burning service).

The Britain and London Visitors Centre ("pink desk") sells long-distance bus tickets and passes, train tickets (convenient for reservations), British Heritage Passes (see page 4), and tickets to plays (20 percent booking fee). They also sell **Fast Track tickets** to some of London's attractions (at no extra cost), allowing you to skip the queue at the sights. These can be worthwhile for places that sometimes have long ticket lines, such as the Tower of London, London Eye Ferris Wheel, and Madame Tussaud's Waxworks. While the Visitors Centre books rooms, you can avoid their £5 booking fee by calling hotels direct (see Sleeping chapter).

The **London Pass** provides free entrance to most of the city's sights, but since many museums are free, it's hard to justify the purchase. Still, fervent sightseers can check the list of covered sights and do the arithmetic (£27/1 day, £42/2 days, £52/3 days, £72/6 days, includes 160-page guidebook, tel. 0870-242-9988 for purchase instructions, www.londonpass.com).

Nearby you'll find the **Scottish Tourist Centre** (Mon–Fri 8:00–20:00, Sat 9:00–17:30, Sun 10:00–16:00, Cockspur Street, tel. 0845-225-5121, www.visitscotland.com) and the slick **French National Tourist Office** (Mon–Fri 10:00–18:00, Sat until 17:00, closed Sun, 178 Piccadilly Street, tel. 0906-824-4123).

Unfortunately, **London's Tourist Information Centres** (which present themselves as TIs at major train and bus stations and airports) are now simply businesses selling advertising space to companies with fliers to distribute. For solid information, visit the Britain and London Visitors Centre, mentioned above.

Local bookstores sell London guides and maps; ***Bensons Map Guide*** is the best (£3, also sold at newsstands).

Helpful Hints

Pedestrian Safety: Cars drive on the left side of the road, so before crossing a street, I always look right, look left, then look right again just to be sure.

Medical Problems: Local hospitals have 24-hour-a-day emergency care centers where any tourist who needs help can drop in and, after a wait, be seen by a doctor. The quality is good and the price is right (free). Your hotel has details. St. Thomas' Hospital, immediately across the river from Big Ben, has a fine reputation.

Daily Reminder

Sunday: Some sights don't open until noon. The Tower of London and British Museum are both especially crowded today. Hyde Park Speakers' Corner rants from early afternoon until early evening. These places are closed: Banqueting House, Sir John Soane's Museum, and legal sights (Houses of Parliament, City Hall, and Old Bailey; the neighborhood called The City is dead). Evensong is at 15:00 at Westminster Abbey (plus free organ recital at 17:45) and 15:15 at St. Paul's (plus free organ recital at 17:00); both churches are open during the day for worship but closed to sightseers. Many stores are closed. There are no plays on Sunday as actors take a day off. Street markets flourish: Camden Lock, Spitalfields, Greenwich, and Petticoat Lane.

Monday: Virtually all sights are open except for Apsley House, the Theatre Museum, Sir John Soane's Museum, and a few others. The St. Martin-in-the-Fields church offers a free 13:00 concert. At Somerset House, the Courtauld Gallery is free until 14:00. Vinopolis is open until 21:00. Houses of Parliament are usually open until 22:30.

Tuesday: All sights are open; the British Library is open until 20:00. St. Martin-in-the-Fields has a free 13:00 concert. On the first Tuesday of the month, St. John Soane's Museum is also open 18:00–21:00.

Wednesday: All sights are open, plus evening hours at Westminster Abbey (until 19:00, but no evensong), the

Theft Alert: The Artful Dodger is alive and well in London. Be on guard, particularly on public transportation and in places crowded with tourists. Tourists, considered naive and rich, are targeted. More than 7,500 handbags are stolen annually at Covent Garden alone.

U.S. Embassy: It's at 24 Grosvenor Square (for passport concerns, open Mon–Fri 8:30–17:30, closed Sat–Sun, Tube: Bond Street, tel. 020/7499-9000).

Changing Money: ATMs are the way to go. While regular banks charge several pounds to change traveler's checks, American Express offices offer a fair rate and will change any brand of traveler's checks for no fee. Handy AmEx offices are at Heathrow's Terminal 4 Tube station (daily 7:00–19:00) and near Piccadilly (Mon–Sat 9:00–18:00, Sun 10:00–17:00, 30 Haymarket, tel. 020/7484-9610; refund office 24-hr tel. 0800-521-313). Marks & Spencer department stores give good rates with no fees.

Avoid changing money at exchange bureaus. Their latest

National Gallery (until 21:00), and Victoria and Albert Museum (until 22:00).

Thursday: All sights are open, British Museum until 20:30 (selected galleries), National Portrait Gallery until 21:00. St. Martin-in-the-Fields hosts a 19:30 evening concert (for a fee).

Friday: All sights are open, British Museum until 20:30 (selected galleries only), National Portrait Gallery until 21:00, Vinopolis until 21:00, Tate Modern and Saatchi Gallery until 22:00. Best street market: Spitalfields. St. Martin-in-the-Fields offers two concerts (13:00-free, 19:30-fee).

Saturday: Most sights are open except legal ones (Old Bailey, City Hall, Houses of Parliament—open summer Sat for tours only; skip The City). Vinopolis is open until 21:00, Tate Modern and Saatchi Gallery until 22:00. Best street markets: Portobello, Camden Lock, Greenwich. Evensong is at 15:00 at Westminster Abbey, 17:00 at St. Paul's. St. Martin-in-the-Fields hosts a concert at 19:30 (fee).

Notes: Evensong occurs daily at St. Paul's (Mon–Sat at 17:00 and Sun at 15:15) and daily except Wednesday at Westminster Abbey (Mon–Tue and Thu–Fri at 17:00, Sat–Sun at 15:00). London by Night Sightseeing Tour buses leave from Victoria Station every evening at 19:30 and 21:30. The London Eye Ferris Wheel spins nightly until 21:00, until 22:00 in summer, until 20:00 in winter (closed Jan).

scam: They advertise very good rates with a same-as-the-banks fee of 2 percent. But the fine print explains that the fee of 2 percent is for buying pounds. The fee for selling pounds is 9.5 percent. Ouch!

Internet Access: The **easyInternetcafé** chain offers up to 500 computers per store and is open long hours daily. Depending on the time of day, a £2 ticket buys anywhere from 80 minutes to six hours of computer time. The ticket is valid for four weeks and multiple visits at any of their branches: Trafalgar Square (456 Strand), Tottenham Court Road (#9–16), Oxford Street (#358, opposite Bond Street Tube station), and Kensington High Street (#160–166). They also sell 24-hour, seven-day, and 30-day passes (www.easyinternetcafe.com). **Access Printers**, across the street from Victoria Station (next to the Apollo Victoria Theatre), has plenty of terminals (£1/30 min, open long hours daily).

Travel Bookstores: Stanfords Travel Bookstore, in Covent Garden, is good and stocks current editions of my books

Tips for Tackling the Self-Guided Tours in this Book

Sightseeing can be hard work. The self-guided tours in this book are designed to help make your visits to London's finest museums meaningful, fun, fast, and painless.

Hours of sights can change without warning. Pick up the latest listing of museum hours at a TI. Don't put off visiting a must-see sight—you never know when a place will close unexpectedly for a holiday, strike, or restoration.

To get the most out of the self-guided tours, read the tour the night before your visit. When you arrive at the sight, use the overview map to get the lay of the land and the basic tour route. Expect a few changes—paintings can be on tour, on loan, out sick, or shifted at the whim of the curator. To adapt, pick up any available free floor plans as you enter, ask an information person to glance at this book's maps to confirm they're current, or if you can't find a particular painting, just ask any museum worker. If the person doesn't recognize the title, show the photograph in this book.

The self-guided tours cover the highlights at sights. You might want to supplement with an audioguide (sometimes free, generally about £2, usually provides excellent recorded descriptions of the art), or a guided tour (about £3 or more). The quality of a tour depends on the guide's knowledge and enthusiasm.

Museums have their rules; if you're aware of them in advance, they're no big deal. Keep in mind that many sights have "last entry" times 30–60 minutes before closing. Guards usher people out before the official closing time.

Cameras are normally allowed, but no flashes or tripods (without special permission). Flashes damage oil paintings and distract others in the room. Even without a flash, a handheld camera will take a decent picture (or buy postcards or posters at the museum bookstore). Video cameras are usually allowed.

For security reasons, you're often required to check even small bags. Many museums have a free checkroom at the entrance. They're safe. If you have something you can't bear to part with, be prepared to stash it in a pocket or purse.

At the museum bookshop, thumb through the biggest guidebook (or scan its index) to be sure you haven't overlooked something that is of particular interest to you. If there's an on-site cafeteria, it's usually a good place to rest and have a snack or light meal. Museum WCs are free and generally clean.

And finally, every sight or museum offers infinitely more than the few stops we cover. Use these tours as an introduction—not the final word.

(Mon–Fri 9:00–19:30, Sat 10:00–19:00, Sun 12:00–18:00, 12 Long Acre, Tube: Covent Garden, tel. 020/7836-1321). Two impressive Waterstone's bookstores have the biggest collection of travel guides in town: on Piccadilly (Mon–Sat 10:00–22:00, Sun 12:00–18:00, 203 Piccadilly, tel. 020/7851-2400) and on Trafalgar Square (Mon–Sat 9:30–21:00, Sun 12:00–18:00, next to Costa Café, tel. 020/7839-4411).

Left Luggage: As security concerns heighten, train stations have replaced their lockers with left-luggage counters. Each bag must go through a scanner (just like at the airport), so lines can be long. Expect a wait to pick up your bags, too (each item-£6/24 hrs, daily 7:00–24:00). You can also check bags at the airports (£5/day). If leaving London and returning later, you may be able to leave a box or bag at your hotel for free—assuming you'll be staying there again.

Time Zone Difference: Britain is one hour earlier than most of continental Europe.

Getting Around London

To travel smart in a city this size, you must get comfortable with public transportation. London's excellent taxis, buses, and subway system make a private car unnecessary. In fact, the "congestion charge" of £8 levied on any private car entering the city center has been effective in cutting down traffic jam delays and bolstering London's public transit. The revenue raised subsidizes the buses, which are now cheaper, more frequent, and even more user-friendly than before. Today, the vast majority of vehicles in the city center are buses, taxis, and service trucks. (Drivers, for all the details on the congestion charge, see page 30 and www.cclondon.com.)

By Taxi

London is the best taxi town in Europe. Big, black, carefully regulated cabs are everywhere. I've never met a crabby cabbie in London. They love to talk, and they know every nook and cranny in town. I ride in one each day just to get my London questions answered. Rides start at £2.20. Connecting downtown sights is quick and easy and will cost you about £5 (for example, St. Paul's to the Tower of London). For a short ride, three people in a cab travel at Tube prices. Groups of four or five should taxi everywhere. While telephoning a cab will get you one in a few minutes, it's generally not necessary; hailing a cab is easy and costs less. If a cab's top light is on, just wave it down. (Drivers flash lights when they see you.) They have a tiny turning radius, so you can wave at cabs going in either direction. If waving doesn't work, ask someone where you can find a taxi stand.

London for Early Birds and Night Owls

Most sightseeing in London is restricted to the hours between 10:00 and 18:00. Here are a few exceptions:

Sights Open Early

British Library: Mon–Sat at 9:30.

Buckingham Palace: Aug–Sept daily at 9:30.

Churchill Museum and Cabinet War Rooms: April–Sept daily at 9:30.

Hampton Court Palace: Tue–Sun at 9:30.

Houses of Parliament: Fri at 9:30.

Kew Gardens: Daily at 9:30.

London Eye Ferris Wheel: Daily at 9:30.

Madame Tussaud's Waxworks: Sat–Sun at 9:30.

Shakespeare's Globe: Mid-May–Sept exhibition opens at 9:00, tours start at 9:30.

Southwark Cathedral: Mon–Fri at 8:00, Sat–Sun at 9:00.

St. Paul's Cathedral: Mon–Sat at 8:30.

Tower of London: Mon–Sat at 9:00 (Tue–Sat in winter).

Westminster Abbey: Mon–Sat at 9:30.

Westminster Cathedral: Daily at 9:30.

Sights Open Late

British Library: Tue until 20:00.

British Museum (some galleries): Thu–Fri until 20:30.

Houses of Parliament (when in session): Mon until 22:30, Tue–Thu until 19:30.

London Eye Ferris Wheel: Daily until 21:00 (22:00 in July–Aug, 20:00 in winter).

National Gallery: Wed until 21:00.

National Portrait Gallery: Thu–Fri until 21:00.

Saatchi Gallery: Mon–Thu until 20:00, Fri–Sat until 22:00.

Sir John Soane's Museum: First Tue of month until 21:00.

Tate Modern: Fri–Sat until 22:00.

Victoria and Albert Museum: Wed and last Fri of month until 22:00.

Vinopolis: Mon and Fri–Sat until 21:00.

Don't worry about meter cheating. British cab meters come with a sealed computer chip and clock that ensures you'll get the regular tariff #1 most of the time, tariff #2 during "unsociable hours" (18:00–6:00 and Sat–Sun), and tariff #3 only on holidays. (Rates only go up about 10 percent with each higher tariff.) All extra charges are explained in writing on the cab wall. The only way a cabbie can cheat you is to take a needlessly long route. Another pitfall is taking a cab when traffic is bad to a destination efficiently served by the Tube. On my last trip to London, I hopped in a taxi at South Kensington for Waterloo Station and hit bad traffic. Rather than spending 20 minutes and £2 on the Tube, I spent 40 minutes and £16 in a taxi.

Tip a cabbie by rounding up (maximum 10 percent). If you over-drink and ride in a taxi, be warned: Taxis charge £40 for "soiling" (a.k.a., pub puke).

By Bus

Riding city buses doesn't come naturally to many travelers, but if you make a point to figure out the system, you'll swing like Tarzan through the urban jungle of London. Pick up the free *Central London Bus Guide* at a transport office or TI for a fine map listing all the bus routes best for sightseeing.

The first step in mastering the bus system is learning how to decipher the bus-stop signs. Find a bus stop and study the signs mounted on the pole next to the stop. You'll see a chart listing (alphabetically) the destinations served by buses that pick up at this spot or nearby; the names of the buses; and alphabet letters that identify exactly where the buses pick up. After locating your destination, remember or write down the bus name and bus stop letter. Next, refer to the neighborhood map (also on the pole) to find your bus stop. Just match your letter with a stop on the map. Make your way to that stop—you'll know it's yours because it will have the same letter on its pole—and wait for the bus with the right name to arrive. Some fancy stops have electric boards indicating the minutes until the next bus arrives; but remember to check the name on the bus before you hop on. Crack the code and you're good to go.

On most buses, you'll pay at a machine at the bus stop (exact change only), then show your ticket (or Tube pass) as you board. On other buses, you can pay the conductor (take a seat, and he'll come and collect £1.20). Any ride in downtown London costs £1.20. A ticket six-pack costs £6 and an all-day bus pass costs £3. If you're staying longer, consider the £8 all-week bus pass. The best views are upstairs.

If you have a Travelcard (see below), get in the habit of hopping buses for quick little straight shots, even just to get to a Tube

Handy Buses

Since the institution of London's "congestion charge" for cars, the bus system is faster, easier, and cheaper than ever. Tube-oriented travelers need to make a point to get over their tunnel vision, learn the bus system, and get around fast and easy.

Here are some of the most useful routes:

Route #9: Harrods to Hyde Park Corner to Piccadilly Circus to Trafalgar Square.

Routes #11 and #24: Victoria Station to Westminster Abbey to Trafalgar Square (#11 continues to St. Paul's).

Route #RV1: Tower of London to Tower Bridge to Tate Modern/Shakespeare's Globe to London Eye/Waterloo Station/County Hall Travel Inn accommodations to Trafalgar Square to Covent Garden (a scenic joyride).

Route #15: Paddington Station to Oxford Circus to Regent Street/TI to Piccadilly Circus to Trafalgar Square to Fleet Street to St. Paul's to Tower of London.

Route #188: Waterloo Station/London Eye to Covent Garden to British Museum.

In addition, several buses (including #6, #12, #13, #15, #23, #139, and #159) make the corridor run from Trafalgar, Piccadilly Circus, and Oxford Circus to Marble Arch.

stop. During bump-and-grind rush hours (8:00–10:00 and 16:00–19:00), you'll go faster by Tube.

By Tube

London's subway system (called the Tube or Underground, but never "subway") is one of this planet's great people-movers and the fastest—and cheapest—long-distance transport in town (runs Mon–Sat about 5:00–24:00, Sun about 7:00–23:00).

Survey a Tube map. At the front of this book, you'll find a complete Tube map with color-coded lines and names. You can also pick up a free Tube map at any station. Each line has a name (such

Handy Bus Routes

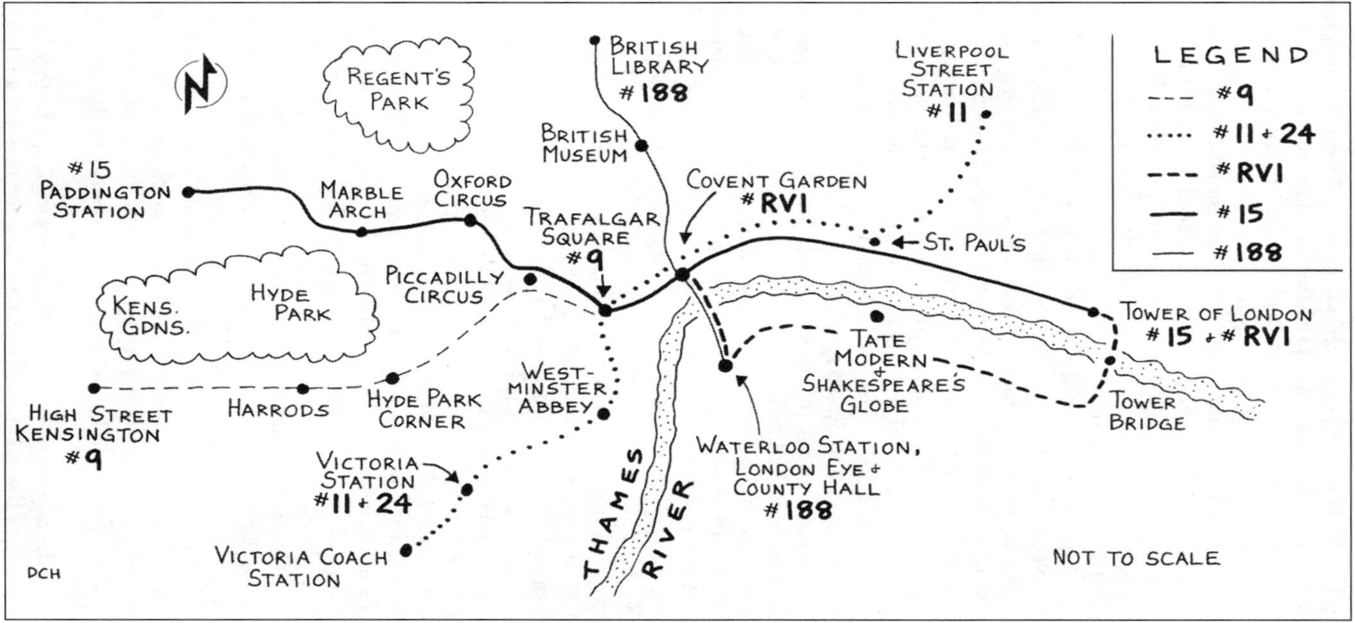

as Circle, Northern, or Bakerloo) and two directions (indicated by the end-of-the-line stop). Find the line that will take you to your destination, and figure out roughly what direction (north, south, east, west) you'll need to go to get there.

In the Tube station, feed your ticket into the turnstile, reclaim it, and hang onto the ticket—you'll need it to get through the turnstile at the end of your journey. Find your train by following signs to your line and the (general) direction it's headed (such as Central Line: east).

Since some tracks are shared by several lines, you'll need to double-check before boarding a train: First, make sure your destination is one of the stops listed on the sign at the platform. Also, check the electronic signboards that announce which train is next, and make sure the destination (the end-of-the-line stop) is the one you want. Some trains, particularly on the Circle and District lines, split off for other directions, but each train has its final destination marked above its windshield. When in doubt, ask a local or a blue-vested staff person for help.

Trains run roughly every three to 10 minutes. If one train is absolutely packed and you notice another to the same destination is coming in three minutes, you can wait to avoid the sardine experience. The system can be fraught with construction delays and breakdowns, so pay attention to signs and announcements explaining necessary detours. The Circle Line is notorious for problems. Rush hours (8:00–10:00 and 16:00–19:00) can be packed and sweaty. Bring something to do to make your waiting time productive. If you get confused, ask for advice at the information window located before the turnstile entry.

You can't leave the system without feeding your ticket to the turnstile. Hang on to your ticket. (The turnstile will either eat your now-expired single-trip ticket, or spit your still-valid pass back out.) Save walking time by choosing the best street exit—check the maps on the walls or ask any station personnel. "Subway" means "pedestrian underpass" in "English." For Tube and bus information, visit www.tfl.gov.uk (and check out the journey planner). And always...mind the gap.

Cost: Any ride in Zone 1 (on or within the Circle Line, including virtually all my recommended sights and hotels) costs £2. Tube tickets are also valid on city buses.

You can avoid ticket-window lines in Tube stations by buying tickets from coin-op or credit-card machines; practice on the punchboard to see how the system works (hit "Adult Single" and your destination). These tickets are valid only on the day of purchase.

The fare for most rides in the center is £2. Go farther, and you owe more. Beware: Overshooting your zone nets you a £10 fine.

If you want to travel a little each day or if you're part of a group, a £17 **Carnet** (CAR-nay) saves £3: You get 10 separate tickets for Tube travel in Zone 1, paying £1.70 per ride rather than £2. Wait for the machine to lay all 10 tickets.

London Tube and Bus Passes: Consider using the following passes, valid on both the Tube and buses. Note that all passes can be purchased as easily as a normal ticket at any Tube station, can get you a 30 percent discount on most Thames cruises (details online at www.tfl.gov.uk, look under "Tickets and Oyster"), and come in a pricier all-zone version.

If you figure you'll take three rides in a day—and many travelers do—a day pass is a good deal. The **One-Day Travelcard,** covering Zones 1 and 2, gives you unlimited travel for a day. The regular price is £6, but an "Off-Peak" version is only £4.70; it's good for travel starting after 9:30 on weekdays and anytime on weekends. A One-Day Travelcard for Zones 1 through 6, which includes Heathrow Airport, costs £12; the restricted "Off-Peak" version (good for travel after 9:30 on weekdays and all day on weekends and holidays) costs £6. Families save with the One-Day Family Travelcard (good for 1–2 adults and 1–4 children, price varies depending on number in family and number of zones).

The **Three-Day Travelcard,** covering Zones 1 and 2 for £15, costs 20 percent less than three "Peak" One-Day Travelcards and is good any time of day. Most travelers staying three days will easily take enough Tube and bus rides to make this worthwhile.

The **7-Day Travelcard** costs £21.40 and covers Zones 1 and 2.

Groups of 10 or more can travel all day on the Tube for £3.70 each (but not on buses).

You'll likely see signs advertising the **Oyster Card,** designed for commuters (or tourists staying a week or more). The prepaid, rechargeable pass is good for Tube and/or bus trips, depending on what version you buy. You'll pay a £3 deposit to use the card (refundable at any Tube station ticket office). For specifics, visit www.oystercard.com.

Tours of London

▲▲▲Hop-on, Hop-off Double-Decker Bus Tours—Two competitive companies (Original and Big Bus) offer essentially the same tours with buses that have either live (English-only) guides or a tape-recorded, dial-a-language narration. This two-hour, once-over-lightly bus tour drives by all the famous sights, providing a stress-free way to get your bearings and at least see the biggies. You can sit back and enjoy the entire two-hour orientation tour (a good idea if you like the guide and the weather), or hop on and hop off at any of the nearly 30 stops and catch a later bus. Buses run about every 10–15 minutes in summer, every 20 minutes in winter.

It's an inexpensive form of transport as well as an informative tour. Buses operate daily (from about 9:00 until early evening in summer, until late afternoon in winter) and stop at Victoria Station, Marble Arch, Piccadilly Circus, Trafalgar Square, and elsewhere.

Both Original and Big Bus offer a core two-hour overview tour, two other routes, and a narrated Thames boat tour covered by the same ticket (buy ticket from driver, credit cards accepted at major stops such as Victoria Station, ticket good for 24 hours, bring a sweater and a camera). Big Bus tours are a little better but more expensive (£20), while Original tours are cheaper (£13.50 with this book) and nearly as good. Pick up a map from any flier rack or from one of the countless salespeople and study the complex system. Note: If you start at Victoria Station at 9:00, you'll finish near Buckingham Palace in time to see the Changing of the Guard at 11:30; ask your driver for the best place to hop off. Sunday morning—when the traffic is light and many museums are closed—is a fine time for a tour. The last full loop leaves Victoria at 17:00. Both companies have entertaining as well as boring guides. The narration is important. If you don't like your guide, jump off and find another. If you like your guide, settle in for the entire loop. Unless you're using the bus tour mainly for hop-on, hop-off transportation, consider saving money with a night tour (described below).

Original London Sightseeing Bus Tour: Live-guided buses have a Union Jack flag and a yellow triangle on the front of the bus. If the front has many flags or a green or red triangle, it's a tape-recorded multilingual tour—avoid it, unless you have kids who'd enjoy the entertaining recorded kids' tour (£16, £2.50 discount with this book, limit 2 discounts per book, they'll rip off the corner of this page—raise bloody hell if they don't honor this discount, ticket good for 24 hours, tel. 020/8877-1722, www.theoriginaltour.com). Your ticket includes a 50-minute round-trip boat tour from Westminster Pier (departs hourly, tape-recorded narration) or a point-to-point boat trip from Embankment Pier to Greenwich, with stops in between (14 departures per day).

Big Bus Hop-on, Hop-off London Tours: For £20 (£18 if you book online), you get the same basic tour plus coupons for several silly one-hour London walks and the scenic and usually entertainingly guided Thames boat ride (normally £5.60) between Westminster Pier and the Tower of London. The pass and extras are valid for 24 hours. Buses with live guides are marked in front with a picture of a red bus; buses with tape-recorded spiels display a picture of a blue bus and headphones. These pricier tours tend to have better, more dynamic guides than Original (daily 8:30–18:00, winter until 16:30, from Victoria Station, tel. 020/7233-9533, www.bigbus.co.uk).

At Night: The London by Night Sightseeing Tour runs basically the same circuit as the other companies, but after hours, with none of the extras (e.g., walks, boat tours), and for half the price. While the narration can be pretty lame, the views at twilight are grand (£9, pay driver or buy tickets at Victoria Station or Paddington Station TI, April–Sept only, 2-hour tour with live guide, normally departs 19:30–21:30 every half hour from Victoria Station, live guides at 19:30, 20:30, and 21:30, Taxi Road, at front of station near end of Wilton Road, tel. 020/8646-1747, www.london-by-night.net). Munch a scenic picnic dinner from the top deck for a memorable and economical evening.

▲▲Walking Tours—Several times a day, top-notch local guides lead (often big) groups through specific slices of London's past. Schedule fliers litter the desks of TIs, hotels, and pubs. *Time Out* lists many, but not all, scheduled walks. Simply show up at the announced location, pay £5.50, and enjoy two chatty hours of Dickens, the Plague, Shakespeare, Legal London, the Beatles, Jack the Ripper, or whatever is on the agenda. Original London Walks, the dominant company, lists its extensive daily schedule in a beefy, plain, black-and-white *The Original London Walks* brochure (walks offered year-round—even Christmas, private tours for £95, tel. 020/7624-3978, for a recorded listing of today's walks call 020/7624-9255, www.walks.com). They also run **Explorer day trips,** a good option for those with limited time and transportation (different trip daily: Stonehenge/Salisbury, Oxford/Cotswolds, York, Bath, and so on).

The Beatles: Fans of the still–Fabulous Four can take one of the Beatles walks (Original London Walks, above, has 5/week; Big Bus, above, has a daily walk included with their bus tour), visit the Beatles Shop (daily, 231 Baker Street, next to Sherlock Holmes Museum, Tube: Baker Street, tel. 020/7935-4464), or go to Abbey Road and walk the famous crosswalk (at intersection with Grove End, Tube: St. John's Wood).

Private Guides—Standard rates for London's registered guides are £100 for four hours, £159 for eight hours (tel. 020/7403-2962, www.touristguides.org.uk, www.blue-badge.org.uk). Robina Brown leads tours of small groups in her Toyota Previa (£220/half-day, £320–400/day, tel. 020/7228-2238, www.driverguidetours.com, robina@driverguidetours.com). Janine Barton provides a similar driver-and-guide tour and similar prices (tel. 020/7402-4600, jbsiis@aol.com) and offers a 15 percent discount to readers of this book. Robina and Janine's services are particularly helpful for wheelchair-bound travelers who want to see more of London. Brit Lonsdale, an energetic mother of twins, is another registered London guide (£100/half-day, £159/day, tel. 020/7386-9907, brittl@ntlworld.com).

London Duck Tours—A bright-yellow amphibious WWII-vintage vehicle (the model that landed troops on Normandy's beaches on D-Day) takes a gang of 30 tourists past some famous sights on land—Big Ben, Trafalgar Square, Piccadilly Circus—then splashes into the Thames for a cruise (£18, 2/hr, daily 10:00–17:30, 75 min—45 min on land and 30 min in the river, these book up in advance, departs from Chicheley Street—you'll see the big ugly vehicle parked 100 yards behind London Eye Ferris Wheel, Tube: Waterloo or Westminster, tel. 020/7928-3132, www.londonducktours.co.uk). All-in-all, it's good fun at a rather steep price; the live guide works hard and it's kid-friendly to the point of goofiness.

▲▲Cruises—Boat tours with entertaining commentaries sail regularly from many points along the Thames. It's confusing, since there are several companies offering essentially the same thing. Your basic options are downstream (to the Tower and Greenwich), upstream (to Kew Gardens and Hampton Court), and round-trip scenic tour cruises. Most people depart from the Westminster Pier (at the base of Westminster Bridge under Big Ben). You can catch most of the same boats (with less waiting) from Waterloo Pier at the London Eye Ferris Wheel across the river. For pleasure and efficiency, consider combining a one-way cruise (to Kew, Greenwich, or wherever) with a Tube ride back. While Tube and bus tickets don't work on the boats, a Travelcard can snare you a 33 percent discount on most cruises (just show the card when you pay for the cruise). Children and seniors get discounts. You can purchase drinks and scant, pricey snacks on board. Buy boat tickets at the small ticket offices on the docks. Clever budget travelers pack a small picnic and munch while they cruise.

Here are some of the most popular cruise options:

To the Tower of London: City Cruises boats sail 30 minutes to the Tower from Westminster Pier (£5.60 one-way, £6.80 round-trip, one-way included with Big Bus London tour; covered by £9 "River Red Rover" ticket that includes Greenwich—see next paragraph; 3/hr during June–Aug daily 9:40–20:40, 2/hr and shorter hours rest of year).

To Greenwich: Two companies head to Greenwich from Westminster Pier. Choose between **City Cruises** (£6.80 one-way, £8.60 round-trip; or get their £9 all-day, hop-on, hop-off "River Red Rover" ticket to have option of getting off at London Eye and Tower of London; June–Aug daily 10:00–17:00, less off-season, every 40 min, 70 min to Greenwich, usually narrated

Thames Boat Piers

While Westminster Pier is the most popular, it's not the only dock in town. Consider all the options:

Westminster Pier, at the base of Big Ben, offers round-trip sightseeing cruises and lots of departures in both directions.

Waterloo Pier, at the base of London Eye Ferris Wheel, is a good, less-crowded alternative to Westminster, with many of the same cruise options.

Embankment Pier is near Covent Garden, Trafalgar Square, and Cleopatra's Needle (the obelisk on the Thames). You can take a round-trip cruise from here, or catch a boat to the Tower of London and Greenwich.

Tower Millennium Pier is at the Tower of London. Boats sail west to Westminster Pier or east to Greenwich.

Bankside Pier (near Tate Modern and Shakespeare's Globe) and **Millbank Pier** (near Tate Britain) are connected to each other by the "Tate to Tate" ferry service.

only downstream—to Greenwich, tel. 020/7740-0400, www.citycruises.com) and **Thames River Services** (£6.80 one-way, £8.60 round-trip, April–Oct daily 10:00–16:00, July–Aug until 17:00, has shorter hours and runs every 40 min rest of year, 2/hr, 50 min, usually narrated only to Greenwich, tel. 020/7930-4097, www.westminsterpier.co.uk).

To Kew Gardens: Westminster Passenger Services Association leaves for Kew Gardens from Westminster Pier (£11 one-way, £17 round-trip, 4/day, generally departing 10:30–14:00, 90 min, narrated for 45 min, tel. 020/7930-2062, www.wpsa.co.uk). Some boats continue on to **Hampton Court Palace** for an additional £3 (and 90 min). Because of the river current, you'll save 30 minutes cruising from Hampton Court back into town.

Round-Trip Cruises: Fifty-minute round-trip cruises of the Thames go hourly from Westminster Pier to the Tower of London (£8, included with Original London Bus tour—listed above, tape-recorded narration, Catamaran Circular Cruises, tel. 020/7987-1185). The London Eye Ferris Wheel operates its own "River Cruise Experience," offering a similar 40-minute live-guided circular tour from Waterloo Pier (£10, £21 with Ferris Wheel, reservations recommended, departures generally :45 past hour, tel. 0870-443-9185, www.ba-londoneye.com).

From Tate to Tate: This boat service for art-lovers connects the Tate Modern and Tate Britain in 18 scenic minutes, stopping at the London Eye Ferris Wheel en route (£4 one-way or £7 for a day ticket; with a Travelcard it's £2.70-one-way/£4.50-day ticket; buy ticket at gallery desk or on board, departing every 40 min from 10:00–17:00, tel. 020/7887-8008).

On Regent's Canal: Consider exploring London's canals by taking a cruise on historic Regent's Canal in north London. The good ship *Jenny Wren* offers 90-minute guided canal boat cruises from Walker's Quay in Camden Town through scenic Regent's Park to Little Venice (£7, March–Oct daily 12:30 and 14:30, Sat–Sun also at 16:30, Walker's Quay, 250 Camden High Street, 3-min walk from Tube: Camden Town, tel. 020/7485-6210, www.walkersquay.com). While in Camden Town, stop by the popular, punky Camden Lock Market to browse through trendy arts and crafts (daily 10:00–18:00, busiest on weekends, a block from Walker's Quay).

SIGHTS

These sights are arranged by neighborhood for handy sightseeing. When you see a ✪ in a listing, it means the sight is covered in much more depth in a self-guided walk or in one of the museum tours.

From Westminster Abbey to Trafalgar Square

✪ These sights are linked by the Westminster Walk on page 74.

▲▲▲Westminster Abbey—The greatest church in the English-speaking world, Westminster Abbey is the place where England's kings and queens have been crowned and buried since 1066. Like a stony refugee camp huddled outside St. Peter's Pearly Gates, this place has a story to tell. You can take a tour (live or audioguide), experience an evensong service (at 17:00 Mon–Tue and Thu–Fri, and at 15:00 on Sat–Sun), listen to a free organ concert (Sun at 17:45), visit several small museums, and even have coffee in the cloister... but you can't take photos (£8, Mon–Fri 9:30–15:45, Wed until 19:00, Sat 9:30–13:45, last admission 60 min before closing, closed Sun to sightseers but open for services, Tube: Westminster or St. James's Park, tel. 020/7222-7110, www.westminster-abbey.org).

✪ See Westminster Abbey Tour on page 215.

▲▲Houses of Parliament (Palace of Westminster)—This neo-Gothic icon of London, the royal residence from 1042 to 1547, is now the meeting place of the legislative branch of government. Tourists are welcome to view debates in either the bickering House of Commons or the genteel House of Lords (in session when a flag flies atop the Victoria Tower). While the actual debates are generally quite dull, it is a thrill to be inside and see the British government inaction (both Houses usually open Mon 14:30–22:30, Tue–Thu 11:30–19:30, Fri 9:30–15:00, closed Sat–Sun, generally less action and no lines after 18:00, use St. Stephen's entrance,

Westminster Abbey to Trafalgar Square

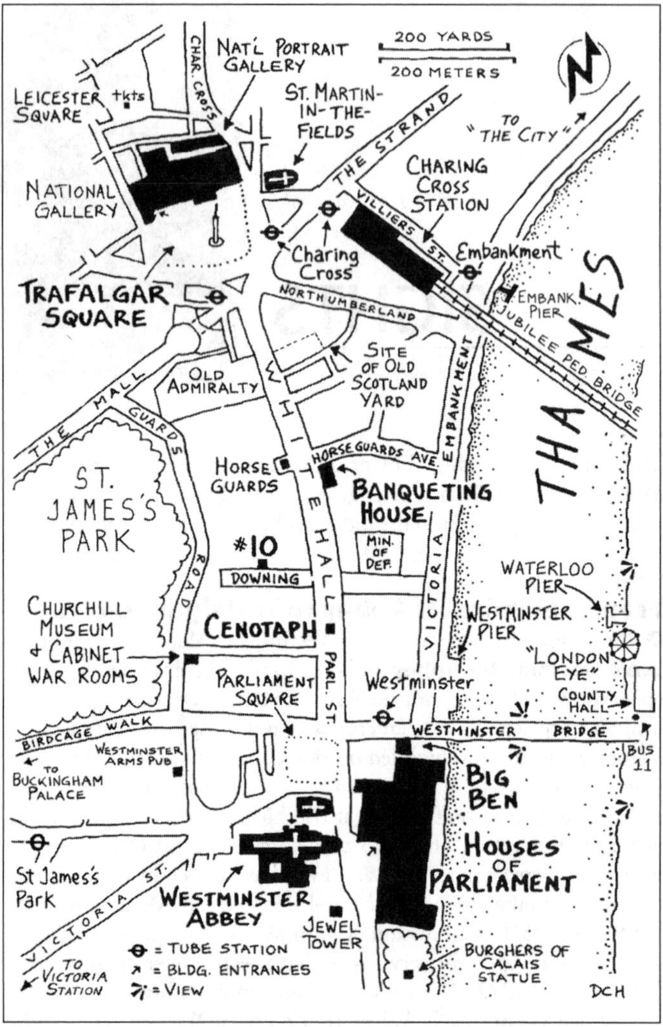

Tube: Westminster, tel. 020/7219-4272 ; see www.parliament.uk for schedule). The House of Lords has more pageantry, shorter lines, and less interesting debates (tel. 020/7219-3107 for schedule, and visit www.parliamentlive.tv for a preview). If there's only one line outside, it's for the House of Commons. Go to the gate and tell the guard you want the Lords (that's the 2nd "line" with no people in it; it just takes a few minutes and both are worth seeing). You may pop right in—that is, after you've cleared the security gauntlet. Once you've seen the Lords (hide your HOL flier), you can often slip directly over to the House of Commons and join the gang waiting in the lobby. Inside the lobby, you'll find an announcement board with the day's lineup for both houses.

Just past security to the left, study the big dark **Westminster Hall,** which survived the 1834 fire. The hall was built in the 11th century and its famous self-supporting hammer-beam roof was added in 1397. The Houses of Parliament are located in what was once the Palace of Westminster, long the palace of England's medieval kings, until it was largely destroyed by fire in 1834. The palace was rebuilt in the Victorian Gothic style (a move away from neoclassicism back to England's Christian and medieval heritage, true to the romantic age). It was completed in 1860.

Houses of Parliament tours are offered in August and September (£7, 75 min; roughly Mon, Tue, Fri, and Sat 9:15–16:30; Wed and Thu 13:15–16:30; to avoid waits, book in advance through First Call, tel. 0870-906-3773, www.firstcalltickets.com, no booking fee). Meet your Blue Badge guide (at the Sovereign's Entrance—far south end) for a behind-the-scenes peek at the royal chambers and both Houses.

The **Jewel Tower** is the only other part of the old Palace of Westminster to survive (besides Westminster Hall). It contains a fine little exhibit on Parliament (1st floor—history, 2nd floor—Parliament today) with a 25-minute video and lonely, picnic-friendly benches (£2, April–Sept daily 10:00–17:00, across street from St. Stephen's Gate, tel. 020/7222-2219).

Big Ben, the clock tower (315 feet high), is named for its 13-ton bell, Ben. The light above the clock is lit when the House of Commons is sitting. The face of the clock is huge—you can actually see the minute hand moving. For a good view of it, walk halfway over Westminster Bridge.

▲▲▲Churchill Museum and Cabinet War Rooms—This is a fascinating walk through the underground headquarters of the British government's fight against the Nazis in the darkest days of the Battle for Britain. The 27-room nerve center of the British war effort was used from 1939 to 1945. Churchill's room, the map room, and other rooms are just as they were in 1945. For all the blood, sweat, toil, and tears details, pick up the excellent and

included audioguide at the entry and follow the 60-minute tour; be patient—it's well worth it. Don't bypass the new Churchill Museum (entrance is a half-dozen rooms into the exhibit), giving a human look at the man behind the famous cigar, bowler hat, and V-for-victory sign. It

London at a Glance

▲▲▲**British Museum** The world's greatest collection of artifacts of Western civilization, including the Rosetta Stone and the Parthenon's Elgin Marbles. **Hours:** Daily 10:00–17:30, Thu–Fri until 20:30 but only a few galleries open after 17:30.

▲▲▲**National Gallery** Remarkable collection of European paintings (1250–1900), including Leonardo, Botticelli, Velázquez, Rembrandt, Turner, van Gogh, and the Impressionists. **Hours:** Daily 10:00–18:00, Wed until 21:00.

▲▲▲**British Library** Impressive collection of the most important literary treasures of the Western world, from the Magna Carta to Handel's *Messiah*. **Hours:** Mon–Fri 9:30–18:00, Tue until 20:00, Sat 9:30–17:00, Sun 11:00–17:00.

▲▲▲**Westminster Abbey** Britain's finest church and the site of royal coronations and burials since 1066. **Hours:** Mon–Fri 9:30–15:45, Wed also until 19:00, Sat 9:30–13:45, closed Sun to sightseers but open for services.

▲▲▲**St. Paul's Cathedral** The main cathedral of the Anglican Church, designed by Christopher Wren, with a climbable dome and daily evensong services. **Hours:** Mon–Sat 8:30–16:30, closed Sun except for worship.

▲▲▲**Tower of London** Historic castle, palace, and prison, today housing the crown jewels and a witty band of Beefeaters. **Hours:** March–Oct Tue–Sat 9:00–18:00, Sun–Mon 10:00–18:00; Nov–Feb Tue–Sat 9:00–17:00, Sun–Mon 10:00–17:00.

▲▲▲**London Eye Ferris Wheel** Enormous observation wheel, dominating—and offering commanding views over—London's skyline. **Hours:** April–mid-Sept daily 9:30–21:00, until 22:00 in July–Aug, mid-Sept–March 9:30–20:00, closed Jan.

▲▲▲**Tate Modern** Works by Monet, Matisse, Dalí, Picasso, and Warhol displayed in a converted powerhouse. **Hours:** Daily 10:00–18:00, Fri–Sat until 22:00.

▲▲▲**Churchill Museum and Cabinet War Rooms** Underground WWII headquarters of Churchill's war effort. **Hours:** Daily April–Sept 9:30–18:00, Oct–March 10:00–18:00.

▲▲**Tate Britain** Collection of British painting from the 16th century through modern times, including works by William Blake, the Pre-Raphaelites, and J.M.W. Turner. **Hours:** Daily 10:00–17:50.

▲▲**Houses of Parliament** London's famous neo-Gothic landmark, topped by Big Ben and occupied by the Houses of Lords and Commons. **Hours** (both Houses): Generally Mon 14:30–22:30, Tue–Thu 11:30–19:30, Fri 9:30–15:00.

▲▲**Imperial War Museum** Examines the military history of the bloody 20th century. **Hours:** Daily 10:00–18:00.

▲▲**National Portrait Gallery** *Who's Who* of British history, featuring portraits of this nation's most important historical figures. **Hours:** Daily 10:00–18:00, Thu–Fri until 21:00.

▲▲**Buckingham Palace** Britain's royal residence with the famous Changing of the Guard. **Hours:** Palace—Aug–Sept only, daily 9:30–17:00; Guard—almost daily in summer at 11:30, every other day all year long.

▲▲**Shakespeare's Globe** Timbered, thatched-roofed reconstruction of the Bard's original wooden "O." **Hours:** Mid-May–Sept exhibition open daily 9:00–18:00, tours go on the half-hour from 9:30, generally until 12:30, until 11:30 on Sun, 17:30 on Mon; Oct–mid-May exhibition open daily 10:00–17:00 with 30-min tours on the half-hour. Plays are also held here; see page 315.

▲▲**Victoria and Albert Museum** The best collection of decorative arts anywhere. **Hours:** Daily 10:00–17:45, Wed and last Fri of the month until 22:00 except mid-Dec–mid-Jan.

▲▲**Somerset House** Grand 18th-century civic palace housing three fine-art museums: Courtauld Gallery (decent painting collection), Hermitage Rooms (rotating exhibits from famous St. Petersburg museum), and the Gilbert Collection (decorative arts). **Hours:** Daily 10:00–18:00.

▲▲**Old Operating Theatre Museum** 19th-century hall where surgeons performed amputations for an audience of aspiring med students. **Hours:** Daily 10:30–17:00.

▲▲**Vinopolis: City of Wine** Offers a breezy history of wine with plenty of tasting opportunities. **Hours:** Daily 12:00–18:00, Fri–Sat and Mon until 21:00.

Winston Churchill
(1874–1965)

As the 20th century dawned, 25-year-old Winston Churchill became famous. Working as a newspaper reporter embedded with British troops in South Africa, his train was attacked by Boers. Churchill was captured and held as a P.O.W. Meanwhile back home, the London papers were praising the young man's heroism for saving fellow train passengers. After two weeks, Churchill escaped from the Boer camp—he slipped through a bathroom window, scaled a wall, walked nonchalantly through an enemy town, hopped a freight train, and was smuggled out of the country. He emerged to find himself famous.

Churchill entered politics. He first followed in his father's (Lord Randolph Churchill) Conservative Party footsteps, but his desire for social reform drove him to switch to the Liberal Party. (He would later flip-flop back to Conservative.) For three decades, Churchill held numerous government posts, serving as Chancellor of This, Undersecretary of That, and Minister of The Other. He earned praise for prison reform and for developing new-fangled airplanes for warfare; he was criticized for heavy-handedly crushing strikes and bungling the pacification of Iraq. During World War I, he took a break from politics to personally command British troops on the Western Front.

In 1929, Churchill-the-career-bureaucrat retired from politics. He wrote books *(History of the English Speaking Peoples)* and spoke out about the growing threat of fascist Germany. When World War II broke out, Prime Minister Chamberlain's appeasement policies were discredited, and—on the day when Germany invaded the Netherlands—the king appointed Churchill as prime minister. Churchill guided the nation through its darkest hour (see "The Blitz," page 231). His greatest contribution may have been his stirring radio speeches that galvanized the will of the British people.

shows his wit, irascibility, work ethic, American ties, writing talents, and drinking habits. A long touch-the-screen timeline lets you zero in on events in his life from birth (November 30, 1874) to his election as Prime Minister in 1940. It's all the more amazing considering that, in the 1930s, the man who became my vote for greatest statesman of the 20th century was considered a washed-up loony ranting about the growing threat of fascism (£10, daily 9:30–18:00, last entry 60 min before closing, on King Charles Street, 200 yards off Whitehall, follow the signs, Tube: Westminster, tel. 020/7930-6961, www.iwm.org.uk). The shop is great for anyone nostalgic for the 1940s.

If you're hungry, get your rations at the Switch Room café (in the museum) or, for a nearby pub lunch, try the Westminster Arms (food served downstairs, on Storeys Gate, a couple of blocks south of War Rooms).

Horse Guards—The Horse Guards change daily at 11:00 (10:00 on Sun), and there's a colorful dismounting ceremony daily at 16:00. The rest of the day, they just stand there—terrible for camcorders (on Whitehall, between Trafalgar Square and #10 Downing Street, Tube: Westminster). While Buckingham Palace pageantry is canceled when it rains, the horse guards change regardless of the weather.

▲Banqueting House—England's first Renaissance building was designed by Inigo Jones around 1620. It's one of the few London landmarks spared by the 1698 fire and the only surviving part of the original Palace of Whitehall. Don't miss its Rubens ceiling, which, at Charles I's request, drove home the doctrine of the legitimacy of the divine right of kings. In 1649—divine right ignored—Charles I was beheaded on the balcony of this building by a Cromwellian Parliament. Admission includes a restful 20-minute audiovisual history, which shows the place in banqueting action; a 30-minute audio tour—interesting only to history buffs; and a look at the exquisite banqueting hall (£4, Mon–Sat 10:00–17:00, closed Sun, last entry at 16:30, subject to closure for government functions, aristocratic WC, immediately across Whitehall from the Horse Guards, Tube: Westminster, tel. 020/7930-4179). Just up the street is Trafalgar Square.

Trafalgar Square

▲▲Trafalgar Square—London's recently renovated central square, the climax of most marches and demonstrations, is a thrilling place to simply hang out. Lord Nelson stands atop his 185-foot-tall fluted granite column, gazing out to Trafalgar, where he lost his life but defeated the French fleet. Part of this 1842 memorial is made from his victims' melted-down cannons. He's surrounded by giant lions, hordes of people, and—until recently—even more pigeons. London's mayor, Ken Livingstone, nicknamed "Red Ken" for his passion for an activist government, decided that London's "flying rats" were a public nuisance and evicted the venerable seed salesmen (Tube: Charing Cross).

▲▲▲National Gallery—Displaying Britain's top collection of European paintings from 1250 to 1900—including works by Leonardo, Botticelli, Velázquez, Rembrandt, Turner, van Gogh, and the Impressionists—this is one of Europe's great galleries. While the collection is huge, following the route suggested on the map on page 148 will give you my best quick visit. The audioguide tour (suggested £4 donation) is one of the best I've used in Europe (free admission,

Affording London's Sights

London is, in many ways, Europe's most expensive city, with lots of pricey sights but—fortunately—lots of freebies, too.

Many of the city's biggest and best museums won't cost you a dime. Free sights include the British Museum, British Library, National Gallery, National Portrait Gallery, Tate Britain, Tate Modern, Wallace Collection, Imperial War Museum, Victoria and Albert Museum, Natural History Museum, Science Museum, National Army Museum, Sir John Soane's Museum, Theatre Museum, the Museum of London, and on the outskirts of town, the Royal Air Force Museum London.

Some museums, such as the British Museum, request a £2–3 donation, but whether you contribute or not is up to you. Many offer essential audioguides for around £3. If I spend the money on an audioguide, I don't feel bad about not donating otherwise.

Other freebies to consider: You can get into the Tower of London by attending the Ceremony of the Keys (which requires a reservation made long in advance—see page 63). You can view the legal action at Old Bailey and the legislature at work in the Houses of Parliament. There are plenty of free concerts, such as the lunch concerts at St. Martin-in-the-Fields. You can also enjoy the pageantry of Changing of the Guard and the wild people-watching scene at Covent Garden.

Smaller churches let worshippers in free (even tourist worshippers), having given up on asking for donations. The big sightseeing churches—Westminster Abbey and St. Paul's—charge £8 for admission, but offer free evensong services virtually daily and a free organ recital on Sunday.

When budgeting your sightseeing money, consider the £5.50 city walking tours as one of the best deals going. The hop-on, hop-off big-bus tours (£16–20), while expensive, provide a great overview, and include boat tours as well as city walks, depending on the company you choose (see page 33). A one-hour Thames ride costs about £7, but generally comes with an entertaining commentary (see page 36).

daily 10:00–18:00, Wed until 21:00, free 1-hour overview tours daily at 11:30 and 14:30 plus Wed at 18:30, photography prohibited, on Trafalgar Square, Tube: Charing Cross or Leicester Square, tel. 020/7839-3321, www.nationalgallery.org.uk).

✪ See National Gallery Tour, page 145.

▲▲National Portrait Gallery—Put off by halls of 19th-century characters who meant

The queen charges big time to open her palace to the public: Buckingham Palace (£14, open Aug–Sept only) and her art gallery and carriage museum (adjacent to the palace, about £7 each) are interesting but expensive. While Kensington Palace (£11) and Hampton Court Palace (£12) are pricey, they are well-presented and a reasonable value if you have a real interest in royal history. Anyone visiting both the Tower of London and Hampton Court Palace saves £6.50 by getting the £20 combo-ticket.

Gimmicky private enterprises can charge sky-high prices, such as the London Dungeon (£14) and the fun, popular, and overpriced Madame Tussaud's Waxworks (£23, but £14 after 17:00). The two privately run £9 museums (Dalí Universe and Saatchi Gallery), which capitalize on their location next to the popular London Eye Ferris Wheel, are both bad values.

Big-ticket sights worth their admission fees are Kew Gardens (£8.50), Shakespeare's Globe Theatre (£9, includes a tour), and the Cabinet War Rooms, with its fine new Churchill Exhibit (£10). The London Eye Ferris Wheel is an unforgettable experience (£12.50), and Vinopolis wine museum provides a classy way to get a buzz and call it museum-going (£12.50 entry includes 5 small glasses of wine).

Many classy smaller museums cost around £5. My favorites include the three Somerset House museums (Courtauld Gallery, Heritage Rooms, and the Gilbert Collection) and the Wellington Museum at Apsley House.

Seek out the freestanding "tkts" booth at Leicester Square to get discounted tickets to London's famous shows. Theater tickets are sold for that day only, and the booth tacks on a £2.50 service charge. But it's still a good deal, offering discounts from 25 to 50 percent (see page 314).

These days, London doesn't come cheap. But with its many free museums and affordable plays, this cosmopolitan, cultured city offers days of sightseeing thrills without requiring you to pinch your pennies (or your pounds).

nothing to me, I used to call this "as interesting as someone else's yearbook." But a selective walk through this 500-year-long *Who's Who* of British history is quick and free, putting faces on the story of England.

Some highlights: Henry VIII and wives; portraits of the "Virgin Queen" Elizabeth I, Sir Francis Drake, and Sir Walter Raleigh; the only real-life portrait of William Shakespeare; Oliver Cromwell and Charles I with his head on; portraits by Gainsborough and Reynolds; the Romantics (William Blake, Lord Byron, William Wordsworth, and company); Queen Victoria and her era; and the present royal family, including the late Princess Diana.

The collection is well-described, not huge, and in historical sequence, from the 16th century on the second floor to today's royal family on the ground floor (free, daily 10:00–18:00, Thu–Fri until 21:00, excellent audioguide, entry 100 yards off Trafalgar Square, around corner from National Gallery, opposite Church of St. Martin-in-the-Fields, Tube: Charing Cross or Leicester Square, tel. 020/7306-0055, www.npg.org.uk).

✪ See National Portrait Gallery Tour, page 164.

▲St. Martin-in-the-Fields—This church, built in the 1720s with a Gothic spire atop a Greek-type temple, is an oasis of peace on the wild and noisy Trafalgar Square (free, donations welcome, open daily, Tube: Charing Cross, www.smitf.com). St. Martin cared for the poor. "In the fields" was where the first church stood on this spot (in the 13th century), between Westminster and the City. Stepping inside, you still feel a compassion for the needs of the people in this community. A free flier provides a brief yet worthwhile self-guided tour. The church is famous for its concerts. Consider a free lunchtime concert (Mon, Tue, and Fri at 13:00) or an evening concert (£8–18, at 19:30 Thu–Sat and on some Tue and Wed, box office tel. 020/7839-8362, church tel. 020/7766-1100). Downstairs, you'll find a ticket office for concerts, a gift shop, a brass-rubbing center, and a fine support-the-church cafeteria (see page 291 of Eating chapter).

Piccadilly, Soho, and Covent Garden

▲▲Piccadilly Circus—London's most touristy square got its name from the fancy ruffled shirts—*picadils*—made in the neighborhood long ago. Today, the square, while pretty grotty, is surrounded by fascinating streets swimming with youth on the rampage. For over-stimulation, drop by the extremely trashy **Pepsi Trocadero Center's** "theme park of the future" for its Segaworld virtual-reality games, nine-screen cinema, and thundering IMAX theater (admission to Trocadero is free; individual attractions cost £2–8; before paying full price for IMAX, look for a discount ticket at brochure racks at the TI or hotels; located between Coventry and Shaftesbury, just off Piccadilly, Tube: Piccadilly Circus). Chinatown, to the east, has swollen since the British colony of Hong Kong gained its independence and was returned to China in 1997. Nearby Shaftesbury Avenue and Leicester Square teem with fun-seekers, theaters, Chinese restaurants, and street singers.

Soho—North of Piccadilly, seedy Soho is becoming trendy and is well worth a gawk (see the West End Walk, page 118). But Soho is also London's red light district, where "friendly models" wait in tiny rooms up dreary stairways and voluptuous con artists sell

Piccadilly, Soho, and Covent Garden

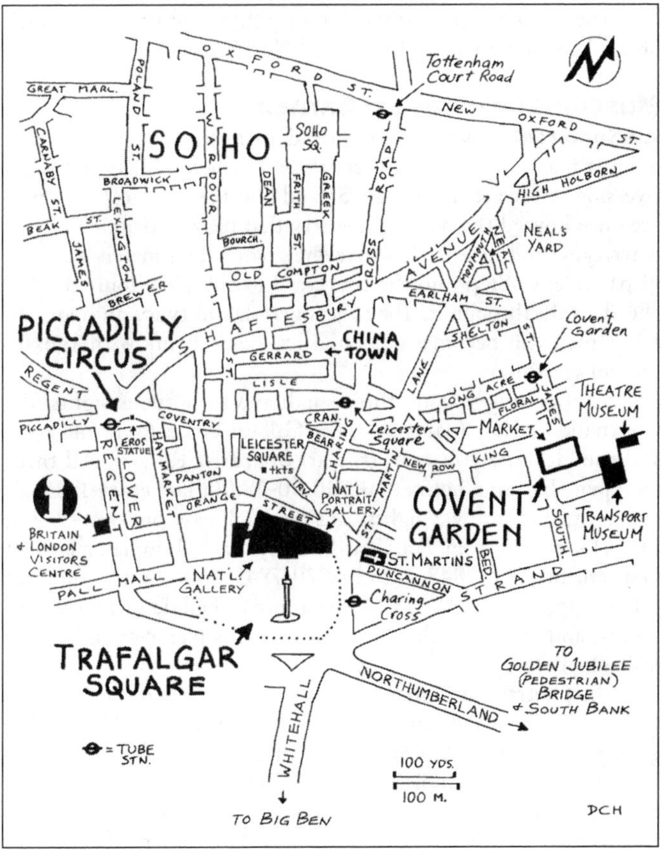

strip shows. While venturing up a stairway to check out a model is interesting, anyone who goes into any one of the shows will be ripped off. Every time. Even a £5 show in a "licensed bar" comes with a £100 cover or minimum (as it's printed on the drink menu) and a "security man." You may accidentally buy a £200 bottle of bubbly. And suddenly, the door has no handle.

Telephone sex is hard to avoid these days in London. Phone booths are littered with racy fliers of busty ladies "new in town." Some travelers gather six or eight phone booths' worth of fliers and take them home for kinky wallpaper.

▲▲Covent Garden—This boutique-ish shopping district is a people-watcher's delight, with cigarette eaters, Punch-and-Judy acts, food that's good for you (but not your wallet), trendy crafts, sweet whiffs of marijuana, two-tone hair (neither natural), and faces that could set off a metal detector (Tube: Covent Garden).

For better Covent Garden lunch deals, walk a block or two away from the eye of this touristic hurricane (check out the places north of the Tube station along Endell and Neal Streets).

Museums near Covent Garden

▲▲**Somerset House**—This grand 18th-century civic palace offers a marvelous public space, three fine art collections, and a riverside terrace (between the Strand and the Thames). The palace once housed the national registry that records Britain's births, marriages, and deaths: "...where they hatch 'em, match 'em, and dispatch 'em." Step into the courtyard to enjoy the fountain. Go ahead...walk through it. The 55 jets get playful twice an hour. (In the winter, this becomes a popular ice-skating rink with a toasty café for viewing.)

Surrounding you are three small and sumptuous sights: the Courtauld Gallery (paintings), the Gilbert Collection (fine arts), and the Hermitage Rooms (the art of czarist Russia). All three are open the same hours (daily 10:00–18:00, last entry 17:15, £5 per sight, £8 for any 2 sights, £12 for all 3, easy bus #6, #9, #11, #13, #15, or #23 from Trafalgar Square, Tube: Temple or Covent Garden, tel. 020/7848-2526 or 020/7845-4600, www.somerset-house.org.uk). The Web site lists a busy schedule of tours, kids' events, and concerts. The riverside terrace is picnic-friendly (deli inside lobby).

The **Courtauld Gallery** is less impressive than the National Gallery, but its wonderful collection of paintings is still a joy. The gallery is part of the Courtauld Institute of Art, and the thoughtful description of each piece of art reminds visitors that the gallery is still used for teaching. You'll see medieval European paintings and works by Rubens, the Impressionists (Manet, Monet, and Degas), Post-Impressionists (such as Cézanne), and more (£5, free Mon until 14:00, downstairs cafeteria, lockers, and WC).

✪ See Courtauld Gallery Tour, page 247.

The **Hermitage Rooms** offer a taste of Romanov imperial splendor. As Russia struggles and tourists are staying away, someone had the bright idea of sending the best of its art to London to raise some hard cash. These five rooms host a different collection every six months, with a standard intro to the czar's winter palace in St. Petersburg (£5, tel. 020/7420-9410). To see what's on, visit www.somerset-house.org.uk/attractions/hermitage.

The **Gilbert Collection** displays 800 pieces of the finest in European decorative arts, from diamond-studded gold snuffboxes to intricate Italian mosaics. Maybe you've seen Raphael paintings and Botticelli frescoes...but this lush collection is refreshingly different (£5, includes free audioguide with a highlights tour and a helpful loaner magnifying glass).

▲London Transport Museum—This wonderful museum is a delight for kids. Whether you're cursing or marveling at the buses and Tube, the growth of Europe's biggest city has been made possible by its public transit system. Watch the growth of the Tube, then sit in the simulator to "drive" a train (£6, kids under 16 free, Sat–Thu 10:00–18:00, Fri 11:00–18:00, in southeast corner of Covent Garden courtyard, Tube: Covent Garden, tel. 020/7379-6344 or recorded info 020/7565-7299).

Theatre Museum—This earnest museum traces British theater from Shakespeare to today (free, Tue–Sun 10:00–18:00, closed Mon, free guided tours at 12:00 and 14:00, a block east of Covent Garden's marketplace down Russell Street, Tube: Covent Garden, tel. 020/7943-4700, www.theatremuseum.org.uk).

✪ See Theatre Museum Tour, page 252.

North London

▲▲▲British Museum—Simply put, this is the greatest chronicle of civilization...anywhere. A visit here is like taking a long hike through Encyclopedia Britannica National Park. The most popular sections of the museum fill the ground floor: Egyptian, Assyrian, and ancient Greek, with the famous Elgin Marbles from the Athenian Parthenon.

While the vast British Museum wraps around its Great Court (the huge entrance hall), its centerpiece is the stately Reading Room, famous as the place where Karl Marx hung out while formulating his ideas on communism and writing *Das Kapital* (free, £3 donation requested, daily 10:00–17:30, Thu–Fri until 20:30—but only a few galleries open after 17:30, tours offered nearly hourly, least crowded weekday late afternoons, Great Russell Street, Tube: Tottenham Court Road, tel. 020/7323-8000 or recorded information 020/7388-2227, www.thebritishmuseum.ac.uk).

✪ See British Museum Tour, page 122.

▲▲▲British Library—Here, in one great room, are the literary treasures of Western civilization, from early Bibles to the Magna Carta to Shakespeare's *Hamlet* to Lewis Carroll's *Alice's Adventures in Wonderland*. You'll see the Lindisfarne Gospels transcribed on an illuminated manuscript, as well as Beatles' lyrics scrawled on the back of a greeting card. The British Empire built its greatest monuments out of paper. And it's with literature that England made her lasting contribution to civilization and the arts (free, Mon–Fri 9:30–18:00, Tue until 20:00, Sat 9:30–17:00, Sun 11:00–17:00; 60-min tours for £6 usually offered Mon, Wed, and Fri–Sun at 15:00, Sat 10:30, and Sun 11:30; call 020/7412-7332 to confirm schedule and reserve; for £3.50 audioguide, leave photo ID or £20 deposit; Tube: King's Cross, turn right out of station and walk a block to 96 Euston Road, library tel. 020/7412-7000, www.bl.uk).

North London

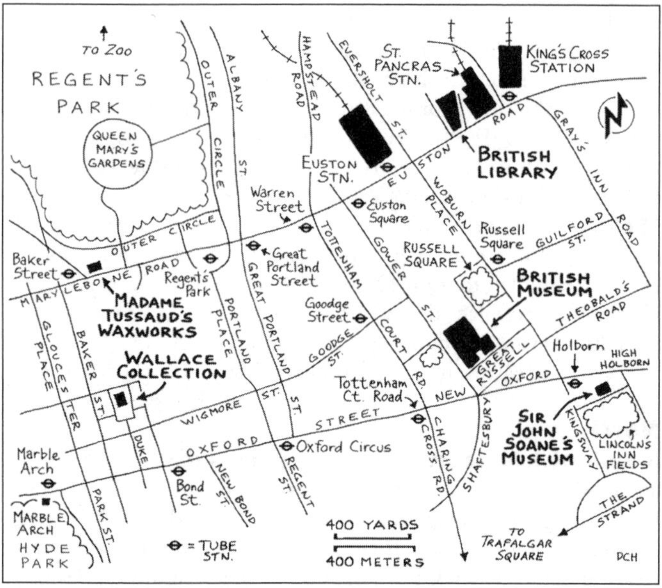

✪ See British Library Tour, page 205.

▲Wallace Collection—Sir Richard Wallace's fine collection of 17th-century Dutch Masters, 18th-century French Rococo, medieval armor, and assorted aristocratic fancies fills the sumptuously furnished Hertford House on Manchester Square. From the rough and intimate Dutch life-scapes of Jan Steen to the pink-cheeked Rococo fantasies of François Boucher, a wander through this little-visited mansion makes you nostalgic for the days of empire (free, Mon–Sat 10:00–17:00, Sun 12:00–17:00, audioguide-£3, just north of Oxford Street on Manchester Square, Tube: Bond Street, tel. 020/7563-9500, www.wallacecollection.org).

▲Madame Tussaud's Waxworks—This is gimmicky and expensive but dang good. The original Madame Tussaud did wax casts of heads lopped off during the French Revolution (such as Marie Antoinette's). She took her show on the road and ended up in London. And now it's much easier to be featured. The gallery is one big *Who's Who* photo-op—a huge hit with the kind of travelers who skip the British Museum. After looking a hundred famous people in their glassy eyes and surviving a silly hall of horror, you'll board

a Disney-type ride and cruise through a kid-pleasing "Spirit of London" time trip. Your last stop is the auditorium for a 15-minute stage show. They've dumped anything really historical (except for what they claim is the blade that beheaded Marie Antoinette) because "there's no money in it and we're a business." Now, it's all about squeezing Brad Pitt's bum, wining and dining with George Clooney, and partying with Beyoncé, Kylie, Britney, and Posh (admission varies with time but about £23, kids-£19; after 17:00 it's £14, kids-£9; children under 5 always free; Mon–Fri 10:00–18:30, Sat–Sun 9:30–18:30, last entry 60 min before closing, Marylebone Road, Tube: Baker Street). The waxworks are popular. Avoid a wait by either booking ahead to get a ticket with an entry time (tel. 0870-400-3000, online at www.madame-tussauds.com for a £2 fee, or at no extra cost at the Britain and London Visitors Centre or the TIs at Victoria and Waterloo train stations) or arriving at 17:00 (avoiding any lines and saving £9 on admission—90 min is plenty of time for the exhibit).

Sir John Soane's Museum—Architects and fans of eclectic knickknacks love this quirky place, as do Martha Stewarts and lovers of Back Door sights. Tour this furnished home on a bird-chirping square and see 19th-century chairs, lamps, and carpets, wood-paneled nooks and crannies, and stained-glass skylights. The townhouse is cluttered with Soane's (and his wife's) collection of ancient relics, curios, and famous paintings, including Hogarth's series on *The Rake's Progress* (read the fun plot) and several excellent Canalettos. In 1833, just before his death, Soane established his house as a museum, stipulating that it be kept as nearly as possible in the state he left it. If he visited today, he'd be entirely satisfied. You'll leave wishing you'd known the man (free, Tue–Sat 10:00–17:00, 1st Tue of the month also 18:00–21:00, closed Sun–Mon, good £1 brochure, £3 guided tours Sat at 14:30, quarter-mile southeast of British Museum, Tube: Holborn, 13 Lincoln's Inn Fields, tel. 020/7405-2107).

Buckingham Palace

▲Buckingham Palace—This lavish home has been Britain's royal residence since 1837. When the queen's at home, the royal standard flies (a red, yellow, and blue flag); otherwise the Union Jack flaps in the wind. Recently, the queen has opened her palace to the public—but only in August and September when she's out of town (£14 for state apartments and throne room, Aug–Sept daily 9:30–18:50, only 8,000 visitors a day—to get an entry time, come early or for £1 extra you can book ahead by phone or online, Tube: Victoria, tel. 020/7766-7300, www.royalcollection.org.uk).

▲Queen's Gallery at Buckingham Palace—Queen Elizabeth's 7,000 paintings make up the finest private art collection in the world, rivaling Europe's biggest national art galleries. It's actually a collection of collections, built on by each successive monarch since the 16th century. She rotates her paintings, enjoying some privately in her many palatial residences while sharing others with her subjects in public galleries in Edinburgh and London. Small, thoughtfully presented, and always exquisite displays fill the handful of rooms open to the public in a wing of Buckingham Palace. As you're in "the most important building in London," security is tight. You'll see a temporary exhibit and the permanent "treasures"—which come with a room full of "antique and personal jewelry." Compared to the crown jewels at the Tower, it may be Her Majesty's bottom drawer—but it's still a dazzling pile of diamonds. Temporary exhibits change about twice a year and are always lovingly described with the included audioguides. While the admissions come with an entry time, this is only enforced during rare days when crowds are a problem (£7.50, £11.50 with Royal Mews, daily 10:00–17:30, last entry 60 min before closing, Tube: Victoria, tel. 020/7766-7301 but Her Majesty rarely answers). Men shouldn't miss the mahogany-trimmed urinals.

Royal Mews—The queen's working stables, or "mews," are open to visitors. The visit is likely to be disappointing (you'll see 2 horses out of the queen's 30, a fancy car, and a bunch of old carriages) unless you follow the included guided tour, in which case it's thoroughly entertaining—especially if you're interested in horses and/or royalty. The 45-minute tours go twice an hour and finish with the Gold State Coach (c. 1760, 4 tons, 4 mph). Queen Victoria said absolutely no cars. When she died, in 1901, the mews got its first Daimler. Today, along with the hay-eating transport, the stable is home to five Rolls-Royce Phantoms (£6, Aug–Sept Sat–Thu 10:00–17:00, March–July and Oct Sat–Thu 11:00–16:00, closed Fri, closed Nov-Feb, Buckingham Palace Road, Tube: Victoria, tel. 020/7766-7302).

▲▲Changing of the Guard at Buckingham Palace—The guards change with much fanfare at around 11:30 almost daily in the summer and, at a minimum, every other day all year long (no band when wet). Each month it's either daily or on odd or even days. Call 020/7321-2233 for the day's plan, or check www.royalresidences.com. Then hop into a big black taxi and say, "Buck House, please" (a.k.a. Buckingham Palace).

Buckingham Palace Area

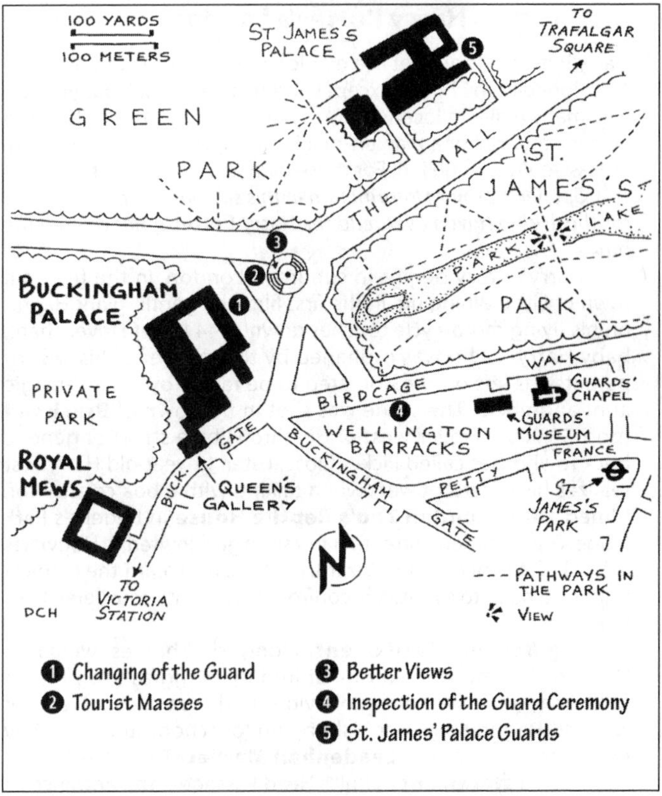

Most tourists just mob the palace gates for a peek at the Changing of the Guard, but those who know the drill will enjoy the event more. Here's the lowdown on what goes down: It's just after 11:00 and the on-duty guards, actually working at nearby St. James's Palace, are ready to finish their shift. At 11:15, these tired guards, along with the band, head out to the Mall, and then take a right turn for Buckingham Palace. Meanwhile, their replacement guards—fresh for the day—gather at 11:00 at their Wellington Barracks, 500 yards east of the palace (on Birdcage Walk), for a review and inspection. At 11:30, they also head for Buckingham Palace. As both the tired and fresh guards converge on the palace, the Horse Guard enters the fray, marching down the Mall from the Horse Guard Barracks on Whitehall. At 11:45, it's a perfect storm of Red Coat pageantry, as all three groups converge. Everyone parades around, the guard changes (passing the regimental flag, or "color") with much shouting, the band plays a happy little concert,

Harry Potter's London

Harry Potter's story is set in a magical Britain, and all of the places mentioned in the books except London are fictional, but you can visit many real film locations. Many of the locations are closed to visitors, though, or are an un-magical disappointment in person, unless you're a huge fan. For those diehards, here's a list.

Spoiler Warning: Information in this sidebar will ruin surprises for those who haven't yet read the Harry Potter *series or seen the movies.*

Harry's story begins in suburban London, in the fictional town of Little Whinging. In the first film, the gentle-giant Hagrid on his flying motorcycle touches down at #4 Privet Drive. There, baby Harry—who was orphaned by the murder of his wizard parents—is left on the doorstep to be raised by an anti-magic aunt and uncle. The scene was shot in the town of **Bracknell** (pop. 50,000, 10 miles west of Heathrow) on a street of generic brick rowhouses called Picket Close. Later, 10-year-old Harry first realizes his wizard powers when talking with a boa constrictor, filmed at the **London Zoo's Reptile House** in Regent's Park (Tube: Great Portland Street). Harry soon gets invited to Hogwarts School of Witchcraft and Wizardry, where he'll learn the magical skills he'll need to eventually confront his parents' murderer, Lord Voldemort.

Big Ben and **Parliament,** along the Thames, welcome Harry to the modern city inhabited by Muggles (non-magic folk). London bustles along oblivious to the parallel universe of wizards. Hagrid takes Harry shopping for school supplies. They enter the glass-roofed **Leadenhall Market** (Tube: Bank), and approach a **storefront** in Bull's Head Passage—the entrance to the Leaky Cauldron pub (which, in the books, is placed among the bookshops of Charing Cross Road). The pub's back wall parts, opening onto the magical Diagon Alley (filmed on a set at Leavesden Studios, north of London), where Harry shops for wands, cauldrons, and wizard textbooks. He pays for it with gold

and then they march out. A few minutes later, fresh guards set up at St. James's Palace, the tired ones dress down at the barracks, and the tourists disperse.

Stake out the high ground on the circular Victoria Monument for the best overall view. Or start early either at St. James's Palace or the Wellington Barracks (the inspection is in full view of the street) and stride in with the band. The marching troops and bands are colorful and even stirring, but the actual Changing of the Guard is a nonevent. It is interesting, however, to see nearly every tourist in London gathered in one place at the same time. Afterwards, stroll through nearby St. James's Park

Galleons from goblin-run Gringotts Bank, filmed in the marble-floored and chandeliered Exhibition Hall of **Australia House** (Tube: Temple), home of the Australian Embassy.

Harry catches the train to Hogwarts at **King's Cross Station**. (The fanciful exterior shot from film #2 is actually of nearby **St. Pancras Station**.) Inside the glass-roofed train station, on a **pedestrian sky bridge** over the tracks, Hagrid gives Harry a train ticket. Harry heads to platform 9¾, actually filmed at **platform 4**. Harry and his new buddy Ron magically push their luggage carts through a brick pillar between the platforms, emerging onto a hidden platform. (For a fun photo-op, find the *Platform 9¾* sign and the luggage cart that appears to be disappearing into the wall.)

A red steam train—the Hogwarts Express—speeds them through the (Scottish) countryside to Hogwarts, where Harry will spend the next seven years. Harry is taught how to wave his wand by tiny Professor Flitwick in a wood-paneled classroom filmed at **Harrow School** in Harrow on the Hill, eight miles northwest of London (Tube: Harrow on the Hill).

In film #3, Harry careens through London's lamplit streets on a purple three-decker bus that dumps him at the Leaky Cauldron. In this film, the pub's exterior was shot on rough-looking Stoney Street at the southeast edge of **Borough Street Market**, by the Market Porter Pub, with trains rumbling overhead (Tube: London Bridge).

Other scenes from the books are set in London—Sirius Black and the Order reside at "Twelve Grimmauld Place" and Harry plumbs the depths of the "Ministry of Magic"—but these places are fictional.

Finally, cinema buffs can visit **Leicester Square** (Tube: Leicester Square), where Daniel Radcliffe and other stars strolled past paparazzi and down red carpets to the Odeon Theater to watch the movies' premieres.

(Tube: Victoria, St. James's Park, or Green Park).

West London

▲Hyde Park and Speakers' Corner—London's "Central Park," originally Henry VIII's hunting grounds, has more than 600 acres of lush greenery, a huge man-made lake, the royal Kensington Palace, and the ornate neo-Gothic Albert Memorial across from the Royal

Albert Hall. Early afternoons on Sunday (until early evening), Speakers' Corner offers soapbox oratory at its best (Tube: Marble Arch). "The grass roots of democracy" is actually a holdover from when the gallows stood here and the criminal was allowed to say just about anything he wanted to before he swung. I dare you to raise your voice and gather a crowd—it's easy to do.

The Princess Diana Memorial Fountain opened in 2004 in honor of the "People's Princess" who once lived in nearby Kensington Palace. The low-key circular stream is in the eastern part of the park, near the Serpentine Gallery. (Don't be confused by signs to the Diana Princess of Wales Children's Playground, also found within the park.)

▲Apsley House (Wellington Museum)—Having beaten Napoleon at Waterloo, the Duke of Wellington was once the most famous man in Europe. He was given London's ultimate address, #1 London. His newly refurbished mansion offers one of London's best palace experiences. An 11-foot-tall marble statue (by Canova) of Napoleon, clad only in a fig leaf, greets you. Downstairs is a small gallery of Wellington memorabilia (including a pair of Wellington boots). The lavish upstairs shows off the duke's fine collection of paintings, including works by Velázquez and Steen (£4.50, Tue–Sun 10:00–17:00, until 16:00 in winter, closed Mon, well-described by included audioguide, 20 yards from Hyde Park Corner Tube station, tel. 020/7499-5676, www.english-heritage.org.uk). Hyde Park's pleasant and picnic-wonderful rose garden is nearby.

▲▲Victoria and Albert Museum—The world's top collection of decorative arts (vases, stained glass, fine furniture, clothing, jewelry, carpets, and more) is a surprisingly interesting assortment of crafts from the West as well as Asian and Islamic cultures. The British Galleries are grand, but there's much more to see, including Raphael's tapestry cartoons and a cast of Trajan's Column that depicts the emperor's conquests (free, possible fee for special exhibits, daily 10:00–17:45, Wed and last Fri of the month until 22:00 except mid-Dec–mid-Jan, free 60-min tours daily, usually on the half-hour from 10:30–15:30, also daily at 13:00, Wed at 16:30, and a half-hour version at 18:30; Tube: South Kensington, a long tunnel leads directly from the Tube station to museum, tel. 020/7942-2000, www.vam.ac.uk).

✪ See Victoria and Albert Museum Tour, page 234.

▲Natural History Museum—Across the street from Victoria and Albert, this mammoth museum is housed in a giant and wonderful Victorian, neo-Romanesque building. Built in the 1870s specifically for the huge collection (50 million specimens), it has two halves: the Life Galleries (creepy-crawlies, human biology, the origin of species, "our place in evolution," and awesome dinosaurs) and

West London

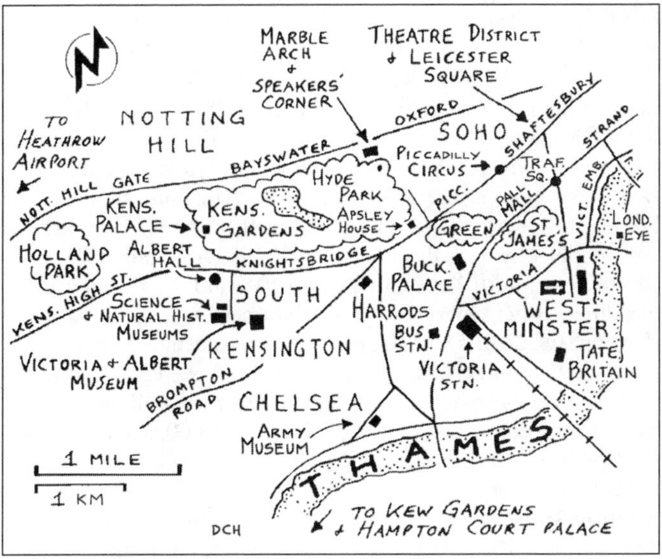

the Earth Galleries (meteors, volcanoes, earthquakes, and so on). Exhibits are wonderfully explained, with lots of creative interactive displays. Pop in, if only for the wild collection of dinosaurs and the roaring Tyrannosaurus rex. Free 45-minute highlights tours occur daily about every hour from 11:00 to 16:00 (free, possible fee for special exhibits, Mon–Sat 10:00–18:00, Sun 11:00–18:00, last entrance 17:30, a long tunnel leads directly from South Kensington Tube station to museum, tel. 020/7942-5000, exhibit info and reservations tel. 020/7942-5011, www.nhm.ac.uk).

▲Science Museum—Next door to the Natural History Museum, this sprawling wonderland for curious minds is kid-perfect. It offers hands-on fun, from moonwalks to deep-sea exploration, with trendy technology exhibits, an IMAX theater (£7–10 tickets for grownups, kids less), cool rotating themed exhibits, and a kids' zone in the basement (free, daily 10:00–18:00, Exhibition Road, Tube: South Kensington, tel. 0870-870-4868, www.sciencemuseum.org.uk).

▲▲Kensington Palace—In 1689, King William and Queen Mary moved their primary residence from Whitehall in central London to the more pristine and peaceful village of Kensington (now engulfed by London). With a little renovation help from Sir Christopher Wren, they turned the existing house into Kensington Palace, which was the center of English court life until 1760, when the royal family moved into Buckingham Palace. Since then, lesser royals have bedded down in Kensington Palace (as Prince Charles and Princess Diana did from their 1981 marriage until her death in 1997). The palace, while still functioning as a royal residence, also welcomes visitors with an impressive string of historic royal apartments and a killer wardrobe of queens' dresses and ceremonial clothing (late 19th and 20th centuries). For the time being, Lady Diana's fashion-statement dresses are also on display. Enjoy a re-created royal tailor and dressmaker's workshop, the 17th-century splendor of the apartments of William and Mary, and the bed where Queen Victoria was born (fully clothed). The displays are wonderfully described by the included audioguide (£11, daily 10:00–18:00, until 17:00 in winter, a 10-min hike through Hyde Park from either Queensway or High Street Kensington Tube station, tel. 0870-751-5170). Garden enthusiasts enjoy popping into the secluded Sunken Garden, 50 yards from the exit. And ladies with fancy hats sip tea at the nearby Orangery, built as a greenhouse for Queen Anne in 1704 (daily 10:00–18:00, à la carte lunch 12:00–15:00, afternoon tea 15:00–18:00, sit indoors or outside overlooking the garden).

Victoria Station—From underneath this station's iron-and-glass canopy, trains depart for the south of England and Gatwick Airport. While Victoria Station is famous and a major Tube stop, few tourists actually take trains from here—most just come to take in the exciting bustle. It's a fun place to just be a "rock in a river" teeming with commuters and services. The station is surrounded by big red buses and taxis, travel agencies, and lousy eateries. It's next to the main bus station (National Express) and the best inexpensive B&Bs in town.

Westminster Cathedral—This largest Catholic church in England, just a block from Victoria Station, is striking but not very historic or important to visit. It opened in 1903 and has a brick neo-Byzantine flavor (surrounded by glassy office blocks). While it's definitely not Westminster Abbey, half the tourists wandering around inside seem to think it is. The highlight is the lift to the viewing gallery atop its bell tower (fine view, £3 for the lift, daily 9:30–17:00, just off Victoria Street, Tube: Victoria).

National Army Museum—This museum is not as awe-inspiring as the Imperial War Museum, but it's still fun, especially for kids into soldiers, armor, and guns. And while the Imperial War Museum is limited to wars of the 20th century, this tells the story of the British Army from 1415 through the Gulf War and Bosnia with lots of Red Coat lore and a good look at Waterloo. Kids enjoy trying on a Cromwellian helmet, seeing the skeleton of Napoleon's horse, and peering out from a WWI trench through a working periscope (free, daily 10:00–17:30, follow arrows in carpet to stay on track, bus #239 from Victoria Station stops at museum's door, Royal Hospital Road, Chelsea, Tube: Sloane Square, tel. 020-7730-0717).

East London: The City

▲▲The City of London—When Londoners say "The City," they mean the one-square-mile business, banking, and journalism center that 2,000 years ago was Roman Londinium. The outline of the Roman city walls can still be seen in the arc of roads from Blackfriars Bridge to Tower Bridge. Within the City are 23 churches designed by Sir Christopher Wren, mostly just ornamentation around St. Paul's Cathedral. Today, while home to only 5,000 residents, the City thrives with more than 500,000 office workers coming and going daily. It's a fascinating district to wander on weekdays, but since almost nobody actually lives there, it's dull in the evenings and on Saturday and Sunday.

✪ See The City Walk, page 100.

▲Old Bailey—To view the British legal system in action—lawyers in little blond wigs speaking legalese with a British accent—spend a few minutes in the visitors' gallery at the Old Bailey, called the "Central Criminal Court." Don't enter under the dome; signs point you to the two visitors' entrances (free, Mon–Fri about 10:30–16:30 depending on caseload, closed Sat–Sun, reduced hours in Aug; no kids under 14; no bags, mobile phones, or cameras, but small purses OK; you can check your bag at Bailey's Sandwich Bar across the street for £2 or at other entrepreneurial places nearby; Tube: St. Paul's, 2 blocks northwest of St. Paul's on Old Bailey Street, follow signs to public entrance, tel. 020/7248-3277).

▲▲▲St. Paul's Cathedral—Wren's most famous church is the great St. Paul's, its elaborate interior capped by a 365-foot dome. Since World War II, St. Paul's has been Britain's symbol of resistance. Despite 57 nights of bombing, the Nazis failed to destroy the cathedral, thanks to the St. Paul's volunteer fire watchmen, who stayed on the dome. Today you can climb the dome for a great city view. The crypt (included with admission) is a world of historic bones and memorials, including Admiral Nelson's tomb and interesting cathedral models (£8, includes church entry and dome climb, Mon–Sat 8:30–16:30, last church entry 16:00, last dome entry 16:15, closed Sun except for worship, no photography allowed, £2.50 tours and £3.50 audioguides, cheery café in crypt, Tube: St. Paul's, tel. 020/7236-4128, www.stpauls.co.uk).

The **evensong** services are free, but nonpaying visitors are not allowed to linger afterward (Mon–Sat at 17:00, Sun at 15:15, 40 min). On Sunday, there's an **organ recital** at 17:00.

✪ See St. Paul's Tour, page 225.

▲Museum of London—London, a 2,000-year-old city, is so littered with Roman ruins that when a London builder finds Roman antiquities, he doesn't stop work. He simply documents the finds, moves the artifacts to a museum, and builds on. If you're asking, "Why did the Romans build their cities underground?" a trip to

The City

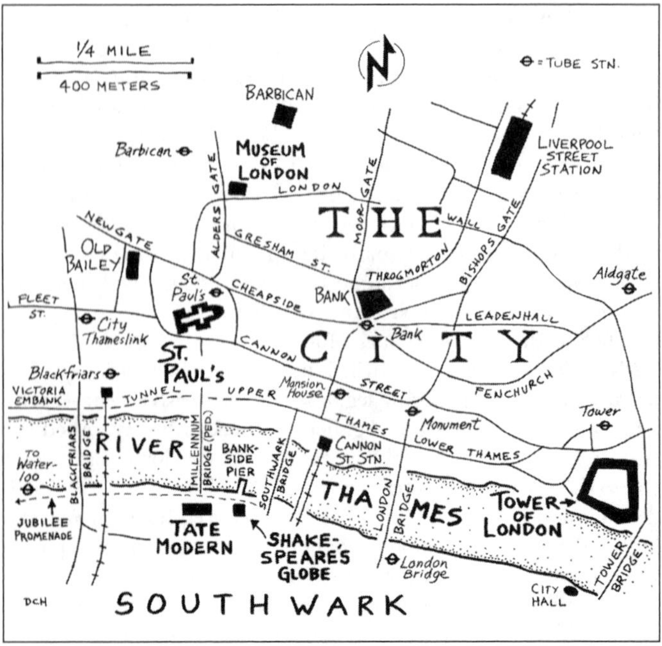

the creative and entertaining London Museum is a must. Stroll through London history from pre-Roman times through the 1920s. This regular stop for the local school kids gives the best overview of London history in town (free, Mon–Sat 10:00–18:00, Sun 12:00–18:00, Tube: Barbican or St. Paul's, tel. 0870-444-3852).

Geffrye Decorative Arts Museum—Walk through a dozen English front rooms dating from 1600 to 1990 (free, Tue–Sat 10:00–17:00, Sun 12:00–17:00, closed Mon, Tube: Liverpool Street, then bus #149 or #242 north, tel. 020/7739-9893).

▲▲▲Tower of London—The Tower has served as a castle in wartime, a king's residence in peace time, and, most notoriously, as the prison and execution site of rebels. You can see the crown jewels, take a witty Beefeater tour, and ponder the executioner's block that dispensed with troublesome heirs to the throne and a couple of Henry VIII's wives (£14.50, 1-day combo-ticket with Hampton Court Palace-£20, March–Oct Tue–Sat 9:00–18:00, Sun–Mon 10:00–18:00; Nov–Feb Tue–Sat 9:00–17:00, Sun–Mon 10:00–17:00; last entry 60 min before closing, the long but fast-moving ticket line is worst on Sun, no photography allowed of jewels or in chapels, Tube: Tower Hill, tel. 0870-751-5177, recorded info: tel. 0870-756-6060, booking: tel. 0870-756-7070, www.hrp.org.uk). You can avoid the long lines by picking up your ticket at any London TI or the Tower Hill Tube station ticket office. Consider taking the boat to Greenwich from here (see cruise info on page 36).

✪ See Tower of London Tour, page 257.

Ceremony of the Keys: Every night at precisely 21:30, with pageantry-filled ceremony, the Tower of London is locked up (as it has been for the last 700 years). To attend this free 30-minute event, you need to request an invitation at least two months before your visit. Write to Ceremony of the Keys, H.M. Tower of London, London EC3N 4AB. Include your name; the addresses, names, and ages of all people attending (up to 6 people, nontransferable, no kids under 8 allowed); requested date; alternative dates; and two international reply coupons (buy at U.S. post office—if your post office doesn't have the $1.75 coupons in stock, they can order them; the turnaround time is a few days).

More Sights Near the Tower—The best remaining bit of London's **Roman Wall** is just north of the tower (at the Tower Hill Tube station). The impressive Tower Bridge is freshly painted and restored; for more information on this neo-Gothic maritime gateway to London, you can visit the **Tower Bridge Experience** for its 1894–1994 history exhibit and a peek at its Victorian engine room (£5.50, family-£10 and up, daily 10:00–1830, last entry at 17:30, good view, poor value, enter at the northwest tower, tel. 020/7403-3761). The chic **St. Katharine Yacht Harbor,** just east of Tower Bridge, has mod shops and the classic old Dickens Inn, fun for a drink or pub lunch. Across the bridge is the South Bank, with the upscale Butlers Wharf area, City Hall, museums, and promenade.

South London, on the South Bank

The South Bank is a thriving arts and cultural center tied together by a riverside path. This popular, pub-crawling walk—called the Jubilee Promenade—stretches from Tower Bridge past Westminster Bridge, where it offers grand views of the Houses of Parliament. (The promenade hugs the river except just east of London Bridge, where it cuts inland for a couple of blocks.)

✪ The Bankside Walk on page 87 connects the following sights (described below): Shakespeare's Globe, Tate Modern, Millennium Bridge, Old Operating Theatre Museum, and Vinopolis.

City Hall—Opened in 2002, the glassy, egg-shaped building near the south end of Tower Bridge is London's City Hall, designed by Sir Norman Foster, the architect who worked on London's Millennium Bridge and Berlin's Reichstag. An interior spiral ramp allows visitors to watch and hear the action below in the Assembly Chamber; ride the lift to the second floor (the highest visitors can go) and spiral down. The Visitors Centre on the lower ground floor has a handy cafeteria. A top-floor observation deck known as

The South Bank

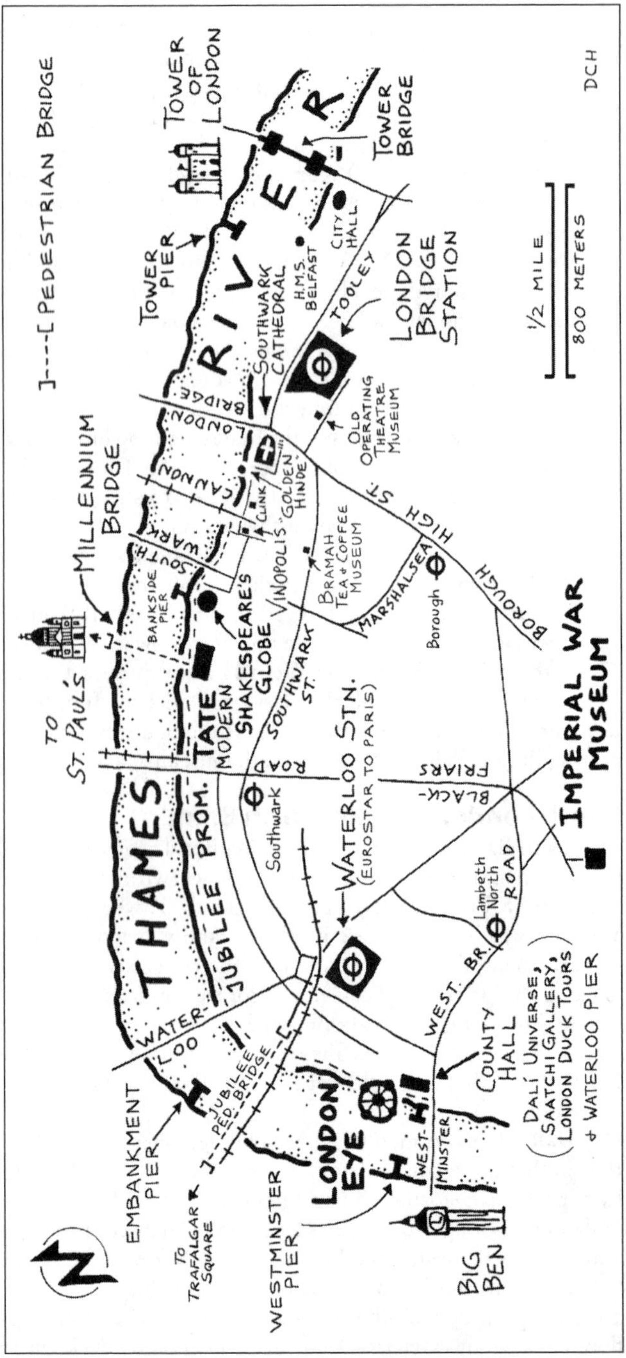

"London's Living Room" is open for tours, usually on Monday morning (phone-in reservation required), and on occasional weekends from 10:00–16:30 (Visitors Centre open Mon–Fri 8:00–20:00, closed Sat–Sun, Tube: London Bridge station plus 10-min walk, or Tower Hill station plus 15-min walk; the Hall occasionally opens up for public tours—call or check Web site to confirm tour times and opening hours, tel. 020/7983-4100, www.london.gov.uk).

▲▲▲**London Eye Ferris Wheel**—Built by British Airways, the wheel towers above London opposite Big Ben. This is the world's highest observational wheel, giving you a chance to fly British Airways without leaving London. Designed like a giant bicycle wheel, it's a pan-European undertaking: British steel and Dutch engineering, with Czech, German, French, and Italian mechanical parts. It's also very "green," running extremely efficiently and virtually silently. Twenty-five people ride in each of its 32 air-conditioned capsules for the 30-minute rotation (each capsule has a bench, but most people stand). From the top of this 450-foot-high wheel—the highest public viewpoint in the city—Big Ben looks small. You go around only once; save a shot on top for the glass capsule next to yours. Its original five-year lease has been extended to 25 years, and it looks like this will become a permanent fixture on the London skyline. Thames boats come and go from here using the Waterloo Pier at the foot of the wheel.

Cost, Hours, Location: £12.50, April–mid-Sept daily 9:30–21:00, until 22:00 in July–Aug, mid-Sept–March 9:30–20:00, often closed Jan for maintenance, Tube: Waterloo or Westminster, www.ba-londoneye.com (10 percent discount for booking online).

Visitors face two lines: one to get your ticket, and the other to board. You can generally just buy your ticket at the wheel (never more than a 30-min wait, worst on weekends and school holidays). If you want to book a ticket (with an assigned time) in advance, call 0870-500-0600 or book online at www.ba-londoneye.com (and save 10 percent). Upon arrival, you either pick up your pre-booked ticket (if you've reserved ahead; use the ATM-type machines to save time—just type in your confirmation number) or wait in the line inside to buy tickets. Then you join the ticket-holders' line at the wheel (starting 10 min before your assigned half-hour time slot).

Dalí Universe—Cleverly located next to the hugely popular London Eye Ferris Wheel, this exhibit features 500 works of mind-bending art by Salvador Dalí. While pricey, it's entertaining if you like Surrealism and want to learn about Dalí (£9, audioguide-£2.50, daily 10:00–18:30, generally summer evenings until 20:00, last entry 1 hour before closing, Tube: Waterloo or Westminster, tel. 020/7620-2720).

▲Saatchi Gallery—The contemporary art gallery at the base of the London Eye features young British artists. Rather than halls of staid canvases, the collection displays many installations, each in their own room, giving the place a kind of funhouse, macabre atmosphere. Exhibits are changed routinely. Here are several I've seen: Damien Hirst's vision of mortality (live insects feeding on a rotting cow's head, then dying on a bug zapper); Ron Mueck's *Dead Dad,* an ultra-realistic (half-size) corpse in silicon and acrylic; and Tracey Emin's installation of her messy bedroom.

Visitors may be put off or simply grossed out. It's "just conceptual art," but the concepts are realized on a large scale, with big money and ultra-modern technical know-how, and displayed in a wood-paneled Edwardian-era setting. You may not like it, you may be offended, you may find it passé—but it's something to e-mail home about (£8.75, daily 10:00–20:00, Fri–Sat until 22:00, last entry 45 min before closing, located next to London Eye, Tube: Waterloo or Westminster).

▲▲Imperial War Museum—This impressive museum covers the wars of the last century, from heavy weaponry to love notes and Vargas Girls, from Monty's Africa campaign tank to Schwartzkopf's Desert Storm uniform. You can trace the development of the machine gun, watch footage of the first tank battles, see one of more than a thousand V2 rockets Hitler rained on Britain in 1944 (each with more than a ton of explosives), hold your breath through the gruesome WWI trench experience, and buy WWII-era toys in the fun museum shop. The "Secret War" section gives a fascinating peek into the intrigues of espionage in World Wars I and II. The section on the Holocaust is one of the best on the subject anywhere. Rather than glorify war, the museum does its best to shine a light on the powerful human side of one of mankind's most persistent traits (free, daily 10:00–18:00, 2 hours is enough time for most visitors, Tube: Lambeth North or bus #12 from Westminster, tel. 020/7416-5000).

The museum is housed in what was the Royal Bethlam Hospital. Also known as "the Bedlam asylum," the place was so wild it gave the world a new word for chaos: "bedlam." Back in

Victorian times, locals—without trash-talk shows and cable TV—came here for their entertainment. The asylum was actually open to the paying public on weekends.

▲▲▲Tate Modern—Dedicated in the spring of 2000, the striking museum across the river from St. Paul's opened the new century with art from the old one. Its powerhouse collection of Monet, Matisse, Dalí, Picasso, Warhol, and much more is displayed in a converted powerhouse. Each year, the main hall features a different monumental installation by a prominent artist (free, fee for special exhibitions, daily 10:00–18:00, Fri–Sat until 22:00—a good time to visit, audioguide-£2, view café on top floor; cross the Millennium Bridge from St. Paul's, or Tube: Southwark plus a 10-min walk; or connect by Tate Boat ferry from Tate Britain for £3.40; tel. 020/7887-8000, www.tate.org.uk).

✪ See Tate Modern Tour, page 192.

▲Millennium Bridge—The pedestrian bridge links St. Paul's Cathedral and the Tate Modern across the Thames. This is London's first new bridge in a century. When it first opened, the $25 million bridge wiggled when people walked on it, so it promptly closed for a $7 million, 20-month stabilization; now it's stable and open again (free). Nicknamed "a blade of light" for its sleek minimalist design—370 yards long, four yards wide, stainless steel with teak planks—it includes clever aerodynamic handrails to deflect wind over the heads of pedestrians.

▲▲Shakespeare's Globe—The original Globe Theater has been rebuilt, half-timbered and thatched, as it was in Shakespeare's time. (This is the first thatched roof in London since they were outlawed after the Great Fire of 1666.) The Globe originally accommodated 2,000 seated and another 1,000 standing. Today, slightly smaller and leaving space for reasonable aisles, the theater holds 900 seated and 600 groundlings. Its promoters brag that the theater melds "the three A's"—actors, audience, and architecture—with each contributing to the play. Open as a museum and a working theater, it hosts authentic old-time performances of Shakespeare's plays. The Globe's exhibition on Shakespeare is the world's largest, with interactive displays and film presentations, a sound lab, a script factory, and costumes. The theater can be toured when there are no plays going on—it's worth planning ahead for these excellent tours (£9 includes exhibition and actor-led guided tour; mid-May–Sept exhibition open daily 9:00–18:00, tours go on the half hour from 9:30, generally until 12:30, until 11:30 on Sun,

Crossing the Thames on Foot

You can cross the Thames on any of the bridges that carry car traffic over the river, but London's two pedestrian bridges are more fun. The Millennium Bridge connects the sedate St. Paul's Cathedral with the great Tate Modern. The Golden Jubilee Bridge (consisting of 2 walkways that flank a railway trestle) links bustling Trafalgar Square on the North Bank with the London Eye Ferris Wheel and Waterloo Station on the South Bank. Replacing the old, run-down Hungerford Bridge, the Golden Jubilee Bridge—well-lit with a sleek, futuristic look—makes this busy route safer and more popular.

17:30 on Mon; Oct–mid-May exhibition open daily 10:00–17:00 with 30-min tours on the half-hour as above; on the South Bank directly across Thames over Southwark Bridge from St. Paul's; Tube: London Bridge plus a 10-min walk; tel. 020/7902-1500; www.shakespeares-globe.org). For details on seeing a play, see the Entertainment chapter on page 312. The Globe Café is open daily (10:00–18:00, tel. 020/7902-1433).

Bramah Tea and Coffee Museum—Aficionados of tea or coffee will find this small museum fascinating. It tells the story of each drink almost passionately. The owner, Mr. Bramah, comes from a big tea family and wants the world to know how the advent of commercial television, with breaks not long enough to brew a proper pot of tea, required a faster hot drink. In came the horrible English instant coffee. Tea countered with finely chopped leaves in tea bags, and it's gone downhill ever since (£4, daily 10:00–18:00, 40 Southwark Street, Tube: London Bridge plus 3-min walk, tel. 020/7403-5650, www.bramahmuseum.co.uk). Its café, which serves more kinds of coffees and teas than cakes, is open to the public (same hours as museum). The #RV1 bus zips you to the museum easily and scenically from Covent Garden.

▲▲Old Operating Theatre Museum and Herb Garret—Climb a tight and creaky wooden spiral staircase to a church attic where you'll find a garret used to dry medicinal herbs, a fascinating exhibit on Victorian surgery, cases of well-described 19th-century medical paraphernalia, and a special look at "anesthesia, the defeat of pain." Then you stumble upon Britain's oldest operating theater, where limbs were sawed off way back in 1821 (£4.75, daily 10:30–

17:00, 9a St. Thomas Street, Tube: London Bridge, tel. 020/7955-4791, www.thegarret.org.uk). ✪ See the Bankside Walk, page 87.

▲▲Vinopolis: City of Wine—While it seems illogical to have a huge wine museum in London, Vinopolis makes a good case. Built over a Roman wine store and filling the massive vaults of an old wine warehouse, the museum offers an excellent audioguide with a light yet earnest history of wine. Sipping various reds and whites, ports, and champagnes—immersed in your headset as you stroll—you learn about the libation from its Georgian origins to Chile, including a Vespa ride through Chianti country in Tuscany. Allow some time, as the included audioguide takes 90 minutes—the sipping can slow things down wonderfully (£12.50 with 5 tastes, only £11 Tue–Thu; don't worry...for £3 you can buy 5 more tastes inside; £15 gets you a premium service with a couple of especially fine wines and tasting lesson, daily 12:00–18:00, Mon and Fri–Sat until 21:00, last entry 2 hours before closing, between the Globe and Southwark Cathedral at 1 Bank End, Tube: London Bridge, tel. 0870-241-4040 or 020/7940-8322, www.vinopolis.co.uk).

Lesser Sights in Southwark, on the South Bank

These sights, while mediocre, are worth knowing about. The area stretching from the Tate Modern to London Bridge, known as Southwark (SUTH-uck), was for centuries the place Londoners would go to escape the rules and decency of the city and let their hair down. Bear-baiting, brothels, rollicking pubs and theater—you name the dream, and it could be fulfilled just across the Thames. A run-down warehouse district through the 20th century, it's been gentrified with classy restaurants, office parks, pedestrian promenades, major sights (such as the Tate Modern and Shakespeare's Globe—described above), and this colorful collection of lesser sights. The area is easy on foot and a scenic—though circuitous—way to connect the Tower of London with St. Paul's.

✪ You'll find more information on these sights (except for HMS *Belfast*) in the Bankside Walk chapter, page 87.

Southwark Cathedral—While made a cathedral only in 1905, it's been the neighborhood church since the 13th century and comes with some interesting history (Mon–Fri 8:00–18:00, Sat–Sun 9:00–18:00, last entry 30 min before close; evensong services weekdays at 17:30, Sat at 16:00, Sun at 15:00, not sung on Wed or alternate Mon, audioguide-£2.50, Tube: London Bridge, tel. 020/7367-6700).

The Clink Prison Museum—Proudly the "original clink," this was where law-abiding citizens threw Southwark troublemakers until 1780. Today, it's a low-tech torture museum filling grotty old rooms with papier-mâché gore. Unfortunately, there's little to seriously deal with the fascinating problem of law and order in Southwark, where 18th-century Londoners went for a good time (overpriced at £5, daily 10:00–18:00, July–Sept until 21:00, 1 Clink Street, Tube: London Bridge, tel. 020/7403-0900, www.clink.co.uk).

***Golden Hinde* Replica**—This is a full-size replica of the 16th-century warship in which Sir Francis Drake circumnavigated the globe from 1577 to 1580. Commanding this ship, Drake earned the reputation as history's most successful pirate. The original is long gone, but this boat has logged more than 100,000 miles, including its own voyage around the world. While the ship is fun to see, its interior is not worth touring (£3.50, daily 10:00–17:30, may be closed if rented out for birthday parties, school groups, or weddings, Tube: London Bridge, tel. 0870-011-8700, www.goldenhinde.co.uk).

HMS *Belfast*—"The last big-gun armored warship of World War II" clogs the Thames just upstream from the Tower Bridge. This huge vessel—now manned with wax sailors—thrills kids who always dreamed of sitting in a turret shooting off their imaginary guns. If you're into WWII warships, this is the ultimate...otherwise, it's just lots of exercise with a nice view of Tower Bridge (£8, daily March–Oct 10:00–18:00, Nov–Feb 10:00–17:00, last entry 45 min before closing, Tube: London Bridge, tel. 020/7940-6300).

South London, on the North Bank

▲▲Tate Britain—One of Europe's great art houses, Tate Britain specializes in British painting from the 16th century through modern times. The museum has a good representation of William Blake's religious sketches, the Pre-Raphaelites' realistic art, and J.M.W. Turner's swirling works (free, £2 donation requested, daily 10:00–17:50, last entry 17:00, fine free and necessary audioguide, free tours: normally Mon–Fri at 11:00—16th, 17th, and 18th centuries; at noon—19th century; at 14:00—Turner; at 15:00—20th century; Sat–Sun at noon and 15:00—highlights; call to confirm schedule; no photography allowed, Tube: Pimlico, then 7-min walk; or arrive directly at museum by taking the Tate Boat ferry from Tate Modern or bus #88 from Oxford Circus or #77A from National Gallery, tel. 020/7887-8000, recorded info tel. 020/7887-8008, www.tate.org.uk).

✪ See Tate Britain Tour, page 177.

Greater London

▲Kew Gardens—For a fine riverside park and a palatial greenhouse jungle to swing through, take the Tube or the boat to every botanist's favorite escape, Kew Gardens. While to most visitors the Royal Botanic Gardens of Kew are simply a delightful opportunity to wander among 33,000 different types of plants, to the hard-working organization that runs the gardens, it's a way to promote

Greater London

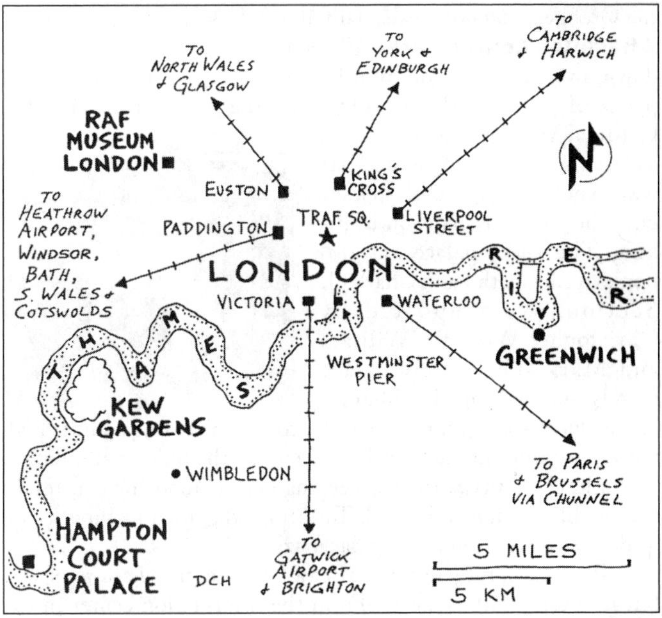

understanding and preservation of the botanical diversity of our planet. The Kew Tube station drops you in an herbal little business community, a two-block walk from Victoria Gate (the main garden entrance). Pick up a map brochure and check at the gate for a monthly listing of best blooms.

Garden-lovers could spend days exploring Kew's 300 acres. For a quick visit, spend a fragrant hour wandering through three buildings: the Palm House, a humid Victorian world of iron, glass, and tropical plants built in 1844; a Waterlily House that Monet would swim for; and the Princess of Wales Conservatory, a modern greenhouse with many different climate zones growing countless cacti, bug-munching carnivorous plants, and more (£8.50, £6 at 15:00 or later, Mon–Fri 9:30–18:30, Sat–Sun 9:30–19:30, until 16:30 or sunset off-season, galleries and conservatories close at 17:30, a £3.50 narrated floral 35-min joyride on little train departs on the hour until 16:00 from Victoria Gate, Tube: Kew Gardens, boats run between Kew Gardens and Westminster Pier—see page 37, tel. 020/8332-5000, www.rbgkew.org.uk).

For a sun-dappled lunch, walk 10 minutes from the Palm House to the Orangery (£6 hot meals, daily 10:00–17:30).

▲Hampton Court Palace—Fifteen miles up the Thames from downtown (£15 taxi ride from Kew Gardens) is the 500-year-old palace of Henry VIII. Actually, it was the palace of his minister, Cardinal Wolsey. When Wolsey, a clever man, realized Henry VIII was experiencing a little palace envy, he gave the mansion to his king. The Tudor palace was also home to Elizabeth I and Charles I. Sections were updated by Christopher Wren for William and Mary. The stately palace stands overlooking the Thames and includes some impressive Tudor rooms, including a Great Hall with a magnificent hammer-beam ceiling. The industrial-strength Tudor kitchen was capable of keeping 600 schmoozing courtesans thoroughly—if not well—fed. The sculpted garden features a rare Tudor tennis court and a popular maze.

The palace, fully restored after a 1986 fire, tries hard to please, but it doesn't quite sparkle. From the information center in the main courtyard, visitors book times for tours with tired costumed guides or pick up audioguides for self-guided tours of various wings of the palace (all free). The Tudor Kitchens, Henry VIII's Apartments, and the King's Apartments are most interesting. The Georgian Rooms are pretty dull. The maze in the nearby garden is a curiosity some find fun (maze free with palace ticket, otherwise £3.50). The palace costs £12 (1-day combo-ticket with Tower of London-£20, kids-£12.50, Mon 10:15–18:00, Tue–Sun 9:30–18:00, Nov–March until 16:30, tel. 0870-751-5175, recorded info tel. 0870-752-7777). Note that there are often discounts available for people riding the train from London to the palace. When you buy your ticket at Waterloo Station, ask for the voucher that gives a second adult 50 percent off and free admission for kids.

The train (2/hr, 30 min) from London's Waterloo station drops you just across the river from the palace. Consider arriving at or departing from the palace by boat (connections with London's Westminster Pier, see page 37); it's a relaxing and scenic three-hour cruise past two locks and a fun new/old riverside mix.

Royal Air Force Museum London—A hit with aviation enthusiasts, this huge aerodrome and airfield contain planes from World War II's Battle of Britain up through the Gulf War. You can climb inside some of the planes, try your luck in a cockpit, and fly with the Red Arrows in a flight simulator (free, daily 10:00–18:00, café, shop, parking, Tube: Colindale—top of Northern Line Edgware branch, Grahame Park Way, tel. 020/8205-2266, www.rafmuseum.org.uk).

Disappointments of London

On the South Bank, the London Dungeon, a much-visited but amateurish attraction, is just a highly advertised, overpriced haunted house—certainly not worth the £20 admission, much less your valuable London time. It comes with long and rude lines. Wait for Halloween and see one in your hometown to support a better cause. "Winston Churchill's Britain at War Experience" (next to the London Dungeon) also wastes your time and money, especially considering the wonderful new Churchill Museum in the Cabinet War Rooms (see page 41). The Jack the Ripper walking tours (by any of several companies) are big sellers, but don't offer much. Anything actually relating to the notorious serial killer was torn down a century ago, and all that's left are a few small sights and lots of bloody stories.

WESTMINSTER WALK

From Big Ben to Trafalgar Square

London is the L.A., D.C., and N.Y.C. of Britain. This walk starts with London's "star" attraction, continues to its "Capitol," passes its "White House," and ends at its "Times Square"...all in about an hour.

Just about every visitor to London strolls the historic Whitehall Boulevard from Big Ben to Trafalgar Square. This quick eight-stop walk gives meaning to that touristy ramble. Under London's modern traffic and big-city bustle lie 2,000 fascinating years of history. You'll get a whirlwind tour as well as a practical orientation to London.

THE WALK BEGINS

• *Start halfway across Westminster Bridge (Tube: Westminster; take the Westminster Pier exit).*

❶ On Westminster Bridge

Views of Big Ben and Parliament

• *First look upstream, toward the Parliament.*

Ding dong ding dong. Dong ding ding dong. Yes, indeed, you are in London. **Big Ben** is actually "not the clock, not the tower, but the bell that tolls the hour." However, since the 13-ton bell is not visible, everyone just calls the whole works Big Ben. Named for a fat bureaucrat, Ben is scarcely older than my great-grandmother, but it has quickly become the city's symbol. The tower is 320 feet high, and the clock faces are 23 feet across. The 13-foot-long minute hand sweeps the length of your body every five minutes.

Big Ben is the north tower of a long building, the **Houses of Parliament,** stretching along the Thames. Britain is ruled from this building, which for five centuries was the home of kings and

queens. Then, as democracy was foisted on tyrants, a parliament of nobles was allowed to meet in some of the rooms. Soon, commoners were elected to office, the neighborhood was shot, and the royalty moved to Buckingham Palace. The current building, though it looks medieval with its prickly flamboyant spires, was built in the 1800s after a fire gutted old Westminster Palace.

Today, the **House of Commons,** which is more powerful than the queen and prime minister combined, meets in one end of the building. The rubber-stamp **House of Lords** grumbles and snoozes in the other end of this 1,000-room complex, and provides a tempering effect on extreme governmental changes. The two houses are very much separate: Notice the riverside tea terraces with the color-coded awnings—royal red for lords, common green for commoners. If a flag is flying from the Victoria Tower, at the far south end of the building, Parliament is in session.

• *Now look north (downstream).*

Views of the London Eye Ferris Wheel, The City, and the Thames

Built in 2000 to celebrate the millennium, the London Eye—known to some as "the London Eyesore"—stands 443 feet tall and slowly spins 32 capsules, each filled with 25 visitors, up to London's best viewpoint (up to 25 miles on a rare clear day). Aside from Big Ben, Parliament, St. Paul's Cathedral (not visible from here), and the wheel itself, London's skyline is not overwhelming; it's a city that wows from within.

Next to the wheel sprawls the huge former **County Hall building,** now a hotel and tourist complex. The London Eye marks the start of the **Jubilee Promenade,** a pleasant one-hour riverside walk along the "South Bank" of the Thames, through London's vibrant, gentrified arts-and-cultural zone. Along the way, you have views across the river of St. Paul's stately dome and the financial district, called "The City."

London's history is tied to the **Thames,** the 210-mile river linking the interior of England with the North Sea. The city got its

Westminster Walk

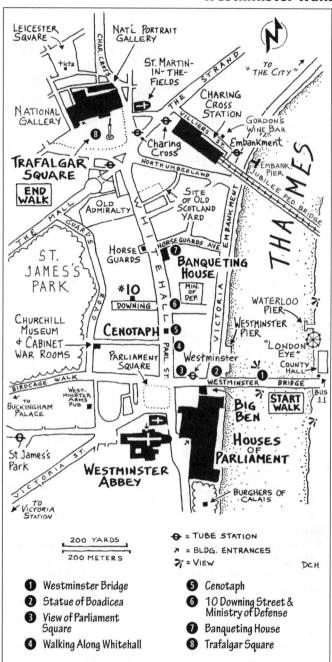

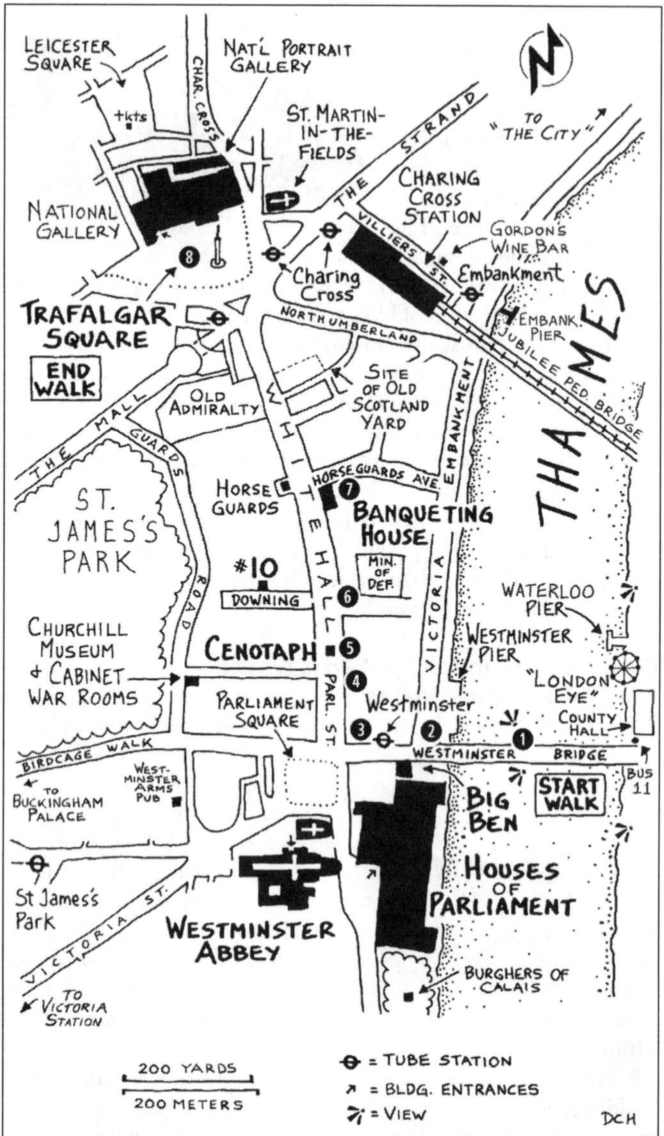

1. Westminster Bridge
2. Statue of Boadicea
3. View of Parliament Square
4. Walking Along Whitehall
5. Cenotaph
6. 10 Downing Street & Ministry of Defense
7. Banqueting House
8. Trafalgar Square

start in Roman times as a trade center along this watery highway. As recently as a century ago, large ships made their way upstream to the city center to unload. Today, the major port is 25 miles downstream.

Look for the piers on the Thames. A 50-minute round-trip **cruise** geared for tourists departs from Waterloo Pier near the base of the Ferris wheel. On the other side of the river, at **Westminster Pier,** boats leave for the Tower of London, Greenwich, and Kew Gardens.

Lining the river, beneath the lamp posts, are little green copper **lions' heads** with rings for tying up boats. Before the construction of the Thames Barrier in 1982 (the world's largest movable flood barrier, downstream near Greenwich), high tides from the nearby North Sea made floods a recurring London problem. The police kept an eye on these lions: "When the lions drink, the city's at risk."

Until 1750, only London Bridge crossed the Thames. Then a bridge was built here. Early in the morning of September 3, 1803, William Wordsworth stood where you're standing and described what he saw:

This city now doth like a garment wear
The beauty of the morning; silent, bare,
Ships, towers, domes, theaters, and temples lie
Open unto the fields, and to the sky;
All bright and glittering in the smokeless air.

• *Walk to Big Ben's side of the river. Near Westminster Pier is a big statue of a lady on a chariot (nicknamed "the first woman driver"...no reins).*

❷ Statue of Boadicea, Queen of the Iceni

Riding in her two-horse chariot, daughters by her side, this Celtic Xena leads her people against Roman invaders. Julius Caesar had been the first Roman to cross the Channel, but even he was weirded out by the island's strange inhabitants, who worshipped trees, sacrificed virgins, and went to war painted blue. Later, Romans subdued and civilized them, building roads and making this spot on the Thames—"Londinium"—into a major urban center.

But Boadicea refused to be Romanized. In A.D. 60, after Roman soldiers raped her daughters, she rallied her people and "liberated" London, massacring its 70,000 Romanized citizens.

However, the brief revolt was snuffed out, and she and her family took poison rather than surrender.

• *There's a civilized public toilet down the stairs behind Boadicea. Continue past Big Ben, one block inland to the busy intersection of Parliament Square.*

❸ View of Parliament Square

To your left is the orange-hued **Parliament.** If Parliament is in session, the entrance is lined with tourists, enlivened by political demonstrations, and staked out by camera crews interviewing Members of Parliament (M.P.s) for the evening news. Kitty-corner across the square, the two white towers of **Westminster Abbey** rise above the trees. The broad boulevard of Whitehall (here called Parliament Street) stretches to your right up to Trafalgar Square.

This is the heart of what was once a suburb of London—the medieval City of Westminster. Like Buda and Pest (later Budapest), London is two cities that grew into one. The City of London, centered near St. Paul's Cathedral and the Tower of London, was the place to live. But King Edward the Confessor decided to build a church (minster) and monastery (abbey) here, west of the city walls—hence Westminster. And to oversee its construction, he moved his court to this spot and built a palace, which gradually evolved into a meeting place for debating public policy. To this day, the Houses of Parliament are known to Brits as the "Palace of Westminster."

Across from Parliament, the cute little church with the blue sundials, snuggling under the Abbey "like a baby lamb under a ewe," is **St. Margaret's Church.** Since 1480, this has been *the* place for politicians' weddings, including Churchill's.

Parliament Square, the small park between Westminster Abbey and Big Ben, is filled with statues of famous Brits. The statue of **Winston Churchill,** the man who saved Britain from Hitler, shows him in the military overcoat he wore as he limped victoriously onto the beaches of Normandy after D-Day. According to tour guides, the statue has a current of electricity running through it to honor Churchill's wish that if a statue were made of him, his head shouldn't be soiled by pigeons.

In 1868, the world's first traffic light was installed on the corner where Whitehall now spills double-decker buses into the square. And speaking of lights, the little yellow lantern atop the concrete post on the street corner closest to Parliament says "Taxi." When an M.P. needs a taxi, this blinks to hail one.

• *Consider touring Westminster Abbey (see page 215). Otherwise, turn right (north), walk away from the Houses of Parliament and the abbey, and continue up Parliament Street, which becomes Whitehall.*

❹ Walking Along Whitehall

Today, Whitehall is choked with traffic, but imagine the effect this broad street must have had on out-of-towners a century ago. In your horse-drawn carriage, you'd clop along a tree-lined boulevard past well-dressed lords and ladies, dodging street urchins. Gazing left, then right, you'd try to take it all in, your eyes dazzled by the bone-white walls of this man-made marble canyon.

Whitehall is now the most important street in Britain, lined with the ministries of finance, treasury, and so on. You may see limos and camera crews as an important dignitary enters or exits. Political demonstrators wave signs and chant slogans—sometimes about issues foreign to most Americans (Britain's former colonies still resent the empire's continuing influence), and sometimes about issues very familiar to us. (In recent years, the war in Iraq has been the catalyst for student walkouts and protest marches here.) Notice the security measures. Iron grates seal off the concrete ditches between the buildings and sidewalks for protection against explosives. The city has been on "orange alert" since long before September 2001, but Londoners refuse to be terrorized, as shown by their determination to continue with life as normal after the bombings of July 2005.

The black, ornamental arrowheads topping the iron fences were once colorfully painted. In 1861, Queen Victoria ordered them all painted black when her beloved Prince Albert ("the only one who called her Vickie") died. Possibly the world's most determined mourner, Victoria wore black for the standard two years of mourning—and tacked on 38 more.

• *Continue toward the tall, square, concrete monument in the middle of the road. On your right is a colorful pub, the Red Lion. Across the street, a 700-foot detour down King Charles Street leads to the Churchill Museum and Cabinet War Rooms, the underground bunker of 21 rooms that was the nerve center of Britain's campaign against Hitler (£10, daily 9:30–18:00; see page 41 for details).*

❺ Cenotaph

This big white stone monument (in the middle of the boulevard) honors those who died in the two events that most shaped modern

Britain—World Wars I and II. The monumental devastation of these wars helped turn a colonial superpower into a cultural colony of an American superpower.

The actual cenotaph is the slab that sits atop the pillar—a tomb. You'll notice no religious symbols on this memorial. The dead honored here came from many creeds and all corners of Britain's empire. It looks lost in a sea of noisy cars, but on each Remembrance Sunday (closest to November 11), Whitehall is closed off to traffic, the royal family fills the balcony overhead in the foreign ministry, and a memorial service is held around the cenotaph.

It's hard for an American to understand the impact of the Great War (WWI) on Europe. It's said that if all the WWI dead from the British Empire were to march four abreast past the cenotaph, the sad parade would last for seven days.

Eternally pondering the cenotaph is an equestrian statue up the street. Earl Haig, commander-in-chief of the British army from 1916 to 1918, was responsible for ordering so many brave and not-so-brave British boys out of the trenches and onto the killing fields of World War I.

• *Just past the cenotaph, on the other (west) side of Whitehall, is an iron security gate guarding the entrance to Downing Street.*

❻ #10 Downing Street and the Ministry of Defense

Britain's version of the White House is where the current prime minister—Tony Blair—and his family live, at #10 (in the black-brick building 300 feet down the blocked-off street, on the right). It looks modest, but the entryway does open up into fairly impressive digs. Blair, who generally prefers persuasive charm to rigid dogma, has tried to build consensus between the "Tories" (Conservatives) and Liberals, but his decision to join the U.S. invasion of Iraq divided the country.

There's not much to see here unless a VIP happens to drive up. Then the bobbies (police officers) snap to and check credentials, the gates open, the traffic barrier midway down the street drops into its bat cave, the car drives in, and...the bobbies go back to mugging for the tourists.

The huge building across Whitehall from Downing Street is the **Ministry of Defense** (MOD), the "British Pentagon." This bleak place looks like a Ministry of Defense should. In front are statues of illustrious defenders of Britain. "Monty" is

Field Marshal Bernard Law Montgomery of World War II, who beat the Nazis in North Africa (defeating Erwin "the Desert Fox" Rommel at El Alamein), giving the Allies a jumping-off point to retake Europe. Along with Churchill, Monty breathed confidence back into a demoralized British army, persuading them they could ultimately beat Hitler.

You may be enjoying the shade of London's **plane trees.** They do well in polluted London: roots that work well in clay, waxy leaves that self-clean in the rain, and bark that sheds and regenerates so the pollution doesn't get into their vascular systems.

• *At the equestrian statue, you'll be flanked by the Welsh and Scottish government offices. At the corner (same side as the Ministry of Defense), you'll find the Banqueting House.*

❼ Banqueting House

This two-story neoclassical building is just about all that remains of what was once the biggest palace in Europe—Whitehall Palace, stretching from Trafalgar Square to Big Ben. Henry VIII started it when he moved out of the Palace of Westminster (now the Parliament) and into the residence of the archbishop of York. Queen Elizabeth I and other monarchs added on as England's worldwide prestige grew. Finally, in 1698, a roaring fire destroyed everything at Whitehall except the name and the Banqueting House.

The kings held their parties and feasts in the Banqueting House's grand ballroom on the first floor. At 112 feet wide by 56 feet tall and 56 feet deep, the Banqueting House is a perfect double cube. Today, the exterior of Greek-style columns and pediments looks rather ho-hum, much like every other white, marble, neoclassical building in London. But in 1620, it was the first—a highly influential building by architect Inigo Jones that sparked London's distinct neoclassical look.

On January 27, 1649, a man dressed in black appeared at one of the Banqueting House's first-floor windows and looked out at a huge crowd that surrounded the building. He stepped out the window and onto a wooden platform. It was **King Charles I**. He gave a short speech to the crowd, framed by the magnificent backdrop of the Banqueting House. His final word was "Remember." Then he knelt and laid his neck on a block as another man in black approached. It was the executioner—who cut off the King's head.

Plop—the concept of divine monarchy in Britain was decapitated. But there would still be kings after **Oliver Cromwell**, the

Protestant anti-monarchist who brought about Charles I's death and then became England's leader. Soon after, the royalty was restored, and Charles' son, **Charles II**, got his revenge here in the Banqueting Hall...by living well. His elaborate parties under the chandeliers celebrated the Restoration of the monarchy. But, from then on, every king knew that he ruled by the grace of Parliament.

Charles I is remembered today with a statue at one end of Whitehall (in Trafalgar Square at the base of the tall column), while his killer, Oliver Cromwell, is given equal time with a statue at the other end (at the Houses of Parliament).

• *Across the street on the left are the* ***Horse Guards,*** *dressed in Charge of the Light Brigade–style cavalry uniforms and swords. Until the Ministry of Defense was created, the Horse Guards was the headquarters of the British army. It's still the home of the queen's private guard. (Changing of the Guard Mon–Sat 11:00, Sun at 10:00, dismounting ceremony daily at 16:00.)*

Continue up Whitehall, passing the ***Old Admiralty,*** *headquarters of the British Navy that once ruled the waves. Across the street, behind the old Clarence Pub, stood the original Scotland Yard, headquarters of London's crack police force in the days of Sherlock Holmes. Finally, Whitehall opens up into the grand, noisy, traffic-filled...*

❽ Trafalgar Square

London's Times Square bustles around world's biggest Corinthian column, where **Admiral Horatio Nelson** stands 170 feet tall in the crow's nest. Nelson saved England at a time as dark as World War II. In 1805, Napoleon was poised on the other side of the Channel, threatening to invade England. Meanwhile, more than 900 miles away, the one-armed, one-eyed, and one-minded Lord Nelson attacked the French fleet off the coast of Spain at Trafalgar. The French were routed, Britannia ruled the waves, and the once-invincible French army was slowly worn down, then defeated at Waterloo. Nelson, while victorious, was shot by a sniper in the battle. He died, gasping, "Thank God, I have done my duty."

At the top of Trafalgar Square (north) sits the domed National

Trafalgar Square

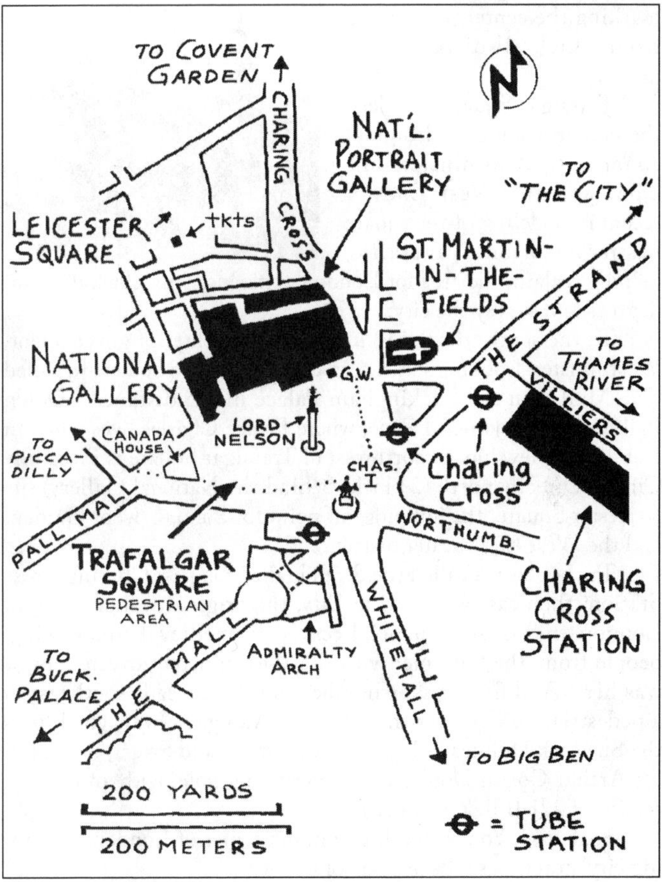

Gallery with its new grand staircase, and to the right, the steeple of **St. Martin-in-the-Fields**, built in 1722, inspiring the steeple-over-the-entrance style of many town churches in New England (free lunch concerts on Mon, Tue, and Fri at 13:00, and evening concerts for a fee at 19:30 Thu–Sat and sometimes Tue or Wed, box office tel. 020/7839-8362). In between is a small statue of America's **George Washington**, looking very much the English gentleman he was. Large statues of important nobodies on pedestals border the four corners of the square. The northwest pedestal remains empty, as Brits debate who should be honored.

At the base of Nelson's column are bronze reliefs cast from melted-down enemy cannons, and four huggable lions dying to have their photo taken with you. In front of the column, Charles I sits on horseback with his head intact. In the pavement in

front of the statue is a plaque marking the center of London, from which all distances are measured.

Trafalgar Square is indeed the center of modern London, connecting Westminster, The City, and the West End. A recent remodeling of the square has rerouted some car traffic, helping reclaim the area for London's citizens. Spin clockwise 360 degrees and survey the city:

To the south (down Whitehall) is the center of government, Westminster. Looking southwest, down the broad boulevard called The Mall, you see Buckingham Palace in the distance. (Down Pall Mall is St. James' Palace, where Prince Charles lives when in London.) A few blocks northwest of Trafalgar Square is Piccadilly Circus. Directly north (2 blocks behind the National Gallery) sits Leicester Square, the jumping-off point for Soho, Covent Garden, and the West End theater district.

The boulevard called the Strand takes you past Charing Cross Station, then eastward to The City, the original walled town of London and today's financial center. In medieval times, when people from The City met with the Westminster government, it was here. And finally, Northumberland Street leads southeast to a pedestrian bridge over the Thames. (Along the way, you'll pass the Sherlock Holmes Pub at 10 Northumberland Street, housed in Sir Arthur Conan Doyle's favorite watering hole, with an upstairs replica of 221-B Baker Street.)

Soak it in. You're smack-dab in the center of London, a thriving city atop thousands of years of history.

BANKSIDE WALK

From London Bridge to Blackfriars Bridge

Bankside—the neighborhood between London Bridge and Blackfriars Bridge—is the historic heart of the newly revamped southern bank of the Thames. For centuries, it was London's red light district. In the 20th century, it became an industrial wasteland of empty warehouses and street crime. Today, the prostitutes and pickpockets are gone, but it's still interesting, with a riverside promenade dotted with pubs, cutesy shops, and historic tourist sights.

Our half-mile walk gives you plenty of history and plenty of sights to choose from—you can see it all, design your own plan, or just enjoy the view of London's skyline across the river.

ORIENTATION

Getting There: Take the Tube to the London Bridge stop to begin the walk. The walk ends near Blackfriars Bridge (closest Tube stops: Blackfriars, just across the bridge on the North Bank, or Southwark, several blocks south of the bridge on the South Bank).

Tourist Information: The Southwark TI is next to Vinopolis (see below), at 1 Bank End, Tue–Sun 10:00–18:00, closed Mon, tel. 020/7357-9168, www.visitsouthwark.com, tourism@southwark.gov.uk.

Old Operating Theatre Museum and Herb Garret: £4.75, daily 10:30–17:00, closed Dec 15–Jan 5, 9a St. Thomas Street, recorded info tel. 020/7955-4791, www.thegarret.org.uk.

Southwark Cathedral: Mon–Fri 8:00–18:00, Sat–Sun 9:00–18:00, last entry 30 min before closing, admission free but £4 suggested donation, audioguide-£2.50, no photo without permission, tel. 020/7367-6700.

***Golden Hinde* Replica:** £3.50, daily 10:00–17:30 (sometimes closed for private events), tel. 0870-011-8700, www.goldenhinde .co.uk.

The Clink Prison Museum: £5 (overpriced), daily 10:00–18:00, July–Sept until 21:00, 1 Clink Street, tel. 020/7403-0900, www.clink.co.uk.

Vinopolis: £12.50 for five tastes (only £11 Tue–Thu), £15 for premium tastes (for £3 you can buy 5 more tastes inside), includes audioguide, daily 12:00–18:00, Mon and Fri–Sat until 21:00, last entry two hours before closing, between the Globe and Southwark Cathedral at 1 Bank End, tel. 0870-241-4040 or 020/7940-8322, www.vinopolis.co.uk.

Shakespeare's Globe: The complex is open 9:00–18:00, but to see the theater interior you must either buy a ticket to a performance (the box office is at the east end of the complex, see Entertainment chapter, page 315) or take a 30-minute guided tour (£9, including exhibit). The tour schedule varies, especially during the summer performance season, when the theater often closes in the afternoon for afternoon or evening shows. (No performances on Mon.) Tours are generally offered on the half-hour mid-May–Sept Mon–Sat 9:00–12:30, Sun 9:30–11:30, and Oct–mid-May daily 10:00–17:00, tel. 020/7902-1500, www.shakespeares-globe.org.

Tate Modern: Free (fee for special exhibitions), daily 10:00–18:00, Fri–Sat until 22:00, audioguide-£2, view restaurant on top floor, tel. 020/7887-8000, recorded info tel. 020/7887-8008, www.tate.org.uk. See page 192 for Tate Modern Tour.

Starring: Shakespeare's world, London Bridge, and historic pubs.

THE WALK BEGINS

• *Start at the south end of London Bridge. From the London Bridge Tube stop, take the "Borough High Street east" exit and turn right (north), walking 100 yards to the bridge.*

❶ London Bridge

The City across the river is to the north, Tower Bridge is east, and the Thames flows from west to east (left to right). Looking to the east (downstream) and turning counterclockwise, you'll see the following.

Downstream

- Tower Bridge (the Gothic-towered drawbridge that many Americans mistakenly call London Bridge).
- The HMS *Belfast* (in the foreground, docked on the southern bank), a WWII cruiser open for tourists. (The new City Hall

Bankside Walk

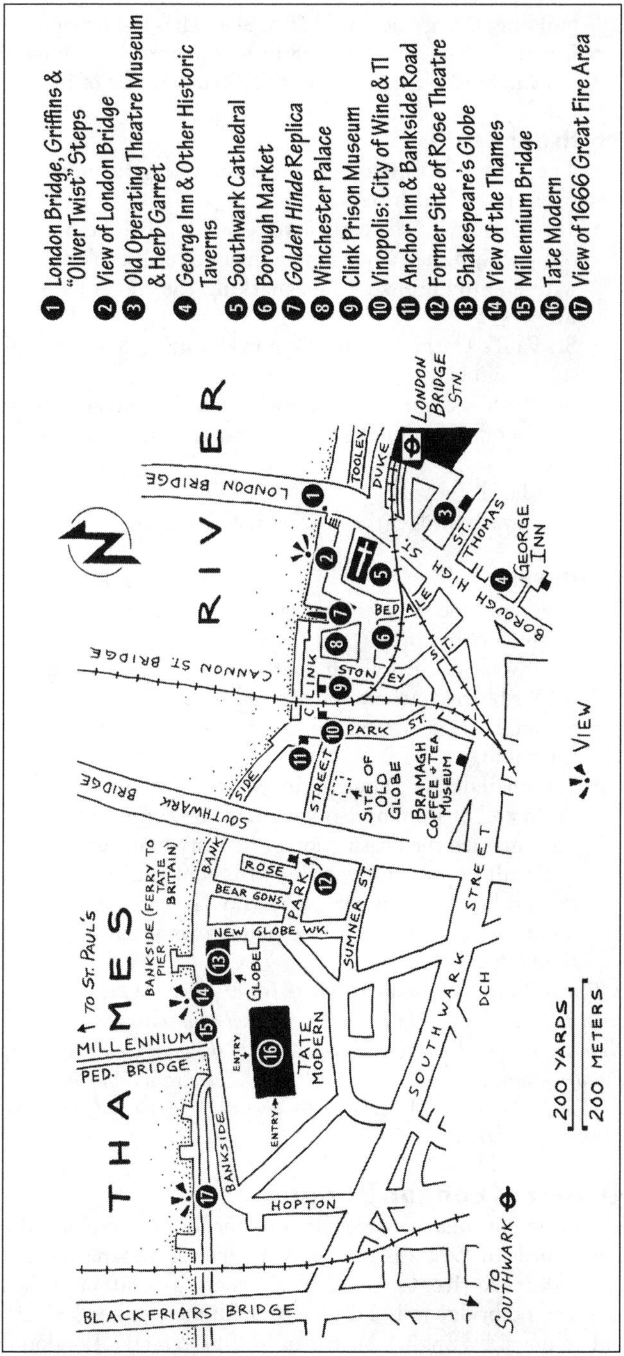

building, though not visible from here, lies just beyond.)
- Canary Wharf (the distant, 800-foot skyscraper with pyramid top and blinking light), built in 1990 on the Isle of Dogs.

North Bank
- The Tower of London (4 spires and a flag rising above the trees on the North Bank).
- The Monument (directly across London Bridge but almost completely buried among modern buildings), a column topped with a shiny bronze knob, marking the start of the Great Fire.
- St. Paul's Cathedral (to the northwest, with a dome like a state capitol and twin spires).
- St. Bride's Church, the pointed, stacked steeple (nestled among office buildings) that supposedly inspired the wedding cake.
- A radio/TV tower.
- Southwark Bridge (the next bridge upstream).

South Bank
- The Tate Modern art museum (square brick smokestack tower on the South Bank).
- Southwark Cathedral (on South Bank, 100 yards away, maybe not visible from where you're standing).
- Borough High Street, the busy street that London Bridge spills into.
- The small dragon statues (winged lions holding shields) at the south end of London Bridge guard the entrance to the City. They marked the jurisdiction of the City to include both sides of the all-important river. Big boats could sail as far inland as this bridge. For centuries, they said, "Neener neener" to late-night partiers who got locked out of town when the gates shut tight at curfew.

• *The best view of London Bridge is not from the bridge itself, but from the riverbank, 50 yards west, reached by a staircase leading down from the bridge. Find the staircase next to the southwest griffin, by the building marked "Two London Bridge." These stairs will impress fans of Charles Dickens'* Oliver Twist*—they're the setting of the infamous "Meeting on the Bridge."*

❷ View of London Bridge

The bridge of today—three spans of boring, traffic-clogged concrete, built in 1972—is (at least) the fourth incarnation of this 2,000-year-old river crossing. The Romans (A.D. 50) built the first wooden footbridge to Londinium (rebuilt many times), which was pulled down by English boatsmen in 1014 to retake London from

Danish invaders. (They celebrated with a song passed down to us as "London Bridge is falling down, my fair lady.")

The most famous version—crossed by everyone from Richard the Lionhearted to Henry VIII to Shakespeare to Newton to Darwin—was built around 1200 and stood for more than six centuries, the only crossing point into this major city. Built of stone on many thick pilings, stacked with houses and shops that arched over the roadway and bulged out over the river, with its own chapel and a fortified gate at each end, it was a neighborhood unto itself (pop. 300). Picture Mel Gibson's head boiled in tar and stuck on a stick along the bridge (like the Scots rebel William Wallace in 1305, depicted in the movie *Braveheart*), and you'll capture the local color of that time.

In 1823, the famous bridge was replaced with a more modern (but less impressive) brick one. In 1967, that brick bridge was sold to an American, dismantled, shipped to Arizona, and reassembled (all 10,000 bricks) in Lake Havasu City. (Humor today's Brits, who'd like to believe the American thought he was buying Tower Bridge.)

• *This walk is a pick-and-choose collection of sights. Those visiting the Old Operating Theatre Museum and Borough High Street inns, described below, will want to see those sights first before heading west: Hike 150 yards south of the bridge (along the left-hand side of Borough High Street) to the Old Operating Theatre Museum (turn left on St. Thomas Street) and the George Inn.*

❸ Old Operating Theatre Museum and Herb Garret

Back when the common cold was treated with a refreshing bloodletting, the Old Operating Theatre—a surgical operating room from the 1800s—was a shining example of "modern" medicine. Today a museum, this is a quirky, sometimes gross, look at that painful transition from folk remedy to clinical health care.

There are three parts to the small museum (reached by a steep, narrow spiral staircase): The Herb Garret displays healing plants used for millennia—different ones for each of the traditional four ailments (melancholic, choleric, sanguine, phlegmatic) to the body's traditional four parts, or "humours" (black bile, yellow bile, blood, and phlegm), corresponding to the earth's traditional four elements (earth, wind, fire, and Ringo). You'll also learn that Florence Nightingale, the nurse famed for saving so many

Crimean War soldiers wounded in Turkey, worked here to improve sanitation and to turn nurses from low-paid domestics into trained doctors' assistants.

The medical instruments section shows crude anesthetics (ether, chloroform, 3 pints of ale), surgical instruments by Black & Decker (drills, knives, saws), and a glaring lack of antiseptics—young Dr. Joseph Lister had yet to discover carbolic acid—which resulted in high rates of mortality and halitosis.

The operating theater is the highlight—a semicircular room surrounded by railings for 150 spectators (truly a "theater"), where patients were operated on and med students observed. The patients were poor women, blindfolded for their own modesty. The doctors donated their time to help, practice, and teach (see the motto *Miseratione non Mercede:* "Out of compassion, not for profit"). The surgeries, usually amputations, were performed under very crude working conditions—under the skylight or by gaslight, with no sink, and only sawdust to sop up blood. The wood still bears bloodstains. Nearly one in three patients died. The informative (if victim-oriented) 75p pamphlet on *Women, St. Thomas' Hospital, and the Old Operating Theatre* draws only a fine line between Victorian male doctors and Jack the Ripper.

• *Farther down Borough High Street (on the left-hand side), you'll find...*

❹ The George Inn and (faint echoes of) Other Historic Taverns

The George is the last of many "coaching inns" that lined the main highway from London to all points south. Like with Greyhound bus lines, each inn was a terminal for far-flung journeys, since coaches were forbidden inside The City. They offered food, drink, beds, and entertainment for travelers—Shakespeare, as a young actor, likely performed in the George's courtyard.

Along Borough High Street are plaques locating the alleyway ("Yard") of long-gone taverns known to book-lovers: **The White Hart** (north of the George), where Shakespeare and Dickens drank and set scenes; **The Tabard** (now called "Talbot," south of George), where Chaucer's band began its fictional trip south in *The Canterbury Tales* ("Befell that in that season on a day/In Southwark at The Tabard as I lay/Ready to wander on my pilgrimage/To Canterbury with full courage"); and **The Queen's Head** (farther south), owned by the mother of John Harvard, of university fame.

• *Southwark Cathedral is near the southwest corner of London Bridge.*

❺ Southwark Cathedral

This neighborhood parish church is where Anne Hathaway would drag husband Will and the Shakespeare girls on Sunday

Southwark Cathedral

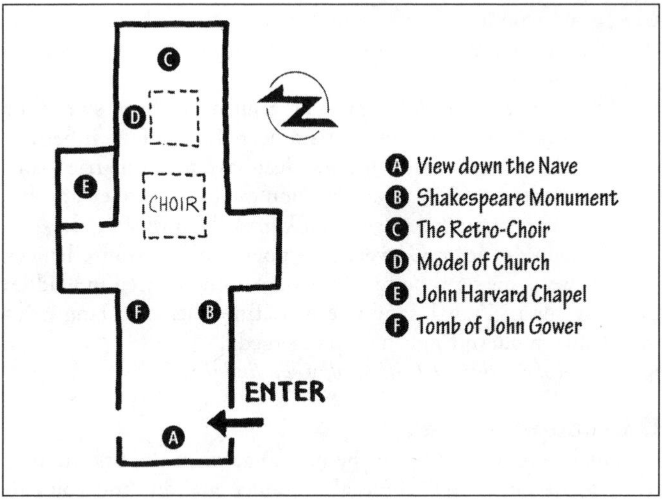

mornings. William prayed while brother Edmund rang the bells. The Southwark (SUTH-uck) church dates back to 1207, though the site has had a church for at least a thousand years and inhabitants for 2,500.

Ⓐ **View down the Nave:** Clean and sparse, with warm golden stone, the church was recently revamped, a symbol of the urban renewal of the whole Bankside/Southwark area. Its WWII damage has been repaired, with new unstained glass windows on the right side. The nave bends slightly to the left (the chandelier, ceiling arches, and altar don't line up until you take 2 baby steps left) as a medieval tribute to Christ's bent body on the cross.

Ⓑ **Shakespeare Monument:** William reclines in front of a backdrop of the 16th-century Bankside skyline (view looking north). Find (left to right) the original Globe Theater, Winchester Palace, Southwark Cathedral, and the old London Bridge with its arched gate. Shakespeare seems to be dreaming about the many characters of his plays, depicted in the stained-glass window above (see Hamlet addressing a skull, right window). To the right is a plaque to the American actor Sam Wanamaker, who spearheaded the building of a replica of Shakespeare's Globe Theatre (see page 96). Shakespeare's brother Edmund is buried in the church, possibly under a marked slab on the floor of the choir area, near the very center of the church. (The Bard lies buried in his hometown of Stratford-upon-Avon.)

Ⓒ **The Retro-Choir:** The 800-year-old crisscross arches and stone tracery in the windows are some of the oldest parts of this historic church.

D Model of Church: Near a reclining stone corpse and a reclining wooden knight, find a model of the church and old Winchester Palace—a helpful reconstruction before we visit the paltry Winchester Palace ruins.

E John Harvard Chapel: The Southwark-born son of an innkeeper (see the record of baptism near the window) inherited money from the sale of the Queen's Head tavern, got married, and sailed to Boston (1637), where he soon died. The money and his 400-book library funded the start of Harvard University.

F Tomb of John Gower: The poet and friend of Chaucer (c. 1400) rests his head on his three books, one written in Middle English, one in French, and one in Latin—the three languages from which modern English soon emerged.

• *Just south of Southwark Cathedral, you'll find the...*

6 Borough Market

Be here weekdays at 2:00 in the morning, when the first trading starts at this open-air wholesale produce market, and you can knock off by sunrise for a pint at the specially licensed Market Porter tavern. On Friday afternoon and all day Saturday, the colorful market opens for retail sales to Londoners seeking trendy specialty and organic foods.

First started a thousand years ago on London Bridge, where country farmers brought fresh goods to the city gates, the market now sits here under a Victorian arcade. Even the railroad rumbling overhead, knifing right through dingy apartment houses (and the Globe Tavern), only adds to the color of London's oldest vegetable market and public gathering spot.

A detour westward through the market leads to Park Street, a popular film set for its old 19th-century ambience. Check out the fragrant cheese shop at Neal's Yard Dairy and the colorful pub.

• *Walk to the river along Cathedral Street, veering left at the Y.*

7 *Golden Hinde* Replica

As we all learned in school, "Sir Francis Drake circumcised the globe with a hundred-foot clipper." Or something like that...

Imagine a hundred men on a boat this size (yes, this replica is full-size) circling the globe on a three-year voyage, sleeping on the wave-swept decks, suffering bad food, floggings, doldrums, B.O., and attacks from foreigners. They explored unknown waters, and were paid only from whatever riches they could find or steal along the way. (I took a bus tour like that once.)

The *Golden Hinde* (see the female deer, or hind, on the prow and stern) was Sir Francis Drake's flagship as he circumnavigated the globe (1577–1580). Drake, a farmer's son who followed the lure of the sea, hated Spaniards. So did Queen Elizabeth I, who hired him to plunder rich Spanish vessels and New World colonies in England's name.

With 164 men on five small ships (the *Hinde* was the largest, at 100 tons and 18 cannons), he sailed southwest, dipping around South America, raiding Spanish ships and towns in Chile, and inching up the coast as far as Canada. By the time it continued across the Pacific to Asia and beyond, the *Hinde* was so full of booty that its crew replaced the rock ballast with gold ingots and silver coins. Three years later, Drake—with only one remaining ship and 56 men—sailed the *Hinde* up the Thames, unloading a fabulously valuable hoard of gold, silver, emeralds, diamonds, pearls, silks, cloves, and spices before the Queen. A grateful Elizabeth knighted Drake on the main deck and kissed him on his *Golden Hinde.*

The *Hinde* was retired gloriously, but rotted away from neglect. Drake received a large share of the wealth, became enormously famous, and later gained more glory defeating the Spanish Armada (aided by "the winds of God") in the decisive battle in the English Channel, off Plymouth (1588)—making England ruler of the waves.

The galleon replica, a working ship that has itself circled the globe, is berthed at St. Mary Overie Dock ("St. Mary's over the river"), a public dock available for free to all Southwark residents. The Thames river trade that used to thrive even this far upstream is now concentrated east of Tower Bridge, a victim of WWII bombing and container ships that require big berths and deep water. Only a few brick warehouses remain (just west of here), waiting to be leveled or yuppified.

• *There's a fine view (with a handy chart to identify things) from the riverside. The beach below is fun for beachcombing—old red roof tiles and little chunks of disposable clay tobacco pipes litter the rocks at low tide. From here, "The Monument" is visible across London Bridge, poking its bristly bronze head above the ugly postwar buildings. Beyond that is the bullet-shaped tip of the modern Swiss Re building. Now turn left, and head west along Pickfords Wharf. About twenty-five yards ahead on the left are the excavated ruins of...*

❽ Winchester Palace

All that remains today is a wall with a medieval rose window, but this was once a lavish 80-acre estate stretching along 200 feet of waterfront. It had a palace, gardens, fountains, stables, tennis courts, a working farm, and a fish-stocked lake. The wall marks the west end of the Great Hall (134 feet by 29 feet), the banquet room for receptions held by the palace's owner, the Bishop of Winchester.

Bishops from 1106 to 1626 lived here as wealthy, worldly rulers of the Bankside area, outside the jurisdiction of The City. They profited from activities illegal across the river, such as prostitution and gambling. They were a law unto themselves, with their own courts and prisons. One famous prison built by the bishops remained, even after its creators were ousted by a Puritan Parliament—the Clink.

• *Fifty yards farther west (along what is now called Clink Street) is...*

❾ The Clink Prison Museum

The prison—now an overpriced and disappointing museum—gave us our expression "thrown in the Clink" from the sound of prisoners' chains. It burned down in 1780, but the underground cells remain, featuring historical information on wall plaques, many torture devices, and a generally creepy, claustrophobic atmosphere.

Originally part of Winchester Palace, it housed troublemakers who upset the smooth running of the bishop's 22 licensed brothels (called "the stews"), gambling dens, and taverns. Bouncers delivered to the Clink drunks who were out of control, johns who couldn't pay, and prostitutes ("women livinge by their bodies") who tried to go freelance or cheated loyal customers. Offending prostitutes had their heads shaved and breasts bared, and were carted through the streets and whipped while people jeered. They might share cells side by side with "heretics"—namely, priests who crossed their bishops.

In 1352, debtors (who'd maxed out their Visa cards) became criminals, housed here among harder criminals in harsh conditions. Prisoners were not fed. They had to bribe guards to get food, to avoid torture, or even to gain their release. (The idea was that you'd brought this on yourself.) Prisoners relied on their families for money, prostituted themselves to guards and other inmates, or reached through the bars at street level, begging from passersby. Murderers, debtors, prostitutes, Protestants, priests, and many innocent people experienced this strange brand of justice...all part of the rough crowd that gave Bankside such a seedy reputation.

• *Continuing west and crossing under the Cannon Street Bridge, you'll find...*

⑩ Vinopolis: City of Wine

This warehouse of wine—with a splash of France, a dash of ancient Rome, and a taste of Italian *vino*—seems out of place in London, but no one's complaining. For more on this wine tasters' paradise, see page 69.

• *Switching from wine to beer, across the street is...*

⑪ Anchor Inn and Bankside Road

The **Anchor** is the last of the original 22 licensed "inns" (tavern/brothel/restaurant/nightclub/casino) of Bankside's red light district heyday in the 1600s. A tavern has stood here for 800 years. The big brick buildings behind the inn were once part of the mass-producing Anchor brewery, with the inn as its brew pub. (Even back in the 1300s, Chaucer wrote, "If the words get muddled in my tale/Just put it down to too much Southwark ale.")

In the cozy, maze-like interior are memories of greats who've drunk here (I did) or indulged in a new drug that hit London in the 1560s—tobacco. Shakespeare, who may have lived along Clink Street, may have tippled here, especially since the original Globe Theatre was right behind the Anchor (see map on page 87). Dr. Samuel Johnson also worked here while writing the famous dictionary that helped codify the English language and spelling. For more on Dr. Johnson, see page 109.

The Anchor Inn marks the start of once-notorious **Bankside Road** that runs along a river retaining wall. In Elizabethan times (16th century), the street was lined with "inns" offering one-stop shopping for addictive personalities. The streets were jammed with sword-carrying punks in tights looking for a fight, prostitutes, gaping tourists from the Borough High Street coaching inns, pick-pockets, river pirates, highwaymen, navy recruiters kidnapping drunks, and many proper ladies and gentlemen who ferried across from the City for an evening's entertainment. And then there were the really seedy people...actors.

• *Crossing under the green-and-yellow Southwark Bridge, notice the metal reliefs depicting London's "Frost Fair" of 1564. Because the old London Bridge was such a wall of stone, the swift-flowing Thames would back up and even freeze over during cold winters. Emerging from under the bridge, die-hard theater fans may wish to detour inland at the first left (the unmarked Bear Gardens Lane) to stop by the site of the Rose Theatre (see map on page 87). But the detour is not highly recommended, since the Rose is almost never open (though private tours can be arranged through the Globe Theatre), and if it is, there's not much to see.*

⓬ Former Site of the Rose Theatre and Bear Gardens (now the Globe Education Centre)

When the 2,200-seat Rose first raised its curtain in 1587, it signaled four decades of phenomenal popularity (centered in Bankside) for a rapidly evolving form of entertainment—theater. Soon there were four great theaters in the area: the Rose, the Hope, the Swan, and...the Globe. (Theatrical types can find the unimpressive plaque marking the site of the original Globe Theater—a half block east of the Rose—and be as disappointed as Sam Wanamaker, who was inspired to build the Shakespeare's Globe replica. More on the Globe when we arrive at the replica.)

It's thought that the young Will Shakespeare, recently arrived from the country, got his start at the Rose tending theatergoers' horses ("What?" he said, "and give up show business?!"). Soon, though, the struggling actor saw his first play *(Henry IV, Part I)* come to life on the Rose stage.

Closer to the river was a theatrical venue called the Bear Gardens (only a plaque marks the spot today). Bankside theaters presented everything from serious drama to light comedy to vaudeville to circus acts to...animal fights. Bearbaiting was the most popular. A bear was chained to a stake while a pack of dogs (mastiffs) attacked, and spectators bet on the winner. The bears, often with teeth filed down or jaws wired shut, fought back with their paws, sweeping dogs into the crowd. Now that's entertainment.

• *Fifty yards farther west on Bankside is...*

⓭ Shakespeare's Globe—1997 Replica of the Original Globe Theatre

All the world's a stage,
And all the men and women merely players.
They have their exits and their entrances,
And one man, in his time, plays many parts.

—*As You Like It*

By 1599, 35-year-old William Shakespeare was a well-known actor, playwright, and businessman in the booming theater trade. His acting company, the Lord Chamberlain's Men, built the 3,000-seat

Globe Theatre, by far the largest of its day (200 yards from today's replica, where only a plaque stands today). The Globe premiered Shakespeare's greatest works—*Hamlet, Othello, King Lear, Macbeth*—in open-air summer afternoon performances, though occasionally at night by light of torches and buckets of tar-soaked ropes.

In 1612, they featured Shakespeare's *All Is True (Henry VIII)*. During Scene 4, a stage cannon boomed, announcing the arrival of King Henry, who started flirting with Anne Boleyn. As the two generated sparks onstage, play-watchers smelled fire. Some stray cannon wadding had sparked a real fire offstage. Within an hour, the wood-and-thatch building had burned completely to the ground, but with only one injury: A man's pants caught on fire and were quickly doused with a bottle of beer.

Built in 1997, the new Globe—round, half-timbered, thatched, using wooden pegs for nails—is a quite realistic replica, though slightly smaller (seating 1,500 spectators) and constructed with fire-repellent materials. They stage performances almost nightly in summer—check at the box office (at the east end of the complex).

Bankside's theater scene vanished in the 1640s, closed by a Parliament dominated by Puritans (hard-line Protestants, like America's Pilgrims). Drama seemed to portray and promote immoral behavior, and actors—men who also played women's roles—parodied and besmirched fair womanhood. Bearbaiting was also outlawed by the outraged moralists (to paraphrase the historian Thomas Macaulay) not because it caused bears pain, but because it gave people pleasure.

⓮ The Thames

From the Cotswolds to the North Sea, the river winds eastward a total of 210 miles. London is close enough to the estuary to be affected by the North Sea's tides, so the river level does indeed rise and fall twice a day. However, after centuries of periodic flooding (spring rains plus high tides), barriers to regulate the tides were built in 1982, east of Tower Bridge. The barriers also slow down the once fast-moving river.

The Thames is still a major commercial artery (again, east of Tower Bridge). In the previous two centuries, it ran brown with Industrial Revolution pollution. Today's it's brown because of estuary silt, and the Thames is one of the cleanest rivers in the industrialized world.

• *Fifty yards west of the Globe, spanning the river, is the...*

⓯ Millennium Bridge

This pedestrian bridge was built in 2000 to connect the Tate Modern with St. Paul's Cathedral and The City. For three glorious days, Londoners made the pleasant seven-minute walk across...before the 25-million-dollar "bridge to the next millennium" started wobbling dangerously (insert your own ironic joke here) and was closed for rethinking. After much work, 20 months, and money ($7 million), the bridge has reopened. Nicknamed "the blade of light," it's designed (partly by Sir Norman Foster, who did the new City Hall downstream) to allow a wide-open view of St. Paul's. Now stabilized and reopened, it links two revitalized sections of London.

⓰ Tate Modern

London's large, impressive modern art collection is housed in a former power station—typical of the whole South Bank's move to renovate empty, ugly Industrial Age hulks. Even if you don't tour the collection, pop inside the north entrance (free) to view the spacious interior, decorated each year with a new industrial-sized sculptural installation by one of the world's top artists.

✪ See Tate Modern Tour, page 192.

• *Bankside—maybe at the Founder's Arms pub along the river—is a great place to contemplate...*

⓱ The Great Fire of 1666

On Sunday, September 2, 1666, stunned Londoners quietly sipped beers in Bankside pubs and watched their City across the river go up in flames. ("When we could endure no more upon the water," wrote Samuel Pepys in his diary, "we went to a little alehouse on the Bankside.") Started in a bakery shop near the Monument (north end of London Bridge) and fanned by strong winds, the fire swept westward, engulfing the mostly wooden city, devouring Old St. Paul's, and moving past what is now Blackfriars Bridge and St. Bride's to Temple Church (near the pointy, black, gold-tipped steeple of the Royal Courts of Justice).

In four days, 80 percent of the City was incinerated, including 13,000 houses and 89 churches. The good news? Incredibly, only nine people died, the fire cleansed a plague-infested city, and Christopher Wren was around to rebuild London's skyline.

The fire also marked the end of Bankside's era as London's naughty playground. Having recently been cleaned up by the Puritans, it now served as a temporary refugee camp for those displaced by the fire. And, with the coming Industrial Age, businessmen demolished the inns and replaced them with brick warehouses, docks, and factories to fuel the economy of a world power.

THE CITY WALK

From Trafalgar Square to London Bridge

In Shakespeare's day, London consisted of a one-square-mile area surrounding St. Paul's. Today, that square mile, the neighborhood known as "The City," is still the financial heart of London, densely packed with history and bustling with business.

This two-mile walk from Trafalgar Square to London Bridge parallels the Thames, on the same main road used for centuries. Allow two to three hours, depending on what you visit. Along the way, you'll see sights from The City's storied past, such as St. Paul's Cathedral, the steeples of other Wren churches, historic taverns, a Crusader church, and narrow alleyways with faint remnants of the London of Shakespeare and Dickens.

But you'll also catch The City in action today, especially if you visit on a weekday at lunchtime, when workers spill into the streets and The City is at its liveliest. See lawyers and judges in robes and wigs taking a cigarette break, brokers in pin-striped power suits buying newspapers from Cockneys, and elderly gentlemen with bowler hats and brollies (umbrellas) browsing for tailored shirts and Cuban cigars. Sip a pint in the same pub where Dickens did, and eavesdrop on a businessmen's power lunch. Use this walk to help resurrect the London that was, then let The City of today surprise you with what is.

ORIENTATION

Getting There: Our walk starts at Trafalgar Square (Tube stops: Charing Cross or Embankment), then heads east on the Strand. The walk ends at London Bridge (where the Bankside Walk, on page 85, begins).

Tourist Information: A TI is next to St. Paul's (daily 9:30–15:00, tel. 020/7332-1456).

Somerset House: Courtauld Gallery-£5, free Mon until 14:00; Hermitage Room-£5; Gilbert Collection-£5; combo-tickets cost £8 for any two sights, £12 for all three; daily 10:00–18:00, last entry 17:15; between the Strand and the Thames, tel. 020/7848-2526 or 020/7845-4600, www.somerset-house.org.uk. ✪ See Courtauld Gallery Tour on page 247.

St. Clement Danes: Free, Mon–Fri 9:00–16:00, Sat 9:30–15:00, Sun 9:30–15:00 but closed to sightseers during worship.

Royal Courts of Justice: Free, Mon–Fri 10:00–16:30, closed Sat–Sun, no photos, Strand, tel. 020/7947-7731.

Prince Henry's Room: Free, Mon–Sat 11:00–14:00, closed Sun, 17 Fleet Street, tel. 020/7936-4004.

Temple Church: Free, Wed–Sat 11:00–16:00, Sun 13:00–15:00, closed Mon–Tue, tel. 020/7353-3470.

Dr. Johnson's House: £4.50, May–Sept Mon–Sat 11:00–17:30, closed Sun; Oct–April Mon–Sat 11:00–17:00, closed Sun, 17 Gough Square, tel. 020/7353-3745.

St. Bride's Church: Free, daily 8:00–16:45 free lunch concerts usually Tue and Fri at 13:15, Sun matinees at 11:00 and evensong at 18:30, just off Fleet Street, tel. 020/7427-0133, www.stbrides.com.

Old Bailey: Free, public galleries only, opening hours depend on court schedule, but are generally Mon–Fri 10:30–16:30, closed Sat–Sun, no kids under 14; no cameras, mobile phones, or bags allowed (check bags across the street at Bailey's Sandwich Bar, £2); tel. 020/7248-3277.

St. Paul's Cathedral: £8, Mon–Sat 8:30–16:30, last entry 16:00, closed Sun except for worship, tel. 020/7236-4128, www.stpauls.co.uk.

St. Mary-le-Bow: Free, Mon–Thu 7:30–18:00, Fri 7:30–16:00, closed Sat–Sun, Cheapside, tel. 020/7248-5139, www.stmarylebow.co.uk.

The Monument: £2, daily 9:30–17:00, tel. 020/7626-2717.

OVERVIEW

The City stretches from Temple Church (near Blackfriars Bridge) to the Tower of London. This was the London of the ancient Romans, William the Conqueror, Henry VIII, Shakespeare, and Elizabeth I.

But The City has been stripped of its history by the Great Fire (1666), the World War II Blitz (1940–1941), and modern economic realities. Today, it's a neighborhood of modern bank buildings and retail stores. Only about 6,000 people actually live here, but on work days, it's packed with hundreds of thousands of commuting bankers, legal assistants, and coffee-shop baristas. By day, The City is a hive of business activity. At night and on weekends, it's a ghost town.

The route is simple—a two-mile walk east along a single street that changes names as you go. The Strand becomes Fleet Street, which becomes Cannon Street.

THE WALK BEGINS

• *From Trafalgar Square (Tube: Charing Cross or Embankment), head east on the Strand. (Some may wish to skip a mile's worth of the Strand by taking the Tube directly to Temple, picking up the walk at St. Clement Danes.)*

The Strand—From Trafalgar Square to The City

This busy boulevard, home to theaters and retail stores, was formerly the high-class riverside promenade, back before the Thames was tamed with retaining walls. **Covent Garden** (see page 119) is just one block left, up Southampton Street.

Ahead on the right is the drive-up entrance to the **Savoy Hotel and Savoy Theatre,** adorned in green neon. The shiny gold knight represents the Earl of Savoy, who built the original riverside palace here in 1245. See the Rolls-Royces, fancy shops, Simpson's Restaurant, Donald Trump luxury, and the doorman in top hat and tails at one of London's ritziest locales. Step inside the Art Deco lobby under the pretext of asking about their afternoon tea (about £25, often booked up a week in advance).

Somerset House is the last of the many great riverside mansions that once lined the Strand. Today, it has a people-friendly courtyard with playful fountains, a riverside terrace, and three separate museums (described on page 101), including the Courtauld Gallery (see tour on page 247).

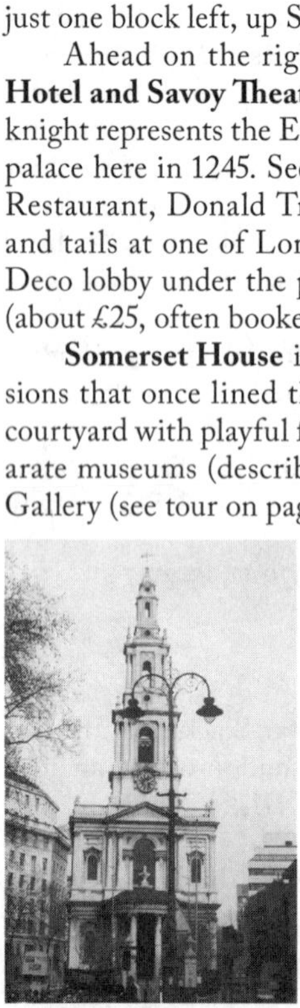

You'll encounter two different churches left Strand-ed in the middle of traffic when the road was widened around them. **St. Mary-le-Strand,** with its clean white interior lit by blue-and-green stained glass, is an oasis of quiet. Charles Dickens' parents got married here. To the left of the church is **BBC World Headquarters,** to the right (a block farther along) is the **Government of Gibraltar Center,** an outpost of one of Britain's last little "colonies," located on the southern tip of Spain.

St. Clement Danes, built by Christopher Wren (1682), was blitzed heavily in World War II. Today, it's dedicated to the

The City Walk

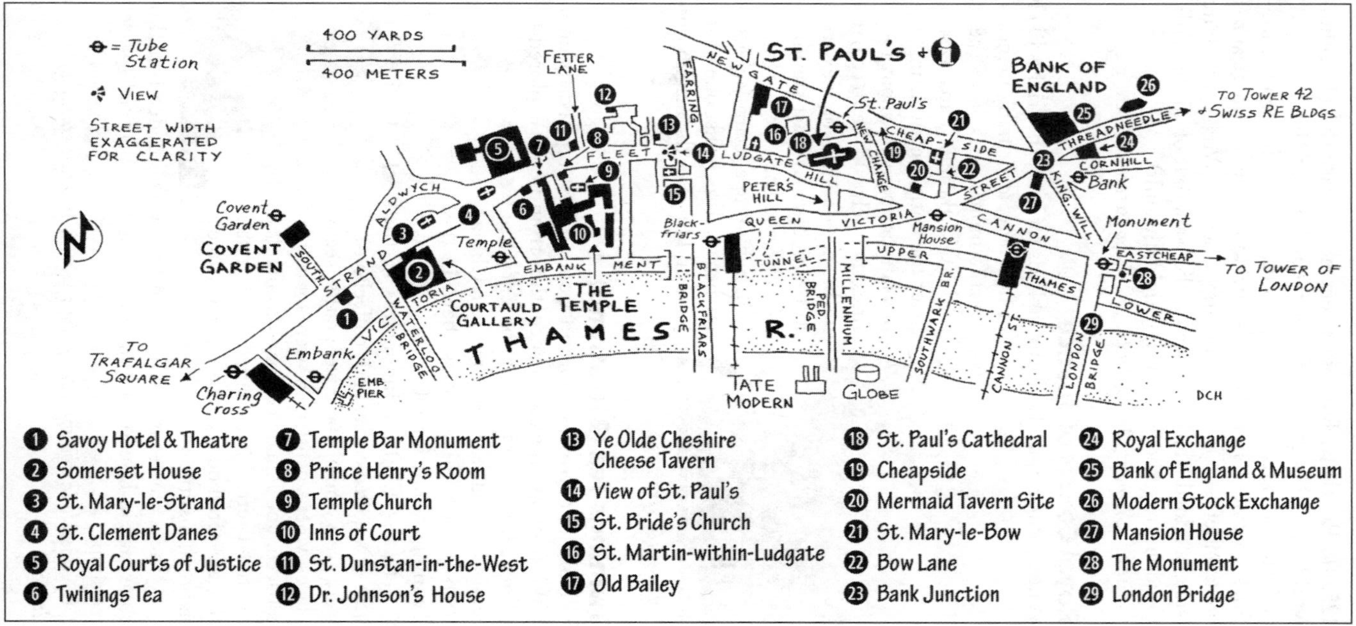

125,000 Royal Air Force servicemen who gave their lives in both world wars. Hundreds of gray medallions in the pavement are dedicated to various squadrons, and Books of Remembrance—10 thick volumes—line the walls, including one to Americans (first book on left side). This is the first of several Wren-built churches (steeple added later) we'll see on the walk, out of 23 that still dot London (from the 50-some he originally built).

• *Past St. Clement Danes, on the left side of street are the...*

Royal Courts of Justice

When former Spice Girls sue tabloids for libel, the trial is likely to be held here, at Britain's highest civil court (criminal cases down the street at the Old Bailey). Paparazzi often litter the entrance, awaiting a celeb or a lawyer (many of whom are celebrities themselves). The 76 courtrooms in this neo-Gothic complex are open to the public. At least step into the lobby to see the vast Gothic entry hall. Submit to a security check to go farther in. This is just one of several legal buildings in the neighborhood.

• *Across the street is...*

Twinings Tea (216 Strand)

When the narrowest store in London first opened its doors in 1706, tea was an exotic concoction from newly explored lands. (The Chinese statues at the entrance remind us that tea came first from China, then India.) This store has been in the Twinings family for 300 years.

In the 1700s, London was in the grip of a coffee craze, and "coffeehouses" were everywhere. These were rather seedy places, where "gentlemen" went for coffee, tobacco, and female companionship. Tea offered a refreshing change of pace, and the late-afternoon "cuppa" soon became a national institution.

These days—as you'll see on this walk—coffee is making a comeback in London in the form of modern, Starbucks-style coffee shops.

• *Up ahead, in the middle of the street, is a small statue of a winged dragon.*

Temple Bar Monument

The mythological dragon marks the official border between the City of Westminster and The City of London. The Queen, who presides over Westminster, does not pass this point without ceremonial permission of The City's Lord Mayor. The relief at its base shows Queen Victoria submitting to this ritual in 1837.

The original Temple Bar gate was built of stone by St. Paul's architect, Christopher Wren, in 1672. But given the increase in traffic and new construction around it, the gate didn't "fit" anymore. It was disassembled in 1878 and carted off to ornament the rural estate of a brewery owner. Finally, in 2004, the 2,700 stones were brought back to The City and painstakingly rebuilt a half-mile away, in Paternoster Square, just north of St. Paul's.

• *Cross the border back at the dragon, leaving Westminster and entering The City. Ahead, on the left (194 Fleet Street), is the Old Bank of England pub—a former bank with a lavish late-Victorian interior that serves lunches to the 9-to-5 crowd. Up a few storefronts, on the right side of the street, find...*

Prince Henry's Room (17 Fleet Street)

This half-timbered, three-story, Tudor-style building (1610) is one of the few to survive the Great Fire. In Shakespeare's day, the entire City was packed, rooftop to rooftop, with wood and plaster buildings like this. Many were five and six stories high, with narrow frontage. Little wonder that a small fire could spread so quickly and become the Great Fire of 1666.

The top floor of the house is "Prince Henry's Room" (which you can visit), once an office of King Charles I's son. Beneath the plaster ceiling is an exhibit on Samuel Pepys (1633–1701). Though not a famous man himself, Pepys (pronounced "peeps") kept a diary chronicling London life and the Great Fire that, even today, makes that time come alive. Pepys lived in the neighborhood, was baptized in nearby St. Bride's Church, and drank in this room when it was a tavern.

• *Pass underneath the house, through the passageway called Inner Temple Lane (if this door is closed, try the wooden doors near #10) that leads a half block to the exotic...*

Temple Church

Exterior: The round, crenellated, castle-turret roof and tiny statue of a knight on horseback (on a pillar in the courtyard) mark this

as a Crusader church (1185), from the days of King Richard the Lionhearted. The church was the headquarters of the Knights Templar, a band of heavily armed, highly trained monks who dressed in long white robes (decorated with red crosses) beneath heavy armor. In their secret rituals, the knights were sworn to chastity and to the protection of pilgrims on their way to the Muslim-held Holy Land.

Interior: Inside (enter along the side), some honored knights lie face-up on the floor under the rotunda of the circular "nave,"

patterned after the Church of the Holy Sepulchre in Jerusalem. A knight's crossed legs indicate that he probably died peacefully at home. Surrounding the serene knights are gargoyle faces, perhaps the twisted expressions seen in distant wars.

By 1300, the Knights Templar's mission of protecting pilgrims had become a corrupt "protection" racket, and they'd grown rich loaning money to kings and popes. Those same kings and popes condemned the monks as heretics and sodomites, and confiscated their lands (1312). The Temple Church was rented to lawyers, who built the Inns of Court around it.

• *Abutting, surrounding, and extending from the Temple Church is a vast complex of buildings covering a full city block between the Strand/Fleet Street and the Thames, known collectively as...*

The Inns of Court

Wander through the peaceful maze of buildings, courtyards, narrow lanes, nooks, gardens, fountains, and century-old gas lamps, where lawyers take a break from the Royal Courts. The complex is a self-contained city of lawyers, with offices, lodgings, courtrooms, chapels, and dining halls. Law students must live here (and are even required to eat a number of meals on the premises) to complete their legal internship.

You'll see barristers in modern business suits and ties, plus a few in traditional wigs and robes, as they prepare to do legal battle. The wigs are a remnant of French manners of the 1700s, when every European gentleman wore one.

• *Get lost. Don't worry, you'll eventually spill back out onto the busy*

The Da Vinci Code in London

Readers of Dan Brown's best-selling novel—a work of fiction encrusted with many real and many fictional facts—will recognize scenes set in London. "In London lies a knight a Pope interred...You seek the orb that ought to be on his tomb." This is one of the cryptic clues Robert Langdon, an American art historian, must follow to solve a murder and, ultimately, find the "Holy Grail." Some stops along his Grail trail (including details that may spoil the plot for those who haven't read it):

Temple Church: The church's stone knights, from the secret society of Templars, seem to be exactly what Langdon seeks. But he finds that there's no "orb," and the knights aren't even "tombs" (containing bodies), but merely effigies. (This isn't the only red herring in the book.)

Westminster Abbey: At the tomb of Isaac Newton (in the nave, see page 223), they find an "orb." (They also find a message summoning them to the Chapter House, where Langdon is surprised to find that a friend is the enemy.)

King's College: Langdon gets research assistance at the building along the Strand, by Somerset House.

Opus Dei Centre: The conservative Catholic organization (also searching for the Grail) has an office near Kensington Gardens.

The novel culminates in Paris, at the Louvre's Pyramide Inversee. If the book turns out to be true, you'll find the Holy Grail in a shopping mall, embedded in concrete under the inverted glass pyramid, next to Virgin Records.

street. Return to Prince Henry's Room, which marks the spot where the Strand becomes...

Fleet Street

"The Street" was the notorious haunt of a powerful combination—lawyers and the media. (You just passed a pub called the "Wig and Pen.") In 1500, Wynkyn de Worde moved here with a newfangled invention, a printing press, making this area the center of an early Information Age. In 1702, the first daily newspaper appeared. Soon you had *The Tatler*, *The Spectator*, and many others pumping out both hard news and paparazzi gossip for the hungry masses. Just past St. Dunstan Church, you'll see a building decorated with mosaic signs with the names of some bygone newspapers: *The Dundee Evening Telegraph*, *The People's Journal*, and so on.

London became the nerve center of a global, colonial empire, and Fleet Street was where every twitch found expression. Hard-drinking, ink-stained reporters gathered in taverns and coffee-houses, pumping lawyers for juicy pretrial information, scrambling for that choice bit of must-read gossip that would make their paper number one. They built an industry that still thrives—Britain supports some 13 national newspapers, selling 14 million papers a day.

Today, busy Fleet Street bustles with almost every business *except* newspapers. The industry made a mass exodus in the 1980s for offices elsewhere, replaced by financial institutions. As you walk along, you'll see the former offices of the the *Daily Telegraph* (135 Fleet Street) and *Daily Express* (#121–28—peek into the lobby to see its classic 1930s Art Deco interior). The last major institution to leave (in the summer of 2005) was the Reuters news agency (#85, opposite the *Daily Express*).

• *Heading east along Fleet Street, you'll find...*

St. Dunstan-in-the-West—The Great Fire of 1666

This church stands where the Great Fire of September 1666 finally ended. The fire started near London Bridge. For three days it swept westward, fanned by hot and blustery weather, leveling everything in its path. As it approached St. Dunstan, 40 theology students battled the blaze, holding it off until the wind shifted, and the fire slowly burned itself out.

From here to the end of our walk (1.5 miles), we'll be passing through the fire's path of destruction. It left London a Sodom-and-Gomorrah wasteland so hot it couldn't be walked on for weeks. (For more on the fire, see page 98 of the Bankside Walk.)

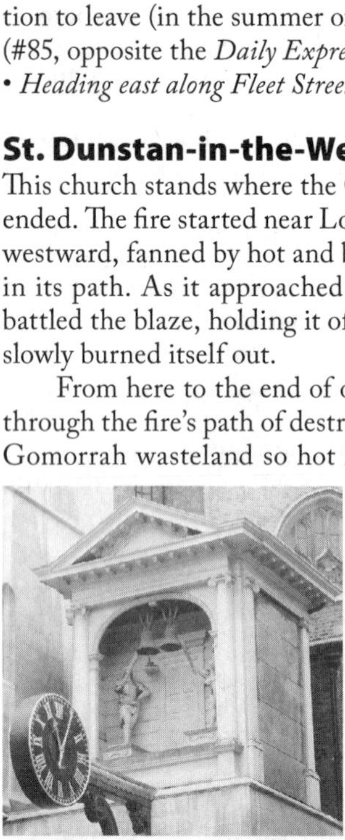

Today, St. Dunstan is one of the few churches with a thriving congregation in this now depopulated and secularized district. It's home to Orthodox Romanians. The clock outside (1670) features London's first minute hand and two slaves gonging two bells four times an hour.

• *Continue east on Fleet Street. A half-block past Fetter Lane, turn left through a covered alleyway (at #167, a few steps beyond Red Lion Court). As the alley ends, turn right at Pemberton Row and follow brown signs directing you to Dr. Johnson's House.*

Narrow Lanes—1700s London

"Sir, if you wish to have a just notion of the magnitude of this city, you must...survey the innumerable little lanes and courts," said the writer Samuel Johnson in 1763 to his young friend and biographer, James Boswell. These twisting alleyways and cramped buildings that house urban hobbits give a glimpse of rebuilt 1700s London, a crowded city of half a million people. After the Great Fire, London was resurrected in brick and stone instead of wood, but they stuck to the same medieval street plan, resulting in narrow lanes of brick buildings like these.

• *The narrow lanes eventually spill into Gough Square, about a block north of Fleet Street, where you'll find...*

Dr. Johnson's House (17 Gough Square)

"When a man is tired of London, he is tired of life," wrote Samuel Johnson, "for there is in London all that life can afford." Johnson (1709–1784) loved to wander these twisting lanes, looking for pungent slices of London street life that he could pass along in his weekly columns called "The Rambler" and "The Idler."

At age 28, Johnson arrived in London with one of his former students, David Garrick, who went on to revolutionize London theater. Doctor Johnson prowled the pubs, brothels, and coffeehouses, and the illicit gaming pits where terriers battled cornered rats while men bet on the outcome. Johnson—described as "tall, stout," and "slovenly in his dress"—became a well-known eccentric and man-about-town, though he always seemed to live on the fringes of poverty.

Johnson inhabited this house from 1748 to 1759. He prayed at St. Clement Danes, drank in Fleet Street pubs, and, in the attic of the house, produced his most famous work. In 1755, he published the first great dictionary of the English language, starring Johnson's 42,773 favorite words culled from all the books he'd read. It took him and six assistants more than six years of sifting through all the alternate spellings and Cockney dialects of the world's most complex language. He standardized spelling and pronunciation, explained the word's etymology, and occasionally put his own droll spin on words. ("Oats: a grain, which is generally given to horses, but in Scotland supports the people.")

Today, the house is a museum (£5) for hard-core Johnson fans (I met one once), featuring period furniture, pictures of Johnson and Boswell, a video, and a first edition of his dictionary.

• *At the other end of Gough Square, turn right at the statue of Johnson's cat Hodge and head back toward Fleet Street, noticing the lists of barristers (trial lawyers) on the doorways. They work not as part of a firm but as freelancers sharing offices and clerks. Stay to the left as you wind through the alleys, and look near Fleet Street for the entrance of...*

Ye Olde Cheshire Cheese Tavern

Johnson often—and I do mean often—popped 'round here for a quick one, sometimes with David Garrick and his sleazy actor friends.

"The Cheese" dates from 1667, when it was rebuilt after the Great Fire, but it's been a tavern since 1538. It's a four-story warren of small, smoky, wood-lined rooms, each offering different menus, from pub grub to white-tablecloth meals. A traditional "chop house," it serves hearty portions of meats to power-lunching businessmen.

Sit in Charles Dickens' favorite seat, next to a coal fireplace (in the "Chop Room," main floor) and order a steak-and-kidney pie and some spotted dick (sponge pudding with currants). Sip a pint of Samuel Smith (the house beer of the current owners) and think of Samuel Johnson, who drank here pondering various spellings: "pint" or "pynte," "color" or "colour," "theater" or "theatre." Immerse yourself in a world largely unchanged for centuries, a world of reporters scribbling the news over lunch, of Alfred Lord Tennyson inventing rhymes and Arthur Conan Doyle solving crimes, of W.B. Yeats, Teddy Roosevelt, and Mark Twain. For more information on pubs, see page 284.

• *Back out on Fleet Street, you're met with a stunning...*

View of St. Paul's—the Blitz, the Great Fire, the Plague, and Christopher Wren

If you were standing here on December 30, 1940, the morning after a German Luftwaffe firebomb raid, you'd see nothing but a flat, smoldering landscape of rubble, with St. Paul's rising above it almost miraculously intact. (For more on the Blitz, see page 231.)

Standing here in September 1666, you'd see nothing but smoke and ruins. The Great Fire razed everything, including the original

The Great Fire

The stones of St. Paul's flew like grenades, the lead melting down the streets in a stream.... God grant mine eyes may never behold the like.... Above 10,000 homes all in one flame, the noise and crackling and thunder of the impetuous flames, the shrieking of women and children, the hurry of the people, the fall of the towers, houses and churches was like an hideous storm.

—John Evelyn, eyewitness

(For more on the Great Fire, see page 98 of the Bankside Walk.)

St. Paul's Cathedral. And standing here in September 1665, you'd hear "Bring out yer dead!" as they carted away 70,000 victims of bubonic plague. After the double-whammy of plague and fire, the architect Christopher Wren was hired to rebuild St. Paul's and The City.

Even today, we see the view that Wren intended—a majestic dome hovering above the hazy rooftops, surrounded by the thin spires of his lesser churches. In the foreground below St. Paul's is the slender, lead-covered steeple of St. Martin-within-Ludgate, perfectly offsetting the more massive dome. Wren's 50-some churches are more than plenty for today's secular ghost town of a City.

• *A half-block east of Ye Olde Cheshire Cheese and a half-block down St. Bride's Avenue, is the stacked-tier steeple of...*

St. Bride's Church (1671–1675)

The 226-foot steeple, Wren's tallest, inspired a local baker to invent the wedding cake. St. Bride's was one of the first of Wren churches to open its doors after the Fire. Inside, the church gleams since its post-Blitz reconstruction, re-creating the squares, circles, and rosettes of Wren's original vision.

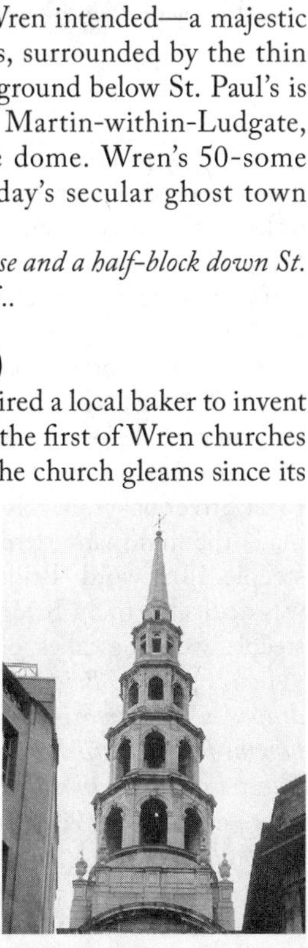

St. Bride's is nicknamed both "The Cathedral of Fleet Street" and "The Printer's Church." It has been home to journalists, scholars, and literati ever since 1500, when Wynkyn de Worde set up his printing press here on church property, in a neighborhood dominated by de Worde's best customers: the literate clergy. The pews bear the names of departed journalists.

Christopher Wren
(1632–1723)

When London burned, King Charles II turned to his old childhood friend, Christopher Wren, to rebuild it. The 33-year-old Wren was not an architect, but he'd proven his ability in every field he touched: astronomy (mapping the moon and building a model of Saturn), medicine (using opium as a general anesthetic, making successful blood transfusions between animals), mathematics (a treatise on spherical trigonometry), and physics (his study of the laws of motion influenced Newton's "discovery" of gravity). Wren also invented a language for the deaf, studied refraction and optics, and built weather-watching instruments.

Though domed St. Paul's is Wren's most famous church, the smaller churches around it better illustrate his distinctive style: a steeple over the west entrance; an uncluttered, well-lit interior; neoclassical (Greek-style) columns; a curved or domed plaster ceiling; geometrical shapes (e.g., round rosettes inside square frames); and fine carved woodwork, often by his favorite whittler, Grinling Gibbons.

Thanks to Hitler's bombs, St. Bride's was instantly excavated down to its sixth-century Saxon foundations, revealing previously unknown history, open to visitors today in the Museum of Fleet Street (free, downstairs in the crypt). You'll see layers of history from six previous churches, including 17th-century tobacco pipes, medieval stained glass, and Roman coins. A facsimile of Ovid's *Metamorphoses* was printed by de Worde's mentor, William Caxton (c. 1422–1491), who also published Chaucer's *Canterbury Tales.* Caxton gave de Worde his training and his printing press.

Also in the crypt is the wedding dress of the wife of the Fleet Street baker, Mr. Rich, who gazed out his shop window and made the first many-tiered wedding cake—inspired by St. Bride's steeple. (The word "Bride" is only coincidental, since the church was dedicated to St. Bridgit—or Bride—of Kildare long before the steeple, wedding cakes, or Mrs. Rich's wedding dress.)

• *A block past St. Bride's Church on Fleet Street is the Punch Tavern, draped with memories of the venerable London political magazine famous for its much-loved "Punch and Judy" cartoons. Peek in to see Punch and his twin wife Judy looking down on a perfectly Victorian scene (good lunches, 99 Fleet Street). The valley between St. Bride's and St. Paul's is the...*

Fleet River and Ludgate

The Fleet River—now covered over with concrete—flows southward, crossing underneath Fleet Street on its way to the Thames at Blackfriars Bridge. In medieval times, the river formed the western boundary of the walled city. Wren's church of St. Martin-within-Ludgate actually incorporates the old city wall into its west wall, at the portal known as Ludgate.

• *After crossing the valley, look left down Old Bailey Street to see...*

Old Bailey—Central Criminal Court

England's nastiest criminals—from the king-killers of the Civil War to the radically religious William Penn, from the criminally homosexual Oscar Wilde to the Yorkshire Ripper—were tried here, in Britain's highest criminal court. On top of the copper dome stands the famous golden Lady who weighs and executes Justice with scale and sword. The Old Bailey is built on the former site of Newgate Prison, with its notorious execution-by-hanging site. Inside, you can visit courtrooms and watch justice doled out the old-fashioned way (see page 61 in Sights chapter, no cameras). Bewigged barristers argue before stern judges while the accused sits in the dock.

• *Continue up Ludgate Hill to...*

St. Paul's Cathedral

The greatest of Wren's creations is the rebuilt St. Paul's, England's national church and the heart of The City. After laboring for over 40 years on the church (and what was then the second-largest dome in the world), an elderly Wren got to look up and see his son place the cross on top of the dome, completing the masterpiece. There's been a church on this spot since 604. St. Paul's was the symbol of London's rise from the Great Fire of 1666 and of the city's survival of the Blitz of 1940.

✪ See St. Paul's Tour on page 225.

• *From St. Paul's, the most direct route to London Bridge is to continue east on what is now called Cannon Street. But we'll go east on Cheapside, located behind St. Paul's. (Note: A right turn at St. Paul's would take you to the Millennium Bridge across the Thames.)*

Cheapside—Shakespeare's London

This was the main east–west street of Shakespeare's London, which had a population of about 200,000. The wide street hosted The City's marketplace ("cheap" meant market), seen today in the

The London Plague of 1665

The Grim Reaper—in the form of the bacteria *Yersinia pestis* (bubonic plague)—rode through London on fleas atop a black rat. It killed one in six people, while leaving the buildings standing. (The next year, the buildings burned.) It started in the spring as "the Poore's Plague," neglected until it spread to richer neighborhoods. During the especially hot summer, 5,000 died each week. By December, St. Bride's congregation was 2,111 souls fewer.

Victims passed through several days of agony: headaches, vomiting, fever, shivering, swollen tongue, and swollen buboes (lumps) on the groin glands. After your skin turned blotchy black (the "Black Death"), you died. "Searchers of the Dead" carted them off to mass graves, including one near St. Bride's. Both the victims and their families were quarantined under house arrest, with a red cross painted on the door and a guard posted nearby, and denied access to food, water, or medical attention for 40 days—a virtual death sentence even for the uninfected.

The disease was blamed on dogs and cats, and paid dog-killers destroyed tens of thousands of pets, bringing even more rats. People who didn't die tried to leave. The Lord Mayor quarantined the whole city within the walls, so the only way out was to produce (or afford) a "certificate of health."

By fall, London was a ghost town, and throughout England, people avoided Londoners like the Plague. It took the Great Fire of 1666 to fully cleanse the city of the disease. Some scholars have suggested that a popular nursery rhyme refers to the dreaded disease (while others brush it off as bunk):

Ring around the rosie (flower garlands to keep the Plague away)
A pocket full of posies (buboes on the groin)
Ashes, ashes (your skin turns black)
We all fall down (dead).

names of the streets that branch off from it: Bread, Milk, Honey. Rebuilt after the war, Cheapside is now the home of cheap shoes, concrete-and-glass banks, and Ye Olde Starbucks.

If you were to detour two blocks south on Bread Street (at the corner of Bread and Cannon streets) you would not see even a trace of the **Mermaid Tavern,** Shakespeare's favorite haunt, but that's where it stood. In the early 1600s, "Sweet Will" would meet Ben Jonson, Sir Walter Raleigh, and John Donne at the Mermaid for food, ale, and literary conversation. Francis Beaumont, one of the group, wrote: "What things have we seen/Done at the Mermaid! heard words that/have been/So nimble, and so full of subtle flame..."

• *A little farther east along Cheapside is...*

St. Mary-le-Bow

From London's earliest Christian times, a church has stood here. The steeple of St. Mary-le-Bow (MAR-ly-bo), rebuilt after the Fire, is one of Wren's most impressive. He incorporated the ribbed-arch design of the former church (a "bow" is an arch) in the steeple's midsection. In the courtyard is a statue of a smiling Captain John Smith, who led an English colony in Jamestown, Virginia, U.S.A. before retiring here near the church. Inside the church, see not one but two pulpits, used today for point-counterpoint debate of moral issues.

The church's bells chime at the very center of old London. This is the "Cockney" neighborhood of plucky streetwise urchins, where a distinctive Eliza Doolittle dialect is still sometimes spoken. Buy a newspaper and see if the man calls you "guv'nah."

• *Behind St. Mary-le-Bow is...*

Bow Lane

Today, pedestrian-only Bow Lane features smart clothing shops, sandwich bars, and pubs. The entire City once had narrow lanes like Bow, Watling, and Bread Streets. Explore this area between Cheapside and Cannon Street.

When Shakespeare bought his tights and pointy shoes in Bow Lane, the shops were wooden, the streets were dirt, and the bathroom was a ditch down the middle of the road. (The garbage brought rats, and rats brought plagues, like the one in 1665.) You bought your water in buckets carted up from the Thames. And at night, the bellman walked the streets, ringing the hour.

(For more Shakespearean ambience, it's a 3-block walk south from St. Paul's to the river, where the Millennium Bridge crosses the Thames to Shakespeare's Globe, a reconstruction of the theater where many of Shakespeare's plays premiered. See page 96 of the Bankside Walk.)

• *Continue east on Cheapside a few blocks to the long, wide intersection where nine streets meet, called Bank Junction (Tube: Bank). Looking east, survey the buildings before you. There may be a historical plaque at the street corner with a helpful diagram of Bank Junction's buildings. A good place to view it all is from in front of Mansion House, the building with the six-columned (not eight-columned) entrance, standing where Victoria Street empties into Bank Junction.*

Bank Junction

You're at the center of financial London. The Square Mile hosts 500 foreign banks. London, centrally located amid the globe's time zones, can find someone around the world to trade with 24 hours a day.

• *Look kitty-corner across the square at the eight-columned entrance to the...*

Royal Exchange: This is where it all began: the original stock exchange, back when "stock" meant whatever could be loaded and unloaded onto a boat in the Thames. Remember, London got its start as a river-trading town. Soon, they were gathering here, trading slips of paper and "futures" in place of live goats and chickens. Traders needed money-changers, who needed bankers...and London's financial district boomed. Today, you can step inside under the *Trading Since 1571* sign to a skylight-covered courtyard lined with traders in retail goods.

• *To the left of the Royal Exchange is the city block–sized Bank of England (main entrance just across Threadneedle Street from the Royal Exchange entrance).*

Bank of England: This 3.5-acre, two-story complex houses the country's national bank. In 1694, it loaned £1.2 million to King William III at 8 percent interest to finance a war with France; it's managed the national debt ever since. It's an investment bank (a banker's bank), loaning money to other financial institutions. Working in tandem with the government (nationalized 1946, independent 1997), "The Old Lady of Threadneedle Street" sets interest rates, prints pound notes, and serves as the country's Fort Knox, housing stacks of gold bars.

The complex has a **Bank Museum** inside (free, enter from far side, on St. Bartholomew Lane). See banknotes from 1699, an old safe, account books, and mannequins of CPAs in powdered wigs. Also see the new pound notes with a foil hologram and numbers visible under UV light (to stay one step ahead of counterfeiters). The museum's highlight is under the rotunda, displaying 59 fake gold bars and one real one. The real gold is worth more than $100,000 (check today's rates nearby) and weighs 28 pounds. Try lifting it.

• *Rising up behind the Bank of England is the...*

Modern Stock Exchange: This gray, concrete, 26-story building on Threadneedle Street now houses the stock exchange, having moved here from the Royal Exchange in 1972.

• *Just behind and to the right of the modern Stock Exchange is...*

Tower 42: The black-capped skyscraper at 600 feet is The City's tallest (but not London's tallest, which is Canary Wharf, far to the east of here).

• *To the right is the bullet-shaped, spiral-ribbed, glass...*

Swiss Re Building: Built in 2003, the 40-story building houses the London office of a Swiss re-insurance company (an insurer's insurer). The building—nicknamed the "erotic gherkin" (pickle)—is ventilated by natural air entering the balconies spiraling around the perimeter.

• *You're standing in front of...*

Mansion House: As the official residence of The City's Lord Mayor, Mansion House carries on centuries of tradition. Until recently, when an all-London mayor was elected, each district was self-governing. Even today, the Lord Mayor holds a prestigious office, presiding from this palatial building.

• *From Bank Junction, turn right on Lombard Street, which turns into King William Street, and head southeast toward London Bridge. Near the northeast corner of the bridge, look to your left and find a lone column poking its bristly bronze head above the modern rooftops.*

The Monument

The 202-foot hollow column is Wren's tribute to the Great Fire

that gave him a blank canvas on which to create modern London. At 2:00 in the morning of September 2, 1666, a small fire broke out in a baker's oven in nearby Pudding Lane. Supposedly, if you tipped the Monument over (to the east), it would fall on the exact spot. Fanned by hot, blustery weather, the fire swept westward, leaping from house to house until The City was a square mile of flame.

You can climb the 311 steps up the column for a view that's still pretty good, despite modern buildings.

• *From here, hike out over the river on...*

London Bridge

End our walk at The City's beginning. (For the history of London Bridge, see page 88 of the Bankside Walk.)

The City was born as a river-trading town. The Thames carried goods east to west, from the interior of England to the open seas. London Bridge, first built by the ancient Romans, established a north–south axis. Soon, goods from every corner of the world were pouring into this, the modern world's first great urban center. Surviving plagues, fires, blitzes, economic changes, and even Thatcherism, with its worldwide financial network and cultural heritage, The City thrives.

• *From here, the Tower of London (see page 257) is a short walk east, down either Eastcheap or Lower Thames Street. The Bankside Walk (page 85) begins across London Bridge. You can return to Trafalgar Square on the Tube (Monument stop nearby) or bus #15 (from Cannon Street).*

WEST END WALK

From Leicester Square to Picadilly Circus

The West End, the area at the west end of the original walled City of London, is London's liveliest neighborhood. Theaters, pubs, restaurants, bookstores, ethnic food, markets, and boutiques attract rock stars, gays, hippies, punks, tourists, and ladies and gentlemen stepping from black cabs for a night on the town.

Allow an hour for this one-mile orientation walk through the neighborhood called "W1" by Londoners. You'll thread through the heart of the West End and the neighborhood of Soho. From Leicester Square (Tube: Leicester Square), we'll head east to Covent Garden, then north on shop-lined Neal Street, then west along Soho's Old Compton Street, ending at Piccadilly Circus. Use the walk to get the lay of the land, then go explore—especially in the evening, when the neon glitters and London gets funky.

THE WALK BEGINS

❶ Leicester Square

Orient yourself from the top (north) end of sloping Leicester (LES-ter) Square. A few blocks to the west is Piccadilly, to the south is Trafalgar Square (and way beyond that, Big Ben), to the east is Covent Garden. The neighborhood north of the square is trendy Soho. Gerrard Street, just two blocks north of Leicester Square, is the center of Chinatown, lined with decent-quality, inexpensive Chinese (mostly Cantonese cuisine) restaurants.

Leicester Square itself is, by day, the central clearinghouse for theater tickets; check out the half-price "tkts" kiosk (see page 314). When the neon ignites after dark, the square hosts red-carpet movie premiers (with publicity appearances by, for example, Tom Cruise and Orlando Bloom), discotheques, and partying teens in town from the suburbs.

West End Walk

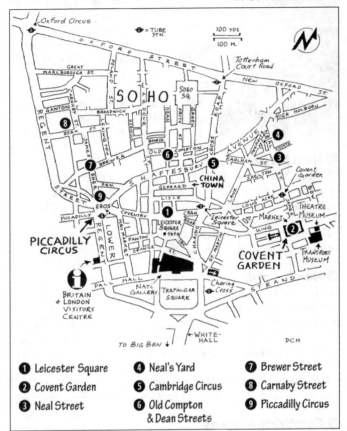

❶ Leicester Square
❷ Covent Garden
❸ Neal Street
❹ Neal's Yard
❺ Cambridge Circus
❻ Old Compton & Dean Streets
❼ Brewer Street
❽ Carnaby Street
❾ Piccadilly Circus

• *To get to Covent Garden, head east on Cranbourn Street. Veer right on Garrick Street, then take your first left onto brick-paved Floral Street, lined with fashionable clothing shops. Turn right on James Street, and you'll enter a large square with a covered marketplace in the center.*

❷ Covent Garden

London's chief produce market until the 1980s, Covent Garden's iron-and-glass arcades were converted to boutiques, cafés, and antiques shops. If you catch a whiff of marijuana smoke, don't call the cops—Britain is moving to decriminalize the substance. When it comes to possession of small amounts for personal use, the British have learned to live and let live.

Surrounding the market are street performers and (working counterclockwise) St. Paul's Church (not the famous cathedral), the London Transport Museum (see page 51), the Theatre Museum

(✪ see tour on page 252), and the Royal Opera House (with entrances on the square and on Bow Street). Two short blocks east down Russell Street is one of London's oldest, biggest, and most historic theaters, the Theatre Royal, on Drury Lane.

• *Head north (uphill) on James Street, which becomes Neal Street.*

❸ Neal Street

This busy pedestrian-only street is lined with clothing shops and boutiques. Look to the left down Earlham Street, with the recommended Belgo Centraal restaurant (see Eating, page 292), cut-flower stands (by day), theaters, and shops.

• *Where Neal Street intersects with Short's Garden Street, you'll find a small courtyard called...*

❹ Neal's Yard

For fun and earthy food, check out the restaurants here and nearby (see page 295). Next door is Neal's Yard Dairy, carrying on the process of traditional cheesemaking into the 21st century. Further west down Short's Garden Street is the "Seven Dials" intersection, where seven sundials atop a pole mark the meeting of seven small streets.

• *Head west on Short's Garden Street, past the Seven Dials. You'll emerge into the heavy traffic of the busy, round intersection called...*

❺ Cambridge Circus

This is the center of the theater district, where Shaftesbury Avenue (running east–west) crosses Charing Cross Road (north–south). The Palace Theatre is the first of five big theaters stretching west along Shaftesbury. Book lovers browse Charing Cross Road, traditional home of bookstores.

• *Cross kitty-corner to the other side of the intersection. Continue west (keeping to the right of the Palace Theatre) on Moor Street, which becomes Old Compton Street.*

❻ Old Compton and Dean Streets

Welcome to Soho, which stretches from Charing Cross Road westward to Regent Street, and from Leicester Square and Piccadilly in the south to Oxford Street in the north. ("Soho" was a hunting cry back when this area consisted of fields.) The restaurants and boutiques here and on adjoining streets (e.g., Greek, Dean, and Wardour streets) are trendy and gay, the kind that attract high society when it feels like slumming it. Private clubs, like the low-profile Groucho Club (#45 Dean Street), cater to the late-night rock crowd. A right on Frith Street leads to the green lawn of (somewhat seedy) Soho Square.

Where Old Compton Street meets Dean Street is perhaps the center of the neighborhood. Just stand and observe the variety of people going by. South of here is Gerrard Street, the center of Chinatown, and you're surrounded by the buzz of Soho.

• *Continue west, to where Old Compton Street squeezes down into a narrow alley (Tisbury Court). Penetrate this sleazy passage of sex shows and blue-video shops, then jog a half-block right and continue west on Brewer Street.*

❼ Brewer Street

Sex shops, video arcades, and (illegal) prostitution mingle with upscale restaurants as we enter the lower-class west Soho. Berwick Street hosts a daily produce market.

• *At Sherwood Street (also called Lower James Street), a left turn takes you south to Piccadilly Circus, a block away. But aging boomers may consider taking a detour right (north) and walking two blocks to...*

❽ Carnaby Street

In the Swinging '60s, when Pete Townsend needed a paisley shirt, or John Lennon a Nehru jacket, or Twiggy a miniskirt, they came here—where those mod fashions were invented.

Today, the street looks like everything else from the '60s — sanitized and co-opted by upscale franchises. (But I do like Lush, a natural bath products store that has somehow spread worldwide while only recently reaching the United States.) From Carnaby Street, it's another block north to the Oxford Circus Tube station.

• *Back at the intersection of Brewer and Sherwood Streets, head south on Sherwood Street one block to...*

❾ Piccadilly Circus

The famous circular intersection spins around the tipsy-but-perfectly-balanced Eros statue in the center. At night, when neon pulses, the 20-foot-high Coke ads paint the classic Georgian facades pink. Black cabs honk, people crowd the attractions, and Piccadilly shows off big-city London at its glitziest.

BRITISH MUSEUM TOUR

In the 19th century, the British flag flew over one-fourth of the world. London was the world's capital, where women in saris walked the streets with men in top hats. And England collected art as fast as it collected colonies.

The British Museum is *the* chronicle of Western civilization. History is a modern invention. Three hundred years ago, people didn't care about crumbling statues and dusty columns. Nowadays, we value a look at past civilizations, knowing that "those who don't learn from history are condemned to repeat it."

The British Museum is the only place I know where you can follow the rise and fall of three great civilizations—Egypt, Assyria, and Greece—in a few hours with a coffee break in the middle. And, while the sun never set on the British Empire, it will on you, so on this tour we'll see just the most exciting two hours.

ORIENTATION

Cost: Free, but £3 donation requested. If you can afford it, donate. There's usually an interesting temporary exhibit that requires separate admission.

Hours: The **British Museum** is open daily 10:00–17:30, plus Thu–Fri until 20:30 (but only selected galleries are open 17:30–20:30). Rainy days and Sundays always get me down because they're most crowded. (The museum is least crowded late on weekday afternoons.)

The **Great Court**—the grand entrance with eateries, gift shops, an exhibit gallery, and the Reading Room—has longer opening hours than the museum (daily 9:00–18:00, Thu–Sat until 23:00).

The **Reading Room,** located within the Great Court, is free and open to the quiet public (daily 10:00–17:30). Computer terminals within the Reading Room allow you to take a virtual tour of the British Museum, delving deeply into whatever interests you (study ahead at www.thebritishmuseum.ac.uk/compass).

Getting There: The main entrance is on Great Russell Street. Take the Tube to Tottenham Court Road, take exit #3, turn right, and follow the brown signs four blocks to the museum. The Holborn and Russell Square Tube stops are also nearby. You have your choice of buses: #7, #8, #10, #19, #24, #25, #29, #38, #55, #68, #73, #91, #98, #134, or #188. Taxis are reasonable if you buddy up.

Information: The information desks just inside the Great Court have museum plans, audioguides, and tour information (tel. 020/7323-8000, recorded info tel. 020/7388-2227, www.thebritishmuseum.ac.uk).

For **books,** consider the main bookstore (tucked behind the Reading Room) or The Museum Bookshop (across the street at 36 Great Russell Street).

Tours: The various Eye-Opener tours are free (nearly hourly 11:00–15:30, 50 min); each one is different, focusing on one particular subject within the museum. The Highlights tours are expensive but meaty (£8, 90 min, at 10:30, 13:00, and 15:00). There are also several different audioguide tours (£3.50, requires leaving photo ID), including Top 50 Highlights (90 min), the Parthenon Sculptures (60 min), and Family Tours (length varies).

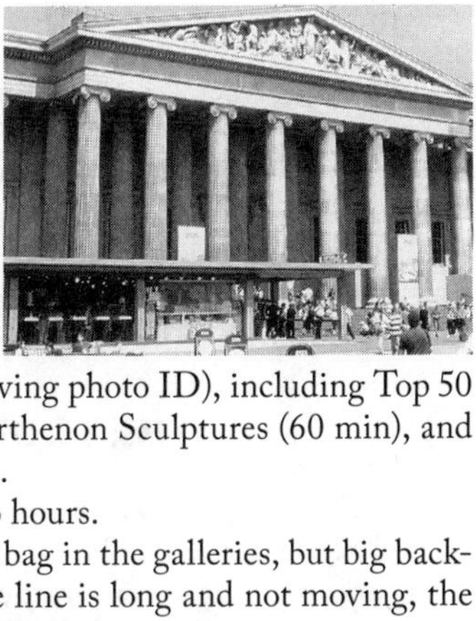

Length of This Tour: Allow two hours.

Cloakroom: You can carry a day bag in the galleries, but big backpacks are not allowed. If the line is long and not moving, the cloakroom may be full (£1 per item).

Photography: Photos allowed without a flash. No tripods.

No-nos: No eating, drinking, smoking, or gum-chewing in the galleries.

Cuisine Art: You have three choices inside the complex. In the Great Court, you'll find the sandwich-and-drink Court Café (on the main level) as well as the pricier Court Restaurant (on the upper floor). Within the museum, the Gallery Café is located off Room 12 (the Greek section). There are lots of fast, cheap, and colorful cafés, pubs, and markets along Great

British Museum Overview

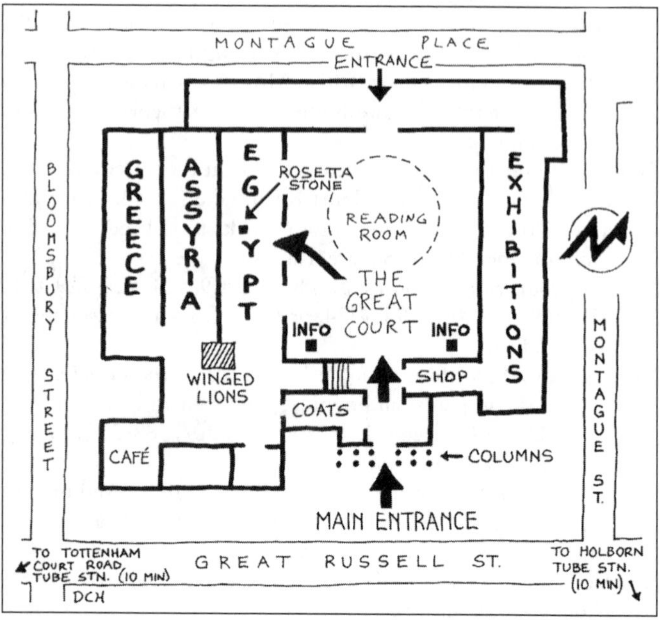

Russell Street. No picnicking is allowed inside the Great Court or the museum, except on weekends and holidays, when they open a family area in the basement under the Great Court. Karl Marx snacked on the benches near the entrance and in Russell Square.

Starring: Rosetta Stone, Egyptian mummies, Assyrian lions, and Elgin Marbles.

THE TOUR BEGINS

Enter through the main entrance on Great Russell Street. Ahead is the Great Court (with the round Reading Room in the center), providing access to all wings. To the left are the exhibits on Egypt, Assyria, and Greece—our tour. You'll notice that this tour does not follow the museum's numbered sequence of rooms. Instead, we'll try to hit the highlights as we work chronologically.

Enjoy the Great Court, Europe's largest covered square, bigger than a football field. This people-friendly court—delightfully spared from the London rain—was for 150 years one

The Ancient World

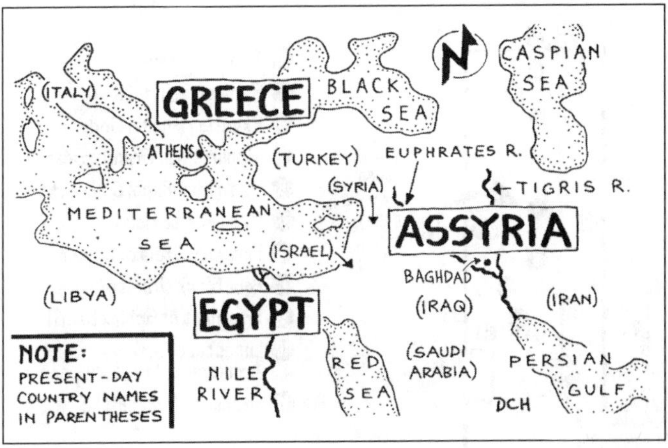

of London's great lost spaces...closed off and gathering dust. Now, ever since the year 2000, it's the 140-foot-wide glass-domed hub of a two-acre cultural complex. Its centerpiece is the stately Reading Room, a study hall for Oscar Wilde, Arthur Conan Doyle, Rudyard Kipling, T.S. Eliot, Virginia Woolf, W.B. Yeats, Mark Twain, V.I. Lenin, and for Karl Marx while formulating his ideas on communism and writing *Das Kapital.*

• *The Egyptian Gallery is in the West Wing, to the left of the round Reading Room. Enter the Egyptian Gallery. The Rosetta Stone is directly in front of you.*

Egypt (3000 B.C.–A.D. 1)

Egypt was one of the world's first "civilizations," that is, a group of people with a government, religion, art, free time, and a written language. The Egypt we think of—pyramids, mummies, pharaohs, and guys who walk funny—lasted from 3000 to 1000 B.C. with hardly any change in the government, religion, or arts.
Imagine two millennia of Eisenhower.

The Rosetta Stone (196 B.C.)

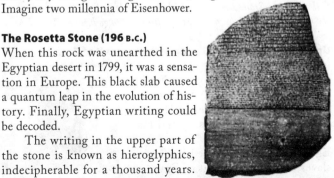

When this rock was unearthed in the Egyptian desert in 1799, it was a sensation in Europe. This black slab caused a quantum leap in the evolution of history. Finally, Egyptian writing could be decoded.

The writing in the upper part of the stone is known as hieroglyphics, indecipherable for a thousand years.

British Museum—Egypt

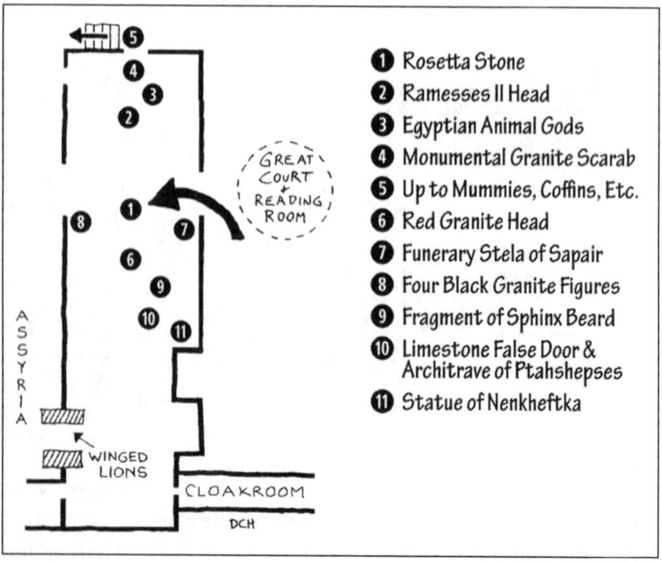

Did a picture of a bird mean "bird"? Or was it a sound, forming part of a larger word, like "burden"? As it turned out, hieroglyphics are a complex combination of the two, surprisingly more phonetic than symbolic. (For example, the hieroglyph that looks like a mouth or eye is the letter "R.")

The Rosetta Stone allowed scientists to break the code. It contains a single inscription repeated in three languages. The bottom third is plain old Greek (find your favorite frat or sorority), while the middle is medieval Egyptian. By comparing the two known languages with the one they didn't know, they figured it out.

The breakthrough came when they discovered that the large ovals (e.g., in the 6th line from the top) represented the name of the ruler, Ptolomy. Simple.

• *The Rosetta Stone sits in the middle of the long Egyptian Gallery. In the Gallery to the right of the Stone, find the huge head of Ramesses.*

Upper Half of Colossal Statue of Ramesses II of Granite (c.1270 B.C.)

When Moses told the king of Egypt, "Let my people go!," this was the stony-faced look he got. Ramesses II ruled 67 years (c. 1290–1223 B.C.) and may have been in power when Moses cursed Egypt with plagues, freed the Israeli slaves, and led them out of Egypt to their homeland in Israel (according to the Bible, but not exactly corroborated by Egyptian chronicles).

This seven-ton statue, made from two different colors of granite, is a fragment from a temple in Thebes. Ramesses was a great builder of temples, palaces, tombs, and statues of himself. There are probably more statues of him in the world than there are cheesy fake *Davids*. He was so concerned about achieving immortality that he even chiseled his own name on other people's statues. Very cheeky.

Picture what the archaeologists saw when they came upon this: a colossal head and torso separated from the enormous legs and toppled into the sand—all that remained of the works of a once-great pharaoh. Kings, megalomaniacs, and workaholics, take note.

• *Say, "Ooh, heavy," and climb the ramp behind Ramesses, looking for animals.*

Various Egyptian Gods as Animals

Before technology made humans the alpha animal on earth, it was easier to appreciate our fellow creatures. Animals were stronger, swifter, or fiercer than puny *Homo sapiens*. The Egyptians worshipped animals as incarnations of the gods.

The powerful ram is the god Amun (king of the gods), protecting a puny pharaoh under his powerful chin. The clever baboon is Thoth, the gods' secretary, who gave writing to man. Horus, the god of the living, is a falcon. The speckled, standing hippo (with lion head) is Tawaret, protectress of childbirth. Her stylized breasts and pregnant belly are supported by ankhs, symbols of life. (Is Tawaret grinning or grimacing in labor?)

• *At the end of the Egyptian gallery is a big stone beetle.*

Monumental Granite Scarab (c.200 B.C.)

This species of beetle would burrow into the ground, then reappear—like the sun rising and setting, or dying and rebirth, a symbol of resurrection. Scarab amulets were placed on mummies' chests to protect the spirit's heart from acting impulsively.

Like the scarab, Egyptian culture was buried—first by Greece, then by Rome. Knowledge of the ancient writing died, condemning the culture to obscurity. But since the discovery of the Rosetta Stone, Egyptology has boomed and Egypt has come back to life.

• *You can't call Egypt a wrap until you visit the mummies upstairs. If you can handle 70 stairs (if not, return to the Rosetta stone and skip ahead to the Red Granite Head, page 129), continue to the end of the gallery past the giant stone scarab (beetle) and up the West Stairs. At the top, take a left into Room 61. Browse through Rooms 61–64, filled with displays in glass cases.*

Rooms 61–64: Mummies, Coffins, Canopic Jars, and Statuettes—The Egyptian Funeral

To mummify a body, disembowel it (but leave the heart inside), pack the cavities with pitch, and dry it with natron, a natural form of sodium carbonate (and, I believe, the active ingredient in Twinkies). Then carefully bandage it head to toe with hundreds of yards of linen strips. Let it sit 2,000 years, and...*voilà!* Or just dump the corpse in the desert and let the hot, dry, bacteria-killing Egyptian sand do the work—you'll get the same results.

The mummy was placed in a wooden coffin, which was put in a stone coffin, which was placed in a tomb. (Remember that the pyramids were just big tombs.) The result is that we now have Egyptian bodies that are as well preserved as Joan Rivers.

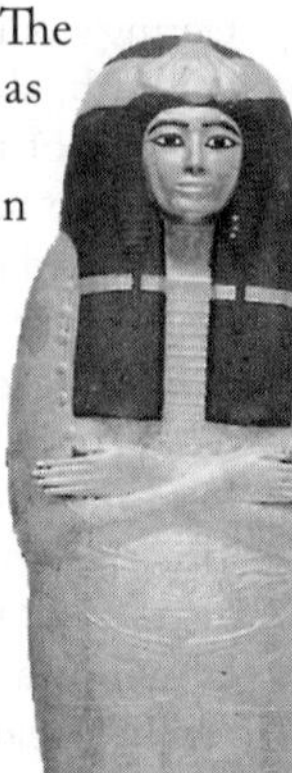

The internal organs were preserved alongside in canopic jars, and small-scale statuettes of the deceased *(shabtis)* were scattered around. Written in hieroglyphs on the coffins and the tomb walls were burial rites from the Book of the Dead. These were magical spells to protect the body and crib notes for the waking soul, who needed to know these passwords to get past the guardians of eternity.

Many of the mummies here are from the time of the Roman occupation, when they painted a fine portrait in wax on the wrapping. X-ray photos in the display cases tell us more about these people.

Don't miss the animal mummies. Cats (Room 62) were incarnations of the goddess Bastet. Worshipped in life as the sun god's allies, preserved in death, and memorialized with statues, cats were given the adulation they've come to expect ever since.

• *Linger in Rooms 62 and 63, but remember that eternity is about the amount of time it takes to see this entire museum. In Room 64, in a glass case, you'll find...*

"Ginger" (Naturally Preserved Body)

This man died 5,400 years ago, a thousand years before the pyramids. His people buried him in the fetal position, where he could "sleep" for eternity. The hot sand naturally dehydrated and protected the body. With him are a few of his possessions: bowls, beads, and the flint blade next to his arm. His grave was covered with stones. Named "Ginger" by scientists for his wisps of red hair, this man from a distant time seems very human.

• *Head back down the stairs to the Egyptian Gallery and backtrack to the Rosetta Stone. Just past it find a huge head with a hat like a bowling pin.*

Red Granite Head from a Colossal Figure of a King (c. 1350 B.C.)

Art also served as propaganda for the pharaohs, kings who called themselves gods on earth. Put this head on top of an enormous body (which still stands in Egypt), and you have the intimidating image of an omnipotent ruler who demands servile obedience. Next to the head is, appropriately, the pharaoh's powerful fist—the long arm of the law.

The crown is actually two crowns in one. The pointed upper half is the royal cap of Upper Egypt. This rests on the flat, fez-like crown symbolizing Lower Egypt. A pharaoh wearing both crowns together is bragging that he rules a combined Egypt. As both "Lord of the Two Lands" and "High Priest of Every Temple," the pharaoh united church and state.

• *On the wall to the left of the Red Granite Head, you'll see three painted stone slabs called stelas. The biggest of these is the...*

Painted Limestone Funerary Stela of Sapair (c. 1400 B.C.)

These people walk like Egyptian statues look—stiff and flat, like they were just run over by a pyramid. We see the torso from the front and everything else—arms, legs, face—in profile, creating the funny walk that has become an Egyptian cliché. But the stiffness is softened by a human touch. It's a family scrapbook; snapshots of loved ones from a happy time to be remembered for all eternity.

In the upper half, Mr. Sapair—now deceased and in the afterlife—worships the god Osiris (with pointed hat). Below, tanned Sapair relaxes with his pale wife while their children prepare a picnic. At Sapair's feet, their tiny son sniffs a lotus flower (with a spiritual scent), and their daughter crouches beneath her parents—a symbol of protection. When Sapair's winged spirit finally left his body (very top of stela), he could look at this painting on the tomb wall and think of his wife just like this...with her arms around him and a smile on her face.

• *On the opposite wall are four black lion-headed statues.*

Four Black Granite Figures of the Goddess Sekhmet (1400 B.C.)

This lion-headed goddess looks pretty sedate here, but she could spring into a fierce crouch when crossed.

The gods ruled the Egyptian cosmos like dictators in a big banana republic (or the American Congress). Egyptians bribed their gods for favors, offering food, animals, or money, or by erecting statues like these to them.

Sekhmet holds an ankh. This key-shaped cross was the hieroglyph meaning "life" and was a symbol of eternal life. Later, it was adopted as a Christian symbol because of its cross shape and religious overtones.

• *Continuing down the Egyptian Gallery, directly in front of you and to the left, find a glass case containing a...*

Limestone Fragment of the Beard of the Sphinx

The Great Sphinx—a statue of a pharaoh-headed lion—crouches in the shadow of the Great Pyramids in Cairo. Time shaved off the sphinx's soft-sandstone, goatee-like beard, and it's now preserved here in a glass case. The beard gives an idea of the scale of the six-story-tall, 200-foot statue.

The sphinx is as old as the pyramids (c. 2500 B.C.), built during the time known to historians as the Old Kingdom (2686–2181 B.C.), but this beard may have been added later, during a restoration (c. 1420 B.C., or perhaps even later under Ramesses II).

• *Ten steps past the Sphinx's "soul patch" is a 10-foot-tall, red-tinted "building" covered in hieroglyphics.*

Limestone False Door and Architrave of Ptahshepses (c. 2400 B.C.)

This "false door" was a ceremonial entrance (never meant to open) for a sealed building called a *mastaba* that marked the grave of a man named Ptahshepses. The hieroglyphs of eyes, birds, and rabbits serve as his epitaph, telling his life story, how he went to school with the pharaoh's kids, became an honored vizier, and married pharaoh's daughter.

The deceased was mummified, placed in a wooden coffin that was encased in a stone coffin, then in a stone sarcophagus (like the **Red-granite sarcophagus with paneled exterior surfaces** from 2400 B.C., in front of Ptahshepses' door), and buried 50 feet beneath the *mastaba* in an underground chamber (see the **diagram of "Old Kingdom Tombs,"** on a nearby wall).

Mastabas like Ptahshepses' were decorated inside and out with **statues, stelas, and frescoes** like those displayed nearby. These pictured the things that the soul could find useful in the next life—magical spells, lists of the deceased's accomplishments, snapshots of the deceased and his family while alive, and secret passwords from the Egyptian Book of the Dead. False doors like this allowed the soul (but not grave robbers) to come and go.

• *Just past Ptahshepses' false door is a glass case with a statue.*

Painted Limestone Statue of Nenkheftka (2400 B.C.)

Originally standing in a "false door" of his *mastaba*, this statue represented the soul of the deceased still active, going in and out of the burial place. This was the image of the departed that greeted his loved ones when they brought food offerings to the *mastaba* to place at his feet to nourish his soul. (In the mummification rites, the mouth was ritually opened, to prepare it to eat soul food.)

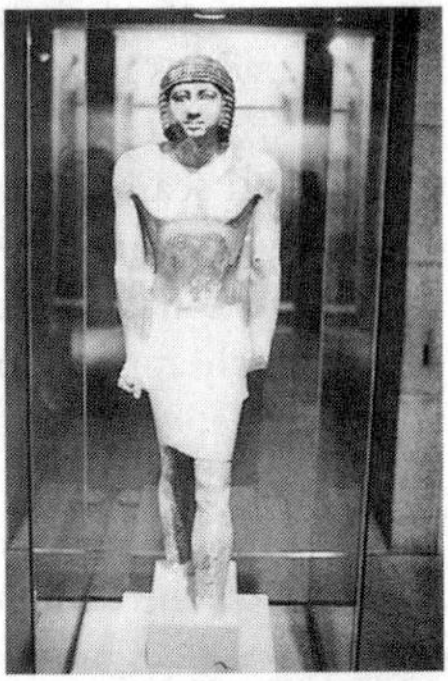

In ancient Egypt, you *could* take it with you. They believed that after you died, your soul lived on, enjoying its earthly possessions—sometimes including servants, who might be walled up alive with their master. (Remember that even the great pyramids were just big tombs for Egypt's most powerful.)

Statues functioned as a refuge for the soul on its journey after death. The rich scattered statues of themselves everywhere, just in case. Statues needed to be simple and easy to recognize, mug shots for eternity: stiff, arms down, chin up, nothing fancy. But this does have all the essential features, like the simplified human figures on international traffic signs. To a soul caught in the fast lane of astral travel, this symbolic statue would be easier to spot than a detailed one.

With their fervent hope for life after death, Egyptians created calm, dignified art that seems built for eternity.

• *At the end of the gallery on your right are two huge, winged Assyrian lions (with bearded human heads) standing guard over the Assyrian exhibit halls.*

Assyria (900–600 B.C.)

Long before Saddam Hussein, Iraq was home to other palace-building, iron-fisted rulers—the Assyrians.

Assyria was the lion, the king of beasts of early Middle Eastern civilizations. This Semitic people from the agriculturally challenged hills of northern Iraq became traders and conquerors, not farmers. They conquered their southern neighbors and dominated the Middle East for 300 years (c. 900–600 B.C.).

Their strength came from a superb army (chariots, mounted cavalry, and seige engines), a policy of terrorism against enemies ("I tied their heads to tree trunks all around the city," reads a royal inscription), ethnic cleansing and mass deportations of the vanquished, and efficient administration (roads and express postal service). They have been called "The Romans of the East."

Two Human-Headed Winged Lions (c. 865–860 B.C.)

These lions guarded an Assyrian palace. With the strength of a lion, the wings of an eagle, the brain of a man, and the beard of ZZ Top, they protected the king from evil spirits, and scared the heck out of foreign ambassadors and left-wing newspaper reporters. (What has five legs and flies? Take a close look. These quintupeds, which appear complete from both the front and the side, could guard both directions at once.)

Carved into the stone between the bearded lions' loins, you can see one of civilization's most impressive achievements—writing. This wedge-shaped (cuneiform) script is the world's first written language, invented 5,000 years ago by the Sumerians (of southern Iraq) and passed down to their less-civilized descendants, the Assyrians.

• *Walk between the lions, glance at the large reconstructed wooden gates from an Assyrian palace, and turn right into the narrow red gallery (Room 7) lined with brown relief panels.*

British Museum—Assyria

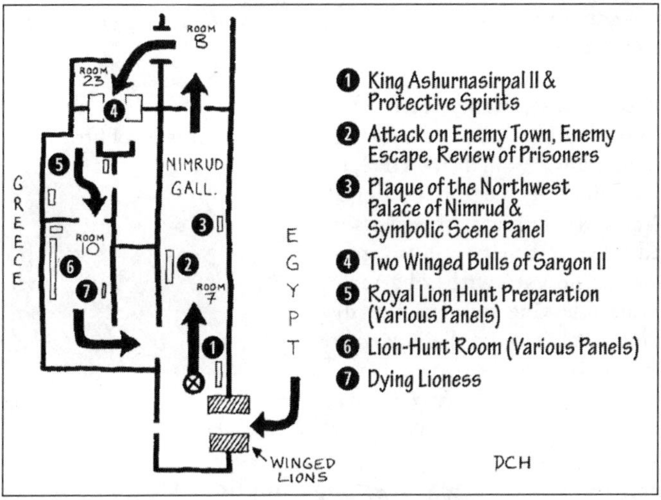

Nimrud Gallery (9th century B.C.)—Palace of Ashurnasirpal II
This gallery is a mini version of the throne room of King Ashurnasirpal II's palace at Nimrud. Entering, you'd see the king on his throne at the far end, surrounded by these pleasant sand-colored gypsum relief panels (which were, however, originally painted and varnished).

That's Ashurnasirpal himself in the **first panel on your right,** with braided beard, earring, and fez-like crown, flanked by his supernatural hawk-headed henchmen, who sprinkle incense on him with pine cones. The bulging forearms tell us that Ashurnasirpal II (r. 883–859 B.C.) was a conqueror's conqueror who enjoyed his reputation as a merciless warrior, using torture and humiliation as part of his distinct management style. The room's panels chronicle his bloody career.

Under his reign, the Assyrians dominated the Mideast from their capital at Nineveh (modern Mosul). Ashurnasirpal II proved his power by building a brand-new palace in nearby Nimrud (called Calah in the Bible).

The cuneiform inscription running through the center of the panel is Ashurnasirpal's résumé: "The king who has enslaved all mankind, the mighty warrior who steps on the necks of his enemies, tramples all foes and shatters the enemy; the weapon of the gods, the mighty king, the King of Assyria, the king of the world, B.A., M.B.A., Ph.D., etc...."

• *A dozen paces farther down, on the left wall, you'll find an upper panel labeled...*

Attack on an Enemy Town

Many "nations" conquered by the Assyrians consisted of little more than a single walled city. Here, the Assyrians lay siege with a crude "tank" that shields them as they advance to the city walls to smash down the gate with a battering ram. The king stands a safe distance away behind the juggernaut and bravely shoots arrows.

• *In the next panel to the right, you'll find...*

Enemy Escape

Soldiers flee the slings and arrows of outrageous Assyrians by swimming across the Euphrates, using inflated animal bladders as life preservers. Their friends in the castle downstream applaud their ingenuity.

• *Below, you'll see...*

Review of Prisoners

The Assyrian economy depended on booty. Here, a conquered nation is paraded before the Assyrian king, who is shaded by a parasol. Ashurnasirpal II sneers and tells the captured chief, "Drop and give me 50." Above the prisoners' heads, we see the rich spoils of war—elephant tusks, metal pots, and so on. The Assyrians depopulated conquered lands by slavery and ethnic cleansing, then repopulated with Assyrian settlers.

• *A few steps farther along, notice the painted reconstruction of the palace on the right wall.*

Plaque of the Northwest Palace of Nimrud, and Symbolic Scene Panel

The plaque shows the king at the far end of the throne room, shaded by a parasol and flanked by winged lions. (In the diagram of the palace's floorplan, the throne room is Room B.) The 30,000-square-foot palace was built atop a 50-acre artificial mound. The new palace was inaugurated with a 10-day banquet (according to an inscription), where the king picked up the tab for 69,574 of his closest friends.

The nearby relief panel labeled **Symbolic Scene** stood behind the throne. It shows the king (and his double) tending the tree of life while reaching up to receive the ring of kingship from the winged sun god.

• *Exit the Nimrud Gallery at the far end, then hang a U-turn left. Pause at the entrance of Room 10 to see...*

Two Winged Bulls from the Khorsabad Palace of Sargon II (c. 710–705 B.C.)

These marble bulls guarded the entrance to the city of Dur-Sharrukin ("Sargonsburg"), a new capital (near Nineveh/Mosul) with vast palaces built by Sargon II (r. 721–705 B.C.). The 30-ton bulls were cut from a single block, tipped on their sides, then dragged to their place by P.O.W.s. (In modern times, when the British transported them here, they had to cut them in half; see the horizontal cracks through the bulls' chests.)

Sargon II gained his reputation as a general subduing the Israelites after a three-year siege of Jerusalem (2 Kings 17:1–6). He solidified his conquest by ethnically cleansing the area, deporting many Israelites (inspiring legends of the "Lost" Ten Tribes).

In 710 B.C., while these bulls were being carved for his palace, Sargon II marched victorious through the streets of Babylon (modern Baghdad), having put down a revolt there against him. His descendants would also have to deal with the troublesome Babylonians.

• *Sneak between these bulls and veer right (into Room 10), where horses are being readied for the big hunt.*

Royal Lion Hunts from the Palace of Ashurbanipal

Lion-hunting was Assyria's sport of kings. On the right wall are horses, on the left are the hunting dogs. And next to them, lions, resting peacefully in a garden, unaware that they will shortly be rousted, stampeded, and slaughtered.

Lions lived in Mesopotamia up until modern times, and it was the king's duty to keep the lion population down to protect farmers and herdsmen. This duty soon became sport, with staged hunts and zoo-bred lions, as the kings of

men proved their power by taking on the king of beasts.
• *Continue ahead into the larger lion-hunt room. Reading the panels like a comic strip, start on the right and gallop counterclockwise.*

The Lion-Hunt Room (c. 650 B.C.)

They release the lions from their cages, then soldiers on horseback herd them into an enclosed arena. The king has them cornered. Let the slaughter begin. The chariot carries King Ashurbanipal, the great-grandson of Sargon II (not to be confused with Ashurnasirpal II, who ruled 200 years earlier, mentioned above).

The last of Assyria's great kings, Ashurbanipal has reigned now for 50 years. Having left a half-dozen corpses in his wake, he moves on, while spearmen hold off lions attacking from the rear.
• *At about the middle of the long wall...*

The fleeing lions, cornered by hounds, shot through with arrows, and weighed down by fatigue, begin to fall. The lead lion carries on even while vomiting blood.

This low point of Assyrian cruelty is, perhaps, the high point of their artistic achievement. It's a curious coincidence that civilizations often produce their greatest art in their declining years. Hmm.
• *On the wall opposite the vomiting lion is the...*

Dying Lioness

A lioness roars in pain and frustration. She tries to run, but her body is too heavy. Her muscular hind legs, once the source of her power, are now paralyzed.

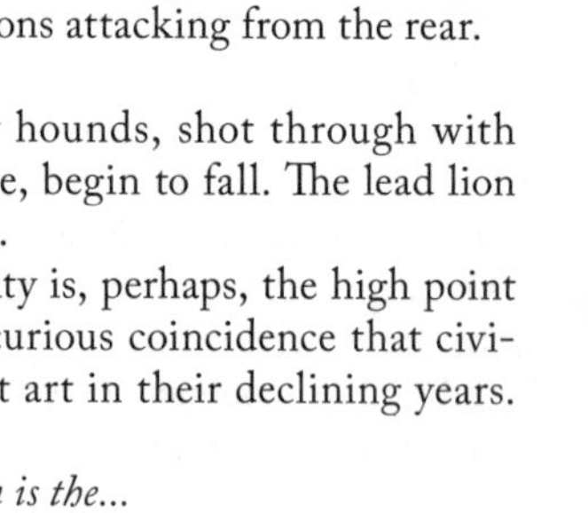

Like these brave, fierce lions, Assyria's once-great warrior nation was slain. Shortly after Ashurbanipal's death, Assyria was conquered, and their capital at Nineveh was sacked and looted by an ascendant Babylon (612 B.C.). The mood of tragedy, dignity, and proud struggle in a hopeless cause makes this dying lioness simply one of the most beautiful of human creations.
• *Return to the huge, winged Assyrian lions by exiting the lion-hunt room at the far end. To reach the Greek section, exit Assyria between the winged lions and make a U-turn right, into Room 11.*

You'll walk past early Greek Barbie and Ken dolls from the Cycladic period (2500 B.C.). Continue into Room 12 (the hungry can go straight to the Gallery Café) and turn right, into Room 13, filled with Greek vases in glass cases.

Greece (600 B.C.–A.D. 1)

The history of ancient Greece could be subtitled "making order out of chaos." While Assyria was dominating the Middle East, "Greece"—a gaggle of warring tribes roaming the Greek peninsula—was floundering in darkness. But by about 700 B.C. these tribes began settling down, experimenting with democracy, forming self-governing city-states, and making ties with other city-states. Scarcely two centuries later, they would be a united community and the center of the civilized world.

During its "Golden Age" (500–430 B.C.), Greece set the tone for all of Western civilization to follow. Democracy, theater, literature, mathematics, philosophy, science, gyros, art, and architecture, as we know them, were virtually all invented by a single generation of Greeks in a small town of maybe 80,000 citizens.

• *Near the middle of Room 13, find case #8, containing a...*

Black-Figured Amphora (Jar): Achilles and Penthesileia (540–530 B.C.)

Greeks poured wine from jars like this one, painted with a man stabbing a woman, a legend from the Trojan War. The Trojan War (c. 1200 B.C.)—part fact but mostly legend—symbolized Greece's long struggle to rise above war and chaos.

Achilles of Greece faces off against the Queen of the Amazons, Penthesileia, who was fighting for Troy. (The Amazons were a legendary race of warrior women who cut off one breast to facilitate their archery skills.) Achilles bears down, plunging a spear through her neck, as the blood spurts. In her dying moment, Penthesileia looks up and her gaze locks on Achilles. His eyes bulge wide, and he falls instantly in love with her. She dies and Achilles is smitten.

Pottery like this (and many others in the room), usually painted red and black, was a popular export product for the sea-trading Greeks. The earliest featured geometric patterns (8th century B.C.), then a painted black silhouette on the natural orange clay, then a red figure on a black background. On this jar, see the names of the two enemies/lovers ("AXILEV" and "PENOESIIEA") as well as the signature of the craftsman, Exekias.

• *Continue to Room 15, then relax on a bench and read, surrounded by statues and vases in glass cases. On the entrance wall, find a...*

Map of the Greek World (500–430 B.C.)

Athens was the most powerful of the city-states and the center of the Greek world. Golden Age Greece was never really a full-fledged empire, but more a common feeling of unity among Greek-speaking people.

A century after the Golden Age, Greek culture was spread still further by Alexander the Great, who conquered the Mediterranean world and beyond. By 300 B.C., the "Greek" world stretched from Italy and Egypt to India (including most of what used to be the Assyrian Empire). Two hundred years later, this Greek-speaking "Hellenistic Empire" was conquered by the Romans.

• *There's a nude male statue on the left side of the room.*

Idealised Youth (*Kouros,* 490 B.C.)

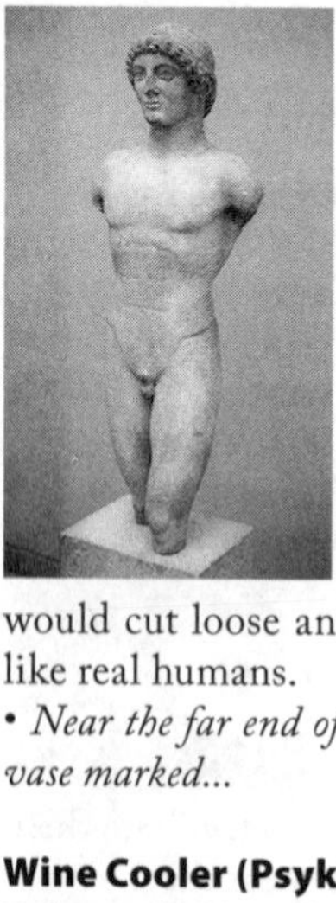

The Greeks saw their gods in human form...and human beings were godlike. With his perfectly round head, symmetrical pecs, and navel in the center, this Boy exemplifies the divine orderliness of the universe. The ideal man was geometrically perfect, a balance of opposites, the "Golden Mean." In a statue, that meant finding the right balance between movement and stillness, between realistic human anatomy (with human flaws) and the perfection of a Greek god. He's still a bit uptight, stiff as the rock from which he's carved. But—as we'll see—in just a few short decades, the Greeks would cut loose and create realistic statues that seemed to move like real humans.

• *Near the far end of Room 15 (on the left) is a glass case containing a vase marked...*

Wine Cooler (Psykter) signed by Douris as Painter (490 B.C.)

This clay vase, designed to float in a bowl of cooling water, shows satyrs at a symposium, or drinking party. These half-man/half-animal creatures (notice their tails) had a reputation for lewd behavior, reminding the balanced and moderate Greeks of their rude roots.

The reveling figures painted on this jar (red on black) are more realistic, more three-dimensional,

British Museum—Greece

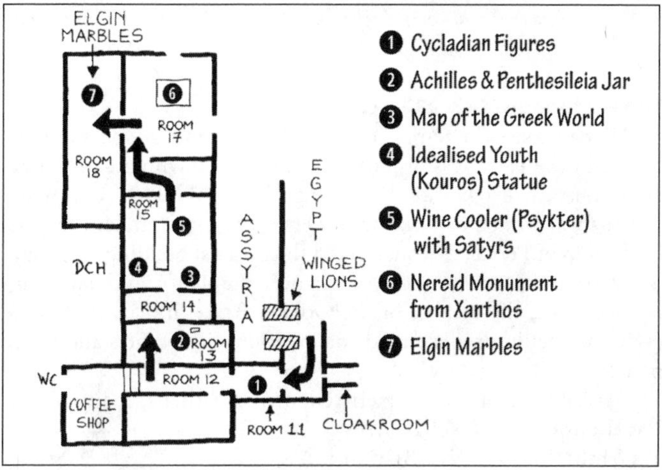

and suggest more natural movements than even the literally three-dimensional but quite stiff *kouros* statue. The Greeks are beginning to conquer the natural world in art. The art, like life, is more in balance. And speaking of "balance," if that's a Greek sobriety test, revel on.

• *Carry on into Room 17 and sit facing the Greek temple at the far end.*

Nereid Monument from Xanthos (c. 390–380 B.C.)

Greek temples (like this reconstruction of a temple-shaped tomb) housed a statue of a god or goddess. Unlike Christian churches, which serve as meeting places, Greek temples were the gods' homes. Worshippers gathered outside, so the most impressive part of the temple was its exterior. Temples were rectangular buildings surrounded by rows of columns and topped by slanted roofs.

The triangle-shaped roof, filled in with sculpture, is called the "pediment." The cross beams that support the pediment are called "metopes" (MET-uh-pees). Now look through the columns to the building itself. Above the doorway is another set of relief panels running around the building (under the eaves) called the "frieze."

Next, we'll see pediment, frieze, and metope decorations from Greece's greatest temple.

• *Leave the British Museum. Take the Tube to Heathrow and fly to Athens. In the center of the old city, on top of the high, flat hill known as the Acropolis, you'll find...*

The Parthenon (447–432 B.C.)

The Parthenon—the temple dedicated to Athena, goddess of wisdom and the patroness of Athens—was the crowning glory of an enormous urban-renewal plan during Greece's Golden Age. After Athens was ruined in a war with Persia, the city—under the bold leadership of Pericles—constructed the greatest building of its day. The Parthenon was a model of balance, simplicity, and harmonious elegance, the symbol of the Golden Age. Phidias, the greatest Greek sculptor, decorated the exterior with statues and relief panels.

While the building itself remains in Athens, many of the Parthenon's best sculptures are right here in the British Museum—the so-called Elgin Marbles (pronounced with a hard "g"), named for the shrewd British ambassador who hammered, chiseled, and sawed them off the Parthenon in 1816.

Though the Greek government complains about losing its marbles, the Brits feel they rescued and preserved the sculptures. The often-bitter controversy continues.

• *Enter through the glass doors labeled The Parthenon Galleries. (The rooms branching off the entryway usually have helpful exhibits that reconstruct the Parthenon.)*

Elgin Marbles (450 B.C.)

The marble panels you see lining the walls of this large hall are part of the frieze that originally ran around the exterior of the Parthenon (under the eaves). The statues at either end of the hall once filled the Parthenon's triangular-shaped pediments. Near the pediment sculptures, we'll also find the relief panels known as metopes. Let's start with the frieze.

The Frieze

These 56 relief panels show Athens' "Fourth of July" parade, celebrating the birth of the city. On this day, citizens marched up the Acropolis to symbolically present a new robe to the 40-foot-tall gold-and-ivory statue of Athena housed in the Parthenon.

• *Start at the panels by the entrance (#136) and work counterclockwise.*

Men on horseback, chariots, musicians, children, animals for sacrifice, and young maidens with offerings are all part of the grand

British Museum—Elgin Marbles

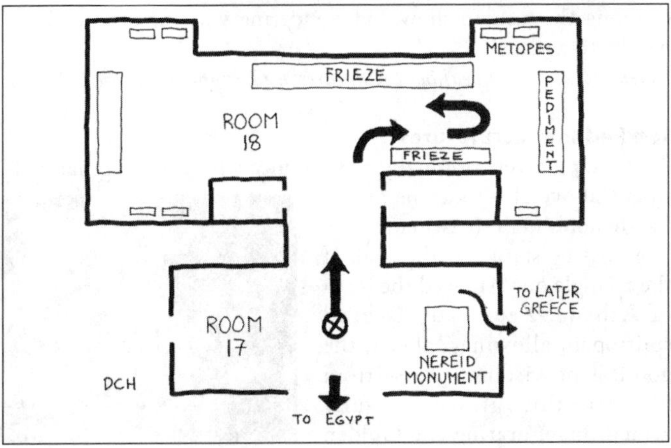

parade, all heading in the same direction—uphill. Prance on.

Notice the muscles and veins in the horses' legs (#130) and the intricate folds in the cloaks and dresses. Some panels have holes drilled in them, where gleaming bronze reins were fitted to heighten the festive look. Of course, all these panels were originally painted in realistic colors. As you move along, notice that, despite the bustle of figures posed every which way, the frieze has one unifying element—all the people's heads are at the same level, creating a single ribbon around the Parthenon.

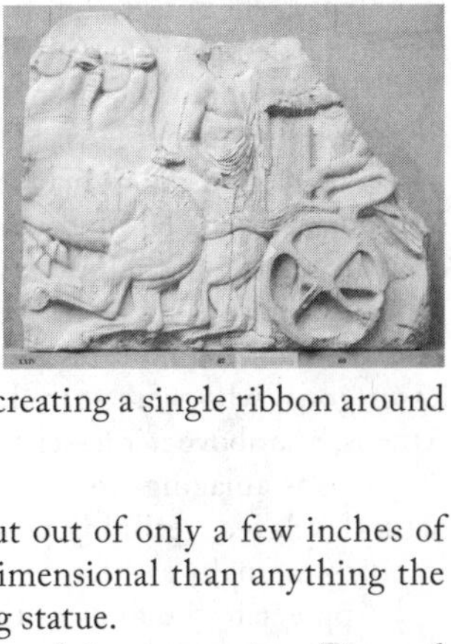

• *Cross to the opposite wall.*

A three-horse chariot (#67) cut out of only a few inches of marble is more lifelike and three-dimensional than anything the Egyptians achieved in a freestanding statue.

Enter the girls (#61), the heart of the procession. Dressed in pleated robes, they shuffle past the parade marshals, carrying incense burners and jugs of wine and bowls to pour out an offering to the thirsty gods.

The procession culminates (#35) in the presentation of the robe to Athena. A man and a child fold the robe for the goddess while the rest of the gods look on. There are Zeus and Hera (#29), the king and queen of the gods, seated, enjoying the fashion show and wondering what length hemlines will be this year.

• *Head for the set of pediment sculptures at the right end of the hall.*

The Pediment Sculptures

These statues were originally nestled nicely in the triangular pediment above the columns at the Parthenon's main (east) entrance. The missing statues at the peak of the triangle once showed the birth of Athena. Zeus had his head split open, allowing Athena, the goddess of wisdom, to rise from his brain fully grown and fully armed, inaugurating the Golden Age of Athens.

The other gods at this Olympian banquet slowly become aware of the amazing event. The first to notice is the one closest to them, Hebe, the cup-bearer of the gods (tallest surviving fragment). Frightened, she runs to tell the others, her dress whipping behind her. A startled Demeter (just left of Hebe) turns toward Hebe.

The only one who hasn't lost his head is laid-back Dionysus (the cool guy further left). He just raises another glass of wine to his lips. Over on the right, Aphrodite, goddess of love, leans back into her mother's lap, too busy admiring her own bare shoulder even to notice the hubbub. A chess-set horse's head screams, "These people are nuts—let me out of here!"

The scene had a message. Just as wise Athena rose above the lesser gods, who were scared, drunk, or vain, so would her city, Athens, rise above her lesser rivals.

This is amazing workmanship. Compare Dionysus, with his natural, relaxed, reclining pose, to all those stiff Egyptian statues standing eternally at attention.

Appreciate the folds of the clothes on the female figures (on the right half), especially Aphrodite's clinging, rumpled robe. Some sculptors would first build a nude model of their figure, put real clothes on it, and study how the cloth hung down before actually sculpting in marble. Others found inspiration at the *taverna* on wet T-shirt night.

Even without their heads, these statues, with their detailed anatomy and expressive poses, speak volumes.

Centaurs Slain Around the World

Dateline 500 B.C.—Greece, China, India: Man no longer considers himself an animal. Bold new ideas are exploding simultaneously around the world. Socrates, Confucius, Buddha, and others are independently discovering a nonmaterial, unseen order in nature and in man. They say man has a rational mind or soul. He's separate from nature and different from the other animals.

Wander behind. The statues originally sat 40 feet above the ground. The backs of the statues, which were never intended to be seen, are almost as detailed as the fronts.

• *The metopes are the panels on the walls to either side. Start with "South Metope XXXI" on the right wall, center.*

The Metopes

In #XXXI, a centaur grabs a man by the throat while the man pulls his hair. The humans have invited some centaurs—wild half-man/half-horse creatures—to a wedding feast. All goes well until the brutish centaurs, the original party animals, get too drunk and try to carry off the women. A battle ensues.

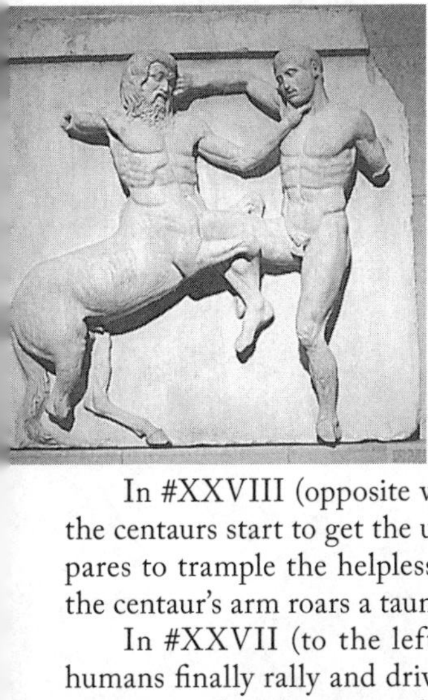

The Greeks prided themselves on creating order out of chaos. Within just a few generations, they went from nomadic barbarism to the pinnacle of early Western civilization. These metopes tell the story of this struggle between the forces of human civilization and animal-like barbarism.

In #XXVIII (opposite wall, center, see photo on next page), the centaurs start to get the upper hand as one rears back and prepares to trample the helpless man. The leopard skin draped over the centaur's arm roars a taunt. The humans lose face.

In #XXVII (to the left—see photo in sidebar above), the humans finally rally and drive off the brutish centaurs. A centaur tries to run, but the man grabs him by the neck and raises his right hand (missing) to run him through. The man's folded cloak sets off his smooth skin and graceful figure.

The centaurs have been defeated. Civilization has triumphed over barbarism, order over chaos, and rational man over his half-animal alter ego.

Why are the Elgin Marbles so treasured? The British of the 19th century saw themselves as the new "civilized" race, subduing "barbarians" in their far-flung empire. Maybe these rocks made them stop and wonder—will our great civilization also turn to rubble?

THE REST OF THE MUSEUM

You've toured only the foundations of Western civilization on the ground floor, West Wing. Upstairs you'll find still more artifacts from these ancient lands, plus Rome and the medieval civilization that sprang from it. Some highlights:

- Lindow Man (a.k.a. the "Bog Man") in Room 50 (upper floor, via east stairs). This victim of a Druid human-sacrifice ritual, with wounds still visible, was preserved for 2,000 years in a peat bog.
- The 7th-century Anglo-Saxon Sutton Hoo Burial Ship (Room 41, upper floor, via east stairs).
- The only existing, complete cartoon by Michelangelo (Room 90, Level 4, via north stairs).

But, of course, history doesn't begin and end in Europe. Look for remnants of the sophisticated, exotic cultures of Asia and the Americas (in North Wing, main floor) and Africa (lower floor)—all part of the totem pole of the human family.

NATIONAL GALLERY TOUR

The National Gallery lets you tour Europe's art without ever crossing the Channel. With so many exciting artists and styles, it's a fine overture to art if you're just starting a European trip and a pleasant reprise if you're just finishing. The "National Gal" is always a welcome interlude from the bustle of London sightseeing.

ORIENTATION

Cost: Free, but temporary (optional) exhibits require an admission fee.

Hours: Daily 10:00–18:00, Wed until 21:00.

Getting There: It's central as can be, overlooking Trafalgar Square, a 15-minute walk from Big Ben and 10 minutes from Piccadilly. The closest Tube stop is Charing Cross or Leicester Square. Take your pick of buses: #3, #6, #9, #11, #12, #13, #15, #23, #24, #29, #53, #77A, #88, #91, #109, #139, #151, #171, or #453.

Information: The information desk in the lobby offers a free, handy floor plan and a schedule of upcoming events and lunchtime lectures (tel. 020/7839-3321, recorded info tel. 020/7747-2885, www.nationalgallery.org.uk).

Tours: Free one-hour overview tours are offered daily at 11:30 and 14:30 (also Wed at 18:00 and 18:30). The excellent audioguide tour—one of the best I've found in Europe—lets you dial up info on any painting in the museum (suggested £4 donation). On the first floor, the "Art Start" computer room lets you study any artist, style, or topic in the museum, and print out a tailor-made tour map.

Length of This Tour: Allow 90 minutes.

Cloakroom: Cloakrooms are at each entrance (free, but £1–2 suggested donation). You can take in a small bag.

Photography: Photos are strictly forbidden.

Cuisine Art: Crivelli's Garden Restaurant (1st floor, Sainsbury Wing), while expensive, is a cool and classy place for a meal. Cheaper eateries abound in and around the museum. On Trafalgar Square, there's a good cafeteria in the crypt of St. Martin-in-the-Fields Church. The Lord Moon of the Mall pub, a block away, offers two meals for the price of one (£7.50, valid Mon–Fri 14:00–21:30, all day Sat–Sun, 18 Whitehall; see Eating chapter, page 282).

Starring: You name it—Leonardo da Vinci, Raphael, Titian, Rembrandt, Monet, and van Gogh.

Overview

The National Gallery offers a quick overview of European art history. We'll stay on one floor, working chronologically through medieval holiness, Renaissance realism, Dutch detail, Baroque excess, British restraint, and the colorful French Impressionism that leads to the modern world. Cruise like an eagle with wide eyes for the big picture, seeing how each style progresses into the next. The new main entrance has just opened, offering visitors a grand first impression of Britain's greatest collection of paintings.

THE TOUR BEGINS

• *Of the two entrances that face Trafalgar Square, enter through the smaller building to the left (as you face it) of the main, domed entrance. Pick up the free map and climb the stairs. At the top, turn left, then left again, entering Room 52.*

Medieval and Early Renaissance (1260–1440)

In Rooms 52 and 53, you see shiny gold paintings of saints, angels, Madonnas, and crucifixions floating in an ethereal gold never-never land. One thing is very clear: Medieval heaven was different from medieval earth. The holy wore gold plates on their heads. Faces were serene and generic. People posed stiffly, facing directly out or to the side, never in between. Saints are recognized by the symbols they carry (a key, a sword, a book), rather than by their human features.

Art in the Middle Ages was religious, dominated by the Church. The illiterate faithful could meditate on an altarpiece and visualize heaven. It's as though they couldn't imagine saints and angels inhabiting the dreary world of rocks, trees, and sky we live in.

• *One of the finest medieval altarpieces is in a glass case in Room 53.*

Anonymous—*The Wilton Diptych* (c. 1395)

Three kings (left panel) come to adore Mary and her rosy-cheeked baby (right panel), surrounded by flame-like angels. Despite the gold-leaf background, a glimmer of human realism peeks through. The kings have distinct, down-to-earth faces. And the back side shows not a saint, not a god, not a symbol, but a real-life deer laying down in the grass of this earth.

Still, the anonymous artist is struggling with reality. John the Baptist (among the kings) is holding a "lamb of God" that looks more like a Chihuahua. Nice try. Mary's exquisite fingers hold an anatomically impossible little foot. The figures are flat, scrawny, and sinless, with cartoon features—far from flesh-and-blood human beings.

• *Walking straight through Room 54 into Room 55, you'll leave this gold-leaf peace and find...*

Uccello—*Battle of San Romano* (c. 1450)

This colorful battle scene shows the victory of Florence over Siena—and the battle for literal realism on the canvas. It's an early Renaissance attempt at a realistic, nonreligious, three-dimensional scene.

Uccello challenges his ability by posing the horses and soldiers at every conceivable angle. The background of farmyards, receding hedges, and tiny soldiers creates an illusion of distance. In the foreground, Uccello the artist actually constructs a grid of fallen lances, then places the horses and warriors within it. Still, Uccello hasn't quite worked out the bugs—the figures in the distance are far too big, and the fallen soldier on the left isn't much bigger than the fallen shield on the right.

• *In Room 56, you'll find...*

Van Eyck—*The Arnolfini Marriage* (1434)

Called by some "The Shotgun Wedding," this painting of a simple ceremony (set in Bruges, Belgium) is a masterpiece of down-to-earth details. The solemn, well-dressed couple take their vows, with hands joined in the center.

National Gallery Highlights

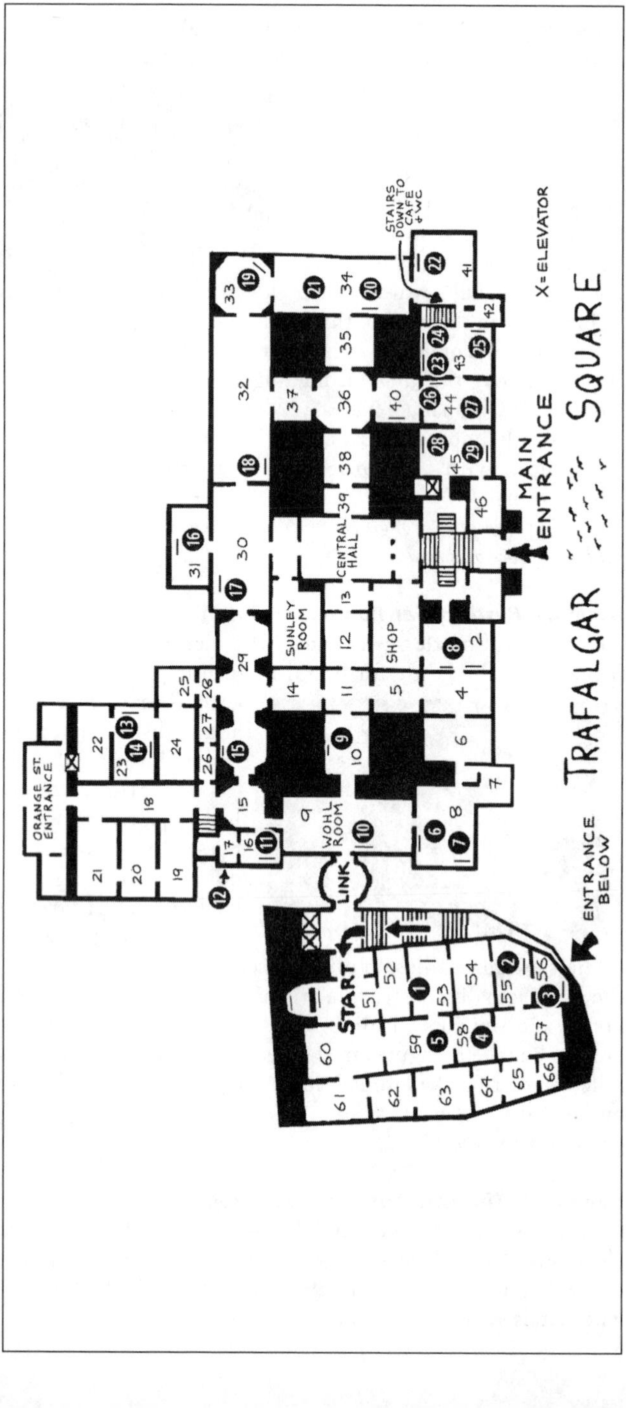

MEDIEVAL & EARLY RENAISSANCE

1. Wilton Diptych
2. UCCELLO – Battle of San Romano
3. VAN EYCK – The Arnolfini Marriage

ITALIAN RENAISSANCE

4. BOTTICELLI – Venus and Mars
5. CRIVELLI – The Annunciation with St. Emidius

HIGH RENAISSANCE

6. MICHELANGELO – Entombment
7. RAPHAEL – Pope Julius II
8. LEONARDO DA VINCI – The Virgin of the Rocks; Virgin and Child with St. John the Baptist and St. Anne

VENETIAN RENAISSANCE

9. TITIAN – Bacchus and Ariadne
10. TINTORETTO – The Origin of the Milky Way

NORTHERN PROTESTANT ART

11. VERMEER – A Young Woman
12. "A PEEPSHOW"
13. REMBRANDT – Belshazzar's Feast
14. REMBRANDT – Self-Portrait

BAROQUE & ROCOCO

15. RUBENS – The Judgment of Paris
16. VAN DYCK – Charles I on Horseback
17. VELÁZQUEZ – The Rokeby Venus
18. CARAVAGGIO – The Supper at Emmaus
19. BOUCHER – Pan and Syrinx

BRITISH

20. CONSTABLE – The Hay Wain
21. TURNER – The Fighting Téméraire
22. DELAROCHE – The Execution of Lady Jane Grey

IMPRESSIONISM & BEYOND

23. MONET – Gare St. Lazare
24. MONET – The Water-Lily Pond
25. MANET – The Waitress (Corner of a Café-Concert)
26. RENOIR – Boating on the Seine
27. SEURAT – Bathers at Asnières
28. VAN GOGH – Sunflowers
29. CEZANNE – Bathers

Van Eyck has built a medieval dollhouse, inviting us to linger over the furnishings. Feel the texture of the fabrics, count the terrier's hairs, trace the shadows generated by the window. Each object is painted at an ideal angle, with the details you'd see if you were standing right in front of it. So, the strings of beads hanging on the back wall are as crystal clear as the bracelets on the bride.

And to top it off, look into the round mirror on the far wall—the whole scene is reflected backward in miniature, showing the loving couple and two mysterious visitors. Is it the concerned parents? The minister? Van Eyck himself at his easel? Or has the artist painted you, the home viewer, into the scene?

The surface detail is extraordinary, but the painting lacks true Renaissance depth. The tiny room looks unnaturally narrow, cramped, and claustrophobic.

In medieval times (this was painted only a generation after *The Wilton Diptych*), everyone could read the hidden meaning of certain symbols—the chandelier with its one lit candle (love), the fruit on the windowsill (fertility), the dangling whisk broom (the bride's domestic responsibilities), and the terrier (Fido—fidelity).

By the way, she may not be pregnant. The fashion of the day was to wear a pillow to look pregnant in hopes you'd soon get that way. At least, that's what they told their parents.

• *Return to Room 55, turn left into Room 57, then turn right into Room 58.*

The Italian Renaissance (1400–1550)

The Renaissance—or "rebirth" of the culture of ancient Greece and Rome—was a cultural boom that changed people's thinking about every aspect of life. In politics, it meant democracy. In religion, it meant a move away from Church dominance and toward the assertion of man (humanism) and a more personal faith. Science and secular learning were revived after centuries of superstition and ignorance. In architecture, it was a return to the balanced columns and domes of Greece and Rome.

In painting, the Renaissance meant realism. Artists rediscovered the beauty of nature and the human body. With pictures of beautiful people in harmonious, 3-D surroundings, they expressed the optimism and confidence of this new age.

Botticelli—*Venus and Mars* (c. 1485)

Mars takes a break from war, succumbing to the delights of love (Venus), while impish satyrs play innocently with the discarded tools of death. In the early spring of the Renaissance, there was an optimistic mood in the air—the feeling that enlightened Man could solve all problems, narrowing the gap between mortals and the Greek gods. Artists felt free to use the pagan Greek gods as symbols of human traits, virtues, and vices. Venus has sapped man's medieval stiffness, and the Renaissance is coming.

• *Continue to Room 59.*

Crivelli—*The Annunciation with Saint Emidius* (1486)

Mary, in green, is visited by the dove of the Holy Ghost, who beams down from the distant heavens in a shaft of light.

Like Van Eyck's wedding, this is a brilliant collection of realistic details. Notice the hanging rug, the peacock, the architectural minutiae that lead you way, way back, then bam—you have a giant pickle in your face.

It combines meticulous detail with Italian spaciousness. The floor tiles and building bricks recede into the distance. We're sucked right in, accelerating through the alleyway, under the arch, and off into space. The Holy Ghost spans the entire distance, connecting heavenly background with earthly foreground. Crivelli creates an Escher-esque labyrinth of rooms and walkways that we want to walk through, around, and into—or is that just a male thing?

Renaissance Italians were interested in—even obsessed with—portraying 3-D space. Perhaps they focused their spiritual passion away from heaven and toward the physical world. With such restless energy, they needed lots of elbowroom. Space, the final frontier.

• *Just two rooms ahead is Room 51, where we first entered. From Room 51, cross to the main building (the West Wing) and enter the large Room 9. We'll return to these big, colorful canvases, but first, turn right into Room 8.*

The High Renaissance (1500)

With the "Big Three" of the High Renaissance—Leonardo, Michelangelo, and Raphael—painters had finally conquered realism. But these three Florence-trained artists weren't content just to copy nature, cranking out photographs-on-canvas. Like Renaissance architects (which they also were), they carefully composed their figures on the canvas, "building" them into geometrical patterns that reflected the balance and order they saw in nature.

Michelangelo—*Entombment* (unfinished, c. 1500–1501)

Michelangelo, the greatest sculptor ever, proves it here in this "painted sculpture" of the crucified Jesus being carried to the tomb.

Like a chiseled Greek god, the muscle-head in red ripples beneath his clothes. Christ's naked body, shocking to the medieval Church, was completely acceptable in the Renaissance world, where classical nudes were admired as an expression of the divine.

Renaissance balance and symmetry reign. Christ is the center of the composition, flanked by two equally leaning people who support his body with strips of cloth. They, in turn, are flanked by two more.

Michelangelo lets the bodies do the talking. The two supporters strain to hold up Christ's body, and in their tension we, too, feel the great weight and tragedy of their dead god. Michelangelo expresses the divine through the human form.

Raphael—*Pope Julius II* (1511)

The new worldliness of the Renaissance even reached the Church. Pope Julius II, who was more a swaggering conquistador than a pious pope, set out to rebuild Rome in Renaissance style, hiring Michelangelo to paint the ceiling of the Vatican's Sistine Chapel.

Raphael gives a behind-the-scenes look at this complex man. On the one hand, the pope is an imposing pyramid of power, with a velvet shawl, silk shirt, and fancy rings boasting of wealth and success. But at the same time, he's a bent and broken man, his throne backed into a corner, with an expression that seems to say, "Is this all there is?"

• *Exit Room 8 at the far end and pass through several rooms until you reach Room 2, with two works by Leonardo.*

Leonardo da Vinci—*The Virgin of the Rocks* (1508)

Mary, the mother of Jesus, plays with her son and little Johnny the Baptist (with cross, at left) while an androgynous angel looks on. Leonardo brings this holy scene right down to earth by setting it among rocks, stalactites, water, and flowering plants. But looking closer, we see that Leonardo has deliberately posed his people into a pyramid shape, with Mary's head at the peak, creating an oasis of maternal stability and serenity amid the hard rock of the earth. Leonardo, who was illegitimate, may have sought in his art the young mother he never knew. Freud thought so.

• *Also in Room 2, you'll find...*

Leonardo da Vinci—*Virgin and Child with St. John the Baptist and St. Anne* (c. 1499–1500)

At first glance, this chalk drawing, or cartoon, looks like a simple snapshot of two loving moms and two playful kids. The two children play—oblivious to the violent deaths they'll both suffer—beneath their mothers' Mona Lisa smiles.

But follow the eyes: Shadowy-eyed Anne turns toward Mary, who looks tenderly down to Jesus, who blesses John, who gazes back dreamily. As your eyes follow theirs, you're led back to the literal and psychological center of the composition—Jesus—the Alpha and Omega. Without resorting to heavy-handed medieval symbolism, Leonardo drives home a theological concept in a natural, human way. Leonardo the perfectionist rarely finished paintings. This sketch—pieced together from two separate papers (see the line down the middle)—gives us an inside peek at his genius.

• *The Renaissance—born in Florence and nurtured in Rome—soon shifted to Venice. Backtrack to the long Room 9 for the following paintings (but note:* Bacchus and Ariadne *may be displayed in Room 10).*

Painting: From Tempera to Tubes

The technology of painting has evolved over the centuries.

1400s Artists used tempera (pigments dissolved in egg yolk) on wood.

1500s Still painting on wood, artists mainly used oil (pigments dissolved in vegetable oil, such as linseed, walnut, or poppy).

1600s Artists applied oil paints to canvases stretched across wooden frames.

1850 Paints in convenient, collapsible tubes are invented, making open-air painting feasible.

The Frames: Although some frames are original, having been chosen by the artist, most are selected by museum curators. Some are old frames from another painting, some are Victorian-era reproductions in wood, and some are recent reproductions made of a composition substance to look like gilded wood.

Venetian Renaissance (1510–1600)

Big change. The canvases are bigger, the colors brighter. Madonnas and saints are being replaced by goddesses and heroes. And there are nudes—not Michelangelo's lumps of noble, knotted muscle, but smooth-skinned, sexy, golden centerfolds.

Venice got wealthy by trading with the luxurious and exotic East. Its happy-go-lucky art style shows a taste for the finer things in life.

Titian—*Bacchus and Ariadne* (1523)

Bacchus, the god of wine, leaps from his leopard-drawn chariot, his red cape blowing behind him, to cheer up Ariadne (far left), who has been jilted by her lover. Bacchus' motley entourage rattles cymbals, bangs on tambourines, and literally shakes a leg.

Man and animal mingle in this pre-Christian orgy, with leopards, a snake, a dog, and the severed head and leg of an ass ready for the barbecue. Man and animal also literally "mix" in the satyrs—part man, part goat. The fat, sleepy guy in the background has had too much.

Titian (see his "Ticianus"

signature on the gold vase, lower left) uses a pyramid composition to balance an otherwise chaotic scene. Follow Ariadne's gaze up to the peak of Bacchus' flowing cape, then down along the snake handler's spine to the lower-right corner. In addition, he balances the picture with harmonious colors—blue sky on the left, green trees on the right, while the two main figures stand out with loud splotches of red.

Tintoretto—*The Origin of the Milky Way* (c. 1575)

In another classical myth, the god Jupiter places his illegitimate son, baby Hercules, at his wife's breast. Juno says, "Wait a minute. That's not my baby!" Her milk spurts upward, becoming the Milky Way.

Tintoretto places us right up in the clouds, among the gods, who swirl around at every angle. Jupiter appears to be flying almost right at us. An X composition unites it all—Juno slants one way while Jupiter slants the other.

• *Exit Room 9 at the far end and turn left into Room 16 for Dutch art.*

Northern Protestant Art (1600–1700)

We switch from CinemaScope to a tiny TV—smaller canvases, subdued colors, everyday scenes, and not even a bare shoulder.

Money shapes art. While Italy had wealthy aristocrats and the powerful Catholic Church to purchase art, the North's patrons were middle-class, hardworking, Protestant merchants. They wanted simple, cheap, no-nonsense pictures to decorate their homes and offices. Greek gods and Virgin Marys were out, hometown folks and hometown places were in—portraits, landscapes, still lifes, and slice-of-life scenes. Painted with great attention to detail, this is art meant not to wow or preach at you, but to be enjoyed and lingered over. Sightsee.

Vermeer—*A Young Woman Standing at a Virginal* (c. 1670)

Inside a simple Dutch home, a prim virgin plays an early piano called a "virginal." We've surprised her and she pauses to look up at us.

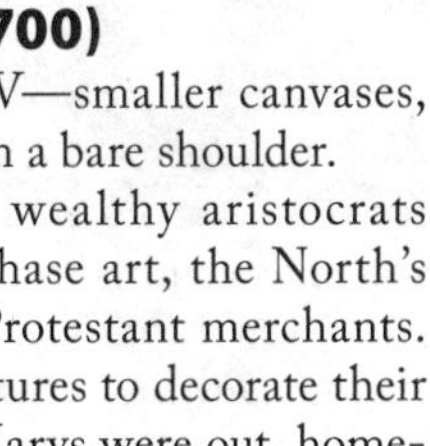

Vermeer, by framing off such a small world to look at—from the blue chair in the foreground to the wall in back—forces us to appreciate the tiniest details, the beauty of everyday things. We can meditate on the tiles lining the floor, the subtle shades of the white wall, and the pale, diffused light that seeps in from the window. Amid straight lines and rectangles, the woman's billowing dress adds a soft touch. The painting of a nude cupid on the back wall only strengthens this virgin's purity.

• *In Room 17 you'll find...*

A Peepshow

Look through the holes at the ends of this ingenious device to make the painting of a house interior come to three-dimensional life. Compare the twisted curves of the painting with the illusion it creates and appreciate the painstaking work of dedicated artists.

• *Get out your floor plan and zigzag your way to Room 23.*

Rembrandt—*Belshazzar's Feast* (c. 1635)

The wicked king has been feasting with God's sacred dinnerware when the meal is interrupted. Belshazzar turns to see the hand of God, burning an ominous message into the wall that Belshazzar's

number is up. As he turns, he knocks over a goblet of wine. We see the jewels and riches of his decadent life.

Rembrandt captures the scene at the most ironic moment. Belshazzar is about to be ruined. We know it, his guests know it, and, judging by the look on his face, he's coming to the same conclusion.

Rembrandt's flair for the dramatic is accentuated by the strong contrast between light and dark. Most of his canvases are a rich, dark brown, with a few crucial details highlighted by a bright light.

Rembrandt—*Self-Portrait* (1669)

Rembrandt throws the light of truth on...himself. This craggy self-portrait was done the year he died, at age 63. Contrast it with one done three decades earlier (hanging nearby). Rembrandt, the greatest Dutch painter, started out as the successful, wealthy young genius of the art world. But he refused to crank out commercial works. Rembrandt painted things that he believed in but no one would invest in—family members, down-to-earth Bible scenes, and self-portraits like these.

Here, Rembrandt surveys the wreckage of his independent life. He was bankrupt, his mistress had just died, and he had also buried several of his children. We see a disillusioned, well-worn, but proud old genius.

• *Backtrack through several rooms to the long Room 29, with mint-green wallpaper.*

Baroque (1600–1700)

Rubens

This room holds big, colorful, emotional works by Peter Paul Rubens and others from Catholic Flanders (Belgium). While Protestant and democratic Europe painted simple scenes, Catholic and aristocratic countries turned to the style called Baroque. Baroque art took what was flashy in Venetian art and made it flashier, gaudy and made it gaudier, dramatic and made it shocking.

Rubens painted anything that would raise your pulse—battles, miracles, hunts, and, especially, fleshy women with dimples on all four cheeks. *The Judgment of Paris,* for instance, is little more than an excuse for a study of the female nude, showing front, back, and profile all on one canvas.

• *Exit Room 29 at the far left end. To the left, in Room 31, you'll see the large canvas of...*

Van Dyck—*Charles I on Horseback* (c. 1637–1638)

King Charles sits on a huge horse, accentuating his power. The horse's small head makes sure that little Charles isn't dwarfed. Charles ruled firmly as a Catholic king in a Protestant country until England's Civil War (1648), when his genteel head was separated from his refined body by Cromwell and company.

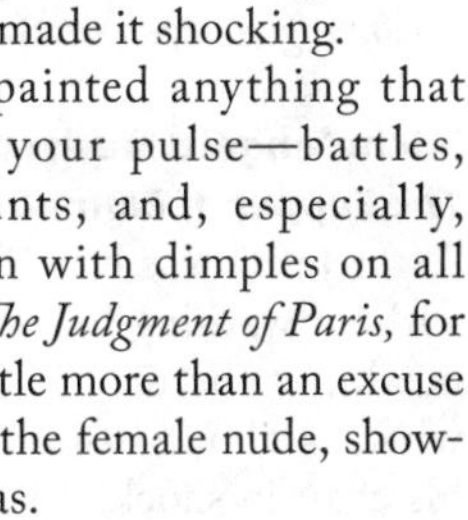

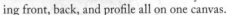

Kings and bishops used the grandiose Baroque style to impress the masses with their power. Van Dyck's portrait style set the tone for all the stuffy, boring portraits of British aristocrats who wished to be portrayed as sophisticated gentlemen—whether they were or not.

• *For the complete opposite of a stuffy portrait, backpedal into Room 30 for...*

Velázquez—*The Rokeby Venus* (c. 1647–1651)

Like a Venetian centerfold, she lounges diagonally across the canvas, admiring herself, with flaring red, white, and gray fabrics to highlight her rosy-white skin and inflame our passion. Horny Spanish kings loved Titian-esque nudes, despite that country's strict Inquisition. This work by the king's personal court painter is the first (and, for over a century, the only) Spanish nude. About the only concession to Spanish modesty is the false reflection in the mirror—if it really showed what the angle should show, Velázquez would have needed two mirrors...and a new job.

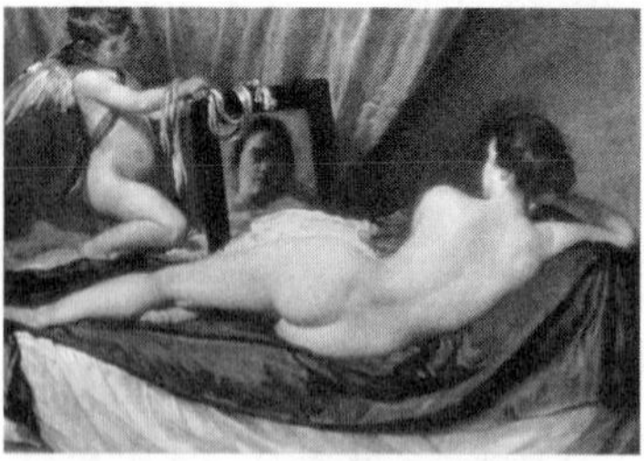

• *Turning your left cheek to hers, tango into Room 32.*

Michelangelo Merisi da Caravaggio—*The Supper at Emmaus* (1601)

After Jesus was crucified, he rose from the dead and appeared without warning to some of his followers. Jesus just wants a quiet meal, but the man in green, suddenly realizing who he's eating with, is about to jump out of his chair in shock. To the right, a man spreads his hands in amazement, bridging the distance between Christ and us by sticking his hand in our face.

Baroque took reality and exaggerated it. Most artists amplified the prettiness, but Caravaggio exaggerated the grittiness, using real, ugly, unhaloed people in Bible scenes. Caravaggio's paintings look like a wet dog smells. Reality.

We've come a long way since the first medieval altarpieces that wrapped holy people in gold foil. From the torn shirts to the five o'clock shadows, from the blemished apples to the uneven part in Jesus' hair, we are witnessing a very human miracle.

• *Leave the Caravaggio Room at the far end, under the sign reading "East Wing, painting from 1700–1900," and enter Room 33.*

French Rococo (1700–1800)

As Europe's political and economic center shifted from Italy to France, Louis XIV's court at Versailles became its cultural hub. Every aristocrat spoke French, dressed French, and bought French paintings. The Rococo art of Louis' successors was as frilly, sensual, and suggestive as the decadent French court. We see their rosy-cheeked portraits and their fantasies: lords and ladies at play in classical gardens where mortals and gods cavort together.

• *One of the finest examples is the tiny...*

Boucher—*Pan and Syrinx* (1739–1759)

Curious Pan seeks a threesome, but Syrinx eventually changes to reeds, leaving him all wet.

Rococo art is like a Rubens that got shrunk in the wash—smaller, lighter pastel colors, frillier, and more delicate than the Baroque style. Same dimples, though.

• *Enter Room 34.*

British (1800–1850)

Constable—*The Hay Wain* (1821)

The more reserved British were more comfortable cavorting with nature than with the lofty gods. Come-as-you-are poets like Wordsworth found the same ecstasy just being outside.

John Constable set up his easel out-of-doors, painstakingly capturing the simple majesty of billowing clouds, billowing trees,

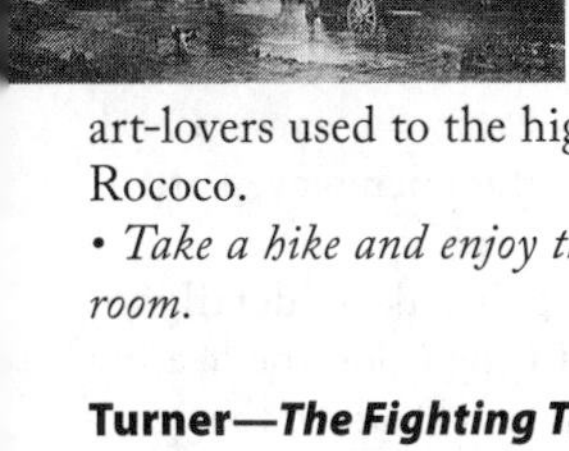

and everyday rural life. Even British portraits (by Thomas Gainsborough and others) placed refined lords and ladies amid idealized greenery.

This simple style—believe it or not—was considered shocking in its day. The rough, thick, earth-toned paint and crude country settings scandalized art-lovers used to the highfalutin, prettified sheen of Baroque and Rococo.

• *Take a hike and enjoy the English-country-garden ambience of this room.*

Turner—*The Fighting Téméraire* (before 1839)

Constable's landscape was about to be paved over by the Industrial Revolution. Soon, machines began to replace humans, factories belched smoke over Constable's hay cart, and cloud-gazers had to punch the clock. Romantics tried to resist it, lauding the forces of nature and natural human emotions in the face of technological "progress." But alas, here a modern steamboat symbolically drags a famous but obsolete sailing battleship off into the sunset to be destroyed.

Turner's messy, colorful style gives us our first glimpse into the modern art world—he influenced the Impressionists. Turner takes an ordinary scene (like Constable), captures the play of light with messy paints (like Impressionists), and charges it with mystery (like, wow).

• *London's Tate Britain (see page 177) has more Constables and an enormous collection of Turner's work. For now, enter Room 41.*

Paul Delaroche—*The Execution of Lady Jane Grey* (1833)

It's 1553. The teenage queen's nine-day reign has reached its curfew. This innocent girl, manipulated into power politics by cunning advisors, is now sent to the execution site in the Tower of London. As her friends swoon with grief, she's blindfolded and forced to kneel at the block. Legend has it that the confused, humiliated girl was left kneeling on the scaffold. She crawled around, groping for the chopping block, crying out, "Where is it? What am I supposed to do?" The executioner in scarlet looks on with as much compassion as he can muster.

Britain's distinct contribution to art history is this Pre-Raphaelite style, showing medieval scenes in luminous realism with a mood of understated tragedy.

• *Exit Room 41 and enter Room 43. The Impressionist paintings are scattered throughout Rooms 43–46.*

Impressionism and Beyond (1850–1910)

For 500 years, a great artist was someone who could paint the real world with perfect accuracy. Then along came the camera and, click, the artist was replaced by a machine. But unemployed artists refused to go the way of *The Fighting Téméraire.*

They couldn't match the camera for painstaking detail, but they could match it—even beat it—in capturing color, the fleeting moment, the candid pose, the play of light and shadow, the quick impression a scene makes on you. A new breed of artists burst out of the stuffy confines of the studio. They donned scarves and berets and set up their canvases in farmers' fields or carried their notebooks into a crowded café, dashing off quick sketches in order to catch a momentary...impression.

• *Start with the misty Monet train station.*

Monet—*Gare St. Lazare* (1877)
Claude Monet, the father of Impressionism, was more interested in the play of light off his subject than the subject itself. He uses smudges of white and gray paint to capture how sun filters through the glass roof of the train station and is refiltered through the clouds of steam.

Monet—*The Water-Lily Pond* (1899)

We've traveled from medieval spirituality to Renaissance realism to Baroque elegance and Impressionist colors. Before you spill out into the 21st century hubbub of London, relax for a second in Monet's garden at Giverny, near Paris. Monet planned an artificial garden, rechanneled a stream, built a bridge, and planted these water lilies—a living work of art, an oasis of order and calm in a hectic world.

Manet—*Corner of a Café-Concert* (a.k.a *The Waitress,* 1878–1880)
Imagine just how mundane (and therefore shocking) Manet's quick "impression" of this café must have been to a public that was raised on Greek gods, luscious nudes, and glowing Madonnas.

- *In Room 44, you'll find...*

Renoir—*Boating on the Seine* (1879–1880)
It's a nice scene of boats on sun-dappled water. Now move in close. The "scene" breaks up into almost random patches of bright colors. The "blue" water is actually separate brushstrokes of blue, green, pink, purple, gray, white, etc. The rower's hat is a blob of green, white, and blue. Up close, it looks like a mess, but when you back up to a proper distance, *voilà!* It shimmers. This kind of rough, coarse brushwork (where you can actually see the brush strokes) is one of the telltale signs of Impressionism. Renoir was not trying to paint the water itself, but the reflection of sky, shore, and boats off its surface.

Seurat—*Bathers at Asnières* (1883–1884)

Viewed from about 15 feet away, this is a bright, sunny scene of people lounging on a riverbank. Up close it's a mess of dots, showing the Impressionist color technique taken to its logical extreme. The "green" grass is a shag rug of green, yellow, red, brown, purple, and white brush strokes. The boy's "red" cap is a collage of red, yellow, and blue.

Seurat has "built" the scene dot by dot, like a newspaper photo, using small points of different, bright colors. Only at a distance do the individual brushstrokes blend together. Impressionism is all about color. Even people's shadows are not dingy black, but warm blues, greens, and purples.

• *In Room 45...*

Van Gogh—*Sunflowers* (1888)

In military terms, van Gogh was the point man of his culture.

He went ahead of his cohorts, explored the unknown, and caught a bullet young. He added emotion to Impressionism, infusing his love of life even into inanimate objects. These sunflowers, painted with characteristic swirling brushstrokes, shimmer and writhe in either agony or ecstasy—depending on your own mood.

Van Gogh painted these during his stay in southern France, a time of frenzied creativity, when he himself hovered between agony and ecstasy, bliss and madness. A year later, he shot himself.

In his day, van Gogh was a penniless nobody, selling only one painting in his whole career. Fairly recently, a *Sunflowers* (he did a half dozen versions) sold for $40 million (a salary of about $2,500 a day for 45 years), and it's not even his highest-priced painting. Hmm.

Cézanne—*Bathers* (*Les Grandes Baigneuses*, c. 1900–1906)

These bathers are arranged in strict triangles à la Leonardo—the five nudes on the left form one triangle, the seated nude on the right forms another, and even the background trees and clouds are triangular patterns of paint.

Cézanne uses the Impressionist technique of building a figure with dabs of paint (though his "dabs" are often larger-sized "cube" shapes) to make solid, 3-D geometrical figures in the style of the Renaissance. In the process, his cube shapes helped inspire a radical new art style—Cube-ism—bringing art into the 20th century.

NATIONAL PORTRAIT GALLERY TOUR

Rock groupies, book-lovers, movie fans, gossipmongers, and even historians all can find at least one favorite celebrity here. From Elizabeth I to Elizabeth II, from Byron to Bowie, the National Portrait Gallery puts a face on 500 years, making "history" the simple story of flesh-and-blood people. It's a great rainy-day museum for serious students, or a quick (and free) peek at the islands' eccentric inhabitants.

ORIENTATION

Cost: Free.

Hours: Daily 10:00–18:00, until 21:00 on Thu and Fri.

Getting There: It's at St. Martin's Place, 100 yards off Trafalgar Square (around the corner from National Gallery and opposite Church of St. Martin-in-the-Fields).

Information: Tel. 020/7306-0055, recorded info tel. 020/7312-2463, www.npg.org.uk.

Tours: The audioguide tours are excellent (free, but £2 donation requested); they describe each room (or era in British history) and more than 300 paintings. You'll learn more about British history than art and can actually hear interviews with 20th-century subjects as you stare at their faces.

Length of This Tour: Allow 90 minutes.

Photography: Photos are not allowed.

Cuisine Art: The elegant Portrait Restaurant on the top floor is pricey but has a fine view. The Portrait Café in the basement is cheaper. The eateries close 30 minutes before the museum closes.

Starring: Royalty (Henry VIII, Elizabeth I, Victoria), writers (Shakespeare, Byron, Wilde), scientists (Newton, Darwin), politicians (Churchill), and musicians (Handel, Bowie).

Overview

The Gallery covers 500 years of history from top to bottom—literally. Start at the top (2nd) floor and work chronologically down to modern times on the ground floor. Historians should linger at the top; celebrity-hunters will lose elevation quickly to the contemporary section. There are many, many famous people from all walks of life, so use this chapter as an overview, then follow your interests, reading more from the museum's informative labels.

THE TOUR BEGINS

• *Ride the long escalator up to the second floor and start in Room 1, marked "The Early Tudors." Find the large black-and-white sketch ("cartoon") of Henry VIII with his hands on his hips.*

SECOND FLOOR

1500s—Debut

The small, isolated island of Britain (pop. 4 million) enters onto the world stage. The Tudor kings—having already settled family feuds (the "Wars of the Roses"), balanced religious factions, and built England's navy—bring wealth from abroad.

Room 1

Henry VIII (1491–1547), The Whitehall Mural Cartoon

Young, athletic, intense, and charismatic, with jeweled hands, gold dagger, and bulging codpiece (the very image of kingly power), Henry VIII carried England on his broad shoulders from political isolation to international power.

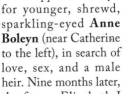

In middle age, he divorced his older, dull-eyed, post-childbearing queen, **Catherine of Aragon** (see her portrait opposite Henry), for younger, shrewd, sparkling-eyed **Anne Boleyn** (near Catherine to the left), in search of love, sex, and a male heir. Nine months later, the future Elizabeth I was born, and the Pope excommunicated adulterous Henry. Defiant, Henry started the (Protestant) Church of England, sparking a century-plus of religious strife between England's Protestants and Catholics.

National Portrait Gallery—Second Floor

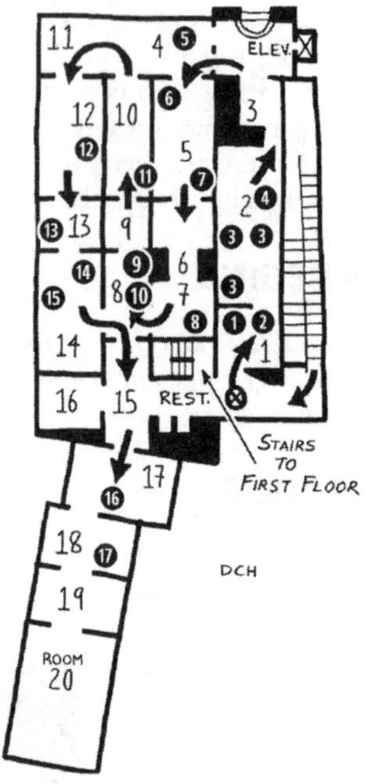

1. Henry VIII & Wives
2. Edward VI
3. Elizabeth I (3 Versions)
4. William Shakespeare
5. James I
6. Charles I
7. Oliver Cromwell
8. Charles II
9. Isaac Newton
10. John Locke
11. Christopher Wren
12. George Frideric Handel
13. James Watt
14. George III
15. George Washington
16. Lord Nelson, Lady Hamilton & the Duke of Wellington
17. The Romantics

By the time Henry died—400 pounds of stinking, pus-ridden paranoia—he had wed six wives (see #6, sweet young **Catherine Parr,** opposite Henry), executed several of them (including Anne Boleyn), killed trusted advisors, pursued costly wars, and produced one male heir, Edward VI.

• *Also in Room 1 is the lo-o-o-ong picture of...*

Edward VI (1537–1553)

Nine-year-old Edward (son of wife #3, Jane Seymour) ruled for only six years before dying young, leaving England in religious and economic turmoil. (View the optical illusion through the hole at the right end to put the enigmatic boy king into perspective.)

Room 2

Elizabeth I (1533–1603), Three Different Portraits on Three Different Walls

Elizabeth I was pale, stern-looking, red-haired (like her father, Henry VIII), and wore big-shouldered power dresses. During her reign, she kept Protestant/Catholic animosity under control and

made England a naval power and cultural capital. The three portraits span her life from age 26 (*Coronation,* the smallest of the three) to age 42 (see photo) to age 60 (*The Ditchley Portrait,* the largest), but she looks ageless, always aware of her public image, resorting to makeup, dye, wigs, showy dresses, and pearls to dazzle courtiers.

The "Virgin Queen" was married only to her country, but she flirtatiously wooed opponents to her side. ("I know I have the body of a weak and feeble woman," she'd coo, "but I have the heart and stomach of a king.") When England's navy sank 72 ships of the Spanish Armada in a single, power-shifting battle (1588), Britannia ruled the waves, feasting on New World spoils. Elizabeth surrounded herself with intellectuals, explorers, and poets.

William Shakespeare (1564–1616)

Though famous in his day, Shakespeare's long hair, beard, earring, untied collar, and red-rimmed eyes make him look less the celebrity and more the bohemian barfly he likely was. This unassuming portrait (reportedly one of only two done in his lifetime) captures 45-year-old Shakespeare just before he retired from his career as actor, poet, and world's greatest playwright. The shiny, domed forehead is a beacon of intelligence. (I suspect Shakespeare liked this plain-spoken portrait.)

Using borrowed plots, outrageous puns, and poetic language, Shakespeare wrote comedies (c. 1590—*Taming of the Shrew, As You Like It*), tragedies (c. 1600—*Hamlet, Othello, Macbeth, King Lear*), and fanciful combinations (c. 1610—*The Tempest*), exploring the full range of human emotions and reinventing the English language.

The museum attributes this portrait to a Shakespeare contemporary, John Taylor, but other scholars insist it was done long after Shakespeare's death.

• *Pass through Room 3, through the stairwell, and into Room 4.*

1600s—Religious and Civil Wars

Catholic kings bickered with an increasingly vocal Protestant Parliament until civil war erupted (1642–1651), killing thousands, decapitating the king, and eventually establishing Parliament as the main power.

Room 4: James I (1566–1625) of England and VI of Scotland

When the Virgin Queen died childless, her Catholic cousin—a rough, unkempt, arrogant Scotsman—moved to genteel London and donned the royal robes. Deeply religious, he launched the "King James" translation of the Bible, but he alienated Anglicans (Church of England), harder-line Protestants (Puritans), and democrats everywhere by insisting that he ruled by divine right, directly from God. He passed this attitude directly to his son, Charles.

• *Enter Room 5 (the doorway is opposite James) with portraits of Civil War veterans.*

Room 5: Charles I (1600–1649)

Picture Charles' sensitive face (with scholar's eyes and artist's long hair and beard) severed from his elegant body (in horse-riding finery), and you've arrived quickly at the heart of the Civil War.

The short, shy, stuttering, and very Catholic Charles had angered Protestants and democrats by dissolving Parliament and raising taxes. Parliament formed an army, fought the king's supporters, arrested and tried Charles, and—outside the Banqueting House on Whitehall—beheaded him.

The man responsible was...

Oliver Cromwell (1599–1658)

Cromwell, with armor, sword, command baton, and a determined look, was the Protestant champion and military leader. The Civil War pitted Parliamentarians (Parliament, Protestant Puritans, industry, and urban areas) against Royalists (King, Catholics, nobles, traditionalists, and rural areas). After Charles' execution, Cromwell led kingless England as "Lord Protector."

Stern Cromwell hated luxury and ordered a warts-and-all portrait (see wart on his left temple and scar between his eyebrows). He has a simple, bowl-cut hairstyle, adorning his 82-ounce brain (49 is average). Speaking of heads, after Cromwell's death, vengeful royalists exhumed his body, cut off the head, stuck it on a stick, and placed it outside Westminster Abbey, where it rotted publicly for 24 years.

• *Pass through Room 6 and into Room 7.*

Room 7: Charles II (1630–1685)

After two decades of wars, Cromwell's harsh rule, and Puritanical excesses (no dancing, theater, or political incorrectness), Parliament welcomed the monarchy back (with tight restrictions) under Charles II. England was ready to party.

Looking completely ridiculous, with splayed legs, puffy face, big-hair wig, garters, and ribbons on his shoes, Charles II became a king with nothing to do, and he did it with grace and a sense of humor. Charles' portrait is sandwiched between portraits of his devoted wife, Catherine of Braganza, and his well-known mistress, the comic actress Nell Gwynn.

• *Make a U-turn right, entering Room 8.*

Room 8: Isaac Newton (1642–1727) and John Locke (1632–1704)

The 1600s, the Age of Enlightenment, saw scientific discoveries suggesting that the world operates in an orderly, rational way. **Isaac Newton** explained the universe's motion with the simplest of formulas (f = ma, etc.), and **John Locke** used human reason to plan a democratic utopia, coining phrases like "life, liberty..." that would inspire America's revolutionaries.

• *Walk straight ahead to...*

Room 10: Christopher Wren (1632–1723)

Christopher Wren—leaning on blueprints with a compass in hand—designed St. Paul's Cathedral, a glorious demonstration of mathematics in stone.

• *In Room 11, make a U-turn left, entering Room 12, with painters, writers, actors, and musicians of the 1700s.*

1700s—Domestic Stability, Wars with France

Blossoming agriculture, the first factories, overseas colonization, and political stability from German-born kings (George I, II, III) allowed the arts to flourish. Overseas, England financed wars against Europe's No. 1 power, France.

Room 12: George Frideric Handel (1685–1759)

In London, an old form of art became something new—modern theater.

Handel, a German writing Italian operas in England, had several smash hits in London (especially with the oratorio *Messiah,* on his desk), making musical theater popular with ordinary folk. Hallelujah.

Room 13: James Watt (1736–1819)

Deep-thinking Watt pores over plans to turn brainpower into work power. His steam engines (with a separate condenser to capture formerly wasted heat energy) soon powered gleaming machines, changing England's economy from grain and ships to iron and coal.

• *In Room 14 you'll find George III over your left shoulder and George Washington along the right wall.*

Room 14: King George III (1738–1820) and George Washington (1732–1799)

Just crowned at 23, George gives little hint in this portrait that he will lead England into the drawn-out, humiliating "American War" (Revolutionary War) against a colony demanding independence. George III, perhaps a victim of an undiagnosed disease, closed out the stuffy "Georgian" era (in Percy Shelley's words) "an old, mad, blind, despised, dying king."

Perhaps it was the war that drove him mad, or perhaps it was that his enemy, **George Washington** (portrait nearby), had the same hairdo. Washington (1732–1799) was born in British-ruled Virginia and fought for Britain in the French and Indian War, but sided with the colonies in what the British called the American War. This famous portrait of Washington is one of several versions of a 1796 portrait by Gilbert Stuart.

1800s—Colonial and Industrial Giant

Britain defeated France (Napoleon) and emerged as the top power. With natural resources from overseas colonies (Australia, Canada, India, West Indies, China), good communications, and a growing population of seven million, Britain became the first industrial power, dotted with smoke-belching factories and laced with railroads.

• *Exit Room 14 into Room 8 and turn right, ending up in Room 17.*

Room 17: Lord Horatio Nelson (1758–1805); Emma, Lady Hamilton (1761–1815); Arthur Wellesley, the Duke of Wellington (1769–1852)

Three heroes in the fight against Napoleon's expansion: the Duke of Wellington on land (the final victory at Waterloo, near Brussels, 1815), Lord Nelson at sea (Battle of Trafalgar, off Spain, 1805), and Lady Hamilton at Nelson's side.

Lady Hamilton, dressed in white with her famously beautiful face tilted coyly, first met dashing Nelson on his way to fight the French in Egypt. She used the influence of her husband, Lord Hamilton, to restock Nelson's ships. Nelson's daring victory *(Nelson Receiving the French Colours)* made him an instant celebrity, though the battle cost him an arm (see sleeveless pose) and an eye (see scar). The hero—a married man—returned home to woo, bed, and impregnate Lady H., with sophisticated Lord Hamilton's patriotic tolerance.

Room 18: The Romantics

Not everyone worshipped industrial progress. Romantics questioned the clinical detachment of science, industrial pollution, and the personal restrictions of modern life. They reveled in strong emotions, non-Western cultures, personal freedom, opium, and the beauties of nature.

• *Scattered around the room, you'll see...*

John Keats (1795–1821) broods over his just-written "Ode to a Nightingale." ("My heart aches, and a drowsy numbness pains/My sense, as though of hemlock I had drunk.")

Samuel Taylor Coleridge (1772–1834), at 23, is open-eyed, open-mouthed, and eager. ("And all should cry, Beware! Beware!/His flashing eyes, his floating hair!/...For he on honey-dew hath fed,/And drunk the milk of Paradise."—from "Kubla Khan")

Mary Wollstonecraft Shelley (1797–1851), in telling ghost stories with husband Percy and friend Lord Byron, conceived a story of science run amok—*Frankenstein*—imitated by many. ("Ahhhhhhh, sweet mystery of life, at last I've found you!")

William Wordsworth (1770–1850): "The world is too much with us.../Little we see in Nature that is ours;/We have given our hearts away, a sordid boon!"

Percy Bysshe Shelley (1792–1822), political radical, sexual explorer (involving Mary and a first wife), traveler, and poet. ("O wild West Wind, thou breath of Autumn's being,.../If Winter comes, can Spring be far behind?")

George Gordon, **Lord Byron** (1788–1824), was athletic, exotic, and passionate about women and freedom. Famous and scandalous in his day, he became a Kerouac-ian symbol of the Romantic movement. ("She walks in beauty, like the night/Of cloudless climes and starry skies...")

• *After browsing Rooms 19 and 20, backtrack to Room 15 and head downstairs to the first floor. Turn right at the bottom of the stairs, and enter a long hall lined with busts (Room 22). Start at the far end of the hall in Room 21.*

FIRST FLOOR

1837–1901—The Victorians

As the wealthiest nation on earth, with a global colonial empire, Britain during Queen Victoria's long reign embraced modern technology, contributing to the development of power looms, railroads, telephones, motorcars, and electric lights. It was a golden age of science, literature, and middle-class morality, though pockets of extreme poverty and vice lurked in the heart of London itself.

• *To either side of a statue, you'll find paintings of...*

Room 21: Queen Victoria (1819–1901) and Prince Albert (1819–1861)

Crowned at 18, the short (5 feet), plump, bug-eyed, quiet girl inherited a world empire. The next year, she proposed marriage (the custom) to the German Prince Albert. They were a perfect match—lovers, friends, and partners—a model for middle-class couples. (See the

white statue of the pair as genteel knight and adoring lady.) Albert co-ruled, especially when "Vickie" was pregnant with their nine kids. "Bertie" promoted education, science, public works, and the Great Exhibition of 1851 in Hyde Park. When Albert died at 42, a heartbroken Victoria moped for 40 years.

National Portrait Gallery—First Floor

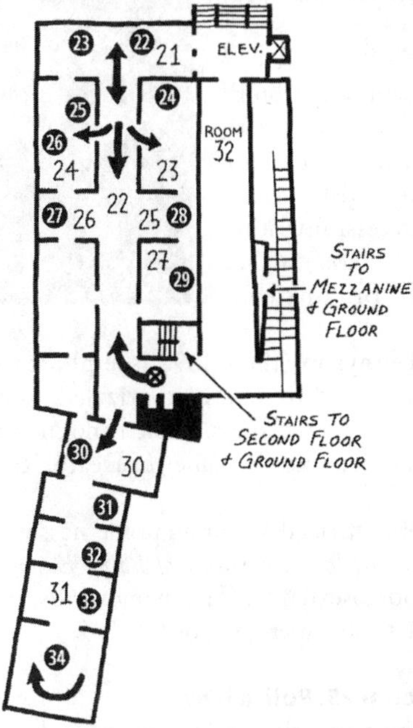

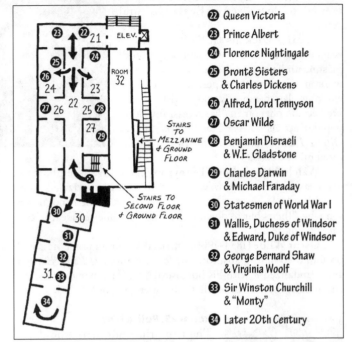

- 22 Queen Victoria
- 23 Prince Albert
- 24 Florence Nightingale
- 25 Brontë Sisters & Charles Dickens
- 26 Alfred, Lord Tennyson
- 27 Oscar Wilde
- 28 Benjamin Disraeli & W.E. Gladstone
- 29 Charles Darwin & Michael Faraday
- 30 Statesmen of World War I
- 31 Wallis, Duchess of Windsor & Edward, Duke of Windsor
- 32 George Bernard Shaw & Virginia Woolf
- 33 Sir Winston Churchill & "Monty"
- 34 Later 20th Century

• *Double-back through the long hall lined with stuffy busts of starched shirts (Room 22), browsing around the rooms branching off it, filled with many prominent Victorians. Here are a few...*

Room 23: Florence Nightingale *(The Mission of Mercy: Florence Nightingale Receiving the Wounded at Scutari)*

Known as "the Lady with the Lamp" for her nightly nursing visits (though she's shown lampless here, in the center, standing, with a piece of paper), Nightingale traveled to Turkey to tend to Crimean War victims. In fact, her forte was not hands-on nursing but efficient hospital administration (sanitation, keeping supplies stocked, transporting wounded) that saved lives and raised public awareness on health issues. To learn more about her, you can visit the Florence Nightingale Museum, just across the Thames from Big Ben (in Gassiot House at 2 Lambeth Palace Road, Tube: Westminster, Waterloo, or Lambeth North).

Room 24: Writers

Anne, Emily, and Charlotte Brontë (left to right, youngest to oldest, painted by brother Branwell), three teenage country girls, grew up to write novels such as *Wuthering Heights* (Emily) and

Jane Eyre (Charlotte), about the complex family and love lives of England's rural gentry.

Charles Dickens (1812–1870) was 12 years old when his dad was sent to a debtor's prison, and young Charles was forced to work in a factory. The experience gave him a working-class perspective on British society. He became phenomenally successful writing popular novels *(Oliver Twist, A Tale of Two Cities, A Christmas Carol)* for Britain's educated middle class.

Watch **Alfred, Lord Tennyson** (1809–1892; see photos in glass case) evolve from wavy-haired Romantic to grizzled, gray-bearded poet laureate of Victorian earnestness. ("Theirs not to reason why,/Theirs but to do and die;/Into the Valley of Death/Rode the six hundred.")

Oscar Wilde (1854–1900) satirized Victorian properness with profound-sounding absurdities *(The Importance of Being Earnest)* and scandalized it with his homosexuality. (His dying words, in a cheap hotel room: "Either that wallpaper goes, or I do.")

Room 25: Politicians

The two prime ministers who dominated politics for two decades, with two completely different personalities and beliefs, now face each other—**Benjamin Disraeli,** a flamboyant novelist, dandy (see his billy-goat goatee), and chum of Victoria, and **William Ewart Gladstone,** a righteous moralizer.

Room 27: Science and Technology

Charles Darwin, with basset-hound eyes and long white beard, looks tired after a lifetime of reluctantly defending his controversial theory of evolution that shocked an entire generation. **Michael Faraday** shocked himself from time to time, harnessing electricity as the work force of the next century.

• *The long hall (Room 22) leads into Room 30, dedicated to World War I.*

1900s—World Wars

Two devastating world wars and an emerging U.S. superpower shrank Britain from global empire to island nation. But Britain remained a cultural giant, producing writers, actors, composers, painters, and Beatles.

Room 30: World War I

Fighting Germans from trenches in France, Britain sent a million-man army to the grave. Among **Some Statesmen of the Great War,** find a bored-looking Winston Churchill.

• *The large Room 31 contains the art described in the following four sections.*

Room 31

Wallis, Duchess of Windsor (painting), and Edward, Duke of Windsor (small statue)

The Duchess' smug smile tells us she got her man.

Edward VIII (1894–1972), great-grandson of Queen Victoria, became king in 1936 as a bachelor dating a common-born (gasp), twice-divorced (double gasp) American (oh no!) named Wallis Simpson (1896–1986). Rather than create a constitutional stink, Edward quietly abdicated, married Wallis, and the two moved to the Continent, living happily ever after. They hosted cocktail parties, played golf, and listened to servants call them "Your Majesty"—though they were now just plain Duke and Duchess of Windsor.

(Edward's brother took over as King George VI, married the "Queen Mum"—who died in 2002—and their daughter became Queen Elizabeth II. Elizabeth snubbed her disgraceful aunt and uncle.)

Writers

George Bernard Shaw (bust)—playwright, critic, and political thinker—brought socialist ideas into popular discussion with plays such as *Man and Superman* and *Major Barbara.* **Virginia Woolf** (1882–1941) wrote feminist essays ("A woman must have money and a room of her own if she is to write fiction") and experimental novels (*Mrs. Dalloway* jumps back and forth in time) before filling her pockets with stones and drowning herself in a river to silence the voices in her head.

World War II

In the darkest days at the beginning of the war, with Nazi bombs raining on a helpless London, **Sir Winston Churchill** (1874–1965, bust) rallied his people with stirring radio speeches from an underground bunker. ("We will fight them on the beaches... We will never surrender!") Britain's military chief, Field Marshall **Bernard Montgomery, 1st Viscount** (1887–1976, known as "Monty") points out the D-Day beaches of the decisive Allied assault.

Later 20th Century

Laurence Olivier (bust), movie and stage actor, played everything from romantic leads and Shakespeare heavies to character parts with funny accents. **Noel Coward** (bust) continued the British tradition of writing witty, sophisticated comedies about the idle rich. **Henry Moore** (see bust), the most famous 20th-century sculptor, combined Michelangelo's grandeur, the raw stone of primitive carvings, and the simplified style of abstract art. **Dylan Thomas** wrote abstract imagery with a Romantic's heart ("Do not go gentle into that good night..."). American-born poet **T.S. Eliot** (bust and Cubist-style portrait) captured the quiet banality of modern life: "This is the way the world ends/Not with a bang but a whimper."

• *Backtrack to the stairs down to the ground floor.*

GROUND FLOOR

Rooms 32–42: 1990 to the Present

London since the Swinging '60s has been a major exporter of pop culture. The contemporary collection changes often depending on who's hot, but you'll likely find royalty **(Queen Elizabeth II, Prince Charles, Princess Diana)**, politicians **(John Major, Tony Blair)**, classic-rock geezers **(Sir Paul McCartney, Sir Elton John, David Bowie)**, and actors **(Michael Caine, Hugh Grant)**...as well as those in lower-profile professions—writers **(Salman Rushdie, Seamus Heaney)**, scientists **(Stephen Hawking)**, composers, painters, and intellectuals.

We've gone from battles to Beatles, seeing Britain's history in the faces of its major players.

TATE BRITAIN TOUR

The "National Gallery of British Art" (a.k.a. the Tate Britain) features the world's best collection of British art—sweeping you from 1500 until today. This is people's art, with realistic paintings rooted in the people, landscape, and stories of the British Isles. You'll see Hogarth's stage sets, Gainsborough's ladies, Blake's angels, Constable's clouds, Turner's tempests, the swooning realism of the Pre-Raphaelites, and the camera-eye portraits of Hockney and Freud. Even if these names are new to you, don't worry. Guaranteed you'll see a few "famous" works you didn't know were British and exit the Tate Britain with at least one new favorite artist.

Since the collection is constantly in motion (visit www.tate.org.uk for the latest), a painting-by-painting tour is impossible. This chapter covers British art chronologically, presenting the essence of each artist and style. Read it beforehand to get the big picture, then let the Tate surprise you with its ever-changing wardrobe of paintings.

ORIENTATION

Cost: Free (£2 donation requested, donate if you can afford it), but temporary exhibits require separate admission.

Hours: Daily 10:00–17:50, last admission 17:00.

Getting There: It's on the River Thames, south of Big Ben and north of Vauxhall Bridge. Take the Tube to Pimlico (and walk 7 min); or hop on the Tate Boat ferry from Tate Modern (£4 one-way or £7 for day ticket, or if you have a Travelcard you pay less: £2.65 one-way/£4.65 for day ticket; buy ticket at gallery desk or on board, departs every 40 min, 18-min trip, ferry also stops at the London Eye); or take bus #88 (from Oxford Circus) or #77A (from National Gallery) directly to the museum; or walk 25 minutes south along the Thames from Big Ben. Other alternatives are buses #2, #3, #C10, #36, #159, #185, or #507. The museum has two entrances: on Millbank, facing the Thames, and on Atterbury Street (accessible for people using wheelchairs).

Information: Pick up a free map at the information desk (tel. 020/7887-8000, recorded info tel. 020/7887-8008, www.tate.org.uk). The bookshop is great.

Tours: Free tours are offered Mon–Fri (normally at 11:00 on the 16th, 17th, and 18th centuries; at 12:00 on 19th century art; at 14:00 on Turner; and at 15:00 on the 20th century). Tours on weekends feature the highlights of the collection (Sat–Sun 12:00 and 15:00). Call to confirm schedule (tel. 020/7887-8000). Good audioguide tours are free and useful. The museum also hosts slide lectures every Sat at 13:00 and games and activities for children (3–12 years) Sat–Sun 12:00–17:00 (for location and details, ask at group desk, tel. 020/7887-8734).

Length of This Tour: Allow one hour.

Cloakroom: Bag and coat check are free (£1 suggested donation).

Photography: Photos are not allowed.

Cuisine Art: Your two options are a café with an affordable gourmet buffet line (daily 10:00–17:40) and a pricey-but-delightful restaurant (Mon–Sat 12:00–15:00, Sun 12:00–14:00).

Starring: Hogarth, Gainsborough, Reynolds, Blake, Constable, Pre-Raphaelites, and Turner.

Orien-Tate: Gallery in Motion

The Tate Britain's large collection of paintings changes every year, but the basic layout stays the same: a roughly chronological walk through British paintings from 1500 in the west half of the building, the 20th century in the east, and the works of J.M.W. Turner in the adjoining Clore Gallery. In addition, there are temporary exhibitions (usually requiring an entrance fee) located in the east wing and in the basement. Note: There are two separate Tate museums in London. The Tate Britain, which this chapter describes, features British art. The Tate Modern (at Bankside, on the South Bank of the Thames across from St. Paul's Cathedral) features modern art.

✪ See the Tate Modern Tour on page 192.

THE TOUR BEGINS

British artists painted people, countrysides, and scenes from daily life, all done realistically and without the artist passing judgment (substance over style). What you won't see here are the fleshy

Tate Britain Overview

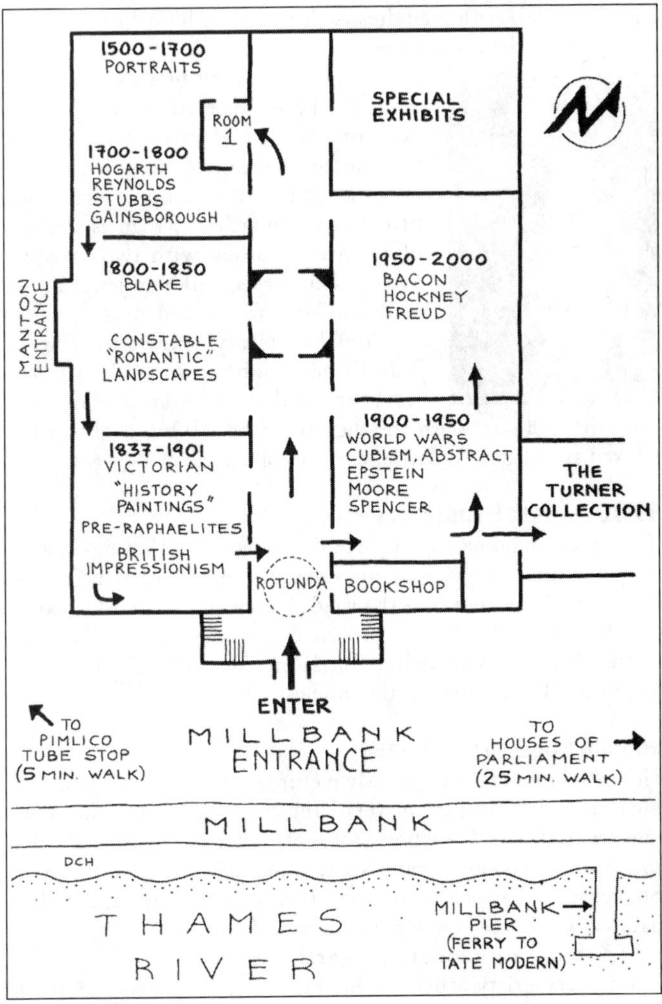

goddesses, naked baby angels, and Madonna-and-child altarpieces so popular elsewhere. The largely Protestant English abhorred the "graven images" of the wealthy Catholic world. Many were even destroyed during the 16th-century Reformation. They preferred portraits of flesh-and-blood English folk.

• *Start in Room 1, in the far left corner (west half) of the museum.*

1500–1700—Portraits of Lord and Lady Whoevertheyare

Stuffy portraits of a beef-fed society try to turn crude country nobles into refined men and delicate women. Men in ruffled collars clutch symbols of power. Women in ruffled collars, puffy sleeves, and elaborately patterned dresses display their lily-white complexions, turning their pinkies out.

English country houses often had a long hall built specially to hang family portraits. You could stroll along and see your noble forebears looking down their noses at you. Britain's upper crust had little interest in art other than as a record of themselves along with their possessions—their wives, children, jewels, furs, ruffled collars, swords, and guns.

You'll see plenty more portraits in the Tate Britain, right up to modern times. Each era had its own style. Portraits from the 1500s are stern and dignified. The 1600s brought a more relaxed and elegant style and more décolletage.

1700s—Art Blossoms

With peace at home (under three King Georges), a strong overseas economy, and a growing urban center in London, England's artistic life began to bloom. As the English grew more sophisticated, so did their portraits. Painters branched out into other subjects, capturing slices of everyday life. The Royal Academy added a veneer of classical Greece to even the simplest subjects.

William Hogarth (1697–1764)

Hogarth loved the theater. "My picture is my stage," he said, "and my men and women my players." The curtain goes up, and we see one scene that tells a whole story, often satirizing English high society. The London theater scene came into its own (after post-Shakespeare censorship) during Hogarth's generation. He often painted series based on popular plays of the time.

A born Londoner, Hogarth loved every gritty aspect of the big city. You'd find him in seedy pubs and brothels, at the half-price ticket booth in Leicester Square, at prize-fights, cockfights, duels, and public executions—sketchbook in hand. An 18th-century Charles Dickens, he exposed the hypocrisy of fat-bellied squires, vain ladies, and gluttonous priests. He also gave the upper classes a glimpse into the hidden poverty of "merry olde England"—poor soldiers with holes in their stockings, overworked servants, and unwed mothers.

Hogarth's portraits (and self-portraits) are unflinchingly honest, quite different from the powdered-wig fantasies of his contemporaries.

George Stubbs—Horses (1724–1806)

Stubbs was the Michelangelo of horse painters. He understood these creatures from the inside out, having dissected them in his studio. He even used machinery to prop the corpses up into lifelike poses. He painted the horses first on a blank canvas, then filled in the background landscape around them (notice the heavy outlines that make them stand out clearly from the countryside). The result is both incredibly natural—from the veins in their noses to their freshly brushed coats—and geometrically posed.

Thomas Gainsborough (1727–1788)

Thomas Gainsborough showcased the elegant, educated women of his generation. He portrayed them as they wished to see themselves: a feminine ideal, patterned after fashion magazines. The cheeks are rosy, the poses relaxed and S-shaped, the colors brighter and more pastel, showing the influence of the refined French culture of the court at Versailles. His ladies tip-toe gracefully toward us, with clear, Ivory-soap complexions that stand out from the swirling greenery of English gardens. Gainsborough worked hard to prettify his subjects, but the results were always natural and never stuffy.

Sir Joshua Reynolds and the "Grand Style" (1723–1792)

Real life wasn't worthy of a painting. So said Sir Joshua Reynolds, the pillar of Britain's Royal Academy. Instead, people, places, and things had to be gussied up with Greek columns, symbolism, and great historic moments, ideally from classical Greece.

In his portraits, he'd pose Lady Bagbody like the Medici Venus, or Lord Milquetoast like Apollo Belvedere. In landscapes, you get Versailles-type settings of classical monuments amid perfectly manicured greenery. Inspired by Rembrandt, Reynolds sometimes used dense, clotted paint to capture the look of the Old Masters.

This art was meant to elevate the viewer, to appeal to his rational nature and fill him with noble sentiment. Sir

Joshua Reynolds, the pillar of England's art establishment, stood for all that was upright, tasteful, rational, brave, clean, reverent, and...and you'll find me in the next room.

History Paintings

Paintings depicting great moments in history—from ancient Greece to medieval knights to Napoleon to Britain's battles abroad—were seen as the classiest form of art, combining the high drama of heroic acts with refined technique.

1800–1850—The Industrial Revolution

Newfangled inventions were everywhere. Railroads laced the land. You could fall asleep in Edinburgh and wake up in London, a trip that used to take days or weeks. But along with technology came factories coating towns with soot, urban poverty, regimentation, and clock-punching. Machines replaced honest laborers, and once-noble Man was viewed as a naked ape.

Strangely, you'll see little of the modern world in paintings of the time—except in reaction to it. Many artists rebelled against "progress" and the modern world. They escaped the dirty cities to commune with nature (Constable and the Romantics). Or they found a new spirituality in intense human emotions (dramatic scenes from history or literature). Or they left the modern world altogether. Which brings us to...

William Blake (1757–1827)

At the age of four, Blake saw the face of God. A few years later, he ran across a flock of angels swinging in a tree. Twenty years later, he was living in a run-down London flat with an illiterate wife, scratching out a thin existence as an engraver. But even in this squalor, ignored by all but a few fellow artists, he still had his heavenly visions, and he described them in poems, paintings, drawings, and prints.

One of the original space cowboys, Blake was also a unique artist who is often classed with the Romantics because he painted in a fit of ecstatic inspiration rather than by studied technique. He painted angels, not the dull material world. While Britain was conquering the world with guns and nature with machines, and while his fellow Londoners were growing rich, fat, and self-important, Blake turned his gaze inward, illustrating the glorious visions of the soul.

Blake's work hangs in a darkened room to protect his

watercolors from deterioration. Enter his mysterious world and let your pupils dilate opium-wide.

His pen and watercolor sketches glow with an unearthly aura. In visions of the Christian heaven or Dante's hell, his figures have superhero musculature. The colors are almost translucent.

Blake saw the material world as bad, trapping the divine spark inside each of our bodies and keeping us from true communion with God. Blake's prints illustrate his views on the ultimate weakness of material, scientific man. Despite their Greek-god anatomy, his men look noble but tragically lost.

A famous poet as well as painter, Blake summed up his distrust of the material world in a poem addressed to "The God of this World," that is, Satan:

Tho' thou art Worship'd by the Names Divine
Of Jesus and Jehovah, thou art still
The Son of Morn in weary Night's decline,
The lost Traveller's Dream under the Hill.

John Constable (1776–1837)

While the Royal Academy thought Nature needed makeup, Constable thought she was just fine. He painted the English landscape as it was, realistically, without idealizing it. With simple earth tones he caught leafy green trees, gathering gray skies, brown country lanes, and rivers the color of the clouds reflected in them.

Clouds are Constable's trademark. Appreciate the effort involved in sketching ever-changing cloud patterns for hours on end—the mix of dark clouds and white clouds, cumulus and stratus, the colors of sunset. A generation before the Impressionists, he actually set up his easel outdoors and painted on the spot, a painstaking process before the invention of ready-made paints-in-a-tube in about 1850.

It's rare to find a Constable (or any British) landscape that doesn't have the mark of man in it—a cottage, hay cart, field hand, or a country road running through the scene. For him, the English countryside and its people were one.

In his later years, Constable's canvases became bigger, the style more "Impressionistic" (messier brushwork), and he worked more from memory than out-of-doors observation.

Constable's commitment to unvarnished nature wasn't fully recognized in his lifetime, and he was forced to paint portraits for his keep. The neglect caused him to ask a friend, "Can it therefore be wondered at that I paint continual storms?"

Other Landscapes

Compare Constable's unpretentious landscapes with others in the Tate Britain. Some artists mixed landscapes with intense human emotion to produce huge, colorful canvases of storms, burning sunsets, towering clouds, and crashing waves, all dwarfing puny humans. Others made supernatural, religious fantasy-scapes. Artists in the Romantic style saw the most intense human emotions reflected in the drama and mystery in nature. God is found within nature, and nature is charged with the grandeur and power of God.

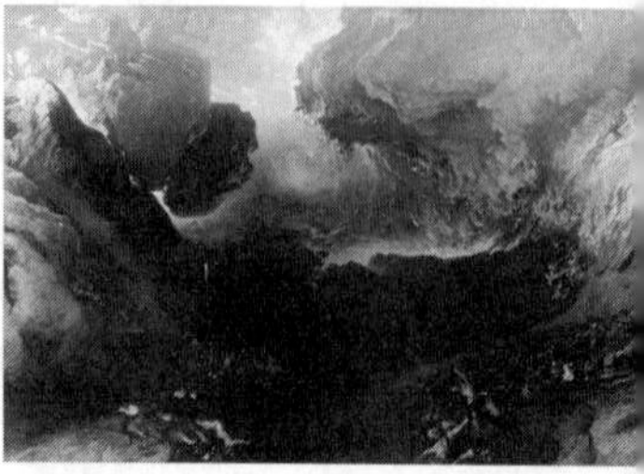

1837–1901—Victorian

In the world's wealthiest nation, the prosperous middle class dictated taste in art. They admired paintings that were realistic (showcasing the artist's talent and work ethic), depicting Norman Rockwell–style slices of everyday life.

We see families and ordinary people eating, working, and relaxing. Some paintings tug at the heartstrings, with scenes of parting couples, the grief of death, or the joy of families reuniting. Dramatic scenes from popular literature get the heart beating. There's the occasional touching look at the plight of the honest poor, reminiscent of Dickens. And many paintings warn us to be good little boys and girls by showing the consequences of a life of sin. Then there are the puppy dogs with sad eyes.

Pre-Raphaelites: Millais, Rossetti, Holman Hunt, Waterhouse, Burne-Jones, etc.

You'll see medieval damsels in dresses and knights in tights, legendary lovers from poetry, and even a very human Virgin Mary as a delicate young woman. The women wear flowing dresses and have long, wavy hair and delicate, elongated, curving bodies. Beautiful.

Overdosed with gushy Victorian sentimentality, a band of 20-year-old artists said, "Enough!" and dedicated themselves to less-saccharine art. Their "Pre-Raphaelite Brotherhood" (you may see the initials P. R. B. by the artist's signature) returned to a style "pre-Raphael," that is, "medieval" in its simple style, in the melancholy mood, and often in subject matter.

"Truth to Nature" was their slogan. Like the Impressionists

who followed, they donned their scarves, barged out of the stuffy studio, and set up outdoors, painting trees, streams, and people, like scientists on a field trip. Still, they often captured nature with such a close-up clarity that it's downright unnatural. And despite the Pre-Raphaelite claim to paint life just as it is, this is so beautiful it hurts.

This is art from the cult of femininity, worshipping Woman's haunting beauty, compassion, and depth of soul. (Proto-feminism or nouveau-chauvinism?) The artists' wives and lovers were their models and muses, and the art echoed their love lives. The people are surrounded by nature at its most beautiful, with every detail painted crystal clear. Even without the people, there is a mood of melancholy.

The Pre-Raphaelites hated overacting. Their subjects—even in the face of great tragedy, high passions, and moral dilemmas—barely raise an eyebrow. Outwardly, they're reflective, accepting their fate. But sinuous postures—with lovers swooning into each other, and parting lovers swooning apart—speak volumes. These volumes are footnoted by the small objects with symbolic importance placed around them: red flowers denoting passion, lilies for purity, pets for fidelity, and so on.

The colors—greens, blues, and reds—are bright and clear, with everything evenly lit, so that we see every detail. To get the luminous color, some painted a thin layer of bright paint over a pure white, still-wet undercoat, which subtly "shines" through. These canvases radiate a pure spirituality, like stained-glass windows.

Stand for a while and enjoy the exquisite realism and human emotions of these Victorian-era works... real people painted realistically. Get your fill, because beloved Queen Victoria is about to check out, the modern world is coming, and with it, new art to express modern attitudes.

British Impressionism

Realistic British art stood apart from the modernist trends in France, but some influences drifted across the Channel. **John Singer Sargent** (American-born) studied with Parisian Impressionists, learning the thick, messy brushwork and play of light at

twilight. **James Tissot** used Degas' snapshot technique to capture a crowded scene from an odd angle. And **James McNeill Whistler** (also born in the United States) composed his paintings like music (see some titles), as collages of shapes and colors that please the eye like a song tickles the ear.

• *To help ease the transition to modern art (in the east half of Tate Britain), first visit the Turner Collection. Pass through the rotunda to the east side of the gallery and just keep going through a few rooms (Rooms 19–20) till you enter "The Clore Gallery/The Turner Collection."*

The Turner Collection: J.M.W. Turner (1775–1851)

The Tate Britain has the world's best collection of Turners. Walking through his life's work, you can trace his progression from a painter of realistic historical scenes, through his wandering years, to Impressionist paintings of color-and-light patterns.

• *Start in Room 35, with biographical info on Turner, his early works, and a display of his paints and brushes. Watch Turner's style evolve from clear-eyed realism to hazy proto-Impressionism. Then browse through Rooms 35–43, seeing how Turner explored different subjects: landscapes, seacapes, Roman ruins, snapshots of Venice, and so on.*

Self-Portrait as a Young Man

At 24, Turner has just been elected the youngest Associate of the Royal Academy. The barber's son now dresses like a gentleman. His full-frontal pose and intense gaze show a young man ready to take on the world.

The Royal Academy Years

Trained in the Reynolds school of grandiose epics, Turner painted the obligatory big canvases of great moments in history—*The Field of Waterloo, Snow Storm: Hannibal and His Army Crossing the Alps, The Destruction of Sodom, The Lost ATM Card, Jason* (and the Argonauts), and various shipwrecks. Not content to crank them out in the traditional staid manner, he sets them in expansive landscapes. Nature's stormy mood mirrors the human events, but is so grandiose it dwarfs them.

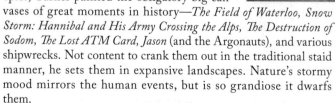

This is a theme we'll see throughout his works: The forces of nature—the burning sun, swirling clouds, churning waves, gathering storms, and the weathering of time—overwhelm men and wear down the civilizations they build.

Travels with Turner

Turner's true love was nature. And he was a born hobo. Oblivious to the wealth and fame that his early paintings gave him, he set out traveling—mostly on foot—throughout England and the Continent, with a rucksack full of sketch pads and painting gear. He sketched the English countryside, not green, leafy, and placid as so many others had done, but churning in motion, hazed over by a burning sunset.

He found the "sublime" not in the studio or in church, but in the overwhelming power of nature. The landscapes throb with life and motion. He sets Constable's clouds on fire.

Italy's Landscape and Ruins

Rick Steves' guidebook in hand, Turner visited the great museums of Italy, drawing inspiration from the Renaissance masters. He painted the classical monuments and Renaissance architecture. He copied masterpieces and learned, assimilated, and fused a great variety of styles—a true pan-European vision. Turner's Roman ruins are not grand; they're dwarfed by the landscape around them and eroded by swirling, misty, luminous clouds.

Stand close to a big canvas of Roman ruins, close enough so that it fills your whole field of vision. Notice how the buildings seem to wrap around you. Turner was a master of using multiple perspectives to draw the viewer in. On the one hand, you're right in the thick of things, looking "up" at the tall buildings. Then again, you're looking "down" on the distant horizon, as though standing on a mountaintop.

Venice

I know what color the palazzo is. But what color is it at sunset? Or through the filter of the watery haze that hangs over Venice? Can I paint the glowing haze itself? Maybe if I combine two different colors and smudge the paint on...

Venice stoked Turner's lust for reflected, golden sunlight. You'll see both finished works and unfinished sketches...uh, which is which?

Seascapes

The ever-changing sea was his specialty, with waves, clouds, mist, and sky churning and mixing together, all driven by the same forces.

Turner used oils like many painters use watercolors. First, he'd lay down a background (a "wash") of large patches of color, then he'd add a few dabs of paint to suggest a figure. The final product lacked photographic clarity, but showed the power and constant change in the forces of nature. He was perhaps the most prolific painter ever, with some 2,000 finished paintings and 20,000 sketches and watercolors.

Late Works

The older Turner got, the messier both he and his paintings became. He was wealthy, but he died in a run-down dive, where he'd set up house with a prostitute. Yet the colors are brighter and the subjects less pessimistic than in the dark and brooding early canvases. His last works—whether landscape, religious, or classical scenes—are a blur and swirl of colors in motion, lit by the sun or a lamp burning through the mist. Even Turner's own creations were finally dissolved by the swirling forces of nature.

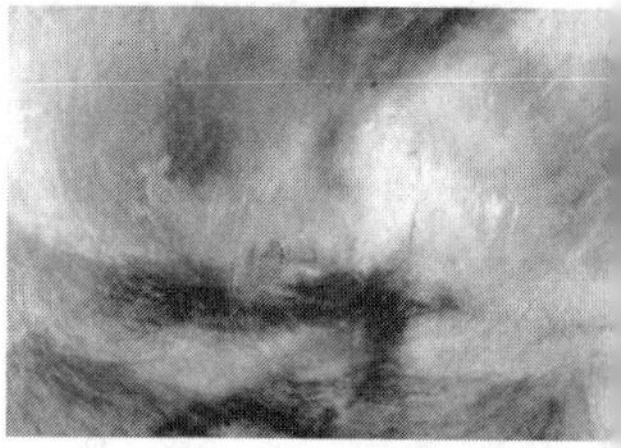

These paintings are "modern" in that the subject is less important than the style. You'll have to read the title to "get" it. You could argue that an Englishman helped invent Impressionism a generation before Monet and his ilk boxed the artistic ears of Paris in the 1880s. Turner's messy use of paint to portray reflected light "Chunneled" its way to France to inspire the Impressionists.

• *The 20th century, found in the east half of the Tate building, starts in Room 19.*

1900–1950—World Wars

As two World Wars whittled the powerful British Empire down, it still remained a major cultural force.

British art mirrored many of the trends and "-isms" pioneered in Paris. You'll see Cubism like Picasso's, abstract art like Mondrian's, and so on. But British artists also continued the British tradition of realistic paintings of people and landscape. (Note: You'll find 20th-century artists' work both here in the Tate Britain and in the Tate Modern.)

World War I, in which Britain lost a million men, cast a long shadow over the land. Artists expressed the horror of war, particularly of dehumanizing battles pitting powerful machines against puny human pawns. **Jacob Epstein's** (1880–1959) gleaming, abstract statues suggest mangled half-human/half-machine forms.

Henry Moore (1898–1986)

Twice a week, young Henry Moore went to the British Museum to sketch ancient statues, especially reclining ones (like in the Parthenon pediment or the Mayan god Chac Mool he saw in a photo). His statues—mostly female, mostly reclining—catch the primitive power of carved stone. Moore almost always carved with his own hands (unlike, say, Rodin, who modeled a small clay figure and let assistants chisel the real thing), capturing the human body in a few simple curves, with minimal changes to the rock itself.

The statues do look vaguely like what their titles say, but it's the stones themselves that are really interesting. Notice the texture and graininess of these mini-Stonehenges; feel the weight, the space they take up, and how the rock forms intermingle.

During World War II, Moore passed time in the bomb shelters sketching mothers with babes in arms, a theme found in later works.

Moore carves the human body with the epic scale and restless poses of Michelangelo but with the crude rocks and simple lines of the primitives.

Stanley Spencer (1891–1959)

Spencer paints unromanticized landscapes, portraits, and hometown scenes. Even the miraculous *Resurrection of the Dead* is portrayed absolutely literally, with the dead climbing out of their Glasgow graves. In fully modern times, Spencer carried on the British tradition of sober realism.

Francis Bacon (1909–1992)

With a stiff upper lip, Britain survived the Blitz, the War, and the loss of hundreds of thousands of men—but at war's end, the bottled-up horror came rushing out. Bacon's 1945 exhibition, opening

just after Holocaust details began surfacing, stunned London with its unmitigated ugliness.

His deformed half-humans/half-animals—caged in a claustrophobic room, with twisted, hunk-of-meat bodies and quadriplegic, smudged-mouth helplessness—can do nothing but scream in anguish and frustration. The scream becomes a blur, as though it goes on forever.

Bacon, largely self-taught, effectively uses "traditional" figurativism to express the existential human predicament of being caught in a world that is not of your making—you feel isolated and helpless to change it.

1950–2000—Modern World

No longer a world power, Britain in the Swinging '60s became a major exporter of pop culture. British art's traditional strengths—realism, portraits, landscapes, and slice-of-life scenes—were redone in the modern style.

David Hockney (b. 1937)

The "British Andy Warhol"—who is bleach-blonde, horn-rimmed, gay, and famous—paints Pop-ular culture with photographic realism. Large, airy canvases of L.A. swimming pools, double portraits of his friends in their stylish homes, or mundane scenes from the artist's own life capture the superficial materialism of the 1970s and 1980s. (Is he satirizing or glorifying it by painting it on a monumental scale with painstaking detail?)

Hockney saturates the canvas with bright (acrylic) paint, eliminating any haze, making distant objects as clear and bright as close ones. This technique, combined with his slightly simplified "cutout" figures, gives the painting the flat look of a billboard.

Lucian Freud (b. 1922)

Sigmund's grandson (who emigrated from Nazi Germany as a boy) puts every detail on the couch for analysis, then reassembles them into works that are still surprisingly realistic. His subjects look you right in the eye, slightly on edge. Even the plants create an ominous mood. Everything is in sharp focus (unlike in real life, where you concentrate on one

thing while your peripheral vision is blurred). Thick brushwork is especially good at capturing the pallor of British flesh.

In the great tradition of British portrait painting, Freud recently did an unflinching (and controversial) portrait of Queen Elizabeth.

Bridget Riley (b. 1931)

The pioneer of Op Art paints patterns of lines and alternating colors that make the eye vibrate (the way a spiral will "spin") when you stare at them. These obscure, scientific experiments in human optics suddenly became trendy in the psychedelic, cannabis-fueled 1960s. Like, wow.

Barbara Hepworth (1903–1975)

Hepworth's small-scale carvings in stone and wood—like "mini-Moores"—make even holes look interesting. Though they're not exactly realistic, it isn't hard to imagine them being inspired by, say, a man embracing a woman (she called it "sex harmony"), or the shoreline encircling a bay near her Cornwall-coast home, or a cliff penetrated by a cave—that is, two forms intermingling.

Gilbert (b. 1943) and George (b. 1942)

The Siegfried and Roy of art satirize the "Me Generation" and its shameless self-marketing by portraying their nerdy, three-piece-suited selves on the monumental scale normally dedicated to kings, popes, and saints.

THE REST OF THE MUSEUM

We've covered 500 years, with social satire from Hogarth to Hockney, from Constable's placid landscapes to Turner's churning scenes, from Blake's inner visions to Pre-Raphaelite fantasies, from realistic portraits to...realistic portraits.

But the Tate's great strength is championing contemporary British art in special exhibitions. There are two exhibition spaces: in the northeast corner of the main floor and the Linbury Gallery downstairs (each usually requiring separate admission). Explore the cutting-edge art from one of the world's thriving cultural capitals—London.

Enough Tate? Great. It's late.

TATE MODERN TOUR

Remember the 20th century? Accelerated by technology and fragmented by war, it was an exciting and chaotic time, with art as turbulent as the world that created it. The Tate Modern lets you walk through the last hundred years with a glimpse at the brave new art of this explosive century.

The Tate Modern is (controversially) displayed by genre—nudes, landscapes, still lifes, and history—rather than by artist and chronology. Unlike the museum, this chapter is neatly chronological. It's not intended as a painting-by-painting tour. Read through this chapter for a general introduction, then take advantage of the Tate's excellent audioguides to focus on specific works.

ORIENTATION

Cost: Free for the permanent collection (but donations are appreciated). Varying costs for temporary exhibits.

Hours: Daily 10:00–18:00, plus Fri–Sat until 22:00. This popular place is especially crowded on weekend days (crowds thin out on Fri and Sat evenings).

Getting There: Located on the South Bank, across from St. Paul's and near the Globe Theatre (Tube: Southwark or Blackfriars plus 10-min walk; or cross the Millennium Bridge from St. Paul's Cathedral; or catch the Tate Boat ferry service from Tate Britain, £4 one-way or £7 for day ticket; if you have a Travelcard, you'll pay less: £2.65 one-way/£4.65 for day ticket; buy ticket at gallery desk or on board, departs every 40 min, 18-min trip, ferry also stops at London Eye).

Information: The museum is also known as "Tate Modern at Bankside" (tel. 020/7887-8000, recorded info tel. 020/7887-8008, www.tate.org.uk). On the ground floor, you'll find the

information desk, baggage check, audioguide rentals, and tickets for temporary exhibits.

Tours: A variety of audioguide tours are available (£2 per audioguide or £3.50 per multimedia handheld device). These include: Director's Tour (highlights of the permanent collection), Collections Tour (all of the permanent collection), and a Children's Tour (geared for 8–12-year-olds). In addition, some individual rooms have free audioguides, and several touch-the-screen computers are scattered throughout.

Length of This Tour: Read this chapter ahead of time, then browse according to your tastes.

Cloakroom: First floor (free, suggested donation £2).

Photography: Photos are only permitted in the entrance hall.

Cuisine Art: View coffee shops are on the second and fourth floors, plus there's a table-service restaurant (with stunning views of St. Paul's—see photo) on the seventh floor. Some fine restaurants are outside, several blocks away, along the street named "the Cut" (near Southwark Tube stop).

Starring: Picasso, Matisse, Dalí, and all the "classic" modern artists, plus the Tate Modern's specialty—British and American artists of the last half of the 20th century.

Overview

The main permanent collection is on the third and fifth floors. Temporary exhibits are on the fourth. (Note: Modern British artists are divided between the Tate Modern and Tate Britain.)

To see the core of the permanent collection, visit the four sections divided by subject: Landscape and Still Life (3rd floor), and Nude and History (5th floor).

THE TOUR BEGINS

Entrance Hall

The grandest entry is from the west entrance. The massive empty space of the former industrial powerhouse dwarfs the art it houses.

(A metaphor for the triumph of 20th-century technology, perhaps?) The Turbine Hall displays major art installations by contemporary artists—always one of the highlights of the art world. Through the spring of 2006, British sculptor Rachel Whiteread—who often casts everyday objects in resin or plaster—gets her turn to try and fill the 4.7-million-cubic-foot blank canvas with appropriately monumental art.

From the Turbine Hall, you can reach the third floor (start of permanent collection) via the escalator near the ground floor cloakroom.

1900—Victoria's Legacy

Anno Domini 1900, a new century dawns. Europe is at peace, Britannia rules the world. Technology is about to usher in a golden age.

Claude Monet (1840–1926)

Monet captures the relaxed, civilized spirit of belle époque France and Victorian England with Impressionist snapshots of peaceful landscapes and middle-class family picnics. But the true subject is the shimmering effect of reflected light, rendered with rough brushstrokes and bright paints that look messy up close, but blend at a distance. The newfangled camera made camera-eye realism obsolete. Artists began placing more importance on *how* something was painted than on *what* was painted.

1905—Colonial Europe

Europe ruled a global empire, tapping its dark-skinned colonials for raw materials, cheap labor, and bold new ways to look at the world. The cozy Victorian world was shattering. Nietzsche murdered God. Darwin stripped off Man's robe of culture and found a naked ape. Primitivism was modern. Ooga-booga.

Henri Matisse (1869–1954)

Matisse was one of the Fauves, or "wild beasts," who tried to inject a bit of the jungle into civilized European society. Inspired by "primitive" African and Oceanic masks and voodoo dolls, the Fauves made modern art that looked primitive: long, mask-like faces with almond eyes; bright, clashing colors; simple figures; and "flat," two-dimensional scenes.

Matisse simplifies. A man is a few black lines and blocks of paint. A snail is a spiral of colored paper. A woman's back is an outline. Matisse's colors are unnaturally bright. The "distant" landscape is as crisp and clear as things close up, and the slanted lines meant to suggest depth are crudely done.

Traditionally, the canvas was like a window that you looked "through" to see a slice of the real world stretching off into the horizon. With Matisse, you look "at" the canvas, like wallpaper, to appreciate the decorative pattern of colors and shapes.

Though fully modern, Matisse built on 19th-century art—the bright colors of van Gogh, the primitive figures of Gauguin, the colorful designs of Japanese wood block prints, and the Impressionist patches of paint that only blend together at a distance.

Paul Cézanne (1839–1906)

Cézanne brings Impressionism into the 20th century. While Monet used separate dabs of different-colored paint to "build" a figure, Cézanne "builds" a man with somewhat larger slabs of paint, giving him a kind of 3-D chunkiness. It's not hard to see the progression from Monet's dabs to Cézanne's slabs to Picasso's cubes—Cubism.

1910—The Moderns

The modern world was moving fast, with automobiles, factories, and mass communication. Motion pictures caught the fast-moving world, while Einstein further explored the fourth dimension, time.

Cubism: Pablo Picasso (1881–1973)

Picasso's Cubist works show the old European world shattering to bits. He pieces the fragments back together in a whole new way, showing several perspectives at once (looking up the left side of a woman's body and down at her right at the same time, for example).

While newfangled motion pictures could capture several perspectives in succession, Picasso does it on a canvas with overlapping images. A single "cube" might contain both an arm (in the foreground) and the window behind (in the background), both painted the same color. The foreground and background are woven together so that the subject dissolves into a pattern.

Born in Spain, Picasso moved to

Paris as a young man. He worked with Georges Braque in poverty so dire they often didn't know where their next bottle of wine was coming from.

Picasso, the most famous and—OK, I'll say it—the greatest artist of the 20th century, constantly explored and adapted his style to new trends. He made collages, tried his hand at "statues" out of wood, wire, or whatever, and even made art out of everyday household objects. These multimedia works, so revolutionary at the time, have become stock-in-trade today. Scattered throughout the museum are works from the many periods of Picasso's life.

Futurism: Férnand Leger (1881–1955) and Umberto Boccioni (1882–1916)

The Machine Age is approaching, and the whole world gleams with promise in cylinder shapes ("Tubism"), like an internal-combustion engine. Or is it the gleaming barrel of a cannon?

1914—World War I

A soldier—shivering in a trench, ankle-deep in mud, waiting to be ordered "over the top," to run through barbed wire, over fallen comrades, and into a hail of machine-gun fire, only to capture a few hundred yards of meaningless territory that would be lost the next day. This soldier was not thinking about art.

World War I left nine million dead. (England sometimes lost more men in a single day than America lost in all of Vietnam.) The war also killed the optimism and faith in mankind that had guided Europe since the Renaissance.

Expressionism: Grosz, Kirchner, Beckmann, Soutine, Dix, and Kokoschka

Cynicism and decadence settled over postwar Europe. Artists "expressed" their disgust by showing a distorted reality that emphasized the ugly. Using the lurid colors and simplified figures of the Fauves, they slapped paint on in thick brushstrokes, depicting a hypocritical, hard-edged, dog-eat-dog world, a civilization watching its Victorian moral foundations collapse.

Dada: Duchamp's Urinal (1917)

When they could grieve no longer, artists turned to grief's giddy twin, laughter. The war made all old values a joke, including artistic ones. The Dada movement, choosing a purposely childish name, made art that was intentionally outrageous: a moustache on the *Mona Lisa*, a shovel hung on the wall, or a modern version of a Renaissance

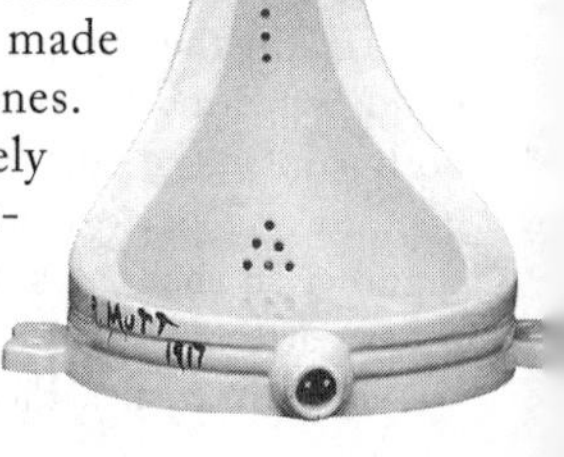

"fountain"—a urinal (by Marcel Duchamp...or was it I. P. Freeley?).

It was a dig at all the pompous prewar artistic theories based on the noble intellect of Rational Women and Men. While the experts ranted on, Dadaists sat in the back of the class and made cultural fart noises.

Hey, I love this stuff. My mind says it's sophomoric, but my heart belongs to Dada.

1920s—Anything Goes

In the Jazz Age, the world turned upside down. Genteel ladies smoked cigarettes. Gangsters laid down the law. You could make a fortune in the stock market one day and lose it the next. You could dance the Charleston with the opposite sex, and even say the word "sex" while talking about Freud over cocktails. It was almost...surreal.

Surrealism: Dalí, Ernst, and Magritte

Artists caught the jumble of images on a canvas. A telephone made from a lobster, an elephant with a heating-duct trunk, Venus sleepwalking among skeletons. Take one mixed bag of reality, jumble in a blender, and serve on a canvas—surrealism.

The artist scatters seemingly unrelated things on the canvas, leaving us to trace the connections in a kind of connect-the-dots without numbers.

Further complicating the modern world was Freud's discovery of the "unconscious" mind that thinks dirty thoughts while we sleep. Surrealists let the id speak. The canvas is an uncensored, stream-of-consciousness "landscape" of these deep urges, revealed in the bizarre images of dreams.

Salvador Dalí (1904–1989)

Salvador Dalí, the most famous surrealist, combined an extraordinarily realistic technique with an extraordinarily twisted mind. He could paint "unreal" scenes with photographic realism, making us believe they could really happen. Dalí's images—crucifixes, political and religious figures, and naked bodies—pack an emotional punch.

1930s—Depression

As capitalism failed around the world, governments propped up their economies with vast building projects. The architecture style was modern, stripped-down (i.e., cheap), and functional. Propagandist campaigns champion noble workers in the heroic Social Realist style.

Piet Mondrian (1872–1944)

Like blueprints for modernism, Mondrian's T-square style boils painting down to its basic building blocks: a white canvas, black lines, and the three primary colors—red, yellow, and blue—arranged in orderly patterns. (When you come right down to it, that's all painting ever has been. A schematic drawing of, say, the *Mona Lisa* shows that it's less about a woman than about the triangles and rectangles she's composed of.)

Mondrian started out painting realistic landscapes of the orderly fields in his native homeland of Holland. Increasingly, he simplified his style into horizontal and vertical patterns. For Mondrian, who was heavily into Eastern mysticism, "up versus down" and "left versus right" were the perfect metaphors for life's dualities: good versus evil, body versus spirit, fascism versus communism, man versus woman. The canvas is a bird's-eye view of Mondrian's personal landscape.

1940s—World War II

World War II was a global war (involving Europe, the Americas, Australia, Africa, and Asia) and a total war (saturation bombing of civilians and ethnic cleansing). It left Europe in ruins.

Alberto Giacometti (1901–1966)

Giacometti's skinny statues have the emaciated, haunted, and faceless look of concentration-camp survivors. In the sweep of world war and overpowering technology, man is frail and fragile. All he can do is stand at attention and take it like a man.

Francis Bacon (1909–1992)

Bacon's caged creatures speak for all of war-torn Europe when they scream, "Enough!" (For more on Bacon, see page 177 of the Tate Britain Tour.)

1950s—America, the Global Superpower

As converted war factories turned swords into kitchen appliances, America helped rebuild Europe, while pumping out consumer goods for a booming population. Prosperity, a stable government, national television broadcasts, and a common fear of Soviet

Abstract Art

Abstract art simplifies. A man becomes a stick figure. A squiggle is a wave. A streak of red expresses anger. Arches

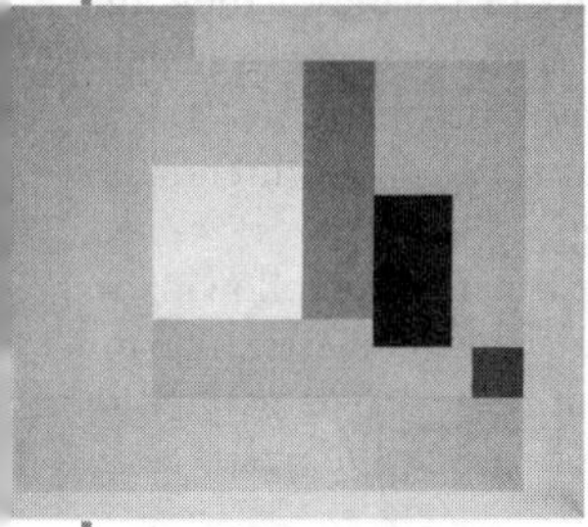

make you want a cheeseburger. These are universal symbols that everyone from a caveman to a banker understands. Abstract artists capture the essence of reality in a few lines and colors, even things a camera can't—emotions, abstract concepts, musical rhythms, and spiritual states of mind.

With abstract art, you don't look "through" the canvas to see the visual world, but "at" it to read the symbolism of lines, shapes, and colors. Most 20th-century paintings are a mix of the real world (representation) and colorful patterns (abstraction).

Communism threatened to turn America into a completely homogeneous society.

Some artists, centered in New York, rebelled against conformity and superficial consumerism. (They'd served under Eisenhower in war and now had to in peace, as well.) They created art that was the very opposite of the functional, mass-produced goods of the American marketplace.

Art was a way of asserting your individuality by creating a completely original and personal vision. The trend was toward bigger canvases, abstract designs, and experimentation with new materials and techniques. It was called "Abstract Expressionism"—expressing emotions and ideas using color and form alone.

Jackson Pollock (1912–1956)

"Jack the Dripper" attacks convention with a can of paint, dripping and splashing a dense web onto the canvas. Picture Pollock in his studio, jiving to the hi-fi, bouncing off the walls, throwing paint in a moment of enlightenment. Of course, the artist loses some control this way—over the paint flying in midair and over himself in an ecstatic trance. Painting becomes a whole-body activity, a "dance" between the artist and his materials.

The intuitive act of creating is what's important, not the final product. The canvas is only a record of that moment of ecstasy.

Big, Empty Canvases

With all the postwar prosperity, artists could afford bigger canvases. But what reality are they trying to show?

In the modern world, we find ourselves insignificant specks in a vast and indifferent universe. Every morning, each of us must confront that big, blank, existential canvas, and decide how we're going to make our mark on it.

Another influence was the simplicity of Japanese landscape painting. A Zen master studies and meditates for years to achieve the state of mind in which he can draw one pure line. These canvases, again, are only a record of that state of enlightenment. (What is the sound of one brush painting?)

On more familiar ground, postwar painters were following in the footsteps of artists such as Mondrian. The geometrical forms here reflect the same search for order, but these artists painted to the musical 5/4 asymmetry of the Dave Brubeck Quartet's jazzy *Take Five.*

Patterns and Textures

Enjoy the lines and colors, but also a new element: texture. Some works have very thick paint piled on, where you can see the brushstrokes clearly. Some have substances besides paint applied to the canvas, or the canvas is punctured so the fabric itself (and the hole) becomes the subject. Artists show their skill by mastering new materials. The canvas is a tray, serving up a delightful buffet of different substances with interesting colors, patterns, shapes, and textures.

Mark Rothko (1903–1970)

Rothko makes two-toned rectangles, laid on their sides, that seem to float in a big, vertical canvas. The edges are blurred, so if you get close enough to let the canvas fill your field of vision (as Rothko intended), the rectangles appear to rise and sink from the cloudy depths like answers in a Magic 8-Ball.

Serious students appreciate the subtle differences in color between the rectangles. Rothko experimented with different bases for the same color and used a single undercoat (a "wash") to unify them. His early works are warmer, with brighter reds, yellows, and oranges; the later works are maroon and brown, approaching black.

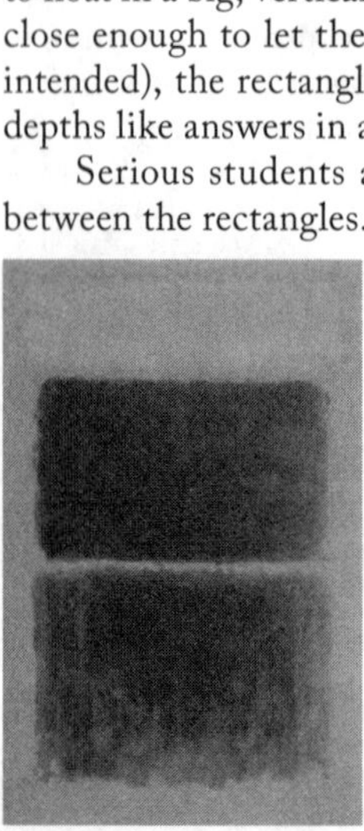

Still, these are not intended to be formal studies in color and form. Rothko was trying to express the most basic human emotions in a pure language. (A "realistic" painting of a person is inherently fake because it's only an illusion of the person.) Staring into these windows onto the soul, you can laugh, cry, or ponder, just as Rothko did when he painted them.

Rothko, the last century's "last serious artist," believed in the power of art to express the human spirit. When he found out that his eight large Seagrams canvases were to be hung in a corporate restaurant, he refused to sell them (and they ended up in the Tate).

In his last years, Rothko's canvases—always rectangles—got bigger, simpler, and darker. When Rothko finally slashed his wrists in his studio, one nasty critic joked that what killed him was the repetition. Minimalism was painting itself into a blank corner.

1960s—The Sixties

The decade began united in idealism—young John F. Kennedy pledged to put a man on the moon, newly launched satellites signaled a united world, the Beatles sang exuberantly, peaceful race demonstrations championed equality, and the Vatican II Council preached liberation. By decade's end, there were race riots, assassinations, student protests, and America's floundering war in distant Vietnam. In households around the world, parents screamed, "Turn that down...and get a haircut!"

Culturally, every postwar value was questioned by a rising, wealthy, populous, baby-boom generation. London—producer of rock-and-roll music, film actors, mod fashions, and Austin Powers' joie de vivre—once again became a world cultural center.

While government-sponsored public art was dominated by big, abstract canvases and sculptures, other artists pooh-poohed the highbrow seriousness of abstract art. Instead, they mocked lowbrow, popular culture by embracing it in a tongue-in-cheek way (Pop art), or they attacked authority with absurd performances to make a political statement (conceptual art).

Pop Art: Andy Warhol (1930–1987)

America's postwar wealth made the consumer king. Pop art is created from the popular objects of that throw-away society—soup can, car fender, tacky plastic statues, movie icons. Take a Sears' product, hang it in a museum, and you have to ask, Is this art? Are mass-produced objects beautiful? Or crap? Why do we work so hard to acquire them? Pop art, like Dadaism, questions our society's values.

Andy Warhol (who coined "15 minutes of fame") concentrated on another mass-produced phenomenon—celebrities. He took publicity photos of famous people and reproduced them. The repetition—like the constant bombardment we get from repeated images on TV—cheapens even the most beautiful things.

Roy Lichtenstein (1923–1997)

Take a comic strip, blow it up, hang it on a wall, and charge a million bucks—wham, Pop art. Lichtenstein supposedly was inspired by his young son, who challenged him to do something as good as Mickey Mouse. The huge newsprint dots never let us forget that the painting—like all commercial art—is an illusionistic fake. The work's humor comes from portraying a lowbrow subject (comics and ads) on the epic scale of a masterpiece.

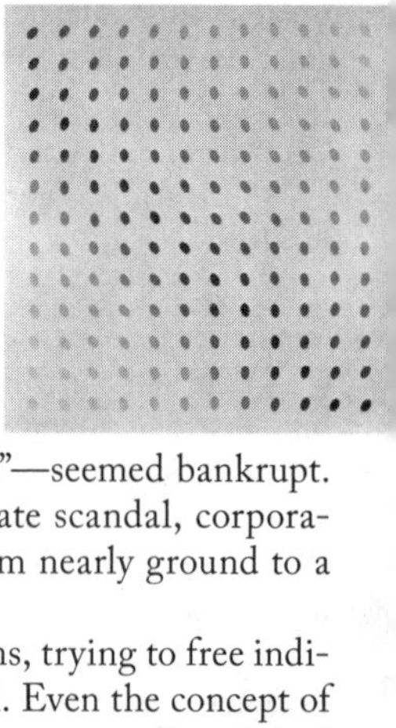

Op Art: Bridget Riley (b. 1931)

Optical illusions play tricks with your eyes, like the way a spiral starts to spin when you stare at it. These obscure scientific experiments in color, line, and optics suddenly became trendy in the psychedelic '60s.

1970s—The "Me Decade"

All forms of authority—"The Establishment"—seemed bankrupt. America's president resigned in the Watergate scandal, corporations were polluting the earth, and capitalism nearly ground to a halt when Arabs withheld oil.

Artists attacked authority and institutions, trying to free individuals to discover their full human potential. Even the concept of "modernism"—that art wasn't good unless it was totally original and progressive—was questioned. No single style could dictate in this postmodern period.

Earth Art

Fearing for the health of earth's ecology, artists rediscovered the beauty of rocks, dirt, trees, even the sound of the wind, using them to create natural art. A rock placed in a museum or urban square is certainly a strange sight.

Joseph Beuys (1921–1986)

The Tate Modern's collection of "sculptures" by Beuys—assemblages of steel, junk, wood, and, especially, felt and animal fat—

20th-Century British Artists

Since 1960, London has rivaled New York as a center for the visual arts. You'll find British artists displayed in both the Tate Modern and Tate Britain. Check out the Tate Britain Tour chapter (page 177) for more on the following artists: David Hockney, Stanley Spencer, Jacob Epstein, Gilbert and George, Henry Moore, Francis Bacon, and Barbara Hepworth.

only hint at his greatest artwork: Beuys himself.

Imagine Beuys (pron. "boyss") walking through the museum, carrying a dead rabbit, while he explains the paintings to it. Or taking off his clothes, shaving his head, and smearing his body with fat.

This charismatic, ex-Luftwaffe art shaman did ridiculous things to inspire others to break with convention and be free. He choreographed "Happenings"—spectacles where people did absurd things while others watched—and pioneered performance art, in which the artist presents himself as the work of art. Beuys inspired a whole generation of artists to walk on stage, cluck like a chicken, and stick a yam up themselves. Beuys will be Beuys.

New Media

Minimalist painting and abstract sculpture were old hat, and there was an explosion of new art forms. Performance art was the most controversial, combining music, theater, dance, poetry, and the visual arts. New technologies brought video, assemblages, installations, artists' books (paintings in book form), and even (gasp!) realistic painting.

Conceptual Art

Increasingly, artists are not creating an original work (painting a canvas or sculpting a stone) but assembling one from premade objects. The *concept* of which object to pair with another to produce maximum effect ("Let's stick a crucifix in a jar of urine," to cite one notorious example) is the key.

1980s—Material Girl

Ronald Reagan in America, Margaret Thatcher in Britain, and corporate executives around the world ruled over a conservative and materialistic society. On the other side were starving Ethiopians, gays with the new disease of AIDS, people of color, and women demanding power. Intelligent, peaceful, straight, white males assumed a low profile.

The art world became big business, with a van Gogh fetching $54 million. Corporations paid big bucks for large, colorful, semi-abstract canvases. Marketing became an art form. Gender and sexual choice were popular themes. Many women picked up paintbrushes, creating bright-colored abstract forms hinting at vulva and penis shapes. Visual art fused with popular music, bringing us installations in dance clubs and fast-edit music videos. The crude style of graffiti art demanded to be included in corporate society.

1990s—Multicultural Diversity

The communist-built Berlin Wall was torn down, ending four decades of a global Cold War between capitalism and communism. The new battleground was the "Culture Wars," the struggle to include all races, genders, and lifestyles within an increasingly corporate-dominated, global society.

Artists looked to Third World countries for inspiration and championed society's outsiders against government censorship and economic exclusion. A new medium arose, the Internet, allowing instantaneous multimedia communication around the world through electronic signals carried by satellites and telephone lines.

2000—?

A new millennium has dawned, with Europe and America at a peak of prosperity unmatched in human history...

BRITISH LIBRARY TOUR

The British Empire built its greatest monuments out of paper. It's with literature that England has made her lasting contribution to history and the arts. These national archives of Britain include more than 12 million books, 180 miles of shelving, and the deepest basement in London. But everything that matters for your visit is in one delightful room labeled "Treasures." We'll concentrate on a handful of documents—literary and historical—that changed the course of history. Start with the top stops (described in this tour), then stray according to your interests.

ORIENTATION

Cost: Free (donations appreciated).

Hours: Mon–Fri 9:30–18:00 (until 20:00 on Tue), Sat 9:30–17:00, Sun 11:00–17:00.

Getting There: Take the Tube to King's Cross. Leaving the station, turn right, and walk a block to 96 Euston Road.

Information: Tel. 020/7412-7000, www.bl.uk.

Tours: One-hour-plus general building tours are usually offered on Mon, Wed, and Fri–Sun at 15:00, and Sat at 10:30 and 15:00 (£7; to confirm schedule and to reserve, call 020/7412-7332). A £3.50 audioguide giving a 45-minute tour of the Treasures is available at the information desk (photo ID or £20 deposit required).

Length of This Tour: Allow one hour.

Cloakroom: Free. Lockers require £1 coin deposit (no large bags).

No-nos: No photography, smoking, or chewing gum.

Cuisine Art: A great cafeteria/restaurant that serves good hot meals is upstairs above the ground-floor café, which is next to a vast and fun pull-out stamp collection. The 50-foot-tall wall of 65,000 books within the cafés was given to the people by King George IV in 1823. This high-tech bookshelf is behind glass and has movable lifts.

Starring: Magna Carta, Bibles, Shakespeare, English Lit 101, and the Beatles.

THE TOUR BEGINS

Entering the library courtyard, you'll see a big statue of a naked Isaac Newton bending forward with a compass to measure the universe. The statue symbolizes the library's purpose: to gather all knowledge and promote our endless search for truth.

Stepping inside, you'll see the information desk and café. The cloakroom and WC are down a short staircase to the right. The reading rooms upstairs are not open to the public. Our tour is in the tiny but exciting area to the left, in the John Ritblat Gallery, under the sign marked Exhibitions.

The priceless literary and historical treasures of the collection are in one carefully designed and well-lit room, called "Treasures." The Turning the Pages computer room (where you can electronically leaf through several rare manuscripts) is in an adjoining room. Down a few steps you'll find the Pearson Gallery, with temporary exhibits sometimes requiring an admission charge.

❶ Maps

Navigate the wall of historic maps from left to right. "A Medieval Map of Britain," from 1250, puts medieval man in an unusual position—looking down on his homeland from 50 miles in the air. "Charting the Seas," from c. 1325, shows a well-defined west coast of Europe as European sailors ventured cautiously out of the Mediterranean. By 1564, you could plan your next trip to Britain with the map of "Mercator's Britain." "The End of a Tradition" (1688) has the world well-mapped, except that the United States has a Miami Beach perspective: Florida plus a lot of unexplored interior inhabited by strange beasts.

❷ Bibles

My favorite excuse for not learning a foreign language is: "If English was good enough for Jesus Christ, it's good enough for me!" I don't know what that has to do with anything, but obviously Jesus didn't speak English—nor did Moses or Isaiah or Paul or any other Bible authors or characters. As a result, our present-day English Bible is not directly from the mouths and pens of these religious figures, but the fitful product of centuries of evolution and translation.

British Library Tour

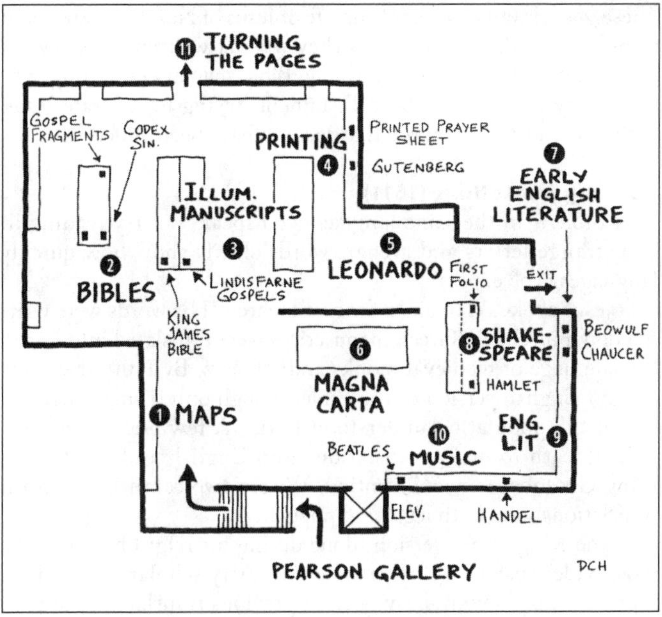

The Bible is not a single book; it's an anthology of books by many authors from different historical periods writing in different languages (usually Hebrew or Greek). So there are three things that editors must consider in compiling the most accurate Bible: 1) deciding which books actually belong, 2) finding the oldest and most accurate version of each book, and 3) translating it accurately.

Codex Sinaiticus **(c. A.D. 350)**

The oldest complete "Bible" in existence (along with one in the Vatican), this is one of the first attempts to collect various books together into one authoritative anthology. It's in Greek, the language in which most of the New Testament was written. The Old Testament portions are Greek translations from the original Hebrew. This particular Bible and the nearby *Codex Alexandrinus* (A.D. 425), contain some books not included in most modern English Bibles. (Even today, Catholic Bibles contain books not found in Protestant Bibles.)

Gospel Fragments

These gospels (an account of the life of Jesus of Nazareth) are about as old as any in existence, but they weren't written until several generations after Jesus died. Today, Bible scholars pore diligently over every word in the New Testament, trying to separate Jesus' authentic words from those that seem to have been added later.

The King James Bible (1611)

This Bible is in the same language you speak, but try reading it. The strange letters and archaic words clearly show how quickly languages evolve.

Jesus spoke Aramaic, a form of Hebrew. His words were written down in Greek. Greek manuscripts were translated into Latin, the language of medieval monks and scholars. By 1400, there was still no English version of the Bible, though only a small percentage of the population understood Latin. A few brave reformers risked death to make translations into English and print them using Gutenberg's new invention. Within two centuries, English translations were both legal and popular.

The King James version (done during his reign) has been the most widely used English translation. Fifty scholars worked for four years, borrowing heavily from previous translations, to produce the work. Its impact on the English language was enormous, making Elizabethan English something of the standard, even after all those *thee*s and *thou*s fell out of fashion in everyday speech.

Many of the most recent translations are both more accurate (based on better scholarship and original manuscripts) and more readable, using modern speech patterns. The late-20th-century debates over God's gender highlight the problems of translating old phrases to fit contemporary viewpoints.

Along the walls are sacred writings from other religious traditions: the Hebrew Torah, Muslim Qur'an, Buddhist sutras, and Hindu Upanishads.

❸ Lindisfarne Gospels (A.D. 698) and Other Illuminated Manuscripts

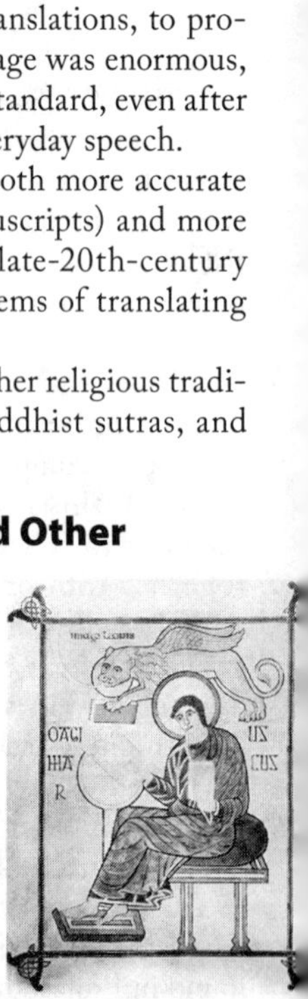

Throughout the Middle Ages, Bibles had to be reproduced by hand. This was a painstaking process, usually done by monks for a rich patron. This beautifully illustrated ("illuminated") collection of the four Gospels is the most magnificent of medieval British monkuscripts. The text is in Latin, the language of scholars ever since the Roman Empire, but the illustrations—with elaborate tracery and interwoven decoration—mix Irish, classical, and even Byzantine forms. (Read an electronic copy in the adjacent Turning the Pages computer room.)

These Gospels are a reminder that Christianity almost didn't make it in Europe. After the fall of Rome (which had established Christianity as the official religion), much of Europe reverted to its pagan ways. This was the time of *Beowulf*, when people worshipped woodland spirits and terrible Teutonic gods. It took dedicated Irish missionaries 500 years to reestablish the faith on the Continent. Lindisfarne, an obscure monastery of Irish monks on an island off the east coast of England, was one of the few beacons of light after the fall of Rome, tending the embers of civilization through the long night of the Dark Ages.

Browse through more illuminated manuscripts (in the cases behind the Lindisfarne Gospels). This is some of the finest art from what we call the Dark Ages. The little intimate details offer a rare and fascinating peek into medieval life.

❹ Printing

Printing was invented by the Chinese (what wasn't?). The Printed Prayer Sheet (c. 618–907) was made seven centuries before the printing press was "invented" in Europe. A bodhisattva (an incarnation of Buddha) rides a lion, surrounded by a prayer in Chinese characters. The faithful gained a blessing by saying the prayer, and so did the printer by reproducing it. Texts such as this were printed using wooden blocks carved with Chinese characters that were dipped into paint or ink.

The Gutenberg Bible (c. 1455)

It looks like just another monk-made Latin manuscript, but it was the first book printed in Europe using movable type. Printing is one of the most revolutionary inventions in history.

Johann Gutenberg (c. 1397–1468), a German silversmith, devised a convenient way to reproduce written materials quickly, neatly, and cheaply—by printing with movable type. You scratch each letter onto a separate metal block, then arrange them into words, ink them up, and

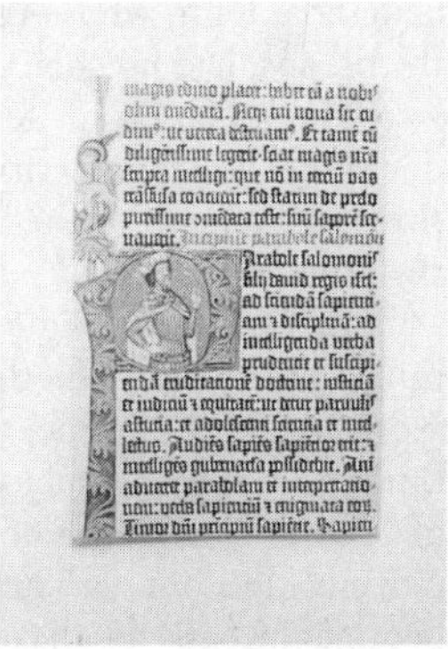

press them onto paper. When one job was done you could reuse the same letters for a new one.

This simple idea had immediate and revolutionary consequences. Suddenly, the Bible was available for anyone to read, fueling the Protestant Reformation. Knowledge became cheap and accessible to a wide audience, not just the rich. Books became the mass medium of Europe, linking people by a common set of ideas.

❺ Leonardo da Vinci's Notebook

Books also spread secular knowledge. Renaissance men turned their attention away from heaven and toward the nuts and bolts of the material world around them. These pages from Leonardo's notebook show his powerful curiosity, his genius for invention, and his famous backward and inside-out handwriting, which makes sense only if you know Italian and have a mirror. Leonardo's restless mind ranged from how birds fly to the flow of the Arno River to military fortifications to the "earthshine" reflecting onto the moon to an early helicopter.

One person's research inspired another's, and books allowed knowledge to accumulate. Galileo championed the counter-commonsense notion that the Earth spun around the sun, and Isaac Newton later perfected the mathematics of those moving celestial bodies.

❻ Magna Carta (1215)

How did Britain, a tiny island with a few million people, come to rule a quarter of the world? Not by force, but by law. The Magna Carta was the basis for England's constitutional system of government. Though historians talk about "the" Magna Carta, there are several different versions of the document on display.

The Articles of the Barons: In 1215, England's barons rose in revolt against the slimy King John. After losing London, John was forced to negotiate. The barons presented him with this list of demands. John, whose rule was worthless without the support of the barons, had no choice but to affix his seal to it.

Magna Carta: A few days after John agreed to this original document, it was rewritten in legal form, and some 35 copies of this final version of the "Great Charter" were distributed around the kingdom.

This was a turning point in the history of government. Before, kings had ruled by God-given authority, above the laws of men. Now, for the first time, there were limits—in writing—on how a king could treat his subjects. More generally, it established the idea of "due process"—the notion that a government can't infringe on citizens' freedom without a legitimate legal reason. This small step became the basis for all constitutional governments, including yours.

So what did this radical piece of paper actually say? Not much, by today's standards. The specific demands had to do with things such as inheritance taxes, the king's duties to widows and orphans, and so on. It wasn't the specific articles that were important, but the simple fact that the king had to abide by them as law.

Nearby are many more historical documents. The displays change frequently, but you may see letters by Queen Elizabeth I, Thomas More, Florence Nightingale, Gandhi, and others. But for now, let's trace the evolution of...

❼ Early English Literature

Four out of every five English words have been borrowed from other languages. The English language, like English culture (and London today), is a mix derived from foreign invaders. Some of the historic ingredients that make this cultural stew:

- The original Celtic tribesmen
- Latin-speaking Romans (A.D. 1–500)
- Germanic tribes called Angles and Saxons (making English a Germanic language and naming the island "Angle-land"—England)
- Vikings from Denmark (A.D. 800)
- French-speaking Normans under William the Conqueror (1066–1250)

Beowulf (c. 1000)

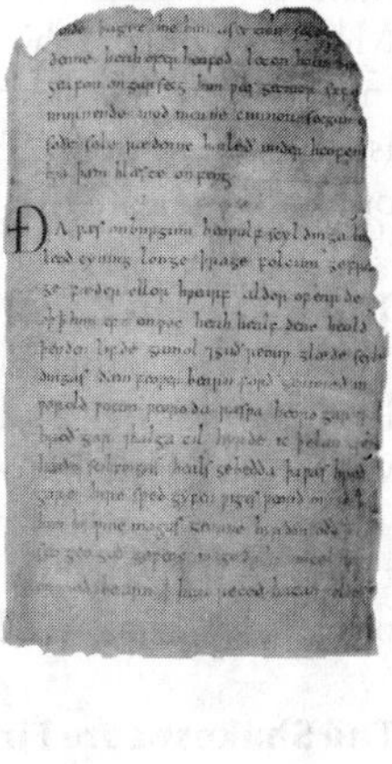

This Anglo-Saxon epic poem, written in Old English, the early version of our language, almost makes the hieroglyphics on the Rosetta Stone look easy. The manuscript here is from A.D. 1000, although the story itself dates to about 750. This is the only existing medieval manuscript of this first English literary masterpiece.

In this epic story, the young hero Beowulf defeats two half-human monsters threatening the kingdom. Beowulf symbolizes England's emergence from the chaos and barbarism of the Dark Ages.

The Canterbury Tales (c. 1410)

Six hundred years later, England was Christian, but it was hardly the pious, predictable, Sunday-school world we might imagine. Geoffrey Chaucer's bawdy collection of stories, told by pilgrims on their way to Canterbury, gives us the full range of life's experiences—happy, sad, silly, sexy, pious. (Late in life, Chaucer wrote an apology for those works of his "that tend toward sin.")

While most serious literature of the time was written in scholarly Latin, the stories in *The Canterbury Tales* were written in Middle English, the language that developed after the French invasion (1066) added a Norman twist to Old English.

❽ Shakespeare (1564–1616)

William Shakespeare is the greatest author in any language.

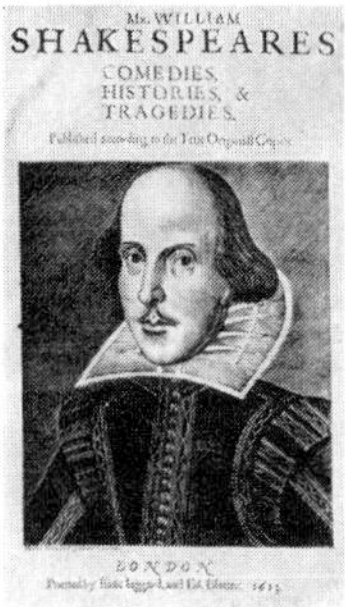

Period. He expanded and helped define modern English. In one fell swoop, he made the language of everyday people as important as Latin. In the process, he gave us phrases like "one fell swoop" that we quote without knowing it's Shakespeare.

Perhaps as important was his insight into humanity. With his stock of great characters—Hamlet, Othello, Macbeth, Falstaff, Lear, Romeo, Juliet—he probed the psychology of human beings 300 years before Freud. Even today, his characters strike a familiar chord.

Shakespeare in Collaboration

Shakespeare co-wrote a play titled *The Booke of Sir Thomas More.* Some scholars have wondered if maybe Shakespeare had help on other plays as well. After all, they reasoned, how could a journeyman actor, with little education, have written so many masterpieces? Modern scholars, though, unanimously agree that Shakespeare did indeed write the plays ascribed to him. This particular manuscript is believed to be in Shakespeare's own handwriting. The crossed-out lines indicate that even geniuses need editing.

The Good and Bad Quartos of *Hamlet*

Shakespeare wrote his plays to be performed, not read. He published a few, but as his reputation grew, unauthorized "bootleg" versions also began to circulate. Some of these were written out by actors who were trying (with faulty memories) to re-create plays they had appeared in years before. Here are two different versions of *Hamlet:* "good" and "bad."

The Shakespeare First Folio (1623)

It wasn't until seven years after his death that this complete collection of Shakespeare's plays came out. The editors were friends and fellow actors.

The engraving of Shakespeare on the title page is one of only two portraits done during his lifetime. Is this what he really looked like? No one knows. The best answer probably comes from his friend and fellow poet Ben Jonson in the introduction on the facing page. Jonson concludes, "Reader, look not on his picture, but his book."

❾ Other Greats in English Literature

The rest of the "*Beowulf*/Chaucer wall" is a greatest-hits sampling of British literature featuring works that have enlightened and brightened our lives for centuries. The displays rotate frequently, but there's always a tasty selection of famous works from Dickens to Austen to Kipling to Woolf to Joyce. Often on display is the original ***Alice's Adventures in Wonderland*** by Lewis Carroll. Carroll (whose real name was Charles L. Dodgson) was a stutterer, which made him uncomfortable around everyone but children. For them he created a fantasy world where grown-up rules and logic were turned upside down.

❿ Music

The Beatles

Future generations will have to judge whether this musical quartet ranks with artists such as Dickens and Keats, but no one can deny their historical significance. The Beatles burst onto the scene in the early 1960s to unheard-of popularity. With their long hair and loud music, they brought counterculture and revolutionary ideas to the middle class, affecting the values of a whole generation. Touring the globe, they served as a link between young people everywhere. Look for photos of John Lennon, Paul McCartney, George Harrison, and Ringo Starr before and after their fame.

Most interesting are the manuscripts of song lyrics written by Lennon and McCartney, the two guiding lights of the group. "I Wanna Hold Your Hand" was the song that launched them to superstardom. "A Hard Day's Night" was the title song of a film capturing their hectic touring schedule. Some call "A Ticket to Ride" the first heavy-metal song. In "Here, There, and Everywhere," notice the changes Paul made searching for just the right rhyme. "Yesterday," by Paul, was recorded with guitar and voice backed by a string quartet—a touch of sophistication by producer George Martin. Also, glance at the rambling, depressed, cynical, but humorous letter by a young John Lennon. Is that a self-portrait at the bottom?

Handel's *Messiah* (1741) and Other Music Manuscripts

Kind of an anticlimax after the Fab Four, I know, but here are manuscripts by Mozart, Beethoven, Schubert, and others. George Frideric Handel's famous oratorio, the *Messiah*, was written in a flash of inspiration—three hours of music in 24 days. Here are the final bars of its most famous tune. Hallelujah.

⓫ Turning the Pages—Virtual-Reality Room

For a chance to page through a few of the most precious books in the collection, drop by the Turning the Pages room. Touch a computer screen and let your fingers do the walking.

WESTMINSTER ABBEY TOUR

Westminster Abbey is the greatest church in the English-speaking world. England's kings and queens have been crowned and buried here since 1066. The histories of Westminster Abbey and England are almost the same. A thousand years of English history—3,000 tombs, the remains of 29 kings and queens, and hundreds of memorials to poets, politicians, and warriors—lie within its stained-glass splendor and under its stone slabs.

ORIENTATION

Cost: £8, includes cloisters and Abbey Museum. Praying is free, thank God, but you must inform the marshal at the door of your purpose. Or, for a free peek inside (without seeing all the historic tombs) and a quiet sit in the nave, you can tell a marshal at the west end (where the tourists exit) that you'd like to pay your respects to Britain's Unknown Soldier, and he will let you slip in.

Hours: The Abbey is open Mon–Fri 9:30–15:45, Wed until 19:00, Sat 9:30–13:45 (last admission 60 min before closing, closed Sun to sightseers but open for services). The Abbey Museum is open daily 10:30–16:00. The cloisters are open daily 8:00–18:00. Special events can shut down all or part of the Abbey.

The main entrance, on the Parliament Square side, often has a sizable line; visit early or late to avoid tourist hordes. Midmornings are most crowded. On weekdays after 15:00 it's less crowded; come then and stay for the 17:00 evensong (see below).

Getting There: Near Big Ben and Houses of Parliament (Tube: Westminster or St. James's Park).

Information: To confirm the times of guided tours, concerts, and services, call 020/7222-7110. Since events and services can shut out sightseers, it's wise to call ahead simply to confirm the Abbey is open. For more information and concert listings, see www.westminster-abbey.org.

Music: Evensong, a stirring experience in a nearly empty church, is on Mon, Tue, Thu, and Fri at 17:00, and Sat and Sun at 15:00. Free organ recitals are held Sun at 17:45 (30 min, look for posted signs with schedules).

Tours: Vergers, the church equivalent of docents, give entertaining guided tours for £4 (up to 6/day, 90 min). Tour themes are the historic church, the personalities buried here, and the great coronations. Informative audioguide tours cost £3 (available weekdays until 15:00, Sat until 13:00, pick up at info desk at north door, can reserve in advance by calling info number, above). Many prefer the audioguide to the vergers' tour because it is self-paced.

Length of This Tour: Allow 90 minutes.

Photography: Photos are prohibited.

Cuisine Art: In good weather, there are sandwich-soup-and-drink kiosks in the cloister courtyard. Or find reasonably priced, cafeteria-style lunches in the basement of Methodist Central Hall, across the street from the west entrance of the Abbey (daily 10:00–16:00). The Westminster Arms pub is near Methodist Hall on Storey's Gate Street.

Starring: Edwards, Elizabeths, Henrys, Annes, Marys, and poets.

THE TOUR BEGINS

You'll have no choice but to follow the steady flow of tourists circling clockwise through the church—in through the north entrance, behind the altar, into Poets' Corner in the south transept, detouring through the cloisters, and, finally, back out through the west end of the nave. It's all one-way, and the crowds can be a real crush. Here are the Abbey's top 10 (plus 1) stops:

• *Walk straight in, entering the North transept. Pick up the map flier that locates the most illustrious tombs, and belly up to the barricade in the center of the church.*

❶ North Transept

You're standing at the center of a cross-shaped church. The main altar (with cross and candlesticks) sits on the platform up the five stairs in front of you. To the right stretches the long, high-ceilinged nave. Nestled in the nave is the elaborately carved wooden seating of the choir (or "quire"), where monks once held intimate

Westminster Abbey Tour

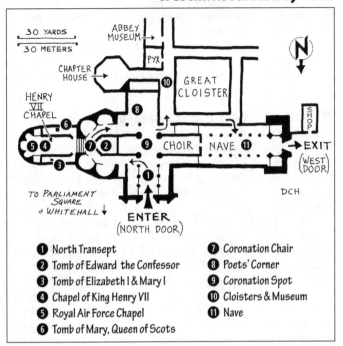

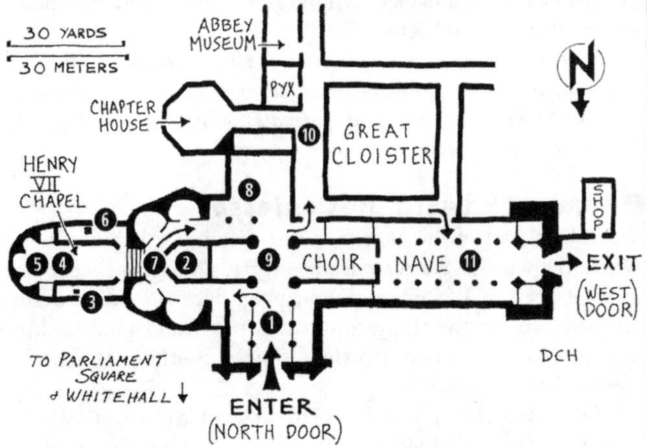

1. North Transept
2. Tomb of Edward the Confessor
3. Tomb of Elizabeth I & Mary I
4. Chapel of King Henry VII
5. Royal Air Force Chapel
6. Tomb of Mary, Queen of Scots
7. Coronation Chair
8. Poets' Corner
9. Coronation Spot
10. Cloisters & Museum
11. Nave

services and where, today, the Abbey boys' choir sings the evensong at 17:00.

Lean over the rail and look down the long and narrow center aisle of the church. Lined with the praying hands of the Gothic arches, glowing with light from the stained glass, it's clear that this is more than a museum. With saints in stained glass, heroes in carved stone, and the bodies of England's greatest under the floor stones, Westminster Abbey is the religious heart of England.

The Abbey was built in 1065. Its name, Westminster, means Church in the West (west of St. Paul's Cathedral). For the next 250 years, the Abbey was redone and remodeled to become essentially the church you see today, notwithstanding an extensive resurfacing in the 19th century. Thankfully, later architects—ignoring building trends of their generation—honored the vision of the original planner, and the building was completed in one relatively harmonious style.

The Abbey's 10-story nave is the tallest in England. The chandeliers, 10 feet tall, look small in comparison (16 were given to the Abbey by the Guinness family).

The north transept (through which you entered) is nicknamed "Statesmen's Corner" and specializes in famous prime ministers.

Find the rival prime ministers, proud William Gladstone and goateed Benjamin Disraeli, who presided over England's peak of power under Queen Victoria.

• *Now turn left and follow the crowd. Walk past Robert ("Bob") Peel, the prime minister whose policemen were nicknamed "bobbies," and stroll a few yards into the land of dead kings and queens. Stop at the wooden staircase on your right.*

❷ Tomb of Edward the Confessor

The holiest part of the church is the raised area behind the altar (where the wooden staircase leads—sorry, no tourist access except with verger tour). Step back and peek over the dark coffin of Edward I to see the tippy-top of the green-and-gold wedding-cake tomb of King Edward the Confessor—the man who built Westminster Abbey.

God had told pious Edward to visit St. Peter's Basilica in Rome. But with the Normans thinking conquest, it was too dangerous for him to leave England. Instead, he built this grand church and dedicated it to St. Peter. It was finished just in time to bury Edward and to crown his foreign successor, William the Conqueror, in 1066. After Edward's death, people prayed at his tomb and, after getting fine results, Pope Alexander III canonized him. This elevated, central tomb—which lost some of its luster when Henry VIII melted down the gold coffin-case—is surrounded by the tombs of eight kings and queens.

• *Continue on. At the top of the stone staircase, veer left into the private burial chapel of Queen Elizabeth I.*

❸ Tomb of Queen Elizabeth I and Mary I

Although there's only one effigy on the tomb (Elizabeth's), there are two queens buried beneath it, both daughters of Henry VIII (by different mothers). Bloody Mary—meek, pious, sickly, and Catholic—enforced Catholicism during her short reign (1553–1558) by burning "heretics" at the stake.

Elizabeth—strong, clever, "virginal," and Protestant—steered England on an Anglican course. She holds a royal orb symbolizing that she's queen of the whole globe. When 26-year-old Elizabeth was crowned in the Abbey, her right to rule was questioned (especially by her Catholic subjects) because she was the bastard seed of Henry VIII's unsanctioned marriage to Anne Boleyn. But Elizabeth's long reign (1559–1603) was one of the greatest in English history, a time when England ruled the seas and Shakespeare explored human emotions. When she died, thousands turned out for the funeral in the Abbey. Elizabeth's face, modeled after her death mask, is considered a very accurate take on this hook-nosed, imperious, virgin queen.

The two half-sisters disliked each other in life—Mary even had Elizabeth locked up in the Tower of London for a short time. Now they lie side by side for eternity—with a prayer for Christians of all persuasions to live peacefully together.

• *Continue into the ornate, flag-draped room behind the main altar.*

❹ Chapel of King Henry VII (a.k.a. the Lady Chapel)

The light from the stained-glass windows, the colorful banners overhead, and the elaborate tracery in stone, wood, and glass give this room the festive air of a medieval tournament. The prestigious Knights of Bath meet here, under the magnificent ceiling studded with gold pendants. The ceiling—of carved stone, not plaster (1519)—is the finest English Perpendicular Gothic and fan vaulting you'll see (unless you're going to King's College Chapel in Cambridge). The ceiling was sculpted on the floor in pieces, then jigsaw-puzzled into place. It capped the Gothic period and signaled the vitality of the coming Renaissance.

The knights sit in the wooden stalls with their coats of arms on the back, churches on their heads, their banner flying above, and the graves of dozens of kings beneath their feet. When the queen worships here, she sits in the southwest corner chair under the carved wooden throne with the lion crown.

Behind the small altar is an iron cage housing tombs of the old warrior Henry VII of Lancaster and his wife, Elizabeth of York. Their love and marriage finally settled the Wars of the Roses between the two clans. The combined red-and-white rose symbol decorates the top band of the ironwork. Henry VII, the first Tudor king, was the father of Henry VIII and the grandfather of Elizabeth I. This exuberant chapel heralds a new optimistic, postwar era as England prepares to step onto the world stage.

• *At the far end of the chapel, stand at the banister in front of the modern set of stained-glass windows.*

❺ Royal Air Force Chapel

Saints in robes and halos mingle with pilots in parachutes and bomber jackets in this tribute to WWII flyers who earned their angel wings in the Battle of Britain (July–Oct 1940). Hitler's air force ruled the skies in the early days of the war, bombing at will, threatening to snuff Britain out without a fight. But while determined Londoners hunkered down underground, British pilots in their Spitfires took advantage of newly-invented radar to get the jump on the more powerful Luftwaffe. These were the fighters about whom Churchill said, "Never...was so much owed by so many to so few."

The Abbey survived the Battle and the Blitz, but this window did not. As a memorial, a bit of bomb damage has been left—the little glassed-over hole in the wall below the windows in the lower left-hand corner. The book of remembrances lists each of the 1,497 airmen (including 1 American) who died in the Battle of Britain.

You're standing on the grave of Oliver Cromwell, leader of the rebel forces in England's Civil War. Or rather, Cromwell was buried here from 1658 to 1661. Then his corpse was exhumed, hanged, drawn, quartered, and decapitated, and the head displayed on a stake as a warning to anarchists.

• *Exit the Chapel of Henry VII. Turn left into a side chapel with the tomb (the central one of three in the chapel).*

❻ Tomb of Mary, Queen of Scots

Historians get dewy-eyed over the fate of Mary, Queen of Scots (1542–1587). The beautiful, French-educated queen was held under house arrest for 19 years by Queen Elizabeth I, who considered her a threat to her sovereignty. Elizabeth got wind of an assassination plot, suspected Mary was behind it, and had her beheaded. When Elizabeth—the "Virgin Queen"—died heirless, Mary's son James I became king of England. James buried his mom here (with her head sewn back on) in the Abbey's most sumptuous tomb.

• *Exit Mary's chapel. Ahead of you, at the foot of the stairs, is the Coronation Chair. Behind the chair, again, is the tomb of the church's founder, Edward the Confessor.*

❼ Coronation Chair

The gold-painted wooden chair waits here—with its back to the high altar—for the next coronation. For every English coronation since 1308 (except two), it's been moved to its spot before the high altar to receive the royal buttocks. The chair's legs rest on lions, England's symbol. The space below the chair originally held a big rock from Scotland called the Stone of Scone (pron. "skoon"), symbolizing Scotland's unity with England's king. Recently, however, Britain gave Scotland more sovereignty, its own Parliament, and the stone. Scotland has agreed to loan the stone to Britain for future coronations.

• *Continue on. Turn left into the south transept. You're in Poets' Corner.*

❽ Poets' Corner

England's greatest artistic contributions are in the written word. Here lie buried the masters of arguably the world's most complex and expressive language. (Many writers are honored with plaques and monuments; relatively few are actually buried here.)

• *Start with Chaucer, buried in the wall under the blue windows, marked with a white plaque reading* "Qui Fuit Anglorum..."

Geoffrey Chaucer (c. 1343–1400) is often considered the father of English literature. Chaucer's *Canterbury Tales* told of earthy people speaking everyday English. He was the first great writer buried in the Abbey (thanks to his job as a Westminster clerk). Later, it became a tradition to bury other writers here, and Poets' Corner was built around his tomb. The blue windows have blank panels awaiting the names of future poets.

• *The plaques on the floor before Chaucer are gravestones and memorials to other literary greats.*

Lord Byron, the great lover of women and adventure: "Though the night was made for loving,/And the day returns too soon,/Yet we'll go no more a roving/By the light of the moon."

Dylan Thomas, alcoholic master of modernism, with a Romantic's heart: "Oh as I was young and easy in the mercy of his means,/Time held me green and dying/Though I sang in my chains like the sea."

W.H. Auden: "May I, composed like them/Of Eros and of dust/Beleaguered by the same/Negation and despair/Show an affirming flame."

Lewis Carroll, creator of *Alice's Adventures in Wonderland:* "'Twas brillig, and the slithy toves/Did gyre and gimble in the wabe..."

T.S. Eliot, American-turned-British author of the influential *The Waste Land:* "April is the cruellest month, breeding/Lilacs out of the dead land, mixing/Memory and desire, stirring/Dull roots with spring rain."

Alfred Lord Tennyson, conscience of the Victorian era: "'Tis better to have loved and lost/Than never to have loved at all."

Robert Browning: "Oh, to be in England/Now that April's there."

• *Farther out in the south transept, you'll find...*

William Shakespeare: Although he's not buried here, this greatest of English writers is honored by a fine statue that stands near the end of the transept, overlooking the others: "Life's but a walking shadow, a poor player that struts and frets his hour upon the stage and then is heard no more."

George Frideric Handel: High on the wall opposite Shakespeare is the German immigrant famous for composing the *Messiah* oratorio: "Hallelujah, hallelujah, hallelujah." The statue's features are modeled on Handel's death mask. Musicians can read the vocal score in his hands for "I Know That My Redeemer Liveth." His actual tomb is on the floor next to...

Charles Dickens, whose serialized novels brought literature to the masses: "It was the best of times, it was the worst of times."

On the floor near Shakespeare, you'll also find the tombs of **Samuel Johnson** (who wrote the first English dictionary) and the great English actor **Laurence Olivier.** (Olivier disdained the "Method" style of experiencing intense emotions in order to portray them. When co-star Dustin Hoffman stayed up all night in order to appear haggard for a scene, Olivier said, "My dear boy, why don't you simply try acting?")

And finally, near the center of the transept, find the small white floor plaque of **Thomas Parr** (marked "THO: PARR"). Check the dates of his life (1483–1635) and do the math. In his (reputed) 152 years, he served 10 sovereigns and was a contemporary of Columbus, Henry VIII, Elizabeth I, Shakespeare, and Galileo.

• *Walk to the center of the church in front of the high altar.*

❾ The Coronation Spot

Here is where every English coronation since 1066 has taken place. Imagine the day when Prince William becomes king:

The nobles in robes and powdered wigs look on from the carved wooden stalls of the choir. The Archbishop of Canterbury stands at the high altar (table with candlesticks, up five steps). The coronation chair is placed before the altar on the round, brown pavement stone representing the earth. Surrounding the whole area are temporary bleachers for 8,000 VIPs, going halfway up the rose windows of each transept, creating a "theater."

Long silver trumpets hung with banners sound a fanfare as the monarch-to-be enters the church. The congregation sings, "I will go into the house of the Lord," as William parades slowly down the nave and up the steps to the altar. After a church service, he sits in the chair, facing the altar, where the crown jewels are placed. William is annointed with holy oil, then receives a ceremonial sword, ring, and cup. The royal scepter is placed in his hands, and—dut, dutta dah—the archbishop lowers the Crown of St. Edward the Confessor onto his royal head. Finally, King William stands up, descends the steps, and is presented to the people. As cannons roar throughout the city, the people cry, "God save the king!"

Royalty are also given funerals here. Princess Diana's coffin lay here before her funeral service. She was then buried on her family estate. The "Queen Mum" (mother of Elizabeth II) had her funeral here, and this is also where Prince Andrew married Sarah Ferguson.

• *Exit the church (temporarily) at the south door, which leads to...*

⑩ Cloisters and Museum

The buildings that adjoin the church housed the monks. (The church is known as the "abbey" because it was the headquarters of the Benedictine Order—until Henry VIII kicked them out in 1540.) Cloistered courtyards gave them a place to meditate on God's creations.

The Chapter House, where the monks had daily meetings, features fine architecture and stained glass with faded but well-described medieval art. The tiny Pyx Chamber has an exhibit about the King's Treasury. Enter the Abbey Museum, formerly the monks' lounge with a cozy fireplace and snacks. Look into the impressively realistic eyes of Henry VII (father of VIII), Elizabeth I, Charles II, Lord Nelson, and a dozen others, part of a compelling series of wax-and-wood statues that, for three centuries, graced coffins during funeral processions. Also see exhibits on royal coronations, funerals, Abbey history, a close-up look at medieval stained glass, and replicas of the Crown Jewels used for coronation practice. Beyond the Abbey Museum, passageways lead to the picturesque College Garden.

As you return to the church, look back through the cloister courtyard to the church exterior, and meditate on the flying buttresses. These stone bridges that push in on the church walls allowed Gothic architects to build so high.

- *Go back into the church for the last stop.*

⑪ Nave

On the floor near the west entrance of the Abbey is the flower-lined Tomb of the Unknown Warrior, one ordinary WWI soldier buried in soil from France with lettering made from melted-down weapons from that war. Think about that million-man army from the Empire and Commonwealth and all those who gave their lives. Hanging on a column next to the tomb is the U.S. Congressional Medal of Honor, presented to England's WWI dead by General Pershing in 1921. Closer to the door is a memorial to the hero of World War II, Winston Churchill.

Near the choir screen is so-called "Scientists' Corner," with memorials to Isaac Newton, Michael Faraday, Charles Darwin, and others. When you leave the church through the west doors, turn around and look up over the doorway to find a statue (5th from the left) of a 20th-century American martyr in the cause of freedom, Martin Luther King Jr.

But first, find the stained-glass window of St. Edward the Confessor (third bay from the left on the north side, marked *"S: Edwardus rex..."*) with crown, scepter, and ring, and thank him for the Abbey.

Look down the nave, filled with the remains of the people who made Britain great—saints, royalty, poets, musicians, scientists, soldiers, politicians. Now step back outside into a city filled with the same kind of poets, saints, and heroes.

ST. PAUL'S TOUR

No sooner was Sir Christopher Wren selected to refurbish Old St. Paul's Cathedral than the Great Fire of 1666 incinerated it. Within a week, Wren had a plan for a whole new building...and for the city around it, complete with some 50 new churches. For the next four decades he worked to achieve his vision—a spacious church, topped by a dome, surrounded by a flock of Wrens.

St. Paul's is England's national church. There's been a church on this spot since 604. It was the symbol of London's rise from the Great Fire of 1666 and of the city's survival of the Blitz of 1940. Today, it's the center of the Anglican faith. Military buffs will find memorials to many great wars and their war heroes.

ORIENTATION

Cost: £8 (free on Sun but officially open only to worshippers); includes dome climb—allow an hour for the climb up and down (dome closed Sun).

Hours: Mon–Sat 8:30–16:30, last entry at 16:00, last dome entry 16:15, closed Sun except for worship.

Getting There: Located in the City in east London, Tube: St. Paul's (Mansion House, Cannon Street, and Blackfriars Tube stops also work). You can take buses: #4, #11, #15, #23, #25, #26, #100, or #242.

Information: Sunday services are at 8:00, 10:15, 11:30 (sung Eucharist), 15:15 (evensong), and 18:00. Free organ recitals are held Sunday at 17:00. Weekday communion is at 8:00 and 12:30. Evensong occurs Mon–Sat at 17:00 and Sun at 15:15 (40 min, free to anyone, though visitors who haven't paid the £8 admission to the church aren't allowed to linger after the service; tel. 020/7236-4128, www.stpauls.co.uk). Major events can cause closures.

Tours: Guided £2.50 90-minute "super tours" of the cathedral and crypt are offered Mon–Sat at 11:00, 11:30, 13:30, and 14:00 (confirm schedule at church or call tel. 020/7236-4128). Audioguide tours cost £3.50 (1 hour to cover 17 stops, available Mon–Sat 9:15–15:30).

Length of This Tour: Allow one hour (2 if you climb dome).

Photography: Photos are forbidden.

Cuisine Art: Good café and a pricier restaurant in the crypt.

Starring: Sir Christopher Wren, Wellington, and World War II.

THE TOUR BEGINS

Even now, as skyscrapers encroach, the 365-foot dome of St. Paul's rises majestically above the rooftops of the neighborhood. The tall dome is set on classical columns, capped with a lantern, topped by a six-foot ball, and iced with a cross. As the first Anglican cathedral built in London after the Reformation, it is Baroque: St. Peter's in Rome filtered through clear-eyed English reason.

• *Enter, buy your ticket, and stand at the back of the nave.*

❶ Nave

Look down the nave through the choir stalls to the stained glass at the far end. This big church feels big. At 515 feet long and 250 feet wide, it's Europe's fourth-largest, after St. Peter's, Sevilla, and Milan. The spaciousness is accentuated by the relative lack of decoration. The simple, cream-colored ceiling and the clear glass in the windows light everything evenly. Wren wanted this: a simple, open church with nothing to hide. Unfortunately, only this entrance area keeps his original vision—the rest was encrusted with Baroque ornamentation after his death.

• *Glance up and behind. The organ trumpets say, "Come to the 17:00 evensong." Ahead and on the left is the towering, black and white...*

❷ Wellington Monument

It's so tall that even Wellington's horse has to duck to avoid bumping his head. Wren would have been appalled, but his church has become so central to England's soul that many national heroes are buried here (in the basement crypt). General Wellington, Napoleon's conqueror at Waterloo and the embodiment of British stiff-upper-lippedness, was honored here in a funeral packed with 13,000 fans.

• *Stroll up the same nave Prince Charles and Lady Diana walked on their 1981 wedding day. Imagine how they felt making the hike to the altar with the world watching. Check out the modern paintings just*

St. Paul's Tour

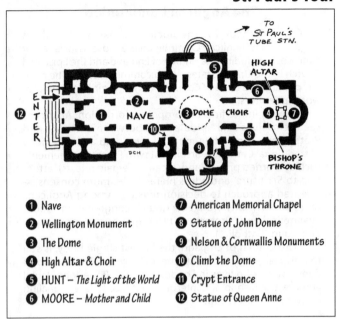

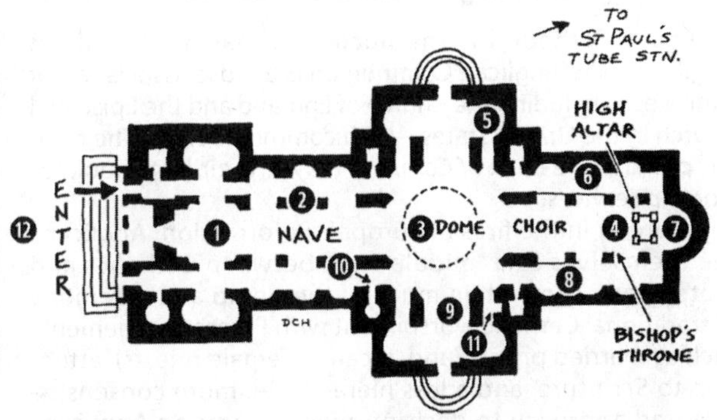

1. Nave
2. Wellington Monument
3. The Dome
4. High Altar & Choir
5. HUNT – *The Light of the World*
6. MOORE – *Mother and Child*
7. American Memorial Chapel
8. Statue of John Donne
9. Nelson & Cornwallis Monuments
10. Climb the Dome
11. Crypt Entrance
12. Statue of Queen Anne

before the dome portraying the Nativity, Public Ministry, Crucifixion, and Resurrection of Jesus. These were painted in 2005 by a Russian artist, Sergei Chepik. The power of these paintings show how Chepik was inspired by his suffering as a Christian under the Soviet system. Grab a chair underneath the dome.

❸ The Dome

The dome you see, painted with scenes from the life of St. Paul, is only the innermost of three. From the painted interior of the first dome, look up through the opening to see the light-filled lantern of the second dome. Finally, the whole thing is covered on the outside by the third and final dome, the shell of lead-covered wood that you see from the street. Wren's ingenious three-in-one design was psychological as well as functional—he wanted a low, shallow inner dome so worshippers wouldn't feel diminished.

You'll see tourists walking around the base of the dome in the Whispering Gallery. The dome is constructed with such acoustic precision that secrets whispered from one side of the dome are heard on the other side, 170 feet away.

Christopher Wren (1632–1723) was the right man at the right time. Though the 31-year-old astronomy professor had never built a major building in his life when he got the commission for St. Paul's, his reputation for brilliance and unique ability to work with

The Anglican Communion

St. Paul's Cathedral is the nucleus of earth's 70 million Anglicans. The Anglican Communion is a loose association of churches—including the Church of England and the Episcopal Church in the United States—with common beliefs. The rallying point is *The Book of Common Prayer,* their handbook for worship services.

Forged in the fires of Europe's Reformation, Anglicans see themselves as a "middle way" between Catholics and Protestants. They retain much of the pomp and ceremony of traditional Catholic worship but with Protestant elements such as married priests (and, recently, female priests), attention to Scripture, and a less hierarchical, more consensus-oriented approach to decision-making. Among Anglicans there are divisions, from Low Church congregations (more evangelical and "Protestant") to High Church (more traditional and "Catholic").

The Church of England, the largest single body, is still the official religion of state, headed by the Archbishop of Canterbury (who lives in London). In 1982, Pope John Paul II and the Archbishop of Canterbury met face to face, signaling a new ecumenical spirit.

others carried him through. The church has the clean lines and geometric simplicity of the age of Newton, when reason was holy and God set the planets spinning in perfect geometrical motion.

For more than 40 years, Wren worked on this site, overseeing every detail of St. Paul's and the 65,000-ton dome. At age 75, he got to look up and see his son place the cross on top of the dome, completing the masterpiece.

On the floor directly beneath the dome is a brass grate—part of a 19th-century attempt to heat the church. Encircling it is Christopher Wren's name and epitaph, written in Latin: *Lector, si monumentum requiris circumspice* (Reader, if you seek his monument, look around you).

Now review the ceiling: Behind is Wren simplicity and ahead is Victorian ornate.

• *The choir area blocks your way to the altar at the far end, but you can see the altar at the far end under a golden canopy.*

❹ The High Altar and Choir

The altar (the marble slab with crucifix and candlesticks—you'll get a close-up look later) was heavily damaged in October 1940 by the bombs of Hitler's Luftwaffe. Today it lies under a huge canopy with corkscrew columns. The canopy looks ancient but was actually built in 1958, in accordance with sketches by Wren.

English churches, unlike most in Europe, often have a central choir area (or quire or chancel), where church officials and the singers sit. St. Paul's—a cathedral since 604—is home to the local Anglican bishop, who presides in the chair nearest the altar on the south or right side (the carved bishop's hat hangs over the chair).

The ceiling above the choir is a riot of glass mosaic representing God (above the altar) and his creation. The mosaics are very Victorian. In fact, Queen Victoria complained that the earlier ceiling was "dark, dingy, and undevotional." The Dean and chapter wisely took note and had it spiffed up with this brilliant mosaic work...textbook late Victorian. In separate spheres eight "Angels of the Morning" hold up creatures of the earth, seas, and sky.

• *In the north transept (to your left as you face the altar), find the big painting of Christ, in a golden wood altarpiece. Glare? Try walking side-to-side to find the best viewing angle.*

❺ *The Light of the World* (1904), by William Holman Hunt

In the dark of night, Jesus—with a lantern, halo, jeweled cape, and crown of thorns—approaches an out-of-the-way home in the woods, knocks on the door, and listens for an invitation to come in. A Bible passage on the picture frame says: "Behold, I stand at the door and knock..." (Revelation 3:20).

In his early twenties, William Holman Hunt (1827–1910) was in the dark night of a spiritual crisis when he heard this verse knocking in his head. He opened his soul to Christ, his life changed forever, and he tried to capture the experience in paint. As one of the Pre-Raphaelites who adored medieval art, he used symbolism, but only images the average Brit-on-the-street could understand. The door is the closed mind, the weeds the neglected soul, the darkness is malaise, while Christ carries the lantern of spiritual enlightenment.

In 1854, Hunt debuted *The Light of the World* (not this version, but a smaller one now at Oxford). The critics savaged it—"syrupy," "too Catholic," "simple"—but the masses lapped it up. It became the most famous painting in Victorian England, a pop icon that inspired sermons, poems, hymns, and countless Christ-at-the-door paintings in churches and homes. Hunt's humble-hippie image of

Christ was stamped forever on the minds of generations of school kids. It was so popular, that late in life Hunt was asked to do this larger version specifically for St. Paul's. Nearly blind, he needed an assistant. (*The Guardian* newspaper recently published "Britain's Ten Worst Paintings." They honored *The Light of the World* as number seven, comparing it to a plastic crucifix.)

• *Return to the area underneath the dome and walk toward the altar, along the left side of the choir, pausing at a modern statue...*

❻ *Mother and Child,* by Henry Moore

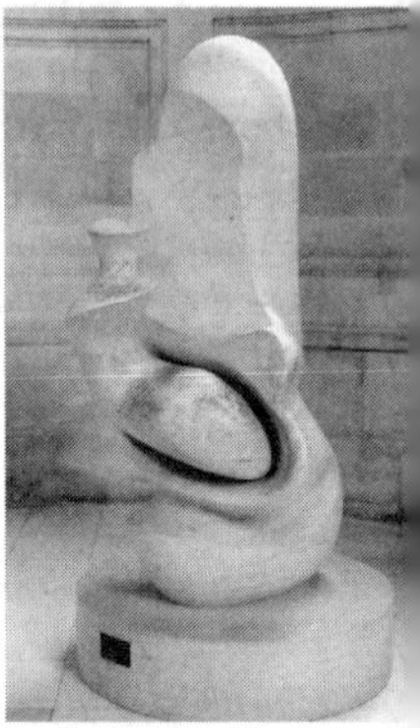

Britain's (and the world's?) greatest modern sculptor, Henry Moore, rendered a traditional subject in an abstract, minimalist way. This Mary and baby Jesus was inspired by the sight of British moms nursing babies in World War II bomb shelters. After donating this sculpture to St. Paul's, Moore was rewarded with a burial spot in the crypt.

• *Continue to the far end of the church, where you'll find three bright and modern stained-glass windows.*

❼ American Memorial Chapel

Each of the three windows has a central core of religious scenes, but the brightly colored panes that arch around them have some unusual iconography: American. Spot the American eagle (center window, to the left of Christ), George Washington (right window, upper right corner), and symbols of all 50 states (find your state seal). In the carved wood beneath the windows, you'll see birds and foliage native to the United States. And at the very far right, check out the tiny tree "trunk" (amid foliage, below the bird)—it's a U.S. rocket ship circa 1958, shooting up to the stars.

Britain is very grateful to its WWII saviors, the Yanks, and remembers them religiously here, immediately behind the altar, with the Roll of Honor. This 500-page book under glass lists the names of 28,000 U.S. servicemen and women based in Britain who gave their lives during the war.

• *Take a close look at the high altar and the view back to the entrance from here, then continue around the altar. Pause here to enjoy a closer look at the Victorian mosaic ceiling above the choir. On the left wall of the aisle, standing white in a black niche, is a statue of...*

❽ John Donne (1573–1631)

This statue survived the Great Fire of 1666. John Donne, shown here wrapped in a burial shroud, was a passionate preacher in old St. Paul's (1621–1631), as well as a great poet.

The Blitz and the Battle of Britain

Often used synonymously, the Blitz and the Battle of Britain are two different phases of the Nazi air raids of 1940–1941. The Battle of Britain (June–Sept 1940) pitted Britain's Royal Air Force against German planes trying to soften Britain up for a land-and-sea invasion. The Blitz (Sept 1940–May 1941) was Hitler's punitive campaign of terror against civilian London.

In the early days of World War II, the powerful, technologically superior Nazi army quickly overran Poland, Belgium, and France. The British Army hightailed it out of France, crossing the English Channel from Dunkirk, and Britain hunkered down, waiting to be invaded. Hitler bombed R.A.F. airfields while his ground troops massed along the Channel. Britain was hopelessly outmatched, but Prime Minister Winston Churchill vowed, "We shall fight on the beaches... we shall fight in the fields and in the streets.... We shall never surrender."

Britain fought back. Though greatly outgunned, they had a new and secret weapon—radar—that allowed them to get the jump on puzzled Nazi pilots. Speedy Spitfires flown by a new breed of young pilots shot down 1,700 German planes. By September 1940, the German land invasion was called off, Britain counterattacked with a daring raid on Berlin...and the Battle of Britain was won.

A frustrated Hitler retaliated with a series of punishing air raids on London itself, known as the Blitz. All through the fall, winter, and spring of 1940–1941, including 57 consecutive nights, Hermann Göring's Luftwaffe pummeled a defenseless London, killing 20,000 and leveling half the city (mostly from St. Paul's eastward). Residents took refuge deep in the Tube stations. From his Whitehall bunker, Churchill made radio broadcasts exhorting his people to give their all, their "blood, toil, sweat, and tears."

Late in the war (1944–1945), Hitler ordered another round of terror-inducing attacks on London (sometimes called the "second Blitz") using car-sized V-1 and V-2 bombs, an early type of cruise missile. But Britain's resolve had returned, the United States had entered the fight, and the pendulum shifted. Churchill could say that even if the Empire lasted a thousand years, Britons would look back and say, "This was their finest hour."

St. Paul's in Wartime

Nazi planes firebombed a helpless London in 1940. While the city around it burned to the ground, St. Paul's survived, giving hope to the citizens. The church took two direct hits, crumbling the altar and collapsing the north transept. On December 29, 1940, some 28 bombs fell on the church. The surrounding neighborhood was absolutely flattened, while the church rose above it, nearly intact. Some swear that many bombs bounced miraculously off Wren's dome, while others credit the heroic work of local firefighters. (There's a memorial chapel to the firefighters who kept watch over St. Paul's with hoses cocked.) Still, it's clear from the damage that St. Paul's was not fully Blitz-proof.

After the war, St. Paul's was the site of a bittersweet remembrance of Britain's victory, when Winston Churchill's state funeral was held here.

Imagine hearing Donne deliver a funeral sermon here, with the huge church bell tolling in the background: "No man is an island....Any man's death diminishes me, because I am involved in Mankind. Therefore, never send to know for whom the bell tolls—it tolls for thee."

• *And also for dozens of people who lie buried beneath your feet, in the crypt where you'll end your tour. But first, in the south transept, find the...*

❾ Horatio Nelson Monument and Charles Cornwallis Monument

Admiral Horatio Nelson (1758–1805) leans on an anchor, his coat draped discreetly over the arm he lost in battle.

In October 1805, England trembled in fear as Napoleon—bent on world conquest—prepared to invade from across the Channel. Meanwhile, hundreds of miles away off the coast of Spain, the daring Lord Nelson sailed the HMS *Victory* into battle against the French and Spanish navies. His motto: England expects that every man shall do his duty.

Nelson's fleet smashed the enemy at Trafalgar, and Napoleon's hopes for a naval invasion of Britain sank. Unfortunately, Nelson took a sniper's bullet in the spine and died, gasping, "Thank God I have done my duty." The lion at Nelson's feet groans sadly, and two little boys gaze up—one at Nelson, one at Wren's dome. You'll find Nelson's tomb directly beneath the dome, downstairs in the crypt.

Opposite Nelson is a monument to another great military

man, Charles Cornwallis (1738–1805), honored here for his service as Governor General of Bengal (India). Yanks know him better as the general who lost the "American War" (the American Revolutionary War) when George Washington—aided by French ships—forced his surrender at Yorktown in 1780.

⑩ Climb the Dome

There are no elevators, but the 409-step climb is worthwhile. First you get to the Whispering Gallery (259 steps, with views of the church interior). Have fun in the gallery and whisper sweet nothings into the wall; your partner (and anyone else) on the far side can hear you. Then, after another set of stairs, you're at the Stone Gallery (with views of London, high enough if you're exhausted). Finally a long, tight, metal staircase takes you to the very top of the cupola (the Golden Gallery) for stunning unobstructed views of the city. A tiny window allows you to peek directly down—350 feet—to the church floor.

⑪ Crypt

Grand tombs of Admiral Nelson (who wore Napoleon down) and General Wellington (who finished him off) dominate the center of Europe's largest crypt.

Facing the chapel altar, you'll find Christopher Wren's tomb in the far right corner. It's only a simple black slab with no statue. ("If you seek his monument..." you'll be disappointed.) Next to it is a hunk of rough Portland stone quarried but unused by Wren while building St. Paul's; see his triangle brand on the left end.

Use the free visitor's map to find the tombs of painters Turner, Reynolds, and others (near Wren); Florence Nightingale (near Wellington); and memorials to many others (including George Washington, who lies buried back in old Virginny). There are models of the dome and interesting exhibits about the building of the cathedral, as well as a fine gift shop, a WC, and the tasty if grim-sounding Crypt Café.

VICTORIA AND ALBERT MUSEUM TOUR

One of the biggest, most eclectic collections of objects anywhere, the Victoria and Albert (V&A) has something for everyone. It bills itself as a museum for the decorative arts, and Martha Stewart types will be in hog heaven. Think of it as two museums. The British Galleries offer a survey of British style, taste, and design from 1500 to 1900. The rest of the museum collects decorative arts from around the world—furniture, glassware, clothing, jewelry, and carpets. Throw in historical artifacts, a few fine-arts masterpieces (painting and sculpture), and a bed that sleeps seven, and you have a museum built for browsing. I've selected a dozen or so objects that I find interesting, but don't limit yourself to those.

The V&A grew out of the Great Exhibition of 1851, that ultimate celebration of the Industrial Revolution. Now "art" could be brought to the masses through modern technology and mass production. The museum was founded on the idealistic Victorian notion that anyone can be continually improved by education and example. After much support from Queen Victoria and Prince Albert, the museum was renamed for the royal couple, and its present building was opened in 1909.

In 2004, the V&A received several grants for refurbishment projects to take place over the next 10 years. During this time, exhibits will likely be rearranged; check with the information desk for current room closures.

ORIENTATION

Cost: Free (£3 donation requested, possible fee for special exhibits).

Hours: Daily 10:00–17:45, open every Wed and last Fri of month until 22:00 except mid-Dec–mid-Jan.

Getting There: It's on Cromwell Road in the South Kensington neighborhood (Tube: South Kensington; a 5-min walk through a tunnel leads directly from the Tube station to the museum).

Information: Pick up the free and much-needed museum map. You could buy the fine £5 *Hundred Highlights* guidebook or the handy £1 *What to See at the V&A* brochure (outlines 5 self-guided, speedy tours). Tel. 020/7942-2000, www.vam.ac.uk.

Tours: Free 60-minute orientation tours are offered daily (usually on the half-hour from 10:30–15:30, also daily at 13:00, Wed at 16:30, and a half-hour version at 18:30).

Length of This Tour: Allow 90 minutes (not counting the British Galleries).

Cloakroom: Free, mandatory for large bags.

Photography: Permitted without tripod (except for special exhibits and works on loan).

Cuisine Art: You can munch a picnic lunch in the Pirelli Garden (when the weather allows), grab tea in the Gamble Room, or lunch in the Café. During summer, they set up a good, inexpensive self-service café in the garden. Many good restaurants are nearby (see page 298).

Overview

The museum is large and gangly, with 150 rooms and more than 12 miles of corridors. Our tour highlights just a few displays, chosen mostly because of their location near the ground-floor entrance. It's a sample of the V&A's range, from fine art to historical objects, interior design, dress, and beautiful objects from around the globe. Look at what's offered, survey a museum map, and see what you want in any order you like.

Don't miss the British Galleries—a one-way tour stretching through 400 years of British lifestyles, almost a museum in itself. You could spend days in this place beyond the British Galleries and our quick tour. The museum's free index of displays allows you to survey things in alphabetical order, from the Ardabil carpet to woven textiles, and track down whatever is of personal interest.

THE TOUR BEGINS

• *If you wish to skip ahead to the British Galleries, go upstairs from the entrance lobby to Room 58. Otherwise, in the lobby, look up.*

❶ Dale Chihuly Chandelier

This modern chandelier/sculpture by an American glass artist epitomizes the spirit of the V&A's collection—beautiful manufactured objects that demonstrate technical skill and innovation, wedding

the old with the new, and blurring the line between arts and crafts.

Each blue and yellow strand of the chandelier is tied with a wire to a central spine. When the chandelier first went up in 2001, Chihuly said "Too small," had it disassembled, and fired up still more glass bubbles.

Dale Chihuly (b. 1941)—face-famous for the eye-patch he's worn since a car accident—studied glass-making in Venice, then set up his own studio/factory in Seattle, creating art as the director of a team effort. He makes an old medium seem fresh and modern, and the V&A keeps his chandelier looking fresh with a long feather duster.

• *From the lobby, look up to the balcony and see the pointed arches of the...*

❷ Hereford Screen (1862)

In the 1800s, just as Britain was steaming into the future on the cutting edge of the Industrial Revolution, the public's taste went retro. This 35-by-35-foot, eight-ton rood screen (for the Hereford Cathedral's sacred altar area) looks medieval, but was created with the most modern materials the Industrial Revolution could produce. The metal parts were not hammered and hand-worked as in olden days,

but are made of electroformed copper. The parts were first cast in plaster, then bathed in molten copper with an electric current running through it, leaving a metal skin around the plaster. The entire project—which might have taken years in medieval times—was done in five months.

George Gilbert Scott (1811–1878), who built the screen, redesigned all of London in the neo-Gothic style, restoring old churches such as Westminster Abbey, renovating the Houses of Parliament, and building new structures like St. Pancras Station and the Albert Memorial—some 700 buildings in all.

The world turns, and a century later (1960s), the Gothic style was "out" again, modernism was in, and this screen was neglected and ridiculed. Considering that the V&A was originally called the Museum of Manufactures (1857), it's appropriate that the

Victoria and Albert Museum Tour

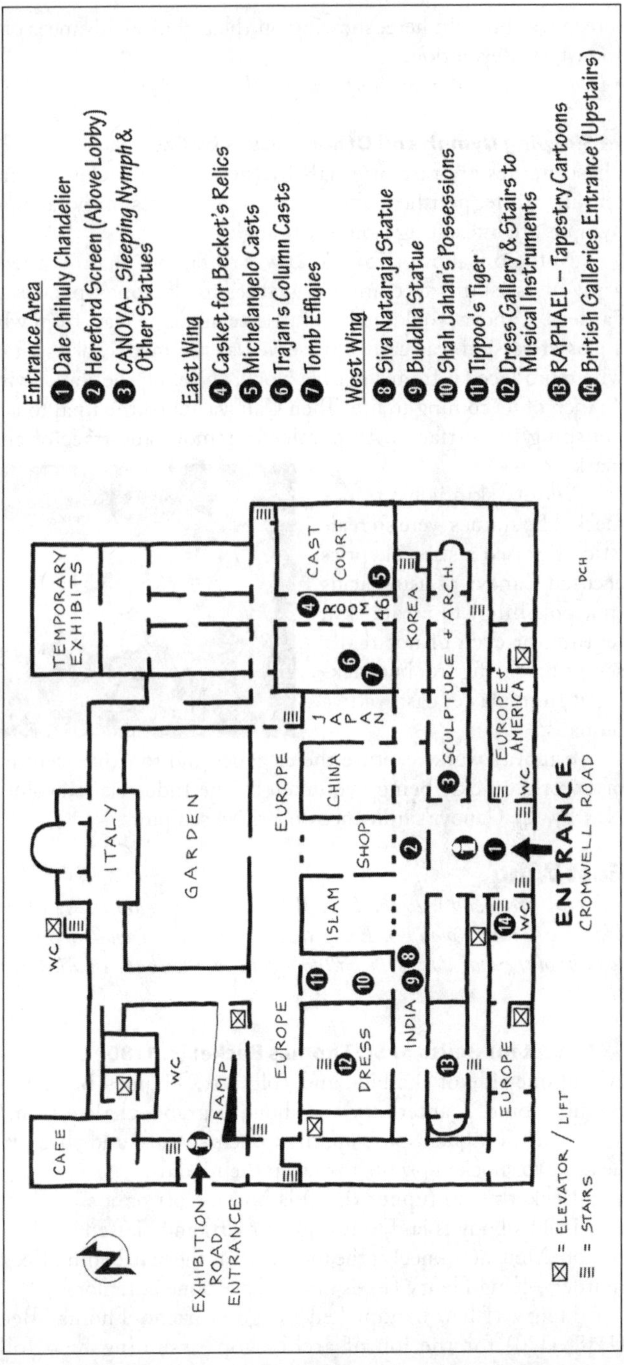
Entrance Area
1 Dale Chihuly Chandelier
2 Hereford Screen (Above Lobby)
3 CANOVA—Sleeping Nymph & Other Statues
East Wing
4 Casket for Becket's Relics
5 Michelangelo Casts
6 Trajan's Column Casts
7 Tomb Effigies
West Wing
8 Siva Nataraja Statue
9 Buddha Statue
10 Shah Jahan's Possessions
11 Tippoo's Tiger
12 Dress Gallery & Stairs to Musical Instruments
13 RAPHAEL – Tapestry Cartoons
14 British Galleries Entrance (Upstairs)
TEMPORARY EXHIBITS
CAST COURT
ROOM 46
KOREA
SCULPTURE + ARCH.
EUROPE + AMERICA
WC
ENTRANCE
CROMWELL ROAD
JAPAN
CHINA
EUROPE
SHOP
ITALY
GARDEN
ISLAM
INDIA
DRESS
EUROPE
WC
RAMP
CAFE
EXHIBITION ROAD ENTRANCE
N
= ELEVATOR / LIFT
= STAIRS
DCH

screen was brought here, showing off the technical advances of the Industrial Revolution.

• *In the big, bright Room 50A, look for the...*

❸ *Sleeping Nymph* and Other Statues by Canova

These statues are rare originals by the Italian neoclassical master. His white, polished, and pretty Greek graces, minotaurs, and nymphs are interesting from every angle.

Antonio Canova (1757–1822) was so famous that he hired an army of assistants to crank out statues for Europe's palaces and gardens. Canova would make a full-size model in clay, from which a plaster version was cast. This served as the model for assistants, who reproduced it from a marble block, chiseling the statue within an inch of its coming to life. Then Canova added the final touches, polishing the surface with pumice to remove any trace of chisel marks.

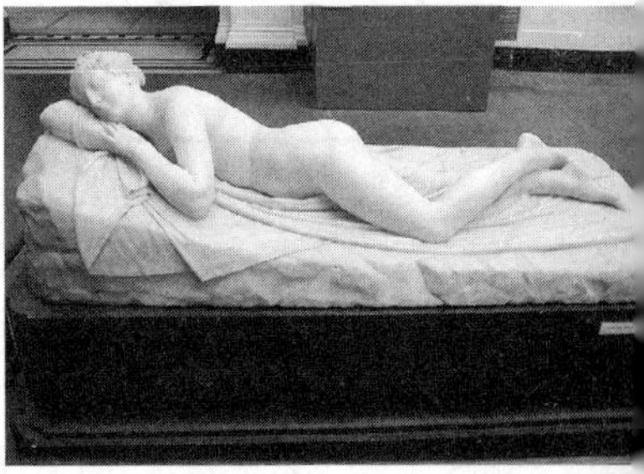

Velvety skin is his trademark. His statues were so realistic, it caused a stir—skeptics accused Canova of using acids (not polishing) to create skin texture, or even of not really sculpting the figure, but making it from plaster casts of live humans.

Canova's works capture the elegance and romantic sentiment of a world quickly being overtaken by the Industrial Revolution. Nearby, see Canova's influence on British sculptors.

East Wing

• *From here, head into the East Wing of the museum. At the far end of the hall, find Room 46. Enter this long room and walk about three-fourths of the way down the hall to a glass case with the small, shoebox-sized...*

❹ Casket for Relics of St. Thomas Becket (c. 1180)

Along one side of the blue and gold box, Thomas Becket—the Archbishop of Canterbury—is about to grab a chalice from the altar, when knights tiptoe up, draw their swords, and slice off his head. Two shocked priests throw up their hands.

Becket's soul (upper right) is borne aloft on a sling by two angels. His body is laid to rest (upper left) and blessed by the new bishop. Mourners kneel at the tomb, just as the man behind Becket's murder—King Henry II—is said to have done in remorse.

Henry II had handpicked his good friend Thomas Becket (1118–1170) for the job of archbishop, assuming he'd follow

the king's orders. In two days, Thomas was made a priest, a bishop, then archbishop—the head of all England's Christians. When Becket proved loyal to the Church and opposed Henry's policies, the king, in a rash fit of anger, ordered Becket killed. Remorseful after the murder, Henry had 80 monks whip him, then he spent all night at the foot of the tomb.

Just three years after his death, Becket was made a saint. This small casket held a relic (a piece of Becket's DNA). The enamel-and-metal work is a specialty of Limoges, France (see similar works nearby).

Elsewhere in Room 43, you'll find stained glass, bishops' robes, old columns, and good descriptions.

• *Along either side of Room 46 are the Cast Courts in Rooms 46A and 46B. Room 46B (to the right) contains plaster-cast replicas of many famous statues, including some...*

❺ Michelangelo Casts

Plaster-cast versions of famous Renaissance statues allowed 19th-century art students who couldn't afford a railpass to go study the classics.

The statues were made by coating the original with a non-stick substance, then laying wet plaster strips over it that dried to form a mold, from which a plaster cast was made. They look solid but are very fragile. In a single glance, you can follow Michelangelo's career, from youthful optimism (*David*), to his never-finished masterpiece (statues from the tomb of Julius II, including *Moses* and two *Slaves*), to full-blown mid-life crisis (while sculpting the brooding Medici Tomb statues of Lorenzo and Giuliano). Compare Michelangelo's monumental *David* with Donatello's girlish *David*, and see Ghiberti's bronze Baptistery doors that inspired the Florentine Renaissance.

David was a gift from Tuscany to Queen Victoria, who immediately donated it to the museum. Circle behind *David* to see the clip-on fig leaf (this was "the Victorian Age") that was hung on him when modest aristocrats visited.

• *In Room 46A, you can't miss...*

❻ Trajan's Column Casts

Rising 140 feet and decorated with a spiral relief of 2,500 figures trumpeting the exploits of the Roman Emperor Trajan (c. A.D. 100), this is a copy of the world's grandest column from antiquity. The original column still stands in Rome, though the V&A's version was cast from a copy in Paris, and they had to cut it in half to fit it here.

The column's relief unfolds like a scroll, telling the story of Trajan's conquest of Dacia (modern-day Romania). It starts at the bottom (the half with the pedestal) with a trickle of water that becomes a river and soon picks up boats full of supplies. Then come the soldiers themselves, who spill out from the gates of the city. A river god surfaces to bless the journey. Along the way (second band), they build roads and forts to sustain the vast enterprise. Trajan himself (fourth band, in military skirt with toga over his arm) mounts a podium to fire up the troops. They hop into a Roman galley ship (fifth band) and head off to fight the valiant Dacians in the middle of a forest (eighth band). Finally, at the very top, the Romans hold a sacrifice to give thanks for the victory, while the captured armor is displayed on the pedestal.

Originally, the entire story was painted in bright colors. If you unwound the scroll, it would stretch the length of two football fields—it's far longer than the frieze around the Greek Parthenon.

• *Near Trajan's column, find several casts of knights and ladies on their backs, staring at the ceiling. Also in Room 46A, see the...*

❼ Tomb Effigies of Henry II and Family (Plaster cast, French, Fontevrault)

This was a remarkable and dysfunctional royal family. King Henry II (1133–1189)—Becket's murderer—lies alongside his wife and their children. Henry's wife, Eleanor of Aquitaine (from southern France), was the ex-wife of the King of France and was renowned as Europe's most sophisticated lady. When Henry and Eleanor wed, it united their two families' large land holdings, creating an "England" that stretched as far south as southern France. It would eventually take a "Hundred Years' War" (1336–1453) to sort out the current border between England and France.

As king, Henry placed church courts under secular control, causing the rift that led to Becket's bloody murder. In Henry's old age, his children rebelled, taking arms against him for their slice of the royal pie. Henry's heir, Richard the Lionhearted, famous as the good guy in the Robin Hood legend, was actually an absentee monarch—a French-speaking dandy allied with the King of France. Younger son John, the "evil" King John of the Robin Hood legend, became a tyrant, prompting English nobles to make him sign the document called the Magna Carta, which established the principle that even kings must follow the law. (You can see a copy of the Magna Carta in the British Library; see page 210.)

West Wing

• *Backtrack toward the entrance lobby. Continue down the hall into the West Wing. In Room 47B, on either side of the hall, find two statues, both from India.*

❽ Siva Nataraja (12th Century)

Life is a dance.

The Hindu god Siva (SHEE-va)—one of the hundreds, if not thousands, of godlike incarnations of Hinduism's eternal being, Brahma—steps lively and creates the world by dancing. His four arms are busy creating, and he treads on the sleepy dwarf of ignorance.

This bronze statue, one of Hinduism's most popular, is loaded with symbolism, summing up where humans came from and where we're going. Surrounded by a ring of fire, he crosses a leg in time to the music. Smiling serenely, he blesses with one hand, while another beats out the rhythm of life with a hand drum. The cobra draped over his arm symbolizes the *Kundalini Sakti,* the cosmic energy inside each of us that can, with the right training, uncoil and bring us to enlightenment.

As long as Siva keeps dancing, the universe will continue. But Siva also holds a flame, reminding us that, at the end of time, he will transform into his female alter ego, Kali, and destroy the world by fire, clearing the slate for another round of existence.

• *Just a few paces ahead is the mellow golden...*

❾ Buddha Offering Reassurance (c. 11th Century)

Besides Hinduism, India also hosts Islam, Jainism, and Buddhism. This Buddha statue—with cape, long ears, and hair tied in a bun—blesses us with a hand stamped with the wheel of dharma, representing the eternal law.

Buddha was a real person who inspired legends and came to be revered as a god. Born in Nepal as Siddhartha (c. 566–486 B.C.), he grew up (according to legend) in a lavish palace, oblivious to suffering. When he was confronted with life's harsh realities, he became an ascetic monk, wandering in search of answers. Finally, after years of fasting and meditation, he reached a moment of enlightenment—the realization that life's suffering can be conquered by mastering your own desires.

Buddhism began in India, but later took root in China and the rest of Asia, where, today, it's more popular than it is in India.

• *In Room 41, a glass case in the center of the room contains small items that were the...*

⑩ Possessions of Emperor Shah Jahan (r. 1628–1658)

Look at the cameo portrait, thumb ring, and wine cup (made of white nephrite jade, 1657) that belonged to one of the world's most powerful men.

Shah Jahan—or "King of the World"—ruled the largest empire of the day, covering Northern India, Pakistan, and Afghanistan. His Mughal Empire was descended from Genghis Khan and the Mongol horde who conquered and then settled in central Asia and converted to Islam.

Shah Jahan was known for his building projects, especially the Taj Mahal (see a watercolor of it nearby), built as a mausoleum for his favorite wife, Mumtaz, who bore him 14 children before dying in childbirth.

His unsuccessful attempts to expand the empire drained the treasury. In his old age, his sons quarreled over the inheritance. Imprisoned by his sons in the Agra fort, Shah Jahan died gazing across the river at the Taj Mahal, where he, too, would be buried. India's glory days were ending.

Then came the British.

• *At the far end of Room 41 is the wood-carved...*

⑪ Tippoo's Tiger (1790s)

This life-size robotic toy, once owned by an oppressed Indian sultan (see Tipu's portrait and belongings nearby), is perhaps better called "India's revenge." The Bengal tiger has a British redcoat down, sinking its teeth into his neck. When you turned the crank, the

The British in India

December 31, 1600—The British East India Company—a multinational trading company owned by stockholders—is founded with a charter from Queen Elizabeth I. They're given a virtual monopoly on trade with India.

1600s—The British trade peacefully with Indian locals on the coast, competing with France, Holland, and Portugal for access to spices, cotton, tea, indigo, and jute (for rope-making).

1700s—As the Mughal (Islamic) Empire breaks down, Britain and France vie for trade ports and inland territory. By the 1750s, Britain is winning. Britain establishes itself in Bombay, Madras, and Calcutta. First they rule through puppet Mughal leaders, then dump local leaders altogether.

1800s—By mid-century, two-thirds of the subcontinent is under British rule, exporting opium and tea (transplanted from its native China) and importing British-made cloth. Britain tries to reform Indian social customs (e.g., outlawing widow suicides) with little long-lasting effect. They build railways, roads, and irrigation systems.

1857–1858—The "Indian Mutiny"—sparked by high taxes, British monopoly of trade, and a chafing against foreign control—is the first of many uprisings that slowly erode British control.

1900s—Two world wars drain and distract Britain while Indians lobby for self-rule.

August 15, 1947—After a decade of peaceful protests led by Mahatma Gandhi, India gains its independence.

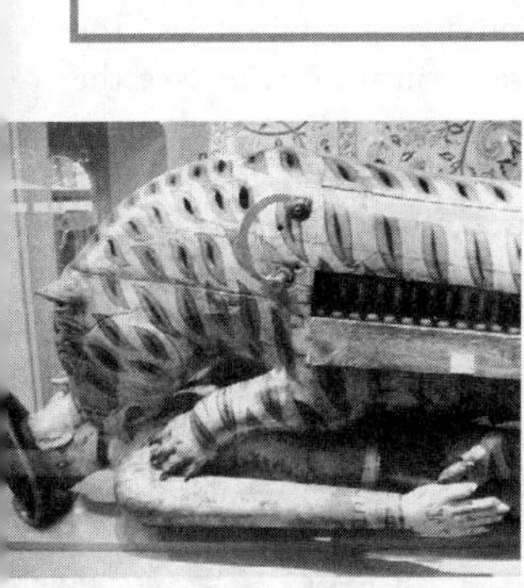

Brit's left arm would flail, and both he and the tiger would roar through organ pipes. (The mechanism still works.)

Tipu, the Sultan of Mysore (1750–1799), called himself "The Tiger of Mysore." He was well educated in several languages and collected a library of 2,000 books. An enlightened ruler, he built roads and dams and promoted new technology. Tipu could see that India was being swallowed up by the all-powerful British East India Company. He allied himself with France and fought several successful wars against the British. But he was eventually defeated and forced to give up half his kingdom to the Brits. Tipu was later killed by the British in battle (1799), his palace was ransacked, and this toy and his other possessions were now owned—like much of India—by the British East India Company.

• *In the southwest corner of the building (to the left of the entrance, at the end of the hall, find Room 40.*

⓬ Dress Gallery and Musical Instruments

Four hundred years of English fashion are corseted into 40 display cases. Each case shows the evolution of a particular article of clothing: formal wear, underwear, men's suits, etc. See the collection chronologically by circling clockwise around the perimeter, then see the contemporary clothes (and temporary exhibits) in the center. For much more on old English fashion, see the British Galleries (described below).

Up a staircase in the middle of Room 40, you'll find the Musical Instruments section, displaying lutes, harpsichords, early flutes, big violins, and strange, curly horns. Some instruments are recognizable, some obsolete.

• *In Room 48A are...*

⓭ Raphael's Tapestry Cartoons

For Christmas, 1519, Pope Leo X unveiled 10 new tapestries in the Sistine Chapel, designed by the famous artist Raphael. The project was one of the largest ever undertaken by a painter—it cost far more than Michelangelo's Sistine Ceiling—and when it was done, the tapestries were a hit, inspiring princes across Europe to decorate their palaces in masterpieces of cloth.

The V&A owns seven of the full-size designs by Raphael (approximately 13 by 17 feet, done in tempera on paper, now mounted on canvas) that were used to produce the tapestries. The cartoons were sent to factories in Brussels, cut into strips (see the lines), and placed on the looms. The scenes are the reverse of the final product—lots of left-handed saints.

Raphael (1483–1520) chose scenes from the Acts of the Apostles, particularly of Peter and Paul, the two early saints most associated with Rome, the seat of the popes. Knowing where the tapestries were to be hung, Raphael was determined to top Michelangelo's famous Sistine Ceiling, with its huge, dramatic figures and subtle color effects. He matched Michelangelo's body-builder muscles (e.g., the fishermen in *The Miraculous Draught of Fishes*), dramatic gestures, and reaction shots (e.g., the busy crowd-scenes in *St. Paul Preaching in Athens*), and

he exceeded Michelangelo in the subtleties of color.

Unfortunately, it was difficult to reproduce Raphael's painted nuances in the tapestry workshop. Traditional tapestries were simple, depicting either set patterns or block figures on a neutral background. Raphael challenged the Flemish weavers. Each brush stroke had to be reproduced by a colored thread woven horizontally. The finished tapestries (which are still in the Vatican) were glorious, but these cartoons capture Raphael's original vision.

• *In Room 48A a staircase leads up (turn left at top of stairs) into the British Galleries, including the Great Bed of Ware and Elizabethan miniatures. But to see the complete British Galleries, chronologically, return to the entrance lobby and take stairs to the first floor (Level 2), beginning in Room 58.*

⓮ British Galleries

The "other half" of the V&A consists of beautifully described exhibits laid out along a series of corridors sweeping you through 400 years of British high-class living. The theme is "taste, fashion, and design from 1500 through 1900." It's all very impressive, but because its exhibits are already so well described, I've included very few specifics here.

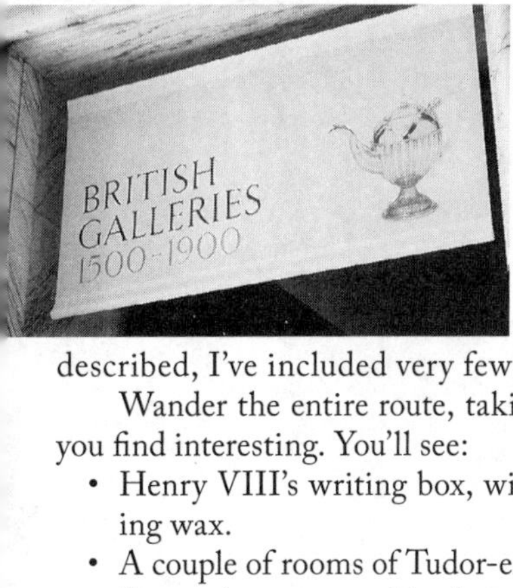

Wander the entire route, taking time to read up on whatever you find interesting. You'll see:

- Henry VIII's writing box, with his quill pens, ink, and sealing wax.
- A couple of rooms of Tudor-era tapestries.
- Fancy dresses so wide that a woman (who showed off her wealth with all that fine fabric) had to enter the room sideways.
- Shoes from an age when they were called "straights," and there was no left or right.
- 400-year-old fans—tools for flirting from an age when "a woman's weapon was a fan and a man's was a sword...and the fan did more damage."
- Room 57 takes us into the era of Queen Elizabeth I. Find rare miniature portraits by Hilliard, a popular

item of the day, and the oft-reproduced "Young Man Among Roses" miniature, capturing the romance of a Shakespeare sonnet. Also in the room is the Great Bed of Ware. Built as a tourist-attracting gimmick by an English inn in about 1600, this four-poster bed still wows. You and six of your favorite friends could bed down here, taking a well-earned rest at the end of this eclectic tour.

COURTAULD GALLERY TOUR

The Courtauld Gallery is just small enough that you can see it all in a single visit, which makes for a pleasant experience. The collection spans the history of Western painting, from medieval altarpieces through Italian Renaissance to the 20th century. But its highlight is Impressionist and Post-Impressionist works, some of which you'll recognize when you see them. Besides the works I've featured, you'll likely see many other well-known Post-Impressionist paintings, part of the museum's rotating collection of loaners. For some, the van Gogh self-portrait alone is worth the price of admission.

ORIENTATION

Cost: £5 (free on Mon until 14:00).

Hours: Daily 10:00–18:00 (last entry 17:15), same hours for Gilbert Collection and Hermitage Rooms.

Getting There: The Courtauld is one of three museums housed in the Somerset House along the Strand. Tube: Temple or Covent Garden, or catch bus #6, #9, #11, #13, #15, or #23 from Trafalgar Square.

The Rest of Somerset House: Two other museums are contained within the Somerset House: the exquisite Gilbert Collection, featuring fine decorative art (£5, free after 16:30), and the Hermitage Rooms, with Russian art (£5). To see any two of the three museums here, just buy a combo-ticket for £8 (or visit all 3 for £12).

Information: Tel. 020/7848-2526, www.somerset-house.org.uk or www.courtauld.ac.uk.
Length of This Tour: Allow one hour.
Cloakroom: Coin-op lockers (free—you get your £1 coin back), and WCs are in the basement.
Photography: It's allowed if you ask when entering, but no flash or tripods.
Cuisine Art: The cafeteria is in the basement.
Starring: Manet, Monet, Degas, Renoir, etc.

Overview

The museum is not arranged chronologically, but by collector—the wealthy people who created this museum by donating their personal collections. Samuel Courtauld (1876–1947), textile magnate and philanthropist, gave his paintings (van Gogh, Manet, Cézanne, and others on the 1st floor) and his name to the budding museum.

THE TOUR BEGINS

• *Start on the ground floor, in Room 1 (a.k.a. Gallery I), filled with religious paintings.*

Bernardo Daddi—*Polyptich with the Crucifixion and Saints* (1348)

Daddi's serene saints stand in their gilded wood frames and ponder Christ's crucifixion (center). Their weighty bodies, flowing robes, and human faces are one small step in the Florentine revolution in realism. Bernardo Daddi (c. 1280–1348) was one of the stronger links in the chain between Giotto (his teacher) and the Florentine Renaissance (1400s). This altarpiece, Daddi's last large-scale work, debuted in Florence the same year as the bubonic plague.
• *Upstairs on the first floor, in Room 3...*

Edouard Manet—*A Bar at the Folies-Bergère* (1881–1882)

While we look at the barmaid and her wares, Manet also shows us the barmaid's-eye-view of the crowded nightclub, reflected in the (slightly tilted) mirror behind her. We see the glittering chandeliers rendered in Impressionist smudges, the bottles of wine, the swirl of activity, and even a trapeze artist (upper left). From the barmaid's own smudgy reflection, we see that she's facing a mustached man in a top hat. This may be a self-portrait,

but whoever he is, he's standing right where we are.

Manet, in his last major painting, places us in the center of the scene, surrounded with glitter. Reflected in the mirror, the gaiety all looks a bit fake, and, judging from her blank expression, that's the way the barmaid sees it.

Edouard Manet—*Le Dejeuner sur l'Herbe* (1863)

This is a smaller, cruder version Manet did of his famous painting (now in Paris' Orsay Museum) that launched the Impressionist revolution. The nude woman in a classical pose wasn't shocking. It was the presence of the fully clothed men in everyday dress that suddenly made the nude naked. Manet and the Impressionists rejected goddesses and romance for the landscapes, café scenes, and still lifes of the real world.

Paul Cézanne—*La Montagne Sainte-Victoire* (c. 1887)

Cézanne could look out his studio window at this 3,300-foot-high mountain in Provence. Over a 20-year span, he painted the same mountain 60 different ways, each with its own color scheme and mood. This one—with a windblown branch framing the mountain from above—may reflect the turmoil of the fortysomething's life (father's death, stalled Impressionist career, shuttling between Paris and hometown Provence, the recent humiliation of having his childhood friend Emile Zola parody him in a novel).

The mountain is realistic, but the scene is carefully composed. The tree branch echoes the curving ridgeline, uniting foreground and background. A patch of paint forming a house (in the foreground) is the same size as a patch depicting a rock formation (in the background), further flattening this "distant" scene into a wall of brushstrokes. (Cézanne's "cube"-shaped brushstrokes inspired the Cubists, a decade later, to build figures using geometric shapes, to mix foreground and background, and to emphasize style over realism.) Cézanne juggles many technical balls of modern painting—a roughed-up surface texture done with thick brushwork, a self-imposed color scheme, abstract composition—and still manages to stay true to his Impressionist roots, painting the mountain he sees.

Paul Gauguin—*Nevermore* (1897)

A nude Tahitian woman lies daydreaming. The curve of her body and of the headboard soften the horizontal lines of the bed and the verticals of the wall.

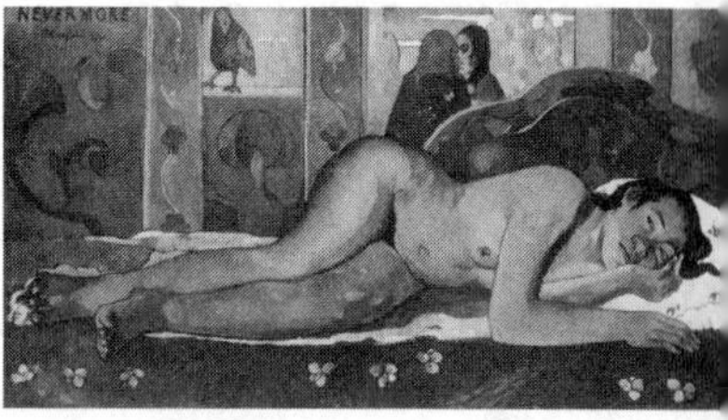

Gauguin—who quit his stockbroker job, abandoned his wife and family, and moved to Tahiti—paints in the primitive style he found there. Like a child, he draws the girl with a thick outline (so different from Impressionists who "built" a figure with a mosaic of brushstrokes), and then fills it in with solid Crayola colors. Gauguin emphasizes only the two dimensions of height and width, so that the women and clouds in the "background" blend into the flowery wallpaper in the "foreground." Gauguin rejected the camera-eye literalness of Western art. His is a simpler style that required the viewer's imagination to fill in the blanks, perhaps evoking the romance of a bygone world that is...nevermore.

By the way, Gauguin insisted that the title and the raven were not from Poe's poem, but "a bird of the devil who watches." Hmm.

• *In Room 4...*

Vincent van Gogh—*Self-Portrait with Bandaged Ear* (1888–1889)

On the night of December 23, 1888, Vincent van Gogh went

ballistic. Drunk, self-doubting, clinically insane, and enraged at his friend Gauguin's smug superiority, he waved a knife in Gauguin's face, then cut off a piece of his own ear and gave it to a prostitute. Gauguin hightailed it back to Paris, and the locals in Arles persuaded the mad Dutchman to get help. A week later, just released from the hospital, Vincent stood in front of a blank canvas and looked at himself in the mirror.

What he saw looking back was a calm man with an unflinching gaze, dressed in a heavy coat (painted with thick, vertical strokes of blue and green) and fur-lined hat. The slightly stained bandage over his ear is neither hidden in shame nor worn as a badge of honor—it's just another accessory. The scene is evenly lit with no melodramatic shadows.

Vincent must have been puzzled and unnerved by his "artist's fit," as he called it. Does this man suspect it was only the first of many he'd suffer over the next year and a half before finally taking his own life?

• *In Room 5...*

Lucas Cranach the Elder—*Adam and Eve* (1526)

Eve takes a bite of Knowledge, gazes to the distance, and passes the forbidden fruit to a puzzled Adam, standing in a lush garden amid peaceful animals. Strategic branches fuzz their genitals, but otherwise they're nude, with the pale, thin bodies of the aristocrats Cranach painted for. (Adam, beware of antlers.) Though the subject is biblical, it captures the worldly spirit of Germany's Renaissance. The northern version of humanism saw humans not as noble Greek gods (as the Italian Renaissance did), but as fallible, lusty, and even a bit cynical.

• *In Room 6...*

Peter Paul Rubens—*The Family of Jan Brueghel the Elder* (c. 1613–1615)

Rubens paints his close friend and occasional collaborator, along with his wife and two kids. Rubens and Brueghel, Antwerp's two best painters, tag-teamed a couple dozen works. Brueghel would do his specialty—background, flowers, animals, and garlands—and Rubens did the people. Also in Room 6 is Rubens' dreamy *Landscape by Moonlight* (c. 1637–1638).

• *Upstairs on the second floor is the sculpture gallery in Room 8.*

Edgar Degas—*Study in the Nude for Dressed Ballet Dancer* (1879–1917)

The naked 14-year-old girl splays her feet out (fourth position), bends her arms back, and turns her face up, exuding the sheer joy of dancing. Like a stripped Barbie doll, this is a smaller-scale, nude version of the famous statue Edgar Degas exhibited in Paris in 1881. The original was made of wax and plaster over a wire frame. (The Courtauld's version is a bronze cast of a wax statue, done after Degas' death.) Degas dressed his original wax statue in a cloth tutu and ballet slippers and attached real human hair to the wax head, creating a modern collage of materials that shocked and intrigued the Parisians. Critics of the day both praised its modernism and lambasted the angular, adolescent body and "ugly" face.

The model for the statue was an aspiring dancer who, like so many adolescent girls then and now, dreamed of finding a career on stage. Degas sketched and painted her many times. Degas, a well-known painter, was a closet sculptor, who fashioned dozens of small-scale statues in the privacy of his studio, especially in his later years as his eyesight failed and painting became more difficult. Only *The Little Fourteen-Year-Old Dancer* was ever exhibited.

• *Rooms 9–14 contain late-19th and early-20th-century paintings, including works by Derain, Dufy, Jawlensky, and members of Britain's own Bloomsbury Group.*

THEATRE MUSEUM TOUR

Yes, the ancient Greeks invented theater, but Londoners took the art form and refined it more than any other people on earth. For five centuries, Londoners from every social level have watched actors pretending to be real people in made-up situations. Theater can express mankind's deepest emotions, elicit belly laughs, or simply titillate the senses.

The Theatre Museum—using paintings, photos, costumes, props, and models—chronicles the great writers, actors, and trends of London's theater scene. True theater fans with low expectations will love this place. As for the rest, hey, it's free.

ORIENTATION

Cost: Free.

Hours: Tue–Sun 10:00–18:00, closed Mon.

Getting There: It's a block east of Covent Garden's marketplace down Russell Street (Tube: Covent Garden).

Information: As you arrive, the helpful staff can inform you of the ever-changing events of the day (like make-up demos and costume workshops). They're also in tune with London's contemporary theater scene. Tel. 020/7943-4700, www.theatremuseum.org.uk.

Tours: Free guided tours are offered at 12:00 and 14:00, giving a sweep through 400 years of English theater history in 30 minutes.

Length of This Tour: Allow 30 minutes.

Starring: Shakespeare, Gilbert and Sullivan, Coward, and Olivier.

Overview

The ground level houses temporary exhibits, and there are often workshops, performances, and special displays scattered throughout the building. This chapter describes the permanent collection (Main Gallery) down the ramp in the basement.

THE TOUR BEGINS

• *Circle the Main Gallery counterclockwise for a chronological display of British theater. Navigate by exhibit numbers in the upper-left corner of the display cases.*

Left Wall, #4: Shakespearean Theatre (1574–1642)

The alpha and omega of English-language theater, Will Shakespeare (1564–1616) hit the London stage just as it became a popular phenomenon. Shakespeare's early comedies, mid-career tragedies, and final fantasies set the tone of dramatic realism that is Britain's forte. In four centuries, his plays have never really fallen out of fashion.

The Globe Theatre (see page 315) seated 3,000 for open-air, daylight performances, and featured a British specialty—a "thrust" stage, jutting out into the audience.

Right Wall, #1: Large Paintings of Brussels' Ommegang Procession

First developed by the ancient Greeks and Romans, theater slumbered during the Middle Ages. But in medieval religious festivals, you'd see mini-plays on portable stages dramatizing, say, the Annunciation of Christ's coming to Mary (center of painting), Diana and her nymphs (lower right), or Jesus' birth (left).

Left Wall, #14: Eleanor "Nell" Gwyn (1642–1687)

After Shakespeare, secular theater was banned by puritanical Puritans. It was "Restored" along with the monarchy, starring "pretty, witty," curly-haired Nell Gwyn. Raised in a Covent Garden brothel, she sold oranges (tasty snack and harmless missile) and her female charms at rowdy Drury Lane Theatre (two blocks east of here) before landing a part onstage. Nell was among the first generation of women to portray women onstage. Small, impish, and saucy, her comic characters epitomized the joyous decadence of the post-Puritan years. Nell became King Charles II's favorite mistress, birthing several royal bastards.

• *Turn the corner.*

Right Wall, #15: George Frideric Handel (1685–1729)

Crafted by a German writing Italian opera in London, this smash hit, *Rinaldo*, brought music to the London stage. But high opera was never as popular in England as it was in Italy. Londoners preferred a show in which the story line unfolds in spoken dialogue punctuated with a big musical number...the style that developed into the modern "musical." Still, opera has a strong tradition in London at the Royal Opera House (a block away).

Right Wall, #19: John Gay's *Beggar's Opera* (1728)

Gay's smash hit—a comic, social satire with hummable tunes—was a forerunner of blockbuster musicals. It featured not goddesses and princesses but ordinary people.

Left Wall, #20–22: David Garrick (1717–1779)

In 1741, the curtain rose, and an unknown actor-playwright named David Garrick strode onstage as Richard III (see porcelain figure with sword). Garrick said, "Now is the winter of our discontent/ Made glorious summer by this sun of York"—and became an overnight sensation. His direct, understated realism was a breath of fresh air after the pompous bombast of actors in the French style. Phenomenally popular, Garrick bought the Drury Lane Theatre (where they're currently showing *The Producers*) and, for the next 30 years, he slowly taught the eating-drinking-jeering vaudeville crowd to shut up and love Shakespeare. He also introduced oil-lamp footlights and sidelights. Garrick is buried in Poets' Corner in Westminster Abbey (see page 221).

Left Wall, #38: Edmund Kean (1787–1833)

England's greatest tragic actor, his offstage life was also troubled. He grew up on London's streets with one goal in life: to be a star. After 10 years of obscurity with a traveling company, he debuted at age 27 at Drury Lane Theatre as Shylock in *The Merchant of Venice.* With flashing eyes, dramatic changes of mood, and magnetic intensity, he oozed evil. Always the heavy—when he once played Romeo, he drew laughs—Kean specialized in Shakespeare's villains and tragic leads (Macbeth, Othello, Hamlet). Kean, who drank heavily, channeled his offstage rage into perfectly choreographed onstage passion. He died onstage, playing Othello at Covent Garden. His son, Charles (who was Iago in that last performance), carried on the family tradition with a triumphant tour of America.

Left Wall, #46: Jenny Lind (1820–1887)

Born in Sweden and trained for opera, the "Swedish Nightingale" wowed London and the United States with her singing. She could do all the vocal acrobatics, but it was her pure presentation of simple songs that created a sensation: "Jenny Lind Mania."

In the Corner, #47: Music Halls of the 1800s

A night at the theater was usually a raucous affair, where the main play or entertainment was interspersed with music, dancing, skits, slapstick, and circus acts while the audience ate, drank, and chatted. (In the United States, it's what we'd call vaudeville.)

• *Turn the corner.*

Right Wall, #51: W.S. Gilbert (1836–1911) and Arthur Sullivan (1842–1900)

Though they reportedly disliked each other, this lyricist and composer teamed up to create sophisticated comic operas (or "operettas," since they were intended as light entertainment). The characters spoofed Victorian pompousness and operatic clichés; the words were witty, and the songs tuneful and memorable. Even today, American amateur companies regularly stage *The Pirates of Penzance*, *The Mikado*, and *H.M.S. Pinafore*.

Right Wall, #58: Henry Irving (1838–1905)

The Victorian era's most famous actor, Irving brought realism to acting, technical innovations to stage sets, and respectability to London theater, becoming the first actor to be knighted. Gaunt, brooding, and haunted-looking, he first skulked onstage playing a guilt-ridden murderer in *The Bells* at the Lyceum Theatre (where *The Lion King* currently roars). As director of the Lyceum, he staged middlebrow melodramas fueled by his star power and awe-inspiring sets. Irving recycled all profits into the latest stage technology—electric lights, machines to rearrange sets quickly between scenes, and devices that could create indoor thunderstorms and supernatural effects. Despite unheard-of popularity (except among highbrows), Irving died broke. (See Irving's statue just southeast of Leicester Square.)

• *Turn the corner.*

Left Wall, #76: Noel Coward (1899–1973)

The generation that lived through World War I—disillusioned and world-weary, but dressing elegantly and sipping cocktails to forget—found comic expression in multitalented Noel Coward. His comedies (*Private Lives*, 1930) and songs ("Mad About the Boy") featured loving-but-bickering couples engaged in sophisticated banter and loose Roaring '20s morality.

Left Wall, #80 & #86: John Gielgud (1904–2000), Laurence Olivier (1907–1989), and Ralph Richardson (1902–1983)

Three superb actors associated with the Old Vic Theatre (across the Thames, Tube: Waterloo) brought the serious Shakespearean tradition to the wider world of motion pictures. Picture young, handsome Gielgud as Romeo, onstage with Olivier as Mercutio—then the next night they'd switch parts. Olivier's versatility ranged from the original production of Coward's *Private Lives* to the 1948 Oscar-winning film *Hamlet* (which he produced, directed, and starred in), to over-the-top Nazi villainy in the movie *Marathon Man* (1976). All three actors received knighthoods (and the title "Sir") for their significant contributions to British life.

Left Wall, #96: Writer's Theatre—*Look Back in Anger* (1956) by John Osborne (1924–1994)

The so-called Angry Young Men of the 1950s—the twentysomethings who had been too young to fight in World War II—were frustrated with a postwar society still dominated by traditional, small-minded, working-class values. Osborne's characters ranted in long tirades perfectly suited to a new breed of angry young British actors such as Richard Burton and Peter O'Toole.

Left Wall, #98: Royal Shakespeare Company

Peter Brook's influential book, *The Empty Space* (1968), stated that you could do riveting theater with just good actors and a bare stage. As director of the Royal Shakespeare Company, he pioneered challenging productions with minimal trappings. After 400 years, Shakespeare lives.

Today's Theater Scene

It's upstairs and out the door—you're right in the thick of it.

TOWER OF LONDON TOUR

William I, still getting used to his new title of "the Conqueror," built the stone "White Tower" (1077–1097) to keep the Londoners in line. The Tower served as an effective lookout for invaders coming up the Thames. His successors enlarged it to its present 18-acre size. Because of the security it provided, it has served over the centuries as the Royal Mint, the Royal Jewel House, and, most famously, as the prison and execution site of those who dared oppose the crown.

Today, while its military purpose is history, it's still home to a beefeating community of 120 (and host to 3 million visitors a year). The Tower's hard stone and glittering jewels represent the ultimate power of the king. So does the executioner's block. You'll find more bloody history per square inch in this original tower of power than anywhere else in Britain.

ORIENTATION

Cost: £14.50, family-£42, £20 for one-day combo-ticket with Hampton Court Palace.

Hours: March–Oct Tue–Sat 9:00–18:00, Sun–Mon 10:00–18:00; Nov–Feb Tue–Sat 9:00–17:00, Sun–Mon 10:00–17:00; last entry one hour before closing.

Upon arrival, pick up the free little map/guide and monthly program flier and check the schedule for a list of events and special demonstrations (such as knights in armor explaining medieval fighting techniques). The audioguide is not worthwhile (£3, plus £10 deposit). And, considering how well-described everything is, neither is the Tower guidebook.

The crowd hits after the 9:30 cheap Tube passes start (worst on Sun). Even though the ticket line moves fast, it can be loooong. To avoid this line, buy your ticket at Tower Hill Tube stop (upon arrival) or at any London TI (in advance) at no extra cost. You can also book online at www.hrp.org.uk (£3 fee). There's a second line inside for the crown jewels, the best on earth. For fewer crowds, arrive when the Tower opens and go straight for the crown jewels, doing the Beefeater tour and White Tower later (or see the jewels after 16:30).

On Sunday, visitors are welcome on the grounds to worship in the Royal Chapel (free, 11:00 service with fine choral music, you get in with no lines and can probably stay after the service).

For information on participating in the evening Ceremony of Keys, see page 63 (advance booking required).

Getting There: The Tower is located in East London (Tube: Tower Hill). For speed, take the Tube there; for romance, take the boat. Boats run between the Tower of London and Westminster Pier near Big Ben (£5.40, included with Big Bus London tour; £6.50 round-trip; daily 9:00–21:00, Nov–March until 15:45, 2/hr, 30 min, tel. 020/7930-9033, see "Tours of London," page 33).

Information: Tel. 0870-751-5177, recorded info tel. 0870-756-6060, booking tel. 0870-756-7070.

Yeoman Warder (Beefeater) Tours: The free, worthwhile, 60-minute Beefeater tours leave every 30 minutes from inside the gate (first one usually at 9:30, last one usually at 15:30, 14:30 off-season). The boisterous Beefeaters are great entertainers. While groups can be huge, the guides are easy to hear and fun to follow. Their talks include lots of bloody anecdotes about the tower and its history and are very entertaining. Check the clock inside the gate. If you just missed a tour, you can join it in progress (just a bit ahead).

Length of This Tour: Allow two hours.

Photography: Photos are allowed, but not of the jewels.

Cuisine Art: The New Armouries Café, inside and beyond the White Tower, is a big, efficient cafeteria.

Starring: Crown jewels, Beefeaters, William the Conqueror, and Henry VIII.

THE TOUR BEGINS

❶ Entrance Gate

Even an army the size of the ticket line couldn't storm this castle. After they pulled the drawbridge up and slammed the iron portcullis down, you'd have to swim a moat; cross an island prowled by wild animals; then swim a second, 40-yard-wide inner moat (eventually drained to be a military parade ground); and finally,

Tower of London Tour

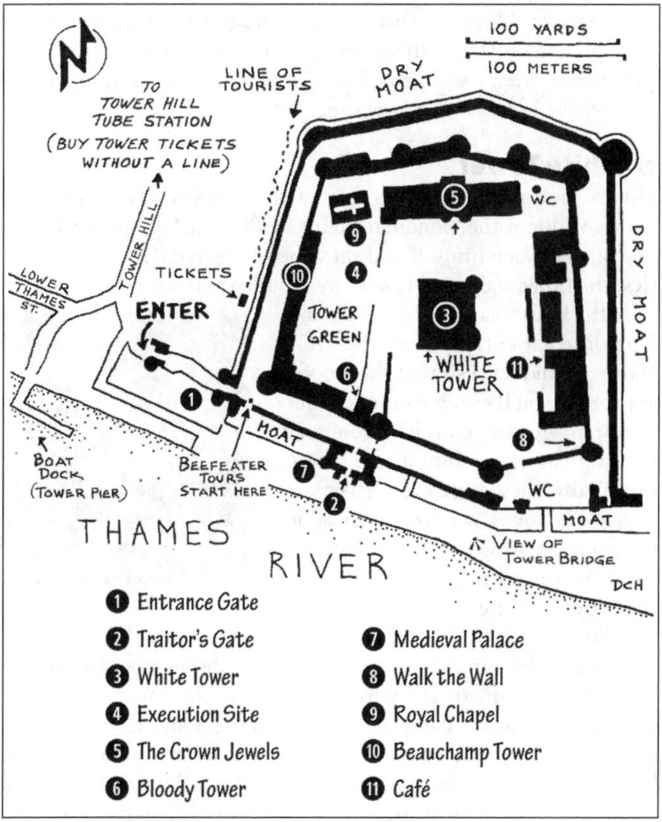

toss a grappling hook onto the wall and climb up while the enemy poured boiling oil on you. Yes, it was difficult to get into the Tower...but it was almost impossible to get out.

• *The entertaining 60-minute tours by the Yeoman Warders (nicknamed "Beefeaters" for the rations of beef they earned) begin just inside the entrance gate (see above). The information booth is nearby, and WCs are 100 yards straight ahead. Otherwise, go 50 yards straight ahead to the...*

❷ Traitor's Gate

This entrance to the Tower was a waterway from the Thames. Princess Elizabeth I, who was a prisoner here before she became queen, was poled through this gate on a barge, thinking about her mom, Anne Boleyn, who had been decapitated inside just a few years earlier. Many English leaders who fell from grace entered through here—Elizabeth was one of the lucky few to walk out.

• *Pass underneath the "Bloody Tower" into the inner courtyard. The big white tower in the middle is the...*

❸ White Tower

This is the tower that gives this castle complex of 20 towers its name. William the Conqueror built it 900 years ago to put 15 feet of stone between himself and those he conquered. Over the centuries, the other walls and towers were built around it.

The keep was a last line of defense. The original entry (on south side) is above ground level so that the wooden approach (you'll climb its modern successor to get in) could be removed, turning the tower into a safe refuge. Originally, there were even fewer windows—the lower windows were added during a Christopher Wren-ovation in 1660. In the 13th century, the tower was painted white.

Standing high above the rest of old London, the White Tower provided a gleaming reminder of the king's absolute power over his subjects. If you made the wrong move here, you could be feasting on roast boar in the banqueting hall one night and chained to the walls of the prison the next. Torture ranged from stretching on the rack to the full monty: hanging by the neck until nearly dead, then "drawing" (cut open to be gutted), and finally quartering, with your giblets displayed on the walls as a warning. (Guy Fawkes, who tried to blow up Parliament, got this treatment.) Any cries for help were muffled by the thick stone walls—15 feet at the base, a mere 11 feet at the top.

Inside today, you can see models of the tower and exhibits re-creating medieval life, as well as suits of armor (including that of Henry VIII, other kings, and one of a 6' 9" giant), guns, swords, and the actual ax and chopping block. The rare and lovely Norman chapel (St. John's Chapel, 1080)—where Lady Jane Grey (see below) offered up a last unanswered prayer—is simple, plain, and moving.

• *Left of the White Tower is the Tower Green, where you'll find a granite-paved square marked "Site of Scaffold."*

❹ Execution Site

Here, enemies of the crown would kneel before the king for the final time and, with their hands tied behind their backs, say a final prayer, then lay their heads on a block, and—*shlit*—the blade would slice through their necks as their heads tumbled to the ground.

The headless corpses were buried in unmarked graves in the Tower Green or under the floor of the stone church ahead of you. The heads were stuck on a stick and displayed at London Bridge. Passersby did not see heads, but spheres of parasites.

Henry VIII axed a couple of his ex-wives here—Anne Boleyn, whom he called a witch and an adulteress, and the forgettable Catherine Howard. Next.

Henry even beheaded his friend, Thomas More (a Catholic), because he refused to recognize (Protestant) Henry as head of the Church of England. (Thomas died at the less-prestigious Tower Hill site just outside the walls—near the Tube stop—where most tower executions took place.)

The most tragic victim was 17-year-old Lady Jane Grey, who was manipulated into claiming the crown for two weeks during the scramble for power after Henry's death, and after the short, six-year reign and death of his sickly young son Edward VI. When "Bloody" Mary took control, she forced her Protestant cousin Jane to kneel at the block. Jane's young husband, locked in the nearby Beauchamp Tower and executed earlier the same day, vented his despair by scratching "Jane" into the tower's stone (in the upstairs room find graffiti #85—"IANE"). Cynics claim he was actually pining for his mother—also named Jane.

A Beefeater, tired of what he called "Hollywood coverage" of the tower, grabbed my manuscript, read it, and told me that in more than 900 years as a fortress, palace, and prison, the place held 8,500 prisoners. But only 120 were executed, and of those, only six were executed inside it. Stressing the hospitality of the tower, he added, "Torture was actually quite rare here."

• *Look past the White Tower on the left to the line leading to the crown jewels. Like a Disney ride, the line is still very long once you get inside. But great videos help pass the time pleasantly. First, you'll pass through a room of wooden chairs and coats of arms—one for every monarch who wore jewels like these, from William the Conqueror (1066) to Elizabeth I, with her lion-and-dragon crest, to Elizabeth II. Next, you'll see a film of the latter Elizabeth's 1953 coronation—a chance to see the jewels in action. You'll also see video close-ups of the jewels. (Get here before 10:00 to avoid the wait, but even if there's no crowd, take your time for the videos about the jewels.) Finally, you pass into a huge vault and reach...*

❺ The Crown Jewels

In the first display case, notice the 12th-century coronation spoon for anointing (used in 1953). Since most of the original crown jewels were lost during the 1648 revolution, this is the most ancient object here. After scepters, robes, trumpets, and wristlets, a moving sidewalk takes you past the most precious of the crown jewels.
• *The crowns are all facing you as you approach them (ride the nearest walkway). You're welcome to circle back and glide by the back side (I did several times) and hang out on the elevated viewing area with the guard. Chat with a guard—they're actually here to provide information. Ask him or her what they'd do if you shot a photo.*

These are the most important pieces (in cases #1, #2, #4, and #5):

St. Edward's Crown, in the first glass case, is placed by the archbishop upon the head of each new monarch in Westminster Abbey on coronation day. It's worn for 20 minutes, then locked away until the next coronation. Although remodeled, this crown is older than the tower itself, dating back to 1061, the time of King Edward the Confessor, "the last English king" before William the Conqueror invaded (1066). Since the gold and 443 precious and semiprecious stones weigh five pounds, weak or frail monarchs have opted not to actually wear it.

The Sovereign's Scepter, in the second case, is encrusted with the world's largest cut diamond—the 530-carat Star of Africa, as beefy as a quarter-pounder. This was one of nine stones cut from the original 3,106-carat diamond. The **orb** (in the same case) symbolized how Christianity rules over the earth; it's a reminder that even a "divine monarch" is not above God's law. The coronation is a kind of marriage between the church and the state in Britain, since the king or queen is head of both, and the ceremony celebrates the monarch's power to do good for the whole of the nation.

The Crown of the Queen Mother (Elizabeth II's famous mum, died in 2002), the highest crown in the fourth case, has the 106-carat Koh-I-Noor diamond glittering on the front. The Koh-I-Noor diamond is considered unlucky for male rulers and, therefore, only adorns the crown of the king's wife. If Charles becomes king, his wife might wear this. This crown was remade in 1937 and given an innovative platinum frame.

The tiny crown to the left was Queen Victoria's. She suffered from migraine headaches, and the last thing someone with a migraine needs is a big crown. This four-ounce job was made in 1870 for £50,000—personally paid for by the queen.

The Imperial Crown, in the fifth and last case, is for when the monarch slips into something a little less formal—for coronation festivities and the annual opening of Parliament. Among its 3,733 jewels are Queen Elizabeth I's former earrings (the hanging pearls), a stunning 13th-century ruby in the center, and Edward the Confessor's ring (the blue sapphire on top). When Edward's tomb was exhumed—a hundred years after he was buried—his body was "incorrupted." The ring on his saintly finger featured this sapphire and ended up on the crown of all future monarchs.

• *Leave the jewels. Back near the Traitor's Gate you'll find sights #6 and #7...*

❻ Bloody Tower

Not all prisoners died at the block. During the Wars of the Roses, the 13-year-old future king Edward V and his kid brother were kidnapped in 1483 by their uncle Richard III ("Now is the winter of our discontent...") and locked in the Bloody Tower, never to be seen again (until 2 centuries later, when two children's skeletons were discovered).

Sir Walter Raleigh—poet, explorer, and political radical—was imprisoned here for 13 years. In 1603, the English writer and adventurer was accused of plotting against King James and sentenced to death. The king commuted the sentence to life imprisonment in the Bloody Tower. While in prison, Raleigh wrote the first volume of his *History of the World.* Check out his rather cushy bedroom, study, and walkway (courtesy of the powerful tobacco lobby?). Raleigh promised the king a wealth of gold if he would release him to search for El Dorado. The expedition was a failure. Upon Raleigh's return, the displeased king had him beheaded in 1618.

More recent prisoners in the complex include Rudolf Hess, Hitler's henchman, who parachuted into Scotland in 1941 (kept in the bell tower). Hess claimed to have dropped in to negotiate a separate peace between Germany and Britain. Hitler denied any such plan.

❼ Medieval Palace

The tower was a royal residence as well as a fortress. These well-described rooms are furnished as they might have been during the reign of Edward I in the 13th century, and come with an actor in medieval garb who explains lifestyles of the medieval rich and royal.

• *Enter near where you leave the Medieval Palace to...*

❽ Walk the Wall

The tower was defended by state-of-the-art walls and fortifications in the 13th century. This walk offers a good look. From the

walls, you also get a good look at the famous bridge straddling the Thames, with the twin towers and blue spans. It's not London Bridge (which is the nondescript bridge just upstream), but **Tower Bridge.** Although it looks medieval, this drawbridge was built in 1894 of steel and concrete. Sophisticated steam engines raise and lower the bridge, allowing tall-masted ships to squeeze through.

Gaze out at the bridge, the river, the new City Hall (the egg-shaped glass building across the river, see page 63), and life-filled London. Turn back and look at the stern stone walls of the Tower. Be glad you can leave.

SLEEPING

I favor accommodations (and restaurants) handy to your sightseeing activities. Rather than list hotels scattered throughout London, I've chosen several favorite neighborhoods and recommended the best accommodations values for each.

I look for places that are friendly; clean; a good value; located in a central, safe, quiet neighborhood; and not mentioned in other guidebooks. I'm more impressed by a handy location and a fun-loving philosophy than hair dryers and shoeshine machines.

London is expensive. Cheaper rooms are relatively dumpy. Don't expect £90 cheeriness in a £60 room. For £70 ($125), you'll get a double with breakfast in a safe, cramped, and dreary place with minimal service and the bathroom down the hall. For £90 ($160), you'll get a basic, clean, reasonably cheery double in a usually cramped, cracked-plaster building with a private bath, or a soulless but comfortable room without breakfast in a huge Motel 6–type place. My London splurges, at £100–150 ($180–270), are spacious, thoughtfully appointed places good for entertaining or romancing. Off-season, it's possible to save money by arriving late without a reservation and looking around. Competition softens prices, especially for multi-night stays.

Hearty English or generous buffet breakfasts are included unless otherwise noted, and TVs are standard in rooms.

Hotels and B&Bs

I've described my recommended hotels and B&Bs using a Sleep Code (see below). Prices listed are for one-night stays in peak season and assume you're booking directly and not through a TI. Some fancy £120 rooms rent for a third off if you arrive late on a slow day and ask for a deal. Official "rack rates" (the highest rates

London's Hotel Neighborhoods

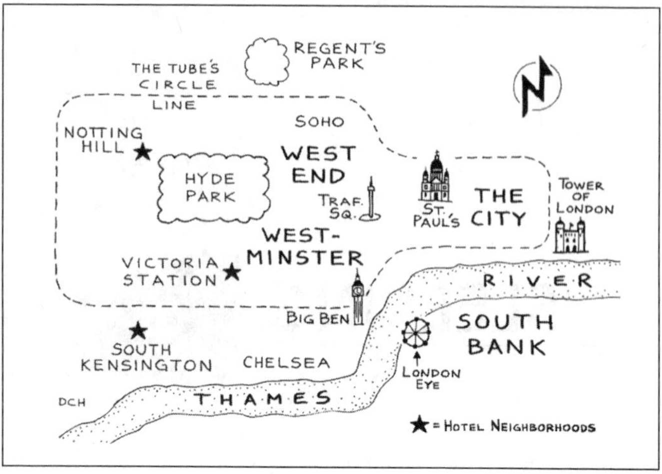

a hotel charges) can be misleading, since they often omit cheaper oddball rooms and special clearance deals.

"Twin" means two single beds, and "double" means one double bed. If you'll take either one, let them know, or you might be needlessly turned away. Most hotels offer family deals, which means that parents with young children can easily get a room with an extra child's bed or a discount for larger rooms. Call to negotiate the price. Teenage kids are generally charged as adults. Kids under five sleep almost free.

Most places listed have three floors of rooms and steep stairs. Elevators are rare except in the larger hotels. If you're concerned about stairs, call and ask about ground-floor rooms or pay for a hotel with a lift (elevator). In this big city, street noise is a fact of life. If concerned, request a room on the back side.

Many places now offer non-smoking rooms (listed in descriptions). Breakfast rooms are nearly always smoke-free.

Rooms have sinks. Any room without a bathroom has access to a free bath or shower in the corridor. Rooms with private plumbing are called "en suite"; rooms that lack private plumbing are "standard." As more rooms go en suite, the hallway bathroom is shared with fewer standard rooms. If money's tight, request standard rooms.

Calling London

To phone London, you'll need to know Britain's country code: 44. To call from the United States or Canada, dial 011-44-20 (includes London's area code without its initial zero) plus the local number. If making the call from another European country,

Sleep Code

(£1 = about $1.80, country code: 44)
To help you easily sort through these listings, I've divided the rooms into three categories, based on the price for a double room with bath:

$$$ **Higher Priced**—Most rooms £100 or more.
$$ **Moderately Priced**—Most rooms between £70–100.
$ **Lower Priced**—Most rooms £70 or less.

To give maximum information in a minimum of space, I use this code to describe accommodations listed in this book. Prices in this book are listed per room, not per person. Unless otherwise noted, credit cards are accepted and breakfast is included.

S = Single room, or price for one person in a double.
D = Double or twin room. (I specify double- and twin-bed rooms only if they are priced differently, or if a place has only one or the other. When reserving, you should specify.)
T = Three-person room (often a double bed with a single).
Q = Four-person room (adding an extra child's bed to a T is usually cheaper).
b = Private bathroom with toilet and shower or tub.
s = Private shower or tub only. (The toilet is down the hall.)

According to this code, a couple staying at a "Db-£70, cash only" hotel would pay a total of £70 (about $125) per night for a room with a private toilet and shower (or tub). This hotel does not accept credit cards—cash only.

dial 00-44-20-local number. If calling from within Britain but outside London, dial 020-local number. To call a London phone number from within London, drop the area code (020) and dial only the local number.

Making Reservations

Reserve your London room as soon as you can commit to a date. It's possible to visit London any time of year without reservations, but given the high stakes, erratic accommodations values, and the quality of the gems we've listed, I recommend booking ahead.

A few national holidays jam things up (especially "bank holiday" Mondays) and merit reservations long in advance. Mark these dates in red on your travel calendar: New Year's Day, Good Friday through Easter Monday (April 14–16 in 2006), the first and last Monday in May (May 1 and 29), the last Monday in August (Aug 28), Christmas, and December 26 (Boxing Day). Just like at home, Monday holidays are preceded by busy weekends, so book the entire weekend in advance.

You can book a room by e-mail, phone, or fax. I've taken great pains to list telephone numbers with long-distance instructions (see "Telephones" in the Introduction). E-mail is preferred. In addition, many hotel Web sites now have online reservation forms. To fax, use the fax form in the appendix (or find it online at www.ricksteves.com/reservation). A two-night stay in August would be "2 nights, 16/8/06 to 18/8/06." (Europeans write the date day/month/year, and hotel jargon uses your day of departure.)

Some places will trust you and hold a room until 16:00 without a deposit, although most places will ask you for a credit-card number. Faxing your credit-card number (rather than emailing it) keeps it safer, more private, and out of cyberspace. The pricier ones sometimes have expensive cancellation policies (you might lose, say, a deposit if you cancel within 2 weeks of your reserved stay, or you might be billed for the entire visit if you leave early); ask about their policies before you book. If your credit card is the deposit, you can pay with your card or cash when you arrive. Honor (or cancel by phone) your reservations. If you don't show up, you'll be billed for one night. Reconfirm your reservations a couple days in advance for safety. Also, don't just assume you can extend. Consider carefully—and well in advance—how long you'll stay.

Looking for Hotel Deals Online

Given the high hotel prices and relatively weak dollar, consider turning to the Internet to help score a hotel deal. Various Web sites list rooms in high-rise, three- and four-star business hotels. You'll give up the charm and warmth of a family-run establishment, and breakfast will probably not be included, but you might find the price is right.

Start by checking the Web sites of several big hotel chains to get an idea of typical rates and to check for online-only deals. Big London hotel chains include: Millennium/Copthorne (www.millenniumhotels.com), Thistle (www.thistlehotels.com), Intercontinental/Holiday Inn (www.ichotelsgroup.com), Radisson (www.radisson.com), and Red Carnation (www.redcarnationhotels.com). For information on the no-frills, more Motel 6–type chains, see "Big, Cheap, Modern Hotels," below.

Auction-type sites (such as www.priceline.com) can be great for matching flexible travelers with empty hotel rooms, often at prices well below the hotel's own rates. Don't feel you have to start as high as the site's suggested opening bid. (For more about the complicated world of online bidding strategies and success stories from other travelers, see www.biddingfortravel.com or www.betterbidding.com.) Warning: Scoring a deal this way may require more patience and flexibility than you have, but if you enjoy shopping for cars, you'll probably like this, too.

Other favorite hotel discount sites mentioned by my readers include www.londontown.com, www.lastminute.com, www.visitlondon.com, www.findlondonrooms.com, and www.eurocheapo.com. Check the "Graffiti Wall" at ricksteves.com for the latest tips and discoveries.

For a good overview on finding London hotel deals, go to smartertravel.com and click on "Hotels," then "City Guides," and finally "Find the best hotel value in London."

Big, Cheap, Modern Hotels

These places—popular with budget tour groups—are well-run and offer elevators and all the modern comforts in a no-frills, practical package. With the notable exception of my second listing, they are often located on busy streets in dreary train-station neighborhoods, so use common sense after dark and wear your money belt. The doubles for £75–100 are a great value for London. Mid-week prices are generally higher than weekend rates. Online bookings are often the easiest way to make reservations, and will get you a discount if you're staying at a Jurys or a Travelodge.

$$$ Jurys Inn Islington rents 200 compact, comfy rooms near King's Cross station (Db/Tb-£100, some discounted rooms available online, 2 adults and 2 kids under age 12 can share 1 room, breakfast extra, non-smoking floors, 60 Pentonville Road, Tube: Angel, tel. 020/7282-5500, fax 020/7282-5511, www.jurysdoyle.com).

$$ Premier Travel Inn London County Hall, literally down the hall from a $400-a-night Marriott Hotel, fills one end of London's massive former County Hall building. This place is wonderfully located near the base of the London Eye Ferris Wheel and across the Thames from Big Ben. Its 300 slick rooms come with all the necessary comforts (Db-£87–90 for 2 adults and up to 2 kids under age 15, couples can request a bigger family room—same price, breakfast extra, book in advance, no-show rooms are released at 15:00, elevator, some smoke-free and easy-access rooms, 500 yards from Westminster Tube stop and Waterloo Station, Belvedere Road, you can call central reservations at 0870-242-8000 or 0870-238-3300, you can fax 020/7902-1619 but you might not get a response, it's easiest to book online at www.premiertravelinn.com).

$$ Premier Travel Inn London Southwark, with 55 rooms, is near Shakespeare's Globe on the South Bank (Db for up to 2 adults and 2 kids-£83–85, Bankside, 34 Park Street, tel. 0870-990-6402, www.premiertravelinn.com).

$$ Premier Travel Inn King's Cross, with 276 rooms, is just east of King's Cross station (Db-£75–85, non-smoking rooms available, breakfast extra, 24-hour reception, elevator, 26–30 York Way, tel. 0870/990-6414, fax 0870/990-6415, www.premiertravelinn.com).

Other **$$ Premier Travel Inns** charging £75–85 per room include **London Euston** (big, blue, Lego-type building packed with families on vacation on handy but noisy street, 141 Euston Road, Tube: Euston, tel. 0870/238-3301), **London Kensington** (11 Knaresboro Place, Tube: Earl's Court or Gloucester Road, tel. 0870/238-3304), and **London Putney Bridge** (farther out, 3 Putney Bridge Approach, Tube: Putney Bridge, tel. 0870-238-3302). Avoid the **Tower Bridge** location, which is an inconvenient, 15-minute walk from the nearest Tube stop. For any of these, call 0870-242-8000, fax 0870-241-9000, or the best option, book online at www.premiertravelinn.com.

$$ Hotel Ibis London Euston, which feels a bit classier than a Premier Travel Inn, is located on a quiet street a block behind and west of Euston Station (380 rooms, Db-£70–80, breakfast extra, no family rooms, non-smoking floor, 3 Cardington Street, tel. 020/7388-7777, fax 020/7388-0001, www.ibishotel.com, h0921@accor-hotels.com).

$ Travelodge London Islington is another typical chain hotel with lots of cookie-cutter rooms just south of King's Cross Station (Db-£60–80, some £26 rooms available online only for scattered dates, breakfast extra, family rooms, non-smoking rooms, 100 Kings Cross Road, tel. 0870-191-1773, fax 020/7833-8261, www.travelodge.co.uk). Other Travelodge London locations are at **King's Cross, Covent Garden, Liverpool Street,** and **Farringdon.** For all the details on each, see www.travelodge.co.uk.

Victoria Station Neighborhood (Belgravia)

The streets behind Victoria Station teem with budget B&Bs. It's a safe, surprisingly tidy, and decent area without a hint of the trashy, touristy glitz of the streets in front of the station. West of the tracks is Belgravia, where the prices are a bit higher and your neighbors include Andrew Lloyd Webber and Margaret Thatcher (her policeman stands outside 73 Chester Square). East of the tracks is Pimlico—cheaper and just as handy, but the rooms can be a bit dowdier. Decent eateries abound (see page 296).

All the recommended hotels are within a five-minute walk of the Victoria Tube, bus, and train stations. On hot summer nights,

Victoria Station Neighborhood

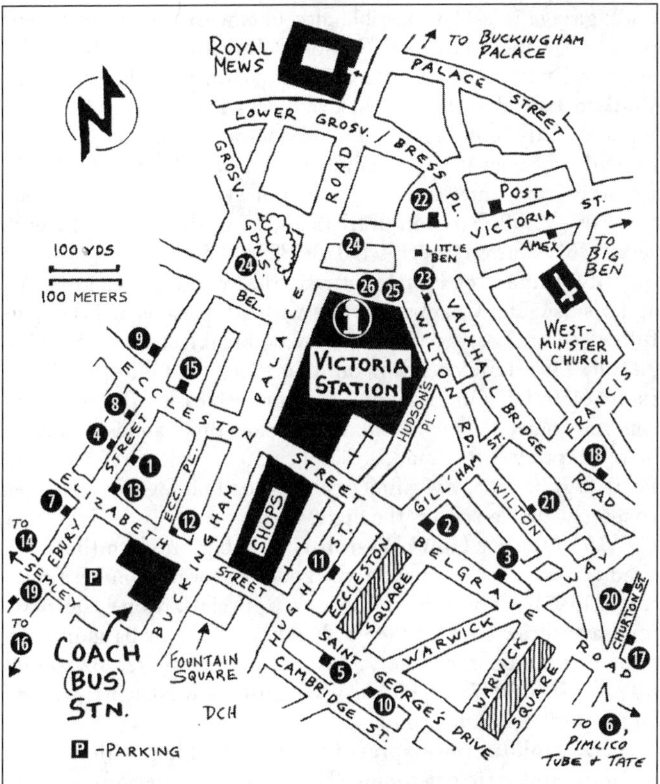

1. Lime Tree Hotel
2. Quality Hotel Westminster
3. Winchester Hotel
4. James House & Cartref House Hotels
5. Elizabeth Hotel & Jubilee Hotel
6. To Holiday Inn Express
7. Morgan House
8. Collin House Hotel
9. Harcourt House
10. Elizabeth House & Bakers Hotel
11. Cherry Court Hotel
12. Goya Spanish Rest. & Tapas Bar
13. Ebury Wine Bar
14. To Duke of Wellington Pub
15. Jenny Lo's Tea House
16. To La Poule au Pot Rest.
17. Grumbles Restaurant
18. The Jugged Hare Pub
19. The Belgravia Pub
20. Chimes English Rest. & Cider Bar
21. Seafresh Fish Restaurant
22. Sainsbury's Local Grocery
23. Internet Café
24. Bus Tours (Day)
25. Bus Tours (Night)
26. TI, Tube, Taxis, City Buses

request a quiet back room. Nearby is the 400-space Semley Place NCP **garage** (£30/day, possible discounts with hotel voucher, just west of the Victoria Coach Station at Buckingham Palace Road and Semley Place, tel. 0870/242-7144, www.ncp.co.uk). The handy **Pimlico Launderette** is about five blocks southwest of Warwick Square (daily 8:00–20:00, self-service or full service, south of Sutherland Street at 3 Westmoreland Terrace, tel. 020/7821-8692). **Launderette Centre** is a block north of Warwick Square (Mon–Fri 8:00–22:00, Sat–Sun until 19:30, £7 wash and dry, £9 with service, 31 Churton Street, tel. 020/7828-6039).

$$$ Lime Tree Hotel, enthusiastically run by David Davies and his daughter Charlotte, comes with 30 spacious and thoughtfully decorated rooms and a fun-loving breakfast room (Sb-£75–80, Db-£105–130 depending on room size, Tb-£140–160, family room-£150–175, £10 discount per night with cash, all rooms non-smoking, quiet garden, David deals in slow times and is creative at helping travelers in a bind, 135 Ebury Street, tel. 020/7730-8191, fax 020/7730-7865, www.limetreehotel.co.uk, info@limetreehotel.co.uk, trusty Alan covers the night shift).

$$$ Quality Hotel Westminster is big, modern (but with tired carpets), well-located, and a good bet for no-nonsense comfort (Db-£130, check for various Web specials, drop-ins can ask for "saver prices" on slow days, breakfast extra or bargained in, non-smoking floor, elevator, 82 Eccleston Square, tel. 020/7834-8042, fax 020/7630-8942, www.hotels-westminster.com, winchester17@hotmail.com).

$$$ Holiday Inn Express fills an old building with 52 fresh, modern, and efficient rooms (Db-£114 rack rate, often £80—especially Sun or if booked online; family rooms, up to 2 kids free, non-smoking floor, elevator, Tube: Pimlico, 106 Belgrave Road, tel. 020/7630-8888, fax 020/7828-0441, www.hiexpressvictoria.co.uk, info@hiexpressvictoria.co.uk).

$$ Winchester Hotel is family-run and perhaps the best value, with 18 fine rooms and a caring management (Db-£85, Tb-£110, Qb-£140, cash only, no groups, no infants, 17 Belgrave Road, tel. 020/7828-2972, fax 020/7828-5191, www.winchester-hotel.net, enquiry@winchester-hotel.net, commanded with panache by irrepressible Jimmy and his crew: Juanita, Andrew, and Frank). The Winchester also rents apartments—with kitchenettes, sitting rooms, and beds on the quiet back side—around the corner (£125–230).

$$ James House and **Cartref House** are two nearly identical, well-run, smoke-free, 10-room places on either side of Ebury Street (S-£52, Sb-£62, D-£70, Db-£85, T-£95, Tb-£110, family bunk-bed Qb-£135, 5 percent discount with cash, all rooms with fans, strictly no smoking, James House at 108 Ebury Street, tel.

020/7730-7338; Cartref House at 129 Ebury Street, tel. 020/7730-6176, www.jamesandcartref.co.uk, info@jamesandcartref.co.uk, Derek and Sharon).

$$ Elizabeth Hotel is a stately old place overlooking Eccleston Square, with fine public spaces and 40 well-worn, slightly overpriced, but spacious and decent rooms (S-£55, Sb-£77, D-£77, small Db-£93, big Db-£105, Tb-£118, Qb-£130, Quint/b-£135, 37 Eccleston Square, tel. 020/7828-6812, fax 020/7828-6814, www.elizabethhotel.com, info@elizabethhotel.com). Be careful not to confuse this hotel with the nearby (cheaper but also recommended) Elizabeth House. Elizabeth Hotel also rents apartments that sleep up to six (£195/night, includes breakfast).

$$ Harcourt House rents 10 newly refurbished, neo-Victorian, smoke-free rooms (Sb-£60, Db-£80, 50 Ebury Street, tel. 020/7730-2722, www.harcourthousehotel.co.uk, harcourthouse@talk21.com, helpful David and Glesni Wood and cute dog Suki).

$$ Morgan House rents 11 good rooms and is entertainingly run, with lots of travel tips and friendly chat—especially about the local rich and famous—by owner Rachel Joplin and manager Davinia (S-£46, D-£66, Db-£86, T-£86, family suites-£110–122 for 3–4 people, 120 Ebury Street, tel. 020/7730-2384, fax 020/7730-8442, www.morganhouse.co.uk, morganhouse@connect.com).

$$ Collin House Hotel, clean, simple, and efficiently-run, offers 12 relatively spacious rooms with woody, modern furnishings (Sb-£55, D-£68, Db-£82, T-£95, non-smoking rooms, 104 Ebury St, tel. & fax 020/7730-8031, www.collinhouse.co.uk, booking@collinhouse.co.uk, absentee owner).

$ Cherry Court Hotel, run by the friendly and industrious Patel family, rents 12 small, basic, air-conditioned rooms in a central location (Sb-£45, Db-£55, Tb-£75, Qb-£90, Quint/b-£105, prices promised with this book through 2006, paying with credit card costs 5 percent extra, fruit-basket breakfast in room, entirely non-smoking, free Internet access with free disk burning, peaceful garden patio, 23 Hugh Street, tel. 020/7828-2840, fax 020/7828-0393, www.cherrycourthotel.co.uk, bookings@cherrycourthotel.co.uk).

$ Jubilee Hotel is a well-run slumber-mill with 26 tiny rooms and many tiny beds—but good prices for London (S-£35, Db-£50, tiny D-£50, tiny Db-£60, Db-£65, Tb-£75, Qb-£95, 5 percent discount with this book through 2006, 31 Eccleston Square, tel. 020/7834-0845, www.jubileehotel.co.uk, reservations@jubileehotel.co.uk). The Jubilee is run by Bob Patel, whose family runs the Cherry Court, listed above.

$ Elizabeth House offers 40 of some of the best cheap—albeit spartan—rooms in town, with a professional reception and a guests' kitchen where you can do your own cooking (S-£35, D-£50, Db-£60, Tb-£70, Q-£80, Qb-£85, Quint/b-£90, includes continental breakfast, avoid some street noise by requesting quiet room in the back, 118 Warwick Way, tel. 020/7630-0741, fax 020/7630-0740, www.elizabethhouse.co.uk, elizabethhouselondon@yahoo.co.uk).

$ Bakers Hotel is a cheapie, with 10 small, tight, and very simple rooms, but it's well-located and offers youth hostel prices and a full breakfast (S-£30, D-£46, T-£55, 126 Warwick Way, tel. 020/7834-0729, www.bakershotel.co.uk, reservations@bakershotel.co.uk, Amin Jamani).

"South Kensington," She Said, Loosening His Cummerbund

To live on a quiet street so classy it doesn't allow hotel signs, surrounded by trendy shops and colorful restaurants, call "South Ken" your London home. Shoppers like being a short walk from Harrods and the designer shops of King's Road and Chelsea. When I splurge, I splurge here. Sumner Place is just off Old Brompton Road, 200 yards from the handy South Kensington Tube station (on Circle Line, 2 stops from Victoria Station, direct Heathrow connection). There's a taxi rank in the median strip at the end of Harrington Road. The handy **Wash & Dry launderette** is on the corner of Queensberry Place and Harrington Road (daily 8:00–21:00, bring 20p and £1 coins).

$$$ Aster House, run by friendly and accommodating Simon and Leonie Tan, has won the "Best B&B in London" award three times in the last five years. It has a sumptuous lobby, lounge, and breakfast room. Its rooms are comfy and quiet, with TV, phone, and air-conditioning. Enjoy breakfast or just lounging in the whisper-elegant Orangery, a Victorian greenhouse (Sb-£90, Db-£130, bigger Db-£160, deluxe 4-poster Db-£175, these prices with this book through 2006, entirely non-smoking, 3 Sumner Place, tel. 020/7581-5888, fax 020/7584-4925, www.asterhouse.com, asterhouse@btinternet.com). Simon and Leonie also offer free Internet access, Wi-Fi, and loaner mobile phones to their guests.

$$$ Five Sumner Place Hotel has received several "Best Small Hotel in London" awards in the last decade. The 13 rooms in this 150-year-old building are tastefully decorated, and the breakfast room is a conservatory/greenhouse (Sb-£100, Db-£155, third bed-£25, ask for 20 percent Rick Steves discount in 2006; TV, phone, and fridge in room by request; non-smoking rooms, elevator, 5 Sumner Place, tel. 020/7584-7586, fax 020/7823-9962, www.sumnerplace.com, reservations@sumnerplace.com).

$$$ Sixteen Sumner Place, for well-heeled travelers, has over-the-top formality and class packed into its 42 rooms, plush lounges, and tranquil garden. It's in a labyrinthine building, with

South Kensington Neighborhood

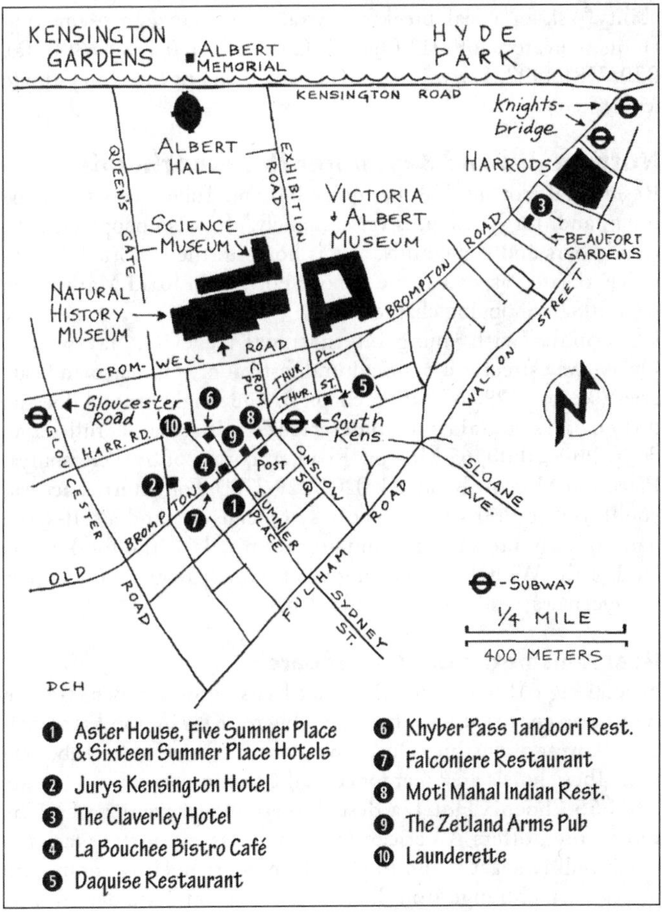

modern decor throughout (Db-£170–250—but soft, breakfast in the garden, elevator, 16 Sumner Place, tel. 020/7589-5232, fax 020/7584-8615, U.S. tel. 800/553-6674, www.firmdale.com, sixteen@firmdale.com).

$$$ The Claverley, two blocks from Harrods, is on a quiet street similar to Sumner Place. The 30 fancy, dark-wood-and-marble rooms come with all the comforts (S-£80, Sb-£100–110, Db-£150, sofa-bed Tb-£190–215, ask for Rick Steves discount, plush lounge, non-smoking rooms, elevator, 13–14 Beaufort Gardens, Tube: Knightsbridge, tel. 020/7589-8541, fax 020/7584-3410, U.S. tel. 800/747-0398, www.claverleyhotel.co.uk, reservations @claverleyhotel.co.uk).

$$$ Jurys Kensington Hotel is big, stately, and impersonal, with a greedy pricing scheme (Db-£100–140 depending on "availability," ask for a deal, breakfast extra, piano lounge, non-smoking floors, elevator, 109–113 Queen's Gate, tel. 020/7589-6300, fax 020/7581-1492, www.jurysdoyle.com, kensington@jurysdoyle.com).

Notting Hill and Bayswater Neighborhoods

Residential Notting Hill has quick bus and Tube access to downtown, and, for London, is very "homely." It's also peppered with trendy bars and restaurants, and is home to the historic Coronet movie theater, as well as the famous Portobello Road Market (see page 308 of Shopping chapter).

Popular with young international travelers, Bayswater's Queensway street is a multicultural festival of commerce and eateries (see page 297 of Eating chapter). The neighborhood does its dirty clothes at **Galaxy Launderette** (£4 self-serve, £8 full-serve, daily 8:00–20:00, 65 Moscow Road, at corner of St. Petersburgh Place and Moscow Road, tel. 020/7229-7771). For **Internet access,** you'll find several stops along busy Queensway and a self-serve bank of easyInternetcafé computer terminals at the food circus level of the Whiteleys Shopping Centre (daily 8:30–24:00, corner of Queensway and Porchester Gardens).

Near Kensington Gardens Square

Several big old hotels line the quiet Kensington Gardens Square (not to be confused with the much bigger Kensington Gardens), a block west of bustling Queensway, north of Bayswater Tube station. These hotels are quiet for central London.

$$$ Phoenix Hotel, a Best Western modernization of a 125-room hotel, offers American business-class comforts; spacious, plush public spaces; and big, fresh, modern-feeling rooms. Its prices—which range from fine value to rip-off—are determined by a greedy computer program, with huge variations according to expected demand. See their Web site and book online to save money (Db-£90–150, elevator, 1–8 Kensington Gardens Square, tel. 020/7229-2494, fax 020/7727-1419, U.S. tel. 800/528-1234, www.phoenixhotel.co.uk, info@phoenixhotel.co.uk).

$$ Garden Court Hotel rents 34 comfortable, smoke-free rooms. It's newly refurbished and has a garden (S-£40, Sb-£62, D-£64, Db-£92, T-£84, Tb-£114, Q-£94, Qb-£135, 10 percent discount with this book through 2006, elevator, 30 Kensington Gardens Square, tel. 020/7229-2553, fax 020/7727-2749, www.gardencourthotel.co.uk, info@gardencourthotel.co.uk, well-run by Edward and his trusty first mate Paul).

$$ Kensington Gardens Hotel laces 16 decent rooms together in a tall, skinny place with lots of stairs and no elevator

Notting Hill Neighborhood

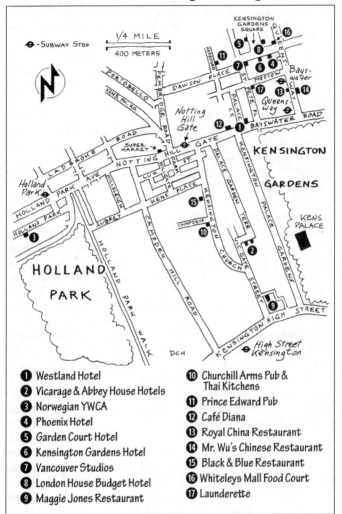

1. Westland Hotel
2. Vicarage & Abbey House Hotels
3. Norwegian YWCA
4. Phoenix Hotel
5. Garden Court Hotel
6. Kensington Gardens Hotel
7. Vancouver Studios
8. London House Budget Hotel
9. Maggie Jones Restaurant
10. Churchill Arms Pub & Thai Kitchens
11. Prince Edward Pub
12. Café Diana
13. Royal China Restaurant
14. Mr. Wu's Chinese Restaurant
15. Black & Blue Restaurant
16. Whiteleys Mall Food Court
17. Launderette

(Ss-£45–50, Sb-£50–55, Db-£75, Tb-£95, book by phone or e-mail rather than through the pricier Web site, 9 Kensington Gardens Square, tel. 020/7221-7790, fax 020/7792-8612, www.kensingtongardenshotel.co.uk, info@kensingtongardenshotel.co.uk, charming Rowshanak).

$$ Vancouver Studios offers 45 modern rooms with fully equipped kitchenettes (utensils, stove, microwave, and fridge) rather than breakfast (small Sb-£60, small Db-£85, big Db-£100, Tb-£120, extra bed-£18, 10 percent discount with week-long stay or more, call to confirm reservation a night or two before, welcoming lounge and garden, near Kensington Gardens Square at 30 Prince's Square, tel. 020/7243-1270, fax 020/7221-8678, www.vancouverstudios.co.uk, info@vancouverstudios.co.uk).

$ London House Budget Hotel is a threadbare, nose-ringed slumber mill renting more than 200 beds in about 80 stark rooms. While their rack rates are high (to hide Web booking commissions for those who don't go direct), their own Web site offers much better prices such as Db-£46 (S-£50, Sb-£56, twin-£54, Db-£60, dorm bed-£16, prices flex downward with demand, includes continental breakfast, lots of school groups, free Internet access in lobby, 81 Kensington Gardens Square, tel. 020/7243-1810, fax 020/7243-1723, www.londonhousehotel.co.uk, londonhousehotel@yahoo.co.uk).

Near Kensington Gardens

$$$ Westland Hotel is comfortable, convenient, and hotelesque, with a fine lounge and spacious rooms. Rooms are recently refurbished and quite plush. Their £105 doubles (less your 10 percent discount—see below) are the best value (Sb-£88–99, Db-£105, deluxe Db-£121, cavernous deluxe Db-£138, sprawling Tb-£132–154, gargantuan Qb-£150–175, Quint/b-£165–187, 10 percent discount with this book if claimed upon arrival; elevator, free garage with 6 spaces; between Notting Hill Gate and Queensway Tube stations; 154 Bayswater Road, tel. 020/7229-9191, fax 020/7727-1054, www.westlandhotel.co.uk, reservations@westlandhotel.co.uk).

$$$ Vicarage Private Hotel, understandably popular, is family-run and elegantly British in a quiet, classy neighborhood. It has 17 rooms furnished with taste and quality, a TV lounge, and facilities on each floor. Mandy, Richard, and Krassi maintain a homey and caring atmosphere (S-£46, Sb-£75, D-£78, Db-£102, T-£95, Tb-£130, Q-£102, Qb-£140, cash only, 6-min walk from Notting Hill Gate and High Street Kensington Tube stations, near Kensington Palace at 10 Vicarage Gate, tel. 020/7229-4030, fax 020/7792-5989, www.londonvicaragehotel.com, reception@londonvicaragehotel.com).

$$ Abbey House Hotel, next door, is basic but its 16 rooms are bright, friendly, and sleepable (S-£45, D-£74, T-£90, Q-£100, Quint-£110, cash only, 11 Vicarage Gate, tel. 020/7727-2594, fax 020/7727-1873, www.abbeyhousekensington.com, abbeyhousedesk@btconnect.com, Rodrigo).

Near Holland Park

$ Norwegian YWCA (Norsk K.F.U.K.) is for women under 30 only (and men under 30 with Norwegian passports). Located on a quiet, stately street, it offers non-smoking rooms, a study, TV room, piano lounge, and an open-face Norwegian ambience (goat cheese on Sundays!). They have mostly quads, so those willing to share with strangers are most likely to get a bed (July–Aug: Ss-£33, shared double-£31/bed, shared triple-£26/bed, shared quad-£23/bed, includes breakfast and sack lunch; includes dinner Sept–June; 52 Holland Park, tel. 020/7727-9346, fax 020/7727-8718, www.kfuk.dial.pipex.com, kfuk.hjemmet@kfuk-kfum.no). With each visit, I wonder which is easier to get—a sex change or a Norwegian passport?

Other Neighborhoods

Near Covent Garden: **$$$ Fielding Hotel,** located on a charming, quiet pedestrian street just two blocks east of Covent Garden, offers 24 no-nonsense rooms, bright orange hallways, and lots of stairs. You're paying about £20 extra for rather small, basic rooms in a very fine location (Db-£100–115, Db with sitting room-£130, no breakfast, no smoking, no kids under 13, 4 Broad Court, Bow Street, tel. 020/7836-8305, fax 020/7497-0064, www.the-fielding-hotel.co.uk).

Downtown near Baker Street: **$$$ The 22 York Street B&B** offers a less hotelesque alternative in the center, renting 18 stark, hardwood, comfortable rooms (Db-£100, Tb-£141, 2-night minimum, strictly smoke-free, social breakfast, inviting lounge; from Baker Street Tube station, walk 2 blocks down Baker Street and take a right, 22 York Street; tel. 020/7224-3990, fax 020/7224-1990, www.22yorkstreet.co.uk, mc@22yorkstreet.co.uk, energetically run by Liz and Michael Callis).

Near Buckingham Palace: **$$ Vandon House Hotel,** run by the Central College in Iowa, is packed with students most of the year, but its 33 rooms are rented to travelers from late May through August at great prices. The rooms, while institutional, are comfy, and the location is excellent (S-£43, D-£68, Db-£84, Tb-£99, Qb-£118, only single beds, non-smoking, elevator, on a tiny road 3-min walk west of St. James's Park Tube station and 7-min walk from Victoria Station, near east end of Petty France Street at 1 Vandon Street, tel. 020/7799-6780, fax 020/7799-1464, www.vandonhouse.com, info@vandonhouse.com).

Euston Station: The **$$ Methodist International Centre,** a modern, youthful, Christian residence, fills its lower floors with international students and its top floor with travelers. Rooms are modern and simple yet comfortable, with fine bathrooms, phones, and desks. The atmosphere is friendly, safe, clean, and controlled; it also has a spacious lounge and game room (Db-£85, 2-course buffet dinner-£13, non-smoking rooms, elevator, on a quiet street a block west of Euston Station, 81–103 Euston Street—not Euston Road, Tube: Euston Station, tel. 020/7380-0001, fax 020/7387-5300, www.micentre.com, acc@micentre.com). In June, July, and August, when the students are gone, they also rent simpler rooms (S-£45, D-£68).

Hostels and Dorms

$ A cluster of three **St. Christopher's Inn** hostels, south of the Thames near London Bridge, rent £16–20 beds (161–165 Borough High Street, Tube: Borough or London Bridge, tel. 020/7407-1856, www.st-christophers.co.uk).

$ The **City of London Youth Hostel,** near St. Paul's, is clean, modern, friendly, and well-run. You'll pay £17 per bed in an 11-bed dorm, about £25 for a bed in their three- to eight-bed rooms, or £32 for a single room (£2 extra if you have no hostel card, 193 beds, cheap meals, open 24 hours, Tube: St. Paul's, 36 Carter Lane, tel. 020/7236-4965, fax 020/7236-7681, www.yha.org.uk, city@yha.org.uk).

$ The **University of Westminster** opens up its dorm rooms to travelers during summer break, from mid-June through mid-September. Located in several high-rise buildings scattered around central London, the rooms—some with private bathrooms, others with shared bathrooms nearby—come with access to well-stocked kitchens and big lounges (S-£27–35, D-£47–56, tel. 020/7834-1169, www.wmin.ac.uk/comserv, comserv@wmin.ac.uk). University College London also has rooms for travelers from mid-June until mid-September; for details see www.ucl.ac.uk/residences.

Near Gatwick and Heathrow Airports

Near Gatwick Airport: **$ London Gatwick Airport Premier Travel Inn** rents cheap rooms at the airport (Db-£58, £2.50 shuttle bus from airport, tel. 0870-238-3305, www.premiertravelinn.com). **$ Gatwick Travelodge** has budget rooms two miles from the airport (Db-£50, £3 shuttle from airport, breakfast extra, Church Road, Lowfield Heath, Crawley, tel. 0870-191-1531, www.travelodge.co.uk).

$ Barn Cottage, a converted 16th-century barn, sits in the peaceful countryside, with a tennis court, small swimming pool, and a good pub within walking distance. It has two wood-beamed rooms, antique furniture, and a large garden that makes you forget Gatwick is 10 minutes away (S-£50, D-£60, cash only, can drive you to airport or train station for £8, Church Road, Leigh, Reigate, Surrey, tel. 01306/611-347, warmly run by Pat and Mike Comer). Do not confuse this place with others of the same name; this Barn Cottage has no Web site.

$ Wayside Manor Farm is another rural alternative to a bland airport hotel. This four-bedroom countryside place is a 10-minute drive from Gatwick (Db-£65, Tb-£80, Norwood Hill, near Charlwood, tel. 01293/862-692, www.wayside-manor.com, info@wayside-manor.com).

Near Heathrow Airport: It's so easy to get to Heathrow from central London, I see no reason to sleep there. But for budget beds near the airport, consider **$ Heathrow Ibis** (Db-£68, Db-£45 on Fri–Sun nights, breakfast extra; £3 shuttle bus to/from terminals except T-4, look for "Hopabus" run by National Express; 112 Bath Road, tel. 020/8759-4888, fax 020/8564-7894, www.ibishotel.com, h0794@accor-hotels.com).

EATING

England's reputation for miserable food is now dated, and the British cuisine scene is lively, trendy, and pleasantly surprising. (Unfortunately, it's also expensive.) Even the basic, traditional pub grub has gone "upmarket," and you'll generally find fresh vegetables rather than soggy fries and mushy peas.

In London, the sheer variety of foods—from every corner of its former empire and beyond—is astonishing. You'll be amazed at the number of hopping, happening new restaurants of all kinds.

If you want to dine (as opposed to eat), drop by a London newsstand to get a weekly entertainment guide or an annual restaurant guide (both have extensive restaurant listings), visit www.london-eating.co.uk for more options...or catch a train for Paris.

The thought of a £40 meal in Britain generally ruins my appetite, so my London dining is limited mostly to easygoing, fun, inexpensive alternatives. I've listed places by neighborhood—handy to your sightseeing or hotel. Considering how expensive London can be, if there's any good place to cut corners to stretch your budget, it's by eating cheaply.

Tips on Budget Eating

You have plenty of inexpensive £7 choices: pub grub, daily specials, ethnic restaurants, cafeterias, fast food, picnics, fish-and-chips, greasy-spoon cafés, or pizza.

Pub grub is the most atmospheric budget option. Many of London's 7,000 pubs serve fresh, tasty buffets under ancient timbers, with hearty lunches and dinners priced at £6–8 (see "Pubs," page 284).

At classier restaurants, look for **early-bird specials,** allowing you to eat well and affordably, but early (about 17:30–19:00, last order by 19:00). A top-end, £25-for-dinner-type restaurant often serves the same quality two-course lunch deals for £10.

Ethnic restaurants from all over the world add spice to England's cuisine scene. Eating Indian or Chinese is cheap (even cheaper if you take it out). Middle Eastern stands sell gyros sandwiches and *shwarmas* (lamb in pita bread). An Indian *samosa* (greasy, flaky meat and vegetable pie) costs £1, can be microwaved, and makes a very cheap, if small, meal.

Most large **museums** (and many churches) have reasonable **cafeterias.**

Fast food places, both American and British, are everywhere. **Cheap chain restaurants**, such as steak houses and pizza places, serve no-nonsense food in a family-friendly setting (steak-house meals about £10; all-you-can-stomach pizza around £5).

Picnicking saves time and money. Fine park benches and polite pigeons abound in most neighborhoods. You can easily get prepared food to go. Munch a relaxed "meal on wheels" picnic during your open-top bus tour or river cruise to save 30 precious minutes for sightseeing.

Bakeries sell yogurt, cartons of "semi-skimmed" milk, pastries, and pasties (PAST-eez). Pasties are "savory" (not sweet) meat pies that originated in the mining country; they had big crust handles so miners with filthy hands could eat them and toss the crust.

Good **sandwich shops** and corner **grocery stores** are a hit with local workers eating on the run. Try boxes of orange juice (pure, by the liter), fresh bread, tasty English cheese, meat, a tube of Colman's English mustard, local eatin' apples, bananas, small tomatoes, a small tub of yogurt (drinkable), trail mix, nuts, plain or chocolate-covered digestive biscuits, and any local specialties. At **open-air markets** and **supermarkets,** you can get produce in small quantities (3 tomatoes and 2 bananas cost me 90p). Supermarkets often have good deli sections, even offering Indian dishes, and sometimes salad bars. Decent packaged sandwiches (£2–3) are sold everywhere. Cheap and cheery chains such as **Pret a Manger, Benjy's,** and **Eat** provide office workers with good, healthful sandwiches and basic food to go. The **Simply Food** chain, with fast, fresh, budget meals and free plasticware, is ideal for picnics.

Breakfast

The traditional "fry" is famous as a hearty way to start the day. Also known as a "heart attack on a plate," the breakfast is especially feast-like if you've just come from the land of the skimpy continental breakfast across the Channel.

Your standard fry gets off to a healthy start with juice and cereal. (Try Weetabix, a soggy English cousin of Shredded Wheat and perhaps the most absorbent material known to man.) Next, with tea or coffee, get a heated plate with a fried egg, lean

Canadian-style bacon, a bad sausage, a grilled tomato, and often a slice of delightfully greasy pan toast and sautéed mushrooms. Toast comes on a rack (to cool quickly and crisply) with butter and marmalade. This meal tides many travelers over until dinner. Order only what you'll eat; hoteliers and B&B hostesses don't like to see food wasted. There's nothing wrong with skipping the fry—few locals actually start their day with this heavy traditional breakfast.

Pubs

Pubs are a basic part of the British social scene, and, whether you're a teetotaler or a beer guzzler, they should be a part of your travel here. "Pub" is short for "public house." It's an extended living room where, if you don't mind the stickiness, you can feel the pulse of London. Smart travelers use the pubs to eat, drink, get out of the rain, watch the latest sporting event, and make new friends.

Pub hours vary. The strict wartime hours (designed to keep the wartime working force sober and productive) ended in 1988, and now pubs generally serve beer Mon–Sat 11:00–23:00 and Sun 12:00–22:30 (though pubs can be open later, particularly on Fri–Sat). As it nears closing time, you'll hear shouts of "Last orders." Then comes the 10-minute warning bell. Finally, they'll call "Time!" to pick up your glass, finished or not, when the pub closes.

A cup of darts is free for the asking. People go to a public house to be social. They want to talk. Get vocal with a local. This is easiest at the bar, where people assume you're in the mood to talk (rather than at a table, where you're allowed a bit of privacy). The pub is the next best thing to having relatives in town. Cheers!

Pub Grub

Pub grub gets better each year. It's London's best eating value. For £6–8, you'll get a basic, budget, hot lunch or dinner in friendly surroundings. The *Good Pub Guide,* published annually by the British Consumers Union, is excellent. Pubs attached to restaurants often have fresher food and a chef who knows how to cook.

Pubs generally serve traditional dishes, like fish-and-chips, vegetables, "bangers and mash" (sausages and mashed potatoes), roast beef with Yorkshire pudding (batter-baked in the oven), and assorted meat pies, such as steak-and-kidney pie or shepherd's pie (stewed lamb topped with mashed potatoes). Side dishes include salads (sometimes even a nice self-serve salad bar), vegetables, and—invariably—"chips" (French fries). "Crisps" are potato chips. A "jacket potato" (baked potato stuffed with fillings of your choice) can almost be a meal in itself. A "ploughman's lunch" is a modern "traditional English meal" of bread, cheese, and sweet pickles that nearly every tourist tries... once. These days, you'll likely find more Italian pasta, curried dishes, and quiche on the menu than "traditional" fare.

"Have You Been Caught Short?"

The full pint of beer is under siege, or so claim supporters of the CAMRA (Campaign for Real Ale) movement. They're referring to being "caught short"—ordering a pint and getting less than a full glass of liquid, topped off with some foam. According to research they cite, eight in 10 pints are short, costing British drinkers £1 million per day. To combat this practice, they've been providing pub-goers with cards to measure the "real price" of their drinks. They've also been encouraging pubs to use oversized glasses, marked with pint and half-pint lines, so pouring a 100-percent full serving is easier and less open to debate. Meanwhile, pub-goers should keep an eye on that costly foam (for more information, see www.camraactionnetwork.org.uk/full_pints).

In a brim measure glass a PINT should come to HERE

HOLD AGAINST THE SIDE OF YOUR NEWLY FILLED PINT GLASS AND READ OFF BY HOW MUCH YOU HAVE BEEN SHORT MEASURED.

PRICE PER PINT

£1.60	£1.70	£1.80	£1.90	£2.00	£2.10	£2.20
8p	8.5p	9p	9.5p	10p	10.5p	11p
14p	15p	16p	16.5p	17.5p	18.5p	19.5p
21p	22p	23.5p	25p	26p	27.5p	28.5p
29.5p	31p	33p	35p	36.5p	38.5p	40p
36p	38.5p	40.5p	43p	45p	47.5p	50p

Prices are rounded to the nearest half pence.
For use with brim measure glasses only. Due to rounding and printing tolerances values should be used as a guide only.

Meals are usually served from 12:00 to 14:00 and from 18:00 to 20:00, not throughout the day. There's usually no table service. Order at the bar, then take a seat and they'll bring the food when it's ready (or sometimes you pick it up at the bar). Pay at the bar (sometimes when you order, sometimes after you eat). Don't tip unless it's a place with full table service. Servings are hearty, service is quick, and you'll rarely spend more than £8. A beer or cider adds another couple of pounds. (Free tap water is always available.) Pubs that advertise their food and are crowded with locals are less likely to be the kinds that serve only lousy microwaved snacks. Because pubs make more money selling drinks than food, many stop cooking fairly early.

Pub Appreciation

The pub is the heart of the people's England, where all manner of folks have, for generations, found their respite from work and a home-away-from-home. England's classic pubs are national treasures, with great cultural value and rich history, not to mention good beer and grub.

The Golden Age for pub-building was in the late Victorian era (c. 1880–1905), when pubs were independently owned and land prices were high enough to make it worthwhile to invest in fixing up pubs. The politics were pro-pub as well: Conservatives, backed by Big Beer, were in, and temperance-minded liberals were out.

Especially in class-conscious Victorian times, traditional pubs were divided into sections by elaborate screens (now mostly gone), allowing the wealthy to drink in a more refined setting, while commoners congregated on the pub's rougher side. These were really "public houses," featuring nooks (snugs) for groups and clubs to meet, friends and lovers to rendezvous, and families to get out of the house at night. Since many pub-goers were illiterate, pubs were simply named for the picture hung outside (e.g., The Crooked Stick, The Queen's Arms—meaning her coat of arms).

Historic pubs still dot the London cityscape. The only place to see the very oldest-style tavern in the "domestic tradition" is at **Ye Olde Cheshire Cheese**, which was rebuilt in 1667 from a 16th-century tavern (see description in The City Walk, page 110; open daily, 145 Fleet Street, located on map on page 287, Tube: Blackfriars, tel. 020/7353-6170). Imagine this place in the pre-Victorian era: With no bar, drinkers gathered around the fireplaces, while tap boys shuttled tankards up from the cellar. (This was long before bar-room taps were connected to casks in the cellar. Oh, and don't say "keg"—that's a gassy modern thing.)

Late Victorian pubs, such as the 1897 **Princess Louise** (open daily, 208 High Holborn, see map on page 293, Tube: Holborn, tel. 020/7405-8816) are more common. These places are fancy, often coming with heavy embossed wallpaper ceilings, decorative tile work, fine-etched glass, ornate carved stillions (the big central hutch for storing bottles and glass), and even urinals equipped with a place to set your glass. London's best Art Nouveau pub is **The Black Friar** (c. 1900–1915), with fine carved capitals, lamp holders, and quirky phrases worked into the decor (open daily,

Historic Pubs

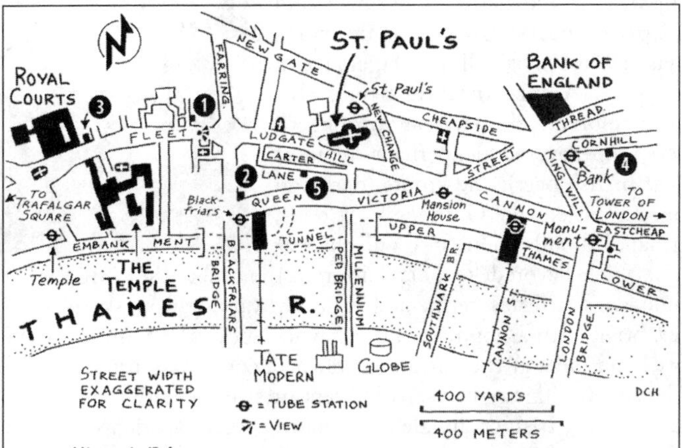

Historic Pubs

1. Ye Olde Cheshire Cheese
2. The Black Friar
3. The Old Bank of England
4. The Counting House

Other Eatery

5. Degustibus Sandwiches

across from Tube: Blackfriars at 174 Queen Victoria Street, tel. 020/7236-5474).

The "former-bank pubs" represent a more modern trend in pub building. As banks increasingly go electronic, they're moving out of lavish, high-rent old buildings. Many of these former banks are being refitted as pubs with elegant bars and free-standing stillions, providing a fine centerpiece. Three such pubs are **The Old Bank of England** (closed Sat–Sun, 194 Fleet Street, Tube: Temple, tel. 020/7430-2255), **The Jugged Hare** (open daily, 172 Vauxhall Bridge Road, see map on page 271, Tube: Victoria, tel. 020/7828-1543; also see listing on page 297) and **The Counting House** (closed Sat–Sun, 50 Cornhill, Tube: Bank, tel. 020/7283-7123; see longer listing on page 299).

Go pubbing in the evening for a lively time, or drop by during the quiet late morning (from 11:00), when the pub is empty and filled with memories. For more information, see Bob Steel's Web site, www.aletrails.com. Bob also offers an historic pubs tour (about £50 for a leisurely half-day walk).

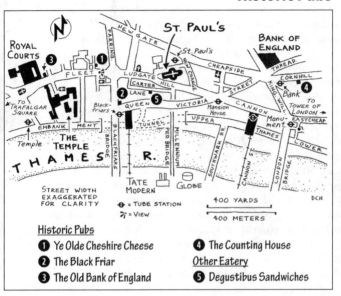

Beer

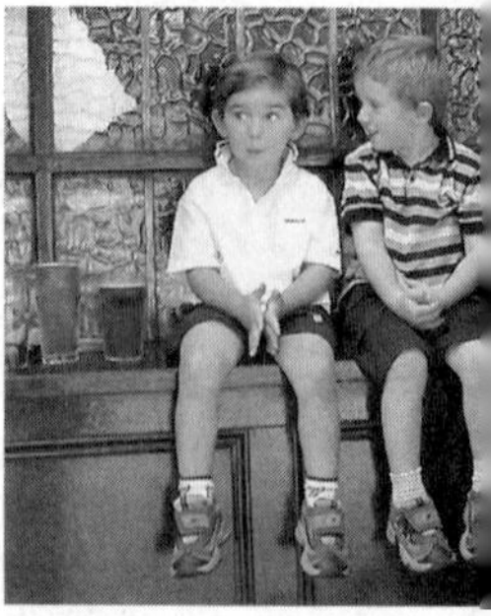

The British take great pride in their beer. Many Brits think that drinking beer cold and carbonated, as Americans do, ruins the taste. Most pubs will have **lagers** (cold, refreshing, American-style beer), **ales** (amber-colored, cellar-temperature beer), **bitters** (hop-flavored ale, perhaps the most typical British beer), and **stouts** (dark and somewhat bitter, like Guinness). At pubs, long-handled pulls are used to pull the traditional, rich-flavored "real ales" up from the cellar. These are the connoisseur's favorites: fermented naturally, varying from sweet to bitter, often with a hoppy or nutty flavor. Notice the fun names. Short-hand pulls at the bar mean colder, fizzier, mass-produced, and less interesting keg beers. Mild beers are sweeter, with a creamy malt flavoring. Irish cream ale is a smooth, sweet experience. Try the draft cider (sweet or dry)...carefully.

Order your beer at the bar and pay as you go, with no need to tip. An average beer costs £2.50. Part of the experience is standing before a line of "hand pulls," or taps, and wondering which beer to choose.

Drinks are served by the pint (20-ounce imperial size) or the half-pint. (It's almost feminine for a man to order just a half; I order mine with quiche.) Proper English ladies like a half-beer and half-lemonade **shandy.**

Besides beer, many pubs actually have a good selection of wines by the glass, a fully stocked bar for the gentleman's "G and T" (gin and tonic), and the increasingly popular bottles of alcohol-plus-sugar (such as Bacardi Breezers) for the younger, working-class set. **Pimm's** is a refreshing and fruity summer cocktail, traditionally popular during Wimbledon. It's an upper-class drink...a rough bloke might insult a pub by claiming it sells more Pimm's than beer. Teetotalers can order from a wide variety of soft drinks.

Indian Food

Eating Indian food is "going local" in cosmopolitan, multi-ethnic London. Take the opportunity to sample food from Britain's former colony. Indian cuisine is as varied as the country itself. In general, they use more exotic spices than we're accustomed to—some hot, some sweet.

As with Chinese food, you build an Indian meal with several dishes. The portions can be quite small, so you'll need at least two dishes per person. A typical meal for one might include **dal** (lentil soup) as a starter; one **meat dish** with sauce (for example, chicken curry, chicken *tikka masala* in a creamy tomato sauce, grilled

English Chocolate

My chocoholic readers are enthusiastic about English chocolates. Like other dairy products, chocolate seems richer and creamier here than it does in the United States, so even the basics like Kit Kat and Twix have a different taste. Some favorites include Cadbury Gold bars (filled with liquid caramel), Cadbury Crunchie bars, Nestle's Lion bars (layered wafers covered in caramel and chocolate), Cadbury's Boost bars (a shortcake biscuit with caramel in milk chocolate), and Galaxy chocolate bars (especially the ones with hazelnuts). Thornton shops (in larger train stations) sell a box of sweets called the Continental Assortment, which comes with a tasting guide. The highlight is the mocha white-chocolate truffle. British M&Ms, called Smarties, are better than American ones. For a few extra pence, adorn your ice cream cone with a "flake"—a chocolate bar stuck right into the middle.

chicken tandoori, or the spicy chicken vindaloo); one **vegetable dish** (in a similar sauce to the meat); **rice** (boiled white basmati rice, fried rice, or *pilau*—cooked in broth with meats); **nan** (a leavened, grilled tortilla, used by Indians to mop up food); and an **Indian beer** (wine and Indian food don't really mix).

A meal like this will set you back about £20. Many restaurants offer a fixed-price combination meal that's simpler and cheaper than ordering à la carte.

Desserts (Sweets)

To the British, the traditional word for dessert is **pudding,** although it's also referred to as **sweets** these days. Sponge cake, cream, fruitcake, and meringue are key players.

Trifle is the best-known British concoction, consisting of sponge cake soaked in brandy or sherry (or orange juice for children), then covered with jam and/or fruit and custard cream. Whipped cream can sometimes put the final touch on this "light" treat.

Castle puddings are sponge puddings cooked in small molds and topped with Golden Syrup (a popular brand and a cross between honey and maple syrup). **Bread and butter pudding** consists of slices of French bread baked with milk, cream, eggs, and raisins (similar to the American preparation), served warm with cold cream. **Hasty pudding,** supposedly the invention of people in a hurry to avoid the bailiff, is made from stale bread with dried fruit and milk. **Queen of puddings** is a breadcrumb pudding topped with warm jam, meringue, and cream. **Treacle pudding** is a popular steamed pudding whose "sponge" mixture combines flour, suet (animal fat), butter, sugar, and milk. **Christmas pudding** (also called plum pudding) is a dense mixture with dried and candied fruit served with brandy butter or hard sauce.

Spotted Dick is a sponge pudding with currants. How did it get its name? Some say it looks like a spotted dog, and dogs were often called Dick. Another theory suggests that "Dick," "duff," and "dog" are all variants of the word "dough." One thing's for sure: The stuff isn't selling very well today, thanks to the name's connotation. Grocers are considering renaming it "Spotted Richard."

The English version of **custard** is a smooth, yellow liquid. Cream tops most everything custard does not. There's **single cream** for coffee. **Double cream** is really thick. **Whipped cream** is familiar, and **clotted cream** is the consistency of butter.

Fool is a dessert with sweetened pureed fruit (such as rhubarb, gooseberry, or black currants) mixed with cream or custard and chilled. Elderflower is a popular flavoring for sorbet.

Scones are tops, and many inns and restaurants have their secret recipes. Whether made with fruit or topped with clotted cream, scones take the cake.

Afternoon Tea

People of leisure punctuate their afternoon with a "cream tea" at a tearoom. You'll get a pot of tea, small finger foods (like cucumber sandwiches), homemade scones, jam, and thick clotted cream. For maximum pinkie-waving taste per calorie, slice your scone thin like a miniature loaf of bread. Tearooms, which often serve appealing light meals, are usually open for lunch and close at about 17:00, just before dinner.

While teatime is still going strong, the new phenomenon is coffee shops: Starbucks and its competitors have sprouted up all over town, providing cushy and social watering holes with comfy chairs, easy WCs, £2 lattes, and a nice break between sights. Many locals are anti-Starbucks, however, claiming the coffee is better and cheaper at London's innumerable Italian cafés.

Tipping

Tipping is an issue only at restaurants and fancy pubs that have waiters and waitresses. If you order your food at a counter, don't tip.

If the menu states that service is included, there's no need to tip beyond that. If service isn't included, tip about 10 percent by rounding up. Leave the tip on the table, or hand it to your server with your payment for the meal and say, "Keep the rest, please."

RESTAURANTS

Near Trafalgar Square

Each of these places is within about 100 yards of Trafalgar Square.

To locate the following restaurants, see the map on page 293.

St. Martin-in-the-Fields Café in the Crypt is just right for a tasty meal on a monk's budget, sitting on somebody's tomb in an ancient crypt. While their enticing buffet line is kept stocked all day, their cheap sandwich bar is generally sold out by 11:30 (£6–8 cafeteria plates, Mon–Wed 10:00–20:00, Thu–Sat 10:00–22:00, Sun 12:00–20:00, profits go to the church, underneath Church of St. Martin-in-the-Fields on Trafalgar Square, Tube: Charing Cross, tel. 020/7839-4342). While here, check out the concert schedule for the busy church upstairs.

The Chandos Pub's Opera Room floats amazingly apart from the tacky crush of tourism around Trafalgar Square. Look for it opposite the National Portrait Gallery (corner of William Street and St. Martin's Lane) and climb the stairs to the Opera Room. This is a fine Trafalgar rendezvous point—smoky, but wonderfully local. They serve traditional, plain-tasting £6–7 pub meals (kitchen open Mon–Wed 11:00–19:00, Thu–Sun until 18:00, order and pay at the bar, tel. 020/7836-1401). The ground-floor pub is a "spit and sawdust" type of pub, with serious beer and some toasted sandwiches.

Gordon's Wine Bar, with a simple, steep staircase leading into a candlelit 15th-century wine cellar, is filled with dusty old bottles, faded British memorabilia, and local nine-to-fivers. At the buffet, choose a hot meal or a fine plate of cheeses and various cold cuts. (One £7 cold plate, which comes with a salad bar and a couple of glasses of wine, provides a light, economical meal for two.) Then step up to the wine bar and consider the many varieties of wine and port available by the glass. This place is passionate about port. The low, carbon-crusted vaulting deeper in the back seems to intensify the Hogarth-painting atmosphere. While it's crowded, you can normally corral two chairs and grab the corner of a table (arrive before 17:30 to get a seat, Mon–Sat 11:00–23:00, Sun 12:00–22:00, 2 blocks from Trafalgar Square, bottom of Villiars Street at #47, Tube: Embankment, tel. 020/7930-1408). On hot days, the crowd spills out into a leafy back patio.

The Lord Moon of the Mall Pub fills a great old former Barclays Bank building a block down Whitehall from Trafalgar Square. They have real ales on tap and good, cheap pub grub, including a two-meals-for-the-price-of-one deal (£7.50, offer valid Mon–Fri 14:00–21:30, all day Sat–Sun). The pub is kid-friendly and smoke-free throughout (daily 10:00–23:00, 18 Whitehall, tel. 020/7839-7701). Nearby are several cheap cafeterias and pizza joints.

Sherlock Holmes Pub has a casual ground-floor section serving cheap grub and a stodgier upstairs restaurant with a spy-theme menu (£10 main courses). Fans of the fictional detective will appreciate sitting next to a wonderful replica of Holmes' 221-B Baker

Street home. The pub is located in the former Northumberland Hotel (featured in Holmes stories). The former Old Scotland Yard was just across the street (daily 11:00–23:00, 10 Northumberland Street, Tube: Charing Cross/Embankment, tel. 020/7930-2644).

Crivelli's Garden Restaurant, serving a classy lunch in the National Gallery, is a good place to treat your palate to pricey, light Mediterranean cuisine (£15 lunches, daily 10:00–17:00, 1st floor of Sainsbury Wing).

Cheap Eating near Piccadilly

Hungry and broke in the theater district? Head for Panton Street (off Haymarket, 2 blocks southeast of Piccadilly Circus) where several hard-working little places compete, all seeming to offer a three-course meal for about £7. Peruse the entire block (vegetarian, Japanese, Pizza Express, Moroccan, Thai, Chinese, and 2 famous London eateries) before making your choice. **Stockpot** is a mushy-peas kind of place, famous and rightly popular for its edible, cheap meals (daily 7:00–22:00, 38 Panton Street). The **West End Kitchen** (across the street at #5, same hours and menu) is a direct competitor that's just as good. Vegetarians prefer the **Woodland South Indian Vegetarian Restaurant**.

The palatial **Criterion Brasserie** serves a special £15 two-course "Anglo-French" menu (or £18 for 3 courses) under gilded tiles and chandeliers in a dreamy Byzantine church setting from 1880. It's right on Piccadilly Circus but a world away from the punk junk. The house wine is great and so is the food (specials available Mon–Sat 12:00–14:30 & 17:30–19:00, closed Sun, tel. 020/7930-0488). After 19:00, the menu becomes really expensive. Anyone can drop in for coffee or a drink.

Hip Eating from Covent Garden to Soho

London has a trendy, Generation X scene that most Beefeater-seekers miss entirely. These restaurants are scattered throughout the hipster, gay, and girlie-bar district, teeming each evening with fun-seekers and theater-goers. Even if you plan to have dinner elsewhere, it's a treat to just wander around this lively area. Beware of the extremely welcoming girls that stand outside the strip bars. But if you're curious, head down Great Windmill Street and stop by the door at each of the three bars. Enjoy the sales pitch, but only fools enter—like a fish attracted to a fancy, well-polished lure, you hardly see the hook. Naive guys bite for the "£5 drink and show" and step in...and then can't get out without emptying their wallets.

Belgo Centraal serves hearty Belgian specialties. It's a seafood, chips, and beer emporium dressed up as a mod-monastic refectory—with noisy acoustics and waiters garbed as Trappist monks. The classy restaurant section is more comfortable and less

Central London Eateries

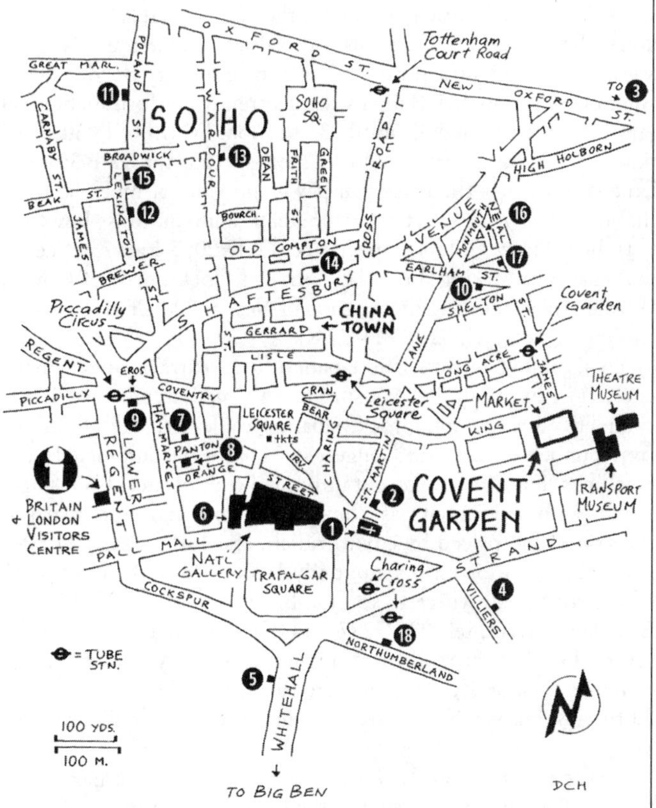

1. St. Martin-in-the-Fields Café in the Crypt
2. The Chandos Pub's Opera Room
3. To The Princess Louise Pub
4. Gordon's Wine Bar
5. The Lord Moon of the Mall Pub
6. Crivelli's Garden Restaurant
7. Pizza Express, Stockpot & West End Kitchen
8. Woodland South Indian Vegetarian Rest.
9. Criterion Brasserie
10. Belgo Centraal
11. Yo! Sushi
12. Wagamama Noodle Bar
13. Soho Spice Indian & Busaba Eathai Thai Rest.
14. Y Ming Chinese Rest.
15. Andrew Edmunds & Mildred's Vegetarian Rest.
16. Neal's Yard Eateries
17. Food for Thought Café
18. Sherlock Holmes Pub

rowdy, but usually requires reservations. It's often more fun to just grab a spot in the boisterous beer hall, with its tight, communal benches (no reservations accepted). The same menu and specials work on both sides. Belgians claim they eat as well as the French and as heartily as the Germans. Specialties include mussels, great fries, and a stunning array of dark, blond, and fruity Belgian beers. Belgo actually makes Belgian things trendy—a formidable feat (£10–14 meals; open daily until 23:00; Mon–Fri 17:00–18:30—or 5 p.m.–6:30 p.m.—"beat the clock" meal specials for £5–6.30—the time you order is the price you pay—and you get mussels, fries, and beer; no meal-splitting after 18:30, and you must buy food with beer; daily £6 lunch special 12:00–17:00; 2 kids eat free for each parent ordering a regular entree; 1 block north of Covent Garden Tube station at intersection of Neal and Shelton streets, 50 Earlham Street, tel. 020/7813-2233).

Yo! Sushi is a futuristic Japanese-food-extravaganza experience. It's not cheap, but it's sure to be a memorable experience, complete with thumping rock, Japanese cable TV, a 195-foot-long conveyor belt—the world's longest sushi bar—and automated sushi machines. For £1 each you get unlimited tea or water (from spigot at bar, with or without gas). Snag a bar stool and grab dishes as they rattle by (priced by color of dish; check the chart: £1.50–5 per dish, £1.50 for miso soup, daily 12:00–24:00, 2 blocks south of Oxford Street, where Lexington Street becomes Poland Street, 52 Poland Street, tel. 020/7287-0443). (If you like Yo!, there are several locations around town, including a handy branch a block from the London Eye on Belvedere Road, as well as outlets within Selfridges, Harvey Nichols department stores, and Whiteleys Mall on Queensway—see below.)

Wagamama Noodle Bar is a noisy, pan-Asian, organic slurpathon. As you enter, check out the kitchen and listen to the roar of the basement, where benches rock with happy eaters. Everybody sucks. Stand against the wall to feel the energy of all this "positive eating" (£12 meals, daily 12:00–23:00, crowded after 20:00, non-smoking, 10-A Lexington Street, tel. 020/7292-0990 but no reservations taken). If you like this place, there are now handy branches all over town, including one near the British Museum (Streatham Street), High Street Kensington (#26), in Harvey Nichols (109 Knightsbridge), Covent Garden (Tavistock Street), Leicester Square (Irving Street), Piccadilly Circus (Norris Street), Fleet Street (#109), and between St. Paul's and the Tower of London (22 Old Broad Street).

Soho Spice Indian is where modern Britain meets Indian tradition—fine cuisine in a trendy, jewel-tone ambience. Unlike many Indian restaurants, when you order an entrée here (£10), it comes with side dishes—nan, dal, rice, and vegetables (£7 lunch special, daily 12:00–22:30, non-smoking, 5 blocks north of Piccadilly Circus at 124 Wardour Street, tel. 020/7434-0808).

Busaba Eathai Thai Restaurant is a hit with locals for its snappy service, casual-yet-high-energy ambience and good, inexpensive Thai cuisine. You'll sit communally around big, square 16-person hardwood tables or in two-person tables by the window—with everyone in the queue staring at your noodles. They don't take reservations, so arrive by 19:00 or line up (£10–14 meals, daily 12:00–23:00, 106 Wardour Street, tel. 020/7255-8686).

Y Ming Chinese Restaurant—across Shaftesbury Avenue from the ornate gates, clatter, and dim sum of Chinatown—has clean European decor, serious but helpful service, and authentic Northern Chinese cooking (good £10 meal deal offered 12:00–18:00—last order at 18:00, Mon–Sat 12:00–23:30, closed Sun, 35 Greek Street, tel. 020/7734-2721).

Andrew Edmunds Restaurant is a tiny, candlelit place where you'll want to hide your camera and guidebook and act as local as possible. This great little place—with a jealous and loyal clientele—is the closest I've found to Parisian quality in a cozy restaurant in London. The modern European cooking with a creative seasonal menu is worth the splurge (£25 meals, daily 12:30–15:00 & 18:00–22:45, come early or call ahead, request ground floor rather than basement, 46 Lexington Street in Soho, tel. 020/7437-5708).

Mildred's Vegetarian Restaurant, across from Andrew Edmunds, has cheap prices, an enjoyable menu, and a plain-yet-pleasant interior filled with happy eaters (£7 meals, Mon–Sat 12:00–23:00, closed Sun, 45 Lexington Street, tel. 020/7494-1634).

Neal's Yard is *the* place for cheap, hip, and healthy eateries near Covent Garden. The neighborhood is a tabouli of fun, hippie-type cafés. One of the best is **Food for Thought,** packed with local health nuts (good £5 vegetarian meals, Mon–Sat 12:00–20:30, Sun 12:00–17:00, non-smoking, 2 blocks north of Covent Garden Tube station, 31 Neal Street, near Neal's Yard, tel. 020/7836-0239).

The Soho "Food is Fun" Three-Course Dinner Crawl: For a multicultural, movable feast, consider eating (or splitting) one course and enjoying a drink at each of these places. Start around 18:00 to avoid lines, get in on early specials, and find waiters willing to let you split a meal. Prices, while reasonable by London standards, add up. Servings are large enough to share. All are open nightly. Arrive before 18:00 at **Belgo Centraal** and split the early-bird dinner special: a kilo of mussels, fries, and dark Belgian beer. At **Yo! Sushi,** have beer or sake and a few dishes. Slurp your last course at **Wagamama Noodle Bar.** Then, for dessert, people-watch at Leicester Square.

Near Recommended Victoria Station Accommodations

Here are places a couple of blocks southwest of Victoria Station where I've enjoyed eating (see map on page 271).

Ebury Wine Bar, filled with young professionals, provides a classy atmosphere, delicious £15–18 meals, and a £14 two-course special from 18:00–19:30. In the delightful back room, the fancy menu features modern European cuisine with an accent on French; at the wine bar, find cheaper food that's still a cut above pub grub. This is emphatically a "traditional wine bar," without a single beer on tap (Mon–Sat 11:00–23:00, Sun 18:00–22:00, reserve after 20:00, 139 Ebury Street, at intersection with Elizabeth Street, near bus station, tel. 020/7730-5447).

Goya Spanish Restaurant and Tapas Bar is popular for its classy, old-church-library ambience and tasty, reasonably priced food (£15 meals, good Spanish wine by the glass, daily 11:30–23:00, 2 Eccleston Place, tel. 020/7730-4299). Several cheap places are around the corner on Elizabeth Street (#23 for take-out or eat-in, super-absorbent fish-and-chips).

The Duke of Wellington pub is good, if somewhat smoky, and dominated by local drinkers. It's the neighborhood place for dinner, with woody sidewalk seating and an inviting interior (£6–7 meals, daily specials, Mon–Sat 11:00–15:00 & 18:00–21:00, closed Sun, 63 Eaton Terrace, at intersection with Chester Row, tel. 020/7730-1782).

The Belgravia Pub is new and more family-friendly than The Duke of Wellington, earning a good reputation for its salads and English and Italian fare (£4–6 meals, beer garden seating or plush interior, open daily, corner of Ebury Street and South Eaton Place).

Jenny Lo's Tea House is a simple, budget place serving up reliably tasty £5–8 eclectic Chinese-style meals to locals in the know. While the menu is small, everything is high quality. Jenny clearly learned from her father, Ken Lo, one of the most famous Cantonese chefs in Britain, whose fancy place is just around the corner (Mon–Fri 11:30–15:00 & 18:00–22:00, Sat 18:00–22:00, closed Sun, cash only, 14 Eccleston Street, tel. 020/7259-0399).

La Poule au Pot, ideal for a romantic splurge, offers a classy, candlelit ambience with well-dressed patrons and expensive but fine country-style French cuisine (£15 lunch, £25 dinners, daily 12:30–14:30 & 18:45–23:00, Sun until 22:00, leafy patio dining, reservations smart, end of Ebury Street at intersection with Pimlico Road, 231 Ebury Street, tel. 020/7730-7763).

Grumbles brags it's been serving "good food and wine at non-scary prices since 1964." Offering a delicious mix of "modern eclectic French and traditional English," this hip and cozy little place is *the* spot to eat well in this otherwise workaday neighborhood

(£12–22 meals, £10 lunch specials, reservations wise, self-serve launderette across the street open evenings, 2 nice sidewalk tables, daily 12:00–14:30 & 18:00–22:30, half a block north of Belgrave Road at 35 Churton Street, tel. 020/7834-0149). While they have seating downstairs, I'd avoid it; call ahead to reserve a spot outside or on the appealing and cozy ground floor.

Chimes English Restaurant and Cider Bar comes with a fresh country farm ambience, serious ciders (rare in London), and very good, traditional English food (2-course meals £13, hearty salads, daily 12:00–14:30 & 17:30–22:15, 26 Churton Street, tel. 020/7821-7456). Experiment with the cider—it's legal here...just barely.

The Jugged Hare is a pub in a lavish old bank building, its vaults replaced by kegs of beer and a fine kitchen. They have a fun, traditional menu with more fresh veggies than fries, and a plush and vivid pub scene good for a meal or just a drink (£7 meals, daily 12:00–21:00, 172 Vauxhall Bridge Road, tel. 020/7828-1543).

Seafresh Fish Restaurant is the neighborhood place for plaice–either take-out on the cheap or eat-in, enjoying a chrome-and-wood mod ambience with classic and creative fish-and-chips cuisine. It feels like the chippie of the 21st century (meals £5 to go, £8–10 to sit, Mon–Sat 12:00–15:00 & 17:00–22:30, closed Sun, 80 Wilton Road, tel. 020/7828-0747).

If you miss America, there's a mall-type **food court** at Victoria Place, upstairs in Victoria Station; **Café Rouge** seems to be the most popular here (£8–11 dinners, daily 9:30–22:30).

Groceries in and near Victoria Station: A large grocery, **Sainsbury's Local,** is on Victoria Street in front of the station, just past the buses (daily 6:00–24:00). In the station you'll find another, smaller Sainsbury's (at rear entrance, on Eccleston Street) and a couple other late-hours mini-markets.

Near Recommended Notting Hill B&Bs and Bayswater Hotels

The road called Queensway is a multi-ethnic food circus, lined with lively and inexpensive eateries. See the map on page 277.

Maggie Jones, exuberantly rustic and very English, serves my favorite £30 London dinner. You'll get fun-loving if brash service, and solid English cuisine, including huge plates of crunchy vegetables—by candlelight. Avoid the stuffy basement on hot summer nights, and request upstairs seating for the noisy but less cramped section. If you eat well once in London, eat here—and do it quick, before it burns down (daily 12:30–14:30 & 18:30–23:00, less expensive lunch menu, reservations recommended, friendly staff, 6 Old Court Place, just east of Kensington Church Street, near High Street Kensington Tube stop, tel. 020/7937-6462).

The **Churchill Arms** pub and **Thai Kitchens** (same location) is a local hangout, with good beer and old-English ambience in front and hearty £6 Thai plates in an enclosed patio in the back. You can eat the Thai food in this tropical hideaway or in the smoky but wonderfully atmospheric pub section. Arrive by 18:00 to avoid a line. During busy times, diners are limited to an hour at the table (daily 12:00–21:30, 119 Kensington Church Street, tel. 020/7792-1246).

Prince Edward Pub serves good pub grub in a quintessential pub setting (£8–10 meals, daily 12:00–15:00 & 18:00–22:00, closed Sun evenings, plush-pubby indoor seating or sidewalk tables, 2 blocks north of Bayswater Road at the corner of Dawson Place and Hereford Road, 73 Prince's Square, tel. 020/7727-2221).

Café Diana is a healthy little eatery serving sandwiches, salads, and Middle Eastern food. It's decorated—almost shrine-like—with photos of Princess Diana, who used to drop by for pita sandwiches (daily 8:00–22:30, 5 Wellington Terrace, on Bayswater Road, opposite Kensington Palace Garden Gates—where Di once lived, tel. 020/7792-9606).

Black and Blue is a trendy bistro serving steaks and burgers to local hipsters. Follow the crowds to the gas torches and patio seating (£10–12 meals, daily 12:00–23:00, 215 Kensington Church Street, tel. 020/7727-0004).

Royal China Restaurant is filled with London's Chinese, who consider this one of the city's best eateries. It's dressy in black, white, and chrome, with candles, brisk waiters, and fine food (£7–10 dishes, dim sum until 17:00, Mon–Sat 12:00–23:00, Sun 11:00–22:00, 13 Queensway, tel. 020/7221-2535).

Mr. Wu's Chinese Restaurant serves a 10-course buffet in a cramped little cafeteria. Just grab a plate and help yourself (£5, daily 12:00–23:00, check quality of buffet—right inside entrance—before committing as pickings can get slim, 54 Queensway, across from Bayswater Tube station, tel. 020/7243-1017).

Whiteleys Mall Food Court offers a fun selection of ethnic and fast-food eateries among Corinthian columns in a delightful mall (open daily long hours; options include Yo! Sushi, good salads at Café Rouge, pizza, Starbucks, and an Internet café; 2nd floor, corner of Porchester Gardens and Queensway).

Supermarket: **Europa** is a half-block from the Notting Hill Gate Tube stop (Mon–Sat 8:00–23:00, Sun 12:00–18:00, 112 Notting Hill Gate, near intersection with Pembridge Road).

Near Recommended Accommodations in South Kensington

Popular eateries line Old Brompton Road and Thurloe Street (Tube: South Kensington). See the map on page 275. The **Tesco Express** grocery store is handy for picnics (daily 7:00–24:00, 54 Old Brompton Road).

La Bouchee Bistro Café is a classy, hole-in-the-wall touch of France—candlelit and woody—serving early-bird, two-course £10 meals daily until 19:00 and £15 *plats du jour* all *jour* (daily 12:00–15:00 & 17:30–23:00, 56 Old Brompton Road, tel. 020/7589-1929). For Italian cuisine, **Falconiere Restaurant,** just down the street, is also popular (£8 pastas, £10 plates, £19 3-course dinner special, closed Sun, 84 Old Brompton Road, tel. 020/7589-2401).

Daquise, an authentic-feeling 1930s Polish time-warp, is ideal if you're in the mood for kielbasa and kraut. It's likeably dreary—fast, cheap, family-run, and a much-appreciated part of the neighborhood (£10 meals, £8 lunch special includes wine, daily 11:30–23:00, non-smoking, 20 Thurloe Street, tel. 020/7589-6117).

The Khyber Pass Tandoori Restaurant is nondescript but handy, serving tasty Indian cuisine. Locals in the know travel to eat here (£12 dinners, daily 12:00–14:30 & 18:00–23:30, 21 Bute Street, tel. 020/7589-7311).

Moti Mahal Indian Restaurant is a new favorite for value, offering Khyber Pass some competition. Find minimalist-yet-classy mod ambience and attentive service (daily 12:00–23:00, 3 Glendower Place, tel. 020/7584-8428).

The Zetland Arms serves good pub meals with a classic pub ambience on the ground floor and a fancier olde English restaurant atmosphere upstairs (same menu throughout, £6–10 meals, hearty £9 specials, table service, Mon–Fri 12:00–22:00, Sat–Sun 13:00–22:30, 2 Bute Street, tel. 020/7589-3813).

Elsewhere in London

Between St. Paul's and the Tower: The **Counting House,** formerly an elegant old bank, offers great £7 meals, nice homemade meat pies, fish, and fresh vegetables (Mon–Fri 12:00–21:00, closed Sat–Sun, gets really busy with the buttoned-down 9-to-5 crowd after 12:15, near Mansion House in the City, 50 Cornhill, tel. 020/7283-7123).

Near St. Paul's: **Degustibus Sandwiches** is where a top-notch artisan bakery meets the public, offering fresh, you-design-it sandwiches, salads, and soups with simple seating or take-out picnic sacks (great parks nearby), just a block below St. Paul's (Mon–Fri 7:00–17:00, closed Sat–Sun, from church steps follow signs to youth hostel a block downhill, 53 Carter Lane, tel. 020/723-60056).

Near the British Library: Drummond Street (running just west of Euston Station) is famous in London for very cheap and good Indian and vegetarian food. Consider **Chutneys** and **Ravi Shankar** for a good *thali.*

LONDON WITH CHILDREN

The key to a successful family trip to London is making everyone happy, including the parents. My family-tested recommendations have this objective in mind. Consider these tips:

- Take advantage of the local newsstand guides. *Time Out*'s family monthly is called *Kids Out*. *Time Out* and *What's On* also have handy kids' calendars listing activities and shows. The *Time Out* guidebook, *London for Children* (£9, is on sale in bookstores and many newsstands) is chock-a-block full of ideas for the serious parent tour guide in London.
- Ask the Britain and London Visitors Centre on Lower Regent Street about kids' events.
- London's big, budget chain hotels allow two kids to sleep for free in their already inexpensive rooms (see page 296).
- Eat dinner early (around 18:00) to miss the romantic crowd. Skip the famous places. Look instead for relaxed cafés, pubs (kids are welcome, though sometimes restricted to restaurant section or courtyard area), or even fast-food restaurants where kids can move around. Picnic lunches and dinners work well.
- Public WCs can be hard to find. Try department stores, museums, and restaurants, particularly fast-food restaurants.
- Follow this book's crowd-beating tips. Kids get antsy standing in a line for a museum. At each sight, ask about a kids' guide or flier.
- Hamleys is the biggest toy store in Britain (Mon–Sat 9:00–20:00, Thu until 21:00, Sun 12:00–18:00, 188 Regent Street, Tube: Oxford Circus, tel. 0870-333-2455, www.hamleys.com). It's also included in my shopping-oriented "Oxford Circus to Piccadilly Walk," page 306.
- Harry Potter fans (and Muggle parents) could visit places in London where scenes from the movies were filmed (see page 300).

SIGHTS AND ACTIVITIES

East London

Tower of London—The crown jewels are awesome, and the Beefeater tour plays off kids in a memorable and fun way. Avoid the long ticket lines by buying your ticket in advance at any London TI or the Tower Hill Tube station ticket office (£14.50, March–Oct Tue–Sat 9:00–18:00, Sun–Mon 10:00–18:00; Nov–Feb Tue–Sat 9:00–17:00, Sun–Mon 10:00–17:00; last entry 60 min before closing, no photos allowed of jewels or in chapels, Tube: Tower Hill, tel. 0870-751-5177).

✪ For Tower of London Tour, see page 257.

Museum of London—A very kid-friendly presentation takes you from the Romans to the 1920s. Parents will learn something, too. The events guide at the entry lists kids' activities (free, Mon–Sat 10:00–18:00, Sun 12:00–18:00, Tube: Barbican or St. Paul's, tel. 0870-444-3852).

Central London

Covent Garden—A great area for people-watching and candy-licking. Kids like the **London Transport Museum** with its interactive zone (£6, kids under 16 free, Sat–Thu 10:00–18:00, Fri 11:00–18:00, in southeast corner of Covent Garden courtyard); see page 51. The **Theatre Museum** is popular for its face painting (free, Tue–Sun 10:00–18:00, closed Mon, free guided tours at 12:00 and 14:00, a block east of Covent Garden's marketplace down Russell Street).

✪ See Theatre Museum Tour, page 252.

Trafalgar Square—The grand square is fun for kids (Tube: Charing Cross). Climb the lions, munch lunch in a crypt (at St. Martin-in-the-Fields, see below), and tour the National Gallery (below).

National Gallery—Begin your visit in the "Art Start" computer room. Your child can list his or her interests (cats, naval battles, and so on) and print out a tailor-made tour map for free. Ask about their Children's Trail fun walks (free admission, daily 10:00–18:00, Wed until 21:00, no photos allowed, on Trafalgar Square, Tube: Charing Cross or Leicester Square).

✪ See National Gallery Tour on page 145.

St. Martin-in-the-Fields—The church on Trafalgar Square has a brass-rubbing center that's fun for kids who'd like a souvenir to show for their efforts (free, donations welcome, open daily; for details, see page 48). The affordable Café in the Crypt has just the right spooky tables-on-tombstones ambience (£6–8 cafeteria plates, Mon–Wed 10:00–20:00, Thu–Sat 10:00–22:00, Sun 12:00–20:00).

London Eye Ferris Wheel—This grand Ferris wheel is a delight for the whole family (£12.50, 10 percent discount for online booking, April–mid-Sept daily 9:30–21:00, until 22:00 in July–Aug, mid-Sept–March 9:30–20:00, often closed Jan for maintenance, Tube: Waterloo or Westminster). For more specifics, including crowd avoidance, see page 65.

Changing of the Guard—Kids enjoy the bands and pageantry of the Buckingham Palace Changing of the Guard, but little ones get a better view at the inspection; they assemble at 11:00 at Wellington Barracks, and march out at 11:30 (see page 54). Horse-lovers enjoy the Horse Guards' colorful dismounting ceremony daily at 16:00 (on Whitehall, between Trafalgar Square and #10 Downing Street, Tube: Westminster); for details, see page 45.

Piccadilly Circus—This titillating district has lots of Planet Hollywood–type amusements, such as Segaworld. Be careful of fast-fingered riffraff. For more information on the district, see page 48. Hamleys toy store is just two blocks up Regent Street at #188 (hours listed above).

Shopping—If your teenager wants to bring home a few chic and cheap London fashions, Oxford Street (at the intersection of Regent Street) is a good place to start. Take the Tube to the Oxford Circus stop, and you'll be surrounded by lots of shops selling inexpensive, trendy clothes for teens. Two big ones—Top Shop and Miss Selfridge (girls only)—are located by the Tube entrance. Other stores such as Zara (#333), two H&M shops (#174–176 and #481–483), and music stores like HMV (#150 and #360) are also within close walking distance. Sandwich-to-go shops and coffeehouses (including a half-dozen Starbucks) offer easy rest stops for families. Also see the more upscale "Oxford Street to Piccadilly Walk" (page 306), which begins at the same Tube stop, but goes down Regent Street.

Theater—Long-running shows such as *The Lion King* (Lyceum) and *Mary Poppins* (Prince Edward) are kid- and parent-pleasers (see Entertainment chapter).

West London

Natural History Museum—This wonderful world of dinosaurs, volcanoes, meteors, and creepy-crawlies offers creative interactive displays (free, possible fee for special exhibits, Mon–Sat 10:00–18:00, Sun 11:00–18:00, last entrance 17:30, a long tunnel leads directly from South Kensington Tube station to museum, tel. 020/7942-5000, exhibit info and reservations tel. 020/7942-5011, www.nhm.ac.uk).

Science Museum—This museum, next door to the Natural History Museum, offers lots of hands-on fun and IMAX shows (also free, daily 10:00–18:00, Exhibition Road, tel. 0870-870-4868, www.sciencemuseum.org.uk). Both the Natural History and Science museums are kid-friendly. Check for special events and rotating exhibits (explained at each museum's entry and on their Web sites).

North London

Madame Tussaud's Waxworks—Despite the lines, the waxworks are popular with kids for gory stuff, pop and movie stars, everyone's favorite royals, and more. For discounted prices, go late (admission varies with time but about £23, kids-£19, after 17:00 it's £14, kids-£9; children under 5 always free; Mon–Fri 10:00–18:30, Sat–Sun 9:30–18:30, last entry 60 min before closing, Marylebone Road, Tube: Baker Street, www.madame-tussauds.com). For details and tips on crowd avoidance, see page 52.

London Zoo—This venerable animal habitat, with more than 8,000 creatures and a fine petting zoo, is one of the best in the world (£14, children-£1.25, family-£26, daily 10:00–17:30, last entry 16:30, in Regent's Park, Tube: Camden Town, then bus #274, tel. 020/7722-3333, www.zsl.org). Call for feeding and event times.

Fun Transportation

Thames Cruise—Young sailors delight in boats. Westminster Pier (near Big Ben) offers a lot of action, with round-trip cruises and boats to the Tower of London, Greenwich, and Kew Gardens. For details, see page 36.

Hop-on, Hop-off London Bus Tours—These two-hour double-decker bus tours, which drive by all the biggies, are fun for kids and stress-free for parents. You can stay on the bus the entire time, or "hop-on and hop-off" at any of the nearly 30 stops and catch a later bus (4–6/hr in summer, 3/hr in winter). To find out how to get a special price with this book, see page 34. The Original London Sightseeing Tour's language bus (marked with lots of flags or a green triangle) has a kids' track on the earphones, but then you miss the live guide.

Day Trip

Legoland Windsor—If your kids are loopy over Legos, they'll love a day trip to Legoland Windsor (£24, children-£22, under 3 free, £10 if you enter during last 2 hours; Windsor TI sells half-price tickets after 13:30; April–Oct daily 10:00–17:00, 18:00, or 19:00 depending upon season and day; closed most Tue–Wed in Sept–Oct, closed Nov–March except Dec 21–Jan 5, tel. 0870-504-0404, www.legoland.co.uk—discount for online bookings). For details, see page 340.

What to Avoid

The London Dungeon's popularity with teenagers makes it one of London's most-visited sights. I enjoy gore and torture as much as the next boy, but this is lousy gore and torture, and I would not waste the time or money on it with my child.

SHOPPING

Most stores are open Monday through Saturday from roughly 10:00 to 18:00, with a late night (until 19:00 or 20:00) on Wednesday or Thursday, depending on the neighborhood. On Sunday, when some stores are closed, shoppers hit the street markets. Consider these five ways to shop in London:

1. If all you need are souvenirs, a surgical strike at any souvenir shop will do.
2. Large department stores offer relatively painless one-stop shopping. Consider the down-to-earth Marks & Spencer (Mon–Sat 9:00–20:00, Thu until 21:00, Sun 12:00–18:00, 173 Oxford Street, Tube: Oxford Circus; another at 458 Oxford Street, Tube: Bond Street or Marble Arch, www.marksandspencer.com).
3. Connect small shops with a pleasant walk (see "Oxford Circus to Piccadilly Walk," below).
4. For flea-market fun, try one of the many street markets.
5. Gawkers as well as serious bidders can attend auctions.

Fancy Department Stores in East London

Harrods—Harrods is London's most famous and touristy department store. With a million square feet of retail space on seven floors, it's a place where some shoppers could spend all day. (To me, it's a department store.) Big yet classy, Harrods has everything from elephants to toothbrushes (Mon–Sat 10:00–19:00, closed Sun, mandatory storage for big backpacks-£2.50, on Brompton Road, Tube: Knightsbridge, tel. 020/7730-1234, www.harrods.com).

Sightseers should pick up the free *Store Guide* at any info post. Here's what I enjoyed: On the Ground and Lower Ground Floors, find the Food Halls, with their Edwardian tiled walls, creative and exuberant displays, and staff in period costumes—not quite like your local supermarket back home.

Descend to the Lower Ground Floor and follow signs to the Egyptian Escalator, where you'll find a memorial to Dodi Fayed and Princess Diana. The huge (and slightly creepy) bronze statue was commissioned by Dodi Fayed's father, Mohamed al-Fayed, who owns Harrods. Photos and flowers honor the late Princess and her lover, who both died in a car crash in Paris in 1997. See the wine glass still dirty from their last dinner, and the engagement ring that Dodi purchased the day before they died.

Ride the Egyptian Escalator—lined with pharaoh-headed sconces, papyrus-plant lamps, and hieroglyphic balconies (Harrods' owner is from Egypt)—to the Fourth Floor. From the escalator, make a U-turn left and head to the far corner of the store (toys) to find child-size luxury cars that actually work. A junior Jaguar or Mercedes will set you back about $13,000. The child's Hummer ($30,000) is as big as my car.

Also on the Fourth Floor is The Georgian Restaurant. Enjoy a fancy tea under a skylight as a pianist tickles the keys of a Bösendorfer, the world's most expensive piano (tea-£19, includes finger sandwiches and pastries, served after 15:45).

Many of my readers report that Harrods is overpriced, snooty, and teeming with American and Japanese tourists. Still, it's the palace of department stores. The nearby Beauchamp Place is lined with classy and fascinating shops.

Harvey Nichols—Once Princess Diana's favorite, "Harvey Nick's" remains the department store *du jour* (Mon–Tue and Sat 10:00–19:00, Wed–Fri until 20:00, Sun 12:00–18:00, near Harrods, Tube: Knightsbridge, 109 Knightsbridge, www.harveynichols.com). Want to pick up a little £20 scarf for the wife? You won't do it here, where they're more like £200. The store's fifth floor is a veritable food fest, with a gourmet grocery store, a fancy (smoky) restaurant, a Yo! Sushi bar, and a lively café. Consider a take-away tray of sushi to eat on a bench in the Hyde Park rose garden two blocks away.

Oxford Circus to Piccadilly Walk

For this walk from Oxford Circus to Piccadilly Street, allow three-quarters of a mile (and only you know how much money and time). If you'd like to stop for high tea at Fortnum & Mason (Tue–Sat 15:00–17:30), begin this walk after lunch. Many stores are open on Sunday from 12:00 to 18:00.

Oxford Circus to Piccadilly Walk

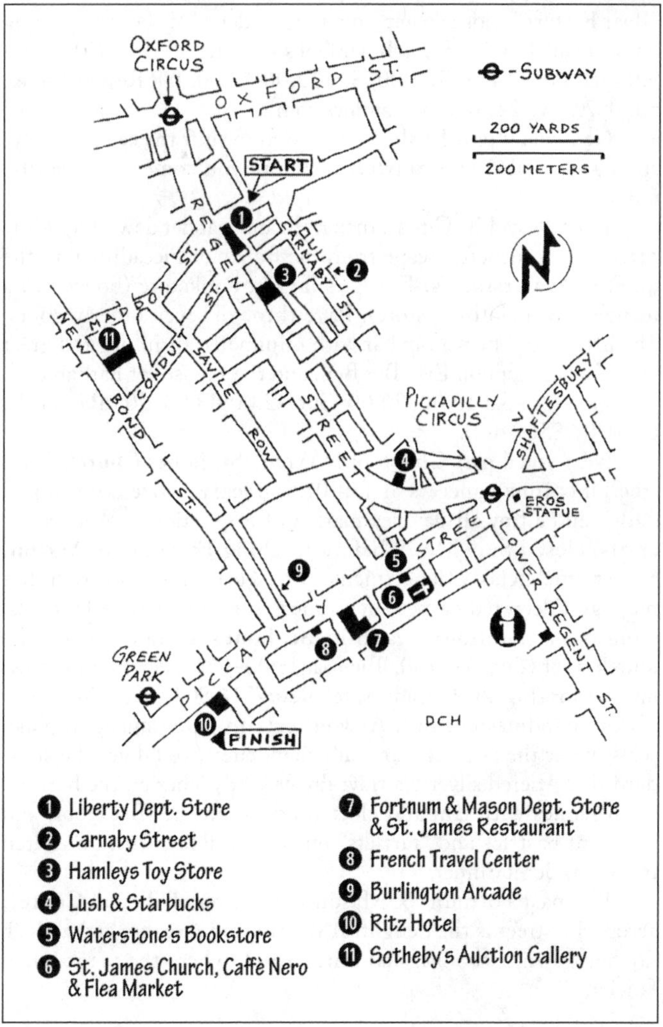

Starting from the Oxford Circus Tube stop, Regent Street leads past a diverse array of places to shop, all on the left-hand (east) side of the street. You'll find the following: **Liberty,** a big, stately, local-favorite department store (Mon–Sat 10:00–19:00, Thu until 20:00, Sun 12:00–18:00, 214 Regent Street, www.liberty.co.uk); the once-hippie-now-hip **Carnaby Street** a block away (with cafés and boutiques selling clothes, shoes, handmade soap, and so on; turn left at first alley after Liberty onto Foubert's Place); and **Hamleys,** the biggest toy store in Britain—seven floors buzzing with 28,000 toys, managed by a staff of 200. At the "Bear Factory," kids can get a made-to-order teddy bear by picking out a "bear skin," and watch while it's stuffed and sewn (Mon–Sat 9:00–20:00, Thu until 21:00, Sun 12:00–18:00, 188 Regent Street, tel. 0870-333-2455, www.hamleys.com).

Next you'll pass **Lush** (#80; stop in to sniff the earthy/fruity/spicy soap slabs) and **Starbucks** before you come to Piccadilly Circus.

From Piccadilly Circus, turn right and wander down Piccadilly Street. On your left, escape from the frenzy of Piccadilly into the quiet of **Waterstone's,** Europe's largest bookstore (housed in a former men's clothing store). Page through seven orderly floors. The fifth floor offers a hip bar with minimalist furniture and great views of the London Eye, Big Ben, and the Houses of Parliament's towers (Mon–Sat 10:00–20:00, Sun 12:00–18:00, 203 Piccadilly, tel. 020/7851-2400).

Next you'll pass Christopher Wren's **St. James Church** (with free lunchtime concerts at 13:00), the leafy **Caffè Nero** (open daily), and a tiny all-day flea market (Tue—antiques, Wed–Sat—crafts, closed Sun–Mon), before reaching **Fortnum & Mason,** an extremely classy department store. Fortnum—with rich displays and deep red carpet—feels more sumptuous than Harrods. Consider a traditional tea in its **St. James Restaurant,** on the fourth floor (£19.50–29.50, Tue–Sat 15:00–17:30, closed Sun, dress up a bit for this, 181 Piccadilly, tel. 020/7734-8040 ext. 2241, www.fortnumandmason.com). As you relax to piano music in plush seats under the elegant tearoom's chandeliers, you'll get the standard three-tiered silver tea tray: finger sandwiches on the bottom, fresh scones with jam and clotted cream on the first floor, and decadent pastries and "tartlets" on the top floor, with unlimited tea. Consider it dinner.

Just past Fortnum & Mason is the **French Travel Center;** across the street is the delightful **Burlington Arcade;** and a block farther down is the original **Ritz Hotel,** where the tea is much fancier.

Street Markets

Antique buffs, people-watchers, and folks who brake for garage sales love London's street markets. There's some good early-morning market activity somewhere any day of the week. The best are Portobello Road and Camden Market. Any London TI has a complete, up-to-date list. If you like to haggle, there are no holds barred in London's street markets. Warning: Markets attract two kinds of people: tourists and pickpockets.

Portobello Road Market—The flea market, with 2,000 stalls (hopping on Sat), has three sections: antiques at the top, produce in the middle, and clothing and books and fleas at the other end. Antiques are featured on Saturday (market open Mon–Wed and Fri–Sat 8:00–18:30, closes at 13:00 on Thu, closed Sun, Tube: Notting Hill Gate, near recommended B&Bs, tel. 020/7229-8354).

Camden Lock Market—This huge, trendy arts-and-crafts festival has become quite punky to many travelers. Still, it's London's fourth-most-popular tourist attraction (daily 10:00–18:00, Tube: Camden Town, tel. 020/7284-2084, www.camdenlock.net).

Brixton Market—Here the food, clothing, records, and hair-braiding throb with an Afro-Caribbean beat (Mon–Tue and Thu–Sat 9:00–18:00, closes at about 13:00 on Wed, closed Sun, Tube: Brixton).

Petticoat Lane Market—Expect budget clothing, leather, shoes, watches, jewelry, and crowds (Sun 9:00–14:00, sometimes later, Tube: Liverpool Street). The Columbia Road flower market is nearby (Sun mornings only).

Spitalfields Market—Housed under an old arcade, this market features more than a hundred merchants daily except Saturday. You'll find a lively organic food market, many ethnic eateries (including Bubba's BBQ), crafts, trendy clothes, bags, and an antique-and-junk market. There's a cutting-edge Fashion Market each Thursday, and a Record and Book Fair on the last Wednesday of each month (Mon–Fri 10:00–16:00, Sun 9:00–17:00, closed Sat, Tube: Liverpool Street; from the Tube stop, take Bishopsgate East exit, turn right, walk 2 blocks, and turn right on Brushfield Street; tel. 020/7377-1496).

Famous Auctions

London's famous auctioneers welcome the curious public for viewing and bidding. You can preview estate catalogs or browse auction calendars online. To ask questions or set up an appointment, contact **Sotheby's** (Mon–Fri 9:00–16:30, closed Sat–Sun, 34–35 New Bond Street, Tube: Oxford Circus, tel. 020/7293-5000, www.sothebys.com) or **Christie's** (Mon–Fri 9:00–16:30, Sun 14:00–17:00, closed Sat, 8 King Street, Tube: Green Park, tel. 020/7839-9060, www.christies.com).

VAT Refunds for Shoppers

Wrapped into the purchase price of your British souvenirs is a Value Added Tax (VAT) that's generally about 17.5 percent. If you make a purchase of more than £20 at a store that participates in the VAT refund scheme, you're entitled to get most of that tax back. Personally, I've never felt that VAT refunds are worth the hassle, but if you do, here's the scoop.

If you're lucky, the merchant will subtract the tax when you make your purchase (this is more likely to occur if the store ships

East End Walk

The East End, a formerly industrial area, has turned into one of London's trendy spots. Take a 30-minute walk around the Spitalfields Market neighborhood (Tube: Liverpool Street) to see the colorful mix of bustling markets, late-night dance clubs, the Bangladeshi ghetto, and tenements of Jack the Ripper's London.

Start at the Spitalfields Market. Across the street (to the east) is **The Ten Bells Pub**, at the intersection of Commercial Street and Brushfield/Fournier. Established in 1753, it was the hangout of one of the Ripper's victims. Across the street from the pub is **Christ Church**, with its impressive 225-foot steeple. Many Ripper witnesses knew the time of the crimes by remembering the church bells' chimes.

Head east a long block on Fournier Street to **Brick Lane**, where you're immediately immersed in "Banglatown," lined with Bangladeshi stores and restaurants—"the curry capital of Europe." At the intersection of Fournier Street and Brick Lane is the not-at-all-obvious neighborhood mosque. Two blocks north on Brick Lane is the former **Truman Brewery**, which now houses a Sunday market and trendy shops (good coffee at Cafe 1001). A half-block farther north, you'll find the old brewery **smokestack** and two trendy **nightclubs**: the Vibe Bar and 93 Feet East.

the goods to your home). Otherwise, here's what you'll need to do:

Get the paperwork. Have the merchant completely fill out the necessary refund document, called a "Tax-Free Shopping Cheque." You'll have to present your passport at the store.

Get your stamp at the border or airport. Have your cheque(s) stamped at your last stop in the European Union (e.g., the airport) by the customs agent who deals with VAT refunds. It's best to keep your purchases in your carry-on for viewing, but if they're too large or dangerous to carry on, then track down the proper customs agent to inspect them before you check your bag. You're not supposed to use your purchased goods before you leave. If you show up at customs wearing your new Wellingtons, officials might look the other way—or deny you a refund.

Collect your refund. You'll need to return your stamped documents to the retailer or its representative. Many merchants work with a service, such as Global Refund or Premier Tax Free, which have offices at major airports, ports, or border crossings. These services, which extract a 4 percent fee, can refund your money

Head south on Brick Lane, and turn right (west) on **Fashion Street**. Though it changes names several times, this road leads straight back to the Liverpool Street Station. Along the way, you'll pass the Islamic-looking **Abraham David Moorish Market**, now housing high-tech businesses. Where Fashion Street becomes White's Row, you could detour a block south to Brune Street to see Industrial Age **tenements**, the "Soup Kitchen for the Jewish Poor," and a nice view of the modern, bullet-shaped Swiss Re building. Also branching off White's Row is **Tenter Ground** street, where weavers once dried cloth "on tenter hooks," giving us the phrase. Continuing west, White's Row becomes narrow **Artillery Passage**, lined with teeny eateries, giving you an idea of how densely packed this neighborhood used to be when it was filled with grimy-faced, 19th-century factory workers. At the intersection with Sandy's Row are the **bollards** (black-white-red stakes in the pavement) alerting you that you're officially leaving the East End and entering the City of London. Continue west one block to busy Middlesex Street, with **Dirty Dick's Pub** (the name has a history, but the pub itself doesn't) and the **Liverpool Street** station and Tube stop (to the left).

At 8:45 on July 7, 2005, a Tube train had just pulled out of Liverpool Street station when it was rocked by a terrorist bomb—the first of four to hit London that day. The next day, Londoners were back on the Tube.

immediately in your currency of choice or credit your card (within 2 billing cycles). If you have to deal directly with the retailer, mail the store your stamped documents and then wait. It could take months.

Customs Regulations

You can take home $800 in souvenirs per person duty-free. The next $1,000 is taxed at a flat 3 percent. After that, you pay the individual item's duty rate. You can also bring in duty-free a liter of alcohol (slightly more than a standard-size bottle of wine), a carton of cigarettes, and up to 100 cigars. As for food, anything in cans or sealed jars is acceptable. Skip dried meats, cheeses, and fresh fruits and veggies. To check customs rules and duty rates, visit www.customs.gov.

ENTERTAINMENT

London bubbles with top-notch entertainment seven days a week: plays, movies, concerts, exhibitions, walking tours, shopping, and children's activities.

For the best list of what's happening and a look at the latest London scene, pick up a current copy of *Time Out* (£2.50, www.timeout.com) or *What's On In London* (£1.60, www.whatsoninlondon.co.uk) at any newsstand. The TI's free, monthly *London Planner* covers sights, events, and plays at least as well. For plays, also visit www.officiallondontheatre.co.uk. For a chatty, *People Magazine*–type Web site on London's entertainment, check www.thisislondon.com.

Choose from classical, jazz, rock, and far-out music, Gilbert and Sullivan, tango lessons, comedy, Baha'i meetings, poetry readings, spectator sports, theater, and the cinema. In Leicester Square, you'll find movies that have yet to be released in the States—if Hugh Grant is attending an opening-night premiere in London, it will likely be at one of the big movie houses here.

Theater (a.k.a. "Theatre")

London's theater rivals Broadway's in quality and beats it in price. Choose from Shakespeare, musicals, comedy, thrillers, sex farces, cutting-edge fringe, revivals starring movie celebs, and more. London does it all well. I prefer big, glitzy—even bombastic—musicals over serious chamber dramas, simply because London can deliver the lights, sound, dancers, and multimedia spectacle I rarely get back home.

Most theaters, marked on tourist maps, are found in the West End between Piccadilly and Covent Garden. Box offices, hotels, and TIs offer a handy free *Theatre Guide* (also at www.londontheatre.co.uk). Performances are nightly except Sunday, usually with one or two matinees a week (Shakespeare's Globe is the rare theater

London's Major Theaters

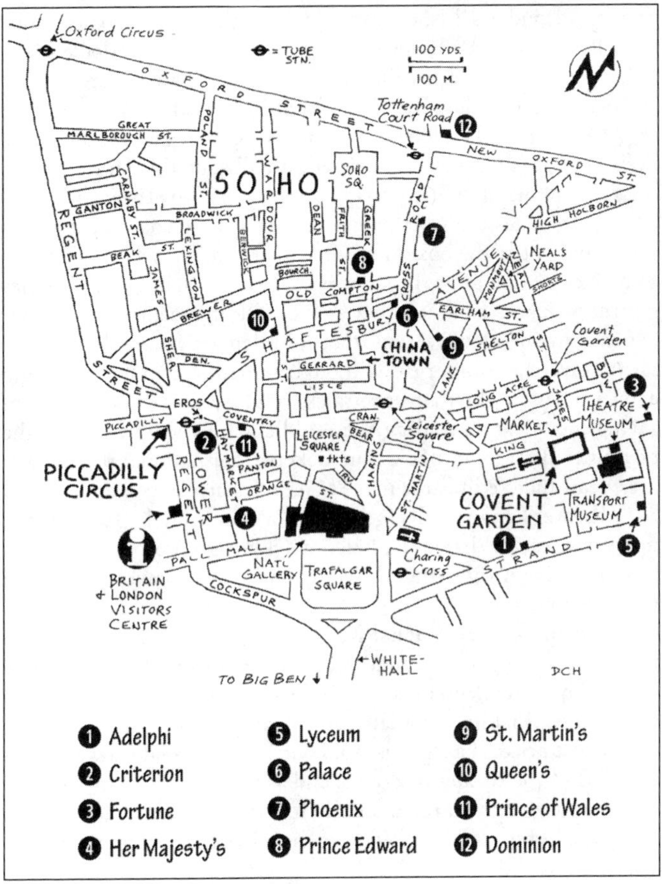

that does offer performances on Sun, mid-May–Sept). Tickets range from about £8 to £40. Matinees are generally cheaper and rarely sell out.

To book a seat, simply call the theater box office directly, ask about seats and available dates, and buy a ticket with your credit card. You can call from the U.S. as easily as from England (check www.officiallondontheatre.co.uk, the American magazine *Variety*, or photocopy your hometown library's London newspaper theater section). Arrive about 30 minutes before the show starts to pick up your ticket and to avoid lines.

For a booking fee, you can reserve online (www.ticketmaster .co.uk or www.firstcalltickets.com) or call Keith Prowse Ticketing, formerly Global Tickets (U.S. tel. 800/223-6108). While booking through an agency is quick and easy, prices are inflated by a standard 25 percent fee. Ticket agencies (whether in the United States, at London's TIs, or scattered throughout the city) are scalpers with an address. If you're buying from an agency, look at the ticket carefully (your price should be no more than 30 percent over the printed face value; the 17.5 percent VAT is already included in the face value) and understand where you're sitting according to the floor plan (if your view is restricted, it will state this on the ticket; for floor plans of the various theaters, see www.theatremonkey.com). Agencies are worthwhile only if a show you've just got to see is sold out at the box office. They scarf up hot tickets, planning to make a killing after the show is sold out. U.S. booking agencies get their tickets from another agency, adding even more to your expense by involving yet another middleman. Many tickets sold on the street are forgeries. Although some theaters have booking agencies handle their advance sales, you'll stand a good chance of saving money and avoiding the middleman by simply calling the box office directly to book your tickets (international phone calls are cheap and credit cards make booking a snap).

Theater Lingo: stalls (ground floor), dress circle (1st balcony), upper circle (2nd balcony), balcony (sky-high 3rd balcony), slips (cheap seats on the fringes). Many cheap seats have a restricted view (behind a pillar).

Cheap Theater Tricks: Most theaters offer cheap returned tickets, standing-room, matinee, and senior or student standby deals. These "concessions" are indicated with a "conc" or "s" in the listings. Picking up a late return can get you a great seat at a cheap-seat price. If a show is "sold out," there's usually a way to get a seat. Call the theater box office and ask how.

Many theaters are so small that there's hardly a bad seat. After the lights go down, scooting up is less than a capital offense. Shakespeare did it.

Half-Price "tkts" Booth: This famous ticket booth at **Leicester Square** sells discounted tickets for top-price seats to shows on the push list the day of the show only (£2.50 service charge per ticket, Mon–Sat 10:00–19:00, Sun 12:00–15:30, matinee tickets from noon, lines often form early, list of shows available online, www.tkts.co.uk). Most tickets are half-price; other shows are discounted 25 percent.

Here are some sample prices: A top-notch seat to *Chicago* costs £40 bought directly from the theater, but only £22.50 at Leicester (LESS-ter) Square. The cheapest balcony seat (bought from the theater) is £15. Half-price tickets can be a good deal, unless you want the cheapest seats or the hottest shows. But check the board; occasionally they sell cheap tickets to good shows. For example, a first-class seat to the long-running *Les Misérables* (which rarely sells out) costs £45 when bought from the theater ticket office, but you'll save 25 percent and pay £36.50 at the tkts booth. Note that the real half-price booth (with its new "tkts" name) is a freestanding kiosk at the edge of the garden in Leicester Square. Several dishonest outfits nearby advertise "official half-price tickets"; avoid these.

A second tkts booth has opened at the Canary Wharf Docklands Light Railway (DLR) Station. The freestanding kiosk is located near platforms #4 and #5 above the DLR concourse (Mon–Sat 11:30–18:00, closed Sun, Tube: Canary Wharf).

West End Theaters: The commercial (non-subsidized) theaters cluster around Soho (especially along Shaftesbury Avenue) and Covent Garden. With a centuries-old tradition of pleasing the masses, these present London theater at its glitziest. See the "What's On in the West End" sidebar.

Royal Shakespeare Company: If you'll ever enjoy Shakespeare, it'll be in Britain. The RSC performs at various theaters around London and in Stratford year-round. To get a schedule, contact the RSC (Royal Shakespeare Theatre, Stratford-upon-Avon, tel. 01789/403-444, www.rsc.org.uk).

Shakespeare's Globe: To see Shakespeare in a replica of the theater for which he wrote his plays, attend a play at the Globe. This round, thatch-roofed, open-air theater performs the plays much as Shakespeare intended (with no amplification). The play's the thing from mid-May through September (usually Tue–Sat 14:00 and 19:30, Sun at either 13:00 and 18:30 or 16:00 only, Mon at 19:30, tickets can be sold out months in advance). You'll pay £5 to stand and £13–29 to sit (usually on a backless bench; only a few rows and the pricier Gentlemen's Rooms have seats with backs; £2 cushions are considered a good investment by many). The £5 "groundling" tickets—while the only ones open to rain—are most fun. Scurry in early to stake out a spot on the stage's edge leaning rail, where the most interaction with the actors occurs. You're a crude peasant. You can lean your elbows on the stage, munch a picnic dinner, or walk around. I've never enjoyed Shakespeare as much as here, performed as it was meant to be in the "wooden O." Plays can be long. Many groundlings leave before the end. If you like, hang out an hour before the finish and beg or buy a ticket from someone leaving early (groundlings are allowed to come and go).

For information on plays or £9 tours (see page 67), contact the theater at tel. 020/7902-1500 (or see www.shakespeares-globe.org). To reserve tickets for plays, call or drop by the box office (Mon–Sat 10:00–18:00, until 20:00 on day of show, at Shakespeare's Globe at New Globe Walk entrance, tel. 020/7401-9919). If you reserve online (www.wayahead.com/shakespeares-globe), be warned: Your ticket price will have an added booking fee.

The theater is on the South Bank, directly across the Thames

What's On in the West End

Here are some of the perennial favorites that you're likely to find among the West End's evening offerings. If spending the time and money for a London play, I like a full-fledged high-energy musical.

Generally you can book tickets for free at the box office or for a £2 fee by telephone or online. See the map on page 313 for locations.

Musicals

Chicago—A chorus-girl-gone-bad forms a nightclub act with another murderess to bring in the bucks (£15–42.50, Mon–Thu and Sat 20:00, Fri 20:30, matinees Fri 17:00 and Sat 15:00, Adelphi Theatre, Strand, Tube: Covent Garden or Charing Cross, booking tel. 020/7344-0055, www.chicagothemusical.com).

Mamma Mia!—This high-energy spandex-and-platform-boots musical weaves together 20 or 30 ABBA hits to tell the story of a bride in search of her real dad as her promiscuous mom plans her Greek Isle wedding. The production has the audience dancing by its happy ending (£25–49, Mon–Thu and Sat 19:30, Fri 20:30, matinees Fri 17:00 and Sat 15:00, Prince of Wales Theatre, Coventry Street, Tube: Piccadilly Circus, booking tel. 0870-850-0393).

Les Misérables—Claude-Michel Schönberg's musical adaptation of Victor Hugo's epic follows the life of Jean Valjean as he struggles with the social and political realities of 19th-century France. This inspiring mega-hit takes you back to the days of France's struggle for a just and modern society (£10–45, Mon–Sat 19:30, matinees Wed and Sat 14:30, Queen's Theatre, Shaftesbury Avenue, Tube: Piccadilly Circus, box office tel. 020/7494-5040, www.lesmis.com).

Phantom of the Opera—A mysterious masked man falls in love with a singer in this haunting Andrew Lloyd Webber musical

over the Millennium Bridge from St. Paul's Cathedral (Tube: Mansion House or London Bridge). The Globe is inconvenient for public transport, but the courtesy phone in the lobby gets a minicab in minutes. (These minicabs have set fees—e.g., £8 to South Kensington—but generally cost less than a metered cab and provide fine and honest service.) During theater season, there's a regular supply of black cabs outside the main foyer on New Globe Walk.

Fringe Theatre: London's rougher evening-entertainment scene is thriving, filling pages in *Time Out.* Choose from a wide range of fringe theater and comedy acts (generally £5).

about life beneath the stage of the Paris Opera (£15–45, Mon–Sat 19:30, matinees Tue and Sat 14:30, Her Majesty's Theatre, Haymarket, Tube: Piccadilly Circus, booking tel. 0870-890-1106, www.thephantomoftheopera.com).

The Lion King—In this Disney extravaganza featuring music by Elton John, Simba the lion learns about the delicately balanced circle of life on the savanna (£17.50–40, Tue–Sat 19:30, matinees Wed and Sat 14:00 and Sun 15:00, Lyceum Theatre, Wellington Street, Tube: Charing Cross or Covent Garden, booking tel. 0870-243-9000 or 020/7344-4444, theater info tel. 020/7420-8112, www.thelionking.co.uk).

We Will Rock You—If you're a Queen fan or not, this musical tribute (more to the band than to Freddie Mercury) is an understandably popular celebration of their work (£23.50–55, Mon–Fri at 19:30, matinees Wed and Sat at 14:30, Dominion Theatre, Tottenham Court Road, Tube: Tottenham Court Road, Ticketmaster tel. 0870-169-0116, www.queenonline.com/wewillrockyou).

Thrillers

The Mousetrap—Agatha Christie's whodunit about a murder in a country house continues to stump audiences after 50 years (£11.50–30, Mon–Sat 20:00, matinees Tue 14:45 and Sat 17:00, St. Martin's Theatre, West Street, Tube: Leicester Square, box office tel. 0870-162-8787).

The Woman in Black—The chilling tale of a solicitor who is haunted by what he learns when he closes a reclusive woman's affairs (£12.50–32.50, Mon–Sat 20:00, matinees Tue 15:00 and Sat 16:00, Fortune Theatre, Russell Street, Tube: Covent Garden, box office tel. 020/7369-1737, www.thewomaninblack.com).

Classical Music

For easy, cheap, or free concerts in historic churches, check the TIs' listings for **lunch concerts,** especially:

- Wren's St. Bride's Church, with free lunch concerts Mon–Fri at 13:15 (church tel. 020/7427-0133, www.stbrides.com).
- St. James at Piccadilly, with concerts on Mon, Wed, and Fri at 13:10 (suggested donation £3, info tel. 020/7381-0441, www.st-james-piccadilly.org).
- St. Martin-in-the-Fields, offering free concerts on Mon, Tue, and Fri at 13:00, church tel. 020/7766-1100, www.smitf.com).

St. Martin-in-the-Fields also hosts fine **evening concerts** by candlelight (£8–18, Thu–Sat at 19:30, sometimes also on Tue or Wed, box office tel. 020/7839-8362).

At St. Paul's Cathedral, **evensong** is held Monday through Saturday at 17:00 and on Sunday at 15:15. At Westminster Abbey, it's sung weekdays at 17:00 (but not on Wed) and Saturday and Sunday at 15:00. Free **organ recitals** are held on Sunday at Westminster Abbey (17:45, 30 min, tel. 020/7222-7110) and at St. Paul's (17:00, 30 min, tel. 020/7236-4128).

For a fun **classical event** (mid-July–early Sept), attend a "Prom Concert" (shortened from "Promenade Concert") during the annual festival at the Royal Albert Hall. Nightly concerts are offered at give-a-peasant-some-culture prices to "Promenaders"—those willing to stand throughout the performance (£4 standing-room spots sold at the door, £7 restricted-view seats, most £22 but depends on performance, Tube: South Kensington, tel. 020/7589-8212, www.royalalberthall.com).

Some of the world's best **opera** is belted out at the prestigious Royal Opera House, near Covent Garden (box office tel. 020/7304-4000, www.royalopera.org), and at the less-formal Sadler's Wells Theatre (Rosebery Avenue, Islington, Tube: Angel, info tel. 020/7863-8198, box office tel. 0870-737-7737, www.sadlerswells.com).

Evening Museum Visits

Many museums are open an evening or two during the week, offering fewer crowds. See "Sights Open Late," page 28.

Tours

Guided **walks** are offered several times a day. Original London Walks is the most established company (tel. 020/7624-3978, www.walks.com). Daytime walks vary: ancient London, museums, legal London, Dickens, Beatles, Jewish quarter, Christopher Wren, and so on. In the evening, expect a more limited choice: ghosts, Jack the Ripper, pubs, or a literary theme. Get the latest from a TI, fliers, or *Time Out*. Show up at the listed time and place, pay £5.50, and enjoy the two-hour tour.

To see the city illuminated at night, consider a **bus** tour. A two-hour London by Night Sightseeing Tour leaves every evening from Victoria Station (see page 35).

Cruises

During the summer, boats sail as late as 21:00 between Westminster Pier (near Big Ben) and the Tower of London. (For details, see page 36.)

A handful of outfits run Thames River evening cruises with

four-course meals and dancing. London Showboat offers the best value (£58, April–Oct Wed–Sun, departs 19:00 from Westminster Pier, Thu–Sat evening cruises throughout the winter, 3.5 hrs, tel. 020/7740-0400, www.citycruises.com). For more on cruising, get the *Thames River Services* brochure from a London TI.

TRANSPORTATION CONNECTIONS

AIRPORTS

Phone numbers and Web sites for London's airports and major airlines are listed on page 402.

Heathrow Airport

Heathrow Airport is the world's fourth busiest. Think about it: 63 million passengers a year on 425,000 flights from 170 destinations riding 90 airlines, like some kind of global maypole dance. While many complain about Heathrow, I think it's a great and user-friendly airport. Read signs, ask questions. For Heathrow's airport, flight, and transfers information, call the switchboard at 0870-000-0123 (www.baa.com). It has four terminals: T-1 (mostly domestic flights, with some European), T-2 (mainly European flights), T-3 (mostly flights from the United States), and T-4 (British Airways transatlantic flights and BA flights to Paris, Amsterdam, and Athens). Taxis know which terminal you'll need.

Each terminal has an airport information desk, car-rental agencies, exchange bureaus, ATMs, a pharmacy, a **VAT refund desk** (tel. 020/8910-3682; you must present the VAT claim form from the retailer here to get your tax rebate on items purchased in Britain, see page 309 for details), and a **baggage-check desk** (£6/day, daily 6:00–23:00 at each terminal). Get online 24 hours a day at Heathrow's **Internet cafés** (T-4, mezzanine level) and at wireless "hotspots" in its departure lounges (T-1, T-3, and T-4). There are **post offices** in T-2 and T-4. Each terminal has cheap **eateries** (such as the cheery Food Village self-service cafeteria in T-3). The **American Express** desk, in the Tube station at Terminal 4 (daily 7:00–19:00), has rates similar to the exchange bureaus upstairs, but doesn't charge a commission (typically 1.5

percent) for cashing any type of traveler's check.

Heathrow's small **TI,** even though it's a for-profit business, is worth a visit to pick up free information: a simple map, the *London Planner*, and brochures (daily 8:30–18:00, 5-min walk from T-3 in Tube station, follow signs to Underground; bypass queue for transit info to reach window for London questions). Have your partner stay with the bags at the terminal while you head over to the TI.

If you're taking the Tube into London, buy a one-day Travelcard pass to cover the ride (see below).

Getting to London from Heathrow Airport

By Tube (Subway): For £3.80, the Tube takes you the 14 miles to downtown London in 50 minutes on the Piccadilly Line, with stops (among others) at South Kensington, Leicester Square, and King's Cross Station (6/hr; depending on your destination, may require a change). Even better, buy a One-Day Travelcard that covers your trip into London and all your Tube travel for the day (£12 covers peak times, £6 "off-peak" card starts at 9:30, less-expensive Travelcards cover the city center only—see page 33 for details). Buy it at the Tube station ticket window. You can generally hop on the Tube at any terminal, but for most of 2006, Terminal 4's Tube station will be closed for renovation. You can still catch the Tube by taking a shuttle bus (from stop D) to the nearest station (allow 15 extra min).

If taking the Tube to the airport, note that Piccadilly Line subway cars post which airlines are served by which terminals.

By Airport Shuttle Bus: The famous Airbus (which shuttled a generation of travelers between the airport and downtown) has finally bit the dust—replaced by the train link and mini-bus shuttles. Hotelink offers door-to-door service (Heathrow-£17 per person, Gatwick-£22 per person, book the day before departure, buy online and save £1–2, tel. 01293/532-244, www.hotelink.co.uk, reservations@hotelink.co.uk).

By Taxi: Taxis from the airport cost about £45 to west and central London (one hour). For four people traveling together, this can be a deal. Hotels can often line up a cab back to the airport for about £30. For the cheapest taxi to the airport, don't order one from your hotel. Simply flag down a few and ask them for their best "off-meter" rate.

By Heathrow Express Train: This slick train service zips you between Heathrow Airport and London's Paddington Station. At Paddington Station, you're in the thick of the Tube system, with

Public Transportation in Southeast England

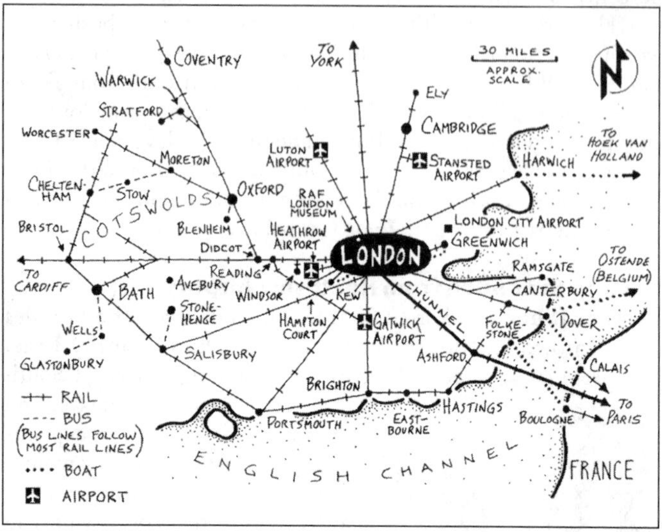

easy access to any of my recommended neighborhoods—Notting Hill Gate is just two stops away. It's only 15 minutes to downtown from Terminals 1, 2, and 3, and 20 minutes from Terminal 4 (at the airport, you can use the Express as a free transfer between terminals). Buy your ticket to London before you board, or pay a £2 surcharge to buy it on the train (£14, but ask about discount promos at Heathrow ticket desk, kids under 16 ride half-price, under 5 ride free, covered by BritRail pass, 4/hr, daily 5:10–23:30, tel. 0845-600-1515, www.heathrowexpress.co.uk). For one person on a budget, combining the Heathrow Express with either a Tube or taxi ride (between your hotel and Paddington Station) is nearly as fast and half the cost of taking a cab directly to (or from) the airport. For groups of three or more, a taxi is faster and easier, as well as cheaper.

Getting to Bath from Heathrow Airport

By Bus: Direct buses run daily from Heathrow to Bath (11/day, 2.5 hrs, £15, tel. 0870-575-7747, www.nationalexpress.com). BritRail passholders may prefer the 2.5-hour Heathrow–Bath bus/train connection via Reading (£10 for bus, rail portion free with pass, otherwise £33 total, payable at desk in terminal): first catch the twice-hourly RailAir Link shuttle bus to Reading (RED-ding), then hop on the hourly express train to Bath.

Most Heathrow buses depart from the common area serving Terminals 1, 2, and 3 (a 5-min walk from any of these terminals), although some depart from T-4 (bus tel. 0870-574-7777).

Gatwick Airport

More and more flights, especially charters, land at Gatwick Airport, halfway between London and the southern coast (recorded airport info tel. 0870-000-2468).

Getting to London: Express trains—clearly the best way into London from here—shuttle conveniently between Gatwick and London's Victoria Station (£13, £24 round-trip, 4/hr during day, 1–2/hr at night, 30 min, runs 5:00–24:00 daily, can purchase tickets on train at no extra charge, tel. 0845-850-1530, www.gatwickexpress.co.uk). If you're traveling with three others, buy your tickets at the station before boarding and you'll travel for the price of two. The only restriction on this impressive deal is that you have to travel together. So if you see another couple in line, get organized and save 50 percent.

You can save a few pounds by taking South Central rail line's slower and less frequent shuttle between Victoria Station and Gatwick (£9, 3/hr, 1/hr midnight–4:00, 45 min, tel. 08457-484-950, www.southcentraltrains.co.uk).

Getting to Bath: To get to Bath from Gatwick, you can catch a bus to Heathrow and the bus to Bath from there. By train, the best Gatwick–Bath connection involves a transfer in Reading (2.5 hrs, irregular schedule; avoid transfer in London, where you'll have to change stations).

London's Other Airports

If you're flying into or out of **Stansted** (airport tel. 0870-0000-303), you can take the National Express bus between the airport and downtown London's Victoria Coach Station (£10, 2/hr, 1.5 hrs, runs 4:00–24:00, picks up and stops throughout London, tel. 0870-575-7747, www.nxairport.com), or take the Stansted Express train (£15, connects to London's Liverpool Station, 40 min, 2–4/hr, 5:00–23:00, tel. 0845-850-0150, www.stanstedexpress.com). Stansted is expensive by cab; figure £80 one-way from central London.

For **Luton** (airport tel. 01582/405-100, www.london-luton.com), here are three choices. You can take the easyJet bus, which runs between the airport and the Baker Street Tube stop (£1, open to non-easyJet passengers as well, 40 min, every 45 min, runs 7:15–20:00, www.easybus.co.uk). Or hop on Green Line's bus #757, which links the airport and London's Victoria Station at Buckingham Palace Road—stop 6 (£10, £9 for easyJet passengers, 2/hr, 1–1.25 hrs depending on time of day, runs 4:30–24:00, tel. 0870-608-7261, www.greenline.co.uk). Or you can connect by rail to London's Kings Cross station (£12, runs 5:00–23:00, 25 min, tel. 0845-748-4950); catch the free 5-minute shuttle from outside the terminal to the Luton Parkway train station.

There's a slim chance you might use **London City Airport** (tel. 020/7646-0088, www.londoncityairport.com). Blue shuttle buses connect the airport to the Liverpool Street Station (£7 one-way, 30 min), a hub for the Tube.

Connecting London's Airports

The **National Express Central Bus Station** offers direct Jetlink bus connections from **Heathrow** to **Gatwick Airport** (2/hr, 70 min or more, depending on traffic), departing just outside arrivals at all terminals (£17 one-way, £22 round-trip). To make a flight connection between Heathrow and Gatwick, allow three hours between flights.

More and more travelers are taking advantage of cheap flights out of London's smaller airports. A handy National Express bus runs between Heathrow, Gatwick, Stansted, and Luton airports—easier than having to cut through the center of London. Buses are frequent (less so between Stansted and Luton) and cheap: Heathrow–Luton is 1.5 hours direct and costs £16. Check schedules at www.nxairport.com.

Discounted Flights from London

Although bmi british midland has been around the longest, the other small airlines generally offer cheaper flights. A visit to www.skyscanner.net sorts the many options offered by the myriad discount airlines, enabling you to see the best schedules for your trip and come up with the best deal.

With **bmi british midland,** you can fly inexpensively to destinations in the U.K. and beyond (fares start at about £30 one-way to Edinburgh, Paris, Brussels, or Amsterdam; or about £50 one-way to Dublin; prices can be higher, but there can also be much cheaper Internet specials—check online). For the latest, call British tel. 0870-607-0555 or U.S. tel. 800-788-0555 (check www.flybmi.com and their subsidiary, bmi baby, at www.bmibaby.com). Book in advance. Although you can book right up until the flight departs, the cheap seats will have sold out long before, leaving the most expensive seats for latecomers.

With no frills and cheap fares, **easyJet** flies from Luton, Stansted, and Gatwick. Prices are based on demand, so the least popular routes make for the cheapest fares, especially if you book early (tel. 0905-821-0905 to book by phone, 65p per minute, or do it free online at www.easyjet.com).

Ryanair is a creative Irish airline that prides itself on offering the lowest fares. It flies from London (mostly Stansted airport) to often obscure airports in Dublin, Glasgow, Frankfurt, Stockholm, Oslo, Venice, Turin, and many others. Sample fares: London–Dublin—£60 round-trip (sometimes as low as £15),

London–Frankfurt—£67 round-trip (Irish tel. 0818-303-030, British tel. 0871-246-0000, www.ryanair.com). Because they offer promotional deals any time of year, you can get great prices on short notice. Be aware of their stiff fees for extra baggage. You can carry on only a small daybag and check 15 kilograms—about 33 pounds—of baggage for free. You'll pay €7 per extra kilo. If you're packing an extra 10 kilos, a cheap €30 flight skyrockets to €100.

Virgin Express is a British-owned company with good rates (book by phone and pick up ticket at airport an hour before your flight, www.virgin-express.com). Virgin Express flies from London Heathrow and Brussels. From its hub in Brussels, you can connect cheaply to Barcelona, Madrid, Nice, Málaga, Copenhagen, Rome, or Milan (round-trip from Brussels to Rome for as little as £105). Their prices stay the same whether or not you book in advance.

TRAINS AND BUSES

London, Britain's major transportation hub, has a different train station for each region. Waterloo handles the Eurostar to Paris. King's Cross covers northeast England and Scotland. Paddington covers west and southwest England (Bath) and South Wales. For information call 0845-748-4950 (or visit www.nationalrail.co.uk or www.eurostar.com; £5 booking fee for telephone reservations). Also see the BritRail Routes map in this chapter. Note that for security reasons, stations offer a left-luggage service (£6/day) rather than lockers.

National Express' excellent bus service is considerably cheaper than trains (call 0870-575-7747, or visit www.nationalexpress.com or the bus station a block southwest of Victoria Station.)

To Bath: Trains leave London's Paddington Station twice every hour between 7:00 and 19:00 (at :15 and :45 after each hour) for the 90-minute ride to Bath (costs £34 if you leave after 9:30 any day but Fri, when it's £40).

To get to Bath via Stonehenge, consider taking a guided bus tour from London to Stonehenge and Bath and abandoning the tour in Bath. Evan Evans' tour for £56 (includes admissions). The tour leaves from the Victoria Coach station every morning at 8:45 (you can stow your bag under the bus), stops in Stonehenge (45 min), and then stops in Bath for lunch and a city tour before returning to London (offered year-round). You can book the tour at the Victoria Coach station, the Evan Evans' office (258 Vauxhall Bridge Road, near Victoria Coach station, tel. 020/7950-1777, U.S. tel. 866-382-6868, www.evanevans.co.uk, reservations@evanevanstours.co.uk), or at the Green Line Travel Office (4a Fountain Square, across from Victoria Coach station, tel. 0870-608-7261, www.greenline.co.uk). Golden Tours also runs a fully guided Stonehenge–Bath

BritRail Routes

London Train Stations

1. Victoria – S. & S.E. England; conn. to Paris & Brussels
2. Charing Cross – S.E. England
3. Waterloo – S. England; Eurostar to Paris & Brussels via Chunnel
4. Liverpool Street – E. England; conn. to Amsterdam
5. King's Cross – E. England, N.E. England, E. Scotland
6. St. Pancras – Central England
7. Euston – N. & N.W. England, N. Wales, W. Scotland
8. Paddington – W. England, S. Wales

London Airports

- A Heathrow
- B Gatwick
- C Luton
- D Stansted
- E City

tour for a similar price (departs from Fountain Square, located across from Victoria Coach Station, tel. 020/7233-7036, U.S. tel. 800/548-7083, www.goldentours.co.uk, reservations@goldentours.co.uk). Another similarly priced day-trip hits Oxford, Stratford, and Warwick.

To Points North: Trains run hourly from London's King's Cross Station, stopping in York (2 hrs), Durham (3 hrs), and Edinburgh (4.5 hrs).

To Dublin, Ireland: The boat/bus journey takes between 9 and 10 hours and goes all day or all night (£29–57, 2/day, tel. 08705-143-219, www.nationalexpress.com or www.eurolines.co.uk). Consider a cheap 70-minute Ryanair flight instead (see above).

CROSSING THE CHANNEL

By Eurostar Train

The fastest and most convenient way to get from the Eiffel Tower to Big Ben is by rail. Eurostar, a joint service of the Belgian, British, and French railways, is the speedy passenger train that zips you (and up to 800 others in 18 sleek cars) from downtown London to downtown Paris (12–15/day, 3 hrs) faster and easier than flying. The actual tunnel crossing is a 20-minute, black, silent, 100-mile-per-hour non-event. Your ears won't even pop. Eurostar trains also run directly from London to Disneyland Paris (1/day direct, more often with transfer at Lille).

Eurostar Fares

Channel fares (essentially the same between London and Paris or Brussels) are reasonable but complicated. Prices vary depending on when you travel, whether you can live with restrictions, and whether you're eligible for any discounts (youth, seniors, and railpass holders all qualify). Rates are lower for round trips and off-peak travel (midday, midweek, low-season, and low-interest). For specifics, visit www.ricksteves.com/rail/eurostar.htm.

As with airfares, the most expensive and flexible option is a **full-fare ticket** with no restrictions on refundability (even refundable after the departure date; for a one-way trip, figure about $375 in first class, $255 in second class). A first-class ticket comes with a meal (a dinner departure nets you more grub than breakfast)—but it's not worth the extra expense.

Eurostar Routes

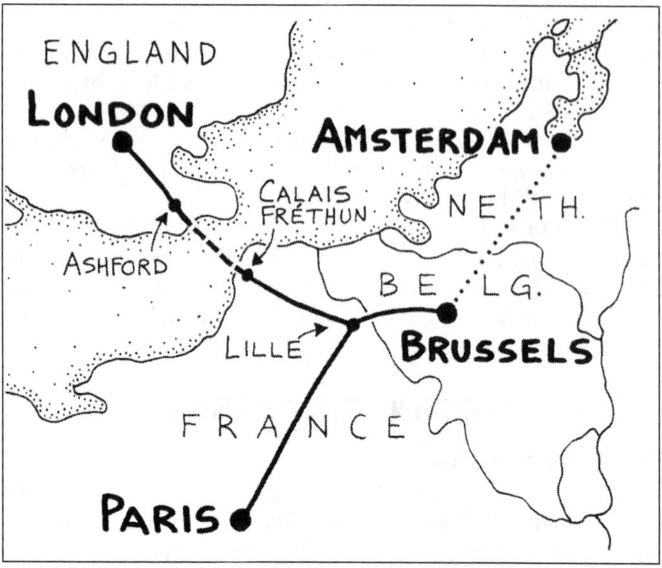

Also like the airlines, **cheaper tickets** come with more restrictions—and are limited in number (so they sell out more quickly; for second-class, one-way tickets, figure $90–200). Non-full-fare tickets have severe restrictions on refundability (best-case scenario: you'll get 25 percent back, but with the cheapest options you'll get nothing). But several do allow you to change the specifics of your trip once before departure.

Those traveling with a railpass for Britain, France, or Belgium should look first at the **passholder** fare, an especially good value for one-way Eurostar trips (about $75). In Britain, passholder tickets can be issued only at the Eurostar office in Waterloo Station or the American Express office in Victoria Station—not at any other stations. You can also order them by phone (see below), then pick them up at Waterloo Station (see below).

Buying Eurostar Tickets

Refund and exchange restrictions are serious, so don't reserve until you're sure of your plans. If you're confident about the time and date of your crossing, order ahead from the U.S. Only the most expensive ticket (full fare) is fully refundable, so if you want to have more flexibility, hold off—keeping in mind that the longer you wait, the more likely the cheapest tickets will sell out. (You might end up having to pay for first class.)

You can check and book fares by phone or online in the U.S. (order online at www.ricksteves.com/rail/eurostar.htm, prices

Building the Chunnel

The toughest obstacle to building a tunnel under the English Channel was overcome in 1986, when long-time rivals Britain and France reached an agreement to build it together. Britain began in Folkestone, France in Calais, planning a rendezvous in the middle.

By 1988, specially made machines three football fields long were boring 26-foot-wide holes under the ground. The dirt they hauled out became landfill in Britain and a hill in France. Crews crept forward 100 feet a day until June 1991, when French and English workers broke through and shook hands midway across the Channel—the tunnel was complete. Rail service began in 1994.

The Chunnel is 31 miles long (24 miles of it underwater) and 26 feet wide. It sits 130 feet below the seabed in a chalky layer of sediment. It's segmented into three separate tunnels—two for trains (one in each direction) and one for service and ventilation. The walls are concrete panels and rebar fixed to the rock around it. Sixteen-thousand-horsepower engines pull 850 tons of railcars and passengers at speeds up to 100 mph through the tunnel.

The ambitious project—the world's longest undersea tunnel—helped to show the European community that cooperation between nations could benefit everyone.

listed in dollars; order by phone at U.S. tel. 800/EUROSTAR) or in Britain (British tel. 0870-518-6186, www.eurostar.com, prices listed in pounds). While tickets are usually cheaper if purchased in the U.S., fares offered in Europe follow different discount rules—so it can be worth it to check www.eurostar.com before buying. If you buy from a U.S. company, you'll pay for ticket delivery in the United States. In Europe, you can buy your Eurostar ticket at any major train station in any country or at any travel agency that handles train tickets (expect a booking fee).

Remember that Britain's time zone is one hour earlier than France's. Times listed on tickets are local times (departure from London is British time, arrival in Paris in French time).

Waterloo Station: Check in at least 30 minutes in advance for your Eurostar trip. It's very similar to an airport check-in: You pass through airport-like security, show your passport to customs officials, and find a TV monitor to locate your departure gate. There are a few airport-like shops, newsstands, horrible snack bars, and cafés (bring food for the trip from elsewhere), pay-Internet terminals, and a currency-exchange booth with rates about the same as you'll find on the other end.

Cheap Passage by Tour: A tour company called Britain Shrinkers sells one- or two-day "Eurostar Tours" to Paris or Brussels, enabling you to side-trip to these cities from London for less than most train tickets alone. For example, a one-day Paris (with Métro pass) tour costs £129—instead of £149 for a regular one-way fare or £249 round-trip (tel. 0800/587-7660 or www.britainshrinkers.com). This can be a particularly good option if you need to get to Paris from London on short notice, when only the costliest fares are available.

Crossing the Channel without Eurostar

The old-fashioned ways of crossing the Channel are cheaper than crossing by Eurostar. They're also twice as romantic, complicated, and time-consuming. You'll get better prices arranging your trip in London than you would in the U.S. Taking the bus is cheapest, and round-trips are a bargain.

By Train and Boat: You'll need to book your own train tickets to Dover; prices are for the ferry only. The **Hoverspeed ferry** runs between Dover, England, and Calais, France (tel. 0870-524-0241, www.hoverspeed.com). Hoverspeed sells London–Paris rail and ferry packages: £44 one-way; £56 round-trip with five-day return; and £67 round-trip over more than five days. You can buy this package deal in person at Waterloo and Charing Cross stations. If you book by phone (number listed above), you must book at least two weeks in advance, and the ticket will be mailed to you (no ticket pickup at station for bookings by phone).

By **P&O Stena Line ferry** runs from Dover to Calais (£18 one-way or round-trip with 5-day return, £36 round-trip over more than 5 days, tel. 0870-520-2020, www.poferries.com).

By Bus: You can take the bus direct to Paris (8 hrs, 5/day), Brussels (9 hrs, 5/day), or Amsterdam (12 hrs, 4/day) from Victoria Coach Station (via boat or Chunnel, day or overnight). Sample prices to Paris for economy fares booked at least two days in advance are: £45 one-way, £62 round-trip (tel. 0870-514-3219; visit www.eurolines.co.uk and look for "fun fares").

By Plane: Check with budget airlines for cheap round-trip fares to Paris (see "Discounted Flights from London," page 324).

DAY TRIPS IN ENGLAND

- *Greenwich*
- *Windsor*
- *Cambridge*
- *Bath*

Greenwich, Windsor, Cambridge, and Bath (listed from nearest to farthest) are four of the best day trip possibilities near London. Greenwich is England's maritime capital; Windsor has the famous castle; Cambridge is England's best university town; and Bath is an elegant spa town dating from Roman times.

Getting Around England

By Bus Tour: Several tour companies take London-based travelers out and back every day. If you're going to Bath and want to stay overnight, consider taking a day tour to Bath and skipping the trip back to London (for details, see page 325 in the Transportation Connections chapter).

By Train: The British rail system uses London as a hub and normally offers round-trip fares (after 9:30) that cost virtually the same as one-way fares. For day trips, "day return" tickets are best (and cheapest). You can save a little money if you purchase Super Advance tickets before 18:00 on the day before your trip.

By Train Tour: Original London Walks offers a variety of Explorer day trips year-round via train for about £10 plus transportation costs (pick up their walking-tour brochures at the TI or hotels, tel. 020/7624-3978, www.walks.com).

Greenwich

Tudor kings favored the palace at Greenwich. Henry VIII was born here. Later kings commissioned Inigo Jones and Christopher Wren to beautify the town and palace. In spite of Greenwich's architectural and royal treats, this is England's sea-going center,

Day Trips from London

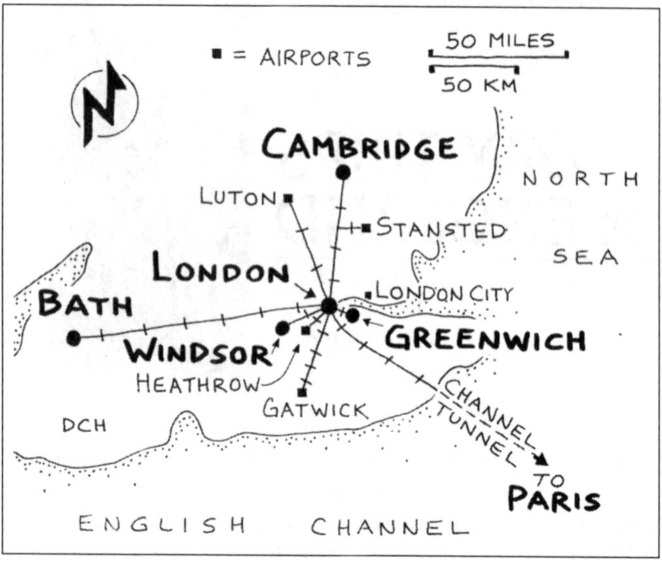

and visitors go for all things salty. Greenwich hosts historic ships, nautical shops, and hordes of tourists.

Planning Your Time

See the two ships—*Cutty Sark* and *Gipsy Moth IV*—upon arrival. Then walk the shoreline promenade, with a possible lunch or drink in the venerable Trafalgar Tavern, before heading up to the National Maritime Museum and the Royal Observatory Greenwich.

Getting to Greenwich

It's a joy by boat or a snap by Tube.

By Boat: From London (50–70 min, 2/hr), cruise down the Thames from central London's piers at Westminster, Embankment, or Tower of London (see "Cruises" on page 36).

By Tube: Take the Tube to Bank and change to the Dockways Light Railway (DLR), which takes you right to the *Cutty Sark* station in Greenwich (1 stop before the main Greenwich station, 20-min ride, all in Zone 2, included with Tube pass). Many DLR trains terminate at Canary Wharf, so make sure you get on one that continues to Lewisham or Greenwich.

By Train: Mainline trains also go from London (Charing Cross, Waterloo East, and London Bridge stations) several times an hour to the Greenwich station (10-min walk from the sights).

ORIENTATION

Covered markets and outdoor stalls make weekends lively. Save time to browse the town. Wander beyond the touristy Church Street and Greenwich High Road to where flower stands spill into the side streets and antique shops sell brass nautical knick-knacks. King William Walk, College Approach, Nelson Road, and Turnpin Lane are all worth a look. If you need pub grub, Greenwich has nearly 100 pubs, with some boasting that they're mere milliseconds from the International Date Line.

Tourist Information

The TI faces the riverside square a few paces from the *Cutty Sark* (daily 10:00–17:00, 2 Cutty Sark Gardens, Pepys House, tel. 0870-608-2000, www.greenwich.gov.uk). Guided walks cover the big sights (£4, daily 12:15 and 14:15, departs from TI).

Helpful Hints

Markets: The town throbs with day-trippers on weekends because of its markets. The arts-and-crafts market is an entertaining mini–Covent Garden between College Approach and Nelson Road (Thu–Sun 10:00–17:00, biggest on Sun), and the antique market sells old odds and ends at high prices on Greenwich High Road, near the post office. To avoid the crowds, visit on a weekday.

Tram: A small tram runs from the National Maritime Museum to the Royal Observatory on top of the hill (free, daily 10:00–16:30, 2/hr, erratic in winter).

Supermarket: If you're picnicking, try the handy Marks & Spencer Simply Food on Church Street, across from the *Cutty Sark*. You can get everything from sandwiches to roast chicken to chocolate sundaes, and they throw in free plastic utensils.

SIGHTS

▲▲***Cutty Sark***—The Scottish-built *Cutty Sark* was the last of the great China tea clippers. Handsomely restored, she was the queen of the seas when first launched in 1869. With 32,000 square feet of sail, she could blow with the wind 300 miles in a day. Below deck, you'll see the best collection of merchant-ship figureheads in Britain and exhibits giving a vivid peek into the lives of Victorian sailors back when Britain ruled the waves. Stand at the big wheel and look up at the still-rigged main mast towering 150 feet above. You may meet costumed storytellers spinning yarns of the high seas and local old salts giving knot-tying demonstrations (£4.50, daily 10:00–17:00, tel. 020/8858-3445, www.cuttysark.org.uk).

▲Gipsy Moth IV—Tiny next to the *Cutty Sark,* the 54-foot *Gipsy Moth IV* is the boat Sir Francis Chichester used for the first solo circumnavigation of the world in 1966 and 1967. Upon Chichester's return, Queen Elizabeth II knighted him in Greenwich, using the same sword Elizabeth I had used to knight Francis Drake in 1581 (free, viewable anytime, but interior not open to public).

Stroll the Thames to Trafalgar Tavern—From the *Cutty Sark* and *Gipsy Moth,* pass the pier and wander east along the Thames on Five Foot Walk (the width of the path) for grand views in front of the Old Royal Naval College (see below). Founded by William III as a naval hospital and designed by Wren, the college was split in two because Queen Mary didn't want the view from Queen's House blocked. The riverside view is good, too, with the twin-domed towers of the college (one giving the time, the other the direction of the wind) framing Queen's House, and the Royal Observatory Greenwich crowning the hill beyond.

Continuing downstream, just past the college, you'll see the **Trafalgar Tavern.** Dickens knew the pub well, and used it as the setting for the wedding breakfast in *Our Mutual Friend.* Built in 1837 in the Regency style to attract Londoners downriver, the tavern is popular with Londoners (and tourists) for its fine lunches. The upstairs Nelson Room is still used for weddings. Its formal moldings and elegant windows with balconies over the Thames are a step back in time (daily 12:00–15:00 & 18:00–22:00, Sun lunch only, smoky, Park Row, tel. 020/8858-2909). From the pub, enjoy views of the white-elephant Millennium Dome a mile downstream.

From the Trafalgar Tavern, you can walk the two long blocks up Park Row and turn right onto the park leading up to the Royal Observatory Greenwich.

Old Royal Naval College—Now that the Royal Navy has moved out, the public is invited in to see the elaborate Painted Hall and Chapel, grandly designed by Wren and completed by other architects in the 1700s (free, Mon–Sun 10:00–17:00, in the two college buildings farthest from river, choral service Sun at 11:00 in chapel—all are welcome).

Queen's House—This building, the first Palladian-style villa in Britain, was designed in 1616 by Inigo Jones for James I's wife, Anne of Denmark. All traces of the queen are now gone, and the Great Hall and Royal Apartments serve as an art gallery for rotating exhibits (free, daily 10:00–17:00, tel. 020/8858-4422).

▲▲National Maritime Museum—Great for anyone remotely interested in the sea, this museum holds everything from *Titanic* tickets and Captain Scott's reindeer-hide sleeping bag (from his 1910 Antarctic expedition) to the uniform Admiral Nelson wore when he was killed at Trafalgar. Under a big glass roof—

Greenwich

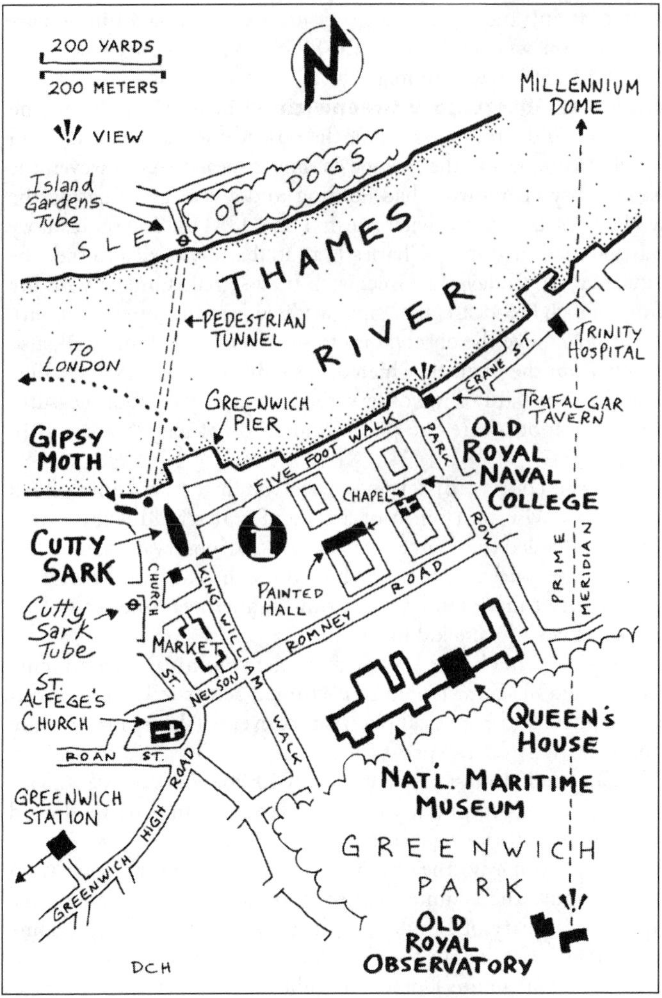

accompanied by the sound of creaking wooden ships and crashing waves—slick, modern displays depict lighthouse technology, a whaling cannon, and a Greenpeace "survival pod."

The Nelson Gallery, while taking up just a fraction of the floor space, deserves at least half your time here. It offers an intimate look at Nelson's life, the Napoleonic threat, Nelson's rise to power, and his victory and death at Trafalgar. Don't miss Turner's *Battle of Trafalgar*—his largest painting and only royal commission.

Kids love the All Hands Gallery, where they can send secret messages by Morse code and operate a miniature dockside crane (free, daily 10:00–17:00, July–Aug 10:00–18:00; look for the events posted at entrance—singing, treasure hunts, storytelling—particularly on weekends; tel. 020/8858-4422, recorded info tel. 020/8312-6565, www.nmm.ac.uk).

▲▲Royal Observatory Greenwich—Located on the prime meridian (0 degrees longitude), the observatory is the point from which the globe and the passage of time is measured. However, the observatory's early work had nothing to do with coordinating the world's clocks to Greenwich Mean Time (GMT). The observatory was founded in 1675 by Charles II to find a way to determine longitude at sea. Today, the Greenwich time signal is linked with the BBC (which broadcasts the "pips" worldwide at the top of the hour).

Look above the observatory to see the orange Time Ball, also visible from the Thames, which drops daily at 13:00. (Nearby, outside the courtyard of the observatory, see how your foot measures up to the foot where the public standards of length are cast in bronze.)

In the courtyard, set your wristwatch to the digital clock showing GMT to a tenth of a second and straddle the prime meridian (called the "Times meridian" at the observatory, in deference to the *London Times,* which paid for the courtyard sculpture and the inset meridian line that runs banner headlines of today's *Times*—I wish I were kidding).

Inside, check out the historic astronomical instruments and camera obscura. Listen to costumed actors tell stories about astronomers and historical observatory events (shows may require small fee, daily July–Sept).

Cost and Hours: Free entry, daily 10:00–17:00, tel. 020/8858-4422, www.rog.nmm.ac.uk. The planetarium will be closed throughout 2007 for renovation.

Before you leave the observatory grounds, enjoy the view from the overlook: the symmetrical royal buildings; the Thames; the square-mile City of London, with its skyscrapers and the dome of St. Paul's Cathedral; the Docklands, with its busy cranes; and the huge Millennium Dome. At night (17:00–24:00), look for the green laser beam the observatory shines in the sky (best viewed in winter), extending along the prime meridian for 15 miles.

Windsor

Windsor, a compact and easy walking town of about 30,000 people, originally grew up around the royal residence. In 1070, William the Conqueror continued his habit of kicking Saxons out of their various settlements, taking over what the locals called "Windlesora" (meaning "riverbank with a hoisting crane"). It would eventually be called "Windsor." William built the first fortified castle on a chalk hill above the Thames; later kings added on to William's early designs, rebuilding and expanding the castle and surrounding gardens.

By setting up primary residence here, modern monarchs increased Windsor's popularity and prosperity—most notably, Queen Victoria, whose statue glares sternly at you as you approach the castle. After her death, Victoria rejoined her beloved husband Albert in the Royal Mausoleum at Frogmore House, a mile south of the castle in a private section of the Home Park (house and mausoleum rarely open; check www.royalcollection.org.uk). The current queen considers Windsor her primary residence, and the one where she feels most at home. You can tell if her majesty is in residence by checking to see which flag is flying above the round tower; if the royal standard (a red, yellow, and blue flag) is flying instead of the Union Jack, the Queen is at home.

While 99 percent of the visitors just come to see the castle and go, some enjoy spending the night. The town's charm is most evident when the tourists are gone. Consider overnighting here, since parking and access to Heathrow Airport are easy; day-tripping into London is feasible; and an evening at the horse races (on Mondays) is hoof-pounding, heart-thumping fun.

Getting to Windsor

By Train: Windsor has two train stations: Windsor Central (5-min walk to palace and TI) and Windsor & Eton Riverside (10-min walk to palace and TI). Thames Trains run between London's Paddington Station and Windsor Central (2/hr, 40 min, change at Slough, www.thamestrains.co.uk). South West Trains run between London's Waterloo Station and the Windsor & Eton Riverside station (2/hr, 50 min, www.nationalrail.co.uk, info tel. 0845-748-4950). If you're day-tripping into London from Windsor, you can save money by buying a One-Day Travelcard at the Windsor train station (£6, good after 9:30, covers rail transportation to and from London with an all-day Tube pass in town; see page 30).

By Bus: Green Line buses #700 and #702 run hourly between London's Victoria Colonnade (between the Victoria train and coach stations) and Windsor, where the bus stops in front of Legoland and near the castle; the castle stop is "Parish Church" (1.5 hrs). Bus info: tel. 0870-608-7261.

By Car: Windsor is 20 miles from London and just off Heathrow airport's landing path. The town (and then the castle and Legoland) is well-signposted from the M4 motorway. It's a convenient stop for anyone arriving at Heathrow, picking up a car, and not going into London.

From Heathrow Airport: Bus #50 makes the 30-minute

trip between Windsor and the airport for £3 (2/hr), dropping you right below the castle near the TI. London black cabs can charge whatever they like from Heathrow to Windsor (and do); avoid them by calling a local Windsor cab (tel. 01753/677-677, £18 ride).

ORIENTATION

You'll find most shops and restaurants around the castle on High and Thames Streets, and down the pedestrian Peascod Street (which runs perpendicular to High Street). The train to Windsor Central station from Paddington (via Slough) will spit you out in a shady shopping pavilion only a few minutes' walk from the castle and TI (see "Getting to Windsor," above). The pleasant pedestrian shopping zone of Windsor litters the approach to its famous palace with fun temptations.

Tourist Information

The TI is on 24 High Street (April–Sept daily 10:00–17:00, Oct–March daily 10:00–16:00, tel. 01753/743-900, www.windsor.gov.uk). The TI sells half-price tickets to Legoland after 13:30.

SIGHTS AND ACTIVITIES

▲▲Windsor Castle—Windsor Castle, the official home of England's royal family for 900 years, claims to be the largest and oldest occupied castle in the world. Thankfully, touring it is simple: You'll see immense grounds, lavish staterooms, a crowd-pleasing dollhouse, an art gallery, and the chapel.

Immediately upon entering, you pass through a simple modern building housing a historical overview of the castle. This excellent intro is worth a close look, since you're basically on your own after this. Inside, you'll find the motte (artificial mound) and bailey (fortified stockade around it) of William the Conqueror's castle still visible. Dating from 1080, this was his first castle in England.

Follow the signs to the staterooms/gallery/dollhouse. Queen Mary's Dollhouse—a palace in miniature (1:12 scale from 1923) and "the most famous dollhouse in the world"—comes with the longest wait. You can skip that line and go immediately into the lavish staterooms. Strewn with history and the art of a long line of kings and queens, it's the best I've seen in Britain—and well-restored after the devastating 1992 fire. Take advantage of the talkative docents in each room, who are happy to answer your questions. The adjacent gallery is a changing exhibit featuring the royal art collection (and some big names, such as Michelangelo and Leonardo). Signs direct you (downhill) to St. George's Chapel. Housing 10 royal tombs, it's a fine example of

Windsor

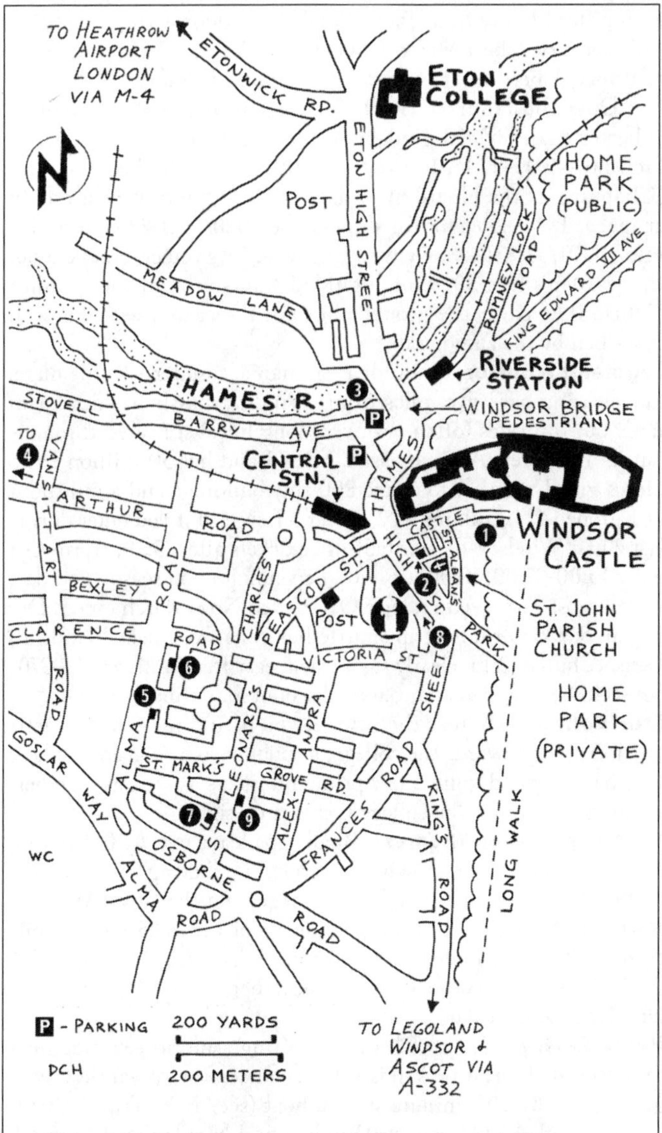

1. Castle Tickets & Entrance
2. Guildhall & Crooked House Tea Rooms
3. Boat Trips
4. To Royal Windsor Racecourse
5. Langton House B&B
6. Dorset Hotel
7. The Netherton Hotel
8. Cornucopia Bistro
9. Blondes Café & Tapas Bar

Perpendicular Gothic, with classic fan vaulting spreading out from each pillar (dating from about 1500). Next door is the sumptuous 13th-century Albert Memorial Chapel, redecorated after the death of Prince Albert in 1861 and dedicated to his memory.

Cost and Hours: £12.50, £32 for family (£3.50 audioguide is better than official guidebook for help throughout). March–Oct daily 9:45–17:15, last entry 16:00, Nov–Feb closes at 16:15 (Changing of the Guard most days at 11:00, nightly evensong in chapel at 17:15—free for worshippers, tel. 020/7321-2233, recorded info tel. 01753/831-118, www.royal.gov.uk). As you enter, ask about the warden's free 30-minute guided walks around the grounds (2/hr). They cover the grounds but not the castle, which is well described by the audioguide.

Legoland Windsor—Fun for Legomaniacs under 12, this huge, kid-pleasing park five miles from Windsor Castle has dozens of tame but fun rides (often with very long lines) scattered throughout its 150 acres. An impressive Mini-Land has 50 million Lego pieces glued together to create 800 tiny buildings and a mini-tour of Europe (£24, children £22, under 3 free, £10 if you enter during last 2 hrs; Windsor TI sells half-price tickets after 13:30; April–Oct daily 10:00–17:00, 18:00, or 19:00 depending upon season and day; closed most Tue–Wed in Sept–Oct, closed Nov–March except Dec 21–Jan 5, £2.50 round-trip shuttle bus runs from near Windsor's Parish Church, 2/hr, clearly signposted, easy free parking, tel. 0870-504-0404, www.legoland.co.uk—discount for online bookings).

Eton College—Across the bridge, you'll find many post-castle tourists filing towards the college, a "public" (our "private") school that has educated quite a few prime ministers as well as members of the royal family. The college is sparse on sights.

Boat Trips on the Thames—Boat trips leave every 30 minutes, ferrying you up and down the river for relaxing views of the castle, the village of Eton, Eton College, and the Royal Windsor Racecourse. Relax onboard and munch a picnic (£4.50, £12 family ticket, 2/hr from 11:00–17:00, 40 min, longer trips available, tel. 01753/851-900, www.boat-trips.co.uk). There's also a longer 2-hour circular trip (£7, 1/day).

Horse Racing—Every Monday evening, the horses race near Windsor at the Royal Windsor Racecourse. The romantic way to get there is by a 10-minute shuttle boat (see "Boat Trips," above; £6 entry, off A308 between Windsor and Maidenhead, info tel. 0870-220-0024, www.windsor-racecourse.co.uk).

SLEEPING

$$ Langton House B&B is a stately Victorian home with three well-appointed rooms lovingly maintained by Paul and Sonja

Fogg (Sb-£63, D-£75, T-£85, Q-£95, prices soft in winter, family-friendly, guest kitchen, Internet access, 5 percent to use credit card, 46 Alma Road, tel. & fax 01753/858-299, www.langtonhouse.co.uk, paul@langtonhouse.co.uk).

$$ Dorset Hotel rents four bright, spacious rooms in an elegant home on a quiet side street (Sb-£65, Db-£80, Tb-£95, parking, 4 Dorset Road, tel. 01753/852-669, Marie Cameron).

$$ The Netherton Hotel is a creaky and tired place with 12 no-personality rooms and lots of stairs (Db-£65, Tb-£85, family room-£95, 96 St. Leonard's Road, tel. 01753/855-508, fax 01753/621-267, netherton@btconnect.com).

EATING

Cornucopia Bistro, a favorite with locals, is a welcoming little place two minutes from the TI and castle, just beyond the tourist crush. They serve tasty international dishes with everything proudly made from scratch. The hardwood floors add a rustic elegance (£7.50 2-course lunches, £9 2-course dinners, Mon–Sat 12:00–14:30 & 18:00–22:00, Sun 12:00–14:30 only, 6 High Street, tel. 01753/833-009, Mark Simmons).

The Crooked House, across from the TI, is a touristy 17th-century, timber-framed teahouse that serves fresh, hearty £6–8 lunches and cream teas in a tipsy interior or outdoors on its cobbled lane (daily 9:30–18:00, 51 High Street, tel. 01753/857-534). The important-looking building next door is the Guildhall, where Charles finally married Camilla in April 2005.

Blondes is a lively café and tapas bar that dishes up good food all day, including breakfast (until 15:00), fresh salads, and steaks (Mon–Fri 9:00–15:30 & 18:00–24:00, Sat 8:00–24:00, Sun 9:00–18:00, 45 St. Leonard's Road, tel. 01753/470-079). While nothing really special, this place is handy to the recommended Windsor accommodations.

Cambridge

Cambridge, 60 miles north of London, is world-famous for its prestigious university. Wordsworth, Isaac Newton, Tennyson, Darwin, and Prince Charles are a few of its illustrious alumni. This historic town of 100,000 people is more pleasant than its rival, Oxford. Cambridge is the epitome of a university town, with busy bikers, stately residence halls, plenty of bookshops, and proud locals who can point out where DNA was modeled, the first atom was split, and electrons were discovered.

In medieval Europe, higher education was the domain of the

Church, and was limited to ecclesiastical schools. Scholars lived in "halls" on campus. This academic community of residential halls, chapels, and lecture halls connected by peaceful garden courtyards survives today in the colleges that make up the universities at Cambridge and Oxford. By 1350 (Oxford is roughly 100 years older), Cambridge had eight colleges, each with a monastic-type courtyard and lodgings. Today, Cambridge has 31 colleges. While a student's life revolves around his or her independent college, the university organizes lectures, presents degrees, and promotes research.

The university dominates—and owns—most of Cambridge. The approximate term schedule is late January to late March (called Lent term), mid-April to mid-June (Easter term), and early October to early December (Michaelmas term). The colleges are closed to visitors during exams, in mid-April and late June, but King's College Chapel and the Trinity Library stay open, and the town is never sleepy.

Planning Your Time

Cambridge is worth most of a day but not an overnight. Arrive in time for the 11:30 walking tour—an essential part of any visit—and spend the afternoon touring King's College Chapel and Fitzwilliam Museum (closed Mon) or simply enjoying the ambience of this stately old college town.

Getting to Cambridge

By Train: It's an easy and economical trip from London, 50 minutes away. Catch the train from London's King's Cross Station (2/hr, fast trains leaving at :15 and :45 past each hour run in each direction, 50 min, one-way £16, cheap day-return for £16.50 if you depart London after 9:30 weekdays or anytime Sat–Sun).

ORIENTATION

Cambridge is congested but small. Everything is within a pleasant walk. There are two main streets, separated from the river by the most interesting colleges. The town center, brimming with tearooms, has a TI and a colorful open-air market (daily 9:30–16:00, on Market Hill Square; arts and crafts Sun 10:30–16:30, clothes and produce rest of week).

Tourist Information

At the station, a City Sightseeing office dispenses free city maps and sells fancier ones. The official TI is well signposted and just off Market Hill Square. They book rooms for £3 and sell a 30p mini-guide/map (Mon–Fri 10:00–17:30, Sat 10:00–17:00, Sun 11:00–16:00, closed Sun Nov–Easter, toll tel. 0906/586-2526

Cambridge

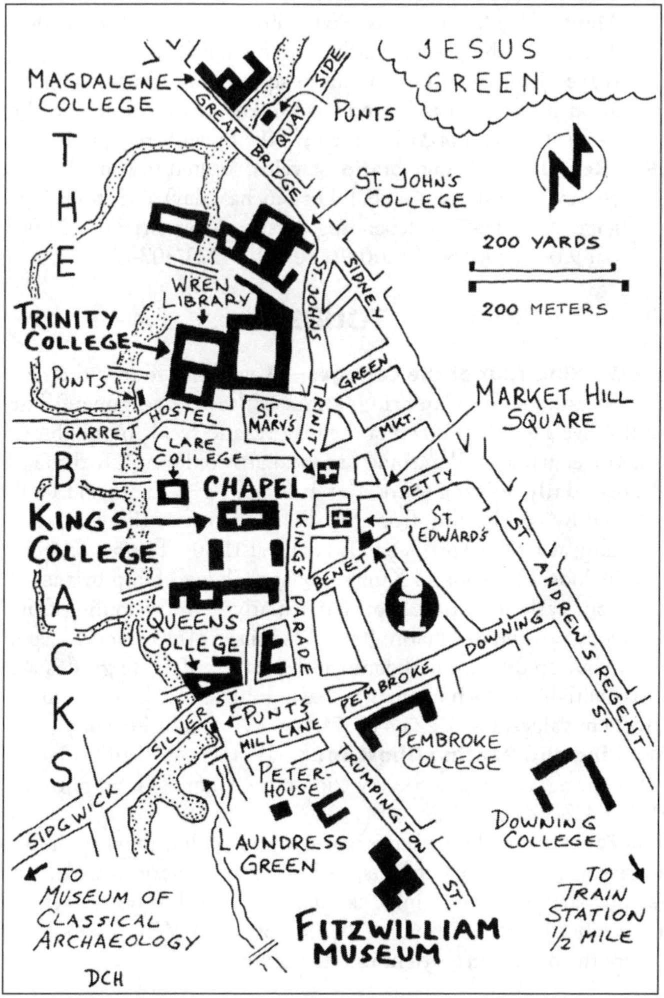

costs 60p/min, room-booking line: tel. 01223/457-581).

Arrival in Cambridge

To get to downtown Cambridge from the train station, take a 20-minute walk (the City Sightseeing map is fine for this), a £4 taxi ride, or bus #C1 or #C3 (£1, every 5–10 min). Drivers can follow signs to any of the handy and central Short Stay Parking Lots.

Helpful Hints

Supermarkets: A Marks & Spencer Simply Food grocery is at the train station; a larger Marks & Spencer is on the main square, Market Hill Square (Mon–Sat 8:30–19:00, Sun 11:00–17:00). The J. Sainsbury supermarket, with slightly longer hours, is three blocks north of the main square on Sidney Street. A good picnic spot is Laundress Green, a grassy park on the river, at the end of Mill Lane near the Silver Street punts.

Bike Rental: Cambridge Station Cycles, located to your right as you exit the station, rents bikes (£6/half day) and stores luggage (£2–3 per bag depending on size, Mon–Fri 7:00–20:00, Sat 9:00–17:00, Sun 10:00–16:00, tel. 01223/307-125).

TOURS

▲▲Walking Tour of the Colleges—A walking tour is the best way to understand Cambridge's mix of "town and gown." The walks give a good rundown of the historic and scenic highlights of the university, as well as some fun local gossip. From July through August, **daily walking tours** start at 10:30, 11:30, 13:30, and 14:30 (offered by and leaving from the TI). The rest of the year, they run daily at 13:30 (April–Oct also daily at 11:30). Tours cost £8.50 and include admission to King's College Chapel. Drop by the TI one hour early to snare a spot. Particularly if you're coming from London, call the day before (tel. 01223/457-574) to reserve a spot with your credit card and confirm departure. **Private guides** are also available (£45/hour for the basic tour, £57/2-hr city tour—excellent values, tel. 01223/457-574, www.visitcambridge.org).

Walking and Punting Ghost Tour—If you're in Cambridge in the evening, consider a spooky trip on the Cam (£14, 90 min, tel. 01223/457-574).

Bus Tours—City Sightseeing hop-on, hop-off bus tours are informative and cover the outskirts, including the American Cemetery (£8, departing every 15 min, can use credit card to buy tickets in their office in train station, tel. 01708/866-000). Walking tours go where the buses can't—right into the center.

SIGHTS AND ACTIVITIES

▲▲King's College Chapel—Built from 1446 to 1515 by Henrys VI through VIII, England's best example of Perpendicular Gothic is the single most impressive building in town. Stand inside, look up, and marvel, as Christopher Wren did, at what was the largest single span of vaulted roof anywhere—2,000 tons of incredible fan vaulting. Wander through the Old Testament, with 25 16th-century stained-glass windows (the most Renaissance stained glass anywhere in one spot; it was taken out for safety during WWII, then painstakingly replaced). Walk to the altar and admire Rubens' masterful *Adoration of the Magi* (£4.50, erratic hours depending on school and events, but usually daily 9:30–16:00). During term, you're welcome to enjoy an evensong service (Mon–Sat at 17:30, Sun at 15:30, tel. 01223/331-447).

▲▲Trinity College—Half of Cambridge's 63 Nobel Prize winners have come from this richest and biggest of the town's colleges, founded in 1546 by Henry VIII. Don't miss the Wren-designed library, with its wonderful carving and fascinating original manuscripts (£2.20, 10p leaflet, Mon–Fri 12:00–14:00, also Sat 10:30–12:30 during term, always closed Sun and during exams; or visit the library for free during the same hours from the riverside entrance by the Garret Hostel Bridge, tel. 01223/338-400). Just outside the library entrance, Sir Isaac Newton, who spent 30 years at Trinity, clapped his hands and timed the echo to measure the speed of sound as it raced down the side of the cloister and back. In the library's display cases (covered with brown cloth that you flip back), you'll see handwritten works by Newton, Milton, Byron, Tennyson, and Housman, alongside Milne's original *Winnie the Pooh* (the real Christopher Robin attended Trinity College).

▲▲Fitzwilliam Museum—Britain's best museum of antiquities and art outside of London is the Fitzwilliam. Enjoy its wonderful paintings (Old Masters and a fine English section featuring Gainsborough, Reynolds, Hogarth, and others, plus works by all the famous Impressionists), old manuscripts, and Greek, Egyptian, and Mesopotamian collections (free, Tue–Sat 10:00–17:00, Sun 12:00–17:00, closed Mon, tel. 01223/332-900, www.fitzmuseum.cam.ac.uk).

Museum of Classical Archaeology—While this museum contains no originals, it offers a unique chance to see accurate copies (19th-century casts) of virtually every famous ancient Greek and Roman statue. More than 450 statues are on display (free, Mon–Fri 10:00–17:00, sometimes also Sat 10:00–13:00 during term, always closed Sun, Sidgwick Avenue, tel. 01223/335-153). The museum is a five-minute walk west of Silver Street Bridge; after crossing the bridge, continue straight until you reach a sign reading *Sidgwick Site* (museum is on your right; the entrance is away from the street).

▲Punting on the Cam—For a little levity and probably more exercise than you really want, try hiring one of the traditional (and inexpensive) flat-bottom punts at the river and pole yourself up and down (around and around, more likely) the lazy Cam. Once you get the hang of it, it's a fine way to enjoy the scenic side of Cambridge. After 17:00 it's less crowded and less embarrassing.

Three places, one at each bridge, rent punts (£60 deposit required, can use credit card) and offer £14 50-minute punt tours. Trinity Punt, at Garrett Hostel Bridge near Trinity College, has the best prices (£8–10/hr rental, ask for free short lesson, tel. 01223/338-483). Scudamore's runs two other locations: the central Silver Street Bridge (£12–14/hr rentals) and the less-convenient Quayside at Great Bridge, at the north end of town (£14–16/hr, tel. 01223/359-750, www.scudamores.com). Depending on the weather, punting season runs daily March through October, with Silver Street open weekends off-season.

TRANSPORTATION CONNECTIONS

From Cambridge by Train to: York (hrly, 2.5 hrs, transfer in Peterborough, about £50), **London** (2/hr, 50 min). Train info: tel. 0845-748-4950.

By Bus to: Heathrow (1 bus/hr, 2.5 hrs). Bus info: tel. 0870-575-7747.

Bath

The best city to visit within easy striking distance of London is Bath—just a 90-minute train ride away. Two hundred years ago, this city of 85,000 was the trendsetting Hollywood of Britain. If ever a city enjoyed looking in the mirror, Bath's the one. It has more "government-listed" or protected historic buildings per capita than any other town in England. The entire city, built of the creamy warm-tone limestone called "Bath stone," beams in its cover-girl complexion. An architectural chorus line, it's a triumph of the Georgian style. Proud locals remind visitors that the town is routinely banned from the "Britain in Bloom" contest to give other towns a chance to win. Bath's narcissism is justified. Even with its mobs of tourists (2 million per year), Bath is a joy to visit.

Long before the Romans arrived in the first century, Bath was known for its hot springs. The importance of Bath has always been shaped by the healing allure of its 116-degree mineral hot springs. Romans called the popular spa town Aquae Sulis. The town's importance carried through Saxon times, when it had a huge church on the site of the present-day abbey and was considered the religious capital of Britain. Its influence peaked in 973 with King Edgar's sumptuous coronation in the abbey. Later Bath prospered as a wool town.

Bath then declined until the mid-1600s, when it was just a

Bath

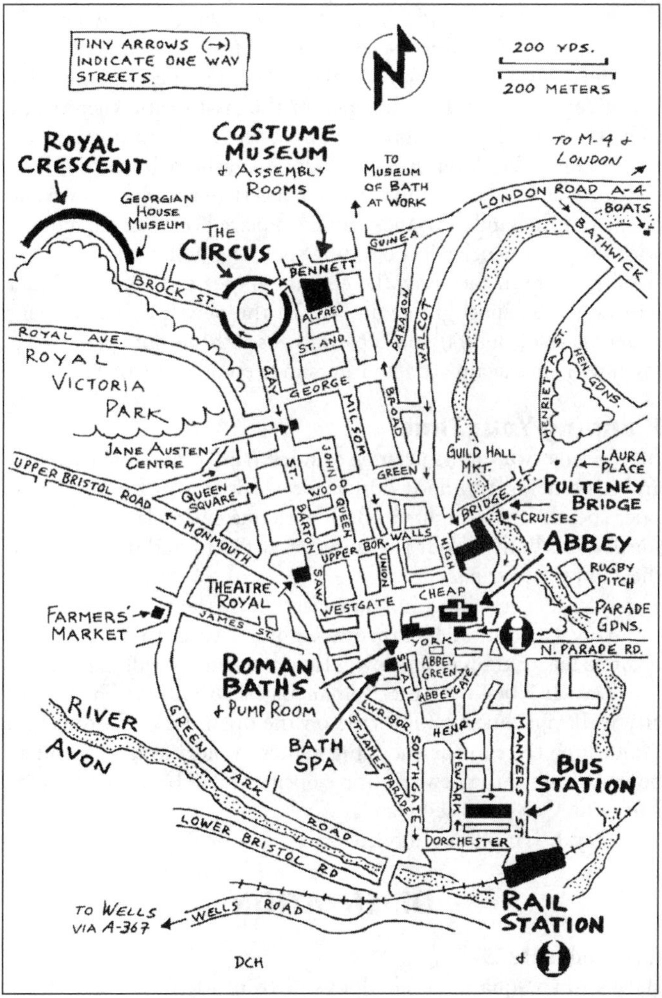

huddle of huts around the abbey, with hot, smelly mud and 3,000 residents, oblivious to the Roman ruins 18 feet below their dirt floors. Then, in 1687, Queen Mary, fighting infertility, bathed here. Within 10 months she gave birth to a son...and a new age of popularity for Bath.

The revitalized town boomed as a spa resort. Ninety percent of the buildings you'll see today are from the 18th century. Local architect John Wood was inspired by the Italian architect Andrea Palladio to build a "new Rome." The town bloomed in the neoclassical style, and streets were lined not with scrawny sidewalks but with wide "parades," upon which the women in their stylishly wide dresses could spread their fashionable tails.

Beau Nash (1673–1762) was Bath's "master of ceremonies." He organized both the daily regimen of the aristocratic visitors and the city, lighting and improving street security, banning swords, and opening the Pump Room. Under his fashionable baton, Bath became a city of balls, gaming, and concerts—the place to see and be seen in England. This most civilized place became even more so with the great neoclassical building spree that followed.

The buzz in the early 21st century is that the venerable baths will be in the spotlight again. When the new spa finally opens (after years of delays) and taps Bath's soothing hot springs, the town will once again attract visitors in need of a cure or a soak.

Planning Your Time

Bath needs two nights even on a quick trip. There's plenty to do, and it's a delight to do it. On a one-week trip to London, consider spending two nights in Bath with one entire day for the city. Ideally, use Bath as your jet-lag recovery pillow and do London at the end of your trip.

Consider starting a London vacation this way:

Day 1: Land at Heathrow. Connect to Bath by National Express bus or train (see below). Take an evening walking tour.

Day 2: 9:00–Tour the Roman Baths; 10:30–Catch the free city walking tour; 12:30–Picnic on the open deck of a tour bus; 14:30–Free time in the shopping center of old Bath, or spend an hour soaking at the new spa (if it's open); 15:30–Tour the Costume Museum. Consider seeing a play.

Day 3: Early train into London.

ORIENTATION

(area code: 01225)

Bath's town square, three blocks in front of the bus and train station, is a bouquet of tourist landmarks, including the abbey, Roman and medieval baths, and the royal Pump Room.

Tourist Information

The TI is in the abbey churchyard (Mon–Sat 9:30–17:00, Sun 10:00–16:00, tel. 0870/420-1278, www.visitbath.co.uk). Pick up the 50p Bath mini-guide (includes a map) and the free, info-packed *This Month in Bath.* Browse through scads of fliers, books, and maps. Skip their room-finding service (£5 fee and your host is nicked 10 percent) and book direct.

Arrival in Bath

The Bath **train station** has small-town charm, a national and international tickets desk, and a privately run tourism office masquerading as a TI. The **bus station** is immediately in front of the train station. To get to the TI from either station, walk two blocks up Manvers Street and turn left at the triangular "square," by following the small TI arrow on a signpost. My recommended B&Bs are all within a 10- to 15-minute walk or a £4 taxi ride from the station.

Helpful Hints

Festivals: The **Bath Literature Festival** is an open book from March 4 to 12 in 2006 (www.bathlitfest.org.uk). The **Bath International Music Festival** bursts into song from May 19 to June 4 in 2006 (classical, folk, jazz, contemporary; for the lineup, see www.bathmusicfest.org.uk), overlapped by the eclectic **Bath Fringe Festival** from May 26 to June 11 (theater, walks, talks, bus trips; www.bathfringe.co.uk). The **Jane Austen Festival** unfolds genteelly mid- to late September (www.janeaustenfestival.co.uk). Bath's festival box office sells tickets for most events, and can tell you exactly what's on tonight (2 Church Street, tel. 01225/463-362, www.bathfestivals.org.uk). Bath's local paper, the *Bath Chronicle,* publishes a "What's On" event listing on Fridays (www.thisisbath.com).

Car Rental: Hertz and **Enterprise** are each handy to central Bath, and have roughly the same rates: £40/day, £80/weekend, and £160/week. Enterprise provides a pickup service for customers to and from their hotels, but doesn't do one-way rentals (at Lower Bristol Road in Bath, tel. 01225/443-311). Hertz is just outside Bath train station (tel. 01225/442-911). **National/Alamo** is a £7 taxi ride from the train station, but often has better rates than Hertz, and will do one-way rentals (at Brass Mill Lane—go west on Upper Bristol Road, tel. 01225/481-898). **Europcar** advertises it's in Bath but is relatively far outside of town. **Avis** is a mile from the Bristol train station; you'd need to rent a car to get there. Most offices close Saturday afternoon and all day Sunday, which complicates weekend pickups. Ideally, take the train or bus from London to Bath and rent a car as you leave Bath, rather than from within London.

Internet Access: Try the Internet place a block in front of the train station (daily 9:00–22:00, on Manvers Street, tel. 01225/443-181).

Laundry: The **Spruce Goose Launderette** is around the corner from the recommended Brock's Guest House on the pedestrian lane called Margaret's Buildings (daily 8:00–21:00, self-service or full-service on same day if dropped off at 8:00, tel. 01225/483-309). Anywhere in town, **Speedy Wash** can pick up your laundry for same-day service (£10/bag, Mon–Fri 7:30–17:30, most hotels work with them, tel. 01225/427-616). East of Pulteney Bridge, the humble **Lovely Wash** is on Daniel Street (daily 9:00–21:00, self-service only).

TOURS

Of Bath

▲▲▲Walking Tours—Free two-hour tours are offered by **The Mayor's Corps of Honorary Guides,** led by volunteers who want to share their love of Bath with its many visitors. Their chatty, historical, and gossip-filled walks are essential for your understanding of this town's amazing Georgian social scene. How else will you learn that the old "chair ho" call for your sedan chair evolved into today's "cheerio" farewell? Tours leave from in front of the Pump Room (free, no tips, year-round Sun–Fri at 10:30 and 14:00, Sun at 10:30 only; evening walks offered May–Sept at 19:00 on Tue, Fri, and Sat). Advice for theater-goers: Guides stop to talk outside the Theatre Royal. You can skip out a moment, pop into the box office, and snare a great deal on a play for tonight (see "Nightlife" on page 359 for details).

For a **private tour,** call the local guides' bureau (£52/2 hrs, tel. 01225/337-111). For **Ghost Walks, Pub Crawls,** and **Bizarre Bath** tours, see "Nightlife," page 359.

Taxi Tours—Local taxis, driven by good talkers, go where big buses can't. A group of up to four can rent a cab for an hour (about £20) and enjoy a fine, informative, and—with the right cabbie—entertaining private joyride. It's probably cheaper to let the meter run than to pay for an hourly rate, but ask the cabbie for advice.

▲▲City Bus Tours—Two companies run hop-on, hop-off bus tours through Bath. Jump on anytime, pay the driver, and climb upstairs. If you're on a Classic City Tour, enjoy the rapid-fire spiel of your live guide; City Sightseeing has taped commentary only (17 signposted pick-up points, generally 4/hr from 9:30–17:00, more frequent and with longer hours in summer). On a sunny day, this is a multitasking tourist's dream-come-true: You can munch a sandwich, work on a tan, snap great photos, and learn a lot all at the same time. Save money by doing the bus tour first—ticket stubs get you minor discounts at many sights. Choose between...

Classic City Tours (red with white stripe): These buses follow the same route as transit buses. (They're required to take passengers across town for the normal £1 fare.) They come with live guides, and are a better value than City Sightseeing (£6.50/2 days, tours run Mon–Sat).

City Sightseeing (red-orange buses): Tickets on this bus line are more expensive (£9, good for 24 hours on either of their routes). But they have two advantages over Classic City Tours: they run on Sundays and they have a second "Skyline" route outside of town, handy for those wanting to visit the American Museum (see page 358).

Of Stonehenge, Avebury, and the Cotswolds

Bath is a good launchpad for visiting Wells, Avebury, Stonehenge, and more.

Mad Max Minibus Tours—Operating daily from Bath, Maddy and Paul offer thoughtfully organized, informative tours that run with a maximum group size of 16 people. Their **Stone Circles and Villages** full-day tour (8:45–16:30) covers 110 miles and visits Stonehenge, the Avebury Stone Circle, and two cute villages—Lacock and Castle Combe. The southernmost Cotswold village, Castle Combe is as sweet as they come (£22.50, cash only, Stonehenge admission not included).

Mad Max also offers the **Cotswold Discovery** full-day tour, a picturesque romp through the countryside, with stops in the Cotswolds' quainter villages, including Stow-on-the-Wold, Bibury, Tetbury, the Coln Valley, and others. If you request this in advance, you can use the tour as transportation to get to Stow or Moreton, and bring your luggage along (£25, runs Sun, Tue, and Thu 8:45–17:15). Their short tour of **Stonehenge and Bradford-on-Avon**—a worthwhile extra stop, with a fascinating Saxon church—leaves daily at 13:30 and ends at 17:15 (£12.50, Stonehenge entry extra).

All tours depart from Bath at the Glass House shop on the corner of Orange Grove, a one-minute walk from the abbey. Arrive a few minutes before your departure time. Only cash is accepted as payment.

It's better to book ahead for these popular tours via e-mail (www.madmaxtours.co.uk, maddy@madmax.abel.co.uk) rather than by phone (Mon–Fri 8:00–18:00, tel. 01225/464-323). Please honor or cancel your seat reservation.

More Bus Tours—If Mad Max is booked up, don't fret. Plenty of companies in Bath offer tours of varying lengths, prices, and destinations. Note that the cost of admission to sites is usually not included with any tour. **Scarper Tours** runs a minibus tour to Stonehenge (£12.50, departs daily Easter–Sept 9:30 and 13:30, Oct–Easter 13:30 only, tel. 07739/644-155, www.scarpertours.com); they also run a Glastonbury and Wells trip (daily, ask at TI or check their Web site). **Heritage City Guided Tour** does a "Stonehenge Express" trip out to the rocks and back (£14, 3.25 hrs, departs from Grand Parade circle behind abbey, daily at 10:00 and 14:00, 01225/444-102).

Bath at a Glance

▲▲▲**Roman and Medieval Baths** Ancient baths that gave the city its name, tourable with good audioguide. **Hours:** Daily April–Sept 9:00–18:00, July–Aug until 22:00, Oct–March 9:00–17:30.

▲▲▲**Costume Museum** 400 years of fashion under one roof, plus opulent Assembly Rooms. **Hours:** Daily March–Oct 11:00–18:00, Nov–March 11:00–17:00.

▲▲▲**Museum of Bath at Work** Gadget-ridden, circa-1900 engineer's shop, foundry, factory, and office, best enjoyed with a live tour. **Hours:** April–Oct daily 10:30–17:00, weekends only in winter.

▲▲**Royal Crescent and the Circus** Stately Georgian (neoclassical) buildings from Bath's late-18th-century glory days. **Hours:** Always viewable.

▲▲**Georgian House at No. 1 Royal Crescent** Best opportunity to explore the interior of one of Bath's high-rent Georgian beauties. **Hours:** Mid-Feb–Oct Tue–Sun 10:30–17:00, closes at 16:00 in Nov, closed Mon and Dec–mid-Feb.

▲**Pump Room** Swanky Georgian hall, ideal for a spot of tea or a taste of unforgettably "healthy" spa water. **Hours:** Daily 9:30–12:00 for coffee, 12:00–14:30 for lunch, 14:30–17:00 for high tea (open for dinner July–Aug only).

Celtic Horizons, run by retired teacher Alan Price, offers tours from Bath to a variety of destinations, such as Stonehenge, Avebury, Wells, and South Wales. He can provide a convenient transfer service (to—or from—London, Heathrow, the Cotswolds, and so on) which can include a tour itinerary en route. He also does personalized genealogy tours. His comfortable minivan seats one to eight people; allow around £20/hr per person. It's best to make arrangements via e-mail at alan@celtichorizons.com (www.celtichorizons.com, tel. 01373/461-784).

SIGHTS

▲▲▲**Roman and Medieval Baths**—In ancient Roman times, high society enjoyed the mineral springs at Bath. From Londinium, Romans traveled so often to Aquae Sulis, as the city was called, to "take a bath" that finally it became known simply as Bath. Today, a fine museum surrounds the ancient bath. It's a one-way system

▲Abbey 500-year-old Perpendicular Gothic church, graced with beautiful fan vaulting and stained glass. **Hours:** Mon–Sat 9:00–18:00, Sun usually 13:00–14:30 & 15:30–17:30, closes at 16:30 in winter.

▲Pulteney Bridge and Parade Gardens Shop-strewn bridge and relaxing riverside gardens. **Hours:** Bridge—always open; gardens—April–Sept daily 10:00–19:00, May–Aug until 20:00, shorter hours off-season.

▲American Museum An insightful look at colonial/early-American lifestyles, with 18 furnished rooms complete with guides eager to talk. **Hours:** April–Oct Tue–Sun 14:00–17:30, closed Mon and Nov–March.

Jane Austen Centre Exhibit on 19th-century Bath-based novelist, best for her fans. **Hours:** Mon–Sat 10:00–17:30, Sun 10:30–17:30.

Building of Bath Museum Architecture buff's guide to Bath. **Hours:** Tue–Sun 10:30–17:00, closed Mon.

Thermae Bath Spa Long-delayed, brand-new relaxation center, putting the bath back in Bath. **Hours:** Should possibly, maybe, finally open in 2006.

leading you past well-documented displays, Roman artifacts, mosaics, a temple pediment, and the actual mouth of the spring, piled high with Roman pennies. Enjoy some quality time looking into the eyes of Minerva, goddess of the hot springs. The included self-guided tour audioguide makes the visit easy and plenty informative. For those with a big appetite for Roman history, in-depth 40-minute tours leave from the end of the museum at the edge of the actual bath (included with ticket, on the hour, a poolside clock is set for the next departure time). The water is greenish because of the lead—don't drink it. You can revisit the museum after the tour (£9.50, £12.50 combo-ticket includes Costume Museum—a £3.25 savings, family combo-£33.50, combo-tickets good for 1 week, April–Sept daily 9:00–18:00, July–Aug until

22:00—last entry an hour before, Oct–March until 17:30, tel. 01225/477-784, www.romanbaths.co.uk). The museum and baths are fun to visit in the evening—romantic, gas-lit, and all yours. After touring the Roman Baths, stop by the attached Pump Room for a spot of tea, or to gag on the water.

▲Pump Room—For centuries, Bath was forgotten as a spa. Then, in 1687, the previously barren Queen Mary bathed here, became pregnant, and bore a male heir to the throne. A few years later Queen Anne found the water eased her gout. Word of its wonder waters spread, and Bath was back on the aristocratic map. High society soon turned the place into one big pleasure palace. The Pump Room, an elegant Georgian hall just above the Roman Baths, offers the visitor's best chance to raise a pinky in this Chippendale grandeur. Drop by to sip coffee or tea or enjoy a light meal (daily 9:30–12:00 for morning coffee, 12:00–14:30 for lunch—£16 2-course menu, 14:30–17:00 for traditional high tea—£12, £7 tea/coffee and pastry available in the afternoons, open for dinner July–Aug only; live music daily—string trio 10:00–12:00, piano 12:00–14:30, string trio 15:00–17:00; tel. 01225/444-477). Above the newspaper table and sedan chairs, a statue of Beau Nash himself sniffles down at you.

The Spa Water: This is your chance to sip a famous (but forgettable) "Bath bun" and split (and spit) a 50p drink of the awful curative water. The water is served from the King's Spring by appropriately attired Martin, who's ready to minuet (but refuses to gavotte). He explains that the water is 10,000 years old, marinated in wonderful minerals, and pumped from nearly 100 yards deep. Convenient public WCs are in the entry hallway that connects the Pump Room with the baths (but are not associated with the spa water).

Thermae Bath Spa—After simmering unused for a quarter-century, Bath's natural thermal springs will possibly once again offer R&R for the masses. The state-of-the-art leisure and curative spa, housed in a complex combining old buildings with controversial new, blocky architecture, is scheduled to open (after numerous delays) in 2006. The only natural thermal spa in the United Kingdom, it will include an open-air rooftop thermal pool and all the "pamper thyself" extras—aromatherapy steam rooms, mud wraps, and various healing-type treatments and classes. Swimwear will be required (if it ever opens, it'll be open daily 9:00–22:00,£17/2 hrs, £23/4 hrs, £35/full day; treatments, massage, and solarium cost extra–ranging from £26–68; 100 yards from Roman and medieval baths on Beau Street, tel. 01225/331-234, www.thermaebathspa.com for the latest).

▲Abbey—The town of Bath wasn't much in the Middle Ages, but an important church has stood on this spot since Anglo-Saxon

times. In 973, Edgar was crowned here. Dominating the town center, the present church—the last great medieval church of England—is 500 years old and a fine example of Late Perpendicular Gothic, with breezy fan vaulting and enough stained glass to earn it the nickname "Lantern of the West." The glass, red-iron gas-powered lamps, and heating grates on the floor are all remnants of the 19th century. The window behind the altar shows 52 scenes from the life of Christ. A window to the left of the altar shows that coronation of Edgar in 973 (worth the £2.50 donation, Mon–Sat 9:00–18:00, Sun usually 13:00–14:30 & 15:30–17:30, closes at 16:30 in winter, handy flyer narrates a self-guided 19-stop tour, www.bathabbey.org). Posted on the door is the schedule for concerts, services, and **evensong** (Sun at 15:30 year-round, plus most Sat in Aug at 17:00). The facade (c. 1500, but mostly restored) is interesting for some of its carvings. Look for the angels going down the ladder. The statue of Peter (to the left of the door) lost his head to mean iconoclasts; it was re-carved out of his once super-sized beard. Take a moment to appreciate the abbey's architecture from the Abbey Green square.

A small but worthwhile exhibit, the abbey's **Heritage Vaults,** tell the story of Christianity in Bath since Roman times (£1, Mon–Sat 10:00–16:00, last entry 15:30, closed Sun, entrance just outside church, south side).

▲Pulteney Bridge, Parade Gardens, and Cruises—Bath is inclined to compare its shop-lined Pulteney Bridge to Florence's Ponte Vecchio. That's pushing it. But to best enjoy a sunny day, pay about £1 to enter the Parade Gardens below the bridge (April–Sept daily 10:00–19:00, May–Aug until 20:00, shorter hours off-season, includes deck chairs, ask about concerts held some Sun at 15:00 in summer, tel. 01225/394-041). Taking a siesta to relax peacefully at the riverside provides a wonderful break (and memory).

Across the bridge at Pulteney Weir, tour boat companies run **cruises** (£7, up to 7/day if the weather's good, 50 min to Bathampton and back, WCs on board). Just take whatever boat is running. Avon Cruisers actually stop in Bathampton (allowing you to hop off and walk back); Pulteney Cruisers come with a sundeck ideal for picnics.

Guildhall Market, located across from Pulteney Bridge, is a frumpy time warp in this affluent place, but it's fun for browsing and picnic shopping. Its cheap Market Café is recommended under "Eating," page 368.

The Victoria Art Gallery, also across from Pulteney Bridge, fills a fine room with paintings from the 18th and 19th centuries (free, includes audioguide, daily 10:00–17:00, WC, next to the Market).

▲▲Royal Crescent and the Circus—If Bath is an architectural cancan, these are the knickers. These first Georgian "condos" by John Wood (the Elder and the Younger) are well-explained in the city walking tours. "Georgian" is British for "neoclassical," or dating from the 1770s. As you cruise the Crescent, pretend you're rich. Pretend you're poor. Notice the "ha ha fence," a drop-off in the front yard that acted as a barrier, invisible from the windows, for keeping out sheep and peasants. The refined and stylish Royal Crescent Hotel sits unmarked in the center of the crescent. You're welcome to (politely) drop in to explore its fine ground floor public spaces. A gracious and traditional cream tea is served in the garden out back (£11, daily 12:00–17:30).

Picture the round Circus as a colosseum turned inside out. Its Doric, Ionic, and Corinthian capital decorations pay homage to its Greco-Roman origin, and are a reminder that Bath (with its 7 hills) aspired to be "the Rome of England." The frieze above the first row of columns has hundreds of different panels, each representing the arts, sciences, and crafts. The first floor was high off the ground, to accommodate aristocrats on sedan chairs and women with Cher-like hairdos. The tiny round windows on the top floors were the servants' quarters. While the building fronts are uniform, the backs are higgledy-piggledy, infamous for their "hanging loos." Stand in the middle of the Crescent among the grand plane trees, on the capped old well. Imagine the days when there was no indoor plumbing, and the servant girls gathered here to fetch water—this was gossip central. Standing on the well, your clap echoes three times around the circle (try it).

▲▲Georgian House at No. 1 Royal Crescent—This museum (corner of Brock Street and Royal Crescent) offers your best look into a period house. It's worth the £4 admission to get behind one of those classy exteriors. The volunteers in each room are determined to fill you in on all the fascinating details of Georgian life...like how high-class women shaved their eyebrows and pasted on carefully trimmed strips of furry mouse skin in their place. On the bedroom dresser sits a bowl of black beauty marks and a hair scratcher from those pre-shampoo days. Fido spent his days in the kitchen treadmill powering the rotisserie (mid-Feb–Oct Tue–Sun 10:30–

17:00, closes at 16:00 in Nov, closed Mon and Dec–mid-Feb, "no stiletto heels, please," tel. 01225/428-126, www.bath-preservation-trust.org.uk).

▲▲▲Costume Museum—One of Europe's great museums, it displays 400 years of fashion—one frilly decade at a time—and is housed within Bath's Assembly Rooms. Follow the excellent included audioguide tour and allow two hours (£6.25, £12.50 combo-ticket covers Roman Baths—saving you £3.25, family combo-£33.50, daily March–Oct 11:00–18:00, Nov–Feb 11:00–17:00, last entry 1 hour before closing, tel. 01225/477-789, www.museumofcostume.co.uk).

The **Assembly Rooms,** which you can see for free en route to the museum, are big, grand, empty rooms. Card games, concerts, tea, and dances were held here in the 18th century, before the advent of fancy hotels with grand public spaces made them obsolete. Note the extreme symmetry (pleasing to the aristocratic eye) and the high windows (which assured their privacy). After the Allies bombed the historical and well-preserved German city of Lübeck, the Germans picked up a Baedeker guide and chose a similarly lovely city to bomb: Bath. The Assembly Rooms—gutted in this wartime tit-for-tat by WWII bombs—have since been restored to their original splendor. (Only the chandeliers are original.)

Below the Costume Museum (left as you leave, 20 yards away) is one of the few surviving sets of iron house hardware. "Link boys" carried torches through the dark streets, lighting the way for big shots in their sedan chairs as they traveled from one affair to the next. The link boys extinguished their torches in the black conical "snuffers." The lamp above was once gas-lit. The crank on the left was used to hoist bulky things to various windows (see the hooks). Few of these sets survived the dark days of the WWII Blitz, when most were collected, melted down, and turned into weapons to power the British war machine.

▲▲▲Museum of Bath at Work—This is the official title for Mr. Bowler's Business, a 1900s engineer's shop, brass foundry, and fizzy-drink factory with a Dickensian office. It's just a pile of meaningless old gadgets until a volunteer guide lovingly resurrects Mr. Bowler's creative genius. Also featured are various Bath creations through the years, including a 1914 car and the versatile plasticine (proto-Play-Doh, handy for clay-mation and more). Don't miss the fine "Story of Bath Stone" in the basement. While there are included audioguides, the live tours are the key (wonderful 45-minute tours go regularly). If rushed, join one already in session (£4, April–Oct daily 10:30–17:00, last entry at 16:00, weekends only in winter, 2 blocks up Russell Street from Assembly Rooms, steep uphill hike, tel. 01225/318-348).

Jane Austen Centre—This exhibition focuses on Jane Austen's five years in Bath (around 1800), and the influence Bath had on her writing. While the exhibit is thoughtfully done and a hit with "Jane-ites," there is little of historic substance here. You'll walk through a Georgian town house that she didn't live in, and see mostly enlarged reproductions of things associated with her writing. The museum describes various places from two novels set in Bath (*Persuasion* and *Northanger Abbey*). After a live intro (15 min, 3/hr) explaining how this romantic but down-to-earth girl dealt with the silly, shallow, and arrogant aristocrat's world where "the doing of nothings all day prevents one from doing anything," you see a 15-minute video and wander through the rest of the exhibit (£4.65; March–Oct Mon–Sat 10:00–17:30, Sun 10:30–17:30; Nov–Feb 11:00–16:30, 40 Gay Street between Queen's Square and the Circus, tel. 01225/443-000, www.janeausten.co.uk). Avid fans gather in mid- to late September for the annual Bath Jane Austen Festival (readings and lectures, www.janeaustenfestival.co.uk).

If you're male and feeling left out, head one door downhill from the museum and look through the window. You'll see a fine delftware-decorated powder bowl designed for men to touch up their wigs.

Building of Bath Museum—This offers an intriguing look behind the scenes at how the Georgian city was actually built. It's just a couple rooms of exhibits, but those interested in construction—inside and out—find it worth the £4 (Tue–Sun 10:30–17:00, closed Mon, above the Circus on a street called "The Paragon," tel. 01225/333-895).

▲American Museum—I know, you need this in Bath like you need a Big Mac. But this museum offers a compelling look at colonial and early-American lifestyles. Each of 18 completely furnished rooms (from the 1600s to the 1800s) is hosted by an eager guide waiting to fill you in on the candles, maps, bedpans, and various religious sects that make domestic Yankee history surprisingly interesting. One room is a quilter's nirvana (£6.50, April–Oct Tue–Sun 14:00–17:30, closed Mon and Nov–March, nice arboretum, at Claverton Manor, tel. 01225/460-503, www.americanmuseum.org). The museum is outside of town and a headache to reach if you don't have a car (10-min walk from bus #18).

ACTIVITIES

Walking—The Bath Skyline Walk is a six-mile wander around the hills surrounding Bath (leaflet at TI). Plenty of other scenic paths are described in the TI's literature. For additional options, get *Country Walks around Bath,* by Tim Mowls (£4.50 at TI).

Hiking the Canal to Bathampton—An idyllic towpath leads

from the Bath train station along an old canal to the sleepy village of Bathampton. Immediately behind the station, cross the footbridge and see where the canal hits the river. Turn left, noticing the series of industrial-age locks, and walk along the towpath, giving thanks that you're not a horse pulling a barge. You'll be in Bathampton in less than an hour, where a classic pub awaits with a nice lunch and cellar-temp beer.

Boating—The Bath Boating Station, in an old Victorian boathouse, rents boats and punts (£5 per person/first hr, then £1.50/additional hr, April–Sept daily 10:00–18:00, Forester Road, 1 mile northeast of center, tel. 01225/312-900).

Swimming—The Bath Sports and Leisure Centre has a fine pool for laps as well as lots of water slides and entertaining gadgets for kids (£3, daily 8:00–22:00 but kids' hours are limited, call for open swim times, just across North Parade Bridge, tel. 01225/462-565).

Shopping—There's great browsing between the abbey and the Assembly Rooms (Costume Museum). Shops close at 17:30, some have longer hours on Thursday, and many are open on Sunday (11:00–17:00). Explore the antique shops lining Bartlett Street just below the Assembly Rooms.

NIGHTLIFE

Events are listed in *This Month in Bath* (free, available at TI) and "What's On," appearing Fridays in the local newspaper, the *Bath Chronicle* (www.thisisbath.com).

▲▲▲Bizarre Bath Street Theater—For an immensely entertaining walking-tour comedy act "with absolutely no history or culture," follow J. J. or Noel Britten on their creative and entertaining Bizarre Bath walk. This 90-minute "tour," which plays off local passersby as well as tour members, is a belly laugh a minute (£5, April–Sept nightly at 20:00, smaller groups Mon–Thu, heavy on magic, careful to insult all minorities and sensitivities, just racy enough but still good family fun, leave from Huntsman pub near the abbey, confirm at TI or call 01225/335-124, www.bizarrebath.co.uk).

▲Plays—The 18th-century Theatre Royal, newly restored and one of England's loveliest, offers a busy schedule of London West End–type plays, including many "pre-London" dress-rehearsal runs (£11–25, generally start at 19:30 or 20:00, box office open Mon–Sat 10:00–20:00, tel. 01225/448-844, www.theatreroyal.org.uk). Forty nosebleed spots on a bench (misnamed "standby seats") go on sale at noon on the day of each performance (£5, pay cash at box office or call and book with credit card, 2 tickets maximum). Or, you can snatch up any unsold seat in the house for £10–15 a half hour before "curtain up."

A handy cheap-sightseers' tip: During the free Bath walking tour, your guide stops here. Pop into the box office, ask what's playing tonight, and see if there are many seats left. If the play sounds good and if plenty of seats remain unsold, you're fairly safe to come back 30 minutes before curtain time to buy a ticket at that £10 price. Oh...and if you smell jasmine, it's the ghost of Lady Grey, a mistress of Beau Nash.

Evening Walks—Take your choice: comedy (Bizarre Bath, described above), history, ghost, or pub crawl. The free city history walks (such a standard every day and described on page 350) are now offered summer evenings (May–Sept 19:00 on Tue, Fri, and Sat, 2 hrs, leave from Pump Room). Ghost Walks are a popular way to pass the after-dark hours (£6, 20:00, 2 hrs, unreliably Mon–Sat April–Oct; in winter Fri only; leave from Garrick's Head pub near Theatre Royal, tel. 01225/350-512, www.ghostwalksofbath.co.uk). York and Edinburgh—which have houses thought to be actually haunted—are better for these walks.

The **Great Bath Pub Crawl,** a relaxed stroll through the town, gives an insight into pubs: "the busy man's recreation, the idle man's business, the melancholy man's sanctuary, and the stranger's welcome" (£5, tours May–Sept nightly at 20:00, depart from outside the centrally located Parade Park Hotel, 10 North Parade, tel. 01225/310-364, www.greatbathpubcrawl.com, info@greatbathpubcrawl.com).

Pubs—Most pubs in the center are very noisy, catering to a rowdy twenty-something crowd. But on the top end of town you can still find some classic, old places with inviting ambience and live music.

The Bell has a jazzy, pierced-and-tattooed, and bohemian feel, but with a mellow older crowd. They serve pizza in the garden out back (live music Mon and Wed evenings and Sun lunch, 103 Walcot Street, tel. 01225/460-426).

The Farmhouse fills its spacious and laid-back interior with live jazz nightly from 21:00 (open mic on Tue, top of Landsdown Road, tel. 01225/316-162).

The **Star Pub** is less inviting and more cramped, but it's much appreciated by local beer lovers for its fine ale and "no machines or music to distract from the chat." It's called a "spit 'n' sawdust" place. And its long bench, nicknamed "death row," still comes with a complimentary pinch of snuff from tins on the ledge (top of Paragon Street, tel. 01225/425-072).

The **Old Green Tree Pub** is a rare, quiet traditional pub right in the town center (locally brewed real ales, non-smoking room, no children, Green Street, tel. 01225/448-259; also recommended under "Eating," page 368, for lunch).

Summer Nights at the Baths—In July and August, you can stretch your sightseeing day at the Roman Baths, open nightly until 22:00 (last admission 21:00), when they're far less crowded and far more atmospheric, with their gas lamps flaming.

SLEEPING

Bath is a busy tourist town. To get a good B&B, make a telephone reservation in advance. Competition is stiff, and it's worth asking any of these places for a weekday, three-nights-in-a-row, or off-season deal. Friday and Saturday nights are tightest, especially if you're staying only one night, since B&Bs favor those staying longer. If staying only Saturday night, you're very bad news to a B&B hostess. At B&Bs (and cheaper hotels), expect lots of stairs and no lifts.

B&Bs near the Royal Crescent

These listings are all a 15-minute uphill walk or an easy £4 taxi ride from the train station. Or take any hop-on, hop-off bus tour from the station, and get off at the stop nearest your B&B (for Brock's, Assembly Rooms, and Marlborough Lane listings hop off at Royal Avenue; confirm with driver), check in, then finish the tour later in the day. All of these B&Bs are non-smoking. Marlborough Lane places have easier parking, but are less centrally located.

$$$ The Town House, overlooking the Assembly Rooms, is genteel and homey, with three fresh, mod rooms that have a hardwood stylishness. In true B&B style, you'll enjoy breakfast at a big family table with the other guests (Db-£80–85, Fri and Sat Db-£90–98, 2-night minimum, prices promised with this book through 2006, 7 Bennett Street, tel. & fax 01225/422-505, www.thetownhousebath.co.uk, stay@thetownhousebath.co.uk, Alan and Brenda Willey).

Sleep Code

(£1 = about $1.80, country code: 44, area code: 01225)
S = Single, **D** = Double/Twin, **T** = Triple, **Q** = Quad, **b** = bathroom, **s** = shower only. Unless otherwise noted, credit cards are accepted.

To help you sort easily through these listings, I've divided the rooms into three categories based on the price for a standard double room with bath:

$$$ Higher Priced—Most rooms £80 or more.
$$ Moderately Priced—Most rooms between £50–80.
$ Lower Priced—Most rooms £50 or less.

Bath Hotels

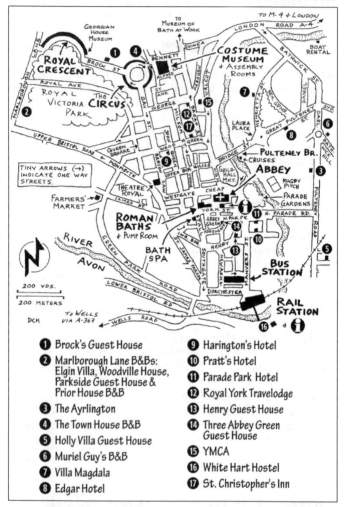

1. Brock's Guest House
2. Marlborough Lane B&Bs: Elgin Villa, Woodville House, Parkside Guest House & Prior House B&B
3. The Ayrlington
4. The Town House B&B
5. Holly Villa Guest House
6. Muriel Guy's B&B
7. Villa Magdala
8. Edgar Hotel
9. Harington's Hotel
10. Pratt's Hotel
11. Parade Park Hotel
12. Royal York Travelodge
13. Henry Guest House
14. Three Abbey Green Guest House
15. YMCA
16. White Hart Hostel
17. St. Christopher's Inn

$$ Elgin Villa rents five comfy, well-maintained rooms (Ss-£38, Sb-£50, Ds-£50, Db-£75–80, Tb-£92, Qb-£112, more expensive for 1 night, discounted for 3 nights, Wi-Fi access, parking, 6 Marlborough Lane, tel. 01225/424-557, www.elginvilla.co.uk, stay@elginvilla.co.uk, friendly Anna Rutherford).

$$ Brock's Guest House puts the bubbles in your Bath experience. Marion Dodd has redone her Georgian townhouse (built by John Wood in 1765) in a way that would make the great architect proud. It's located between the prestigious Royal Crescent and the courtly Circus (6 rooms, Db-£70–80, deluxe Db-£90, Tb-£95, reserve with credit card far in advance, little library on top floor, 32 Brock Street, tel. 01225/338-374, fax 01225/334-245, www.brocksguesthouse.co.uk, marion@brocksguesthouse.co.uk).

$$ Parkside Guest House has five thoughtfully appointed Edwardian rooms and a spacious back garden (Db-£69, 11 Marlborough Lane, tel. & fax 01225/429-444, www.parksidebandb.co.uk, post@parksidebandb.co.uk, Erica and Inge Lynall).

$$ Prior House B&B, with four well-kept rooms, is run by hardworking Lynn Shearn (D-£50, Db-£55, serve-yourself breakfast at a common table, 3 Marlborough Lane, tel. 01225/313-587, www.greatplaces.co.uk/priorhouse, priorhouse@greatplaces.co.uk).

$ Woodville House, warmly run by Anne Toalster, is a grandmotherly little house with three tidy, charming rooms sharing two WCs and a TV lounge. Breakfast is served at a big, family-style table (D-£45, 2-night minimum, cash only, some parking, below the Royal Crescent at 4 Marlborough Lane, tel. 01225/319-335, matoalster@freenet.co.uk).

B&Bs East of the River

These smoke-free listings are a 10-minute walk from the city center and generally a better value (but are less conveniently located).

$$$ The Ayrlington, next door to a lawn-bowling green, has attractive rooms with Asian decor, and hints of a more genteel time. Though this well-maintained hotel fronts a busy street, it's quiet and tranquil. Rooms in the back have pleasant views of sports greens and Bath beyond. For the best value, request a standard double with a view of Bath (huge price range due to varying sizes of rooms and policy of charging 30 percent more on Fri–Sun, Db-£75–175—see Web site for specifics; fine garden, easy parking, 24–25 Pulteney Road, tel. 01225/425-495, fax 01225/469-029, www.ayrlington.com, mail@ayrlington.com).

$$ Holly Villa Guest House, with a cheery garden, six bright rooms, and a cozy TV lounge, is enthusiastically and thoughtfully run by Jill and Keith McGarrigle (Ds-£55, small Db-£55, big Db-£60–65, Tb-£85, cash only, easy parking; 8-min walk from station and city center—walk over North Parade Bridge, take the 1st right, and then take the 2nd left; 14 Pulteney Gardens, tel. 01225/310-331, www.hollyvilla.com, jill@hollyvilla.com).

$$ Muriel Guy's B&B is another good value, mixing Georgian glamour with homey warmth and modern, artistic taste within its five rooms. Muriel is a fun and endearing live wire who serves organic food (S-£35, Db-£60, Tb-£70, cash only; go over bridge on North Parade Road, left on Pulteney Road, cross to church, Raby Place is 1st row of houses on hill; 14 Raby Place, tel. 01225/465-120).

B&Bs East of Pulteney Bridge

These B&Bs are a five-minute walk from the city center.

$$$ Villa Magdala rents 18 rooms in a freestanding Victorian town house opposite a park. It's hotelesque and sparkles with elegance (Db-£95–160, depending on size of room and type of bed, less off-season; in quiet residential area, inviting lounge, smoke-free, parking, Henrietta Street, tel. 01225/466-329, fax 01225/483-207, www.villamagdala.co.uk, enquiries@villamagdala.co.uk, Roy and Lois).

$$ Edgar Hotel, with 18 simple rooms and lots of stairs, gives you a budget-hotel option in this smart Georgian neighborhood (Sb-£40–50, Db-£60–85 depending on room, Tb-£100, Qb-£120, less in winter, smaller rooms on top, avoid #18 on ground level, pleasant sitting room with old organ and gramophones, 64 Great Pulteney Street, tel. 01225/420-619, fax 01225/466-916, www.edgar-hotel.co.uk, edgar-hotel@breathe.com).

In the City Center

$$$ Three Abbey Green Guest House is newly renovated, bright, fresh, and located in a quiet courtyard only 50 yards from the abbey and the Roman Baths. Its spacious rooms are a fine value (Sb-£65, Db-£75–85, Tb-£95–110, Qb-£125, families welcome, tel. 01225/428-558, www.threeabbeygreen.com, stay@threeabbeygreen.com). It's managed by Sue and Derek, who also run the Henry Guest House (see below).

$$$ Harington's Hotel rents 13 fresh and newly refurbished rooms on a quiet street in the town center (Sb-£68–114, Db-£88–124, high prices are for Fri–Sat; smoke-free, lots of stairs, attached restaurant-bar open all day, 10 Queen Street, tel. 01225/461-728, fax 01225/444-804, www.haringtonshotel.co.uk, post@haringtonshotel.co.uk). Melissa and Peter offer a 5 percent discount with this book for two-night stays except on Fridays, Saturdays, and holidays.

$$$ Pratt's Hotel is as proper and old English as you'll find in Bath. Its creaks and frays are aristocratic. Its public places make you want to sip a brandy, and its 46 rooms are bright and spacious (Sb-£85, Db-£130, advance reservations get highest rate, drop-ins after 16:00 often snare Db for £75, dogs-£7.50 but children free, attached restaurant-bar, elevator, 4 blocks from station on South Parade, tel. 01225/460-441, fax 01225/448-807, www.forestdale.com, pratts@forestdale.com).

$$ Parade Park Hotel rents 35 modern, basic rooms in a very central location (S-£38, D-£55, small Db-£65, large Db-£90, Tb-£95, Qb-£120, smoke-free, lots of stairs, lively bar downstairs and noisy seagulls, 10 North Parade, tel. 01225/463-384, fax 01225/442-322, www.paradepark.co.uk, info@paradepark.co.uk).

$$ Royal York Travelodge—which offers 66 American-style, characterless yet comfortable rooms—worries B&Bs with its reasonable prices (Db-£70, Tb-same price, up to 2 kids sleep free, breakfast extra, non-smoking rooms available, as low as £26 if you book online in advance, 1 York Building, George Street, tel. 01225/448-999, central reservation tel. 0870/085-0950, www.travelodge.co.uk). This is especially economic for families of four (who enjoy the Db price).

$$ Henry Guest House is a plain, newly redecorated, clean, vertical, eight-room place. It's two blocks in front of the train station on a quiet side street, run by a couple who genuinely cares about your travel experience (S-£35, D-£50–60, T-£75, family deals, lots of narrow stairs, 3 showers and 2 WCs for everybody, 6 Henry Street, tel. 01225/424-052, fax 01225/316-669, www.thehenry.com, stay@thehenry.com, helpful Sue and Derek).

Dorms

$ The **YMCA,** central on a leafy square, has 200 beds in industrial-strength rooms (S-£23.50, twin-£36, beds in big dorms-£12–13, £2 more per person on Fri and Sat, includes continental breakfast, cheap lunches, lockers, Internet access in lobby, dorms closed 10:00–14:00, down a tiny alley off Broad Street on Broad Street Place, tel. 01225/325-900, fax 01225/462-065, www.bathymca.co.uk, reservations@bathymca.co.uk).

$ White Hart Hostel is a simple place offering adults and families good, cheap beds in two- to six-bed dorms (£14/bed, D-£40, Db-£60, family rooms, smoke-free, kitchen, 5-min walk behind train station at Widcombe—where Widcombe Hill hits Claverton Street, tel. 01225/313-985, www.whitehartbath.co.uk, run by Jo).

$ St. Christopher's Inn, in a prime, central location, is part of a chain of low-priced, high-energy hubs for backpackers looking for beds and brews (60 beds in 4- to 12-bed rooms-£16–19.50, deals available online; lively and affordable restaurant and bar downstairs, Internet access, smoke-free bedrooms, laundry, lounge with video, 9 Green Street, tel. 01225/481-444, www.st-christophers.co.uk). Their beds are so cheap because they know you'll spend money on their beer.

EATING

Bath is bursting with quaint and stylish eateries. There's something for every appetite and budget—just stroll around the center of town. A picnic dinner of deli food or take-out fish-and-chips in the Royal Crescent Park is ideal for aristocratic hoboes. Reserve a table on Friday and Saturday evenings. Save money by eating before 19:00.

Near the Abbey

Three fine and popular places share North Parade Passage, a block south of the abbey:

Tilley's Bistro, popular with locals, serves healthy French, English, and vegetarian meals with candlelit ambience. Their fun menu lets you build your meal, choosing from an interesting array of £7 starters (Mon–Sat 12:00–14:30 & 18:30–23:00, closed Sun, reservations smart, non-smoking, North Parade Passage, tel. 01225/484-200).

Sally Lunn's House is a cutesy, quasi-historic place for traditional English meals, tea, pink pillows, and lots of lace (£15–20, £10 early-bird 2-course dinner 17:00–19:00, nightly, smoke-free, 4 North Parade Passage, tel. 01225/461-634). Their forte is a variety of cream teas and buns (£7, until 18:00). Lunch customers get a free peek at the basement Kitchen Museum (otherwise 30p).

Crystal Palace Pub, with typical pub grub under rustic timbers or in the sunny courtyard, is a handy standby (meals-£7, meals Mon–Sat 11:00–21:00, Sun 12:00–20:00, smoke-free, children welcome on patio until 16:30 but not indoors, 11 Abbey Green, tel. 01225/482-666).

Near the Train Station

These two places are two blocks up from the train station on Pierrepont Street.

Mai Thai Restaurant is a favorite with locals. It's cheap and crowded, serves good curry, and also does take-out food (£5–7 meals, daily 12:00–14:00 & 18:00–22:30, 6 Pierrepont Street, tel. 01225/445-557).

The Wife of Bath serves hearty English and French cuisine in a creaky, wood-beamed restaurant. They have an extensive wine selection, good "banoffee" (very sweet banana/toffee) pie, and a friendly waitstaff (£12–15 meals, £10 lunch and early-bird dinner special, Tue–Sat 12:00–14:00 & 17:30–22:00, Sun–Mon 17:30–22:00 only, down the stairs across the street from the Mai Thai on Pierrepont Street, tel. 01225/461-745).

Between the Abbey and the Circus

George Street is lined with cheery eateries: Thai, Italian, wine bars, and so on.

Loch Fyne Restaurant, a Scottish fish place with a bright, airy, and youthful atmosphere, fills a former bank. The fish is fresh, prices are reasonable (£10–14), the energy is high, and it doesn't feel like a chain (daily 12:00–22:00, 24 Milsom Street, tel. 01225/750-120).

Martini Restaurant, a hopping, purely Italian place, has class and jovial waiters (entrées-£12, pizzas-£7, plenty of veggie

Bath Restaurants

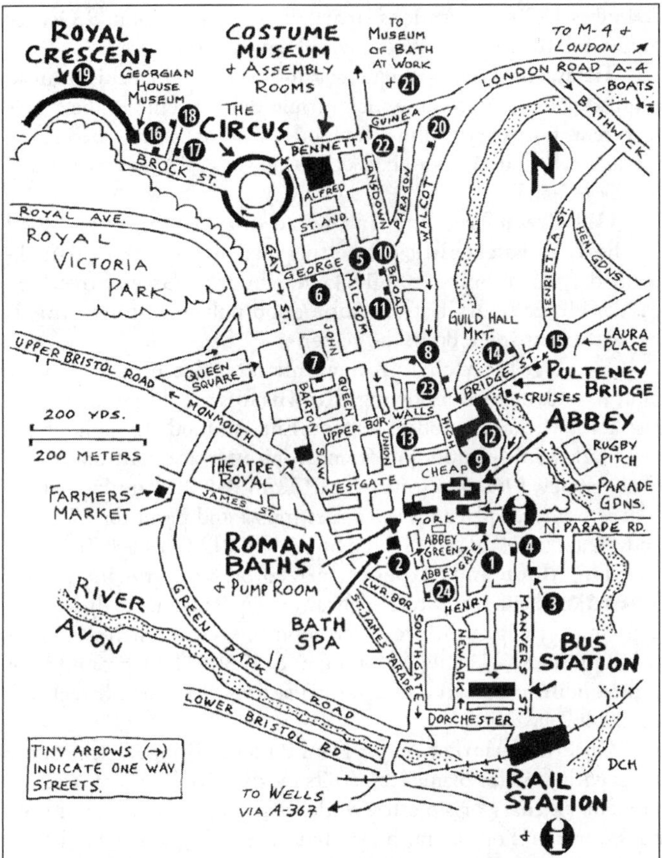

1. Tilley's Bistro & Sally Lunn's House
2. Crystal Palace Pub
3. Mai Thai Restaurant
4. The Wife of Bath
5. Loch Fyne Restaurant
6. Martini Restaurant
7. The Eastern Eye
8. Old Green Tree Pub
9. Browns Restaurant
10. Ask Restaurant
11. The Moon and Sixpence
12. Guildhall Market
13. Cornish Bakehouse
14. No. 5 Restaurant & Rajpoot Tandoori
15. Pastiche Bistro, Yak Yeti Yak & Boater Pub
16. Circus Restaurant
17. Papillon Bistro
18. Pinch of Salt Restaurant
19. Royal Crescent Hotel (Cream Teas)
20. The Bell Pub
21. To The Farmhouse Pub
22. Star Pub
23. Waitrose Supermarket
24. Marks & Spencer

options, daily fish specials, extensive wine list, daily 12:00–14:30 & 18:00–22:30, reservations smart, smoke-free section, 9 George Street, tel. 01225/460-818, Nunzio, Franco, and Luigi).

The Eastern Eye is unique, serving decent Indian cuisine in an exquisite Georgian room under a triple-domed ceiling. The architecture almost overwhelms the food—and that's not a bad thing (£7 lunches, daily 12:00–14:30 & 18:00–23:00, 8 Quiet Street, tel. 01225/422-323).

Old Green Tree Pub, in the old town center, serves good lunches in a characteristic pub setting (real ales on tap, non-smoking room, lunch only 12:00–14:45, no children, Green Street, tel. 01225/448-259). As Bath is not a good pub-grub town, this is likely the best you'll do in the center.

Two big, noisy chain restaurants offer decent, inexpensive food to a loyal local following: **Browns** fills an old police station just across from the abbey, serving English food throughout the day (daily 12:00–23:00, kid-friendly, nice terrace, half-block east of the abbey, Orange Grove, tel. 01225/461-199). Family-friendly **Ask** is a similar place up the street (pizza and pasta for £7, noisy and cheap, good salads, George Street, tel. 01225/789-997).

The Moon and Sixpence, prized by locals for its quality international cuisine, is tucked away on a quiet lane. It's dressy and a bit smoky, with well-presented food (2-course lunch-£8.50, 3-course dinner-£27, daily 12:00–14:30 & 17:30–22:30, ground floor is preferable to upstairs, fine garden seating, 6a Broad Street, tel. 01225/460-962).

Guildhall Market, across from Pulteney Bridge, has produce stalls with food for picnickers. At its inexpensive Market Café, you can slurp a curry or sip a tea while surrounded by stacks of used books, bananas on the push list, and honest-to-goodness old-time locals (£4 meals, Mon–Sat 7:45–17:00, closed Sun, a block north of the abbey, on High Street).

The **Cornish Bakehouse,** near the Guildhall Market, has good take-away pasties (open until 17:30, 11a The Corridor, off High Street, tel. 01225/426-635).

Supermarkets: **Waitrose,** at the Podium shopping center, is great for picnics, with a good salad bar (Mon–Fri 8:30–20:00, Sat 8:30–19:00, Sun 11:00–17:00, just west of Pulteney Bridge and across from post office on High Street). **Marks & Spencer,** near the train station, has a grocery at the back of its department store (Mon–Sat 9:00–20:00, Sun 11:00–17:00, Stall Street).

East of Pulteney Bridge

No. 5 Restaurant serves classic French and Mediterranean cuisine in a stylish, intimate setting (main courses with vegetables-£16, daily 12:00–14:30 & 18:30–22:00, Mon–Tue are "bring your own bottle of wine" nights—no corkage fee, smart to reserve, smoke-free, just over Pulteney Bridge at 5 Argyle Street, tel. 01225/444-499).

Rajpoot Tandoori, next door to No. 5, serves—by all assessments—the best Indian food in Bath. You'll hike down deep into a cellar where the plush Indian atmosphere and award-winning cooking makes paying the extra pounds palatable. The seating is tight and the ceilings low, but it's smoke-free and air-conditioned (£8 3-course lunch special, £10 plates, daily 12:00–14:30 & 18:00–23:00, 4 Argyle Street, tel. 01225/466-833).

Yak Yeti Yak Restaurant, a fun Nepali place, is run by a cheerful, hardworking Nepali family that cooks up great traditional food at prices a Sherpa could handle (open daily, plenty of vegetarian plates, 12A Argyle Street, tel. 01225/442-299).

The Boater Pub offers a £5 lunch in its pleasant beer garden overlooking the river. It's popular with rowdy twentysomethings for its good ales and riverside perch (lunch only 12:00–15:00, otherwise snacks, Mon–Sat 11:00–23:00, Sun 12:00–20:30, 9 Argyle Street, tel. 01225/464-211).

The feisty **Pastiche Bistro** offers inexpensive English food (2-course lunch-£6, 2-course dinner-£11, just east of Pulteney Bridge at 16 Argyle Street, tel. 01225/442-323).

Between the Circus and Royal Crescent

Circus Restaurant, a good value, gives modern English cuisine a Mediterranean twist. You'll get meat, fish, or veggies with an intimate, candlelit, Mozartean ambience. The three-course dinner special for £20 includes tasty vegetables and a selection of fine desserts (Wed–Sun 12:00–14:00 & 18:30–22:00, closed Tue lunch and all day Mon, reservations smart, 34 Brock Street, tel. 01225/318-918, Natasha serves while Adrian cooks).

Papillon Bistro is small, fun, and unpretentious, dishing up "modern-rustic cuisine from the south of France." It has cozy indoor and outdoor seating on a fine pedestrian lane (2-course meal-£8.50 from 12:00–18:30, 2-course dinners-£15–20, closed Sun–Mon, smart to reserve, 2 Margaret's Buildings, tel. 01225/310-064).

Pinch of Salt is a splurge, offering "world cuisine" in an uppity space—tight and trendy with mod decor—just off Brock Street (Mon–Sat 12:00–14:00 and 19:00–22:00 main courses-£14–17, closed Sun, 11 Margaret's Buildings, tel. 01225/421-251).

TRANSPORTATION CONNECTIONS

Bath's train station is called Bath Spa (train info: tel. 08457-484-950). The National Express bus office (Mon–Sat 8:00–17:30, closed Sun, bus info: tel. 0870/580-8080) is one block in front of the train station.

From London to Bath: To get from London to Bath and see Stonehenge to boot, consider an all-day organized **bus tour** from London (and skip out of the return trip; see page 325 in the London chapter).

From Bath to London: You can catch a **train** to London's Paddington Station (2/hr, 90 min, £34 one-way after 9:30 but £40 on Fri), or save money—but not time—by taking the National Express **bus** to Victoria Station (nearly hourly, a little more than 3 hrs, one way-£15, round trip-£22, www.nationalexpress.com).

From Heathrow to Bath: See page 322. Also consider taking a minibus with Alan Price; see "Celtic Horizons" on page 352.

From Bath to London's Airports: You can reach **Heathrow** by a train-and-bus combination (take train to Reading—runs hourly, catch airport shuttle bus from there—runs twice hourly, allow 2.5 hrs, £33, cheaper for BritRail passholders) or by National Express bus (11/day, 2.5 hrs, £15, tel. 0870-575-7747). Or take the Celtic Horizons minibus to Heathrow; see page 352. You can get to **Gatwick** by bus (nearly twice hourly, 4.5 hrs, £24) or by train (hrly, 3 hrs, £30, transfer in Reading or Clapham Junction).

DAY TRIP TO PARIS

The most exciting single day trip from London is Paris, just a three-hour journey by Eurostar train. Paris offers sweeping boulevards, sleepy parks, world-class art galleries, chatty crêpe stands, sleek shopping malls, the Eiffel Tower, and people-watching from outdoor cafés. Climb Notre-Dame and the Eiffel Tower, master the Louvre, and cruise the grand Champs-Elysées. Many fall in love with Paris, one of the world's most romantic cities.

This chapter is excerpted from *Rick Steves' France 2006,* by Rick Steves and Steve Smith.

Planning Your Time

Ideally, spend the night in Paris; see the accommodations listed at the end of this chapter.

But if all you have is a day, here's the plan: about 7:10–Depart London (about 7:40 on Sat); about 11:00–Arrive in Paris, take a taxi or the Métro to Notre-Dame; 11:30–Explore Notre-Dame and Sainte-Chapelle; 14:00–Taxi or Métro to the Arc de Triomphe; 14:30–Walk down the Champs-Elysées and through the Tuileries Garden; 16:00–Tour the Louvre (open until 18:00, until 21:45 Wed and Fri, closed Tue); 18:00–Taxi or Métro to Trocadero stop, walk to Eiffel Tower (if you ascend, allow plenty of time for delays); take a taxi or the Métro back to Paris' Gare du Nord train station one hour before departure; catch late train back to London (usually 20:40, or 21:10 on Fri); arrive in London (usually 22:30, or 23:00 on Fri). Confirm train times when you purchase your ticket.

Getting to Paris

For information on taking the Eurostar (3 hours to Paris), see the Transportation Connections chapter. Note that Britain's time zone is one hour earlier than the Continent's; the departure and arrival times listed on Eurostar tickets are local times (i.e., the British time you depart London and the French time you arrive in Paris).

ORIENTATION

(€1 = about $1.20; €1 = about £0.70; country code: 33)
Paris is split in half by the Seine River. You'll find Paris easier to navigate if you know which side of the river you're on, and which subway stop (abbreviated "Mo") you're closest to. If you're north of the river (above on any city map), you're on the Right Bank *(rive droite)*. If you're south of it, you're on the Left Bank *(rive gauche)*.

Tourist Information

Avoid the Paris TIs—long lines, short information, and a charge for maps. This chapter and a map (cheap at newsstands or free from any hotel) are all you need for a short visit. If you're staying longer than a day, pick up a copy of *Pariscope* (or one of its clones, €0.40 at any newsstand, in French), which lists museum hours, concerts, plays, movies, nightclubs, and art exhibits.

If you really need a TI, try TIs at the **Pyramides** Métro stop between the Louvre and Opéra (daily 9:00–19:00) or the **Eiffel Tower** (May–Sept daily 11:00–18:42, closed Oct–April). Paris' TIs share a single phone number: 08 92 68 30 00 (from the U.S., dial 011 33 8 92 68 30 00) and the same Web site (www.parisinfo.com).

Arrival in Paris

Paris has six major train stations, each serving a different region. The Eurostar train from London zips you to Paris' **Gare du Nord** train station. You'll find handy train information booths near track 8. Change offices, the Métro, and taxis are easy to find. You'll need currency in euros to function in Paris, available from any ATM. There's an ATM in the station, and one outside (go straight out the doors from track 8, then walk 50 yards down the street—it's on the left-hand side).

Passengers departing for London on the Eurostar must check in on the second level, opposite track 6. A peaceful waiting area overlooks the tracks.

Helpful Hints

Closed Days: On Monday, the Orsay and Rodin Museums are closed. The Louvre and Eiffel Tower are more crowded because of this. On Tuesday, when the Louvre is closed, the Eiffel Tower, and Orsay Museum can be jammed.

Paris Museum Pass: Serious sightseers save time and money by getting this pass. Sold at museums, major Métro stations, and TIs, it pays for itself in three admissions and gets you into

Paris

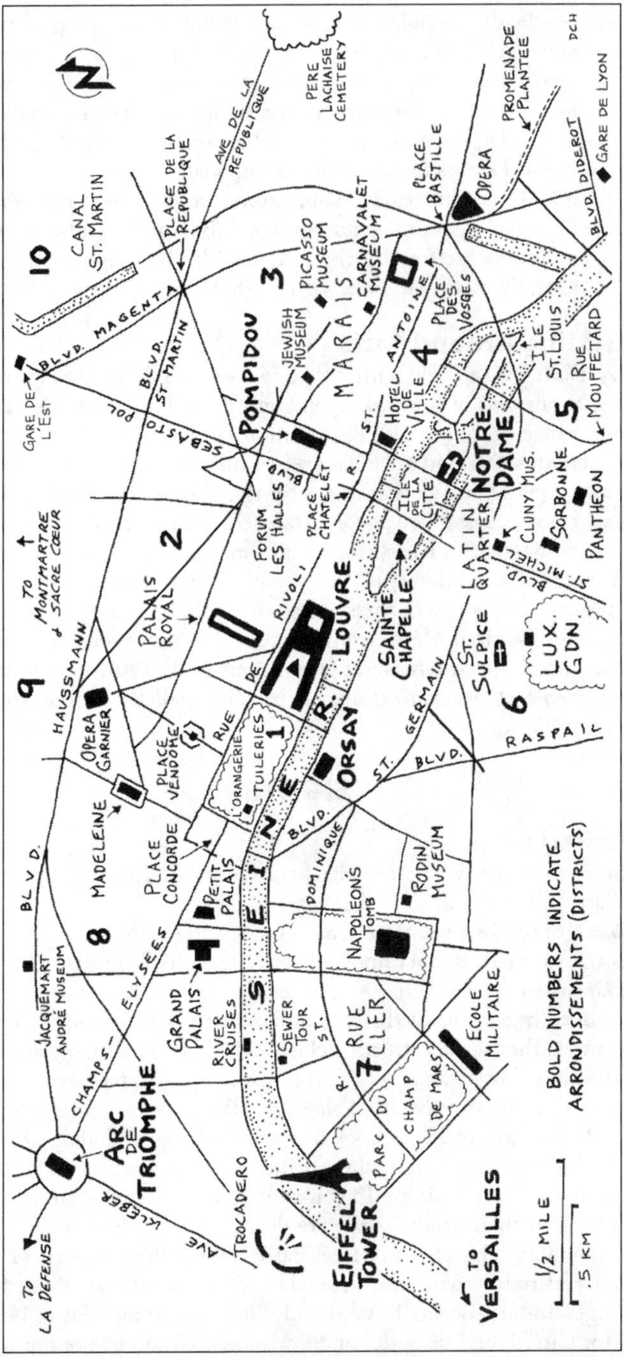

TO LA DEFENSE
AVE KLEBER
ARC DE TRIOMPHE
TROCADERO
EIFFEL TOWER
CHAMPS-ELYSEES
JACQUEMART ANDRÉ MUSEUM
BLVD.
HAUSSMANN
TO MONTMARTRE & SACRE COEUR
GARE DE L'EST
BLVD. MAGENTA
CANAL ST. MARTIN
10
9
8
MADELEINE
OPERA GARNIER
PLACE VENDOME
PLACE CONCORDE
GRAND PALAIS
PETIT PALAIS
RIVER CRUISES
SEWER TOUR
SEINE R.
L'ORANGERIE
TUILERIES
1
RUE DE RIVOLI
PALAIS ROYAL
LOUVRE
ORSAY
2
FORUM LES HALLES
PLACE CHATELET
BLVD. SEBASTOPOL
BLVD. ST MARTIN
PLACE DE LA REPUBLIQUE
AVE. DE LA REPUBLIQUE
PERE LACHAISE CEMETERY
POMPIDOU
JEWISH MUSEUM
PICASSO MUSEUM
3
MARAIS
CARNAVALET MUSEUM
R. ST. ANTOINE
HOTEL DE VILLE
PLACE DES VOSGES
PLACE BASTILLE
OPERA
PROMENADE PLANTEE
4
ILE DE LA CITE
SAINTE CHAPELLE
NOTRE-DAME
ILE ST. LOUIS
BLVD. DIDEROT
GARE DE LYON
LATIN QUARTER
CLUNY MUS.
SORBONNE
PANTHEON
RUE MOUFFETARD
5
BLVD. ST. MICHEL
LUX. GDN.
ST. SULPICE
6
BLVD. ST. GERMAIN
RASPAIL
BLVD. ST. DOMINIQUE
RODIN MUSEUM
NAPOLEON'S TOMB
R. ST.
RUE CLER
7
ECOLE MILITAIRE
PARC DU CHAMP DE MARS
TO VERSAILLES
BOLD NUMBERS INDICATE ARRONDISSEMENTS (DISTRICTS)
1/2 MILE
.5 KM
DCH

nearly all the sights (exceptions: Eiffel Tower, Notre-Dame treasury). The Museum Pass allows you to skip to the front of lines at many sights, saving hours of waiting in summer—though everyone must pass through the slow-moving metal-detector lines at some sights, and a few places, such as Notre-Dame's tower, can't accommodate a bypass lane (1 day-€18, 3 consecutive days-€36, 5 consecutive days-€54; no youth or senior discounts, and not worth buying for kids, as most museums are free for those under 18; if the sight is free for kids, they can skip lines with passholder parents).

Getting Around Paris

By Taxi: Two people with only one day should taxi everywhere. You'll save lots of time and spend only a few bucks per ride (a 10-min ride costs about €10; €5.20 minimum per ride). Parisian cabs are comfortable and have hassle-free meters. You can try waving down a taxi, but it's easier to ask for the nearest taxi stand (*"Où est une station de taxi?"*; oo ay toon stah-see-ohn duh taxi).

By Métro: In Paris, you're never more than a 10-minute walk from a Métro station (runs daily 5:30–00:30). One ticket (€1.40) takes you anywhere in the system with unlimited transfers. These are your essential Métro words: *direction*, *correspondance* (transfer), *sortie* (exit), *carnet* (cheap set of 10 tickets for €10.70), and *Donnez-moi mon porte-monnaie!* (Give me back my wallet!). Thieves thrive in the Métro.

SIGHTS

In Paris

Start your visit where the city began—on the Ile de la Cité (the island of the city), facing the Notre-Dame.

▲▲Notre-Dame Cathedral—This 700-year-old cathedral is packed with history and tourists. Study its sculpture (Notre-Dame's forte) and windows, eavesdrop on guides, and walk all around the outside of the church dedicated to Our Lady (Notre-Dame). The facade is worth a close look. Mary, cradling Jesus and surrounded by the halo of the rose window, is center stage. Adam is on the left, and Eve is on the right. Below Mary and above the arches is a row of 28 statues known as the Kings of Judah. During the French Revolution, these Biblical kings were mistaken for the hated French kings. The citizens stormed the church, crying, "Off with their heads." All were decapitated but have since been recapitated (church entry free, daily 7:45–19:00; treasury-€2.50, not covered by Museum Pass, daily 9:30–17:30; ask about free English tours, normally Wed and Thu at 12:00 and Sat at 14:30; Mo: Cité, Hôtel de Ville, or St. Michel). Climb to the top for a

Heart of Paris

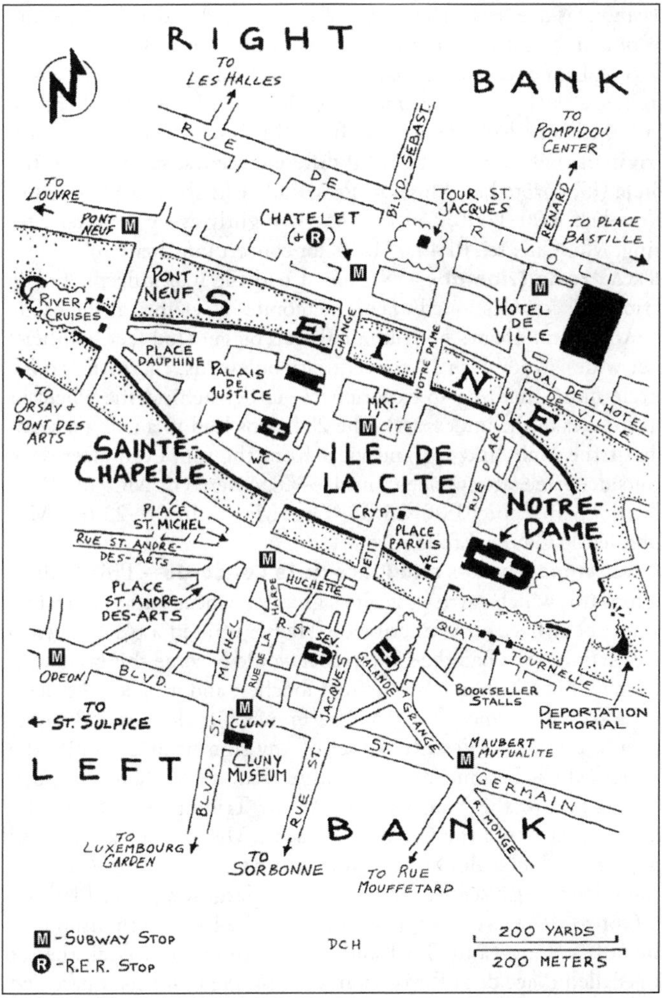

great gargoyle's-eye view of the city; you get 400 steps for only €7 (July–Aug Mon–Fri 9:00–19:30, Sat–Sun 9:00–23:00, April–June and Sept daily 9:30–19:30, Oct–March daily 10:00–17:30, last entry 45 min before closing, covered by Museum Pass though you can't bypass line, arrive early to avoid long lines). Clean toilets are in front of the church near Charlemagne's statue. Two blocks west of Notre-Dame is the...

▲▲▲Sainte-Chapelle—The triumph of Gothic church architecture is a cathedral of glass like no other. It was speedily built from 1242 to 1248 for St. Louis IX (the only French king who is now a saint) to house the supposed Crown of Thorns. Its architectural harmony is due to the fact that it was completed under the direction of one architect in only five years—unheard of in Gothic times. (Notre-Dame took more than 200 years to build.) Climb the spiral staircase to the *Chapelle Haute* and "let there be light." There are 15 huge stained-glass windows (two-thirds of them 13th-century originals) with more than 1,100 different scenes, mostly from the Bible (€7, covered by Museum Pass, daily March–Oct 9:30–18:00, Nov–Feb 9:00–17:00, concerts nearly nightly every summer evening, Mo: Cité, tel. 01 44 07 12 38 for concert information).

▲▲▲Arc de Triomphe—Napoleon had the magnificent Arc de Triomphe commissioned to commemorate his victory at the battle of Austerlitz. There's no triumphal arch bigger (164 feet high, 130 feet wide). And, with 12 converging boulevards, there's no traffic circle more thrilling to experience—either behind the wheel or on foot (take the underpass). The 284 steps lead to a cute museum about the arch, and a grand view from the top, even after dark (outside—free, always open; inside—€8, covered by Museum Pass, daily April–Sept 10:00–23:00, Oct–March 10:00–22:00, Mo: Charles de Gaulle-Etoile).

▲▲Champs-Elysées and Place de la Concorde—This famous boulevard, which carries the city's greatest concentration of traffic, came about because Catherine de Medici wanted a place to drive her carriage. She had the swamp that would become this boulevard drained. Napoleon put on the final touches, and it's been the place to be seen ever since. The Tour de France bicycle race ends here, as do all parades (French or foe) of any significance. While the boulevard has become a bit hamburgerized, a walk here is a must. Take a taxi or the Métro to the Arc de Triomphe (Mo: Etoile) and saunter down the Champs-Elysées (Métro stops are located every few blocks along the boulevard: Etoile, George V, FDR). The Champs-Elysées leads to the city's largest square, Place de la Concorde. Here the guillotine took the lives of thousands—including King Louis XVI and Marie-Antoinette. Back then it was called Place de la Révolution. Continuing past this square and through the Tuileries Garden brings you to the...

▲▲▲Louvre—This is Europe's oldest, biggest, greatest, and possibly most crowded museum. It's packed with ancient Greek and Roman masterpieces, medieval jewels, Michelangelo statues, and paintings by the greatest artists from the Renaissance to the Romantic movement of the mid-1800s.

Pick up the free English-language *Louvre Plan Information* at the information desk under the pyramid as you enter. Don't try to cover the huge museum thoroughly; be selective. Start in the Denon wing and visit these highlights in this order: Ancient Greek and Roman art (Parthenon frieze, *Venus de Milo,* Pompeii mosaics,

Etruscan sarcophagi, Roman portrait busts, *Nike of Samothrace*); French and Italian paintings in the Grand Gallery (a quarter-mile long and worth the hike); the *Mona Lisa* and her Italian Renaissance roommates; the neoclassical collection (J. L. David's *Coronation of Napoleon*); the Romantic collection (Delacroix's *Liberty at the Barricades* and Géricault's *Raft of the Medusa*); and Michelangelo's *Slaves*.

Cost: €8.50, €6 after 18:00 on Wed and Fri, free on first Sun of month, covered by Museum Pass. Tickets good all day; re-entry allowed. Optional additional charges apply for temporary exhibits.

Hours: Wed–Mon 9:00–18:00, closed Tue. Most wings open Wed and Fri until 21:45. Galleries start closing 30 minutes early. Evening visits are peaceful and the pyramid glows after dark. Galleries start shutting down 30 minutes early. The last entry is 45 minutes before closing. Crowds are worst on Sun, Mon, Wed, and mornings (tel. 01 40 20 53 17, recorded info tel. 01 40 20 51 51, www.louvre.fr).

Tours: The 90-minute English-language tours (for €5 plus your entry ticket), which leave three times daily except Sunday (normally at 11:00, 14:00, and 15:45), boil this overwhelming museum down to size (tour tel. 01 40 20 52 63, www.louvre.fr). Sign up for tours at the *Acceuil des Groupes* area. Digital audioguides (available for €5 at entries to the 3 wings, at top of escalators) give you a receiver and a directory of about 130 masterpieces, allowing you to dial an interesting commentary on included works as you stumble upon them.

Getting There: The Métro stop Palais Royal–Musée du Louvre is closer to the entrance than the stop called Louvre–Rivoli. From the Palais Royal–Musée du Louvre stop, you can stay underground to enter the Louvre, or exit above ground if you want to enter the Louvre through the pyramid (possibly longer lines; see below).

There is no grander entry than through the main entrance at the pyramid in the central courtyard, but metal detectors (not ticket-buying lines) create a long line at times. There are several ways to avoid the line:

Museum Pass–holders can use the group entrance in the pedestrian passageway between the pyramid and rue de Rivoli (under the arches, a few steps north of the pyramid, find the uniformed guard at the entrance, with the escalator down).

Otherwise, you can enter the Louvre from its (usually less-crowded) underground entrance, accessed through the "Carrousel du Louvre" shopping mall. Enter the mall at 99 rue de Rivoli (the door with the red awning, daily 8:30–23:00) or directly from the Métro stop Palais Royal–Musée du Louvre (stepping off the train, exit to the left, following signs to Carrousel du Louvre–Musée du Louvre).

▲▲▲**Eiffel Tower**—It may be crowded and expensive, but it's worth the trouble. The Eiffel Tower is 1,000 feet tall (6 inches taller in hot weather), covers 2.5 acres, and requires 50 tons of paint. Its 7,000 tons of metal are spread out so well at the base that it's no heavier per square inch than a linebacker on tiptoes.

Built a hundred years after the French Revolution (and in the midst of an industrial one), the tower served no function but to impress. To a generation hooked on technology, the tower was the marvel of the age, a symbol of progress and of human ingenuity.

There are three observation platforms, at 200, 400, and 900 feet; the higher you go, the more you pay. Each requires a separate elevator (and a line), so plan on at least 90 minutes if you want to go to the top and back. The view from the 400-foot-high second level is plenty. It costs €4 to go to the first level, €7.50 to the second, and €11 to go all the way for the 1,000-foot view (not covered by Museum Pass, daily March–Sept 9:00–24:00, Oct–Feb 9:30–23:00, last entry 1 hour before closing, shorter lines at night, Mo: Trocadero, tel. 01 44 11 23 23, www.tour-eiffel.fr). To avoid most crowds, go early (arrive by 8:45) or late in the day (after 18:00, after 20:00 in summer); weekends are the worst.

The best place to view the tower is from the **Trocadéro** square to the north (a 10-min walk across the river and a happening scene at night). Another great viewpoint is the long, grassy field, **Parc du Champ de Mars,** to the south (ideal for picnics). Arrive at the Trocadéro Métro stop for the view, then walk toward the tower. However impressive it may be by day, it's an awesome thing to see at twilight, when the tower becomes engorged with light, and virile Paris lies back and lets night be on top. When darkness fully envelops the city, the tower seems to climax at the top of each hour...for 10 minutes. (It's been doing this since the Millennium festivities, when it was wired with thousands of special lights.)

▲▲▲**Orsay Museum**—The Orsay boasts Europe's greatest collection of Impressionist works. It's housed in a former train station (Gare d'Orsay) across the river and a 15-minute walk downstream from the Louvre (Mo: Solférino, 3 blocks south of Orsay).

This museum picks up where the Louvre leaves off: the second half of the 19th century. Begin on the ground floor, featuring conservative art of the mid-1800s. Then glide up the escalator to the late 1800s, when the likes of Manet, Monet, Degas, and Renoir jolted the art world with their colorful, lively new invention, Impressionism. You'll also see the works of their artistic descendents, Vincent van Gogh, Paul Cézanne, and other Post-Impressionists (Rousseau, Gauguin, Seurat, and Toulouse-Lautrec). On the mezzanine level, waltz through the Grand Ballroom, Art Nouveau exhibits, and Rodin sculptures. The second-floor restaurant, pricey but *très* elegant, serves tea and coffee from 15:00–17:30. A simple fifth-floor café is sandwiched between the Impressionists; above it is an easy self-service place.

Cost: €7.50; €5.50 after 16:15 and on Sun, free first Sun of month, covered by Museum Pass. Tickets are good all day. Museum Pass–holders can enter quickly on the right side of the building; ticket-buyers enter along the left (river) side. The booth inside the entrance gives free floor plans in English. Tel. 01 40 49 48 41, www.musee-orsay.fr.

Free Entry near Closing: Right when the ticket booth stops selling tickets (17:00 on Tue–Wed and Fri–Sun, 20:45 on Thu), you're welcome to scoot in free of charge. (They won't let you in much after that, however.) For one hour, you'll have the art mostly to yourself before the museum closes. Immediately head upstairs to the Impressionism galleries because they shut down first.

Tours: Audioguides are €5. English-language guided tours are usually offered Mon–Sat at 11:30 (90-min tours-€6). Tours in English focusing on the Impressionists are offered Tuesdays at 14:30 (€6, sometimes also on other days).

Hours: June 20–Sept 20 Tue–Sun 9:00–18:00, Sept 21–June 19 Tue–Sat 10:00–18:00, Sun 9:00–18:00, Thu until 21:45 year-round, always closed Mon. Last entry one hour before closing. The Impressionist galleries start closing at 17:15, frustrating unwary visitors. Note that the Orsay is crowded on Tuesday, when the Louvre is closed.

▲▲Napoleon's Tomb and the Army Museums—The emperor lies majestically dead inside several coffins under a grand dome glittering with 26 pounds of gold—a goose-bumping pilgrimage for historians. Napoleon is surrounded by the tombs of other French war heroes. Follow signs to the "crypt" to find Roman Empire–style reliefs that list the accomplishments of Napoleon's administration. Check out the interesting World War II wing. The Army Museums' West Wing (with a focus on World War I) should reopen in 2006 while the East Wing (starring Napoleon) will likely close for renovation (€7, covered by Museum Pass, April–Sept daily 10:00–18:00, summer Sun until 19:00, Oct–March daily 10:00–17:00, closed the first Mon of every month except July–Sept; Mo: La Tour-Maubourg or Varenne, tel. 01 44 42 37 72, www.invalides.org).

▲▲Rodin Museum (Musée Rodin)—This user-friendly museum is filled with works by the greatest sculptor since Michelangelo. See *The Kiss, The Thinker, The Gates of Hell,* and many more. Don't miss the room full of work by Rodin's student and mistress, Camille Claudel (€5, €3 on Sun, free first Sun of month, covered by Museum Pass; €1 for gardens only—perhaps Paris' best deal, as many works are well displayed in the beautiful gardens; April–Sept Tue–Sun 9:30–17:45, closed Mon, gardens close 18:45; Oct–March Tue–Sun 9:30–16:45, closed Mon, gardens close 17:00;

near Napoleon's Tomb, 77 rue de Varennes, Mo: Varennes, tel. 01 44 18 61 10, www.musee-rodin.fr). The gardens are picnic-perfect (BYO), but there's also a pleasant, if pricey, café on site.

▲Latin Quarter—The Left Bank neighborhood just opposite Notre-Dame is the Latin Quarter, named for the scholarly language of the neighborhood's university. This was a center of Roman Paris, but its touristic fame relates to the Latin Quarter's intriguing artsy, bohemian character. This was Europe's leading university district in the Middle Ages—home, since the 13th century, to the prestigious Sorbonne College. In more recent times, this was the center of Paris' café culture. The neighborhood's main boulevards (St. Michel and St. Germain) are lined with cafés—once the haunts of great poets and philosophers, but now just places where tired tourists can hang out. While still youthful and artsy, the area has become a tourist ghetto filled with cheap North African eateries. The neighborhood merits a wander, but you're better off focusing on the area around boulevard St. Germain and rue de Buci, and on the streets around the Maubert-Mutualité Métro stop.

▲▲Sacré-Cœur and Montmartre—This Byzantine-looking church, while only 130 years old, is impressive. It was built as a "praise the Lord anyway" gesture after the French were humiliated by the Germans in a brief war in 1871. The church is open daily until 23:00. One block from the church, the square called the Place du Tertre was the haunt of Henri de Toulouse-Lautrec and the original bohemians. Today, it's mobbed by tourists and unoriginal bohemians, but it's still fun. Either use the Anvers Métro stop (from the stop, you can either take the stairs up the hill or take the funicular, which costs one Métro ticket) or get off at the closer but less scenic Abbesses Métro stop. A taxi to the top of the hill saves time and avoids sweat.

SLEEPING

In the Rue Cler Neighborhood

(7th district, Mo: Ecole Militaire or La Tour-Maubourg)

Rue Cler, a village-like pedestrian street, is safe, tidy, and makes me feel like I must have been a poodle in a previous life. How such coziness lodged itself between the high-powered government/business district and the expensive Eiffel Tower area, I'll never know. Living here ranks with the top museums as one of the city's great experiences.

The street called rue Cler is the glue that holds this pleasant neighborhood together. On rue Cler, you can eat and browse your way through a street full of tart shops, cheeseries, and colorful outdoor produce stalls.

Sleep Code

(€1 = about $1.20, country code: 33)
S = Single, **D** = Double/Twin, **T** = Triple, **Q** = Quad, **b** = bathroom, **s** = shower only, * = French hotel rating system (0–4 stars). For more information on the rating system, see "Sleeping" in this book's Introduction. Unless otherwise noted, credit cards are accepted and English is spoken (in fact, hotels with 2 or more stars are required to have an English-speaking staff).

To help you sort easily through these listings, I've divided the rooms into three categories based on the price for a standard double room with bath:

$$$ **Higher Priced**—Most rooms €150 or more.
$$ **Moderately Priced**—Most rooms between €100–150.
$ **Lower Priced**—Most rooms €100 or less.

If you're calling Paris from the U.S., dial 011-33 (from Britain dial 00-33) and then dial the local number without the initial zero.

$$$ Hôtel Relais Bosquet*** is modern, spacious, and a bit upscale, with snazzy, air-conditioned rooms, electric darkness blinds, and big beds. Gerard and his friendly staff are politely formal and offer free breakfasts to anyone booking direct with this book in 2006 (standard Db-€150, spacious Db-€170, ask about occasional promotional rates and off-season discounts, claim free Rick Steves breakfast at time of booking, extra bed-€20, family suites, free Internet in lobby, parking-€14, 19 rue du Champ de Mars, tel. 01 47 05 25 45, fax 01 45 55 08 24, www.relaisbosquet.com, hotel@relaisbosquet.com).

$$ Hôtel la Motte Picquet***, at the end of rue Cler, is elaborately decorated and feminine-feeling. Most of its 18 adorable and spendy rooms face a busy street, but the twins are on the quieter side (Sb-€115–125, standard Db-€145, bigger Db with air-con-€180, 30 avenue de la Motte-Picquet, tel. 01 47 05 09 57, fax 01 47 05 74 36, www.hotelmottepicquetparis.com, book@hotelmottepicquetparis.com).

$$ Hôtel Beaugency***, a particularly good value on a quieter street a short block off rue Cler, has 30 small, cookie-cutter rooms, a helpful staff, and a lobby you can stretch out in (Db-€105–110, these special rates promised in 2006 with this book, air-con, 21 rue Duvivier, tel. 01 47 05 01 63, fax 01 45 51 04 96, www.hotel-beaugency.com, info@hotel-regency.com, Christelle).

Warning: The next two hotels listed here are busy with my readers (reserve long in advance).

$ Grand Hôtel Lévêque** is ideally located, with a helpful staff (Christophe and Pascale), a singing maid, and a slow-dance elevator. The simple but well-designed rooms have all the comforts, including air-conditioning and ceiling fans (S-€57, Db-€87–110 depending on views and beds, Tb-€125 for 2 adults and 1 child only, first breakfast free for readers of this book in 2006, additional breakfasts aren't worth the €8 price, 29 rue Cler, tel. 01 47 05 49 15, fax 01 45 50 49 36, www.hotel-leveque.com, info@hotel-leveque.com).

$ Hôtel du Champ de Mars**, with charming pastel rooms and helpful owners Françoise and Stephane, is a homier rue Cler option. This plush little hotel has a Provence-style, small-town feel from top to bottom. Rooms are small but comfortable, and an excellent value. Single rooms can work as tiny doubles (Sb-€73, Db-€79–83, Tb-€100, 30 yards off rue Cler at 7 rue du Champ de Mars, tel. 01 45 51 52 30, fax 01 45 51 64 36, www.hotelduchampdemars.com, reservation@hotelduchampdemars.com).

TRANSPORTATION CONNECTIONS

To London: The sleek Eurostar train makes the trip in 3 hours, with frequent departures daily in each direction. For details and prices, see page 327 of the Transportation Connections chapter.

To Other Destinations: Paris is Europe's transportation hub. The city has six central rail stations, each serving a different region. You'll find trains (day and night) to almost any French or European destination. For schedule information, check Germany's excellent all-Europe Web site: http://bahn.hafas.de/bin/query.exe/en.

ENGLISH HISTORY

FOUR MILLENNIA IN FOUR PAGES

Invasions (2000 B.C.–A.D. 1000)

The mysterious Stonehenge builders were replaced by the Celts, whose Druid priests made human sacrifices and worshipped trees.

The Romans brought 500 years of peace and stability, establishing London (Londinium) as a major city. Then civilization fell for a thousand years, to German pirates (Angles and Saxons), Danish Vikings, and, finally, William the Conqueror (A.D. 1066). During these Dark Ages, Christians had to battle pagan gods for supremacy of the island.

People and Sights

People: Boadicea, Julius Caesar, "King Arthur," "Beowulf," Alfred the Great

Sights: Boadicea statue, Roman Wall, Lindisfarne Gospels

Wars with France, Wars of the Roses (1066–1500)

French-speaking kings ruled England, and English-speaking kings invaded France as the two budding nations defined their modern borders. In the 1400s, feuding English nobles duked it out for control of the country.

People and Sights

People: Richard the Lionhearted, Robin Hood, Eleanor of Aquitaine, Chaucer, Joan of Arc

Sights: Tower of London, Magna Carta, Westminster Abbey, Temple Church

The Tudor Renaissance (1500s)

Powerful Henry VIII thrust England onto the world stage by defying the pope and sparking a century of Protestant/Catholic warfare. His daughter, Elizabeth I, reigned over a cultural renaissance of sea exploration, scientific discovery, and literature known as the "Elizabethan Age."

People and Sights

People: Anne Boleyn, Thomas More, "Bloody Mary," William Shakespeare, Sir Francis Drake, Sir Walter Raleigh

Sights: Shakespeare folios and Shakespeare's Globe, Tower of London execution site, Chapel of Henry VII and Elizabeth I's tomb in Westminster Abbey, portraits of Henry VIII's wives and daughter Elizabeth in the National Portrait Gallery.

Catholic Kings vs. Protestant Parliament (1600s)

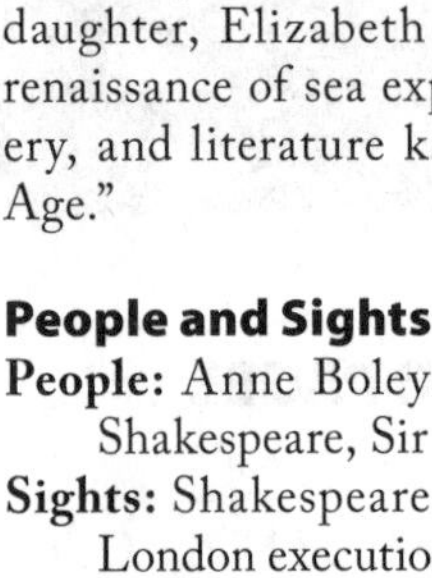

The "Virgin Queen" Elizabeth died without heirs, and the crown passed to the Catholic Stuart family. Their arrogant, divine-right management style sparked a Civil War, led by the commoner Oliver Cromwell, who beheaded the king and briefly established a Commonwealth. The monarchy returned, along with back-to-back disasters—first the Great Plague (1665), and then the Great Fire (1666) that leveled London.

People and Sights

People: King James I (Bible), Charles I (headless), Christopher Wren (St. Paul's), Isaac Newton (apple)

Sights: St. Paul's and other Wren churches, Fire Monument, City of London, Banqueting House, Crown Jewels, King James Bible

Colonial Expansion (1700s)

Britannia ruled the waves and became a world power, exploiting the wealth of India, Africa, Australia, and America...at least until the Yanks revolted in the "American War."

People and Sights

People: King George III, James Cook, Handel, Lord Nelson, Duke of Wellington

Sights: Portraits by Reynolds and Gainsborough in the Tate Britain

Victorian Gentility and the Industrial Revolution (1800s)

Britain under Queen Victoria reigned supreme, steaming into the modern age with railroads, factories, electricity, telephones, and the first Underground. Meanwhile, Romantic poets longed for the innocence of Nature, Charles Dickens questioned the social order, and Rudyard Kipling criticized the colonial system.

People and Sights

People: Byron, Wordsworth, Keats, Shelley, Coleridge, Blake, Brontë Sisters, Jane Austen, James Watt, Charles Darwin, Tennyson, "Sherlock Holmes," Jack the Ripper

Sights: Big Ben and Halls of Parliament, Buckingham Palace, The Mall, Hyde Park, the Tube, writers' manuscripts in the British Library, Poets' Corner in Westminster Abbey

World Wars and Recovery (20th Century)

Two world wars whittled Britain down from a world empire to an island chain struggling to compete in a global economy. The German Blitz in World War II leveled London. Colonies rebelled and gained their independence, then flooded London with immigrants. Longtime residents fled on the Tube for London's suburbs.

In the 1960s, "Swinging London" became a center for rock music, film, theater, youth culture, and Austin Powers–style *joie de vivre*. The 1970s brought massive unemployment and a conservative reaction in the 1980s and early 1990s.

People and Sights

People: T. E. Lawrence (of Arabia), Winston Churchill, Edward VIII and Wallis Simpson, T. S. Eliot (American-turned-British), Virginia Woolf, Dylan Thomas, John–Paul–George–Ringo, The Rolling Stones, The Who, Elton John, David Bowie, Margaret Thatcher, John Major

Sights: Cabinet War Rooms, Cenotaph, Westminster Abbey tombs, Blitz photos at St. Paul's, Beatles memorabilia in British Library, Rock Circus at Piccadilly Circus

London Today

London is one of the world's major cultural capitals, an exporter of art, science, and technology.

People and Sights

People: Tony Blair, Hugh Grant, soccer star David Beckham and wife (former "Posh" Spice Girl) Victoria Beckham, Monty Python alumni, Anthony Hopkins, Martin Amis, Tom Stoppard, Prince William

Sights: The London Eye Ferris Wheel, West End theaters, Tate Modern contemporary art exhibits

TIMELINE OF LONDON HISTORY

c. 1700 B.C. Stone slabs erected to create ceremonial site... Stonehenge.

A.D. 43 Romans defeat the Celtic locals and establish Londinium as a seaport. They build the original London Bridge and a city wall, encompassing one square mile, which sets the city boundaries for 1,500 years.

c. 60 Boadicea defies the Romans and burns Londinium before the revolt is squelched.

c. 200 London is the thriving, river-trading, walled, Latin-speaking capital of Roman-dominated England.

410 The city of Rome is looted by invaders, and the Europe-wide Roman infrastructure crumbles. England is soon overrun by "barbarian" Anglo-Saxon invaders from Germany. This begins 500 years of Viking invasions, poverty, ignorance, superstition, and hand-me-down leotards—the Dark Ages.

886 King Alfred the Great liberates London from Danish Vikings; he helps reunite England, reestablish Christianity, and encourage learning.

1052 King Edward the Confessor builds his palace and abbey a mile and a half from London at Westminster.

1066 England is conquered by Norman invaders under William the Conqueror, beginning two centuries of rule by French-speaking kings. London reasserts itself as a trade center.

1215 King John, under pressure from barons and London's

powerful trade guilds, signs the Magna Carta, establishing that even kings must follow the rule of law.

1209 London Bridge—the famous stone version, topped with houses—is built. It stands until 1832.

1280 Old St. Paul's Cathedral is finished.

1337 Start of the Hundred Years' War with France.

1348 The Black Death (bubonic plague) kills half of London.

1415 British victory over the French at Battle of Agincourt.

1455–1485 Prosperous London plays kingmaker in the Wars of the Roses, helping determine which noble becomes king.

1500 London's population swells to 50,000.

1534 Henry VIII breaks with Rome and dissolves monasteries, bringing religious strife. Generally speaking, London leans to the Protestant side.

1558 Elizabeth I is crowned, with London's backing. Her reign brings a renaissance of theater (Shakespeare), literature, science, discovery, and manners to the city.

1588 England's navy defeats the powerful Spanish Armada and now rules the waves. Overseas trade brings the world's wealth directly to London's wharves.

1600 London, population 200,000, is Europe's largest city, expanding beyond the medieval walls, stretching westward along the river to Charing Cross.

1649 King Charles I is beheaded outside Whitehall as London backs the Protestant Parliament in England's Civil War (1642–1648). Oliver Cromwell heads a democratic Commonwealth (1649–1653) and then becomes Lord Protector (1653–1659).

1660 Charles II, son of Charles I, is invited to restore the monarchy.

1665 The Great Plague kills 100,000.

1666 The Great Fire rages for four days, destroying the wooden city. The city is rebuilt in stone, including Christopher Wren's new St. Paul's Cathedral and other churches.

1700 London's population is 500,000 and growing fast. One in seven Brits lives in London.

1702 London's first daily newspapers hit the streets.

1776 Britain fights one of its colonies in the American War of Independence (1775–1783).

1789 The French Revolution sparks decades of war with France.

1805 Lord Nelson defeats the French navy at Trafalgar (Spain), ending the threat of invasion by Napoleon.

1815 The Duke of Wellington defeats Napoleon for good at Waterloo (Belgium). Britain becomes Europe's No. 1 power.

c. 1830 Railroads lace the country together. The Industrial Revolution kicks into high gear.

1837 Eighteen-year-old Victoria becomes Queen, soon marries Prince Albert, and presides over an era of peace and middle-class values.

1851 With Britain at the peak of prosperity from its worldwide colonial empire, London—population one million—hosts a Great Exhibition in Hyde Park, trumpeting the latest triumphs of science and technology.

1863 First Underground line is built.

1914–1918 World War I. Britain, France, and other allies battle Germany from trenches dug in the open fields of France and Belgium. A million British men die.

1936 King Edward VIII abdicates to marry an American commoner.

1939–1945 World War II.

1940–1941 The Blitz. Preparing to invade the Isle, Nazi Germany air-bombs Britain, and particularly London. Despite enormous devastation, Britain holds firm.

1945 Postwar recovery begins, aided by the United States. Many cheap, concrete (ugly) buildings rise from the rubble. Britain begins granting independence to many foreign colonies.

1964 The Beatles tour America, spreading "Swinging London" hipness to the world.

1970s Labor strikes, unemployment, and recession.

1980s Conservative government of Margaret Thatcher.

1981 Prince Charles marries Lady Diana Spencer.

1982 Britain battles Argentina over the Falkland Islands. Britain claims victory.

1992 Britain is part of the European Union, but maintains her distance.

1994 Channel Tunnel opens, linking London with Paris and Brussels.

1997 Tony Blair becomes Prime Minister, signaling a shift toward moderate liberalism.

1997 Princess Diana dies in a car crash in Paris. The nation and the world mourn.

2000 London hosts big millennium celebration, building a Ferris wheel, the Millennium Bridge, and the Millennium Dome exhibition.

2002 Many E.U. nations adopt the euro currency, but Britain sticks with pounds sterling. Queen Elizabeth II celebrates her 50-year Jubilee.

2003 Britain joins America's "Coalition of the Willing," and invades Iraq, dividing the British people.

2005 Four terrorist bombs rock London.

2006 You visit Britain and make your own history.

London's History is Britain's History

When Julius Caesar landed on the misty and mysterious isle of Britain in 55 B.C., England entered the history books. The primitive Celtic tribes he conquered were themselves invaders, who had earlier conquered the even more mysterious people who built Stonehenge. The Romans built towns and roads and established their capital at Londinium. The Celtic natives in Scotland and Wales, consisting of Gaels, Picts, and Scots, were not subdued so easily. The Romans built Hadrian's Wall near the Scottish border as protection against their troublesome northern neighbors. Even today, the Celtic language and influence are strongest in these far reaches of Britain.

As Rome fell, so fell Roman Britain, a victim of invaders and internal troubles. Barbarian tribes from Germany and Denmark, called Angles and Saxons, swept through the southern part of the island, establishing Angle-land. These were the days of the real King Arthur, possibly a Christianized Roman general fighting valiantly, but in vain, against invading barbarians. The island was plunged into 500 years of Dark Ages—wars, plagues, and poverty—lit only by the dim candle of a few learned Christian monks and missionaries trying to convert the barbarians. The sightseer sees little from this Saxon period.

Modern England began with yet another invasion. William the Conqueror and his Norman troops crossed the English Channel from France in 1066. William crowned himself king in Westminster Abbey (where all subsequent coronations would take place) and began building the Tower of London. French-speaking Norman kings ruled the country for two centuries. Then followed two centuries of civil wars, with various noble families vying for the crown. In one of the most bitter feuds, the York and Lancaster families fought the Wars of the Roses, so-called because of the white and red flowers the combatants chose as their symbols.

Royal Families: Past and Present

Royal Lineage

802–1066	Saxon and Danish kings
1066–1154	Norman invasion (William the Conqueror), Norman kings
1154–1399	Plantagenet (kings with French roots)
1399–1461	Lancaster
1462–1485	York
1485–1603	Tudor (Henry VIII, Elizabeth I)
1603–1649	Stuart (civil war and beheading of Charles I)
1649–1653	Commonwealth, no royal head of state
1653–1659	Protectorate, with Cromwell as Lord Protector
1660–1714	Restoration of Stuart monarchy
1714–1901	Hanover (four Georges, Victoria)
1901–1910	Edward VII
1910–present	Windsor (George V, Edward VIII, George VI, Elizabeth II)

The Royal Family Today

It seems you can't pick up a London newspaper without some mention of the latest scandal or oddity involving the royal family. Here they are:

Queen Elizabeth II wears the traditional crown of her great-great grandmother, Victoria. Her husband is **Prince Phillip** (he's not considered king).

Their son, **Prince Charles** (the Prince of Wales), is next in

Battles, intrigues, kings imprisoned and nobles executed in the Tower of London—it's a wonder the country survived its rulers.

England was finally united by the "third-party" Tudor family. Henry VIII, a Tudor, was England's Renaissance king. He was handsome, athletic, highly sexed, a poet, a scholar, and a musician. He was also arrogant, cruel, gluttonous, and paranoid. Henry married six wives in 40 years, and divorced, imprisoned, or beheaded five of them when they no longer suited his needs. Henry's last wife (Catherine Parr) was fortunate enough to outlive him

Henry also "divorced" England from the Catholic Church, establishing the Protestant Church of England (the Anglican Church) and setting in motion years of religious squabbles. He also "dissolved" the monasteries (about 1540), leaving just the shells of many formerly glorious abbeys dotting the countryside and pocketing their land and wealth for the crown.

line to become king. In 1981, Charles married Lady Diana Spencer (**"Princess Di"**) who, after their bitter divorce, died in a car crash in 1997. Their two sons, **William** and **Harry,** are next in line to the throne after their father. In 2005, Charles married his long-time girlfriend, **Camilla Parker Bowles,** who is trying to gain respectability with the Queen and the public.

The **Queen Mother** (or "Queen Mum") is the late mother of Queen Elizabeth II. Prince Charles' siblings are often in the news for their marital or dating escapades: **Princess Anne, Prince Andrew** (who married and divorced **Sarah "Fergie" Ferguson**), and **Prince Edward** (who married Di look-alike **Sophie Rhys-Jones**). For more on the monarchy, see www.royal.gov.uk.

Royal Sightseeing

You can see the trappings of royalty at **Buckingham Palace** (the Queen's residence) with its Changing of the Guard; **Kensington Palace,** where members of the extended royal family keep apartments; **St. James' Palace,** the London home of Prince Charles and sons; **Althorp Estate** (80 miles from London), the childhood home and burial place of Princess Diana; **Windsor Castle,** a royal country home near London; and the **Crown Jewels** in the Tower of London.

Your best chances to actually see the Queen are on three public occasions: Opening of Parliament (late October), Remembrance Sunday (early November, at the Cenotaph), or Trooping the Colour (one Saturday in mid-June, parading down Whitehall and at Buckingham Palace).

Otherwise, check daily papers for the "Court Circular," which lists all public engagements of the royal family.

Henry's daughter, Queen Elizabeth I, who reigned for 45 years, made England a great trading and naval power (defeating the Spanish armada) and presided over the Elizabethan era of great writers (such as Shakespeare) and scientists (such as Sir Francis Bacon).

The long-standing quarrel between England's divine-right kings and the nobles in Parliament finally erupted into a civil war (1642). Parliament forces under the Protestant Puritan farmer Oliver Cromwell defeated—and beheaded—King Charles I. This civil war left its mark on much of what you'll see in England. Eventually, Parliament invited Charles' son to take the throne. This "restoration of the monarchy" was accompanied by a great colonial expansion and the rebuilding of London (including Christopher Wren's St. Paul's Cathedral), which had been devastated by the Great Fire of 1666.

Britain grew as a naval superpower, colonizing and trading with all parts of the globe. Admiral Horatio Nelson's victory over Napoleon's fleet at the Battle of Trafalgar secured her naval superiority ("Britannia rules the waves"). Ten years later, the Duke of Wellington stomped Napoleon on land at Waterloo. Nelson and Wellington—both buried in London's St. Paul's Cathedral—are memorialized by many arches, columns, and squares throughout England.

Economically, Britain led the world into the Industrial Age with her mills, factories, coal mines, and trains. By the time of Queen Victoria's reign (1837–1901), Britain was at the zenith of her power, with a colonial empire that covered one-fifth of the world.

The 20th century was not kind to Britain. Two world wars devastated the population. The Nazi blitzkrieg reduced much of London to rubble. The colonial empire dwindled to almost nothing, and Britain was no longer an economic superpower. The "Irish Troubles" were constant, as the Catholic inhabitants of British-ruled Northern Ireland fought for the independence their southern neighbors won decades ago. The war over the Falkland Islands in 1982 showed how little of the British Empire was left—and how determined the British were to hang on to what remained.

But the tradition (if not the substance) of greatness continues, presided over by Queen Elizabeth II, her husband Prince Philip, and their son, Prince Charles. With economic problems, the turmoil between Charles and the late Princess Diana, and a relentless popular press, the royal family has had a tough time. But the Queen has stayed above it all, and most British people still jump at an opportunity to see royalty. The massive outpouring of grief over the death of Princess Diana made it clear that the concept of royalty was still alive and well when Britain entered the third millennium.

Queen Elizabeth marked her 50th year on the throne in 2002 with a flurry of Golden Jubilee festivities. While many wonder who will succeed her, the case is fairly straightforward: The queen sees her job as a lifelong position, and legally, Charles (who wants to be king) cannot be skipped over for his son, William. Given the longevity in the family (the Queen's mum, born in August of 1900, made it to 101 before she died in April 2002), Charles is in for a long wait.

Thumbnail Sketches of Famous Brits

Albert, Prince (1819–1861)—German-born husband of Queen Victoria, whose support of the arts and sciences enriched London. (See National Portrait Gallery Tour.)

Arthur, King (c. 600?)—A character of legend, perhaps based on a Roman Christian general battling barbarians after the Fall of Rome.

Boadicea (d. 61)—A queen of the isle's indigenous people, who defied Roman occupation, burning Londinium to the ground before being defeated. (See Westminster Walk.)

Beatles (1960s)—Rock music quartet (John Lennon, Paul McCartney, George Harrison, Ringo Starr) whose worldwide popularity brought counterculture ideas to the middle class. (See British Library Tour.)

Charles I (1600–1649)—King beheaded after England's Civil War, which pitted a Catholic aristocracy against a Protestant Parliament. Parliament won. (See Westminster Walk, National Gallery Tour, and National Portrait Gallery Tour.)

Charles II (1630–1685)—Son of Charles I who was invited to restore the monarchy under supervision by the Parliament. (See National Portrait Gallery Tour.)

Cromwell, Oliver (1599–1658)—Leader of the Protestant Parliament that deposed the king in England's Civil War, briefly establishing a Parliament-run Commonwealth. (See National Portrait Gallery Tour and Westminster Walk.)

Chaucer, Geoffrey (c. 1340–1400)—Poet, author of *The Canterbury Tales,* which popularized common English. (See Westminster Abbey Tour and Bankside Walk.)

Churchill, Sir Winston (1874–1965)—As prime minister during World War II, his resolve and charismatic speeches rallied Britain during its darkest hour. (See Westminster Walk, St. Paul's Tour, and The City Walk.)

Constable, John (1776–1837)—Painter of the English countryside, specializing in cloudy skies. (See Tate Britain Tour and National Gallery Tour.)

Dickens, Charles (1812–1870)—Popular novelist, bringing literature to the masses and educating them about Britain's harsh social and economic realities. (See Bankside Walk and Westminster Abbey Tour.)

Edward the Confessor (c. 1002–1066)—The English king who built Westminster Abbey, his death prompted the Norman invasion by William the Conqueror. (See Westminster Abbey Tour.)

Elizabeth I (1533–1603)—Daughter of Henry VIII and Anne Boleyn, she ruled England when its navies gained mastery of the seas, bringing prosperity and a renaissance of the arts (Shakespeare). (See National Portrait Gallery Tour and Tower of London Tour.)

Garrick, David (1717–1779)—Actor and theater manager whose naturalism on the stage and business sense off it greatly enhanced the blossoming theater scene. (See National Portrait Gallery Tour, Theatre Museum Tour, and The City Walk.)

Henry VIII (1491–1547)—Charismatic king during an era of expansion whose marital choices forced a break with the pope in

Get It Right

Americans tend to use "England," "Britain," and "United Kingdom" interchangeably, but they're not quite the same:

- England is the country occupying the southeast part of the island.
- **Britain** is the name of the island.
- **Great Britain** is the political union of the island's three countries: England, Scotland, and Wales.
- **The United Kingdom** adds a fourth country, Northern Ireland.
- **The British Isles** (not a political entity) also includes the independent nation of Ireland.
- **The British Commonwealth** is a loose association of possessions and former colonies (including Canada, Australia, and India) that profess at least symbolic loyalty to the Crown.

You can call the modern nation either the United Kingdom ("the U.K.") or simply "Britain."

Rome, leading to centuries of religious division. (See National Portrait Gallery Tour and Tower of London Tour.)

Hogarth, William (1697–1764)—Painter of realistic slices of English life. (See Tate Britain Tour.)

Holmes, Sherlock (late 1800s)—Fictional detective living at fictional 221-B Baker Street, who solved fictional crimes that the real Scotland Yard couldn't.

Jack the Ripper (late 1800s)—Serial killer of prostitutes in east London; his or her identity remains unknown.

Johnson, Dr. Samuel (1709–1784)—Writer of a magazine column on everyday London life, compiler of the first great English dictionary, known to us today for witty remarks captured by his friend and biographer, James Boswell. (See The City Walk and Westminster Abbey Tour.)

Keats, John (1795–1821)—Romantic poet (in the company of Percy Shelley, Lord Byron, and William Wordsworth) who pondered mortality before dying young. (See National Portrait Gallery Tour.)

Nelson, Horatio (1758–1805)—Admiral who defeated the French navy at Trafalgar (Spain), ending Napoleon's plans to invade England. (See Westminster Walk, National Portrait Gallery Tour, and St. Paul's Tour.)

Pepys, Samuel (1633–1701)—Not a famous man himself, Pepys (pronounced "Peeps") kept a diary chronicling London life and the Great Fire that, even today, makes that time come alive. (See The City Tour.)

Richard the Lionhearted (1157–1199)—Not a great king, he preferred speaking French and spent his energy on distant Crusades.

Robin Hood (1100s)—Fictional (or perhaps real) bandit.

Shakespeare, William (1564–1616)—Earth's greatest playwright. Born in Stratford, he lived most of his adult life in London, writing and acting. (See Bankside Walk, British Library Tour, National Portrait Gallery Tour, and Westminster Abbey Tour.)

Thatcher, Margaret (b. 1925)—Prime minister during the conservative 1980s, known as the "Iron Lady." (See Westminster Walk and National Portrait Gallery Tour.)

Victoria, Queen (1819–1901)—During her 64-year reign, the worldwide British Empire reached its height of power and prosperity. "Victorian" has come to describe the prim middle-class morality of the time. (See National Portrait Gallery Tour.)

Wellington, Duke of (1769–1852)—General who defeated Napoleon at Waterloo and later served as a domineering prime minister. (See National Portrait Gallery Tour and St. Paul's Tour.)

William the Conqueror (c. 1027–1087)—Duke of Normandy in northern France, he invaded England (1066), built the Tower of London, and initiated two centuries of rule by French-speaking kings. (See Tower of London Tour.)

Wren, Christopher (1632–1723)—Architect who rebuilt London after the Great Fire of 1666, designing more than 20 churches, including his masterpiece, St. Paul's Cathedral. (See St. Paul's Tour and The City Walk.)

What's So Great about Britain?

Regardless of the revolution we had 200 years ago, many American travelers feel that they "go home" to Britain. This most popular tourist destination has a strange influence and power over us. The more you know of Britain's roots, the better you'll get in touch with your own.

Geographically, the Isle of Britain is small (about the size of Uganda or Idaho)—600 miles long and 300 miles at its widest point. Its highest mountain is 4,400 feet, a foothill by our standards. The population is a fifth that of the United States. At its peak in the mid-1800s, Britain owned one-fifth of the world and accounted for more than half the planet's industrial output. Today, the Empire is down to the Isle of Britain itself and a few token, troublesome scraps, such as the Falklands, Gibraltar, and Northern Ireland.

Economically, Great Britain's industrial production is about five percent of the world's total. For the first time in history, Ireland has a higher per-capita income than Britain. Still, the economy is booming, and inflation, unemployment, and interest rates are all low.

Culturally, Britain is still a world leader. Her heritage, culture, and people cannot be measured in traditional units of power. London is a major exporter of actors, movies, and theater, of rock and classical music, and of writers, painters, and sculptors.

Ethnically, the British Isles are a mix of the descendants of the early Celtic natives (like Scots and Gaels in Scotland, Ireland, and Wales), descendants of the invading Anglo-Saxons who took southeast England in the Dark Ages, and descendants of the conquering Normans of the 11th century. Cynics call the United Kingdom an English Empire ruled by London, whose dominant Anglo-Saxon English (49 million) far outnumber their Celtic brothers and sisters (8 million).

Politically, Britain is ruled by the House of Commons, with some guidance from the mostly figurehead Queen and House of Lords. Just as the United States Congress is dominated by Democrats and Republicans, Britain's Parliament is dominated by two parties: Labour and Conservative ("Tories"). (George W. Bush would fit the Conservative Party and Bill Clinton the Labour Party like political gloves.)

The prime minister is the chief executive. He's not elected directly by voters; rather, he assumes power as the head of the party that wins a majority in Parliamentary elections.

In the 1980s, Conservatives were in charge under Prime Minister Margaret Thatcher and Prime Minister John Major. As proponents of traditional, Victorian values—community, family, hard work, thrift, and trickle-down economics—they took a Reaganesque approach to Britain's serious social and economic problems.

In 1997, a huge Labour victory brought Tony Blair to the prime ministership. Labour began shoring up a social-service system (health care, education, the minimum wage) undercut by years of Conservative rule. Blair's Labour Party is "New Labour"—akin to Clinton's "New Democrats"—meaning they're fiscally conservative but attentive to the needs of the people. Conservative Party fears of old-fashioned, big-spending, bleeding-heart, Union-style liberalism have proved unfounded. The Liberal Parliament is more open to integration with Europe.

Tony Blair—relatively young, family-oriented, personable, easy-going, and forever flashing his toothy grin—has been a respected and well-liked PM, but his popularity took a dive after he propelled the country into a war with Iraq. The 2005 elections were a virtual referendum on whether Blair could be trusted after joining America's attack on Iraq based on faulty evidence. His Labour party won a slim majority, but some wonder whether Blair will have sufficient support to finish his term.

The morning of July 7, 2005, London's commuters were

rocked by four different bombs that killed dozens across the city. The bombers (who died in the attacks) were British citizens of Pakistani descent, leaving the country to ponder how well it has incorporated its Muslim population. Also in 2005, London won its bid to host the 2012 Olympic Games.

APPENDIX

Let's Talk Telephones

Here's a primer on making phone calls. For information specific to Britain, see "Telephones" in the Introduction.

Making Calls within a European Country: About half of all European countries—including Britain—use area codes; the other half uses a direct-dial system without area codes.

In countries that use area codes (such as Britain, Austria, Finland, Germany, Ireland, the Netherlands, and Sweden), you dial the local number when calling within a city, and you add the area code if calling long distance within the country.

To make calls within a country that uses a direct-dial system (Belgium, the Czech Republic, Denmark, France, Italy, Portugal, Norway, Spain, and Switzerland), you dial the same number whether you're calling across the country or across the street.

Making International Calls: You always start with the international access code (011 if you're calling from America or Canada, or 00 from Europe), then dial the country code of the country you're calling (see chart below).

What you dial next depends on the phone system of the country you're calling. If the country uses area codes, drop the initial 0 of the area code, then dial the rest of the number.

Countries that use direct-dial systems (no area codes) vary in how they're accessed internationally by phone. For instance, if you're making an international call to the Czech Republic, Denmark, Italy, Norway, Portugal, or Spain, simply dial the international access code, country code, and phone number. But if you're calling Belgium, France, or Switzerland, drop the initial 0 of the phone number. Example: To call a Paris hotel (tel. 01 47 05 49 15) from London, dial 00, 33 (France's country code), then 1 47 05 49 15 (phone number without the initial 0).

European Calling Chart

Just smile and dial, using this key:
AC = Area Code, LN = Local Number.

European Country	Calling long distance within...	Calling from the U.S.A./ Canada to...	Calling from a European country to...
Austria	AC + LN	011 + 43 + AC (without the initial zero) + LN	00 + 43 + AC (without the initial zero) + LN
Belgium	LN	011 + 32 + LN (without initial zero)	00 + 32 + LN (without initial zero)
Britain	AC + LN	011 + 44 + AC (without initial zero) + LN	00 + 44 + AC (without initial zero) + LN
Croatia	AC + LN	011 + 385 + AC (without initial zero) + LN	00 + 385 + AC (without initial zero) + LN
Czech Republic	LN	011 + 420 + LN	00 + 420 + LN
Denmark	LN	011 + 45 + LN	00 + 45 + LN
Finland	AC + LN	011 + 358 + AC (without initial zero) + LN	00 + 358 + AC (without initial zero) + LN
France	LN	011 + 33 + LN (without initial zero)	00 + 33 + LN (without initial zero)
Germany	AC + LN	011 + 49 + AC (without initial zero) + LN	00 + 49 + AC (without initial zero) + LN
Greece	LN	011 + 30 + LN	00 + 30 + LN
Hungary	06 + AC + LN	011 + 36 + AC + LN	00 + 36 + AC + LN
Ireland	AC + LN	011 + 353 + AC (without initial zero) + LN	00 + 353 + AC (without initial zero) + LN
Italy	LN	011 + 39 + LN	00 + 39 + LN

European Country	Calling long distance within...	Calling from the U.S.A./ Canada to...	Calling from a European country to...
Netherlands	AC + LN	011 + 31 + AC (without initial zero) + LN	00 + 31 + AC (without initial zero) + LN
Norway	LN	011 + 47 + LN	00 + 47 + LN
Poland	AC + LN	011 + 48 + AC (without initial zero) + LN	00 + 48 + AC (without initial zero) + LN
Portugal	LN	011 + 351 + LN	00 + 351 + LN
Slovakia	AC + LN	011 + 421 + AC (without initial zero) + LN	00 + 421 + AC (without initial zero) + LN
Slovenia	AC + LN	011 + 386 + AC (without initial zero) + LN	00 + 386 + AC (without initial zero) + LN
Spain	LN	011 + 34 + LN	00 + 34 + LN
Sweden	AC + LN	011 + 46 + AC (without initial zero) + LN	00 + 46 + AC (without initial zero) + LN
Switzerland	LN	011 + 41 + LN (without initial zero)	00 + 41 + LN (without initial zero)
Turkey	AC (if no initial zero is included, add one) + LN	011 + 90 + AC (without initial zero) + LN	00 + 90 + AC (without initial zero) + LN

The instructions above apply whether you're calling a fixed phone or mobile phone.

The international access codes (the first numbers you dial when making an international call) are 011 if you're calling from the U.S.A./Canada, or 00 if you're calling from anywhere in Europe.

To call the U.S.A. or Canada from Europe, dial 00, then 1 (the country code for the U.S.A. and Canada), then the area code and number. In short, 00 + 1 + AC + LN = Hi, Mom!

Country Codes

After you've dialed the international access code (00 if you're calling from Europe, 011 if calling from the U.S. or Canada), dial the code of the country you're calling.

Austria—43
Belgium—32
Britain—44
Canada—1
Croatia—385
Czech Rep.—420
Denmark—45
Estonia—372
Finland—358
France—33
Germany—49
Gibraltar—350
Greece—30
Ireland—353
Italy—39
Morocco—212
Netherlands—31
Norway—47
Poland—48
Portugal—351
Slovakia—421
Slovenia—386
Spain—34
Sweden—46
Switzerland—41
Turkey—90
U.S.A.—1

Useful Numbers in Britain

Emergency (police and ambulance): tel. 999
Operator Assistance: tel. 100
Directory Assistance: tel. 192 (20p from phone booth, otherwise expensive)
International Info: tel. 153 (20p from phone booth, £1.50 otherwise)
International Assistance: tel. 155
United States Embassy: tel. 020/7499-9000
Eurostar (Chunnel Info): tel. 08705-186-186 (www.eurostar.com)
Trains to all points in Europe: tel. 08705-848-848 (www.raileurope.com)
Train information for trips within England: tel. 0845-748-4950
Note: Understand the various prefixes—09 numbers are telephone-sex–type expensive. The prefixes 0845 (4p/min, 2p evenings and weekends) and 0870 (8p/min, 4p evenings and weekends) are local calls nationwide. And 0800 numbers are toll-free. If you have questions about a prefix, call 100 for free help.

Airports

For online information on the first three airports, check www.baa.co.uk.
Heathrow (flight info): tel. 0870-000-0123
Gatwick (general info): tel. 0870-000-2468 for all airlines, except British Airways–tel. 0870-551-1155 (flights) or tel. 0870-850-9850 (booking)

Stansted (general info): tel. 0870-000-0303
Luton (general info): tel. 01582/405-100 (www.london-luton.com)
London City Airport (general info): tel. 020/7646-0088 (www.londoncityairport.com)

Airlines
Aer Lingus: tel. 0845-084-4444 (www.aerlingus.com)
Air Canada: tel. 0871-220-1111 (www.aircanada.com)
Alitalia: reservations tel. 0870-544-8259, Heathrow tel. 020/8745-5812 (www.alitalia.it)
American: tel. 0845-789-0890 (www.aa.com)
British Airways: reservations tel. 0870-850-9850, flight info tel. 0870-551-1155 (www.ba.com), cool voice-activated system
bmi british midland: reservations tel. 0870-607-0555, info tel. 020/8745-7321 (www.flybmi.com)
Continental Airlines: tel. 0845-607-6760 (www.continental.com)
easyJet (cheap fares): www.easyjet.com
KLM Royal Dutch Airlines: tel. 0870-507-4074 (www.klm.com)
Lufthansa: tel. 0870-837-7747 (www.lufthansa.com)
Ryanair (cheap fares): tel. 0871-246-0000 (www.ryanair.com)
Scandinavian Airlines (SAS): tel. 0870-607-27727 (www.flysas.com)
United Airlines: tel. 0845-844-4777 (www.unitedairlines.co.uk)
US Airways: tel. 0845-600-3300 (www.usair.com)
Virgin Express: tel. 0870-730-1134 (www.virgin-express.com)

Heathrow Airport Car-Rental Agencies
Avis: tel. 0870-0100-287
Budget: tel. 0870-156-5656
Europcar: tel. 0870-607-5000 or 020/8897-0811
Hertz: tel. 0870-599-6699 or 020/8897-2072
National/Alamo: tel. 0870-600-6666 or 020/8750-2800

Festivals and Holidays in 2006
This list includes major festivals in London, plus national holidays observed throughout Great Britain. Many sights and banks close down on national holidays—keep it in mind when planning your itinerary. Note that this isn't a complete list; holidays often strike without warning.

Included in this list are events in the nearby towns of Bath and Cambridge. Both towns are an easy train ride from the city (see Day Trips in England chapter).

For specifics and a more comprehensive list of festivals, contact the Visit Britain office in the United States (see page 6) and visit www.whatsonwhen.com, www.travelbritain.org, or www.londontouristboard.com.

2006

JANUARY

S	M	T	W	T	F	S
1	2	3	4	5	6	7
8	9	10	11	12	13	14
15	16	17	18	19	20	21
22	23	24	25	26	27	28
29	30	31				

FEBRUARY

S	M	T	W	T	F	S
			1	2	3	4
5	6	7	8	9	10	11
12	13	14	15	16	17	18
19	20	21	22	23	24	25
26	27	28				

MARCH

S	M	T	W	T	F	S
			1	2	3	4
5	6	7	8	9	10	11
12	13	14	15	16	17	18
19	20	21	22	23	24	25
26	27	28	29	30	31	

APRIL

S	M	T	W	T	F	S
						1
2	3	4	5	6	7	8
9	10	11	12	13	14	15
16	17	18	19	20	21	22
23/30	24	25	26	27	28	29

MAY

S	M	T	W	T	F	S
	1	2	3	4	5	6
7	8	9	10	11	12	13
14	15	16	17	18	19	20
21	22	23	24	25	26	27
28	29	30	31			

JUNE

S	M	T	W	T	F	S
				1	2	3
4	5	6	7	8	9	10
11	12	13	14	15	16	17
18	19	20	21	22	23	24
25	26	27	28	29	30	

JULY

S	M	T	W	T	F	S
						1
2	3	4	5	6	7	8
9	10	11	12	13	14	15
16	17	18	19	20	21	22
23/30	24/31	25	26	27	28	29

AUGUST

S	M	T	W	T	F	S
		1	2	3	4	5
6	7	8	9	10	11	12
13	14	15	16	17	18	19
20	21	22	23	24	25	26
27	28	29	30	31		

SEPTEMBER

S	M	T	W	T	F	S
					1	2
3	4	5	6	7	8	9
10	11	12	13	14	15	16
17	18	19	20	21	22	23
24	25	26	27	28	29	30

OCTOBER

S	M	T	W	T	F	S
1	2	3	4	5	6	7
8	9	10	11	12	13	14
15	16	17	18	19	20	21
22	23	24	25	26	27	28
29	30	31				

NOVEMBER

S	M	T	W	T	F	S
			1	2	3	4
5	6	7	8	9	10	11
12	13	14	15	16	17	18
19	20	21	22	23	24	25
26	27	28	29	30		

DECEMBER

S	M	T	W	T	F	S
					1	2
3	4	5	6	7	8	9
10	11	12	13	14	15	16
17	18	19	20	21	22	23
24/31	25	26	27	28	29	30

Jan 1: New Year's Day

March 4–March 12: Literature Festival, Bath (www.bathfestivals.org.uk)

April 14: Good Friday

April 16–17: Easter Sunday and Monday

May 1: May Day (Bank Holiday)

Early May: Spring Flower Show, Bath

May 19–June 4: International Music Festival, Bath (www.bathfestivals.org.uk)

May 23–27: Chelsea Flower Show, London (book tickets ahead for this popular event at www.rhs.org.uk/chelsea)

May 26–June 11: Fringe Festival, Bath (alternative music, dance, and theater; www.bathfringe.co.uk)

May 29: Spring Bank Holiday

June: Trooping the Color, London (military bands and pageantry, Queen's birthday parade)
June 26–July 9: Wimbledon Tennis Championship, London (www.wimbledon.org)
July: Cambridge Folk Festival, Cambridge (buy tickets early at www.cam-folkfest.co.uk)
Aug: Notting Hill Carnival, London (costumes, Caribbean music)
Aug 28: Late Summer Holiday
Nov 1: All Saints' Day
Nov 5: Guy Fawkes Day (fireworks, effigy burning of traitor Guy Fawkes)
Dec 24–26: Christmas holidays

London's Climate

The first line is the average low, the second line is the average high, and the third line is number of days with no rain.

J	F	M	A	M	J	J	A	S	O	N	D
36°	36°	38°	42°	47°	53°	56°	56°	52°	46°	42°	38°
43°	44°	50°	56°	62°	69°	71°	71°	65°	58°	50°	45°
16	15	20	18	19	19	19	20	17	18	15	16

Metric Conversion (approximate)

1 inch = 25 millimeters
1 foot = 0.3 meter
1 yard = 0.9 meter
1 mile = 1.6 kilometers
1 centimeter = 0.4 inch
1 meter = 39.4 inches
1 kilometer = .62 mile
32° F = 0° C
82° F = about 28° C
1 ounce = 28 grams
1 kilogram = 2.2 pounds
1 quart = 0.95 liter
1 square yard = 0.8 square meter
1 acre = 0.4 hectare

Numbers and Stumblers

- The British write a couple of their numbers differently than we do: 1 = 1 and 4 = 4.
- In Europe, dates appear as day/month/year, so Christmas is 25/12/06.
- When pointing, use your whole hand, palm down.
- When counting with fingers, start with your thumb. If you hold up your first finger to request one item, you'll probably get two.
- What Americans call the second floor of a building is the first floor in Europe.
- Europeans keep the left "lane" open for passing on escalators and moving sidewalks. Keep to the right.
- And please...don't call your waist pack a "fanny pack."

Converting Temperatures: Fahrenheit and Celsius

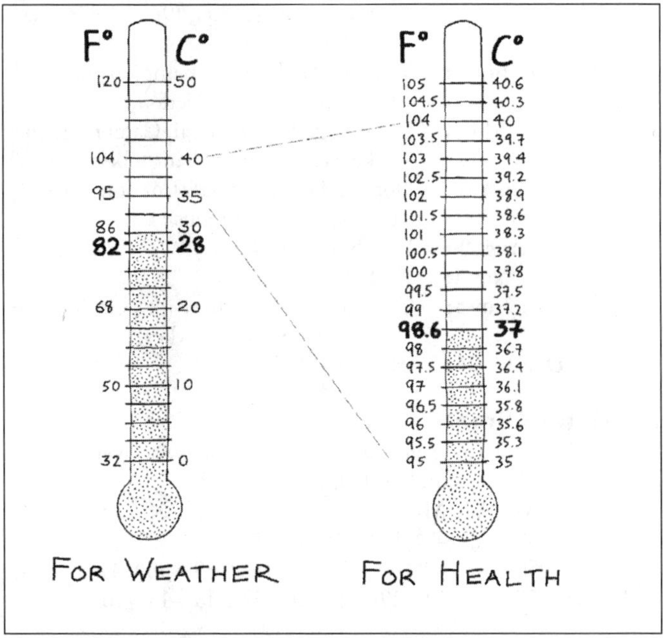

Europe takes its temperature using the Celsius scale, while we opt for Fahrenheit. For weather, remember that 28° C is 82° F—perfect. For health, 37° C is just right.

British–Yankee Vocabulary

advert–advertisement
afters–dessert
anticlockwise–counterclockwise
aubergine–eggplant
banger–sausage
bangers and mash–sausage and mashed potatoes
bank holiday–legal holiday
bap–hamburger-type bun
bespoke–custom
billion–a thousand of our billions (a million million)
biro–ballpoint pen
biscuit–cookie
black pudding–sausage made from dried blood
bloody–damn
blow off–fart
bobby–policeman ("copper" is more common)
Bob's your uncle–there you go (with a shrug), naturally
boffin–nerd
bolshy–argumentative
bomb–success
bonnet–car hood
boot–car trunk
braces–suspenders
bridle way–path for walkers, bikers, and horse riders
brilliant–cool
brolly–umbrella
bubble and squeak–cold meat fried with cabbage and potatoes
bum–bottom or "backside"
candy floss–cotton candy
caravan–trailer
car boot sale–temporary flea market with car trunk displays (a good place to buy back your stolen goods)
casualty–emergency room
cat's eyes–road reflectors
ceilidh (KAY-lee)–informal evening of song and folk fun (Scottish and Irish)
cheap and cheerful–budget but adequate
cheap and nasty–cheap and bad quality
cheers–good-bye or thanks
chemist–pharmacist
chicory–endive
chips–French fries
chock-a-block–jam-packed
chuffed–pleased
cider–alcoholic apple cider
clearway–road where you can't stop
coach–long-distance bus
concession–discounted admission
cos–romaine lettuce
cotton buds–Q-tips
courgette–zucchini
craic (pronounced "crack")–fun, good conversation (Irish and spreading to England)
crisps–potato chips
cuppa–cup of tea
dear–expensive
dicey–iffy, risky
digestives–round graham cookies
dinner–lunch or dinner
diversion–detour
donkey's years–ages, long time
draughts–checkers
draw–marijuana
dual carriageway–divided highway (four lanes)
elvers–baby eels
elevens–snack time before lunch

face flannel–washcloth
fag–cigarette
fagged–exhausted
faggot–meatball
fanny–vagina
fell–hill or high plain
first floor–second floor
flutter–a bet
football–soccer
force–waterfall (Lake District)
fortnight–two weeks
fringe–hair bangs
Frogs–French people
fruit machine–slot machine
full Monty–whole shebang; everything
gallery–balcony
gammon–ham
gangway–aisle
gaol–jail (same pronunciation)
gateau (or gateaux)–cake
give way–yield
glen–narrow valley
goods wagon–freight truck
grammar school–high school
half eight–8:30 (not 7:30)
heath–open treeless land
holiday–vacation
homely–likable or cozy
hoover–vacuum cleaner
ice lolly–Popsicle
interval–intermission
ironmonger–hardware store
jacket potato–baked potato
jelly–Jell-O
Joe Bloggs–John Doe
jumble–sale, rummage sale
jumper–sweater
just a tick–just a second
keep your pecker up–be brave
kipper–smoked herring
knackered–exhausted (Cockney: cream crackered)
knickers–ladies' panties
knocking shop–brothel
knock up–wake up or visit
ladybird–ladybug
lady fingers–flat, spongy cookie; also okra
left luggage–baggage check
lemon squash–lemonade
let–rent
listed–protected historic building
loo–toilet or bathroom
lorry–truck
mac–mackintosh raincoat
mate–buddy (boy or girl)
mangetout–snow peas
mean–stingy
mews–courtyard stables, often used as cottages
mobile (MOH-bile)–mobile phone
moggie–cat
naff–dorky
napkin–sanitary pad
nappy–diaper
natter–talk and talk
neep–Scottish for turnip
nought–zero
noughts & crosses–tic-tac-toe
off license–store selling take-away liquor
on offer–on sale
pants–underwear, briefs
pasty (PASS-tee)–crusted savory (usually meat) pie
pavement–sidewalk
pear-shaped–messed up, gone wrong
petrol–gas
pillar box–postbox
pissed (rude), paralytic, bevvied, wellied, popped up, trollied, ratted, rat-arsed, pissed as a newt–drunk
pitch–playing field
plaster–Band-Aid
publican–pub manager
public convenience–toilets

public school–private "prep" school (Eton)
pudding–dessert in general
punter–customer
put a sock in it–shut up
queue–line
queue up–line up
quid–pound (money, worth about $1.80)
randy–horny
rasher–slice of bacon
redundant, made–fired
Remembrance Day–Veterans' Day
return ticket–round trip
ring up–call (telephone)
roundabout–traffic circle
rubber–eraser
sausage roll–sausage wrapped in a flaky pastry
Scotch egg–hard-boiled egg wrapped in sausage meat
self-catering–apartment with kitchen
sellotape–Scotch tape
serviette–napkin
shag–intercourse
silencer–car muffler
single ticket–one-way ticket
skip–Dumpster
sleeping policeman–speed bumps
smalls–underwear
snogging–kissing, cuddling
solicitor–lawyer
spanner–wrench
spend a penny–urinate
starkers–buck naked
starters–appetizers
state school–public school
sticking plaster–Band-Aid
sticky tape–Scotch tape
stone–14 pounds (weight)
stroppy–bad-tempered
subway–underground pedestrian passageway
sultanas–golden raisins
surgical spirit–rubbing alcohol
suspenders–garters
suss out–figure out
swede–rutabaga
ta–thank you
take the mickey–tease
tatty–worn out or tacky
taxi rank–taxi stand
telly–TV
theatre–live stage
tick–a check mark
tight as a fish's bum–cheapskate (water-tight)
tights–panty hose
tin–can
tip–public dump
tipper lorry–dump truck
to let–for rent
top hole–first rate
to pull–to attract romantic attention
top up–refill a drink
torch–flashlight
towel, press-on–panty liner
towpath–path along a river
trousers–pants
Tube–subway
twee–quaint, cute
twitcher–bird watcher
Underground–subway
vegetable marrow–summer squash
verge–grassy edge of road
verger–church official
way out–exit
wee–urinate
Wellingtons, wellies–rubber boots
whacked–exhausted
whinge (rhymes with hinge)–whine
witter on–gab and gab
yob–hooligan
zebra crossing–crosswalk
zed–the letter Z

Making Your Hotel Reservation

Faxing or e-mailing are the preferred methods for reserving a room. They're more accurate than telephoning and much faster than writing a letter. Use this handy form for your fax or find it online at www.ricksteves.com/reservation. Photocopy and fax away.

One-Page Fax

To: ______________________ @ ______________________
hotel *fax*

From: ______________________ @ ______________________
name *fax*

Today's date: _____ /_____ /_____
day *month* *year*

Dear Hotel ______________________________,
Please make this reservation for me:

Name: ______________________________

Total # of people: _________ # of rooms: _________ # of nights: _________

Arriving: _____ /_____ /_____ My time of arrival (24-hr clock): _________
day *month* *year* (I will telephone if I will be late)

Departing: _____ /_____ /_____
day *month* *year*

Room(s): Single _____ Double ___ Twin _____ Triple ___ Quad _____

With: Toilet _____ Shower _____ Bath _____ Sink only _____

Special needs: View ___ Quiet ___ Cheapest ___ Ground Floor ___

Please fax, mail, or e-mail confirmation of my reservation, along with the type of room reserved and the price. Please also inform me of your cancellation policy. After I hear from you, I will quickly send my credit-card information as a deposit to hold the room. Thank you.

____
Signature

____
Name

____
Address

____
City **State** **Zip Code** **Country**

____
E-mail Address

INDEX

CREDITS

Researcher

Darbi Macy

Darbi Macy, who has worked for Rick Steves for five years, spends summers in Britain and Ireland researching guidebooks, guiding tours, learning to speak Irish, and eating banoffee pie. When not in Europe, Darbi works in the HR department at Rick Steves' Europe Through the Back Door.

Travel smart...carry on!

The latest generation of Rick Steves' carry-on travel bags is easily the best—benefiting from two decades of on-the-road attention to what really matters: maximum quality and strength; practical, flexible features; and no unnecessary frills. You won't find a better value anywhere!

Convertible, expandable, and carry-on-size:

Rick Steves' Back Door Bag $99

This is the same bag that Rick Steves lives out of for three months every summer. It's made of rugged water-resistant 1000 denier Cordura nylon, and best of all, it converts easily from a smart-looking suitcase to a handy backpack with comfortably-curved shoulder straps and a padded waistbelt.

This roomy, versatile 9" x 21" x 14" bag has a large 2600 cubic-inch main compartment, plus three outside pockets (small, medium and huge) that are perfect for often-used items. And the cinch-tight compression straps will keep your load compact and close to your back—not sagging like a sack of potatoes.

Wishing you had even more room to bring home souvenirs? Pull open the full-perimeter expando-zipper and its capacity jumps from 2600 to 3000 cubic inches. When you want to use it as a suitcase or check it as luggage (required when "expanded"), the straps and belt hide away in a zippered compartment in the back.

Attention travelers under 5'4" tall: This bag also comes in an inch-shorter version, for a compact-friendlier fit between the waistbelt and shoulder straps.

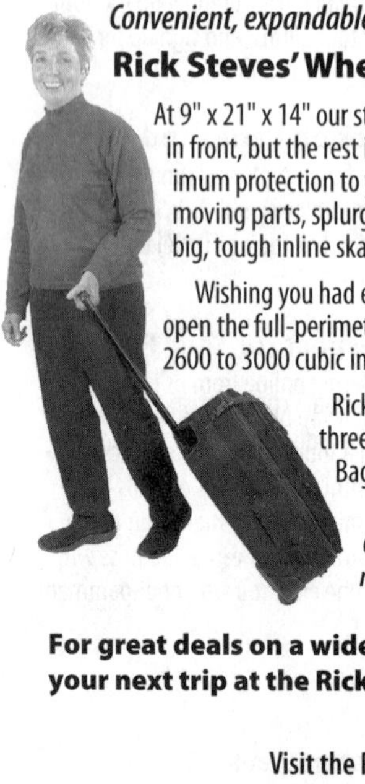

Convenient, expandable, and carry-on-size:

Rick Steves' Wheeled Bag $129

At 9" x 21" x 14" our sturdy Rick Steves' Wheeled Bag is rucksack-soft in front, but the rest is lined with a hard ABS-lexan shell to give maximum protection to your belongings. We've spared no expense on moving parts, splurging on an extra-long button-release handle and big, tough inline skate wheels for easy rolling on rough surfaces.

Wishing you had even more room to bring home souvenirs? Pull open the full-perimeter expando-zipper and its capacity jumps from 2600 to 3000 cubic inches.

Rick Steves' Wheeled Bag has exactly the same three-outside-pocket configuration as our Back Door Bag, plus a handy "add-a-bag" strap and full lining.

Our Back Door Bags and Wheeled Bags come in black, navy, blue spruce, evergreen and merlot.

For great deals on a wide selection of travel goodies, begin your next trip at the Rick Steves Travel Store!

Visit the Rick Steves Travel Store at
www.ricksteves.com

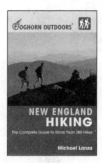

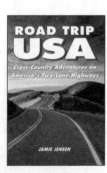

For a complete list of Rick Steves' guidebooks, see page 7.

Avalon Travel Publishing
1400 65th Street, Suite 250
Emeryville, CA 94608

AVALON
publishing group incorporated

Avalon Travel Publishing is an Imprint of Avalon Publishing Group, Inc.

Printed in the U.S.A. by Worzalla. First printing December 2005.
Distributed by Publishers Group West.

ISBN (10) 1-56691-729-8
ISBN (13) 978-1-56691-729-2
ISSN 1522-3280

For the latest on Rick's lectures, books, tours, public radio show, and public television series, contact Europe Through the Back Door, Box 2009, Edmonds, WA 98020, tel. 425/771-8303, fax 425/771-0833, www.ricksteves.com, rick@ricksteves.com.

Europe Through the Back Door Managing Editor: Risa Laib
ETBD Editors: Kevin Yip, Jennifer Hauseman, Lauren Mills
Avalon Travel Publishing Series Manager: Patrick Collins
Avalon Travel Publishing Project Editor: Madhu Prasher
Copy Editor: Matthew Reed Baker
Indexer: Laura Welcome
Research Assistance: Darbi Macy
Production & Typesetting: Patrick David Barber, Holly McGuire
Cover Design: Kari Gim, Laura Mazer
Interior Design: Jane Musser, Amber Pirker, Laura Mazer
Maps and Graphics: David C. Hoerlein, Laura VanDeventer, Lauren Mills, Mike Morgenfeld
Photography: Leo de Wys Inc. provided p. 39 (Steve Vidler), p. 282 (Sylvain Grandadam); all others: Rick Steves, Dominic Bonuccelli, Gene Openshaw, Elizabeth Openshaw, Bruce VanDeventer, Lauren Mills
Front Matter Color Photos: p. i, Tower Bridge and River Thames, © Laurence Parent; p. viii, Guards outside Buckingham Palace, © Dominic Bonuccelli
Cover Photos: Front cover images: front image, St Stephen's Tower © Doug McKinlay/Lonely Planet Images; back image: Trafalgar Square © Dennis Johnson/Lonely Planet Images